WRITERS OF MODERN AMERICA

THE COLUMBIA UNIVERSITY COURSE IN LITERATURE

BASED ON

THE WORLD'S BEST LITERATURE

The Columbia University Course in Literature

WRITERS OF MODERN AMERICA

VOLUME I

COSMO PUBLICATIONS
2010 New Delhi

WRITERS OF MODERN AMERICA

THIS VOLUME IS A PART OF THE SERIES

THE COLUMBIA UNIVERSITY COURSE IN LITERATURE

INDIVIDUAL VOLUMES BEING RELEASED TO FULFILL CONSTANT DEMAND FROM THE READERS

First published by COSMO 2010

ISBN 978-81-307-0934-5 (Set)
ISBN 978-81-307-0847-8 (Volume 1)

Published by
COSMO PUBLICATIONS
for
GENESIS PUBLISHING PVT. LTD.
24-B, Ansari Road, Darya Ganj,
New Delhi-110 002,
INDIA

Printed in India

TABLE OF CONTENTS

FRANCIS RICHARD STOCKTON, 1834–1902

PAGE

Critical Essay 1
The Casting Away of Mrs. Lecks and Mrs. Aleshine 2

JOHN MUIR, 1837–1914

Critical Essay 19
A Wind-Storm in the Forests 20

SAMUEL LANGHORNE CLEMENS (MARK TWAIN), 1835–1910

Critical Essay, by Brander Matthews 27
The Notorious Jumping Frog of Calaveras County 36
The Child of Calamity 41
A Steamboat Landing at a Small Town 44
The High River: And a Phantom Pilot 46
An Enchanting River Scene 50
The Lightning Pilot 52
An Expedition against Ogres 55
The True Prince and the Feigned One 60

THOMAS BAILEY ALDRICH, 1837–1907

Critical Essay 66
Destiny 68
Identity 69
Broken Music 69
Tennyson (1890) 70
Prescience 71
Memory 71
Père Antoine's Date-Palm 71

CELIA THAXTER, 1836–1894

Critical Essay 76
Sorrow 77
Seaward 78

PAGE
The Sandpiper . . . 79
Impatience . . . 80
Wild Geese . . . 80

EDWARD EGGLESTON, 1837–1902

Critical Essay . . . 82
Roger Williams: The Prophet of Religious Freedom . . . 84

JOHN BURROUGHS, 1837–1921

Critical Essay . . . 89
Sharp Eyes . . . 92
Waiting . . . 101

WILLIAM DEAN HOWELLS, 1837–1920

Critical Essay, by Carl Van Doren . . . 102
Society . . . 108
Another Day . . . 109
A Midsummer-Day's Dream . . . 110
Arrival and First Days in Venice . . . 118

JOHN HAY 1838–1905

Critical Essay . . . 125
Lincoln's Death and Fame . . . 126
When Phyllis Laughs . . . 132
Night in Venice . . . 133
Jim Bludso of the Prairie Belle . . . 133

HENRY ADAMS, 1838–1918

Critical Essay . . . 135
The Auspices of the War of 1812 . . . 137
What the War of 1812 Demonstrated . . . 141
The Battle between the Constitution and the Guerrière . . . 146

HENRY GEORGE, 1839–1897

Critical Essay, by Robert Murray Haig . . . 150
The Problem . . . 154
The Remedy . . . 160

BRET HARTE, 1839–1902

Critical Essay, by William Henry Hudson . . . 164
Jim . . . 167

PAGE

The Society upon the Stanislaus . . . 168
Plain Language from Truthful James . . . 169
Dickens in Camp . . . 171
The Luck of Roaring Camp . . . 172

EDWARD ROWLAND SILL, 1841–1887

Critical Essay . . . 181
Opportunity . . . 183
Home . . . 183
The Fool's Prayer . . . 184
A Morning Thought . . . 185
Strange . . . 186

JOAQUIN MILLER, 1841–1913

Critical Essay . . . 187
Kit Carson's Ride . . . 188
Good and Bad . . . 192

SIDNEY LANIER, 1842–1881

Critical Essay, by Richard Burton . . . 193
Song of the Chattahoochee . . . 197
Tampa Robins . . . 199
Evening Song . . . 199
Life and Song . . . 200
From 'The Marshes of Glynn' . . . 200
From the Flats . . . 202
A Ballad of Trees and the Master . . . 202

WILLIAM JAMES, 1842–1910

Critical Essay, by H. M. Kallen . . . 204
The Moral Equivalent of War . . . 207

HENRY JAMES, 1843–1916

Critical Essay, by Stuart P. Sherman . . . 218
The Madonna of the Future . . . 234

GEORGE W. CABLE, 1844–1925

Critical Essay . . . 262
"Posson Jone'" . . . 264

JOEL CHANDLER HARRIS, 1848–1908 PAGE

Critical Essay . . . 279
Why Brother Wolf Didn't Eat the Little Rabbits . . . 281
Brother Mud Turtle's Trickery . . . 284
Uncle Remus at the Telephone . . . 288

SARAH ORNE JEWETT, 1849–1909

Critical Essay . . . 291
Miss Tempy's Watchers . . . 293
The Brandon House . . . 301

JAMES WHITCOMB RILEY, 1849–1916

Critical Essay, by W. D. Howe . . . 303
When She Comes Home . . . 307
A Song . . . 308
Knee-Deep in June . . . 308
Out to Old Aunt Mary's . . . 311
Little Orphant Annie . . . 315
When the Frost is on the Punkin . . . 316
A Life Lesson . . . 317
Away . . . 318
Nothin' to Say . . . 319

LAFCADIO HEARN, 1850–1904

Critical Essay . . . 320
My First Day in the Orient . . . 321
Impressions and Memories . . . 325
The Temple at Kwannon . . . 326
The Shintō Faith . . . 327

JAMES LANE ALLEN, 1849–1925

Critical Essay . . . 329
A Courtship . . . 330

BRANDER MATTHEWS, 1852–1929

Critical Essay, by Ernest Hunter Wright . . . 339
American Character . . . 342

HENRY CUYLER BUNNER, 1855–1896

Critical Essay . . . 356
Triolet . . . 358
The Love-Letters of Smith . . . 358

GEORGE EDWARD WOODBERRY, 1855– PAGE

Critical Essay, by John Erskine 367
At Gibraltar 368
Lines 369
Sodoma's 'Christ Scourged' 369
Song 370

WOODROW WILSON, 1856–1924

Critical Essay, by Roscoe C. E. Brown 372
Address of the President of the United States 378

THEODORE ROOSEVELT, 1858–1919

Critical Essay, by Brander Matthews 385
Citizenship in a Republic 390

OWEN WISTER, 1860–

Critical Essay, by Mary Leland Hunt 406
Specimen Jones 407

WILLIAM SYDNEY PORTER (O. HENRY), 1862–1910

Critical Essay, by Stephen Leacock 423
The Cop and the Anthem 428

MARY WILKINS FREEMAN, 1862–

Critical Essay 433
The Revolt of "Mother" 435

EDITH WHARTON, 1862–

Critical Essay, by Mary Leland Hunt 448
From 'The Reef' 450

FINLEY PETER DUNNE, 1867–

Critical Essay, by Jefferson Butler Fletcher 464
Our Cuban Allies 466
On the Dreyfus Case 468

JACK LONDON, 1876–1916

Critical Essay, by Leland Hall 470
From 'The Sea Wolf' 472

FRANK NORRIS, 1870–1902

PAGE

CRITICAL ESSAY, by Carl Van Doren 481
From 'The Octopus' 483

BOOTH TARKINGTON, 1869–

CRITICAL ESSAY 493
A Boy and His Dog 494
From 'The Turmoil' 498

RICHARD WATSON GILDER, 1844–1909

CRITICAL ESSAY 504
Two Songs from 'The New Day' 505
"Rose-Dark the Solemn Sunset" 505
The Sonnet 506
America 506
On the Life-Mask of Abraham Lincoln 507
"Call Me Not Dead" 507
After-Song 508
From 'Non Sine Dolore' 508

EUGENE FIELD, 1850–1895

CRITICAL ESSAY, by Richard Burton 509
To the Passing Saint 510
Dutch Lullaby 511
Ipswich 513

AMERICAN POETRY SINCE 1900, by Allan Abbott 515

MODERN FICTION, by Blanche Colton Williams 528

MODERN AMERICAN DRAMA, by Frank W. Chandler . . . 538

RECENT AMERICAN HISTORICAL WRITING, by David Saville Muzzey 544

THE NEW ART OF BIOGRAPHY, by Raymond Weaver . . . 555

IN bringing to a conclusion the volumes of the COLUMBIA UNIVERSITY COURSE IN LITERATURE, the Board of Editors desire to express their appreciation of the contribution made not only by those scholars who have prepared the several articles that bear their signatures, but still more those who have exercised expert supervision of one or another of the literatures represented. Volume I, 'The Wisdom of the East,' owes something on every page and a great deal in the aggregate to the editorial care of Professor Louis H. Gray of Columbia University. Similar acknowledgments for expert supervision are due to Professor Carroll N. Brown of the College of the City of New York for Volume II, 'The Glory That Was Greece,' and Volume III, 'The Power of Rome'; to Professors Jefferson B. Fletcher and Arthur Livingston, both of Columbia University, for Volume V, 'The Voice of Italy'; to Professor Bayard Quincy Morgan of the University of Wisconsin for Volume IX, 'The German Mind'; to Professor Clarence A. Manning of Columbia University for the Slavonic section and to Professor Anders Orbeck of the University of Rochester for the Scandinavian section of Volume X, 'Scandinavian and Slavonic Literature'; and to Professor A. Smillie Noad of McGill University for Volume VI, 'Old France and the Revolution,' Volume VII, 'Romance and Realism in Modern France,' and Volume VIII, 'The Great Literature of Small Nations.' Of the members of the Editorial Board, Professor Harry Morgan Ayres undertook more direct supervision of Volume IV, 'Medieval Song and Story'; Professor John W. Cunliffe of Volume XI, 'Shakespeare to Dryden,' Volume XII, 'Pope to Burns,' Volume XIII, 'The Romantic Revival in England,' Volume XIV, 'The Great Victorians,' and Volume XV, 'Writers of Modern England'; and Professor Franklin T. Baker of Volume XVI, 'Early Days in America,' Volume XVII, 'The American Tradition in Letters,' and Volume XVIII, 'Writers of Modern America.'

FRANCIS RICHARD STOCKTON

STOCKTON'S name is commonly associated with a certain quizzical type of story best represented by 'The Lady or the Tiger.' It was, however, an earlier story, 'Rudder Grange,' that gave him his national reputation. His favorite theme is an unusual, almost fantastic, situation carried out in a natural, matter-of-fact way by ordinary and matter-of-fact people.

'The Lady or the Tiger' presents and leaves unanswered a provocative riddle: Would the barbaric princess, who could not have her lover, give him to the tiger or to her rival? Women of gentle nurture have been disagreeing on the matter ever since the story appeared. Stockton always refused to give his own answer to the riddle; from which it may be inferred that he knew something of human nature.

'Rudder Grange' introduces a young married pair and their servant Pomona, living, like the Peggotty family, in an old boat beached and fitted up as a house. Their guilelessness, their naïve optimism, their adjustments to life and to each other are the theme of the story. Its serious way of presenting absurd ideas and ridiculous situations, the freshness and kindliness of its humor, and especially the novelty of the setting for this old theme of comedy — the inexperienced married pair — won for the book a wide and enthusiastic set of readers.

Stockton's best piece of work is 'The Casting Away of Mrs. Lecks and Mrs. Aleshine.' The two village-bred heroines are clearly imagined and drawn without a false line. Into all their startling adventures they carry the same cool though limited judgment, the same practical foresight, the same small-town measure of values. No crises can upset them or make them other than they were when they left home.

He has written also stories of pure adventure. 'The Adventures of Captain Horn' is a tale of treasure trove. The scene is a desert coast of Peru; the gold, hidden from the Spaniards by the Incas of Peru, is found by accident by a group of shipwrecked Americans, and in quantities immense enough to satisfy the most insatiable appetite for romance.

During Stockton's earlier literary period he was on the staff of St. Nicholas. Some of his stories for children have passed into the courses of reading recommended in schools, and bid fair to outlast his other work. Particularly fine are: 'The Bee Man of Orme,' 'Old Pipes and the Dryad,' and 'The Clocks of Rondaine,' which are included in the collection called 'Fanciful Tales.' In their human interest, inventiveness, delicacy of imagination and feeling, and their urbanity and restraint in hinting a moral, they are among the best things in the juvenile literature of the last half century. Here, as in the tales for older people, Stockton is no moralist, but a humorist, a teller of tales with an agile fancy and an engaging style.

THE CASTING AWAY OF MRS. LECKS AND MRS. ALESHINE

From the novel so named. Copyright, 1886, 1892, by Frank R. Stockton. Reprinted by permission of The Century Co., publishers

I WAS on my way from San Francisco to Yokohama, when in a very desultory and gradual manner I became acquainted with Mrs. Lecks and Mrs. Aleshine. The steamer, on which I was making a moderately rapid passage toward the land of the legended fan and the lacquered box, carried a fair complement of passengers, most of whom were Americans; and among these, my attention was attracted from the very first day of the voyage to two middle-aged women who appeared to me very unlike the ordinary traveler or tourist. At first sight they might have been taken for farmers' wives who, for some unusual reason, had determined to make a voyage across the Pacific; but on closer observation, one would have been more apt to suppose that they belonged to the families of prosperous tradesmen in some little country town, where, besides the arts of rural housewifery, there would be opportunities of becoming acquainted in some degree with the ways and manners of the outside world. They were not of that order of persons who generally take first-class passages on steamships, but the state-room occupied by Mrs. Lecks and Mrs. Aleshine was one of the best in the vessel; and although they kept very much to themselves and showed no desire for the company or notice of the other passengers, they evidently considered themselves quite as good as any one else, and with as much right to voyage to any part of the world in any manner or style which pleased them.

Mrs. Lecks was a rather tall woman, large-boned and muscular; and her well-browned countenance gave indications of that conviction of superiority which gradually grows up in the minds of those who, for a long time, have had absolute control of the destinies of a state, or the multifarious affairs of a country household. Mrs. Aleshine was somewhat younger than her friend, somewhat shorter, and a great deal fatter. She had the same air of reliance upon her individual worth that characterized Mrs. Lecks; but there was a certain geniality about her which indicated that she would have a good deal of forbearance for those who never had had the opportunity or the ability of becoming the thoroughly good housewife which she was herself.

These two worthy dames spent the greater part of their time on deck, where they always sat together in a place at the stern of the vessel which was well sheltered from wind and weather. As they sat thus they were generally employed in knitting; although this occupation did not prevent them from keeping up what seemed to me, as I passed them in my walks about the deck, a continuous conversation. From a question which Mrs. Lecks once asked me about a distant sail, our acquaintance began. There was no one on board for whose society I particularly cared; and as there was something quaint and odd about these countrywomen on the ocean which interested me, I was glad to vary my solitary promenades by an occasional chat with them. They were not at all backward in giving me information about themselves. They were both widows, and Mrs. Aleshine was going out to Japan to visit a son who had a position there in a mercantile house. Mrs. Lecks had no children, and was accompanying her friend because, as she said, she would not allow Mrs. Aleshine to make such a voyage as that by herself; and because, being quite able to do so, she did not know why she should not see the world as well as other people.

These two friends were not educated women. They made frequent mistakes in their grammar, and a good deal of Middle States provincialism showed itself in their pronunciation and expressions. But although they brought many of their rural ideas to sea with them, they possessed a large share of that common-sense which is available anywhere, and they frequently made use of it in a manner which was very amusing to me. I think also that they found in me a quarry of information concerning nautical matters, foreign countries, and my own affairs, the working of which helped to make us very good ship friends.

Our steamer touched at the Sandwich Islands; and it was a little more than two days after we left Honolulu, that about nine o'clock in the evening we had the misfortune to come into collision with an eastern-bound vessel. The fault was entirely due to the other ship; the lookout on which, although the night was rather dark and foggy, could easily have seen our lights in time to avoid collision, if he had not been asleep or absent from his post. Be this as it may, this vessel, which appeared to be a small steamer, struck us with great force near our bows, and then backing disappeared into the fog, and we never saw or heard of her again. The general opinion was that she was injured very much more than we were, and that she probably sank not very long after the accident; for when the fog cleared away, about an hour afterward, nothing could be seen of her lights.

As it usually happens on occasions of accidents at sea, the damage to our vessel was at first reported to be slight; but it was soon discovered that our injuries were serious, and indeed disastrous. The hull of our steamer had been badly shattered on the port bow, and the wa[illegible]me in at a most alarming rate. For nearly two hours the crew and man[illegible] the passengers worked at the pumps, and everything possible was done to stop the enormous leak: but all labor to save the vessel was found to be utterly unavailing; and a little before midnight the captain announced that it was impossible to keep the steamer afloat, and that we must all take to the boats. The night was now clear, the stars were bright, and as there was but little wind, the sea was comparatively smooth. With all these advantages, the captain assured us there was no reason to apprehend danger; and he thought that by noon of the following day we could easily make a small inhabited island, where we could be sheltered and cared for until we should be taken off by some passing vessel.

There was plenty of time for all necessary preparations, and these were made with much order and subordination. Some of the ladies among the cabin passengers were greatly frightened, and inclined to be hysterical. There were pale faces also among the gentlemen. But everybody obeyed the captain's orders, and all prepared themselves for the transfer to the boats. The first officer came among us, and told each of us what boats we were to take, and where we were to place ourselves on deck. I was assigned to a large boat which was to be principally occupied by steerage passengers; and as I came up from my state-room, where I had gone to secure my money and some portable valuables, I met on the companion-way Mrs. Lecks and Mrs. Aleshine, who expressed considerable dissatisfaction when they found that I was not going in the boat with them. They however hurried below, and I went on deck; where in about ten minutes I was joined by Mrs. Lecks, who apparently had been looking for me. She told me she had something very particular to say to me, and conducted me toward the stern of the vessel; where, behind one of the deck-houses, we found Mrs. Aleshine.

"Look here," said Mrs. Lecks, leading me to the rail and pointing downward, "do you see that boat there? It has been let down, and there is nobody in it. The boat on the other side has just gone off, full to the brim. I never saw so many people crowded into a boat. The other ones will be just as packed, I expect. I don't see why we shouldn't take this empty boat, now we've got a chance, instead of squeezin' ourselves into those crowded ones. If any of the other people come afterward, why, we shall have our choice of seats; and that's considerable of a p'int, I should say, in a time like this."

"That's so," said Mrs. Aleshine, "and me and Mrs. Lecks would 'a' got right in when we saw the boat was empty, if we hadn't been afraid to be there without any man — for it might have floated off, and neither of us don't know nothin' about rowin'. And then Mrs. Lecks she thought of you, supposin' a young man who knew so much about the sea would know how to row."

"Oh, yes," said I, "but I cannot imagine why this boat should have been left empty. I see a keg of [illegible] in it, and the oars, and some tin cans; and so I suppose it has been made [illegible] for somebody. Will you wait here a minute until I run forward and see how things are going on there?"

Amidships and forward I saw that there was some confusion among the people who were not yet in their boats, and I found that there was to be rather more crowding than at first was expected. People who had supposed that they were to go in a certain boat found there no place, and were hurrying to other boats. It now became plain to me that no time should be lost in getting into the small boat which Mrs. Lecks had pointed out, and which was probably reserved for some favored persons, as the officers were keeping the people forward and amidships, the other stern-boat having already departed. But as I acknowledged no reason why any one should be regarded with more favor than myself and the two women who were waiting for me, I slipped quietly aft, and joined Mrs. Lecks and Mrs. Aleshine.

"We must get in as soon as we can," said I in a low voice, "for this boat may be discovered, and then there will be a rush for it. I suspect it may have been reserved for the captain and some of the officers, but we have as much right in it as they."

"And more too," replied Mrs. Lecks; "for we had nothin' to do with the steerin' and smashin'."

"But how are we goin' to get down there?" said Mrs. Aleshine. "There's no steps."

"That is true," said I. "I shouldn't wonder if this boat is to be taken forward when the others are filled. We must scramble down as well as we can by the tackle at the bow and stern. I'll get in first and keep her close to the ship's side."

"That's goin' to be a scratchy business," said Mrs. Lecks; "and I'm of the opinion we ought to wait till the ship has sunk a little more, so we'll be nearer to the boat."

"It won't do to wait," said I, "or we shall not get in at all."

"And goodness gracious!" exclaimed Mrs. Aleshine, "I can't stand here and feel the ship sinkin' cold-blooded under me, till we've got where we can make an easy jump!"

"Very well, then," said Mrs. Lecks, "we won't wait. But the first thing to be done is for each one of us to put on one of these life-preservers. Two of them I brought from Mrs. Aleshine's and my cabin, and the other I got next door, where the people had gone off and left it on the floor. I thought if anythin' happened on the way to the island, these would give us a chance to look about us; but it seems to me we'll need 'em more gettin' down them ropes than anywhere else. I did intend puttin' on two myself to make up for Mrs. Aleshine's fat; but you must wear one of 'em, sir, now that you are goin' to join the party."

As I knew that two life-preservers would not be needed by Mrs. Lecks, and would greatly inconvenience her, I accepted the one offered me; but declined to put it on until it should be necessary, as it would interfere with my movements.

"Very well," said Mrs. Lecks, "if you think you are safe in gettin' down without it. But Mrs. Aleshine and me will put ours on before we begin sailor-scramblin'. We know how to do it, for we tried 'em on soon after we started from San Francisco. And now, Barb'ry Aleshine, are you sure you've got everythin' you want? for it'll be no use thinkin' about anythin' you've forgot after the ship has sunk out of sight."

"There's nothin' else I can think of," said Mrs. Aleshine — "at least nothin' I can carry; and so I suppose we may as well begin, for your talk of the ship sinkin' under our feet gives me a sort o' feelin' like an oyster creepin' up and down my back."

Mrs. Lecks looked over the side at the boat, into which I had already descended. "I'll go first, Barb'ry Aleshine," said she, "and show you how."

The sea was quiet, and the steamer had already sunk so much that Mrs. Leck's voice sounded frightfully near me, although she spoke in a low tone.

"Watch me," said she to her companion. "I'm goin' to do just as he did, and you must follow in the same way."

So saying, she stepped on a bench by the rail; then, with one foot on the rail itself, she seized the ropes which hung from one of the davits to the bow of the boat. She looked down for a moment, and then she drew back.

"It's no use," she said. "We must wait until she sinks more, an' I can get in easier."

This remark made me feel nervous. I did not know at what moment there might be a rush for this boat, nor when indeed the steamer might go down. The boat amidships on our side had rowed away some minutes before, and through the darkness I could distinguish another boat, near the bows, pushing off. It would be too late now for us to try to get into any other boat, and I did not feel that there was time enough for me to take this one to a place where the two women could more easily descend to her. Standing upright, I urged them not to delay.

"You see," said I, "I can reach you as soon as you swing yourself off the ropes, and I'll help you down."

"If you're sure you can keep us from comin' down too sudden, we'll try it," said Mrs. Lecks, "but I'd as soon be drowned as to get to an island with a broken leg. And as to Mrs. Aleshine, if she was to slip she'd go slam through that boat to the bottom of the sea. Now then, be ready! I'm comin' down!"

So saying, she swung herself off, and she was then so near me that I was able to seize her and make the rest of her descent comparatively easy. Mrs. Aleshine proved to be a more difficult subject. Even after I had a firm grasp of her capacious waist she refused to let go the ropes, for fear that she might drop into the ocean instead of the boat. But the reproaches of Mrs. Lecks and the downward weight of myself made her loosen her nervous grip; and although we came very near going overboard together, I safely placed her on one of the thwarts.

I now unhooked the tackle from the stern; but before casting off at the bow, I hesitated, for I did not wish to desert any of those who might be expecting to embark in this boat. But I could hear no approaching footsteps; and from my position, close to the side of the steamer, I could see nothing. Therefore I cast off, and taking the oars, I pushed away and rowed to a little distance, where I could get whatever view was possible of the deck of the steamer. Seeing no forms moving about, I called out, and receiving no answer, I shouted again at the top of my voice. I waited for nearly a minute; and hearing nothing and seeing nothing, I became convinced that no one was left on the vessel.

"They are all gone," said I, "and we will pull after them as fast as we can."

And I began to row toward the bow of the steamer, in the direction which the other boats had taken.

"It's a good thing you can row," said Mrs. Lecks, settling herself comfortably in the stern-sheets, "for what Mrs. Aleshine and me would ha' done with them oars, I am sure I don't know."

"I'd never have got into this boat," said Mrs. Aleshine, "if Mr. Craig hadn't been here."

"No, indeed," replied her friend. "You'd ha' gone to the bottom, hangin' for dear life to them ropes."

When I had rounded the bow of the steamer, which appeared to me to be rapidly settling in the water, I perceived at no great distance several lights which of course belonged to the other boats; and I rowed as hard as I could, hoping to catch up with them, or at least to keep sufficiently near. It might be my duty to take off some of the people who had crowded into the other boats, probably supposing that this one had been loaded and gone. How such a mistake could have taken place I could not divine, and it was not my business to do so. Quite certain that no one was left on the sinking steamer, all I had to do was to row after the other boats, and to overtake them as soon as possible. I thought it would not take me very long to do this; but after rowing for half an hour, Mrs. Aleshine remarked that the lights seemed as far off as, if not farther than, when we first started after them. Turning, I saw that this was the case, and was greatly surprised. With only two passengers I ought soon to have come up with those heavily laden boats; but after I had thought over it a little, I considered that as each of them was probably pulled by half a dozen stout sailors, it was not so very strange that they should make as good or better headway than I did.

It was not very long after this that Mrs. Lecks said that she thought the lights on the other boats must be going out; and that this, most probably, was due to the fact that the sailors had forgotten to fill their lanterns before they started. "That sort of thing often happens," she said, "when people leave a place in a hurry."

But when I turned around, and peered over the dark waters, it was quite plain to me that it was not want of oil, but increased distance, which made those lights so dim. I could now perceive but three of them; and as the surface was agitated only by a gentle swell, I could not suppose that any of them were hidden from our view by waves. We were being left behind, that was certain; and all I could do was to row on as long and as well as I could in the direction which the other boats had taken. I had been used to rowing, and thought I pulled a good oar, and I certainly did not expect to be left behind in this way.

"I don't believe this boat has been emptied out since the last rain," said Mrs. Aleshine; "for my feet are wet, though I didn't notice it before."

At this I shipped my oars, and began to examine the boat. The bottom was covered with a movable floor of slats, and as I put my hand down I could feel the water welling up between the slats. The flooring was in sections; and lifting the one beneath me, I felt under it, and put my hand into six or eight inches of water.

The exact state of the case was now as plain to me as if it had been posted up on a bulletin-board. This boat had been found to be unseaworthy, and its use had been forbidden, all the people having been crowded into the others. This had caused confusion at the last moment, and of course we were supposed to be on some one of the other boats.

And now, here was I, in the middle of the Pacific Ocean, in a leaky boat with two middle-aged women!

"Anythin' the matter with the floor?" asked Mrs. Lecks.

I let the section fall back into its place and looked aft. By the starlight I could see that my two companions had each fixed upon me a steadfast gaze. They evidently felt that something was the matter, and wanted to know what it was. I did not hesitate for a moment to inform them. They appeared to me to be women whom it would be neither advisable nor possible to deceive in a case like this.

"This boat has a leak in it," I said. "There is a lot of water in her already, and that is the reason we have got along so slowly."

"And that is why," said Mrs. Aleshine, "it was left empty. We ought to have known better than to expect to have a whole boat just for three of us. It would have been much more sensible, I think, if we had tried to squeeze into one of the others."

"Now, Barb'ry Aleshine," said Mrs. Lecks, "don't you begin findin' fault with good fortune when it comes to you. Here we've got a comfortable boat, with room enough to set easy and stretch out if we want to. If the water is comin' in, what we've got to do is to get it out again just as fast as we can. What's the best way to do that, Mr. Craig?"

"We must bail her out, and lose no time about it," said I. "If I can find the leak I may be able to stop it."

I now looked about for something to bail with, and the two women aided actively in the search. I found one leather scoop in the bow; but as it was well that we should all go to work, I took two tin cans that had been put in by some one who had begun to provision the boat, and proceeded to cut the tops from them with my jack-knife.

"Don't lose what's in 'em," said Mrs. Lecks; "that is, if it's anythin' we'd be likely to want to eat. If it's tomatoes, pour it into the sea, for nobody ought to eat tomatoes put up in tins."

I hastily passed the cans to Mrs. Lecks, and I saw her empty the contents of one into the sea, and those of the other on a newspaper which she took from her pocket and placed in the stern.

I pulled up the movable floor and threw it overboard, and then began to bail.

"I thought," said Mrs. Aleshine, "that they always had pumps for leaks."

"Now, Barb'ry Aleshine," said Mrs. Lecks, "just gether yourself up on one of them seats and go to work. The less talkin' we do and the more scoopin', the better it'll be for us."

I soon perceived that it would have been difficult to find two more valuable assistants in the bailing of a boat than Mrs. Lecks and Mrs. Aleshine. They were evidently used to work, and were able to accommodate themselves to the unusual circumstances in which they were placed. We threw out the water very rapidly, and every little while I stopped bailing and felt about to see if I could discover where it came in. As these attempts met with no success, I gave them up after a time, and set about bailing with new vigor, believing that if we could get the boat nearly dry, I should surely be able to find the leak.

But after working half an hour more, I found that the job would be a long one; and if we all worked at once, we should all be tired out at once, and that might be disastrous. Therefore I proposed that we should take turns in resting, and Mrs. Aleshine was ordered to stop work for a time. After this Mrs. Lecks took a rest, and when she went to work I stopped bailing and began again to search for the leak.

For about two hours we worked in this way, and then I concluded it was useless to continue any longer this vain exertion. With three of us bailing we were able to keep the water at the level we first found it; but with only two at work it slightly gained upon us, so that now there was more water in the boat than when we first discovered it. The boat was an iron one, and the leak in it I could neither find nor remedy. It had probably been caused by the warping of the metal under a hot sun; an accident which, I am told, frequently occurs to iron boats. The little craft, which would have been a life-boat had its air-boxes remained intact, was now probably leaking from stem to stern; and in searching for the leak without the protection of the flooring, my weight had doubtless assisted in opening the seams, for it was quite plain that the water was now coming in more rapidly than it did at first. We were very tired; and even Mrs. Lecks, who had all along counseled us to keep at work and not to waste one breath in talking, now admitted that it was of no use to try to get the water out of that boat.

It had been some hours since I had used the oars, but whether we had drifted or remained where we were when I stopped rowing, of course I could not know; but this mattered very little — our boat was slowly sinking beneath us, and it could make no difference whether we went down in one spot or another. I sat and racked my brain to think what could be done in this fearful emergency. To bail any longer was useless labor, and what else was there that we could do?

"When will it be time," asked Mrs. Lecks, "for us to put on the life-preservers? When the water gets nearly to the seats?"

I answered that we should not wait any longer than that, but in my own mind I could not see any advantage in putting them on at all. Why should we wish to lengthen our lives by a few hours of helpless floating upon the ocean?

"Very good," said Mrs. Lecks: "I'll keep watch on the water. One of them cans was filled with lobster, which would be more than likely to disagree with us, and I've throwed it out; but the other had baked beans in it, and the best thing we can do is to eat some of these right away. They are mighty nourishin', and will keep up strength as well as anythin'; and then, as you said there's a keg of water in the boat, we can all take a drink of that, and it'll make us feel like new creatur's. You'll have to take the beans in your hands, for we've got no spoons nor forks."

Mrs. Lecks and Mrs. Aleshine were each curled up out of reach of the water, the first in the stern, and the other on the aft thwart. The day was now beginning to break, and we could see about us very distinctly. Before reaching out her hands to receive her beans, Mrs. Aleshine washed them in the water in the boat, remarking at the same time that she might as well make use of it since it was there. Having then wiped her hands on some part of her apparel, they were filled with beans from the newspaper held by Mrs. Lecks, and these were passed over to me. I was very hungry; and when I had finished my beans, I agreed with my companions that although they would have been a great deal better if heated up with butter, pepper, and salt, they were very comforting as they were. One of the empty cans was now passed to me; and after having been asked by Mrs. Lecks to rinse it out very carefully, we all satisfied our thirst from the water in the keg.

"Cold baked beans and lukewarm water ain't exactly company victuals," said Mrs. Aleshine, "but there's many a poor wretch would be glad to get 'em."

I could not imagine any poor wretch who could be glad of the food together with the attending circumstances; but I did not say so.

"The water is just one finger from the bottom of the seat," said Mrs. Lecks, who had been stooping over to measure, "and it's time to put on the life-preservers."

"Very good," said Mrs. Aleshine: "hand me mine."

Each of us now buckled on a life-preserver; and as I did so, I stood up upon a thwart and looked about me. It was quite light now, and I could see for a long distance over the surface of the ocean, which was gently rolling in wide, smooth swells. As we rose upon the summit of one of these I saw a dark spot upon the water, just on the edge of our near horizon. "Is that the steamer?" I thought; "and has she not yet sunk?"

At this there came to me a glimmering of courageous hope. If the steamer had remained afloat so long, it was probable that on account of water-tight compartments, or for some other reason, her sinking had reached its limit, and that if we could get back to her we might be saved. But alas, how were we to get back to her? This boat would sink long, long before I could row that distance.

However, I soon proclaimed the news to my companions, whereupon Mrs. Aleshine prepared to stand upon a thwart and see for herself. But Mrs. Lecks restrained her.

"Don't make things worse, Barb'ry Aleshine," said she, "by tumblin' overboard. If we've got to go into the water, let us do it decently and in order. If that's the ship, Mr. Craig, don't you suppose we can float ourselves to it in some way?"

I replied that by the help of a life-preserver a person who could swim might reach the ship.

"But neither of us can swim," said Mrs. Lecks; "for we've lived where the water was never more'n a foot deep — except in time of freshets, when there's no swimmin' for man or beast. But if we see you swim perhaps we can follow, after a fashion. At any rate, we must do the best we can, and that's all there is to be done."

"The water now," remarked Mrs. Aleshine, "is so near to the bottom of my seat that I've got to stand up, tumble overboard or no."

"All right," remarked Mrs. Lecks: "we'd better all stand up, and let the boat sink under us. That will save our jumpin' overboard, or rollin' out any which way, which might be awkward."

"Goodness gracious me!" exclaimed Mrs. Aleshine. "You set the oysters creepin' over me again! First you talk of the ship sinkin' under us, and now it's the boat goin' to the bottom under our feet. Before any sinkin' 's to be done I'd ruther get out."

"Now, Barb'ry Aleshine," said Mrs. Lecks, "stand up straight and don't talk so much. It'll be a great deal better to be let down gradual than to flop into the water all of a bunch."

"Very well," said Mrs. Aleshine. "It may be best to get used to it by degrees, but I must say I wish I was home."

As for me, I would have much preferred to jump overboard at once, instead of waiting in this cold-blooded manner; but as my companions had so far preserved their presence of mind, I did not wish to do anything which might throw them into a panic. I believed there would be no danger from the suction caused by the sinking of a small boat like this; and if we took care not to entangle ourselves with it in any way, we might as well follow Mrs. Lecks's advice as not. So we all stood up, Mrs. Lecks in the stern, I in the bow, and Mrs. Aleshine on a thwart between us. The last did not appear to have quite room enough for a steady footing; but as she remarked, it did not matter very much, as the footing, broad or narrow, would not be there very long.

I am used to swimming, and have never hesitated to take a plunge into river or ocean; but I must admit that it was very trying to my nerves to stand up this way and wait for a boat to sink beneath me. How the two women were affected I do not know. They said nothing; but their faces indicated that something disagreeable was about to happen, and that the less that was said about it the better.

The boat had now sunk so much that the water was around Mrs. Aleshine's feet, her standing-place being rather lower than ours. I made myself certain that there were no ropes nor any other means of entanglement near my companions or myself, and then I waited. There seemed to be a good deal of buoyancy in the bow and stern of the boat, and it was a frightfully long time in sinking. The suspense became so utterly unendurable that I was tempted to put one foot on the edge of the boat, and by tipping it, put an end to this nerve-rack; but I refrained, for I probably should throw the women off their balance, when they might fall against some part of the boat and do themselves a hurt. I had just relinquished this intention, when two little waves seemed to rise one on each side of Mrs. Aleshine; and gently flowing over the side of the boat, they flooded her feet with water.

"Hold your breaths!" I shouted. And now I experienced a sensation which must have been very like that which comes to a condemned criminal at the first indication of the pulling of the drop. Then there was a horrible sinking, a gurgle, and a swash; and the ocean, over which I had been gazing, appeared to rise up and envelop me.

In a moment, however, my head was out of the water; and looking hastily about me, I saw close by the heads and shoulders of Mrs. Lecks and Mrs. Aleshine. The latter was vigorously winking her eyes and blowing from her mouth some sea-water that had got into it; but as soon as her eyes fell upon me she exclaimed, "That was ever so much more suddint than I thought it was goin' to be!"

"Are you both all right?"

"I suppose I am," said Mrs. Aleshine; "but I never thought that a person with a life-preserver on would go clean under the water."

"But since you've come up again, you ought to be satisfied," said Mrs. Lecks. "And now," she added, turning her face toward me, "which way ought we to try to swim? and have we got everythin' we want to take with us?"

"What we haven't got we can't get," remarked Mrs. Aleshine; "and as for swimmin', I expect I'm goin' to make a poor hand at it."

I had a hope, which was not quite strong enough to be a belief, that, supported by their life-preservers, the two women might paddle themselves along; and that by giving them in turn a helping hand, I might eventually get them to the steamer. There was a strong probability that I should not succeed, but I did not care to think of that.

I now swam in front of my companions, and endeavored to instruct them in the best method of propelling themselves with their arms and their hands. If they succeeded in this, I thought I would give them some further lessons in striking out with their feet. After watching me attentively, Mrs. Lecks did manage to move herself slowly through the smooth water; but poor Mrs. Aleshine could do nothing but splash.

"If there was anythin' to take hold of," she said to me, "I might get along; but I can't get any grip on the water, though you seem to do it well enough. Look there! " she added in a higher voice. "Isn't that an oar floatin' over there? If you can get that for me, I believe I can row myself much better than I can swim."

This seemed an odd idea; but I swam over to the floating oar, and brought it to her. I was about to show her how she could best use it, but she declined my advice.

"If I do it at all," she said, "I must do it in my own way." And taking the oar in her strong hands, she began to ply it on the water, very much in the way in which she would handle a broom. At first she dipped the blade too deeply, but correcting this error, she soon began to paddle herself along at a slow but steady rate.

"Capital! " I cried. "You do that admirably! "

"Anybody who's swept as many rooms as I have," she said, "ought to be able to handle anythin' that can be used like a broom."

"Isn't there another oar? " cried Mrs. Lecks, who had now been left a little distance behind us. "If there is, I want one."

Looking about me, I soon discovered another floating oar, and brought it to Mrs. Lecks; who, after holding it in various positions, so as to get "the hang of it," as she said, soon began to use it with as much skill as that shown by her friend. If either of them had been obliged to use an oar in the ordinary way, I fear they would have had a bad time of it; but considering the implement in the light of a broom, its use immediately became familiar to them, and they got on remarkably well.

I now took a position a little in advance of my companions, and as I swam slowly they were easily able to keep up with me. Mrs. Aleshine, being so stout, floated much higher out of the water than either Mrs. Lecks or I, and this permitted her to use her oar with a great deal of freedom. Sometimes she would give such a vigorous brush to the water that she would turn herself almost entirely around; but after a little practice she learned to avoid undue efforts of this kind.

I was not positively sure that we were going in the right direction, for my position did not allow me to see very far over the water; but I remembered that when I was standing up in the boat and made my discovery, the sun was just about to rise in front of me, while the dark spot on the ocean lay to my left. Judging, therefore, from the present position of the sun, which was not very high, I concluded that we were moving toward the north, and therefore in the right direction. How far off the steamer might be, I had no idea, for I was not accustomed to judging distances at sea; but I believed that if we were careful of our strength, and if the ocean continued as smooth as it now was, we might eventually reach the vessel, provided she were yet afloat.

"After you are fairly in the water," said Mrs. Aleshine, as she swept along, although without the velocity which that phrase usually implies, "it isn't half so bad as I thought it would be. For one thing, it don't feel a bit salt, although I must say it tasted horribly that way when I first went into it."

"You didn't expect to find pickle-brine, did you?" said Mrs. Lecks. "Though if it was, I suppose we could float on it settin'."

"And as to bein' cold," said Mrs. Aleshine, "the part of me that's in is actually more comfortable than that which is out."

"There's one thing I would have been afraid of," said Mrs. Lecks, "if we hadn't made preparations for it, and that's sharks."

"Preparations!" I exclaimed. "How in the world did you prepare for sharks?"

"Easy enough," said Mrs. Lecks. "When we went down into our room to get ready to go away in the boats, we both put on black stockin's. I've read that sharks never bite colored people, although if they see a white man in the water they'll snap him up as quick as lightnin'; and black stockin's was the nearest we could come to it. You see, I thought as like as not we'd have some sort of an upset before we got through."

"It's a great comfort," remarked Mrs. Aleshine; "and I'm very glad you thought of it, Mrs. Lecks. After this I shall make it a rule: Black stockin's for sharks."

"I suppose in your case," said Mrs. Lecks, addressing me, "dark trousers will do as well."

To which I answered that I sincerely hoped they would.

"Another thing I'm thankful for," said Mrs. Aleshine, "is that I thought to put on a flannel skeert."

"And what's the good of it," said Mrs. Lecks, "when it's soppin' wet?"

"Flannel's flannel," replied her friend, "whether it's wet or dry; and if you'd had the rheumatism as much as I have, you'd know it."

To this Mrs. Lecks replied with a sniff, and asked me how soon I thought we would get sight of the ship; for if we were going the wrong way, and had to turn round and go back, it would certainly be very provoking.

I should have been happy indeed to be able to give a satisfactory answer to this question. Every time that we rose upon a swell I threw a rapid glance around the whole circle of the horizon; and at last, not a quarter of an hour after Mrs. Lecks's question, I was rejoiced to see, almost in the direction in which I supposed it ought to be, the dark spot which I had before discovered. I shouted the glad news, and as we rose again my companions strained their eyes in the direction to which I pointed. They both saw it, and were greatly satisfied.

"Now then," said Mrs. Aleshine, "it seems as if there was somethin' to work for"; and she began to sweep her oar with great vigor.

"If you want to tire yourself out before you get there, Barb'ry Aleshine," said Mrs. Lecks, "you'd better go on in that way. Now what I advise is, that we stop rowin' altogether and have somethin' to eat; for I'm sure we need it to keep up our strength."

"Eat!" I cried. "What are you going to eat? Do you expect to catch fish?"

"And eat 'em raw?" said Mrs. Lecks. "I should think not. But do you suppose, Mr. Craig, that Mrs. Aleshine and me would go off and leave that ship without takin' somethin' to eat by the way? Let's all gether here in a bunch, and see what sort of a meal we can make. And now, Barb'ry Aleshine, if you lay your oar down there on the water, I recommend you to tie it to one of your bonnet-strings, or it'll be floatin' away, and you won't get it again."

As she said this, Mrs. Lecks put her right hand down into the water and fumbled about, apparently in search of a pocket. I could not but smile, as I thought of the condition of food when for an hour or more it had been a couple of feet under the surface of the ocean; but my ideas on the subject were entirely changed when I saw Mrs. Lecks hold up in the air two German sausages, and shake the briny drops from their smooth and glittering surfaces.

"There's nothin'," she said, "like sausages for shipwreck and that kind o' thing. They're very sustainin'; and bein' covered with a tight skin, water can't get at 'em, no matter how you carry 'em. I wouldn't bring these out in the boat, because havin' the beans we might as well eat them. Have you a knife about you, Mr. Craig?"

I produced a dripping jack-knife; and after the open blade had been waved in the air to dry it a little, Mrs. Lecks proceeded to divide one of the sausages, handing the other to me to hold meanwhile.

"Now don't go eatin' sausages without bread, if you don't want 'em to give you dyspepsy," said Mrs. Aleshine, who was tugging at a submarine pocket.

"I'm very much afraid your bread is all soaked," said Mrs. Lecks.

To which her friend replied that that remained to be seen, and forthwith produced with a splash a glass preserve-jar with a metal top.

"I saw this nearly empty as I looked into the ship's pantry, and I stuffed into it all the soft biscuits it would hold. There was some sort of jam left at the bottom, so that the one who gets the last biscuit will have somethin' of a little spread on it. And now, Mrs. Lecks," she continued triumphantly, as she unscrewed the top, "that rubber ring has kept 'em as dry as chips. I'm mighty glad of it, for I had trouble enough gettin' this jar into my pocket — and gettin' it out, too, for that matter."

Floating thus, with our hands and shoulders above the water, we made a very good meal from the sausages and soft biscuit.

"Barb'ry Aleshine," said Mrs. Lecks, as her friend proceeded to cut the second sausage, "don't you lay that knife down when you've done with it, as if 't was an oar; for if you do it'll sink, as like as not, about six miles. I've read that the ocean is as deep as that in some places."

"Goodness gracious me!" exclaimed Mrs. Aleshine, "I hope we are not over one of them deep spots."

"There's no knowin'," said Mrs. Lecks; "but if it's more comfortin' to think it's shallerer, we'll make up our minds that way. Now then," she continued, "we'll finish off this meal with a little somethin' to drink. I'm not given to takin' spirits; but I never travel without a little whisky, ready mixed with water, to take if it should be needed."

So saying, she produced from one of her pockets a whisky flask tightly corked, and of its contents we each took a sip; Mrs. Aleshine remarking that leaving out being chilled or colicky, we were never likely to need it more than now.

Thus refreshed and strengthened, Mrs. Lecks and Mrs. Aleshine took up their oars, while I swam slightly in advance, as before. When, with occasional intermissions of rest, and a good deal of desultory conversation, we had swept and swam for about an hour, Mrs. Lecks suddenly exclaimed, "I can see that thing ever so much plainer now, and I don't believe it's a ship at all. To me it looks like bushes."

"You're mighty long-sighted without your specs," said Mrs. Aleshine, "and I'm not sure but what you're right."

For ten minutes or more I had been puzzling over the shape of the dark spot, which was now nearly all the time in sight. Its peculiar form had filled me with a dreadful fear that it was the steamer, bottom upward; although I knew enough about nautical matters to have no good reason to suppose that this could be the case. I am not far-sighted; but when Mrs. Lecks suggested bushes, I gazed at the distant object with totally different ideas, and soon began to believe that it was not a ship, either right side up or wrong side up, but that it might be an island. This belief I proclaimed to my companions; and for some time we all worked with increased energy, in the desire to get near enough to make ourselves certain in regard to this point.

"As true as I'm standin' here," said Mrs. Lecks, who, although she could not read without spectacles, had remarkably good sight at long range, "them is trees and bushes that I see before me, though they do seem to be growin' right out of the water."

"There's an island under them; you may be sure of that!" I cried. "And isn't this ever so much better than a sinking ship?"

"I'm not so sure about that," said Mrs. Aleshine. "I'm used to the ship, and as long as it didn't sink I'd prefer it. There's plenty to eat on board of it, and good beds to sleep on, which is more than can be expected on a little bushy place like that ahead of us. But then the ship might sink all of a suddint — beds, victuals, and all."

"Do you suppose that is the island the other boats went to?" asked Mrs. Lecks.

This question I had already asked of myself. I had been told that the island to which the captain intended to take his boats lay about thirty miles south of the point where we left the steamer. Now, I knew very well that we had not come thirty miles; and had reasons to believe, moreover, that the greater part of the progress we had made had been toward the north. It was not at all probable that the position of this island was unknown to our captain; and it must therefore have been considered by him as an unsuitable place for the landing of his passengers. There might be many reasons for this unsuitableness: the island might be totally barren and desolate; it might be the abode of unpleasant natives; and more important than anything else, it was in all probability a spot where steamers never touched.

But whatever its disadvantages, I was most wildly desirous to reach it; more so, I believe, than either of my companions. I do not mean that they were not sensible of their danger, and desirous to be freed from it; but they were women who had probably had a rough time of it during a great part of their lives, and on emerging from their little circle of rural experiences accepted with equanimity, and almost as a matter of course, the rough times which come to people in the great outside world.

"I do not believe," I said, in answer to Mrs. Lecks, "that that is the island to which the captain would have taken us; but whatever it is, it is dry land, and we must get there as soon as we can."

"That's true," said Mrs. Aleshine, "for I'd like to have ground nearer to my feet than six miles; and if we don't find anythin' to eat and any place to sleep when we get there, it's no more than can be said of where we are now."

"You're too particular, Barb'ry Aleshine," said Mrs. Lecks, "about your comforts. If you find the ground too hard to sleep on when you get there, you can put on your life-preserver, and go to bed in the water."

"Very good," said Mrs. Aleshine; "and if these islands are made of coral, as I've heard they was, and if they're as full of small p'ints as some coral I've got at home, you'll be glad to take a berth by me, Mrs. Lecks."

I counseled my companions to follow me as rapidly as possible, and we all pushed vigorously forward. When we had approached near enough to the island to see what sort of place it really was, we perceived that it was a low-lying spot, apparently covered with verdure, and surrounded, as far as we could see as we rose on the swells, by a rocky reef, against which a tolerably high surf was running. I knew enough of the formation of these coral islands to suppose that within this reef was a lagoon of smooth water, into which there were openings through the rocky barrier. It was necessary to try to find one of these; for it would be difficult and perhaps dangerous to attempt to land through the surf.

Before us we could see a continuous line of white-capped breakers; and so I led my little party to the right, hoping that we should soon see signs of an opening in the reef.

We swam and paddled, however, for a long time, and still the surf rolled menacingly on the rocks before us. We were now as close to the island as we could approach with safety; and I determined to circumnavigate it, if necessary, before I would attempt with these two women to land upon that jagged reef. At last we perceived, at no great distance before us, a spot where there seemed to be no breakers; and when we reached it we found, to our unutterable delight, that here was smooth water flowing through a wide opening in the reef. The rocks were piled up quite high, and the reef, at this point at least, was a wide one; for as we neared the opening we found that it narrowed very soon and made a turn to the left, so that from the outside we could not see into the lagoon.

I swam into this smooth water, followed close by Mrs. Lecks and Mrs. Aleshine — who, however, soon became unable to use their oars, owing to the proximity of the rocks. Dropping these useful implements, they managed to paddle after me with their hands; and they were as much astonished as I was when, just after making the slight turn, we found stretched across the narrow passage a great iron bar about eight or ten inches above the water. A little farther on, and two or three feet above the water, another iron bar extended from one rocky wall to the other. Without uttering a word I examined the lower bar, and found one end of it fastened by means of a huge padlock to a great staple driven into the rock. The lock was securely wrapped in what appeared to be tarred canvas. A staple through an eyehole in the bar secured the other end of it to the rocks.

"These bars were put here," I exclaimed, "to keep out boats, whether at high or low water. You see they can only be thrown out of the way by taking off the padlocks."

"They won't keep us out," said Mrs. Lecks, "for we can duck under. I suppose whoever put 'em here didn't expect anybody to arrive on life-preservers."

JOHN MUIR

JOHN MUIR, an explorer and naturalist, whose field of work was particularly the western and northwestern mountain regions of America — where at least one great glacier now bears his name — was born at Dunbar, Scotland, in 1837. With his parents and a large flock of brothers and sisters, he came to the United States in 1850, after some good common-schooling in Dunbar. He began his study of nature in the region near Fort Winnebago, Wisconsin, with an ever increasing interest and delight in whatever belongs to the world of creatures, plants, and stones, particularly in the waving solitudes of forests and rock-and-snow tracts of the northwestern Sierras.

Muir's freedom to devote himself to a life of observation and record was delayed: and in the story of his years of manual work as a farmer, mechanic, lumberman, sheep-herder, and what not besides, there comes surprise at his power to find time and energy for other pursuits in the nature of an avocation; and with the surprise we have a sense of pleasure that a man of untiring muscles and mind could win free of all that checked his natural preferences. He studied grammar and mathematics while a farm hand, and read through a library of books when in the fields. He earned enough as a young man to give himself four years of special scientific study in the University of Wisconsin. Then began an independent life, in which he alternated seasons of hard work, wholly or much alone; partly through the circumstances of his wanderings, partly by his own choice. It is said that during ten years of mountaineering in the remoter Sierras, he met no men except one band of Mono tribesmen.

For some ten summers and winters prior to 1876, Muir was settled near the Yosemite district. In the year named he became a member of the Geodetic Survey of the Great Basin, and attempted much botanical work. During 1879 and subsequently, after he reached Alaska, he explored and charted its vast mountain ranges, discovered Glacier Bay and the Muir Glacier system; and with that expedition and the two succeeding tours he became the foremost authority on Alaska's geologic and other natural aspects. He also visited the Yukon and Mackenzie Rivers, and traversed the cañon country of California. He was of the party on board the Corwin in 1881, sent out to trace the lost Jeannette, which enterprise added largely to his sketches and notes for scientific use. After 1879, the year of his marriage, Muir had his home in California; but to find him in it at other than a given time, was somewhat an accident, so indefatigable was his industry as a naturalist. He died in 1914.

Muir wrote much less than his explorations would suggest: but as a contributor to the highest class of American and foreign periodicals, and the author of volumes dealing with his experiences, impressions, and discoveries, he was a writer of distinct and unusual individuality. He was less a man of letters in his manner than he was the direct, graphic, and sincere observer, whose aim was to write down simply what he saw or felt, to put the reader in the quickest and closest touch with a topic or a scene. But the simplicity and personal effect of his style give it a peculiar vigor and eloquence, and he has won wide favor through descriptive pages which are splendid for spontaneous and vivid prose pictures of great scenery — studies of the wind's movement of a pine forest, or a delicate flower of California, or a wild-bird's lonely nest.

A WIND-STORM IN THE FORESTS

From 'The Mountains of California.' Copyright, 1894, by The Century Company

THE mountain winds, like the dew and rain, sunshine and snow, are measured and bestowed with love on the forests, to develop their strength and beauty. However restricted the scope of other forest influences, that of the winds is universal. The snow bends and trims the upper forests every winter, the lightning strikes a single tree here and there, while avalanches mow down thousands at a swoop as a gardener trims out a bed of flowers. But the winds go to every tree, fingering every leaf and branch and furrowed bole; not one is forgotten: the Mountain Pine towering with outstretched arms on the rugged buttresses of the icy peaks, the lowliest and most retiring tenant of the dens — they seek and find them all, caressing them tenderly, bending them in lusty exercise, stimulating their growth, plucking off a leaf or limb as required, or removing an entire tree or grove, now whispering and cooing through the branches like a sleepy child, now roaring like the ocean; the winds blessing the forests, the forests the winds, with ineffable beauty and harmony as the sure result.

After one has seen pines six feet in diameter bending like grasses before a mountain gale, and ever and anon some giant falling with a crash that shakes the hills, it seems astonishing that any, save the lowest thick-set trees, could ever have found a period sufficiently stormless to establish themselves; or once established, that they should not sooner or later have been blown down. But when the storm is over, and we behold the same forests tranquil again, towering fresh and unscathed in erect majesty, and consider what centuries of storms have fallen upon them since they were first planted: hail, to break the tender seedlings; lightning, to scorch and shatter; snow, winds, and avalanches, to crush and overwhelm — while the manifest result of all this wild storm-culture is the glorious perfection we behold: then faith in Nature's forestry is established, and we cease to deplore the violence of her most destructive gales, or of any other storm implement whatsoever.

There are two trees in the Sierra forests that are never blown down, so long as they continue in sound health. These are the Juniper and the Dwarf Pine of the summit peaks. Their stiff, crooked roots grip the storm-beaten ledges like eagles' claws; while their lithe, cord-like branches bend round compliantly, offering but slight holds for winds, however violent. The other alpine conifers — the Needle Pine, Mountain Pine, Two-leaved Pine, and Hemlock Spruce — are never thinned out by this agent to any destructive extent, on account of their admirable toughness and the closeness of their growth. In general the same is true of the giants of the lower zones. The kingly Sugar Pine, towering aloft to a height of more than two hundred feet, offers a fine mark to storm-winds; but it is not densely foliaged, and its long horizontal arms swing round compliantly in the blast, like tresses of green, fluent algæ in a brook: while the Silver Firs in most places keep their ranks well together in united strength.

The Yellow or Silver Pine is more frequently overturned than any other tree on the Sierra, because its leaves and branches form a larger mass in proportion to its height; while in many places it is planted sparsely, leaving open lanes through which storms may enter with full force. Furthermore, because it is distributed along the lower portion of the range, which was the first to be left bare on the breaking up of the ice-sheet at the close of the glacial winter, the soil it is growing upon has been longer exposed to post-glacial weathering, and consequently is in a more crumbling, decayed condition than the fresher soils farther up the range, and therefore offers a less secure anchorage for the roots. While exploring the forest zones of Mount Shasta, I discovered the path of a hurricane strewn with thousands of pines of this species. Great and small had been uprooted or wrenched off by sheer force, making a clean gap, like that made by a snow avalanche. But hurricanes capable of doing this class of work are rare in the Sierra; and when we have explored the forests from one extremity of the range to the other, we are compelled to believe that they are the most beautiful on the face of the earth, however we may regard the agents that have made them so.

There is always something deeply exciting, not only in the sounds of winds in the woods, which exert more or less influence over every mind, but in their varied water-like flow as manifested by the movements of the trees, especially those of the conifers. By no other trees are they rendered so extensively and impressively visible; not even by the lordly tropic palms or tree-ferns responsive to the gentlest breeze. The waving of a forest of the giant Sequoias is indescribably impressive and sublime; but the pines seem to me the best interpreters of winds. They are mighty waving golden-rods, ever in tune, singing and writing wind-music all their long century lives. Little, however, of this noble tree-waving and tree-music will you see or hear in the strictly alpine portion of the forests. The burly Juniper, whose girth sometimes more than equals its height, is about as rigid as the rocks on which it grows. The slender lash-like sprays of the Dwarf Pine stream out in wavering ripples, but the tallest and slenderest are far too unyielding to wave even in the heaviest gales. They only shake in quick, short vibrations. The Hemlock Spruce, however, and the Mountain Pine, and some of the tallest thickets of the Two-leaved species, bow in storms with considerable scope and gracefulness. But it is only in the lower and middle zones that the meeting of winds and woods is to be seen in all its grandeur.

One of the most beautiful and exhilarating storms I ever enjoyed in the Sierra occurred in December 1874, when I happened to be exploring one of the tributary valleys of the Yuba River. The sky and the ground and the trees had been thoroughly rain-washed and were dry again. The day was intensely pure: one of those incomparable bits of California winter, warm and balmy and full of white sparkling sunshine, redolent of all the purest influences of the spring, and at the same time enlivened with one of the most bracing wind-storms conceivable. Instead of camping out, as I usually do, I then chanced to be stopping at the house of a friend. But when the storm began to sound, I lost no time in pushing out into the woods to enjoy it. For on such occasions Nature has always something rare to show us, and the danger to life and limb is hardly greater than one would experience crouching deprecatingly beneath a roof.

It was still early morning when I found myself fairly adrift. Delicious sunshine came pouring over the hills, lighting the tops of the pines, and setting free a steam of summery fragrance that contrasted strangely with the wild tones of the storm. The air was mottled with pine-tassels and bright green plumes, that went flashing past in the sunlight like birds pursued. But there was not the slightest dustiness; nothing less pure than leaves, and ripe pollen, and flecks of withered bracken and moss. I heard trees falling for hours at the rate of one every two or three minutes: some uprooted, partly on account of the loose, water-soaked condition of the ground; others broken straight across, where some weakness caused by fire had determined the spot. The gestures of the various trees made a delightful study. Young Sugar Pines, light and feathery as squirrel-tails, were bowing almost to the ground; while the grand old patriarchs, whose massive boles had been tried in a hundred storms, waved solemnly above them, their long, arching branches streaming fluently on the gale, and every needle thrilling and ringing and shedding off keen lances of light like a diamond. The Douglas Spruces, with long sprays drawn out in level tresses, and needles massed in a gray, shimmering glow, presented a most striking appearance as they stood in bold relief along the hilltops. The Madroños in the dells, with their red bark and large glossy leaves tilted every way, reflected the sunshine in throbbing spangles like those one so often sees on the rippled surface of a glacier lake. But the Silver Pines were now the most impressively beautiful of all. Colossal spires two hundred feet in height waved like supple golden-rods chanting and bowing low as if in worship; while the whole mass of their long, tremulous foliage was kindled into one continuous blaze of white sun-fire. The force of the gale was such that the most steadfast monarch of them all rocked down to its roots, with a motion plainly perceptible when one leaned against it. Nature was holding high festival, and every fiber of the most rigid giants thrilled with glad excitement.

I drifted on through the midst of this passionate music and motion, across many a glen, from ridge to ridge; often halting in the lee of a rock for shelter, or to gaze and listen. Even when the grand anthem had swelled to its highest pitch, I could distinctly hear the varying tones of individual trees — Spruce, and Fir, and Pine, and leafless Oak — and even the infinitely gentle rustle of the withered grasses at my feet. Each was expressing itself in its own way — singing its own song, and making its own peculiar gestures — manifesting a richness of variety to be found in no other forest I have yet seen. The coniferous woods of Canada and the Carolinas and Florida are made up of trees that resemble one another about as nearly as blades of grass, and grow close together in much the same way. Coniferous trees, in general, seldom possess individual character, such as is manifest among Oaks and Elms. But the California forests are made up of a greater number of distinct species than any other in the world. And in them we find, not only a marked differentiation into special groups, but also a marked individuality in almost every tree, giving rise to storm effects indescribably glorious.

Toward midday, after a long, tingling scramble through copses of hazel and ceanothus, I gained the summit of the highest ridge in the neighborhood; and then it occurred to me that it would be a fine thing to climb one of the trees, to obtain a wider outlook and get my ear close to the Æolian music of its topmost needles. But under the circumstances the choice of a tree was a serious matter. One whose instep was not very strong seemed in danger of being blown down, or of being struck by others in case they should fall; another was branchless to a considerable height above the ground, and at the same time too large to be grasped with arms and legs in climbing; while others were not favorably situated for clear views. After cautiously casting about, I made choice of the tallest of a group of Douglas Spruces that were growing close together like a tuft of grass, no one of which seemed likely to fall unless all the rest fell with it. Though comparatively young, they were about a hundred feet high, and their lithe, brushy tops were rocking and swirling in wild ecstasy. Being accustomed to climb trees in making botanical studies, I experienced no difficulty in reaching the top of this one; and never before did I enjoy so noble an exhilaration of motion. The slender tops fairly flapped and swished in the passionate torrent, bending and swirling backward and forward, round and round, tracing indescribable combinations of vertical and horizontal curves, while I clung with muscles firm braced, like a bobolink on a reed.

In its widest sweeps my tree-top described an arc of from twenty to thirty degrees; but I felt sure of its elastic temper, having seen others of the same species still more severely tried — bent almost to the ground indeed, in heavy snows — without breaking a fiber. I was therefore safe, and free to take the wind into my pulses and enjoy the excited forest from my superb outlook. The view from here must be extremely beautiful in any weather. Now my eye roved over the piny hills and dales as over fields of waving grain, and felt the light running in ripples and broad swelling undulations across the valleys from ridge to ridge, as the shining foliage was stirred by corresponding waves of air. Oftentimes these waves of reflected light would break up suddenly into a kind of beaten foam, and again, after chasing one another in regular order, they would seem to bend forward in concentric curves, and disappear on some hillside, like sea waves on a shelving shore. The quantity of light reflected from the bent needles was so great as to make whole groves appear as if covered with snow, while the black shadows beneath the trees greatly enhanced the effect of the silvery splendor.

Excepting only the shadows, there was nothing somber in all this wild sea of pines. On the contrary, notwithstanding this was the winter season, the colors were remarkably beautiful. The shafts of the pine and libocedrus were brown and purple, and most of the foliage was well tinged with yellow; the laurel groves, with the pale under sides of their leaves turned upward, made masses of gray; and then there was many a dash of chocolate color from clumps of manzanita, and jet of vivid crimson from the bark of the madroños; while the ground on the hillsides, appearing here and there through openings between the groves, displayed masses of pale purple and brown.

The sounds of the storm corresponded gloriously with this wild exuberance of light and motion. The profound bass of the naked branches and boles booming like waterfalls; the quick, tense vibrations of the pine-needles, now rising to a shrill, whistling hiss, now falling to a silky murmur; the rustling of laurel groves in the dells, and the keen metallic click of leaf on leaf — all this was heard in easy analysis when the attention was calmly bent.

The varied gestures of the multitude were seen to fine advantage, so that one could recognize the different species at a distance of several miles by this means alone, as well as by their forms and colors and the way they reflected the light. All seemed strong and comfortable, as if really enjoying the storm, while responding to its most enthusiastic greetings. We hear much nowadays concerning the universal struggle for existence, but no struggle in the common meaning of the word was manifest here; no recognition of danger by any tree; no deprecation: but rather an invincible gladness, as remote from exultation as from fear.

I kept my lofty perch for hours, frequently closing my eyes to enjoy the music by itself, or to feast quietly on the delicious fragrance that was streaming past. The fragrance of the woods was less marked than that produced during warm rain, when so many balsamic buds and leaves are steeped like tea; but from the chafing of resiny branches against each other, and the incessant attrition of myriads of needles, the gale was spiced to a very tonic degree. And besides the fragrance from these local sources, there were traces of scents brought from afar. For this wind came first from the sea, rubbing against its fresh, briny waves, then distilled through the redwoods, threading rich ferny gulches, and spreading itself in broad undulating currents over many a flower-enameled ridge of the coast mountains, then across the golden plains, up the purple foot-hills, and into these piny woods with the varied incense gathered by the way.

Winds are advertisements of all they touch, however much or little we may be able to read them; telling their wanderings even by their scents alone. Mariners detect the flowery perfume of land-winds far at sea and sea-winds carry the fragrance of dulse and tangle far inland, where it is quickly recognized, though mingled with the scents of a thousand land-flowers. As an illustration of this, I may tell here that I breathed sea-air on the Firth of Forth, in Scotland, while a boy; then was taken to Wisconsin, where I remained nineteen years: then, without in all this time having breathed one breath of the sea, I walked quietly, alone, from the middle of the Mississippi Valley to the Gulf of Mexico, on a botanical excursion; and while in Florida, far from the coast, my attention wholly bent on the splendid tropical vegetation about me, I suddenly recognized a sea-breeze, as it came sifting through the palmettos and blooming vine-tangles, which at once awakened and set free a thousand dormant associations, and made me a boy again in Scotland, as if all the intervening years had been annihilated.

Most people like to look at mountain rivers, and bear them in mind; but few care to look at the winds, though far more beautiful and sublime, and though they become at times about as visible as flowing water. When the north winds in winter are making upward sweeps over the curving summits of the High Sierra, the fact is sometimes published with flying snow-banners a mile long. Those portions of the winds thus embodied can scarce be wholly invisible, even to the darkest imagination. And when we look around over an agitated forest, we may see something of the wind that stirs it, by its effects upon the trees. Yonder it descends in a rush of water-like ripples, and sweeps over the bending pines from hill to hill. Nearer, we see detached plumes and leaves, now speeding by on level currents, now whirling in eddies, or escaping over the edges of the whirls, soaring aloft on grand, upswelling domes of air, or tossing on flame-like crests. Smooth, deep currents, cascades, falls, and swirling eddies, sing around every tree and leaf, and over all the varied topography of the region with telling changes of form, like mountain rivers conforming to the features of their channels.

After tracing the Sierra streams from their fountains to the plains, marking where they bloom white in falls, glide in crystal plumes, surge gray and foam-filled in boulder-choked gorges, and slip through the woods in long, tranquil reaches — after thus learning their languages and forms in detail, we may at length hear them chanting all together in one grand anthem, and comprehend them all in clear inner vision, covering the range like lace. But even this spectacle is far less sublime and not a whit more substantial than what we may behold of these storm-streams of air in the mountain woods.

We all travel the Milky Way together, trees and men; but it never occurred to me until this stormy day, while swinging in the wind, that trees are travelers, in the ordinary sense. They make many journeys; not extensive ones, it is true; but our own little journeys, away and back again, are only little more than tree-wavings — many of them not so much.

When the storm began to abate, I dismounted and sauntered down through the calming woods. The storm-tones died away, and turning toward the east, I beheld the countless hosts of the forests hushed and tranquil, towering above one another on the slopes of the hills like a devout audience. The setting sun filled them with amber light, and seemed to say, while they listened, "My peace I give unto you."

As I gazed on the impressive scene, all the so-called ruin of the storm was forgotten; and never before did these noble woods appear so fresh, so joyous, so immortal.

SAMUEL LANGHORNE CLEMENS (MARK TWAIN)

THE career of Mark Twain was as characteristically American as that of Benjamin Franklin; and like Franklin's it was a career possible only in America. In the eighteenth century Franklin began life in Boston, the son of a poor man who could give him no educational advantages; before he had grown to manhood he removed to Philadelphia where he set up as a printer; he prospered and found leisure for scientific discovery, practical invention, and public service; he came at last to be recognized as the first citizen of the town of his adoption; he was sent to represent Pennsylvania in London, and then to represent the United States in Paris; and when at last in the fullness of years he died, he was, of all Americans born before George Washington, the best known abroad and the best beloved at home. In the nineteenth century Mark Twain saw the light in a struggling little town in Missouri; he had scant schooling; after wide wanderings as a journeyman printer, he became a river pilot, then a miner in Nevada, a journalist in California, a correspondent in Europe, a lecturer throughout the United States; in his maturity he turned story-teller and won immediate popularity on all the shores of all the Seven Seas; and when he had attained to threescore years and ten, he had become an international figure, known and loved far beyond the boundaries of his native land and of his native language.

Like Franklin again Mark Twain was as American in his character as he was in his career, indisputably indigenous to the soil of his nativity. Like Franklin he was a humorist who was far more than a mere humorist, who was shrewd, independent, individual, erect on his own feet, and doing his own thinking, who could develop into a citizen of the world, a cosmopolitan in outlook, without surrender of his standing in the country of his birth, retaining to the end the homely directness of thought and of speech which was his inalienable inheritance.

I

Samuel Langhorne Clemens was born in the overgrown village of Florida, Missouri, on November 30, 183[illegible]. Four years later the family moved to Hannibal on the Mississippi River, where young Clemens spent his boyhood in the atmosphere that he was later to recreate lovingly in 'Tom Sawyer.' When he was sixteen he learned to set type; and when he was eighteen he started out as a journeyman printer, straying as far east as New York. In 1857, when he was twenty-two, he fulfilled an early ambition and became a Mississippi pilot, only to have this calling prohibited four years later when the Civil War broke out and traffic on the mighty stream ceased abruptly. After a few days of service in a company training for the Confederate army, he went out to Nevada, accompanying his elder brother; and his experiences in this expanding community he has narrated in 'Roughing It.' He was twenty-seven when he turned reporter on a Virginia City paper; and he was twenty-eight when he adopted the pen-name of Mark Twain. The next year, 1864, found him in San Francisco contributing frequently to its newspapers and infrequently to weeklies in Philadelphia and New York. The 'Jumping Frog,' printed in a New York journal in 1865, was instantly appreciated; and it gave the title to a volume of comic sketches published in 1867.

The year before this first book appeared he had taken a voyage to the Sandwich Islands; and he had made his first appearance as a lecturer. In 1867, he came east again to find that his reputation as a humorist had preceded him, and that he could attract to hear him talk on the platform an audience which filled Cooper Union. And in that year he made his first visit to Europe in the chartered steamer and in the selected company which he described in the letters he had been engaged to write for a California journal. On his return to America he revised this newspaper correspondence, and the resulting volume called 'Innocents Abroad' was published in 1869. Mark Twain was thirty-four years old when the success of this book gave him immediate celebrity, established his position as a writer to be reckoned with, and assured him of an income.

Although he continued to lecture, he still thought of himself as a newspaper man; and after his marriage in 1870, he bought an interest in a Buffalo daily. Yet only two years later he sold out at a loss, giving up journalism, and removing to Hartford, which was to be the family home for a score of years — although he was frequently to leave it for long visits to Europe. It was in 1872, the first year of his residence in Hartford, that he published 'Roughing It'; and in 1873 he collaborated with Charles Dudley Warner in writing 'The Gilded Age,' which was the first of his longer fictions. To this tale told in partnership, Mark Twain contributed the character of Colonel Mulberry Sellers; and this character he made the central figure of a fortuitously constructed play, acted with popular approval all over the United States for several seasons. It may be noted here that a little later he collaborated with Bret Harte in the composition of another piece, 'Ah Sin,' which failed to please the public.

The character of Colonel Sellers was the result of memory rather than of invention; and Mark was encouraged to draw again on the experiences of his youth; 'The Adventures of Tom Sawyer' was published in 1875. In the next three or four years he issued two or three collections of his humorous sketches. In 1879 he took his family over to Europe for a long visit in the course of which he collected the material for another book of travels, 'A Tramp Abroad,' issued in 1880. Then, after he had settled down again in Hartford, he returned to fiction, writing his first historical novel — if this is a fit term to describe the invented adventures of 'The Prince and the Pauper' published in 1882. At the solicitation of Howells, then the editor of the Atlantic, he had contributed to that magazine half a dozen years earlier half a dozen papers in which he had narrated his adventures and described his emotions when he was a cub-pilot "learning the river"; and these papers, supplemented by observations gathered on a more recent voyage down the river, were put forth in 1883 as 'Life on the Mississippi.'

And it was life on the Mississippi which supplied both the background and the substance of his next venture in fiction, 'The Adventures of Huckleberry Finn,' which is a sequel to the earlier 'Adventures of Tom Sawyer,' and which appeared in 1884; it was acclaimed then and it is recognized now as his masterpiece. Not for five years thereafter did he put forth another work of fiction — 'A Connecticut Yankee at King Arthur's Court,' a daring fantasy which was even less historical than 'The Prince and the Pauper.' Then he revived the attractive figure of Colonel Sellers in one of his least attractive stories, 'The American Claimant,' issued in 1892; and he followed it two years later by the equally unsuccessful revival of another attractive figure in the artificial story called 'Tom Sawyer Abroad.' Yet in 1894, the year in which this more or less negligible tale appeared, he published his third long study of life on the Mississippi, 'Pudd'n-Head Wilson,' in some of its episodes worthy to take its place beside 'Tom Sawyer' and 'Huckleberry Finn.'

These had been years of prosperity; his books were very profitable and the income from them was augmented by occasional lecturing. But Mark Twain had been successful in depicting Colonel Sellers only because he himself possessed the financial incapacity and the invincible hopefulness with which he had endowed his pathetically humorous character. He made many ill-advised investments; he sank two hundred thousand dollars in a typesetting machine; and then, like Sir Walter Scott, he became the chief supporter of a publishing house. This new enterprise began magnificently with the publication of the 'Personal Memoirs of Grant,' which was so well received by the American people that the widow of the author was paid four hundred thousand dollars in copyright royalties. This first success was not followed by many others; and the later business ventures of Charles L. Webster & Co. were ill-managed and unprofitable; the house accumulated a heavy burden of debt and a few months after the panic of 1893 it had to give up the unavailing struggle. At the age of fifty-eight Mark Twain found himself bereft of all he had made and loaded with a huge debt.

Sir Walter Scott was nearly as old when the same misfortune befell him; and like Scott, Mark Twain made no effort to evade his responsibilities. He reduced his indebtedness by realizing on the assets of the bankrupt firm, and he set out to make the many thousands needed to enable him to be again a free man. Although he had tired of lecturing, he started in 1895 on a tour around the world, talking to huge audiences whenever and wherever he appeared on the platform. His account of this circumnavigation of the globe was called 'Following the Equator' and it was published in 1897. The lecture tour itself and this record of its varied aspects had been so profitable that he was able to pay off the last of his creditors early in 1898, less than five years after the failure. In those years, it must also be noted, the 'Personal Recollections of Joan of Arc' had appeared anonymously as a serial and had been issued as a book with his signature attached.

This painful period of struggle and of financial redemption was also saddened by the sudden death of his eldest daughter; and the stricken family felt it impossible ever to settle down again in the old Hartford home. Not until the fall of 1900 did they return to America; and Mark Twain's homecoming was the occasion of a spontaneous outpouring of appreciation and affection from his fellow-countrymen. For the next years of his life he was an intermittent resident of New York City, removing to the new home he built at Redding, Connecticut, only a year or two before his death. He made occasional visits to Europe, on one of which in 1904 Mrs. Clemens died; and it must be here recorded that the married life of Mark Twain had been unbroken in its happiness. Five years later, in 1909, the youngest of his three daughters was found dead; and this deepened the melancholy which had always sustained and intensified his humor and which manifested itself more abundantly and more openly in the final years of his life, when he found himself bereft and lonely, despite the warmth of the many friendships which encompassed him.

Yet even in these years of his disillusion and of darkness there were consolations of one kind or another. There was a unanimous recognition of the commanding position which he had won as a man of letters — a recognition which was not confined to the United States, the British Islands, and the British Empire, but which transcended the boundaries of language and extended to Germany and to France. He was not only an international figure, he was even more emphatically a national figure, inexpugnably American and by that fact the more heartily appreciated by his own country. In 1904 he was one of the seven men chosen by the National Institute of Arts and Letters to found an American Academy of Arts and Letters which should include the leaders in literature, in music, and in the fine arts. In 1905 his seventieth birthday evoked manifold testimonies to the high position he held in the affectionate esteem of his fellow-men of letters in all parts of the English-speaking community. And in 1907 the University of Oxford invited him to cross the Atlantic again to receive the degree of Doctor of Letters, an unexpected honor which greatly gratified him. He delighted in the red gown with which he was entitled thereafter to adorn himself, for he retained to the end a Tom Sawyer-like pleasure in being conspicuous.

A uniform library edition of his works began to be published in 1900, seemly tomes in which what he had written could be read without distraction by disfiguring illustrations. His literary activity seems to have been stimulated by the expansion of his fame; and in these final years he produced more abundantly than ever before. He wrote or dictated an autobiography, although he decided to allow only a few passages of this to appear during his lifetime. The same reserve led him to issue only in a privately printed edition a book called 'What is Man?' His Swift-like parable, 'The Man That Corrupted Hadleyburg,' one of the most incisive of moral tales, gave its name to a volume of shorter pieces; and he issued half a dozen other books long and short, including 'Extracts from Adam's Diary' (1904) and 'Eve's Diary' (1903).

Early in 1910 his health began to fail. He took a trip to Bermuda, where he had several painful attacks and where his condition became serious. He survived to return to Stormfield, his new home at Redding; and there on April 21, he died at the ripe age of seventy-four.

II

From the foregoing record of the salient facts in Mark Twain's life, the titles of not a few of his books were omitted. He edited a 'Library of Humor' (1888). He collected into one volume, 'How to Tell a Story' (1897), a selection from his essays and literary criticisms. He found keen enjoyment in analyzing mercilessly the pretensions of 'Christian Science,' falsely so-called (1907). He convinced himself that the plays attributed to Shakespeare were really written by Bacon; and he tried to convert the public to his view by an elaborate argument, 'Is Shakespeare Dead?' (1909) — an unfortunate tome which only confirmed the evidence supplied by his repeated failure as a playwright that, although he could be on occasion superbly dramatic, he was lacking in intimate understanding of the theater and of its necessary and unchanging conditions.

Since his death a selection of his speeches has been issued in one volume; and a curious tale entitled 'The Mysterious Stranger' was posthumously published in 1916. An ample and admirable biography by Albert Bigelow Paine (1912) contained a few of his letters, as characteristic and as self-revelatory as his more formal writings. He was an indefatigable correspondent, often finding vent for the feelings of the moment in an impulsive missive that he never sent. For thirty years or more he kept up a constant interchange of letters with Howells; and the publication of the complete correspondence between the two foremost figures in American literature at the beginning of the twentieth century would be most cordially received. A collection of his general correspondence was published in 1917, and in 1924 the much heralded 'Autobiography' appeared, with an introduction by Albert Bigelow Paine.

Yet nothing which has been published since his death has materially altered our conception of Mark Twain derived from the books he sent forth in his lifetime. These books reveal him completely at every stage of his development as a man of letters and of his evolution as a man. They are in many departments of literature, for in his own way he was multifarious. At one time or another he gave to the public comic sketches of many kinds, short stories, literary criticisms, travels, reminiscences, plays, tales of his youth, and historical novels. We can find in them manifold aspects of human life and human character as the panorama of existence unrolled itself before his piercing insight. And the entire body of his work, various as it may seem at first sight, is unified by the fact that it is all of it warranted by his sign-manual, instantly recognizable as his, as his only, so individual as to be impossible to any other man of letters. Even the 'Joan of Arc,' from which he deliberately excluded his bolder humor and which he wished to have judged on its own merits without the preconceptions necessarily created by his signature — even this serious historical evocation could have come from no other pen than his.

His widespread popularity with all sorts and conditions of men was due in a measure to the breadth of his appeal and to the many-sidedness of his work. Not a few of those who were moved by the sincerely reverent treatment of the noble figure of Joan of Arc were repelled by the frolicsome iconoclasm of his 'Connecticut Yankee at King Arthur's Court,' and were perhaps shocked at its insistence on the "glorious gospel of equality," as Howells has suggested. In 'Huckleberry Finn' the frank veracity of his portrayal of melancholy conditions of life along the Mississippi in the slave-holding states was offensive to some sensitive souls who sought to have that Odyssey of the great river excluded from public libraries; and yet this very book was held by Robert Louis Stevenson to be the most important contribution to the fiction of our language which had appeared in the decade of its publication. The merciless analysis of human frailty which characterizes 'The Man That Corrupted Hadleyburg' — one of the austerest and most uncompromising apologues in all literature — disconcerted many of the unthinking who had reveled in the free and spontaneous fun of the 'Jumping Frog' and in the rollicking playfulness of 'Innocents Abroad.'

Now that we can at last survey the work of Mark Twain in the perspective of time, we cannot fail to discover that it is as unequal in merit as it is varied in topic. Sublimated autobiography like 'Roughing It' and 'Life on the Mississippi' is not more remote in manner from a quasi-historical fantasy such as 'The Prince and the Pauper' than is 'Tom Sawyer' — an imaginative transcript from actuality as the facts on which it was founded were glimpsed through the haze of memory — differentiated from the unconvincing unreality of its sorry sequel, 'Tom Sawyer Abroad,' not rooted in fact but made out of whole cloth, compounded with arbitrary artificiality. Even in a masterpiece of sustained realism like 'Huckleberry Finn' there are passages of exaggerated caricature and of broad burlesques, wherein we are pained to perceive that the King and the Duke are clowning on purpose to evoke our inexpensive laughter.

Probably there is no author attaining at times to the lofty level of Mark Twain's finest work who is as unequal and as uncertain. Nor is this inequality and uncertainty due to any carelessness of composition. So far as style is concerned he was always doing his best; he is always conscientious, even meticulous. The defect lies below the surface; it is contained in the topic itself and in the treatment imposed by the topic. The most obvious explanation of this distressing fact is that Mark Twain had no solid standard for the evaluation of his own work and that he could not rely on his own judgment. His taste was wavering; and it was sometimes at the mercy of his tricksy fancy. He was modest in self-criticism and he often let those in whose opinions he had confidence, Mrs. Clemens or Howells, decide against the publication of articles and even of books which he had written with keen satisfaction. But there is another explanation going deeper than this: it is that Mark Twain, rich as he was in interpretative imagination, was more or less insufficiently equipped with the subordinate faculty of invention. When he had to make up a story out of his own head, he was not at his best. He needed to be sustained by the validity of the actual fact, either observed by himself or narrated by an eyewitness. Once possessed of this fact he could make it his own, absorb it, expand it, and set his imagination at work interpreting it. The poet is never prone to invent his myths, preferring apparently to take over the old tales and to bring out their latent beauty and their human significance. In his own way, Mark Twain was a poet, never seen at his best when he was relying solely on his invention, the result of which was likely to reveal the mechanical quality of mere invention. The basis of the 'Jumping Frog' was a tale told him in Nevada; and the basis of the Blue Jay chapter in the 'Tramp Abroad' was another tale which came to him by word of mouth. These transmitted narratives were the raw material out of which he could make his profit in due season. Out of the transfigured memories of his own boyhood he put together 'Tom Sawyer,' that self-revelatory portrayal of the perennial boy. In 'Life on the Mississippi' he set down various particulars of a vendetta which ended in the destruction of two families; and then in 'Huckleberry Finn' we see how these bare facts have taken on color and have been made to surrender their ultimate significance in the account of the Shepherdson-Grangerford feud, wherein Mark borrowed the eternal Romeo and Juliet situation to intensify the poignant pathos of a commonplace quarrel often paralleled in many a Southern community.

III

Although the uncertainties and the inequalities are as evident and as frequent in his later books as in his earlier, a consideration of his writings in chronological sequence instantly reveals his steady progress in his mastery of the art of writing and in his knowledge of the art of life. At the very beginning he was little more than a newspaper fun-maker, a more or less docile pupil of John Phœnix and of Artemus Ward, although he was never tempted to the too easy trick of misfit spelling to which the earlier manufacturers of comic copy had been unduly addicted. He contented himself with what Howells has neatly termed "the established absurdities of English orthography." But the paper pattern of Derby and Browne was too thin to be serviceable for long to a writer with the potentiality of Mark Twain; and it was in 'Innocents Abroad' that he began to reveal his own characteristics more amply and to disclose himself as something more than a funny man content to scratch at the surface of life. A humorist he remained to the end, the greatest humorist of his age as well as of his country, yet already giving warnings that he was far more than a mere laughter-evoker.

As he gained experience, so he gained confidence, if that had ever been lacking. He sank his shaft deeper into the fundamentals of human nature and he ran out his galleries on all sides to disclose the rambling inconsistencies of humanity. He contrived to make us laugh but he also made us think. He gave us that true comedy of life, which in Meredith's phrase arouses "thoughtful laughter"; and the reader is to be pitied who finds nothing more in the 'Connecticut Yankee' or in 'Huckleberry Finn' than a succession of highly amusing episodes. A humorist first of all, Mark Twain was a moralist last of all, with an ethical understanding that penetrated directly down to bed-rock and unerringly found the vein of pure gold. Very early in his work he let us see his scorn for snobbishness, for sham, for pretense, for affectation, for meanness, for cruelty — a scorn that in time burned as hot within him and played forth as volcanically as Molière's hatred for these same perennially contemptible characteristics.

He had the fecundity of the affluent; and yet it did not need more than a few of his multifarious volumes in half a dozen different departments of literature to make it plain that the concocter of comic copy for a country weekly had developed into a humorist made of sterner stuff, and equipped to conduct an austere inquest into human frailty and human folly. The foundations of his humor were below frost — as Lowell said of Shakespeare's; and elsewhere the same keen critic declared that "real wit keeps, real humor is of the same nature in Aristophanes and in Mark Twain." And Howells is as keen and as emphatic when he declares that "Mark Twain's humor is as simple in form and as direct as the statesmanship of Lincoln or the generalship of Grant."

The obvious reason for this validity of Mark Twain's humor is that it is rooted in pathos. It may be only a step from the sublime to the ridiculous; but it is less than a step from the comic to the tragic. "Everything human is pathetic," so one may read at the head of a chapter in 'Following the Equator,' one of many instances of the author's self-confession: "Everything human is pathetic. The secret source of humor itself is not joy but sorrow. There is no humor in heaven." Cheerful as Mark Twain might seem, bravely as he might bear himself before men, he was as sorrowful as Cervantes or as Molière; and perhaps at the end he had a deeper despair and a bitterer grief than either of these mighty predecessors in what one of them called the "strange task of making people laugh." Their American successor had understanding and sympathy and loving-kindness, yet even Swift scarcely ever achieved the misanthropic melancholy of 'The Man That Corrupted Hadleyburg.'

To dwell unduly on the fact that the humorist was also a moralist may be a little unfair to the humorist that Mark Twain never ceased to be. He was far more than a fun-maker, but he was an exuberant and inexhaustible fun-maker first of all. The laughter he continuously compelled might also provoke thought, but it had no need to do this to justify itself; it was its own excuse for being. He was an immitigable humorist, wielding all the weapons of comedy, satire, irony, and even on occasion, parody. He was a humorist who could create characters which etched themselves unforgettably on the memory of every reader. He was a humorist who was a supreme story-teller and who could handle situation with the simple certainty of the masters; and Robinson Crusoe's thrill at the discovery of the human footprint on the sand is not finer in its kind than Tom Sawyer's shrinking back into his recess in the cave when the candle that gleamed hopefully in the distance illuminated the dark hand of Indian Joe. He was a humorist who was also a man of letters, nourishing himself on the strong meat of literature, sitting at the feet of the masters of the written word from Suetonius to Saint-Simon.

As a reader he was as discriminating as he was insatiable, seeking ever a first-hand interpretation of life and therefore preferring to the writers of fiction, the writers of biography and of autobiography. He was as piercing a critic of books as he was of men; and as a critic he was never the bond slave of tradition, being always irreconcilably unacademic and conscientiously individual in his likes and in his dislikes. About books as about men he had his frank and frequent prejudices and his habitual violences of expression. Himself a master of English, ever alert in the quest for the necessary noun and the indispensable adjective, he had no patience with the verbal flatting and sharping of Cooper or with the mincing orotundity of Dowden, dismissing the style of this British critic's 'Shelley' as a "literary cakewalk."

His own style was indisputably his own, free and flexible, direct and exact, never bookish, always racy with the flavor of the soil, unconsciously American —like Franklin's and Lincoln's. He had at his command an enormous vocabulary, from which only the dead words had been excluded; and he could compel it to do his bidding with effortless ease. The passage describing the Sphinx in 'Innocents Abroad' is worthy to be set by the side of the passage describing the Jungfrau in the 'Tramp Abroad'; and they are passages unsurpassed in the work of any other master of English prose.

Mark Twain was a stylist and a story-teller, an artist in words and an artist in narration, a fertile creator of character and a lively critic of books and of men, a militant moralist, but above and beyond all these things he was a humorist who made men laugh even if he also on occasion made them think.

BRANDER MATTHEWS

THE NOTORIOUS JUMPING FROG OF CALAVERAS COUNTY

IN compliance with the request of a friend of mine, who wrote me from the East, I called on good-natured, garrulous old Simon Wheeler, and inquired after my friend's friend, Leonidas W. Smiley, as requested to do, and I hereunto append the result. I have a lurking suspicion that *Leonidas W.* Smiley is a myth; that my friend never knew such a personage; and that he only conjectured that if I asked old Wheeler about him, it would remind him of his infamous *Jim* Smiley, and he would go to work and bore me to death with some exasperating reminiscence of him as long and as tedious as it should be useless to me. If that was the design, it succeeded.

I found Simon Wheeler dozing comfortably by the bar-room stove of the dilapidated tavern in the decayed mining camp of Angel's, and I noticed that he was fat and baldheaded, and had an expression of winning gentleness and simplicity upon his tranquil countenance. He roused up, and gave me good day. I told him a friend of mine had commissioned me to make some inquiries about a cherished companion of his boyhood named *Leonidas W.* Smiley — *Rev. Leonidas W.* Smiley, a young minister of the Gospel, who he had heard was at one time a resident of Angel's Camp. I added that if Mr. Wheeler could tell me anything about this Rev. Leonidas W. Smiley, I would feel under many obligations to him.

Simon Wheeler backed me into a corner and blockaded me there with his chair, and then sat down and reeled off the monotonous narrative which follows this paragraph. He never smiled, he never frowned, he never changed his voice from the gentle-flowing key to which he tuned his initial sentence, he never betrayed the slightest suspicion of enthusiasm; but all through the interminable narrative there ran a vein of impressive earnestness and sincerity, which showed me plainly that, so far from his imagining that there was anything ridiculous or funny about his story, he regarded it as a really important matter, and admired its two heroes as men of transcendent genius and *finesse.* I let him go on his own way, and never interrupted him once.

"Rev. Leonidas W. H'm, Reverend Le — well, there was a feller here once by the name of Jim Smiley, in the winter of '49 — or maybe it was the spring of '50 — I don't recollect exactly, somehow, though what makes me think it was one or the other is because I remember the big flume warn't finished when he first come to the camp; but any way, he was the curiosest man about always betting on anything that turned up you ever see, if he could get anybody to bet on the other side; and if he couldn't he'd change sides. Any way that suited the other man would suit *him* — any way just so's he got a bet, *he* was satisfied. But still he was lucky, uncommon lucky; he most always come out winner. He was always ready and laying for a chance; there couldn't be no solit'ry thing mentioned but that feller'd offer to bet on it, and take ary side you please, as I was just telling you. If there was a horse-race, you'd find him flush or you'd find him busted at the end of it; if there was a dog-fight, he'd bet on it; if there was a cat-fight, he'd bet on it; if there was a chicken-fight, he'd bet on it; why, if there was two birds setting on a fence, he would bet you which one would fly first; or if there was a camp meeting, he would be there reg'lar to bet on Parson Walker, which he judged to be the best exhorter about here, and so he was too, and a good man. If he even see a straddle-bug start to go anywheres, he would bet you how long it would take him to get to — to wherever he was going to, and if you took him up, he would foller that straddle-bug to Mexico but what he would find out where he was bound for and how long he was on the road. Lots of boys here has seen that Smiley, and can tell you about him. Why, it never made no difference to *him* — he'd bet on *any*thing — the dangdest feller. Parson Walker's wife laid very sick once, for a good while, and it seemed as if they warn't going to save her; but one morning he come in, and Smiley up and asked him how she was and he said she was considerable better — thank the Lord for his inf'nit mercy — and coming on so smart that with the blessing of Prov'dence she'd get well yet; and Smiley, before he thought, says, 'Well, I'll resk two-and-a-half she don't anyway.'

"Thish-yer Smiley had a mare — the boys called her the fifteen-minute nag, but that was only in fun, you know, because of course she was faster than that — and he used to win money on that horse, for all she was so slow and always had the asthma, or the distemper, or the consumption, or something of that kind. They used to give her two or three hundred yards' start, and then pass her under way; but always at the fag-end of the races she'd get excited and desperate-like, and come cavorting and straddling up, and scattering her legs around limber, sometimes in the air, and sometimes out to one side amongst the fences, and kicking up m-o-r-e dust and raising m-o-r-e racket with her coughing and sneezing and blowing her nose — and *always* fetch up at the stand just about a neck ahead, as near as you could cipher it down.

"And he had a little small bull-pup, that to look at you'd think he warn't worth a cent but to set around and look ornery and lay for a chance to steal something. But as soon as money was up on him he was a different dog; his under-jaw'd begin to stick out like the fo'castle of a steamboat, and his teeth would uncover and shine like the furnaces. And a dog might tackle him and bully-rag him, and bite him, and throw him over his shoulder two or three times, and Andrew Jackson — which was the name of the pup — Andrew Jackson would never let on but what *he* was satisfied, and hadn't expected nothing else — and the bets being doubled and doubled on the other side all the time, till the money was all up; and then all of a sudden he would grab that other dog jest by the j'int of his hind leg and freeze to it — not chaw, you understand, but only just grip and hang on till they throwed up the sponge, if it was a year. Smiley always come out winner on that pup, till he harnessed a dog once that didn't have no hind legs, because they'd been sawed off in a circular saw, and when the thing had gone along far enough, and the money was all up, and he come to make a snatch for his pet holt, he see in a minute how he'd been imposed on, and how the other dog had him in the door, so to speak, and he 'peared surprised, and then he looked sorter discouraged-like, and didn't try no more to win the fight, and so he got shucked out bad. He give Smiley a look, as much as to say his heart was broke, and it was *his* fault, for putting up a dog that hadn't no hind legs for him to take holt of, which was his main dependence in a fight, and then he limped off a piece and laid down and died. It was a good pup, was that Andrew Jackson, and would have made a name for hisself if he'd lived, for the stuff was in him and he had genius — I know it, because he hadn't no opportunities to speak of, and it don't stand to reason that a dog could make such a fight as he could under them circumstances if he hadn't no talent. It always makes me feel sorry when I think of that last fight of his'n, and the way it turned out.

"Well, thish-yer Smiley had rat-tarriers, and chicken cocks, and tomcats, and all them kind of things, till you couldn't rest, and you couldn't fetch nothing for him to bet on but he'd match you. He ketched a frog one day, and took him home, and said he cal'lated to educate him; and so he never done nothing for three months but set in his back yard and learn that frog to jump. And you bet you he *did* learn him, too. He'd give him a little punch behind, and the next minute you'd see that frog whirling in the air like a doughnut — see him turn one summerset, or may be a couple, if he got a good start, and come down flat-footed and all right, like a cat. He got him up so in the matter of catching flies, and kep' him in practice so constant, that he'd nail a fly every time as fur as he could see him. Smiley said all a frog wanted was education, and he could do 'most anything — and I believe him. Why, I've seen him set Dan'l Webster down here on this floor — Dan'l Webster was the name of the frog — and sing out, 'Flies, Dan'l, flies!' and quicker'n you could wink he'd spring straight up and snake a fly off'n the counter there, and flop down on the floor ag'in as solid as a gob of mud, and fall to scratching the side of his head with his hind foot as indifferent as if he hadn't no idea he'd been doing any more'n any frog might do. You never see a frog so modest and straightfor'ard as he was, for all he was so gifted. And when it come to fair and square jumping on a dead level, he could get over more ground at one straddle than any animal of his breed you ever see. Jumping on a dead level was his strong suit, you understand; and when it came to that, Smiley would ante up money on him as long as he had a red. Smiley was monstrous proud of his frog, and well he might be, for fellers that had traveled and been everywheres, all said he laid over any frog that ever *they* see.

"Well, Smiley kep' the beast in a little lattice box, and he used to fetch him down town sometimes and lay for a bet. One day a feller — a stranger in the camp, he was — come acrost him with his box, and says: —

"'What might it be that you've got in the box?'

"And Smiley says, sorter indifferent-like, 'It might be a parrot, or it might be a canary, maybe, but it ain't — it's only just a frog.'

"And the feller took it, and looked at it careful, and turned it round this way and that, and says 'H'm — so 'tis. Well, what's *he* good for?'

"'Well,' Smiley says, easy and careless, 'he's good enough for *one* thing, I should judge — he can outjump any frog in Calaveras County.'

"The feller took the box again, and took another long, particular look, and give it back to Smiley, and says, very deliberate, 'Well,' he says, 'I don't see no p'ints about that frog that's any better'n any other frog.'

"'Maybe you don't,' Smiley says. 'Maybe you understand frogs and maybe you don't understand 'em; maybe you've had experience, and maybe you ain't only a amature, as it were. Anyways I've got my opinion and I'll resk forty dollars that he can outjump any frog in Calaveras County.'

"And the feller studied a minute, and then says, kinder sad like, 'Well, I'm only a stranger here, and I ain't got no frog; but if I had a frog, I'd bet you.'

"And then Smiley says, 'That's all right — that's all right — if you'll hold my box a minute, I'll go and get you a frog.' And so the feller took the box, and put up his forty dollars along with Smiley's, and set down to wait.

"So he set there a good while thinking and thinking to hisself, and then he got the frog out and pried his mouth open and took a teaspoon and filled him full of quail shot — filled him pretty near up to his chin — and set him on the floor. Smiley he went to the swamp and slopped around in the mud for a long time, and finally he ketched a frog, and fetched him in, and give him to this feller, and says:

"'Now, if you're ready, set him alongside of Dan'l, with his forepaws just even with Dan'l's, and I'll give the word.' Then he says, 'One — two —

three — *git!* ' and him and the feller touched up the frogs from behind, and the new frog hopped off lively, but Dan'l give a heave, and hysted up his shoulders — so — like a Frenchman, but it warn't no use — he couldn't budge; he was planted as solid as a church, and he couldn't no more stir than if he was anchored out. Smiley was a good deal surprised, and he was disgusted too, but he didn't have no idea what the matter was, of course.

"The feller took the money and started away; and when he was going out at the door, he sorter jerked his thumb over his shoulder — so — at Dan'l, and says again, very deliberate, 'Well,' he says, '*I* don't see no p'ints about that frog that's any better'n any other frog.'

"Smiley he stood scratching his head and looking down at Dan'l a long time, and at last he says, 'I do wonder what in the nation that frog throw'd off for — I wonder if there ain't something the matter with him — he 'pears to look mighty baggy, somehow.' And he ketched Dan'l by the nap of the neck, and hefted him, and says, 'Why blame my cats if he don't weigh five pound!' and turned him upside down and he belched out a double handful of shot. And then he see how it was, and he was the maddest man — he set the frog down and took out after that feller, but he never ketched him. And — "

Here Simon Wheeler heard his name called from the front yard, and got up to see what was wanted and turning to me as he moved away, he said: "Just set where you are, stranger, and rest easy — I ain't going to be gone a second."

But, by your leave, I did not think that a continuation of the history of the enterprising vagabond *Jim* Smiley would be likely to afford me much information concerning the *Rev. Leonidas W.* Smiley and so I started away.

At the door I met the sociable Wheeler returning, and he button-holed me and recommenced:

"Well, thish-yer Smiley had a yaller one-eyed cow that didn't have no tail, only just a short stump like a bannanner, and — "

However, lacking both time and inclination, I did not wait to hear about the afflicted cow, but took my leave.

NOTE. — The story of the Jumping Frog was told to Mark Twain by Ben Coon in the bar-room of Angel's Camp in the winter of 1864–5. Mark's version of the story entitled 'Jim Smiley and his Jumping Frog' appeared in the Saturday Press of New York on November 18, 1865. The story went the rounds of the newspapers and captured the public. It gave the title to Mark Twain's first book, 'The Celebrated Jumping Frog of Calaveras County, and Other Sketches' (1867), and made the beginning of his national reputation.

THE CHILD OF CALAMITY

From 'Life on the Mississippi.' Copyright, 1883, by James R. Osgood and Company

BY way of illustrating keelboat talk and manners, and that now departed and hardly remembered raft life, I will throw in, in this place, a chapter from a book which I have been working at by fits and starts during the past five or six years, and may possibly finish in the course of five or six more. The book is a story which details some passages in the life of an ignorant village boy, Huck Finn, son of the town drunkard of my time out West there. He has run away from his persecuting father, and from a persecuting good widow who wishes to make a nice truth-telling respectable boy of him; and with him a slave of the widow's has also escaped. They have found a fragment of a lumber raft (it is high water and dead summer-time), and are floating down the river by night and hiding in the willows by day — bound for Cairo — whence the negro will seek freedom in the heart of the free States. But in a fog, they pass Cairo without knowing it. By-and-by they begin to suspect the truth, and Huck Finn is persuaded to end the dismal suspense by swimming down to a huge raft which they have seen in the distance ahead of them, creeping aboard under cover of the darkness, and gathering the needed information by eavesdropping: —

But you know a young person can't wait very well when he is impatient to find a thing out. We talked it over, and by-and-by Jim said it was such a black night now that it wouldn't be no risk to swim down to the big raft and crawl aboard and listen — they would talk about Cairo, because they would be calculating to go ashore there for a spree, maybe, or anyway they would send boats ashore to buy whisky or fresh meat or something. Jim had a wonderful level head, for a nigger: he could 'most always start a good plan when you wanted one.

I stood up and shook my rags off and jumped into the river, and struck out for the raft's light. By-and-by, when I got down nearly to her, I eased up and went slow and cautious. But everything was all right — nobody at the sweeps. So I swum down along the raft till I was 'most abreast the camp-fire in the middle, then I crawled aboard and inched along and got in amongst some bundles of shingles on the weather side of the fire. There was thirteen men there — they was the watch on deck, of course. And a mighty rough-looking lot too. They had a jug, and tin cups, and they kept the jug moving. One man was singing — roaring, you may say; and it wasn't a nice song — for a parlor anyway. He roared through his nose, and strung out the last word of every line very long. When he was done they all fetched a kind of Injun war-whoop, and then another was sung. It begun: —

"There was a woman in our towdn,
In our towdn did dwed'l (dwell),
She loved her husband dear-i-lee,
But another man twyste as wed'l.

"Singing too, riloo, riloo, riloo,
Ri-loo, riloo, rilay - - - e,
She loved her husband dear-i-lee,
But another man twyste as wed'l."

And so on — fourteen verses. It was kind of poor, and when he was going to start on the next verse one of them said it was the tune the old cow died on; and another one said, "Oh, give us a rest." And another one told him to take a walk. They made fun of him till he got mad and jumped up and begun to cuss the crowd, and said he could lam any thief in the lot.

They was all about to make a break for him, but the biggest man there jumped up and says: —

"Set whar you are, gentlemen. Leave him to me; he's my meat."

Then he jumped up in the air three times and cracked his heels together every time. He flung off a buckskin coat that was all hung with fringes, and says, "You lay thar tell the chawin-up's done"; and flung his hat down, which was all over ribbons, and says, "You lay thar tell his sufferins is over."

Then he jumped up in the air and cracked his heels together again and shouted out: —

"Whoo-oop! I'm the old original iron-jawed, brass-mounted, copper-bellied corpse-maker from the wilds of Arkansaw! — Look at me! I'm the man they call Sudden Death and General Desolation! Sired by a hurricane, dam'd by an earthquake, half-brother to the cholera, nearly related to the small-pox on the mother's side! Look at me! I take nineteen alligators and a bar'l of whisky for breakfast when I'm in robust health, and a bushel of rattlesnakes and a dead body when I'm ailing! I split the everlasting rocks with my glance, and I squench the thunder when I speak! Whoo-oop! Stand back and give me room according to my strength! Blood's my natural drink, and the wails of the dying is music to my ear! Cast your eye on me, gentlemen! — and lay low and hold your breath, for I'm 'bout to turn myself loose!"

All the time he was getting this off, he was shaking his head and looking fierce and kind of swelling around in a little circle, tucking up his wristbands and now and then straightening up and beating his breast with his fist, saying, "Look at me, gentlemen!" When he got through he jumped up and cracked his heels together three times, and let off a roaring "Whoo-oop! I'm the bloodiest son of a wildcat that lives!"

Then the man that had started the row tilted his old slouch hat down over his right eye; then he bent stooping forward, with his back sagged and his south end sticking out far, and his fists a-shoving out and drawing in in front of him, and so went around in a little circle about three times, swelling himself up and breathing hard. Then he straightened, and jumped up and cracked his heels together three times before he lit again (that made them cheer), and he begun to shout like this: —

"Whoo-oop! bow your neck and spread, for the kingdom of sorrow's a-coming! Hold me down to the earth, for I feel my powers a-working! whoo-oop! I'm a child of sin; *don't* let me get a start! Smoked glass, here, for all! Don't attempt to look at me with the naked eye, gentlemen! When I'm playful I use the meridians of longitude and parallels of latitude for a seine, and drag the Atlantic Ocean for whales! I scratch my head with the lightning and purr myself to sleep with the thunder! When I'm cold I bile the Gulf of Mexico and bathe in it; when I'm hot I fan myself with an equinoctial storm; when I'm thirsty I reach up and suck a cloud dry like a sponge; when I range the earth hungry, famine follows in my tracks! Whoo-oop! Bow your neck and spread! I put my hand on the sun's face and make it night in the earth; I bite a piece out of the moon and hurry the seasons; I shake myself and crumble the mountains! Contemplate me through leather — *don't* use the naked eye! I'm the man with a petrified heart and biler-iron bowels! The massacre of isolated communities is the pastime of my idle moments, the destruction of nationalities the serious business of my life! The boundless vastness of the great American desert is my inclosed property, and I bury my dead on my own premises!" He jumped up and cracked his heels together three times before he lit (they cheered him again), and as he came down he shouted out: "Whoo-oop! bow your neck and spread, for the pet child of calamity's a-coming!"

Then the other one went to swelling around and blowing again — the first one — the one they called Bob; next, the Child of Calamity chipped in again, bigger than ever; then they both got at it at the same time, swelling round and round each other and punching their fists 'most into each other's faces, and whooping and jawing like Injuns; then Bob called the Child names, and the Child called him names back again: next, Bob called him a heap rougher names, and the Child come back at him with the very worst kind of language; next, Bob knocked the Child's hat off, and the Child picked it up and kicked Bob's ribbony hat about six foot; Bob went and got it and said never mind, this warn't going to be the last of this thing, because he was a man that never forgot and never forgive, and so the Child better look out; for there was a time a-coming, just as sure as he was a living man, that he would have to answer to him with the best blood in his body. The Child said no man was willinger than he was for that time to come, and he would give Bob fair warning, *now*, never to cross his path again, for he could never rest till he had waded in his blood; for such was his nature, though he was sparing him now on account of his family, if he had one.

Both of them was edging away in different directions, growling and shaking their heads and going on about what they was going to do; but a little black-whiskered chap skipped up and says: —

"Come back here, you couple of chicken-livered cowards, and I'll thrash the two of ye!"

And he done it, too. He snatched them, he jerked them this way and that, he booted them around, he knocked them sprawling faster than they could get up. Why, it warn't two minutes till they begged like dogs — and how the other lot did yell and laugh and clap their hands all the way through, and shout "Sail in, Corpse-Maker!" "Hi! at him again, Child of Calamity!" "Bully for you, little Davy!" Well, it was a perfect pow-wow for a while. Bob and the Child had red noses and black eyes when they got through. Little Davy made them own up that they was sneaks and cowards, and not fit to eat with a dog or drink with a nigger; then Bob and the Child shook hands with each other very solemn, and said they had always respected each other and was willing to let bygones be bygones. So then they washed their faces in the river; and just then there was a loud order to stand by for a crossing, and some of them went forward to man the sweeps there, and the rest went aft to handle the after-sweeps.

A STEAMBOAT LANDING AT A SMALL TOWN

From 'Life on the Mississippi.' Copyright, 1883, by James R. Osgood and Company

ONCE a day a cheap gaudy packet arrived upward from St. Louis, and another downward from Keokuk. Before these events, the day was glorious with expectancy; after them, the day was a dead and empty thing. Not only the boys but the whole village felt this. After all these years I can picture that old time to myself now, just as it was then: the white town drowsing in the sunshine of a summer's morning; the streets empty, or pretty nearly so; one or two clerks sitting in front of the Water Street stores, with their splint-bottomed chairs tilted back against the wall, chins on breasts, hats slouched over their faces, asleep — with shingle-shavings enough around to show what broke them down; a sow and a litter of pigs loafing along the sidewalk, doing a good business in watermelon rinds and seeds; two or three lonely little freight piles scattered about the "levee"; a pile of "skids" on the slope of the stone-paved wharf, and the fragrant town drunkard asleep in the shadow of them; two or three wood flats at the head of the wharf, but nobody to listen to the peaceful lapping of the wavelets against them; the great Mississippi, the majestic, the magnificent Mississippi, rolling its mile-wide tide along, shining in the sun; the dense forest away on the other side; the "point" above the town and the "point" below, bounding the river-glimpse and turning it into a sort of sea, and withal a very still and brilliant and lonely one. Presently a film of dark smoke appears above one of those remote "points"; instantly a negro drayman, famous for his quick eye and prodigious voice, lifts up the cry, "S-t-e-a-m-boat a-comin'!" and the scene changes! The town drunkard stirs, the clerks wake up, a furious clatter of drays follows, every house and store pours out a human contribution, and all in a twinkling the dead town is alive and moving. Drays, carts, men, boys, all go hurrying from many quarters to a common center, the wharf. Assembled there, the people fasten their eyes upon the coming boat, as upon a wonder they are seeing for the first time. And the boat *is* rather a handsome sight too. She is long and sharp and trim and pretty; she has two tall fancy-topped chimneys, with a gilded device of some kind swung between them; a fanciful pilot-house, all glass and "gingerbread," perched on top of the "texas" deck behind them; the paddle-boxes are gorgeous with a picture or with gilded rays above the boat's name; the boiler deck, the hurricane deck, and the texas deck are fenced and ornamented with clean white railings; there is a flag gallantly flying from the jack-staff; the furnace doors are open and the fires glaring bravely; the upper decks are black with passengers; the captain stands by the big bell, calm, imposing, the envy of all; great volumes of the blackest smoke are rolling and tumbling out of the chimneys — a husbanded grandeur created with a bit of pitch-pine just before arriving at a town; the crew are grouped on the forecastle; the broad stage is run far out over the port bow, and an envied deck hand stands picturesquely on the end of it with a coil of rope in his hand; the pent steam is screaming through the gage-cocks; the captain lifts his hand, a bell rings, the wheels stop; then they turn back, churning the water to a foam, and the steamer is at rest. Then such a scramble as there is to get aboard, and to get ashore, and to take in freight and to discharge freight, all at one and the same time; and such a yelling and cursing as the mates facilitate it all with! Ten minutes later the steamer is under way again, with no flag on the jack-staff and no black smoke issuing from the chimneys. After ten more minutes the town is dead again, and the town drunkard asleep by the skids once more.

THE HIGH RIVER: AND A PHANTOM PILOT

From 'Life on the Mississippi.' Copyright, 1883, by James R. Osgood and Company

DURING this big rise these small-fry craft were an intolerable nuisance. We were running chute after chute — a new world to me — and if there was a particularly cramped place in a chute, we would be pretty sure to meet a broad-horn there; and if he failed to be there, we would find him in a still worse locality, namely, the head of the chute, on the shoal water. And then there would be no end of profane cordialities exchanged.

Sometimes, in the big river, when we would be feeling our way cautiously along through a fog, the deep hush would suddenly be broken by yells and a clamor of tin pans, and all in an instant a log raft would appear vaguely through the webby veil, close upon us; and then we did not wait to swap knives, but snatched our engine bells out by the roots and piled on all the steam we had, to scramble out of the way! One doesn't hit a rock or a solid log raft with a steamboat when he can get excused.

You will hardly believe it, but many steamboat clerks always carried a large assortment of religious tracts with them in those old departed steamboating days. Indeed they did. Twenty times a day we would be cramping up around a bar, while a string of these small-fry rascals were drifting down into the head of the bend away above and beyond us a couple of miles. Now a skiff would dart away from one of them, and come fighting its laborious way across the desert of water. It would "ease all," in the shadow of our forecastle, and the panting oarsmen would shout, "Gimme a pa-a-per!" as the skiff drifted swiftly astern. The clerk would throw over a file of New Orleans journals. If these were picked up *without comment*, you might notice that now a dozen other skiffs had been drifting down upon us without saying anything. You understand, they had been waiting to see how No. 1 was going to fare. No. 1 making no comment, all the rest would bend to their oars and come on now; and as fast as they came the clerk would heave over neat bundles of religious tracts, tied to shingles. The amount of hard swearing which twelve packages of religious literature will command when impartially divided up among twelve raftsmen's crews, who have pulled a heavy skiff two miles on a hot day to get them, is simply incredible.

As I have said, the big rise brought a new world under my vision. By the time the river was over its banks we had forsaken our old paths and were hourly climbing over bars that had stood ten feet out of water before; we were shaving stumpy shores, like that at the foot of Madrid Bend, which I had always seen avoided before; we were clattering through chutes like that of 82, where the opening at the foot was an unbroken wall of timber till our nose was almost at the very spot. Some of these chutes were utter solitudes. The dense untouched forest overhung both banks of the crooked little crack, and one could believe that human creatures had never intruded there before. The swinging grapevines, the grassy nooks and vistas, glimpsed as we swept by, the flowering creepers waving their red blossoms from the tops of dead trunks, and all the spendthrift richness of the forest foliage, were wasted and thrown away there. The chutes were lovely places to steer in; they were deep, except at the head; the current was gentle; under the "points" the water was absolutely dead, and the invisible banks so bluff that where the tender willow thickets projected you could bury your boat's broadside in them as you tore along, and then you seemed fairly to fly.

Behind other islands we found wretched little farms and wretcheder little log cabins; there were crazy rail fences sticking a foot or two above the water, with one or two jeans-clad, chills-racked, yellow-faced male miserables roosting on the top rail, elbows on knees, jaws in hands, grinding tobacco and discharging the result at floating chips through crevices left by lost teeth; while the rest of the family and the few farm animals were huddled together in an empty wood flat riding at her moorings close at hand. In this flatboat the family would have to cook and eat and sleep for a lesser or greater number of days (or possibly weeks), until the river should fall two or three feet and let them get back to their log cabin and their chills again — chills being a merciful provision of an all-wise Providence to enable them to take exercise without exertion. And this sort of watery camping out was a thing which these people were rather liable to be treated to a couple of times a year: by the December rise out of the Ohio, and the June rise out of the Mississippi. And yet these were kindly dispensations, for they at least enabled the poor things to rise from the dead now and then, and look upon life when a steamboat went by. They appreciated the blessing too, for they spread their mouths and eyes wide open and made the most of these occasions. Now what *could* these banished creatures find to do to keep from dying of the blues during the low-water season!

Once in one of these lovely island chutes we found our course completely bridged by a great fallen tree. This will serve to show how narrow some of the chutes were. The passengers had an hour's recreation in a virgin wildernes while the boat hands chopped the bridge away; for there was no such thing as turning back, you comprehend.

From Cairo to Baton Rouge, when the river is over its banks, you have no particular trouble in the night, for the thousand-mile wall of dense forest that guards the two banks all the way is only gapped with a farm or woodyard opening at intervals, and so you can't "get out of the river" much easier than you could get out of a fenced lane; but from Baton Rouge to New Orleans it is a different matter. The river is more than a mile wide, and very deep — as much as two hundred feet, in places. Both banks, for a good deal over a hundred miles, are shorn of their timber and bordered by continuous sugar plantations, with only here and there a scattering sapling or row of ornamental China-trees. The timber is shorn off clear to the rear of the plantations, from two to four miles. When the first frost threatens to come, the planters snatch off their crops in a hurry. When they have finished grinding the cane, they form the refuse of the stalks (which they call *bagasse*) into great piles and set fire to them, though in other sugar countries the bagasse is used for fuel in the furnaces of the sugar-mills. Now the piles of damp bagasse burn slowly, and smoke like Satan's own kitchen.

An embankment ten or fifteen feet high guards both banks of the Mississippi all the way down that lower end of the river, and this embankment is set back from the edge of the shore from ten to perhaps a hundred feet, according to circumstances; say thirty or forty feet as a general thing. Fill that whole region with an impenetrable gloom of smoke from a hundred miles of burning bagasse piles, when the river is over the banks, and turn a steamboat loose along there at midnight and see how she will feel. And see how you will feel too! You find yourself away out in the midst of a vague dim sea that is shoreless, that fades out and loses itself in the murky distances; for you cannot discern the thin rib of embankment, and you are always imagining you see a straggling tree when you don't. The plantations themselves are transformed by the smoke and look like a part of the sea. All through your watch you are tortured with the exquisite misery of uncertainty. You hope you are keeping in the river, but you do not know. All that you are sure about is that you are likely to be within six feet of the bank *and* destruction, when you think you are a good half-mile from shore. And you are sure also that if you chance suddenly to fetch up against the embankment and topple your chimneys overboard, you will have the small comfort of knowing that it is about what you were expecting to do. One of the great Vicksburg packets darted out into a sugar plantation one night, at such a time, and had to stay there a week. But there was no novelty about it: it had often been done before.

I thought I had finished this chapter, but I wish to add a curious thing while it is in my mind. It is only relevant in that it is connected with piloting. There used to be an excellent pilot on the river, a Mr. X., who was a somnambulist. It was said that if his mind was troubled about a bad piece of river, he was pretty sure to get up and walk in his sleep and do strange things. He was once fellow pilot for a trip or two with George Ealer, on a great New Orleans passenger packet. During a considerable part of the first trip George was uneasy, but got over it by-and-by, as X. seemed content to stay in his bed when asleep. Late one night the boat was approaching Helena, Arkansas; the water was low, and the crossing above the town in a very blind and tangled condition. X. had seen the crossing since Ealer had, and as the night was particularly drizzly, sullen, and dark, Ealer was considering whether he had not better have X. called to assist in running the place, when the door opened and X. walked in. Now on very dark nights, light is a deadly enemy to piloting; you are aware that if you stand in a lighted room on such a night, you cannot see things in the street to any purpose; but if you put out the lights and stand in the gloom you can make out objects in the street pretty well. So on very dark nights pilots do not smoke; they allow no fire in the pilot-house stove if there is a crack which can allow the least ray to escape; they order the furnaces to be curtained with huge tarpaulins and the skylights to be closely blinded. Then no light whatever issues from the boat. The undefinable shape that now entered the pilot-house had Mr. X.'s voice. This said: —

"Let me take her, George; I've seen this place since you have, and it is so crooked that I reckon I can run it myself easier than I could tell you how to do it."

"It is kind of you, and I swear *I* am willing. I haven't got another drop of perspiration left in me. I have been spinning around and around the wheel like a squirrel. It is so dark I can't tell which way she is swinging till she is coming around like a whirligig."

So Ealer took a seat on the bench, panting and breathless. The black phantom assumed the wheel without saying anything, steadied the waltzing steamer with a turn or two, and then stood at ease, coaxing her a little to this side and then to that, as gently and as sweetly as if the time had been noonday. When Ealer observed his marvel of steering, he wished he had not confessed! He stared and wondered, and finally said: —

"Well, I thought I knew how to steer a steamboat, but that was another mistake of mine."

X. said nothing, but went serenely on with his work. He rang for the leads; he rang to slow down the steam; he worked the boat carefully and neatly into invisible marks, then stood at the center of the wheel and peered blandly out into the blackness, fore and aft, to verify his position; as the leads shoaled more and more, he stopped the engines entirely, and the dead silence and suspense of "drifting" followed; when the shoalest water was struck, he cracked on the steam, carried her handsomely over, and then began to work her warily into the next system of shoal marks; the same patient, heedful use of leads and engines followed, the boat slipped through without touching bottom, and entered upon the third and last intricacy of the crossing; imperceptibly she moved through the gloom, crept by inches into her marks, drifted tediously till the shoalest water was cried, and then, under a tremendous head of steam, went swinging over the reef and away into deep water and safety!

Ealer let his long-pent breath out in a great relieving sigh, and said: —

"That's the sweetest piece of piloting that was ever done on the Mississippi River! I wouldn't believed it could be done, if I hadn't seen it."

There was no reply, and he added: —

"Just hold her five minutes longer, partner, and let me run down and get a cup of coffee."

A minute later Ealer was biting into a pie, down in the "texas," and comforting himself with coffee. Just then the night watchman happened in, and was about to happen out again, when he noticed Ealer and exclaimed: —

"Who is at the wheel, sir?"

"X."

"Dart for the pilot-house, quicker than lightning!"

The next moment both men were flying up the pilot-house companion way, three steps at a jump! Nobody there! The great steamer was whistling down the middle of the river at her own sweet will! The watchman shot out of the place again; Ealer seized the wheel, set the engine back with power, and held his breath while the boat reluctantly swung away from a "tow-head" which she was about to knock into the middle of the Gulf of Mexico!

By-and-by the watchman came back and said: —

"Didn't that lunatic tell you he was asleep when he first came up here?"

"No."

"Well, he was. I found him walking along on top of the railings, just as unconcerned as another man would walk a pavement; and I put him to bed; now just this minute there he was again, away astern, going through that sort of tight-rope deviltry the same as before."

"Well, I think I'll stay by, next time he has one of those fits. But I hope he'll have them often. You just ought to have seen him take this boat through Helena crossing. *I* never saw anything so gaudy before. And if he can do such gold-leaf, kid-glove, diamond-breastpin piloting when he is sound asleep, what *couldn't* he do if he was dead!"

AN ENCHANTING RIVER SCENE

From 'Life on the Mississippi.' Copyright, 1883, by James R. Osgood and Company

THE face of the water in time became a wonderful book — a book that was a dead language to the uneducated passenger, but which told its mind to me without reserve, delivering its most cherished secrets as clearly as if it uttered them with a voice. And it was not a book to be read once and thrown aside, for it had a new story to tell every day. Throughout the long twelve hundred miles there was never a page that was void of interest, never one that you could leave unread without loss, never one that you would want to skip, thinking you could find higher enjoyment in some other thing. There never was so wonderful a book written by man; never one whose interest was so absorbing, so unflagging, so sparklingly renewed with every re-perusal. The passenger who could not read it was charmed with a peculiar sort of faint dimple on its surface (on the rare occasions when he did not overlook it altogether); but to the pilot that was an *italicized* passage; indeed it was more than that — it was a legend of the largest capitals, with a string of shouting exclamation-points at the end of it; for it meant that a wreck or a rock was buried there, that could tear the life out of the strongest vessel that ever floated. It is the faintest and simplest expression the water ever makes, and the most hideous to a pilot's eye. In truth, the passenger who could not read this book saw nothing but all manner of pretty pictures in it, painted by the sun and shaded by the clouds; whereas to the trained eye these were not pictures at all, but the grimmest and most dead-earnest of reading matter.

Now when I had mastered the language of this water and had come to know every trifling feature that bordered the great river as familiarly as I knew the letters of the alphabet, I had made a valuable acquisition. But I had lost something too. I had lost something which could never be restored to me while I lived. All the grace, the beauty, the poetry had gone out of the majestic river! I still kept in mind a certain wonderful sunset which I witnessed when steamboating was new to me. A broad expanse of the river was turned to blood; in the middle distance the red hue brightened into gold, through which a solitary log came floating, black and conspicuous; in one place a long slanting mark lay sparkling upon the water; in another the surface was broken by boiling tumbling rings that were as many-tinted as an opal; where the ruddy flush was faintest, was a smooth spot that was covered with graceful circles and radiating lines, ever so delicately traced; the shore on our left was densely wooded, and the somber shadow that fell from this forest was broken in one place by a long ruffled trail that shone like silver; and high above the forest wall a clean-stemmed dead tree waved a single leafy bough, that glowed like a flame in the unobstructed splendor that was glowing from the sun. There were graceful curves, reflected images, woody heights, soft distances; and over the whole scene, far and near, the dissolving lights drifted steadily, enriching it every passing moment with new marvels of coloring.

I stood like one bewitched. I drank it in, in a speechless rapture. The world was new to me, and I had never seen anything like this at home. But as I have said, a day came when I began to cease from noting the glories and the charms which the moon and the sun and the twilight wrought upon the river's face; another day came when I ceased altogether to note them. Then, if that sunset scene had been repeated, I should have looked upon it without rapture and should have commented upon it inwardly after this fashion: This sun means that we are going to have wind tomorrow; that floating log means that the river is rising, small thanks to it; that slanting mark on the water refers to a bluff reef which is going to kill somebody's steamboat one of these nights, if it keeps on stretching out like that; those tumbling "boils" show a dissolving bar and a changing channel there; the lines and circles in the slick water over yonder are a warning that that troublesome place is shoaling up dangerously; that silver streak in the shadow of the forest is the "break" from a new snag, and he has located himself in the very best place he could have found to fish for steamboats; that tall dead tree, with a single living branch, is not going to last long, and then how is a body ever going to get through this blind place at night without the friendly old landmark?

No, the romance and the beauty were all gone from the river. All the value any feature of it had for me now was the amount of usefulness it could furnish toward compassing the safe piloting of a steamboat. Since those days I have pitied doctors from my heart. What does the lovely flush in a beauty's cheek mean to a doctor but a "break" that ripples above some deadly disease? Are not all her visible charms sown thick with what are to him the signs and symbols of hidden decay? Does he ever see her beauty at all, or doesn't he simply view her professionally and comment upon her unwholesome condition all to himself? And doesn't he sometimes wonder whether he has gained most or lost most by learning his trade?

THE LIGHTNING PILOT

From 'Life on the Mississippi.' Copyright, 1883, by James R. Osgood and Company

NEXT morning I felt pretty rusty and low-spirited. We went booming along, taking a good many chances, for we were anxious to "get out of the river" (as getting out to Cairo was called) before night should overtake us. But Mr. Bixby's partner, the other pilot, presently grounded the boat, and we lost so much time getting her off that it was plain the darkness would overtake us a good long way above the mouth. This was a great misfortune; especially to certain of our visiting pilots, whose boats would have to wait for their return, no matter how long that might be. It sobered the pilot-house talk a good deal. Coming up-stream, pilots did not mind low water or any kind of darkness; nothing stopped them but fog. But down-stream work was different; a boat was too nearly helpless, with a stiff current pushing behind her; so it was not customary to run down-stream at night in low water.

There seemed to be one small hope, however: if we could get through the intricate and dangerous Hat Island crossing before night, we could venture the rest, for we would have plainer sailing and better water. But it would be insanity to attempt Hat Island at night. So there was a deal of looking at watches all the rest of the day, and a constant ciphering upon the speed we were making; Hat Island was the eternal subject; sometimes hope was high, and sometimes we were delayed in a bad crossing, and down it went again. For hours all hands lay under the burden of this suppressed excitement; it was even communicated to me, and I got to feeling so solicitous about Hat Island, and under such an awful pressure of responsibility, that I wished I might have five minutes on shore to draw a good full relieving breath, and start over again. We were standing no regular watches. Each of our pilots ran such portions of the river as he had run when coming up-stream, because of his greater familiarity with it; but both remained in the pilot-house constantly.

An hour before sunset, Mr. Bixby took the wheel and Mr. W —— stepped aside. For the next thirty minutes every man held his watch in his hand and was restless, silent, and uneasy. At last somebody said with a doomful sigh: —

"Well, yonder's Hat Island — and we can't make it."

All the watches closed with a snap, everybody sighed and muttered something about its being "too bad, too bad — ah, if we could *only* have got here half an hour sooner!" and the place was thick with the atmosphere of disappointment. Some started to go out, but loitered, hearing no bell-tap to land. The sun dipped behind the horizon, the boat went on. Inquiring looks passed from one guest to another; and one who had his hand on the door-knob and had turned it, waited, then presently took away his hand and let the knob turn back again. We bore steadily down the bend. More looks were exchanged, and nods of surprised admiration — but no words. Insensibly the men drew together behind Mr. Bixby, as the sky darkened and one or two dim stars came out. The dead silence and sense of waiting became oppressive. Mr. Bixby pulled the cord, and two deep mellow notes from the big bell floated off on the night. Then a pause, and one more note was struck. The watchman's voice followed, from the hurricane deck: —

"Labboard lead, there! Stabboard lead!"

The cries of the leadsmen began to rise out of the distance, and were gruffly repeated by the word-passers on the hurricane deck.

"M-a-r-k three! . . . M-a-r-k three! . . . Quarter-less-three! . . . Half twain! . . . Quarter twain! . . . M-a-r-k twain! . . . Quarter-less —"

Mr. Bixby pulled two bell-ropes, and was answered by faint jinglings far below in the engine-room, and our speed slackened. The steam began to whistle through the gage-cocks. The cries of the leadsmen went on — and it is a weird sound always in the night. Every pilot in the lot was watching now, with fixed eyes, and talking under his breath. Nobody was calm and easy but Mr. Bixby. He would put his wheel down and stand on a spoke, and as the steamer swung into her (to me) utterly invisible marks — for we seemed to be in the midst of a wide and gloomy sea — he would meet and fasten her there. Out of the murmur of half-audible talk one caught a coherent sentence now and then, such as: —

"There; she's over the first reef all right!"

After a pause, another subdued voice: —

"Her stern's coming down just *exactly* right, by *George!*"

"Now she's in the marks; over she goes!"

Somebody else muttered: —

"Oh, it was done beautiful — *beautiful!*"

Now the engines were stopped altogether, and we drifted with the current. Not that I could see the boat drift, for I could not, the stars being all gone by this time. This drifting was the dismalest work; it held one's heart still. Presently I discovered a blacker gloom than that which surrounded us. It was the head of the island. We were closing right down upon it. We entered its deeper shadow, and so imminent seemed the peril that I was likely to suffocate; and I had the strongest impulse to do *something*, anything, to save the vessel. But still Mr. Bixby stood by his wheel, silent, intent as a cat, and all the pilots stood shoulder to shoulder at his back.

"She'll not make it!" somebody whispered.

The water grew shoaler and shoaler, by the leadsman's cries, till it was down to —

"Eight-and-a-half! . . . E-i-g-h-t feet! . . . E-i-g-h-t feet! . . . Seven-and —"

Mr. Bixby said warningly through his speaking-tube to the engineer: —

"Stand by, now!"

"Ay-ay, sir!"

"Seven-and-a-half! Seven feet! *Six*-and —"

We touched bottom! Instantly Mr. Bixby set a lot of bells ringing, shouted through the tube, "*Now* let her have it — every ounce you've got!" then to his partner, "Put her hard down! snatch her! snatch her!" The boat rasped and ground her way through the sand, hung upon the apex of disaster a single tremendous instant, and then over she went! And such a shout as went up at Mr. Bixby's back never loosened the roof of a pilot-house before!

There was no more trouble after that. Mr. Bixby was a hero that night; and it was some little time, too, before his exploit ceased to be talked about by river men.

AN EXPEDITION AGAINST OGRES

From 'A Connecticut Yankee in King Arthur's Court.' Copyright, 1889, by Charles L. Webster and Company

MY expedition was all the talk that day and that night, and the boys were very good to me, and made much of me, and seemed to have forgotten their vexation and disappointment, and come to be as anxious for me to hive those ogres and set those ripe old virgins loose as if it were themselves that had the contract. Well, they *were* good children — but just children, that is all. And they gave me no end of points about how to scout for giants, and how to scoop them in; and they told me all sorts of charms against enchantments, and gave me salves and other rubbish to put on my wounds. But it never occurred to one of them to reflect that if I was such a wonderful necromancer as I was pretending to be, I ought not to need salves, or instructions, or charms against enchantments, and least of all arms and armor, on a foray of any kind — even against fire-spouting dragons and devils hot from perdition, let alone such poor adversaries as these I was after, these common-place ogres of the back settlements.

I was to have an early breakfast, and start at dawn, for that was the usual way; but I had the demon's own time with my armor, and this delayed me a little. It is troublesome to get into, and there is so much detail. First you wrap a layer or two of blanket around your body for a sort of cushion, and to keep off the cold iron; then you put on your sleeves and shirt of chain-mail — these are made of small steel links woven together, and they form a fabric so flexible that if you toss your shirt on to the floor it slumps into a pile like a peck of wet fish-net; it is very heavy and is nearly the uncomfortablest material in the world for a night-shirt, yet plenty used it for that — tax collectors and reformers, and one-horse kings with a defective title, and those sorts of people; then you put on your shoes — flatboats roofed over with interleaving bands of steel — and screw your clumsy spurs into the heels. Next you buckle your greaves on your legs and your cuisses on your thighs; then come your backplate and your breastplate, and you begin to feel crowded; then you hitch on to the breastplate the half-petticoat of broad overlapping bands of steel which hangs down in front but is scalloped out behind so you can sit down, and isn't any real improvement on an inverted coal-scuttle, either for looks, or for wear, or to wipe your hands on; next you belt on your sword; then you put your stove-pipe joints on to your arms, your iron gauntlets on to your hands, your iron rat-trap on to your head, with a rag of steel web hitched on to it to hang over the back of your neck — and there you are, snug as a candle in a candle-mold. This is no time to dance. Well, a man that is packed away like that is a nut that isn't worth the cracking, there is so little of the meat, when you get down to it, by comparison with the shell.

The boys helped me, or I never could have got in. Just as we finished, Sir Bedivere happened in, and I saw that as like as not I hadn't chosen the most convenient outfit for a long trip. How stately he looked; and tall and broad and grand. He had on his head a conical steel casque that only came down to his ears, and for visor had only a narrow steel bar that extended down to his upper lip and protected his nose; and all the rest of him, from neck to heel, was flexible chain-mail, trousers and all. But pretty much all of him was hidden under his outside garment, which of course was of chain-mail, as I said, and hung straight from his shoulders to his ankles; and from his middle to the bottom, both before and behind, was divided, so that he could ride and let the skirts hang down on each side. He was going grailing, and it was just the outfit for it, too. I would have given a good deal for that ulster, but it was too late now to be fooling around. The sun was just up; the king and the court were all on hand to see me off and wish me luck; so it wouldn't be etiquette for me to tarry. You don't get on your horse yourself; no, if you tried it you would get disappointed. They carry you out, just as they carry a sun-struck man to the drug-store, and put you on, and help get you to rights, and fix your feet in the stirrups; and all the while you do feel so strange and stuffy and like somebody else — like somebody that has been married on a sudden, or struck by lightning, or something like that, and hasn't been quite fetched around yet, and is sort of numb, and can't just get his bearings. Then they stood up the mast they called a spear in its socket by my left foot, and I gripped it with my hand; lastly they hung my shield around my neck, and I was all complete and ready to up anchor and get to sea. Everybody was as good to me as they could be, and a maid of honor gave me the stirrup-cup her own self. There was nothing more to do now but for that damsel to get up behind me on a pillion, which she did, and put an arm or so around me to hold on.

And so we started; and everybody gave us a good-by and waved their handkerchiefs or helmets. And everybody we met, going down the hill and through the village, was respectful to us except some shabby little boys on the outskirts. They said: —

"Oh, what a guy!" and hove clods at us.

In my experience boys are the same in all ages. They don't respect anything, they don't care for anything or anybody. They say "Go up, baldhead!" to the prophet going his unoffending way in the gray of antiquity; they sass me in the holy gloom of the Middle Ages; and I had seen them act the same way in Buchanan's administration; I remember, because I was there and helped. The prophet had his bears and settled with his boys; and I wanted to get down and settle with mine, but it wouldn't answer, because I couldn't have got up again. I hate a country without a derrick.

Straight off, we were in the country. It was most lovely and pleasant in those sylvan solitudes in the early cool morning in the first freshness of autumn. From hilltops we saw fair green valleys lying spread out below, with streams winding through them, and island groves of trees here and there, and huge lonely oaks scattered about and casting black blots of shade; and beyond the valleys we saw the ranges of hills, blue with haze, stretching away in billowy perspective to the horizon, with at wide intervals a dim fleck of white or gray on a wave-summit, which we knew was a castle. We crossed broad natural lawns sparkling with dew, and we moved like spirits, the cushioned turf giving out no sound of footfall; we dreamed along through glades in a mist of green light that got its tint from the sun-drenched roof of leaves overhead, and by our feet the clearest and coldest of runlets went frisking and gossiping over its reefs and making a sort of whispering music comfortable to hear; and at times we left the world behind and entered into the solemn great deeps and rich gloom of the forest, where furtive wild things whisked and scurried by and were gone before you could even get your eye on the place where the noise was; and where only the earliest birds were turning out and getting to business, with a song here and a quarrel yonder and a mysterious far-off hammering and drumming for worms on a tree-trunk away somewhere in the impenetrable remoteness of the woods. And by-and-by out we would swing again into the glare.

About the third or fourth or fifth time that we swung out into the glare — it was along there somewhere, a couple of hours or so after sun-up — it wasn't as pleasant as it had been. It was beginning to get hot. This was quite noticeable. We had a very long pull, after that, without any shade. Now it is curious how progressively little frets grow and multiply after they once get a start. Things which I didn't mind at all at first, I began to mind now — and more and more, too, all the time. The first ten or fifteen times I wanted my handkerchief I didn't seem to care; I got along, and said never mind, it isn't any matter, and dropped it out of my mind. But now it was different: I wanted it all the time; it was nag, nag, nag, right along, and no rest: I couldn't get it out of my mind; and so at last I lost my temper, and said hang a man that would make a suit of armor without any pockets in it. You see I had my handkerchief in my helmet, and some other things; but it was that kind of a helmet that you can't take off by yourself. That hadn't occurred to me when I put it there; and in fact I didn't know it. I supposed it would be particularly convenient there. And so now the thought of its being there, so handy and close by, and yet not get-at-able, made it all the worse and the harder to bear. Yes, the thing that you can't get is the thing that you want, mainly; every one has noticed that. Well, it took my mind off from everything else; took it clear off and centered it in my helmet; and mile after mile there it stayed, imagining the handkerchief, picturing the handkerchief; and it was bitter and aggravating to have the salt sweat keep trickling down into my eyes, and I couldn't get at it. It seems like a little thing on paper, but it was not a little thing at all; it was the most real kind of misery. I would not say it if it was not so. I made up my mind that I would carry along a reticule next time, let it look how it might and people say what they would. Of course these iron dudes of the Round Table would think it was scandalous, and maybe raise sheol about it, but as for me, give me comfort first and style afterwards. So we jogged along, and now and then we struck a stretch of dust, and it would tumble up in clouds and get into my nose and make me sneeze and cry; and of course I said things I oughtn't to have said — I don't deny that. I am not better than others. We couldn't seem to meet anybody in this lonesome Britain, not even an ogre; and in the mood I was in then, it was well for the ogre; that is, an ogre with a handkerchief. Most knights would have thought of nothing but getting his armor; but so I got his bandana, he could keep his hardware for all of me.

Meantime it was getting hotter and hotter in there. You see the sun was beating down and warming up the iron more and more all the time. Well, when you are hot, that way, every little thing irritates you. When I trotted I rattled like a crate of dishes, and that annoyed me; and moreover I couldn't seem to stand that shield slatting and banging, now about my breast, now around my back; and if I dropped into a walk my joints creaked and screeched in that wearisome way that a wheelbarrow does, and as we didn't create any breeze at that gait, I was like to get fried in that stove; and besides, the quieter you went the heavier the iron settled down on you, and the more and more tons you seemed to weigh every minute. And you had to be always changing hands and passing your spear over to the other foot, it got so irksome for one hand to hold it long at a time.

Well, you know when you perspire that way, in rivers, there comes a time when you — when you — well, when you itch. You are inside, your hands are outside; so there you are; nothing but iron between. It is not a light thing, let it sound as it may. First it is one place; then another; then some more; and it goes on spreading and spreading, and at last the territory is all occupied, and nobody can imagine what you feel like, nor how unpleasant it is. And when it had got to the worst, and it seemed to me that I could not stand anything more, a fly got in through the bars and settled on my nose, and the bars were stuck and wouldn't work, and I couldn't get the visor up; and I could only shake my head, which was baking hot by this time, and the fly — well, you know how a fly acts when he has got a certainty: he only minded the shaking enough to change from nose to lip, and lip to ear, and buzz and buzz all around in there, and keep on lighting and biting in a way that a person already so distressed as I was simply could not stand. So I gave in, and got Alisande to unship the helmet and relieve me of it. Then she emptied the conveniences out of it and fetched it full of water, and I drank and then stood up and she poured the rest down inside the armor. One cannot think how refreshing it was. She continued to fetch and pour until I was well soaked and thoroughly comfortable.

It was good to have a rest — and peace. But nothing is quite perfect in this life at any time. I had made a pipe a while back, and also some pretty fair tobacco; not the real thing, but what some of the Indians use: the inside bark of the willow, dried. These comforts had been in the helmet, and now I had them again, but no matches.

Gradually, as the time wore along, one annoying fact was borne in upon my understanding — that we were weather-bound. An armed novice cannot mount his horse without help and plenty of it. Sandy was not enough; not enough for me, anyway. We had to wait until somebody should come along. Waiting in silence would have been agreeable enough, for I was full of matter for reflection, and wanted to give it a chance to work. I wanted to try and think out how it was that rational or even half-rational men could ever have learned to wear armor, considering its inconveniences; and how they had managed to keep up such a fashion for generations when it was plain that what I had suffered today they had had to suffer all the days of their lives. I wanted to think that out; and moreover I wanted to think out some way to reform this evil and persuade the people to let the foolish fashion die out: but thinking was out of the question in the circumstances. You couldn't think where Sandy was. She was a quite biddable creature and good-hearted, but she had a flow of talk that was as steady as a mill and made your heard sore like the drays and wagons in a city. If she had had a cork she would have been a comfort. But you can't cork that kind; they would die. Her clack was going all day, and you would think something would surely happen to her works by-and-by; but no, they never got out of order; and she never had to slack up for words. She could grind and pump and churn and buzz by the week, and never stop to oil up or blow out. And yet the result was just nothing but wind. She never had any ideas, any more than a fog has. She was a perfect blatherskite; I mean for jaw, jaw, jaw, talk, talk, talk, jabber, jabber, jabber; — but just as good as she could be. I hadn't minded her mill that morning, on account of having that hornet's nest of other troubles; but more than once in the afternoon I had to say: —

"Take a rest, child; the way you are using up all the domestic air, the kingdom will have to go to importing it by tomorrow, and it's a low enough treasury without that."

By permission of S. L. Clemens and his publishers

THE TRUE PRINCE AND THE FEIGNED ONE

From 'The Prince and the Pauper.' Copyright, 1889, by Charles L. Webster and Company

AT last the final act was at hand. The Archbishop of Canterbury lifted up the crown of England from its cushion and held it out over the trembling mock king's head. In the same instant a rainbow radiance flashed along the spacious transept; for with one impulse every individual in the great concourse of nobles lifted a coronet and poised it over his or her head — and paused in that attitude.

A deep hush pervaded the Abbey. At this impressive moment a startling apparition intruded upon the scene — an apparition observed by none in the absorbed multitude, until it suddenly appeared, moving up the great central aisle. It was a boy, bare-headed, ill-shod, and clothed in coarse plebeian garments that were falling to rags. He raised his hand with a solemnity which ill comported with his soiled and sorry aspect, and delivered this note of warning: —

"I forbid you to set the crown of England upon that forfeited head. *I* am the king!"

In an instant several indignant hands were laid upon the boy, but in the same instant Tom Canty, in his regal vestments, made a swift step forward and cried out in a ringing voice: —

"Loose him and forbear! He *is* the king!"

A sort of panic of astonishment swept the assemblage, and they partly rose in their places and stared in a bewildered way at one another and at the chief figures in this scene, like persons who wondered whether they were awake and in their senses or asleep and dreaming. The Lord Protector was as amazed as the rest, but quickly recovered himself and exclaimed in a voice of authority: —

"Mind not his Majesty, his malady is upon him again — seize the vagabond!"

He would have been obeyed, but the mock king stamped his foot and cried out: —

"On your peril! Touch him not, he is the king!"

The hands were withheld; a paralysis fell upon the house; no one moved, no one spoke; indeed no one knew how to act or what to say, in so strange and surprising an emergency. While all minds were struggling to right themselves, the boy still moved steadily forward, with high port and confident mien; he had never halted from the beginning; and while the tangled minds still floundered helplessly, he stepped upon the platform, and the mock king ran with a glad face to meet him, and fell on his knees before him and said: —

"O my lord the king, let poor Tom Canty be first to swear fealty to thee, and say, 'Put on thy crown and enter into thine own again!'"

The Lord Protector's eye fell sternly upon the new-comer's face; but straightway the sternness vanished away, and gave place to an expression of wondering surprise. This thing happened also to the other great officers. They glanced at each other, and retreated a step by a common and unconscious impulse. The thought in each mind was the same: "What a strange resemblance!"

The Lord Protector reflected a moment or two in perplexity; then he said, with grave respectfulness: —

"By your favor, sir, I desire to ask certain questions which —"

"I will answer them, my lord."

The duke asked him many questions about the court, the late king, the prince, the princesses — the boy answered them correctly and without hesitating. He described the rooms of state in the palace, the late king's apartments, and those of the Prince of Wales.

It was strange; it was wonderful; yes, it was unaccountable — so all said that heard it. The tide was beginning to turn, and Tom Canty's hopes to run high, when the Lord Protector shook his head and said: —

"It is true it is most wonderful — but it is no more than our lord the king likewise can do." This remark, and this reference to himself as still the king, saddened Tom Canty, and he felt his hopes crumbling under him. "These are not *proofs*," added the Protector.

The tide was turning very fast now, very fast indeed — but in the wrong direction; it was leaving poor Tom Canty stranded on the throne, and sweeping the other out to sea. The Lord Protector communed with himself — shook his head; the thought forced itself upon him, "It is perilous to the State and to us all, to entertain so fateful a riddle as this; it could divide the nation and undermine the throne." He turned and said: —

"Sir Thomas, arrest this — No, hold!" His face lighted, and he confronted the ragged candidate with this question: —

"Where lieth the Great Seal? Answer me this truly, and the riddle is unriddled; for only he that was Prince of Wales *can* so answer! On so trivial a thing hang a throne and a dynasty!"

It was a lucky thought, a happy thought. That it was so considered by the great officials was manifested by the silent applause that shot from eye to eye around their circle in the form of bright approving glances. Yes, none but the true prince could dissolve the stubborn mystery of the vanished Great Seal — this forlorn little imposter had been taught his lesson well, but here his teachings must fail, for his teacher himself could not answer *that* question — ah, very good, very good indeed; now we shall be rid of this troublesome and perilous business in short order! And so they nodded invisibly and smiled inwardly with satisfaction, and looked to see this foolish lad stricken with a palsy of guilty confusion. How surprised they were, then, to see nothing of the sort happen — how they marveled to hear him answer up promptly in a confident and untroubled voice and say: —

"There is naught in this riddle that is difficult." Then, without so much as a by-your-leave to anybody, he turned and gave this command with the easy manner of one accustomed to doing such things: "My lord St. John, go you to my private cabinet in the palace — for none knoweth the place better than you — and close down to the floor, in the left corner, remotest from the door that opens from the ante-chamber, you shall find in the wall a brazen nail-head; press upon it and a little jewel-closet will fly open, which not even you do know of — no, nor any soul else in all the world but me and the trusty artisan that did contrive it for me. The first thing that falleth under your eye will be the Great Seal — fetch it hither."

All the company wondered at this speech, and wondered still more to see the little mendicant pick out this peer without hesitancy or apparent fear of mistake, and call him by name with such a placidly convincing air of having known him all his life. The peer was almost surprised into obeying. He even made a movement as if to go, but quickly recovered his tranquil attitude and confessed his blunder with a blush. Tom Canty turned upon him and said sharply: —

"Why dost thou hesitate? Hast not heard the king's command? Go!"

The lord St. John made a deep obeisance — and it was observed that it was a significantly cautious and non-committal one, it not being delivered at either of the kings, but at the neutral ground about half-way between the two — and took his leave.

Now began a movement of the gorgeous particles of that official group which was slow, scarcely perceptible, and yet steady and persistent — a movement such as is observed in a kaleidoscope that is turned slowly, whereby the components of one splendid cluster fall away and join themselves to another — a movement which little by little, in the present case, dissolved the glittering crowd that stood about Tom Canty and clustered it together again in the neighborhood of the new-comer. Tom Canty stood almost alone. Now ensued a brief season of deep suspense and waiting — during which even the few faint-hearts still remaining near Tom Canty gradually scraped together courage enough to glide, one by one, over to the majority. So at last Tom Canty, in his royal robes and jewels, stood wholly alone and isolated from the world, a conspicuous figure, occupying an elegant vacancy.

Now the lord St. John was seen returning. As he advanced up the mid-aisle, the interest was so intense that the low murmur of conversation in the great assemblage died out and was succeeded by a profound hush, a breathless stillness, through which his footfalls pulsed with a dull and distant sound. Every eye was fastened upon him as he moved along. He reached the platform, paused a moment, then moved toward Tom Canty with a deep obeisance, and said: —

"Sire, the Seal is not there!"

A mob does not melt away from the presence of a plague-patient with more haste than the band of pallid and terrified courtiers melted away from the presence of the shabby little claimant of the crown. In a moment he stood all alone, without friend or supporter, a target upon which was concentrated a bitter fire of scornful and angry looks. The Lord Protector called out fiercely: —

"Cast the beggar into the street, and scourge him through the town — the paltry knave is worth no more consideration!"

Officers of the guard sprang forward to obey, but Tom Canty waved them off and said: —

"Back! Whoso touches him perils his life!"

The Lord Protector was perplexed in the last degree. He said to the lord St. John: —

"Searched you well? — but it boots not to ask that. It doth seem passing strange. Little things, trifles, slip out of one's ken, and one does not think it matter for surprise; but how so bulky a thing as the Seal of England can vanish away and no man be able to get track of it again — a massy golden disk —"

Tom Canty, with beaming eyes, sprang forward and shouted:

"Hold, that is enough! Was it round? — and thick? — and had it letters and devices graved upon it? — Yes? Oh, *now* I know what this Great Seal is, that there's been such worry and pother about! An ye had described it to me, ye could have had it three weeks ago. Right well I know where it lies; but it was not I that put it there — first."

"Who then, my liege?" asked the Lord Protector.

"He that stands there — the rightful king of England. And he shall tell you himself where it lies — then you will believe he knew it of his own knowledge. Bethink thee, my king — spur thy memory — it was the last, the very *last* thing thou didst that day before thou didst rush forth from the palace, clothed in my rags, to punish the soldier that insulted me."

A silence ensued, undisturbed by a movement or a whisper, and all eyes were fixed upon the new-comer, who stood with bent head and corrugated brow, groping in his memory among a thronging multitude of valueless recollections for one single little elusive fact, which, found, would seat him upon a throne — unfound, would leave him as he was for good and all — a pauper and an outcast. Moment after moment passed — the moments built themselves into minutes — still the boy struggled silently on, and gave no sign. But at last he heaved a sigh, shook his head slowly, and said, with a trembling lip and in a despondent voice: —

"I call the scene back — all of it — but the Seal hath no place in it." He paused, then looked up, and said with gentle dignity, "My lords and gentlemen, if ye will rob your rightful sovereign of his own for lack of this evidence which he is not able to furnish, I may not stay ye, being powerless. But —"

"Oh folly, oh madness, my king!" cried Tom Canty in a panic; "wait! — think! Do not give up! — the cause is not lost! nor *shall* be, neither! List to what I say — follow every word — I am going to bring that morning back again, every hap just as it happened. We talked — I told you of my sisters, Nan and Bet — ah yes, you remember that; and about my old grandam — and the rough games of the lads of Offal Court — yes, you remember these things also; very well, follow me still, you shall recall everything. You gave me food and drink, and did with princely courtesy send away the servants, so that my low breeding might not shame me before them — ah yes, this also you remember."

As Tom checked off his details, and the other boy nodded his head in recognition of them, the great audience and the officials stared in puzzled wonderment; the tale sounded like true history, yet how could this impossible conjunction between a prince and a beggar boy have come about? Never was a company of people so perplexed, so interested, and so stupefied before.

"For a jest, my prince, we did exchange garments. Then we stood before a mirror; and so alike were we that both said it seemed as if there had been no change made — yes, you remember that. Then you noticed that the soldier had hurt my hand — look! here it is, I cannot yet even write with it, the fingers are so stiff. At this your Highness sprang up, vowing vengeance upon that soldier, and ran toward the door — you passed a table — that thing you call the Seal lay on that table — you snatched it up and looked eagerly about, as if for a place to hide it — your eye caught sight of — "

"There, 'tis sufficient! — and the dear God be thanked!" exclaimed the ragged claimant, in a mighty excitement. "Go, my good St. John — in an arm-piece of the Milanese armor that hangs on the wall, thou'lt find the Seal!"

"Right, my king! right!" cried Tom Canty; "*now* the scepter of England is thine own; and it were better for him that would dispute it that he had been born dumb! Go, my lord St. John, give thy feet wings!"

The whole assemblage was on its feet now, and well-nigh out of its mind with uneasiness, apprehension, and consuming excitement. On the floor and on the platform a deafening buzz of frantic conversation burst forth, and for some time nobody knew anything or heard anything or was interested in anything but what his neighbor was shouting into his ear, or he was shouting into his neighbor's ear. Time — nobody knew how much of it — swept by unheeded and unnoted. — At last a sudden hush fell upon the house, and in the same moment St. John appeared upon the platform and held the Great Seal aloft in his hand. Then such a shout went up!

"Long live the true king!"

For five minutes the air quaked with shouts and the crash of musical instruments, and was white with a storm of waving handkerchiefs; and through it all a ragged lad, the most conspicuous figure in England, stood, flushed and happy and proud, in the center of the spacious platform, with the great vassals of the kingdom kneeling around him.

Then all rose, and Tom Canty cried out: —

"Now, O my king, take these regal garments back, and give poor Tom thy servant his shreds and remnants again."

The Lord Protector spoke up: —

"Let the small varlet be stripped and flung into the Tower."

But the new king, the true king, said: —

"I will not have it so. But for him I had not got my crown again — none shall lay a hand upon him to harm him. And as for thee, my good uncle, my Lord Protector, this conduct of thine is not grateful toward this poor lad, for I hear he hath made thee a duke" — the Protector blushed — "yet he was not a king; wherefore, what is thy fine title worth now? Tomorrow you shall sue to me, *through him*, for its confirmation, else no duke, but a simple earl, shalt thou remain."

Under this rebuke his Grace the Duke of Somerset retired a little from the front for the moment. The king turned to Tom, and said kindly: —

"My poor boy, how was it that you could remember where I hid the Seal, when I could not remember it myself?"

"Ah, my king, that was easy, since I used it divers days."

"Used it — yet could not explain where it was?"

"I did not know it was *that* they wanted. They did not describe it, your Majesty."

"Then how used you it?"

The red blood began to steal up into Tom's cheeks, and he dropped his eyes and was silent.

"Speak up, good lad, and fear nothing," said the king. "How used you the Great Seal of England?"

Tom stammered a moment in a pathetic confusion, then got it out: —

"To crack nuts with!"

Poor child, the avalanche of laughter that greeted this nearly swept him off his feet. But if a doubt remained in any mind that Tom Canty was not the king of England and familiar with the august appurtenances of royalty, this reply disposed of it utterly.

Meantime the sumptuous robe of state had been removed from Tom's shoulders to the king's, whose rags were effectually hidden from sight under it. Then the coronation ceremonies were resumed; the true king was anointed and the crown set upon his head, whilst cannon thundered the news to the city, and all London seemed to rock with applause.

THOMAS BAILEY ALDRICH

A POET in verse often becomes a poet in prose also, in composing novels; although the novelist may not, and in general does not, possess the faculty of writing poems. The poet-novelist is apt to put into his prose a good deal of the same charm and the same picturesque choice of phrase and image that characterize his verse; while it does not follow that the novelist who at times writes verse — like George Eliot, for example — succeeds in giving a distinctly poetic quality to prose, or even wishes to do so. Among authors who have displayed peculiar power and won fame in the dual capacity of poet and of prose romancer or novelist, Sir Walter Scott and Victor Hugo no doubt stand pre-eminent; and in American literature, Edgar Allan Poe and Oliver Wendell Holmes very strikingly combine these two functions. Another American author who has gained a distinguished position both as a poet and as a writer of prose fiction and essays is Thomas Bailey Aldrich.

It is upon his work in the form of verse, perhaps, that Aldrich's chief renown is based; but some of his short stories in especial have contributed much to his popularity, no less than to his repute as a delicate and polished artificer in words. A New Englander, he has infused into some of his poems the true atmosphere of New England, and has given the same light and color of home to his prose, while imparting to his productions in both kinds a delightful tinge of the foreign and remote. In addition to his capacities as a poet and a romancer, he is a wit and humorist of sparkling quality. In reading his books one seems also to inhale the perfumes of Arabia and the farther East, blended with the salt sea-breeze and the pine-scented air of his native state, New Hampshire.

He was born in the old seaside town of Portsmouth, New Hampshire, November 11, 1837; but moved to New York City in 1854, at the age of seventeen. There he remained until 1866; beginning his work quite early; forming his literary character by reading and observation, by the writing of poems, and by practice and experience in writing prose sketches and articles for journals and periodicals. During this period he entered into associations with the poets Stedman, Stoddard, and Bayard Taylor, and was more or less in touch with the group that included Walt Whitman, Fitz-James O'Brien, and William Winter. Removing to Boston in January, 1866, he became the editor of Every Saturday, and remained in that post until 1874, when he resigned. In 1875 he made a long tour in Europe, plucking the first fruits of foreign travel, which were succeeded by many rich and dainty gatherings from the same source in later years. In the intervals of these wanderings he lived in Boston and Cambridge; occupying for a time James Russell Lowell's historic house of Elmwood, in the semi-rural university city; and then established a pretty country house at Ponkapog, a few miles south of Boston. This last suggested the title for a charming book of travel papers, 'From Ponkapog to Pesth.' In 1881 he was appointed editor of the Atlantic Monthly, and continued to direct that famous magazine for nine years, frequently making short trips to Europe, extending his tours as far as the heart of Russia, and gathering fresh materials for essay or song. Much of his time after giving up the Atlantic Monthly editorship was passed in voyaging, and in 1894–5 he made a journey around the world.

From the beginning he struck with quiet certainty the vein that was his by nature in poetry; and this was broadened almost continually, yielding richer results, which were worked out with an ever increasing refinement of skill. His predilection was for the picturesque; for romance combined with simplicity, purity, and tenderness of feeling, touched by fancy and by occasional lights of humor so reserved and dainty that they never disturb the pictorial harmony. The capacity for unaffected utterance of feeling on matters common to humanity reached a climax in the poem of 'Baby Bell,' which by its sympathetic and delicate description of a child's advent and death gave the author a claim to the affections of a wide circle; and this remained for a long time probably the best known among his poems. 'Friar Jerome's Beautiful Book' is another of the earlier favorites. 'Spring in New England' has since come to hold high rank both for its vivid and graceful description of the season, for its tender fervor of patriotism, and for its sentiment of reconciliation between North and South. The lines on 'Piscataqua River' remain one of the best illustrations of boyhood memories, and have something of Whittier's homely truth. In his longer narrative pieces, 'Judith' and 'Wyndham Towers,' cast in the mold of blank-verse idyls, Aldrich does not seem so much himself as in many of his briefer flights. An instinctive dramatic tendency finds outlet in 'Pauline Pavlovna' and 'Mercedes' — the latter of which, a two-act piece in prose, has found representation in the theater; yet in these, also, he is less eminently successful than in his lyrics and society verse.

No American poet has wrought his stanzas with greater faithfulness to an exacting standard of craftsmanship than Mr. Aldrich, or has known better when to leave a line loosely cast, and when to reinforce it with correction or with a syllable that might seem, to an ear less true, redundant. This gives to his most carefully chiseled productions an air of spontaneous ease, and has made him eminent as a sonneteer. The conciseness and concentrated aptness of his expression also — together with a faculty of bringing into conjunction subtly contrasted thoughts, images, or feelings — has issued happily in short, concentrated pieces and in a number of pointed and effective quatrains. Without overmastering purpose outside of art itself, his is the poetry of luxury rather than of deep passion or conviction; yet, with the freshness of bud and tint in springtime, it still always relates itself effectively to human experience.

If we perceive in his verse a kinship with the dainty ideals of Théophile Gautier and Alfred de Musset, this does not obscure his originality or his individual charm; and the same thing may be said with regard to his prose. The first of his short fictions that made a decided mark was 'Marjorie Daw.' The fame which it gained, in its separate field, was as swift and widespread as that of Hawthorne's 'The Gentle Boy' or Bret Harte's 'Luck of Roaring Camp.' It is a bright and half-pathetic little parody on human life and affection; or perhaps we should call it a parable symbolizing the power which imagination wields over real life, even in supposedly unimaginative people. The covert smile which it involves, at the importance of human emotions, may be traced to a certain extent in some of Mr. Aldrich's longer and more serious works of fiction: his three novels, 'Prudence Palfrey,' 'The Queen of Sheba,' and 'The Stillwater Tragedy.' 'The Story of a Bad Boy,' frankly but quietly humorous in its record of the pranks and vicissitudes of a healthy average lad (with the scene of the story localized at old Portsmouth, under the name of Rivermouth), a less ambitious work, still holds a secure place in the affections of many mature as well as younger readers. Besides these books, Mr. Aldrich published a collection of short descriptive, reminiscent, and half-historic papers on Portsmouth — 'An Old Town by the Sea'; with a second volume of short stories entitled 'Two Bites at a Cherry.' The character-drawing in his fiction is clear-cut and effective, often sympathetic, and nearly always suffused with an agreeable coloring of humor.

His later publications included 'A Sea Turn' (1902), 'Ponkapog Papers' (1903), the poetical drama 'Judith of Methulia' (1904), 'Pauline Pavlovna' (1907), and 'Songs and Sonnets' (1907). Until the end his work continued to show the same fastidious art. Aldrich died in Boston on March 19, 1907. His last poetical work was his exquisite tribute to Longfellow written for the Centenary celebration in Cambridge, which was penned only a few weeks prior to his death. His 'Life' by Ferris Greenslet appeared in 1908.

DESTINY

THREE roses, wan as moonlight, and weighed down
Each with its loveliness as with a crown,
Drooped in a florist's window in a town.

The first a lover bought. It lay at rest,
Like flower on flower, that night, on Beauty's breast.

The second rose, as virginal and fair,
Shrunk in the tangles of a harlot's hair.

The third, a widow, with new grief made wild
Shut in the icy palm of her dead child.

IDENTITY

SOMEWHERE — in desolate wind-swept space —
In Twilight-land — in No man's land —
Two hurrying Shapes met face to face,
And bade each other stand.

"And who are you?" cried one, agape,
Shuddering in the gloaming light.
"I know not," said the second Shape,
"I only died last night!"

BROKEN MUSIC

"A note
All out of tune in this world's instrument."

AMY LEVY

I KNOW not in what fashion she was made,
Nor what her voice was, when she used to speak,
Nor if the silken lashes threw a shade
On wan or rosy cheek.

I picture her with sorrowful vague eyes,
Illumed with such strange gleams of inner light
As linger in the drift of London skies
Ere twilight turns to night.

I know not; I conjecture. 'Twas a girl
That with her own most gentle desperate hand
From out God's mystic setting plucked life's pearl —
'Tis hard to understand.

So precious life is! Even to the old
The hours are as a miser's coins, and she —
Within her hands lay youth's unminted gold
And all felicity.

The winged impetuous spirit, the white flame
That was her soul once, whither has it flown?
Above her brow gray lichens blot her name
Upon the carven stone.

This is her Book of Verses — wren-like notes,
Shy franknesses, blind gropings, haunting fears;
At times across the chords abruptly floats
A mist of passionate tears.

A fragile lyre too tensely keyed and strung,
A broken music, weirdly incomplete:
Here a proud mind, self-baffled and self-stung,
Lies coiled in dark defeat.

TENNYSON (1890)

I

SHAKESPEARE and Milton — what third blazoned name
Shall lips of after ages link to these?
His who, beside the wild encircling seas,
Was England's voice, her voice with one acclaim,
For threescore years; whose word of praise was fame,
Whose scorn gave pause to man's iniquities.

II

What strain was his in that Crimean war?
A bugle-call in battle; a low breath,
Plaintive and sweet, above the fields of death!
So year by year the music rolled afar,
From Euxine wastes to flowery Kandahar,
Bearing the laurel or the cypress wreath.

III

Others shall have their little space of time,
Their proper niche and bust, then fade away
Into the darkness, poets of a day;
But thou, O builder of enduring rhyme,
Thou shalt not pass! Thy fame in every clime
On earth shall live where Saxon speech has sway.

IV

Waft me this verse across the winter sea,
Through light and dark, through mist and blinding sleet,
O winter winds, and lay it at his feet;
Though the poor gift betray my poverty,
At his feet lay it; it may chance that he
Will find no gift, where reverence is, unmeet.

PRESCIENCE

THE new moon hung in the sky, the sun was low in the west,
And my betrothed and I in the churchyard paused to rest —
Happy maiden and lover, dreaming the old dream over:
The light winds wandered by, and robins chirped from the nest.

And lo! in the meadow-sweet was the grave of a little child,
With a crumbling stone at the feet and the ivy running wild —
Tangled ivy and clover folding it over and over:
Close to my sweetheart's feet was the little mound up-piled.

Stricken with nameless fears, she shrank and clung to me,
And her eyes were filled with tears for a sorrow I did not see:
Lightly the winds were blowing, softly her tears were flowing —
Tears for the unknown years and a sorrow that was to be!

MEMORY

MY mind lets go a thousand things,
Like dates of wars and deaths of kings,
And yet recalls the very hour —
'T was noon by yonder village tower,
And on the last blue noon in May —
The wind came briskly up this way,
Crisping the brook beside the road;
Then, pausing here, set down its load
Of pine-scents, and shook listlessly
Two petals from that wild-rose tree.

PÈRE ANTOINE'S DATE-PALM

NEAR the Levée, and not far from the old French Cathedral in the Place d'Armes, at New Orleans, stands a fine date-palm, thirty feet in height, spreading its broad leaves in the alien air as hardily as if its sinuous roots were sucking strength from their native earth.

Sir Charles Lyell, in his 'Second Visit to the United States,' mentions this exotic: — "The tree is seventy or eighty years old; for Père Antoine, a

Roman Catholic priest, who died about twenty years ago, told Mr. Bringier that he planted it himself, when he was young. In his will he provided that they who succeeded to this lot of ground should forfeit it if they cut down the palm."

Wishing to learn something of Père Antoine's history, Sir Charles Lyell made inquiries among the ancient Creole inhabitants of the faubourg. That the old priest, in his last days, became very much emaciated, that he walked about the streets like a mummy, that he gradually dried up, and finally blew away, was the meager and unsatisfactory result of the tourist's investigations. This is all that is generally told of Père Antoine.

In the summer of 1861, while New Orleans was yet occupied by the Confederate forces, I met at Alexandria, in Virginia, a lady from Louisiana — Miss Blondeau by name — who gave me the substance of the following legend touching Père Antoine and his wonderful date-palm. If it should appear tame to the reader, it will be because I am not habited in a black ribbed-silk dress, with a strip of point-lace around my throat, like Miss Blondeau; it will be because I lack her eyes and lips and Southern music to tell it with.

When Père Antoine was a very young man, he had a friend whom he loved as he loved his life. Émile Jardin returned his passion, and the two, on account of their friendship, became the marvel of the city where they dwelt. One was never seen without the other; for they studied, walked, ate, and slept together.

Thus began Miss Blondeau, with the air of Fiammetta telling her prettiest story to the Florentines in the garden of Boccaccio.

Antoine and Émile were preparing to enter the Church; indeed, they had taken the preliminary steps, when a circumstance occurred which changed the color of their lives. A foreign lady, from some nameless island in the Pacific, had a few months before moved into their neighborhood. The lady died suddenly, leaving a girl of sixteen or seventeen, entirely friendless and unprovided for. The young men had been kind to the woman during her illness, and at her death — melting with pity at the forlorn situation of Anglice, the daughter — swore between themselves to love and watch over her as if she were their sister.

Now Anglice had a wild, strange beauty that made other women seem tame beside her; and in the course of time the young men found themselves regarding their ward not so much like brothers as at first. In brief, they found themselves in love with her.

They struggled with their hopeless passion month after month, neither betraying his secret to the other; for the austere orders which they were about to assume precluded the idea of love and marriage. Until then they had dwelt in the calm air of religious meditations, unmoved except by that pious fervor which in other ages taught men to brave the tortures of the rack and to smile amid the flames. But a blonde girl, with great eyes and a voice like the soft notes of a vesper hymn, had come in between them and their ascetic dreams of heaven. The ties that had bound the young men together snapped silently one by one. At last each read in the pale face of the other the story of his own despair.

And she? If Anglice shared their trouble, her face told no story. It was like the face of a saint on a cathedral window. Once, however, as she came suddenly upon the two men and overheard words that seemed to burn like fire on the lip of the speaker, her eyes grew luminous for an instant. Then she passed on, her face as immobile as before in its setting of wavy gold hair.

"Entre or et roux Dieu fit ses longs cheveux."

One night Émile and Anglice were missing. They had flown — but whither, nobody knew, and nobody save Antoine cared. It was a heavy blow to Antoine — for he had himself half resolved to confess his love to Anglice and urge her to fly with him.

A strip of paper slipped from a volume on Antoine's *prie-dieu,* and fluttered to his feet.

"*Do not be angry,*" said the bit of paper, piteously; "*forgive us, for we love.*" ["*Pardonnez-nous, car nous aimons.*"]

Three years went by wearily enough. Antoine had entered the Church, and was already looked upon as a rising man; but his face was pale and his heart leaden, for there was no sweetness in life for him.

Four years had elapsed, when a letter, covered with outlandish postmarks, was brought to the young priest — a letter from Anglice. She was dying; — would he forgive her? Émile, the year previous, had fallen a victim to the fever that raged on the island; and their child, Anglice, was likely to follow him. In pitiful terms she begged Antoine to take charge of the child until she was old enough to enter the convent of the Sacré-Cœur. The epistle was finished hastily by another hand, informing Antoine of Madame Jardin's death; it also told him that Anglice had been placed on board a vessel shortly to leave the island for some Western port.

The letter, delayed by storm and shipwreck, was hardly read and wept over when little Anglice arrived.

On beholding her, Antoine uttered a cry of joy and surprise — she was so like the woman he had worshiped.

The passion that had been crowded down in his heart broke out and lavished its richness on this child, who was to him not only the Anglice of years ago, but his friend Émile Jardin also.

Anglice possessed the wild, strange beauty of her mother — the bending, willowy form, the rich tint of skin, the large tropical eyes, that had almost made Antoine's sacred robes a mockery to him.

For a month or two Anglice was wildly unhappy in her new home. She talked continually of the bright country where she was born, the fruits and flowers and blue skies, the tall, fan-like trees, and the streams that went murmuring through them to the sea. Antoine could not pacify her.

By and by she ceased to weep, and went about the cottage in a weary, disconsolate way that cut Antoine to the heart. A long-tailed paroquet, which she had brought with her in the ship, walked solemnly behind her from room to room, mutely pining, it seemed, for those heavy orient airs that used to ruffle its brilliant plumage.

Before the year ended, he noticed that the ruddy tinge had faded from her cheek, that her eyes had grown languid, and her slight figure more willowy than ever.

A physician was consulted. He could discover nothing wrong with the child, except this fading and drooping. He failed to account for that. It was some vague disease of the mind, he said, beyond his skill.

So Anglice faded day after day. She seldom left the room now. At last Antoine could not shut out the fact that the child was passing away. He had learned to love her so!

"Dear heart," he said once, "what is't ails thee?"

"Nothing, mon père," for so she called him.

The winter passed, the balmy spring had come with its magnolia blooms and orange blossoms, and Anglice seemed to revive. In her small bamboo chair, on the porch, she swayed to and fro in the fragrant breeze, with a peculiar undulating motion, like a graceful tree.

At times something seemed to weigh upon her mind. Antoine observed it, and waited. Finally she spoke.

"Near our house," said little Anglice — "near our house, on the island, the palm-trees are waving under the blue sky. Oh, how beautiful! I seem to lie beneath them all day long. I am very, very happy. I yearned for them so much that I grew ill — don't you think it was so, mon père?"

"Hélas, yes!" exclaimed Antoine, suddenly. "Let us hasten to those pleasant islands where the palms are waving."

Anglice smiled. "I am going there, mon père."

A week from that evening the wax candles burned at her feet and forehead, lighting her on the journey.

All was over. Now was Antoine's heart empty. Death, like another Émile, had stolen his new Anglice. He had nothing to do but to lay the blighted flower away.

Père Antoine made a shallow grave in his garden, and heaped the fresh brown mold over his idol.

In the tranquil spring evenings, the priest was seen sitting by the mound, his finger closed in the unread breviary.

The summer broke on that sunny land; and in the cool morning twilight, and after nightfall, Antoine lingered by the grave. He could never be with it enough.

One morning he observed a delicate stem, with two curiously shaped emerald leaves, springing up from the center of the mound. At first he merely noticed it casually; but presently the plant grew so tall, and was so strangely unlike anything he had ever seen before, that he examined it with care.

How straight and graceful and exquisite it was! When it swung to and fro with the summer wind, in the twilight, it seemed to Antoine as if little Anglice were standing there in the garden.

The days stole by, and Antoine tended the fragile shoot, wondering what manner of blossom it would unfold, white, or scarlet, or golden. One Sunday, a stranger, with a bronzed, weather-beaten face like a sailor's, leaned over the garden rail, and said to him, "What a fine young date-palm you have there, sir!"

"*Mon Dieu!*" cried Pere Antoine starting, "and is it a palm?"

"Yes, indeed," returned the man. "I didn't reckon the tree would flourish in this latitude."

"Ah, *mon Dieu!*" was all the priest could say aloud; but he murmured to himself, "*Bon Dieu, vous m'avez donné cela!*"

If Père Antoine loved the tree before, he worshiped it now. He watered it, and nurtured it, and could have clasped it in his arms. Here were Émile and Anglice and the child, all in one!

The years glided away, and the date-palm and the priest grew together — only one became vigorous and the other feeble. Père Antoine had long passed the meridian of life. The tree was in its youth. It no longer stood in an isolated garden; for pretentious brick and stucco houses had clustered about Antoine's cottage. They looked down scowling on the humble thatched roof. The city was edging up, trying to crowd him off his land. But he clung to it like lichen and refused to sell.

Speculators piled gold on his doorsteps, and he laughed at them. Sometimes he was hungry, and cold, and thinly clad; but he laughed none the less.

"Get thee behind me, Satan!" said the old priest's smile.

Père Antoine was very old now, scarcely able to walk; but he could sit under the pliant, caressing leaves of his palm, loving it like an Arab; and there he sat till the grimmest of speculators came to him. But even in death Père Antoine was faithful to his trust: the owner of that land loses it if he harm the date-tree.

And there it stands in the narrow, dingy street, a beautiful, dreamy stranger, an exquisite foreign lady whose grace is a joy to the eye, the incense of whose breath makes the air enamoured. May the hand wither that touches her ungently!

"*Because it grew from the heart of little Anglice,*" said Miss Blondeau tenderly.

CELIA THAXTER

THE poetry of Celia Thaxter suggests the happy results for literature when a poetic nature draws inspiration from some imaginative stimulus, and lets that inspiration dominate without confusing or weakening it with others. With Mrs. Thaxter such a stimulus was the sea. It was on the northern sea-coast of New England that she lived, knew joy and sorrow, and wrote out of her heart experiences. Her verse reflects the impressions upon a sensitive soul of the sea-birds and the island blooms, of the glory and tragedy of the illimitable ocean, and the overarch of the more illimitable sky; while the drama of human existence, interwoven of good and ill, is always present, lending pathos to the beauty of nature, and imbuing with a tender melancholy the tonic of sea air and free communion with fair created things.

Celia Leighton was born June 29, 1836, at Portsmouth, New Hampshire. Her father was a disappointed politician who became keeper of the White Island Light, Isles of Shoals; so that Celia grew up companioned by sea and sky. In her maturity she established her residence upon Appledore Island, one of the Isles of Shoals. There she married Levi Lincoln Thaxter in 1851; and for many years she wrote poetry, painted, enjoyed music, tended her garden; and at last, on August 26, 1894, passed away, having won a distinct reputation as a singer of sincerity, charm, and power. When Lowell, as editor of the Atlantic, printed her first poem, 'Landlocked,' he recognized hers as a new voice, not an echo. 'The Sandpiper' is as well known and loved as any verse written by an American woman. In the finest of Mrs. Thaxter's lyrics, felicitous description, a deep human sympathy, and sense of the dramatic are to be noted. Her verse is strong as well as sweet; it can be objective and have narrative interest, as well as be purely lyrical. Its movement and vigor preserve it from weakness or sentimentality. The didactic and moral creep in at times to the injury of the work as art, but this is only occasionally a defect. There is in much of Mrs. Thaxter's poetry an undertone of sadness — easily explained by events in the poet's life, for she was not unacquainted with grief. In poems like 'The Watch of Boon Island' or 'The Tryst,' her sense of the gloom and doom of life comes boldly out. She was naturally, however, of a buoyant, sanguine temperament, and the mood of faith and hope prevails in her verse. The love of the sea and the love of flowers were passions with her; music was dear to her heart, and as a motive it is found in some of her loveliest poems — 'Beethoven,' 'Schumann's Sonata in A Minor,' and others. She was widely receptive to the arts. She wrote charming prose, but it is as a poet that she will survive in American literature.

Mrs. Thaxter's first volume of poems appeared in 1872; the next year, 'Among the Isles of Shoals,' a prose history with autobiographic touches, was published. 'Drift-weed' (1879), 'Poems for Children' (1884), 'The Cruise of The Mystery, and Other Poems' (1886), and 'An Island Garden,' a prose diary of her Appledore life, printed in a beautiful illustrated edition in the year of her death, complete the list of this genuine singer's works.

[The following poems of Celia Thaxter are copyrighted, and are reprinted here by permission of Houghton Mifflin Company, publishers.]

SORROW

UPON my lips she laid her touch divine,
And merry speech and careless laughter died;
She fixed her melancholy eyes on mine,
And would not be denied.

I saw the West Wind loose his cloudlets white
In flocks, careering through the April sky;
I could not sing, though joy was at its height,
For she stood silent by.

I watched the lovely evening fade away;
A mist was lightly drawn across the stars:
She broke my quiet dream — I heard her say,
"Behold your prison bars!

"Earth's gladness shall not satisfy your soul;
This beauty of the world in which you live,
The crowning grace that sanctifies the whole —
That, I alone can give."

I heard, and shrank away from her afraid:
But still she held me, and would still abide;
Youth's bounding pulses slackened and obeyed,
With slowly ebbing tide.

"Look thou beyond the evening star," she said,
"Beyond the changing splendors of the day;
Accept the pain, the weariness, the dread —
Accept, and bid me stay!"

I turned and clasped her close with sudden strength:
And slowly, sweetly, I became aware
Within my arms God's angel stood at length,
White-robed and calm and fair.

And now I look beyond the evening star,
Beyond the changing splendors of the day —
Knowing the pain He sends more precious far,
More beautiful than they.

SEAWARD

TO ——

HOW long it seems since that mild April night,
When, leaning from the window, you and I
Heard, clearly ringing from the shadowy bight,
The loon's unearthly cry!

Southwest the wind blew, million little waves
Ran rippling round the point in mellow tune,
But mournful, like the voice of one who raves,
That laughter of the loon!

We called to him, while blindly through the haze
Uprose the meager moon behind us, slow —
So dim the fleet of boats we scarce could trace,
Moored lightly just below.

We called, and lo, he answered! Half in fear
We sent the note back. Echoing rock and bay
Made melancholy music far and near,
Sadly it died away.

That schooner, you remember? Flying ghost!
Her canvas catching every wandering beam,
Aërial, noiseless, past the glimmering coast
She glided like a dream.

Would we were leaning from your window now,
Together calling to the eerie loon,
The fresh wind blowing care from either brow,
This sumptuous night of June!

So many sighs load this sweet inland air,
'Tis hard to breathe, nor can we find relief:
However lightly touched, we all must share
This nobleness of grief.

But sighs are spent before they reach your ear;
Vaguely they mingle with the water's rune.
No sadder sound salutes you than the clear,
Wild laughter of the loon.

THE SANDPIPER

ACROSS the narrow beach we flit,
One little sandpiper and I;
And fast I gather, bit by bit,
The scattered driftwood bleached and dry.
The wild waves reach their hands for it,
The wild wind raves, the tide runs high,
As up and down the beach we flit —
One little sandpiper and I.

Above our heads the sullen clouds
Scud black and swift across the sky;
Like silent ghosts in misty shrouds
Stand out the white light-houses high.
Almost as far as eye can reach
I see the close-reefed vessels fly,
As fast we flit along the beach —
One little sandpiper and I.

I watch him as he skims along
Uttering his sweet and mournful cry.
He starts not at my fitful song,
Or flash of fluttering drapery;
He has no thought of any wrong;
He scans me with a fearless eye:
Stanch friends are we, well tried and strong,
The little sandpiper and I.

Comrade, where wilt thou be tonight
When the loosed storm breaks furiously?
My driftwood fire will burn so bright!
To what warm shelter canst thou fly?

I do not fear for thee, though wroth
  The tempest rushes through the sky:
For are we not God's children both,
  Thou, little sandpiper, and I?

IMPATIENCE

ONLY to follow you, dearest, only to find you!
  Only to feel for one instant the touch of your hand;
Only to tell you once of the love you left behind you —
  To say the world without you is like a desert of sand;

That the flowers have lost their perfume, the rose its splendor,
  And the charm of nature is lost in a dull eclipse;
That joy went out with the glance of your eyes so tender,
  And beauty passed with the lovely smile on your lips.

I did not dream it was you who kindled the morning,
  And folded the evening purple in peace so sweet;
But you took the whole world's rapture without a warning,
  And left me naught save the print of your patient feet.

I count the days and the hours that hold us asunder;
  I long for Death's friendly hand which shall rend in twain,
With the glorious lightning flash and the golden thunder,
  These clouds of the earth, and give me my own again!

WILD GEESE

AFAR, strange sound through the night,
  A dauntless and resolute cry,
Clear in the tempest's despite,
  Ringing so wild and so high!

Darkness and tumult and dread,
  Rain and the battling of gales,
Yet cleaving the storm overhead,
  The wedge of the wild geese sails:

Pushing their perilous way,
Buffeted, beaten, and vexed;
Steadfast by night and by day,
Weary, but never perplexed;

Sure that the land of their hope
Waits beyond tempest and dread,
Sure that the dark where they grope
Shall glow with the morning red!

Clangor that pierces the storm
Dropped from the gloom of the sky!
I sit by my hearth-fire warm
And thrill to that purposeful cry.

Strong as a challenge sent out,
Rousing the timorous heart
To battle with fear and with doubt,
Courageously bearing its part.

O birds in the wild, wild sky!
Would I could so follow God's way
Through darkness, unquestioning why,
With only one thought — to obey!

EDWARD EGGLESTON

EDWARD EGGLESTON was born at Vevay, Indiana, December 10, 1837. His father was a native of Amelia County, Virginia, and was of a family which migrated from England to Virginia in the seventeenth century, and which became one of much distinction in the state. He was a sufferer from ill health as a child. He had repeatedly to be removed from school for this cause, and he spent a considerable part of his boyhood on farms in Indiana, where he made acquaintance with that rude backwoods life which he has described in 'The Hoosier Schoolmaster' and other stories. An important incident of his youth was a visit of thirteen months which he paid to his relations in Virginia in 1854. This opportunity of making acquaintance under such favorable circumstances with slave society, must have been of great value to one who was to make American history the chief pursuit of his life. In 1856 he went to Minnesota, and there lived a frontier life to the great improvement of his health. The accounts we have of him show him to have had the ardent and energetic character which belongs to the youth of the West. When not yet nineteen years old he became a Methodist preacher in that state. Later, ill health forced him again to Minnesota, where with the enthusiasm of a young man he traveled on foot, shod in Indian moccasins, in winter and summer preaching to the mixed Indian and white populations on the Minnesota River.

Eggleston's literary career began, while he was still preaching, with contributions to Western periodicals. Having written for the New York Independent, he was offered in 1870 the place of literary editor of that paper, and the following year became its editor-in-chief. He was afterwards editor of Hearth and Home, to the columns of which journal he contributed 'The Hoosier Schoolmaster,' a story that has been very popular. He wrote a number of other novels, 'The End of the World,' 'The Mystery of Metropolisville,' 'The Circuit Rider,' 'Roxy,' etc. In January 1880, while on a visit to Europe, he began to make plans for a 'History of Life in the United States.' He had always had a strong taste for this subject, a keen natural interest in history being evident here and there in his stories. His historical researches were carried on in many of the chief libraries of Europe and the United States. A result of these studies was the thirteen articles on 'Life in the Colonial Period' published in The Century Magazine. These, however, were but preliminary studies to the work which he intended should be the most important of his life. The first volume of this work, 'The Beginners of a Nation,' was published in 1896.

This work does not pretend to be a particular account of colonial history. It is an attempt rather to describe the colonial individual and colonial society, to state the succession of cause and effect in the establishment of English life in North America, and to describe principles rather than details — giving, however, as much detail as is necessary to illustrate principles. The volume of 1896 contains chapters on 'The James River Experiments' and 'The Procession of Motives' which led to colonization. Book II of this volume is upon the Puritan migration, and has chapters on the rise of Puritanism in England, on the Pilgrim migration, and the great Puritan exodus. Book III receives the name of 'Centrifugal Forces in Colony Planting,' and contains accounts of Lord Baltimore's Maryland colony, of Roger Williams, and the "New England Dispersions," by which is meant the establishment of communities in Connecticut and elsewhere.

The candor and fair-mindedness of this work is one of its special merits. We have an indication of this quality in the author's refusal to accept the weak supposition, common among writers upon American history, that the faults of our ancestors were in some way more excusable than those of other people. Nor is the work wanting in an adequate literary merit. The style, especially in the later chapters, is free, simple, nervous, and rhythmical.

Little has been said of Eggleston's novels in the course of these remarks. But the qualities of his historical writing appear in his novels. The qualities of the realistic novelist are of great use to the historian, when the novelist has the thoroughness and the industry which characterized Eggleston. By the liveliness of his imagination, he succeeds in making history as real as fiction should be. Eggleston's novels deserve the popularity they have attained. They are themselves, particularly those which describe Western life, valuable contributions to history. The West, we may add, was Eggleston's field. 'The Faith Doctor,' one of his latest novels, the scene of which is laid in New York, is inferior to his Western stories. Of these novels probably the best is 'The Graysons,' a book full of its author's reality and warmth of human sympathy; of this book the reader will follow every word with the same lively interest with which he reads 'The Beginners of a Nation.' In 1900 Eggleston published 'The Transit of Civilization from England to America.' His death occurred at Lake George, New York, September 3, 1902.

ROGER WILLIAMS: THE PROPHET OF RELIGIOUS FREEDOM

From 'The Beginners of a Nation.' Copyright, 1896, by Edward Eggleston

LOCAL jealousy and sectarian prejudice have done what they could to obscure the facts of the trial and banishment of Williams. It has been argued by more than one writer that it was not a case of religious persecution at all, but the exclusion of a man dangerous to the State. Cotton, with characteristic verbal legerdemain, says that Williams was "enlarged" rather than banished. The case has even been pettifogged in our own time by the assertion that the banishment was only the action of a commercial company excluding an uncongenial person from its territory. But with what swift indignation would the Massachusetts rulers of the days of Dudley and Haynes have repudiated a plea which denied their magistracy! They put so strong a pressure on Stoughton, who said that the assistants were not magistrates, that he made haste to renounce his pride of authorship and to deliver his booklet to be officially burned; nor did even this prevent his punishment. The rulers of "the Bay" were generally frank advocates of religious intolerance; they regarded toleration as a door set open for the Devil to enter. Not only did they punish for unorthodox expressions, they even assumed to inquire into private beliefs. Williams was only one of scores bidden to depart on account of opinion.

The real and sufficient extenuation for the conduct of the Massachusetts leaders is found in the character and standards of the age. A few obscure and contemned sectaries — Brownists, Anabaptists, and despised Familists — in Holland and England had spoken more or less clearly in favor of religious liberty before the rise of Roger Williams, but nobody of weight or respectable standing in the whole world had befriended it. All the great authorities in Church and State, Catholic and Protestant, prelatical and Puritan, agreed in their detestation of it. Even Robinson, the moderate pastor of the Leyden Pilgrims, ventured to hold only to the "toleration of tolerable opinions." This was the toleration found at Amsterdam and in some other parts of the Low countries. Even this religious sufferance, which did not amount to liberty, was sufficiently despicable in the eyes of that intolerant age to bring upon the Dutch the contempt of Christendom. It was a very qualified and limited toleration, and one from which Catholics and Arminians were excluded. It seems to have been that practical amelioration of law which is produced more effectually by commerce than by learning or religion. Outside of some parts of the Low Countries, and oddly enough of the Turkish Empire, all the world worth counting decried toleration as a great crime. It would have been wonderful indeed if Massachusetts had been superior to the age. "I dare aver," says

Nathaniel Ward, the New England lawyer-minister, "that God doth nowhere in his Word tolerate Christian States to give tolerations to such adversaries of his Truth, if they have power in their hands to suppress them." To set up toleration was "to build a sconce against the walls of heaven to batter God out of his chair," in Ward's opinion.

This doctrine of intolerance was sanctioned by many refinements of logic, such as Cotton's delicious sophistry that if a man refused to be convinced of the truth, he was sinning against conscience, and therefore it was not against the liberty of conscience to coerce him. Cotton's moral intuitions were fairly suffocated by logic. He declared that men should be compelled to attend religious service, because it was "better to be hypocrites than profane persons. Hypocrites give God part of his due, the outward man, but the profane person giveth God neither outward nor inward man." To reason thus is to put subtlety into the *cathedra* of common-sense, to bewilder vision by legerdemain. Notwithstanding his natural gift for devoutness and his almost immodest godliness, Cotton was incapable of high sincerity. He would not specifically advise Williams's banishment, but having labored with him round a corner according to his most approved ecclesiastical formula, he said, "We have no more to say in his behalf, but must sit down"; by which expression of passivity he gave the signal to the "secular arm" to do its worst, while he washed his hands in innocent self-complacency. When one scrupulous magistrate consulted him as to his obligation in Williams's case, Cotton answered his hesitation by saying, "You know they are so much incensed against his course that it is not your voice, nor the voice of two or three more, that can suspend the sentence." By such shifty phrases he shirked responsibility for the results of his own teaching. Of the temper that stands alone for the right, nature had given him not a jot. Williams may be a little too severe, but he has some truth when he describes Cotton on this occasion as "swimming with the stream of outward credit and profit," though nothing was further from Cotton's conscious purpose than such worldliness. Cotton's intolerance was not like that of Dudley and Endicott, the offspring of an austere temper; it was rather the outgrowth of his logic and his reverence for authority. He sheltered himself behind the examples of Elizabeth and James I, and took refuge in the shadow of Calvin, whose burning of Servetus he cites as an example, without any recoil of heart or conscience. But the consideration of the character of the age forbids us to condemn the conscientious men who put Williams out of Massachusetts theocracy as they would have driven the Devil out of the garden of Eden. When, however, it comes to judging the age itself, and especially to judging the Puritanism of the age, these false and harsh ideals are its sufficient condemnation. Its government and its very religion were barbarous; its Bible, except for mystical and ecclesiastical uses, might as well have closed with the story of the Hebrew judges and the imprecatory Psalms. The Apocalypse of John, grotesquely interpreted, was the one book of the New Testament that received hearty consideration, aside from those other New Testament passages supposed to relate to a divinely appointed ecclesiasticism. The humane pity of Jesus was unknown not only to the laws, but to the sermons of the time. About the time of Williams's banishment the lenity of John Winthrop was solemnly rebuked by some of the clergy and rulers as a lax imperiling of the safety of the gospel; and Winthrop, overborne by authority, confessed, explained, apologized, and promised amendment. The Puritans substituted an unformulated belief in the infallibility of "godly" elders acting with the magistrates, for the ancient doctrine of an infallible Church.

In this less scrupulous but more serious age it is easy to hold Williams up to ridicule. Never was a noble and sweet-spirited man bedeviled by a scrupulosity more trivial. Cotton aptly dubbed him "a haberdasher of small questions." His extant letters are many of them vibrant with latent heroism; there is manifest in them an exquisite charity and a pathetic magnanimity: but in the midst of it all the writer is unable to rid himself of a swarm of scruples as pertinacious as the buzzing of mosquitoes in the primitive forest about him. In dating his letters, where he ventures to date at all, he never writes the ordinary name of the day of the week or the name of the month, lest he should be guilty of etymological heathenism. He often avoids writing the year, and when he does insert it he commits himself to the last two figures only and adds a saving clause. Thus 1652 appears "52 (so called)," and other years are tagged with the same doubting words, or with the Latin "*ut vulgo*." What quarrel the tender conscience had with the Christian era it is hard to guess. So too he writes to Winthrop, who had taken part in his banishment, letters full of reverential tenderness and hearty friendship. But his conscience does not allow him even to seem to hold ecclesiastical fellowship with a man he honors as a ruler and loves as a friend. Once at least he guards the point directly by subscribing himself "Your worship's faithful and affectionate in all *civil* bonds." It would be sad to think of a great spirit so enthralled by the scrupulosity of his time and his party, if these minute restrictions had been a source of annoyance to him. But the cheerful observance of little scruples seems rather to have taken the place of a recreation in his life; they were to him perhaps what bric-à-brac is to a collector, what a well-arranged altar and candlesticks are to a ritualist.

Two fundamental notions supplied the motive power of every ecclesiastical agitation of that age. The notion of a succession of churchly order and ordinance from the time of the apostles was the mainspring of the High Church movement. Apostolic primitivism was the aim of the Puritan, and still more the goal of the Separatist. One party rejoiced in a belief that a mysterious apostolic virtue had trickled down through generations of bishops and priests to its own age; the other rejoiced in the destruction of institutions that had grown up in the ages, and in getting back to the primitive nakedness of the early Christian conventicle. True to the law of his nature, Roger Williams pushed this latter principle to its ultimate possibilities. If we may believe the accounts, he and his followers at Providence became Baptists that they might receive the rite of baptism in its most ancient Oriental form. But in an age when the fountains of the great deep were utterly broken up, he could find no rest for the soles of his feet. It was not enough that he should be troubled by the Puritan spirit of apostolic primitivism: he had now swung round to where this spirit joined hands with its twin, the aspiration for apostolic succession. He renounced his baptism because it was without apostolic sanction, and announced himself of that sect which was the last reduction of Separatism. He became a Seeker.

Here again is a probable influence from Holland. The Seekers had appeared there long before. Many Baptists had found that their search for primitivism, if persisted in, carried them to this negative result; for it seemed not enough to have apostolic rites in apostolic form unless they were sanctioned by the "gifts" of the apostolic time. The Seekers appeared in England as early as 1617, and during the religious turmoils of the Commonwealth period the sect afforded a resting-place for many a weather-beaten soul. As the miraculous gifts were lost, the Seekers dared not preach, baptize, or teach; they merely waited, and in their mysticism they believed their waiting to be an "upper room" to which Christ would come. It is interesting to know that Williams, the most romantic figure of the whole Puritan movement, at last found a sort of relief from the austere externalism and ceaseless dogmatism of his age by traveling the road of literalism, until he had passed out on the other side into the region of devout and contented uncertainty.

In all this, Williams was the child of his age, and sometimes more childish than his age. But there were regions of thought and sentiment in which he was wholly disentangled from the meshes of his time, and that not because of intellectual superiority — for he had no large philosophical views — but by reason of elevation of spirit. Even the authority of Moses could not prevent him from condemning the harsh severity of the New England capital laws. He had no sentimental delusions about the character of the savages — he styled them "wolves endued with men's brains"; but he constantly pleads for a humane treatment of them. All the bloody precedents of Joshua could not make him look without repulsion on the slaughter of women and children in the Pequot war, nor could he tolerate dismemberment of the dead or the selling of Indian captives into perpetual slavery. From bigotry and resentment he was singularly free. On many occasions he joyfully used his ascendancy over the natives to protect those who kept in force against him a sentence of perpetual banishment. And this ultra-Separatist, almost alone of the men of his time, could use such words of catholic charity as those in which he speaks of "the people of God wheresoever scattered about Babel's banks, either in Rome or England."

Of his incapacity for organization or administration we shall have to speak hereafter. But his spiritual intuitions, his moral insight, his genius for justice, lent a curious modernness to many of his convictions. In a generation of creed-builders which detested schism, he became an individualist. Individualist in thought, altruist in spirit, secularist in governmental theory, he was the herald of a time yet more modern than this laggard age of ours. If ever a soul saw a clear-shining inward light, not to be dimmed by prejudices or obscured by the deft logic of a disputatious age, it was the soul of Williams. In all the region of petty scrupulosity the time-spirit had enthralled him; but in the higher region of moral decision he was utterly emancipated from it. His conclusions belong to ages yet to come.

This union of moral aspiration with a certain disengagedness constitutes what we may call the prophetic temperament. Bradford and Winthrop were men of high aspiration, but of another class. The reach of their spirits was restrained by practical wisdom, which compelled them to take into account the limits of the attainable. Not that they consciously refused to follow their logic to its end, but that, like other prudent men of affairs, they were, without their own knowledge or consent, turned aside by the logic of the impossible. Precisely here the prophet departs from the reformer. The prophet recks nothing of impossibility; he is ravished with truth disembodied. From Elijah the Tishbite to Socrates, from Socrates to the latest and perhaps yet unrecognized voice of our own time, the prophetic temperament has ever shown an inability to enter into treaty with its environment. In the seventeenth century there was no place but the wilderness for such a John Baptist of the distant future as Roger Williams. He did not belong among the diplomatic builders of churches, like Cotton, or the politic founders of States, like Winthrop. He was but a babbler to his own time; but the prophetic voice rings clear and far, and ever clearer as the ages go on.

Reprinted by consent of the author, and of D. Appleton & Company, publishers, New York.

JOHN BURROUGHS

JOHN BURROUGHS was born in Roxbury, New York, April 3, 1837, and like many other American youths who later in life became distinguished, he went to school winters and worked on the farm in summer. He grew up among people who neither read books nor cared for them, and he considers this circumstance best suited to his development. Early intercourse with literary men would, he believes, have dwarfed his original faculty.

He began to write essays at the age of fourteen, but these early literary efforts give little hint of his later work, of that faculty for seeing, and commenting on all that he saw in nature, which became his chief characteristic. He was especially fond of essays; one of his first purchases with his own money was a full set of Dr. Johnson, and for a whole year he lived on 'The Idler' and 'The Rambler' and tried to imitate their ponderous prose. His first contributions to literature, modeled on these essays, were promptly returned. By chance he picked up a volume of Emerson, the master who was to revolutionize his whole manner of thinking; and as he had fed on Dr. Johnson he fed on the 'Essays and Miscellanies,' until a paper he wrote at nineteen on 'Expressions' was accepted by the editor of the Atlantic, with a lurking doubt whether it had not come to him on false pretenses, as it was very much like an early essay of Emerson.

His first volume, 'Notes on Walt Whitman as a Poet and a Person' (1867), was followed by a long series of books on themes drawn from the world of nature. Their very titles give a hint of their charm; as 'Wake Robin' (1871); 'Birds and Poets' (1877); 'Locusts and Wild Honey' (1879); 'Fresh Fields' (1884); 'Ways of Nature' (1905); and a volume of poems, 'Bird and Bough' (1906). In 1916 he was awarded the gold medal of the National Academy of Arts and Letters for eminence as an essayist. He died in 1921.

The literary quality of his writings from the first captivates the reader. He has the interpretative power which makes us see what he sees and invites us to share his enjoyment in his strange adventures. The stories of the wary trout and the pastoral bee, the ways of sylvan folk, their quarrels and their lovemaking, are so many character sketches on paper, showing a most intimate acquaintance with nature.

He is a born naturalist. He tells us that from childhood he was familiar with the homely facts of the barn, the cattle and the horses, the sugar-making and the work of the corn-field, the hay-field, the threshing, the planting, the burning of fallows. He "loved nature in those material examples and subtle expressions, with a love passing all the books in the world." But he also loved and knew books, and this other love gives to his works their literary charm.

His account of a bird, a flower, or an open-air incident, however painstaking and minute the record, teems with literary memories. The sight of the Scotch hills recalls Shakespeare's line,

> The tufty mountains where lie the nibbling sheep.

The plane-tree vocal with birds' voices recalls Tennyson — "The pillared dusk of sounding sycamores"; he hears the English chaffinch, and remembers with keen delight that Drayton calls it "the throstle with sharp thrills," and Ben Jonson "the lusty throstle." After much wondering, he finds out why Shakespeare wrote

> The murmuring surge
> That on the unnumbered idle pebbles chafes,

his own experience being that sea-shores are sandy; but the pebbled cliffs of Folkestone, with not a grain of sand on the chalk foundation, justified the poet.

This lover of nature loves not only the beautiful things he sees, but he loves what they suggest, what they remind him of, what they bid him aspire to. Like Wordsworth, he "looks on the hills with tenderness, and makes deep friendship with the streams and groves." He notes what he divines by observation. And what an observer he is! He discovers that the bobolink goes south in the night. He scraped an acquaintance with a yellow-rumped warbler who, taking the reflection of the clouds and blue sky in a pond for a short cut to the tropics, tried to cross it; with the result of his clinging for a day and night to a twig that hung down in the water.

Burroughs has found that whatever bait you use in a trout stream — grasshopper, grub, or fly — there is one thing you must always put on your hook; namely, your heart. It is a morsel they love above everything else. He tells us that man has sharper eyes than a dog, a fox, or any of the wild creatures except the birds, but not so sharp an ear or a nose; he says that a certain quality of youth is indispensable in the angler, a certain unworldliness and readiness to invest in an enterprise that does not pay in current coin. He says that nature loves to enter a door another hand has opened: a mountain view never looks better than when one has been warmed up by the capture of a big trout. Like certain wary game, she is best taken by seeming to pass her by, intent on other matters. What he does not find out for himself, people tell him. From a hedge-cutter he learns that some of the birds take an earth-bath and some a water-bath, while a few take both; a farmer boy confided to him that the reason we never see any small turtles is because for two or three years the young turtles bury themselves in the ground and keep hidden from observation. From a Maine farmer he heard that both male and female hawks take part in incubation. A barefooted New Jersey boy told him that "lampers" die as soon as they have built their nests and laid their eggs. How apt he is in similes! The pastoral fields of Scotland are "stall-fed," and the hillsides "wrinkled and dimpled, like the forms of fatted sheep."

And what other bird-lover has such charming fancies about birds, in whom he finds a hundred human significances? "The song of the bobolink," he says, "expresses hilarity; the sparrow sings faith, the bluebird love, the catbirds pride, the white-eyed fly-catchers self-consciousness, that of the hermit thrush spiritual serenity, while there is something military in the call of the robin." Burroughs has been compared with Thoreau, but he seems closer to White of Selborne, whom he has commemorated in one of his most charming essays. Like White, he is a literary man who is a born naturalist in close intimacy with his brute neighbors and "rural nature's varied shows." In both, the moral element is back of nature and the source of her value and charm. Never nature for her own sake, but for the sake of the soul that is above all and over all. Like White, too, though by nature solitary, Burroughs is on cordial terms with his kind. He is an accurate observer, and he takes Bryant to task for giving an odor to the yellow violet, and Coleridge for making a lark perch on the stalk of a foxglove. He gloats over a felicitous expression, like Arnold's "blond meadow-sweet" and Tennyson's "little speedwell's darling blue"; though in commenting on another poet he waives the question of accuracy, and says "his happy literary talent makes up for the poverty of his observation."

And again as with White, he walks through life slowly and in a ruminating fashion, as though he had leisure to linger with the impression of the moment. Incident he uses with reserve, but with picturesque effects; figures do not dominate his landscape but humanize it.

As a critic Burroughs most fully reveals his personality. In his sketches of nature we see what he sees; in his critiques, what he feels and thinks. The cry of discovery he made when 'Leaves of Grass' fell into his hands found response in England and was re-echoed in this country till Burroughs' strange delight in Whitman seemed no longer strange, but an accepted fact in the history of poetry. The essay on Emerson, his master, shows the same discriminating mind. But as a revelation of both author and subject there are few more delightful papers than Burroughs' essay on Thoreau. In manner it is as pungent and as racy as Thoreau's writings, and as epigrammatic as Emerson's; and his defense of Thoreau against the English reviewer who dubbed him a "skulker" has the sound of the trumpet and the martial tread of soldiers marching to battle.

SHARP EYES

From 'Locusts and Wild Honey.' Copyright by Houghton Mifflin Company, Boston

NOTING how one eye seconds and reinforces the other, I have often amused myself by wondering what the effect would be if one could go on opening eye after eye, to the number, say, of a dozen or more. What would he see? Perhaps not the invisible — not the odors of flowers or the fever germs in the air — not the infinitely small of the microscope or the infinitely distant of the telescope. This would require not so much more eyes as an eye constructed with more and different lenses; but would he not see with augmented power within the natural limits of vision? At any rate, some persons seem to have opened more eyes than others, they see with such force and distinctness; their vision penetrates the tangle and obscurity where that of others fails, like a spent or impotent bullet. How many eyes did Gilbert White open? how many did Henry Thoreau? how many did Audubon? how many does the hunter, matching his sight against the keen and alert senses of a deer, or a moose, or a fox, or a wolf? Not outward eyes, but inward. We open another eye whenever we see beyond the first general features or outlines of things — whenever we grasp the special details and characteristic markings that this mask covers. Science confers new powers of vision. Whenever you have learned to discriminate the birds, or the plants, or the geological features of a country, it is as if new and keener eyes were added.

Of course one must not only see sharply, but read aright what he sees. The facts in the life of nature that are transpiring about us are like written words that the observer is to arrange into sentences. Or, the writing is a cipher and he must furnish the key. A female oriole was one day observed very much preoccupied under a shed where the refuse from the horse stable was thrown. She hopped about among the barn fowls, scolding them sharply when they came too near her. The stable, dark and cavernous, was just beyond. The bird, not finding what she wanted outside, boldly ventured into the stable, and was presently captured by the farmer. What did she want? was the query. What but a horse-hair for her nest, which was in an apple-tree near by? and she was so bent on having one that I have no doubt she would have tweaked one out of the horse's tail had he been in the stable. Later in the season I examined her nest, and found it sewed through and through with several long horse-hairs, so that the bird persisted in her search till the hair was found.

Little dramas and tragedies and comedies, little characteristic scenes, are always being enacted in the lives of the birds, if our eyes are sharp enough to see them. Some clever observer saw this little comedy played among some English sparrows, and wrote an account of it in his newspaper. It is too good not to be true: A male bird brought to his box a large, fine goose-feather, which is a great find for a sparrow and much coveted. After he had deposited his prize and chattered his gratulations over it, he went away in quest of his mate. His next-door neighbor, a female bird, seeing her chance, quickly slipped in and seized the feather — and here the wit of the bird came out, for instead of carrying it into her own box she flew with it to a near tree and hid it in a fork of the branches, then went home, and when her neighbor returned with his mate, was innocently employed about her own affairs. The proud male, finding his feather gone, came out of his box in a high state of excitement, and with wrath in his manner and accusation on his tongue, rushed into the cot of the female. Not finding his goods and chattels there as he had expected, he stormed around awhile, abusing everybody in general and his neighbor in particular, and then went away as if to repair the loss. As soon as he was out of sight, the shrewd thief went and brought the feather home and lined her own domicile with it. . . .

The bluebird is a home bird, and I am never tired of recurring to him. His coming or reappearance in the spring marks a new chapter in the progress of the season; things are never quite the same after one has heard that note. The past spring the males came about a week in advance of the females. A fine male lingered about my grounds and orchard all that time, apparently awaiting the arrival of his mate. He called and warbled every day, as if he felt sure she was within earshot and could be hurried up. Now he warbled half angrily or upbraidingly; then coaxingly; then cheerily and confidently, the next moment in a plaintive and far-away manner. He would half open his wings, and twinkle them caressingly as if beckoning his mate to his heart. One morning she had come, but was shy and reserved. The fond male flew to a knot-hole in an old apple-tree and coaxed her to his side. I heard a fine confidential warble — the old, old story. But the female flew to a near tree and uttered her plaintive, homesick note. The male went and got some dry grass or bark in his beak and flew again to the hole in the old tree, and promised unremitting devotion; but the other said "Nay," and flew away in the distance. When he saw her going, or rather heard her distant note, he dropped his stuff and cried out in a tone that said plainly enough, "Wait a minute: one word, please!" and flew swiftly in pursuit. He won her before long, however, and early in April the pair were established in one of the four or five boxes I had put up for them, but not until they had changed their minds several times. As soon as the first brood had flown, and while they were yet under their parents' care, they began to nest in one of the other boxes, the female as usual doing all the work and the male all the complimenting. A source of occasional great distress to the mother-bird was a white cat that sometimes followed me about. The cat had never been known to catch a bird, but she had a way of watching them that was very embarrassing to the bird. Whenever she appeared, the mother bluebird set up that pitiful melodious plaint. One morning the cat was standing by me, when the bird came with her beak loaded with building material, and alighted above me to survey the place before going into the box. When she saw the cat she was greatly disturbed, and in her agitation could not keep her hold upon all her material. Straw after straw came eddying down, till not half her original burden remained. After the cat had gone away the bird's alarm subsided; till presently, seeing the coast clear, she flew quickly to the box and pitched in her remaining straws with the greatest precipitation, and without going in to arrange them as was her wont, flew away in evident relief.

In the cavity of an apple-tree but a few yards off, and much nearer the house than they usually build, a pair of high-holes, or golden-shafted woodpeckers, took up their abode. A knot-hole which led to the decayed interior was enlarged, the live wood being cut away as clean as a squirrel would have done it. The inside preparations I could not witness, but day after day as I passed near I heard the bird hammering away, evidently beating down obstructions and shaping and enlarging the cavity. The chips were not brought out, but were used rather to floor the interior. The woodpeckers are not nest-builders, but rather nest-carvers.

The time seemed very short before the voices of the young were heard in the heart of the old tree — at first feebly, but waxing stronger day by day, until they could be heard many rods distant. When I put my hand upon the trunk of the tree they would set up an eager, expectant chattering; but if I climbed up it toward the opening, they soon detected the unusual sound and would hush quickly, only now and then uttering a warning note. Long before they were fully fledged they clambered up to the orifice to receive their food. As but one could stand in the opening at a time, there was a good deal of elbowing and struggling for this position. It was a very desirable one, aside from the advantages it had when food was served; it looked out upon the great shining world, into which the young birds seemed never tired of gazing. The fresh air must have been a consideration also, for the interior of a high-hole's dwelling is not sweet. When the parent birds came with food, the young one in the opening did not get it all; but after he had received a portion, either on his own motion or on a hint from the old one, he would give place to the one behind him. Still, one bird evidently outstripped his fellows, and in the race of life was two or three days in advance of them. His voice was the loudest and his head oftenest at the window. But I noticed that when he had kept the position too long, the others evidently made it uncomfortable in his rear, and after "fidgeting" about awhile he would be compelled to "back down." But retaliation was then easy, and I fear his mates spent few easy moments at the outlook. They would close their eyes and slide back into the cavity as if the world had suddenly lost all its charms for them.

This bird was of course the first to leave the nest. For two days before that event he kept his position in the opening most of the time, and sent forth his strong voice incessantly. The old ones abstained from feeding him almost entirely, no doubt to encourage his exit. As I stood looking at him one afternoon and noticing his progress, he suddenly reached a resolution — seconded, I have no doubt, from the rear — and launched forth upon his untried wings. They served him well, and carried him about fifty yards up-hill the first heat. The second day after, the next in size and spirit left in the same manner; then another, till only one remained. The parent birds ceased their visits to him, and for one day he called and called till our ears were tired of the sound. His was the faintest heart of all: then he had none to encourage him from behind. He left the nest and clung to the outer bole of the tree, and yelped and piped for an hour longer; then he committed himself to his wings and went his way like the rest.

A young farmer in the western part of New York sends me . . . some interesting observations about the cuckoo. He says a large gooseberry-bush, standing in the border of an old hedge-row in the midst of the open fields, and not far from his house, was occupied by a pair of cuckoos for two seasons in succession; and after an interval of a year, for two seasons more. This gave him a good chance to observe them. He says the mother-bird lays a single egg and sits upon it a number of days before laying the second, so that he has seen one young bird nearly grown, a second just hatched, and a whole egg all in the nest at once. "So far as I have seen, this is the settled practice — the young leaving the nest one at a time, to the number of six or eight. The young have quite the look of the young of the dove in many respects. When nearly grown they are covered with long blue pin-feathers as long as darning needles, without a bit of plumage on them. They part on the back and hang down on each side by their own weight. With its curious feathers and misshapen body the young bird is anything but handsome. They never open their mouths when approached, as many young birds do, but sit perfectly still, hardly moving when touched." He also notes the unnatural indifference of the mother-bird when her nest and young are approached. She makes no sound, but sits quietly on a near branch in apparent perfect unconcern.

These observations, together with the fact that the egg of the cuckoo is occasionally found in the nest of other birds, raise the inquiry whether our bird is slowly relapsing into the habit of the European species, which always foists its egg upon other birds; or whether on the other hand it be not mending its manners in this respect. It has but little to unlearn or forget in the one case, but great progress to make in the other. How far is its rudimentary nest — a mere platform of coarse twigs and dry stalks of weeds — from the deep, compact, finely woven, and finely modeled nest of the goldfinch or king-bird, and what a gulf between its indifference toward its young and their solicitude! Its irregular manner of laying also seems better suited to a parasite like our cowbird, or the European cuckoo, than to a regular nest-builder.

This observer, like most sharp-eyed persons, sees plenty of interesting things as he goes about his work. He one day saw a white swallow, which is of rare occurrence. He saw a bird, a sparrow, he thinks, fly against the side of a horse and fill his beak with hair from the loosened coat of the animal. He saw a shrike pursue a chickadee, when the latter escaped by taking refuge in a small hole in a tree. One day in early spring he saw two hen-hawks that were circling and screaming high in air, approach each other, extend a claw, and grasping them together, fall toward the earth flapping and struggling as if they were tied together; on nearing the ground they separated and soared aloft again. He supposed that it was not a passage of war but of love, and that the hawks were toying fondly with each other.

When the air is damp and heavy, swallows frequently hawk for insects about cattle and moving herbs in the field. My farmer describes how they attended him one foggy day, as he was mowing in the meadow with a mowing-machine. It had been foggy for two days, and the swallows were very hungry and the insects stupid and inert. When the sound of his machine was heard, the swallows appeared and attended him like a brood of hungry chickens. He says there was a continual rush of purple wings over the "cutter-bar," and just where it was causing the grass to tremble and fall. Without his assistance the swallows would have gone hungry yet another day.

Of the hen-hawk he has observed that both the male and female take part in incubation. "I was rather surprised," he says, "on one occasion, to see how quickly they change places on the nest. The nest was in a tall beech, and the leaves were not yet fully out. I could see the head and neck of the hawk over the edge of the nest, when I saw the other hawk coming down through the air at full speed. I expected he would alight near by, but instead of that he struck directly upon the nest, his mate getting out of the way barely in time to avoid being hit; it seemed almost as if he had knocked her off the nest. I hardly see how they can make such a rush on the nest without danger to the eggs."

The kingbird will worry the hawk as a whiffet dog will worry a bear. It is by his persistence and audacity, not by any injury he is capable of dealing with his great antagonist. The kingbird seldom more than dogs the hawk keeping above and between his wings and making a great ado; but my correspondent says he once "saw a kingbird riding on a hawk's back. The hawk flew as fast as possible, and the kingbird sat upon his shoulders in triumph until they had passed out of sight" — tweaking his feathers, no doubt, and threatening to scalp him the next moment.

That near relative of the kingbird, the great crested flycatcher, has one well-known peculiarity: he appears never to consider his nest finished until it contains a cast-off snake-skin. My alert correspondent one day saw him eagerly catch up an onion skin and make off with it, either deceived by it or else thinking it a good substitute for the coveted material.

One day in May, walking in the woods, I came upon the nest of a whippoorwill, or rather its eggs — for it builds no nest — two elliptical whitish spotted eggs lying upon the dry leaves. My foot was within a yard of the mother-bird before she flew. I wondered what a sharp eye would detect curious or characteristic in the ways of the bird, so I came to the place many times and had a look. It was always a task to separate the bird from her surroundings, though I stood within a few feet of her, and knew exactly where to look. One had to bear on with his eye, as it were, and refuse to be baffled. The sticks and leaves, and bits of black or dark-brown bark, were all exactly copied in the bird's plumage. And then she did sit so close and simulate so well a shapeless decaying piece of wood or bark! Twice I brought a companion, and guiding his eye to the spot, noted how difficult it was for him to make out there, in full view upon the dry leaves, any semblance to a bird. When the bird returned after being disturbed, she would alight within a few inches of her eggs and then, after a moment's pause, hobble awkwardly upon them.

After the young had appeared, all the wit of the bird came into play. I was on hand the next day, I think. The mother-bird sprang up when I was within a pace of her, and in doing so fanned the leaves with her wings till they sprang up too; as the leaves started the young started, and, being of the same color, to tell which was the leaf and which the bird was a trying task to any eye. I came the next day, when the same tactics were repeated. Once a leaf fell upon one of the young birds and nearly hid it. The young are covered with a reddish down like a young partridge, and soon follow their mother about. When disturbed they gave but one leap, then settled down, perfectly motionless and stupid, with eyes closed. The parent bird, on these occasions, made frantic efforts to decoy me away from her young. She would fly a few paces and fall upon her breast, and a spasm like that of death would run through her tremulous outstretched wings and prostrate body. She kept a sharp eye out the meanwhile to see if the ruse took, and if it did not she was quickly cured, and moving about to some other point tried to draw my attention as before. When followed she always alighted upon the ground, dropping down in a sudden peculiar way. The second or third day both old and young had disappeared.

The whippoorwill walks as awkwardly as a swallow, which is as awkward as a man in a bag, and yet she manages to lead her young about the woods. The latter, I think, move by leaps and sudden spurts, their protective coloring shielding them most effectively. Wilson once came upon the mother-bird and her brood in the woods, and though they were at his very feet, was so baffled by the concealment of the young that he was about to give up the search, much disappointed, when he perceived something "like a slight moldiness among the withered leaves, and, on stooping down, discovered it to be a young whippoorwill, seemingly asleep." Wilson's description of the young is very accurate, as its downy covering does look precisely like a "slight moldiness." Returning a few moments afterward to the spot to get a pencil he had forgotten, he could find neither old nor young.

It takes an eye to see a partridge in the woods, motionless upon the leaves: this sense needs to be as sharp as that of smell in hounds and pointers, and yet I know an unkempt youth that seldom fails to see the bird and shoot it before it takes wing. I think he sees it as soon as it sees him, and before it suspects itself seen. What a training to the eye is hunting! To pick out the game from its surroundings, the grouse from the leaves, the gray squirrel from the mossy oak limb it hugs so closely, the red fox from the ruddy or brown or gray field, the rabbit from the stubble, or the white hare from the snow, requires the best powers of this sense. A woodchuck motionless in the fields or upon a rock looks very much like a large stone or boulder, yet a keen eye knows the difference at a glance, a quarter of a mile away.

A man has a sharper eye than a dog, or a fox, or than any of the wild creatures; but not so sharp an ear or nose. But in the birds he finds his match. How quickly the old turkey discovers the hawk, a mere speck against the sky, and how quickly the hawk discovers you if you happen to be secreted in the bushes, or behind the fence near which he alights! One advantage the bird surely has; and that is, owing to the form, structure, and position of the eye, it has a much larger field of vision — indeed, can probably see in nearly every direction at the same instant, behind as well as before. Man's field of vision embraces less than half a circle horizontally, and still less vertically; his brow and brain prevent him from seeing within many degrees of the zenith without a movement of the head; the bird, on the other hand, takes in nearly the whole sphere at a glance.

I find I see, almost without effort, nearly every bird within sight in the field or wood I pass through (a flit of the wing, a flirt of the tail, are enough, though the flickering leaves do all conspire to hide them), and that with like ease the birds see me, though unquestionably the chances are immensely in their favor. The eye sees what it has the means of seeing, truly. You must have the bird in your heart before you can find it in the bush. The eye must have purpose and aim. No one ever yet found the walking-fern who did not have the walking-fern in his mind. A person whose eye is full of Indian relics picks them up in every field he walks through.

One season I was interested in the tree-frogs, especially the tiny pipers that one hears about the woods and brushy fields — the hylas of the swamps become a denizen of trees; I had never seen him in this new rôle. But this season having them in mind, or rather being ripe for them, I several times came across them. One Sunday, walking amid some bushes, I captured two. They leaped before me as doubtless they had done many times before, but though not looking for or thinking of them, yet they were quickly recognized, because the eye had been commissioned to find them. On another occasion, not long afterward, I was hurriedly loading my gun in the October woods in hopes of overtaking a gray squirrel that was fast escaping through the treetops, when one of these Lilliput frogs, the color of the fast-yellowing leaves, leaped near me. I saw him only out of the corner of my eye, and yet bagged him, because I had already made him my own.

Nevertheless, the habit of observation is the habit of clear and decisive gazing; not by a first casual glance, but by a steady, deliberate aim of the eye are the rare and characteristic things discovered. You must look intently and hold your eye firmly to the spot, to see more than do the rank and file of mankind. The sharpshooter picks out his man and knows him with fatal certainty from a stump, or a rock, or a cap on a pole. The phrenologists do well to locate not only form, color, weight, etc., in the region of the eye, but a faculty which they call individuality — that which separates, discriminates, and sees in every object its essential character. This is just as necessary to the naturalist as to the artist or the poet. The sharp eye notes specific points and differences — it seizes upon and preserves the individuality of the thing.

We think we have looked at a thing sharply until we are asked for its specific features. I thought I knew exactly the form of the leaf of the tulip-tree, until one day a lady asked me to draw the outlines of one. A good observer is quick to take a hint and to follow it up. Most of the facts of nature, especially in the life of the birds and animals, are well screened. We do not see the play, because we do not look intently enough.

Birds, I say, have wonderfully keen eyes. Throw a fresh bone or a piece of meat upon the snow in winter, and see how soon the crows will discover it and be on hand. If it be near the house or barn, the crow that first discovers it will alight near it, to make sure that he is not deceived; then he will go away and soon return with a companion. The two alight a few yards from the bone, and after some delay, during which the vicinity is sharply scrutinized, one of the crows advances boldly to within a few feet of the coveted prize. Here he pauses, and if no trick is discovered, and the meat be indeed meat, he seizes it and makes off.

One midwinter I cleared away the snow under an apple-tree near the house, and scattered some corn there. I had not seen a blue jay for weeks, yet that very day they found my corn, and after that they came daily and partook of it, holding the kernels under their feet upon the limbs of the trees and pecking them vigorously.

Of course the woodpecker and his kind have sharp eyes. Still I was surprised to see how quickly Downy found out some bones that were placed in a convenient place under the shed to be pounded up for the hens. In going out to the barn I often disturbed him making a meal off the bits of meat that still adhered to them.

"Look intently enough at anything," said a poet to me one day, "and you will see something that would otherwise escape you." I thought of the remark as I sat on a stump in the opening of the woods one springy day. I saw a small hawk approaching; he flew to a tall tulip-tree and alighted on a large limb near the top. He eyed me and I eyed him. Then the bird disclosed a trait that was new to me; he hopped along the limb to a small cavity near the trunk, when he thrust in his head and pulled out some small object and fell to eating it. After he had partaken of it some minutes he put the remainder back in his larder and flew away. I had seen something like feathers eddying slowly down as the hawk ate, and on approaching the spot found the feathers of a sparrow here and there clinging to the bushes beneath the tree. The hawk then — commonly called the chicken hawk — is as provident as a mouse or squirrel, and lays by a store against a time of need; but I should not have discovered the fact had I not held my eye to him.

An observer of the birds is attracted by any unusual sound or commotion among them. In May and June, when other birds are most vocal, the jay is a silent bird; he goes sneaking about the orchards and the groves as silent as a pickpocket; he is robbing birds' nests and he is very anxious that nothing should be said about it, but in the fall none so quick and loud to cry "Thief, thief," as he. One December morning a troop of them discovered a little screech-owl secreted in the hollow trunk of an old apple-tree near my house. How they found the owl out is a mystery, since it never ventures forth in the light of day; but they did, and proclaimed the fact with great emphasis. I suspect the bluebirds first told them, for these birds are constantly peeping into holes and crannies, both spring and fall. Some unsuspecting bird probably entered the cavity, prospecting for a place for next year's nest, or else looking out a likely place to pass a cold night, when it has rushed out with very important news. A boy who should unwittingly venture into a bear's den when Bruin was at home could not be more astonished and alarmed than a bluebird would be on finding itself in the cavity of a decayed tree with an owl. At any rate, the bluebirds joined the jays, in calling the attention of all whom it might concern to the fact that a culprit of some sort was hiding from the light of day in the old apple-tree. I heard the notes of warning and alarm and approached to within eyeshot. The bluebirds were cautious, and hovered about uttering their peculiar twittering calls; but the jays were bolder, and took turns looking in at the cavity and deriding the poor shrinking owl. A jay would alight in the entrance of the hole, and flirt and peer and attitudinize, and then fly away crying "Thief, thief, thief," at the top of his voice.

I climbed up and peered into the opening, and could just descry the owl clinging to the inside of the tree. I reached in and took him out, giving little heed to the threatening snapping of his beak. He was as red as a fox and as yellow-eyed as a cat. He made no effort to escape, but planted his claws in my forefinger and clung there with a grip that soon grew uncomfortable. I placed him in the loft of an out-house in hopes of getting better acquainted with him. By day he was a very willing prisoner, scarcely moving at all even when approached and touched with the hand, but looking out upon the world with half-closed sleepy eyes. But at night what a change; how alert, how wild, how active! He was like another bird; he darted about with wild fearful eyes, and regarded me like a cornered cat. I opened the window, and swiftly, but as silently as a shadow, he glided out into the congenial darkness, and perhaps ere this has revenged himself upon the sleeping jay or bluebird that first betrayed his hiding-place.

WAITING

SERENE, I fold my hands and wait,
  Nor care for wind, or tide, or sea;
I rave no more 'gainst time or fate,
  For lo! my own shall come to me.

I stay my haste, I make delays,
  For what avails this eager pace?
I stand amid the eternal ways,
  And what is mine shall know my face.

Asleep, awake, by night or day,
  The friends I seek are seeking me;
No wind can drive my bark astray,
  Nor change the tide of destiny.

What matter if I stand alone?
  I wait with joy the coming years,
My heart shall reap where it has sown,
  And garner up its fruit of tears.

The waters know their own, and draw
  The brook that springs in yonder height;
So flows the good with equal law
  Unto the soul of pure delight.

The stars come nightly to the sky;
  The tidal wave unto the sea;
Nor time, nor space, nor deep, nor high,
  Can keep my own away from me.

[Republished by courtesy of John Burroughs.]

WILLIAM DEAN HOWELLS

NOT yet made the subject of a formal biography, William Dean Howells has been revealed, however, by his own books with a fullness rare in writers so essentially modest. 'A Boy's Town' (1890), 'My Literary Passions' (1895), 'Literary Friends and Acquaintance' (1900), and 'Years of My Youth' (1916) are openly autobiographical, but all his travels and essays, as well as his criticisms, speak the same candid language. From them it is easy to discover the main facts of his life. He was born in 1837 at Martin's Ferry, Ohio, the grandson of a pious Welsh Quaker who came to America early in the nineteenth century, and the son of a country editor and printer with a passion for books. The Howellses were a reading family; the eager, sensitive, delicate child, who was to become one of the great American writers, read from the first with an ardor which lends an astonishing glow and haste to the quiet pages of 'My Literary Passions.' Goldsmith, Cervantes, and Irving were his earliest loves, at a time long before he was conscious of their art but when he was already susceptible, perhaps also unconsciously, to their gentleness and humanity. That he did not always read, the mellow memories of his childhood in 'A Boy's Town' attest, and yet his growth may better be measured by the books he loved than by more outward facts. His first literary ambition was to write verse, and he devoted months to studying Pope, with a kind of fanaticism for regularity and exactness. From the worship of these traits he was partly won, at about sixteen or seventeen, by Shakespeare, to whose histories Howells was particularly drawn. Chaucer was another great passion, loved for his sense of earth in human life, and Dickens, who overwhelmed the youth by what he nevertheless knew was a rough magic. Criticism he first learned to like from Macaulay, and he revised his own style to fit his new liking. Thackeray, Longfellow, Tennyson followed in their turn.

Having taught himself some Latin and Greek and more French and Spanish, Howells took up German and came under the spell of Heine, who not only dominated him longer than any other author but was the first to teach him that the expression of literature is not different from the expression of life and that that is the best literature which most closely and most naturally utters reality. Poems in the manner of Heine won Howells a place in the Atlantic Monthly, then edited by Lowell, and in 1860 he made the reverent pilgrimage to New England about which he tells with such winning grace in 'Literary Friends and Acquaintance.' This journey, in more ways than one, had a large hand in his future. Although he was already a journalist of promise and had published, with John James Piatt, the pleasant 'Poems of Two

Friends' (1860), he was now finally confirmed in his literary ambition; he made friends wherever he found acquaintances; and he captured certain impressions of scenery and manners upon which he later founded his first novels.

Neither verse nor fiction, however, had a chance to claim him entirely. Having written a campaign biography of Lincoln, whom, to his lasting regret, he did not go to Illinois to see as he might have done, and being known to John G. Nicolay and John Hay, Lincoln's secretaries, Howells was appointed United States consul at Venice in 1861. He had asked for a similar post at Munich, hoping that he might continue his studies in German poetry, but he was so little disappointed at what he received that he eventually called it "the beginning of the best luck I have had in the world" — a hint at the fact that he was married at Venice to Miss Elinor Mead of Vermont in 1862. So far as literature was concerned, however, his good fortune was not so apparent. The verses he wrote won no favor with the magazines to which he offered them. It was journalism, not poetry, that served him, for his defeat in verse turned him to prose, and he began that study of Italian life which bore fruit directly in 'Venetian Life' (1866) and 'Italian Journeys' (1867), and indirectly in the stories with an Italian setting, such as 'A Foregone Conclusion,' 'A Fearful Responsibility,' and 'Indian Summer.' From the first he had the gift of a ripe easy style and a temper singularly genial. Of the Italian writers he read in these four years, Howells felt his truest passion for Dante, whom he found often dull and tough and dry but still the great authentic voice of an age, and Goldoni, whom he called "the first of the realists."

Realism, indeed, had practically won Howells by the time he returned to the United States. The romantic world of Europe on which his eyes had long been bent had turned out to be actual when he came to it, and now, once more in his native land, he found it not only more dear, as many men find it after a foreign residence, but more real. He had taken a new hold upon life by his marriage, and after his return he had the steadying experience of regular tasks, first as editorial contributor to the Nation for a few months, and then for fifteen years as assistant editor and editor of the Atlantic. Gradually, by the due process of growth, rather than by any deliberate thought, he came to his mature creed, the realism of which he is the chief American exponent. It was not solely an artistic or esthetic matter with him. He derived his principles from a general philosophy of life in which the plain facts of the human story had come to seem the truest concern. From his childhood he had been intensely humane, sensitive himself, and charitable toward others. His deepening sympathies now made him still more aware of human problems, and his delicate imagination made him aware of fine distinctions in character and feeling. Some bias toward actuality had compelled him when he read Hawthorne, more truly a passion with him than any other American writer, to like best of all Hawthorne's novels the realistic 'Blithedale Romance.' On his return from Italy, Howells met the books of John W. De Forest, who taught him much about realism before the thing had a name. Perhaps Howells had his realistic bent before he knew it; certainly he had thought it out in most of its bearings before he practised it. It is important to understand that his realism was the fruit of his own growth and not some alien graft. His first novel, 'Their Wedding Journey' (1871), offers proof. Strictly speaking, the book hardly deserves the term novel, for it is very near to the books of travel which he had already written; it takes a bridal couple on a late honeymoon over much the same route, in a reverse order, that Howells had traveled between Ohio and Boston in 1860. It has no structure beside that given by the simplest thread of narrative, no complication, no suspense. The aim of the author is clearly stated: "to talk of some ordinary traits of American life as these appeared to them [the travelers], to speak a little of well-known and easily accessible places, to present now a bit of landscape and now a sketch of character." And he justified his choice of such unromantic material by certain remarks here and there in the volume which have an air of zeal about them and would hardly have appeared in any of his later books:

"Ah! poor Real Life, which I love, can I make others share the delight I find in thy foolish and insipid face? . . . As in literature the true artist will shun the use even of real events if they are of an improbable character, so the sincere observer of man will not desire to look upon his heroic or occasional phases, but will seek him in his habitual moods of vacancy and tiresomeness. . . . Do I pitch the pipe too low? We poor honest men are at a sad disadvantage; and now and then I am minded to give a loose to fancy, and attribute something really fine and grand to my people, in order to make them worthier the reader's respected acquaintance. But again, I forbid myself in a higher interest."

Howells' first novel, in the stricter sense of the word, was 'A Chance Acquaintance' (1873), which made use again of a group of American travelers in Canada, three of whom had already appeared in 'Their Wedding Journey.' A pretty, intelligent, inexperienced girl from western New York, traveling with her brother and his wife, becomes acquainted with a young man who is perhaps the most unlovely of all Howells' unlovely Bostonians. The two are thrown much together and fall in love, but his love, though full of passion, cannot overcome his ingrained provincial snobbishness. In the end, the lover, who has steadily condescended to the girl because of her inland simplicity, suddenly sees, as she sees, that he has played a hopelessly ignoble and vulgar part. The subtle turn by which their relative positions are reversed is as convincing as their consequent separation is final. Howells had shown that he could not only present landscape and sketch character but could also organize a plot with delicate skill. At thirty-six he thus decisively became a novelist, and entered upon what might be called his middle period, during which he produced his richest work. For that period 'A Chance Acquaintance' is prophetic and representative. Its style is more assured and crisp than that of his earlier books but not less graceful. The central idea is clearly conceived and the outlines sharp without being in any way cruel or cynical. The descriptions are exquisite, the dialogue both natural and revealing, and over and through all is that lambent mirth, that undeceived kindliness of wisdom, which was to remain Howells' essential quality.

The study of the conflict between differing manners or grades of sophistication, which Howells and Henry James thus took up almost at the same time, concerned Howells largely in the next dozen years. 'A Foregone Conclusion' (1874) is of a fine-spirited Venetian priest, tutor to an American girl, who falls in love with her, confesses his desire to leave his uncongenial profession for a new career in America, mistakes her friendly interest for affection, and finds her, when he declares himself, only horrified at an outcome she had never once dreamed of. Had he known more of America or she more of Italy, the error need not have been made. 'The Lady of the Aroostook' (1879) recounts another courtship of a village girl by a more worldly man, who in this case loves her enough to disregard the superficial differences between them. 'A Fearful Responsibility' (1881) shows how an American in Italy, from too rigid an insistence upon European decorum, which in this case is quite unnecessary, mismanages the affairs of a young girl placed in his wife's charge. 'Dr. Breen's Practice' (1881) is the story of a woman's struggle to make a place for herself in the medical profession against the stupid resistance of a public which has no objection except that women are new in that profession. 'A Modern Instance' (1881) presents, with disconcerting truthfulness, the moral descent of a Boston journalist under the influence of success. 'The Rise of Silas Lapham' (1885), generally thought Howells' greatest novel, aims to prove that a sturdy, virtuous countryman from Vermont, who is not at all a gentleman according to the standards of Boston, might have moral qualities sufficient to outweigh his fatal defect. 'Indian Summer' (1885) illustrates the hardships which a man of forty must go through to remain comfortably engaged to a girl half his age.

'Silas Lapham' marked the culmination of Howells' art. But he had not yet shaped his final philosophy. In 1881 he had withdrawn from the Atlantic. In 1886 he began to write for "The Editor's Study" in Harper's Magazine, and produced during five years a series of monthly articles, chiefly discussions of current books, which it would be hard to surpass for good temper and sane judgment and ripe style anywhere in the world of literary criticism. Avoiding whatever was metaphysical, he confined himself principally to poetry, history, biography, but above all to fiction. It was these columns that had most to do with encouraging the growth of realism in America, and it was they that most eloquently commended to native readers such Latin realists as Valera, Valdes, Galdos, and Verga, and the great Russians, Turgenev, Dostoyevsky, and Tolstoy.

It will not do to say that these Russians molded Howells, for his development, whatever his readiness to assimilate, was always from within outward, but it helps to distinguish between the Howells who lived before about 1886 and the one who lived after that date, to say that the earlier man had one of his supreme literary passions for the art of Turgenev, and that the later Howells, knowing Tolstoy, had become impatient of even the most secret artifice. For Tolstoy was Howells' great passion. "As much as one merely human being can help another, I believe that he has helped me; he has not influenced me in esthetics only, but in ethics, too, so that I can never again see life in the way I saw it before I knew him." Tolstoy's novels seemed as perfect to Howells as his doctrine.

"To my thinking they transcend in truth, which is the highest beauty, all other works of fiction that have been written. . . . He has not only Turgenev's transparency of style, unclouded by any mist of the personality which we mistakenly value in style, and which ought no more to be there than the artist's personality should be in a portrait; but he has a method which not only seems without artifice, but is so. . . . I believe if I had not turned the corner of my fiftieth year, when I first knew Tolstoy, I should not have been able to know him as fully as I did. He has been to me that final consciousness, which he speaks of so wisely in his essay on Life. I came in it to the knowledge of myself in ways I had not dreamt of before, and began at least to discern my relations to the race, without which we are each nothing. The supreme art in literature had its highest effect in making me set art forever below humanity."

This was said in 1895, some ten years after Howells had first read Tolstoy, about whom he has written at length in an essay published in another volume of this Course. In the interval he had not reverted to the preacher, as he saw Tolstoy doing, and he had indeed published his merry farces and had begun to be reminiscent in 'A Boy's Town.' But, though too much himself to be greatly changed, Howells had broadened his field to include new problems. 'A Hazard of New Fortunes' (1889), in which Mr. and Mrs. Basil March, the bridal couple of 'Their Wedding Journey,' now grown middle aged, leave Boston for a future in New York, is not content merely to point out the unfamiliar fashions of life which they meet but is full of conscience regarding certain evils of the modern social order. Or rather, Howells had turned from representing the clash of those lighter manners which belong to comedy and had set himself to discuss the deeper manners of the race which belong to sociology and ethics and religion. Such concerns appear most frankly in his two Utopian tales, 'A Traveler from Altruria' (1894) and 'Through the Eye of the Needle' (1907), in which he compares America with the remote and lovely land of Altruria, where all work is honorable and servants are unknown, where capital and usury are only memories, where equality is complete, and men and women, in the midst of beauty, lead lives that are just, temperate, and kind. Howells has neither the languor of William Morris nor the bitter satire of Swift, and yet his socialistic books are full of peace and alive with gentle irony.

The stern tones of Tolstoy Howells never learned, or at least never used, for he could not lose his habitual kindness, even when he spoke most firmly. It was kindness, not timidity, however, for though he held steadily to his art he did not keep silence before even the most popular injustices. He defended the Chicago anarchists and he condemned the annexation of the Philippines in brave, just terms; no good cause lacked the support of his voice.

After 1892 he succeeded George William Curtis in "The Editor's Easy Chair" of Harper's and wrote monthly articles which, less exclusively literary than "The Editor's Study" pieces, carried on the same tradition. Nor did he give up fiction. To this period belong 'The World of Chance' (1893), 'The Coast of Bohemia' (1893), 'The Day of Their Wedding' (1895), 'A Parting and a Meeting' (1896), 'The Landlord at Lion's Head' (1897), 'An Open-Eyed Conspiracy' (1897), 'The Story of a Play' (1898), 'Ragged Lady' (1899), 'A Pair of Patient Lovers' (1901), 'The Kentons' (1902), 'The Flight of Pony Baker' (1902), 'Questionable Shapes' (1903), 'The Son of Royal Langbrith' (1903), 'Miss Bellard's Inspiration' (1905), 'Between the Dark and the Daylight' (1907), 'Fennel and Rue' (1908), 'The Mother and the Father' (1909), 'New Leaf Mills' (1913), 'The Daughter of the Storage' (1916), 'The Leatherwood God' (1916). That he could produce such an array of fiction is sign enough that he had not been overpowered by Tolstoy's humanitarianism. And there is further proof in the fact that these later novels, though they open up a wider world, are even kinder, gayer, mellower than the early ones. Their range of theme and setting is very great, from the solid realism of 'The Landlord at Lion's Head' to the subtle explorations into psychic phenomena in 'Questionable Shapes.' If they have been less read, as a rule, than 'A Modern Instance' and 'The Rise of Silas Lapham,' it is because they lack the important tang of malice, the sharp edge, of those books. It is a question how far realism can ever be impressive unless it bites and stings now and then.

Reminiscences and travels assume a large place in Howells' later work. After 'My Literary Passions' he wrote 'Literary Friends and Acquaintance,' of all accounts of the classic age of Boston and Cambridge one of the best. He revisited Europe, and left records in 'London Films' (1905), 'Certain Delightful English Towns' (1906), 'Roman Holidays' (1908), 'Seven English Cities' (1909), 'Familiar Spanish Travels' (1913), in which, indeed, he occasionally drew his matter out thin but in which he was never for a page dull, or untruthful, or sour, after the ancient habit of travelers. 'My Mark Twain' (1910) is a golden book, incomparably the finest of all the interpretations of Howells' great friend, while 'Years of My Youth' (1916), written when the author was almost eighty, was the work of a master whom age had made wise and kept strong. He died in 1920.

To a remarkable degree Howells' life and work seem always of a piece.

No writer was ever more wholly devoted to his calling, but in this case the creed of realism prevented the growth of any barrier which might have shut so devoted an author away from the world of reality upon which his whole art was based. If his poems, his fiction, his farces, his essays, his criticisms, his biographical writings, his travels contain what is clearly the most considerable transcript of American life yet made by one man, they are still full of a personality which, try as it might, could not withhold itself from the record. That personality, not American life, explains why Howells' world is so free from whatever is savage, sordid, illicit, bloody. His own essential gentleness and reserve, rather than the decorous American tradition of his time, kept him from the violent frankness often associated with realism. "I think," he said, "that the books of Zola are not immoral, but they are indecent through the facts that they nakedly represent. . . . I do not mind owning that he has been one of my great literary passions." What Howells practised was a kind of selective realism, choosing his material as a sage chooses his words, decently. He knew, too, that "in matters of art one must do what one likes if one would do it well." His gentle nature, which thus limited his subjects, also limited his treatment, and he is seldom best in impassioned or tragic moments. He preferred, indeed, not to make too much of them, believing that the true bulk of life is to be represented by its commonplaces. Few have written more engaging commonplaces and Howells cannot justly be charged with a failure to produce effects at which he never aimed, but the charge must stand that his work lacks the intensity which appears in such of his contemporaries as Flaubert, Tolstoy, and Thomas Hardy. The mere mention of such names makes it necessary to look elsewhere for authors with whom Howells may reasonably be classed, and one goes back to his first boyish passions, Goldsmith, Cervantes, Irving, men who please less by depth or intensity than by ease, grace, and charm in their art, and in themselves by kind wisdom and thoughtful mirth.

CARL VAN DOREN

SOCIETY

From 'Stops of Various Quills.' Copyright, 1895, by Harper & Brothers

I LOOKED, and saw a splendid pageantry
Of beautiful women and of lordly men,
Taking their pleasure in a flowery plain,
Where poppies and the red anemone,
And many another leaf of cramoisy,
Flickered about their feet, and gave their stain
To heels of iron or satin, and the grain
Of silken garments floating far and free,

As in the dance they wove themselves, or strayed
  By twos together, or lightly smiled and bowed,
Or curtsied to each other, or else played
At games of mirth and pastime, unafraid
  In their delight; and all so high and proud
  They seemed scarce of the earth whereon they trod.

I looked again, and saw that flowery space
  Stirring, as if alive, beneath the tread
  That rested now upon an old man's head,
And now upon a baby's gasping face,
Or mother's bosom, or the rounded grace
  Of a girl's throat; and what had seemed the red
  Of flowers was blood, in gouts and gushes shed
From hearts that broke under that frolic pace.
And now and then from out the dreadful floor
  An arm or brow was lifted from the rest,
As if to strike in madness, or implore
  For mercy; and anon some suffering breast
Heaved from the mass and sank; and as before
  The revelers above them thronged and prest.

ANOTHER DAY

From 'Stops of Various Quills.' Copyright, 1895, by Harper & Brothers

ANOTHER day, and with it that brute joy,
Or that prophetic rapture of the boy
Whom every morning brings as glad a breath
As if it dawned upon the end of death!

All other days have run the common course,
And left me at their going neither worse
Nor better for them; only a little older,
A little sadder, and a little colder.

But this — it seems as if this day might be
The day I somehow always thought to see,
And that should come to bless me past the scope
And measure of my farthest-reaching hope.

To-day, maybe, the things that were concealed
Before the first day was, shall be revealed;
The riddle of our misery shall be read,
And it be clear whether the dead are dead.

Before this sun shall sink into the west
The tired earth may have fallen on his breast,
And into heaven the world have passed away. . . .
At any rate, it is another day!

A MIDSUMMER-DAY'S DREAM

From 'Their Wedding Journey.' Copyright, 1871 and 1894, by W. D. Howells. Reprinted by permission of the author, and of Houghton Mifflin Company, publishers

THEY had waited to see Leonard, in order that they might learn better how to find his house in the country; and now, when they came in upon him at nine o'clock, he welcomed them with all his friendly heart. He rose from the pile of morning's letters to which he had but just sat down; he placed them the easiest chairs; he made a feint of its not being a busy hour with him, and would have had them look upon his office, which was still damp and odorous from the porter's broom, as a kind of down-town parlor: but after they had briefly accounted to his amazement for their appearance then and there, and Isabel had boasted of the original fashion in which they had that morning seen New York, they took pity on him and bade him adieu till evening.

They crossed from Broadway to the noisome street by the ferry, and in a little while had taken their places in the train on the thither side of the water.

"Don't tell me, Basil," said Isabel, "that Leonard travels fifty miles every day by rail going to and from his work!"

"I must, dearest, if I would be truthful."

"Then, darling, there *are* worse things in this world than living up at the South End, aren't there?" And in agreement upon Boston as a place of the greatest natural advantages, as well as all acquirable merits, with after-talk that need not be recorded, they arrived in the best humor at the little country station near which the Leonards dwelt.

I must inevitably follow Mrs. Isabel thither, though I do it at the cost of the reader, who suspects the excitements which a long description of the movement would delay. The ladies were very old friends, and they had not met since Isabel's return from Europe and renewal of her engagement. Upon the news of this, Mrs. Leonard had swallowed with surprising ease all that she had said in blame of Basil's conduct during the rupture, and exacted a promise from her friend that she should pay her the first visit after their marriage. And now that they had come together, their only talk was of husbands, whom they viewed in every light to which husbands could be turned, and still found an inexhaustible novelty in the theme. Mrs. Leonard beheld in her friend's joy the sweet reflection of her own honeymoon, and Isabel was pleased to look upon the prosperous marriage of the former as the image of her future. Thus, with immense profit and comfort, they reassured one another by every question and answer, and in their weak content lapsed far behind the representative women of our age when husbands are at best a necessary evil, and the relation of wives to them is known to be one of pitiable subjection. When these two pretty fogies put their heads of false hair together, they were as silly and benighted as their great-grandmothers could have been in the same circumstances, and as I say, shamefully encouraged each other in their absurdity. The absurdity appeared too good and blessed to be true. "Do you really suppose, Basil," Isabel would say to her oppressor, after having given him some elegant extract from the last conversation upon husbands, "that we shall get on as smoothly as the Leonards when we have been married ten years? Lucy says that things go more hitchily the first year than ever they do afterwards, and that people love each other better and better, just because they've got used to it. Well, our bliss does seem a little crude and garish compared with their happiness; and yet" — she put up both her palms against his, and gave a vehement little push — "there *is* something agreeable about it, even at this stage of the proceedings."

"Isabel," said her husband with severity, "this is bridal!"

"No matter! I only want to seem an old married woman to the general public. But the application of it is that you must be careful not to contradict me, or cross me in anything, so that we can be like the Leonards very much sooner than they became so. The great object is not to have any hitchiness; and you know you *are* provoking — at times."

They both educated themselves for continued and tranquil happiness by the example and precept of their friends; and the time passed swiftly in the pleasant learning, and in the novelty of the life led by the Leonards. This indeed merits a closer study than can be given here, for it is the life led by vast numbers of prosperous New Yorkers who love both the excitement of the city and the repose of the country, and who aspire to unite the enjoyment of both in their daily existence. The suburbs of the metropolis stretch landward fifty miles in every direction; and everywhere are handsome villas like Leonard's, inhabited by men like himself, whom strict study of the time-table enables to spend all their working hours in the city and all their smoking and sleeping hours in the country.

The home and the neighborhood of the Leonards put on their best looks for our bridal pair, and they were charmed. They all enjoyed the visit, said guests and hosts, they were all sorry to have it come to an end; yet they all resigned themselves to this conclusion. Practically, it had no other result than to detain the travelers into the very heart of the hot weather. In that weather it was easy to do anything that did not require an active effort, and resignation was so natural with the mercury at ninety, that I am not sure but there was something sinful in it.

They had given up their cherished purpose of going to Albany by the day boat, which was represented to them in every impossible phase. It would be dreadfully crowded, and whenever it stopped the heat would be insupportable. Besides, it would bring them to Albany at an hour when they must either spend the night there, or push on to Niagara by the night train. "You had better go by the evening boat. It will be light almost till you reach West Point, and you'll see all the best scenery. Then you can get a good night's rest, and start fresh in the morning." So they were counseled, and they assented, as they would have done if they had been advised: "You had better go by the morning boat. It's deliciously cool, traveling; you see the whole of the river; you reach Albany for supper, and you push through to Niagara that night and are done with it."

They took leave of Leonard at breakfast and of his wife at noon, and fifteen minutes later they were rushing from the heat of the country into the heat of the city, where some affairs and pleasures were to employ them till the evening boat should start.

Their spirits were low, for the terrible spell of the great heat brooded upon them. All abroad burned the fierce white light of the sun, in which not only the earth seemed to parch and thirst, but the very air withered, and was faint and thin to the troubled respiration. Their train was full of people who had come long journeys from broiling cities of the West, and who were dusty and ashen and reeking in the slumbers at which some of them still vainly caught. On everyone lay an awful languor. Here and there stirred a fan, like the broken wing of a dying bird; now and then a sweltering young mother shifted her hot baby from one arm to another; after every station the desperate conductor swung through the long aisle and punched the ticket, which each passenger seemed to yield him with a tacit malediction; a suffering child hung about the empty tank, which could only gasp out a cindery drop or two of ice-water. The wind buffeted faintly at the windows; when the door was opened, the clatter of rails struck through and through the car like a demoniac yell.

Yet when they arrived at the station by the ferry-side, they seemed to have entered its stifling darkness from fresh and vigorous atmosphere, so close and dead and mixed with the carbonic breath of the locomotives was the air of the place. The thin old wooden walls that shut out the glare of the sun transmitted an intensified warmth; the roof seemed to hover lower and lower, and in its coal-smoked, raftery hollow to generate a heat deadlier than that poured upon it from the skies.

In a convenient place in the station hung a thermometer, before which every passenger, on going aboard the ferry-boat, paused as at a shrine, and mutely paid his devotions. At the altar of this fetich our friends also paused, and saw that the mercury was above ninety; and, exulting with the pride that savages take in the cruel might of their idols, bowed their souls to the great god Heat.

On the boat they found a place where the breath of the sea struck cool across their faces, and made them forget the thermometer for the brief time of the transit. But presently they drew near that strange irregular row of wooden buildings and jutting piers which skirts the river on the New York side; and before the boat's motion ceased the air grew thick and warm again, and tainted with the foulness of the street on which the buildings front. Upon this the boat's passengers issued, passing up through the gangway, on one side of which a throng of return passengers was pent by a gate of iron bars, like a herd of wild animals. They were streaming with perspiration, and according to their different temperaments had faces of deep crimson or deadly pallor.

"Now the question is, my dear," said Basil, when free of the press they lingered for a moment in the shade outside, "whether we had better walk up to Broadway, at an immediate sacrifice of fiber, and get a stage there, or take one of these cars here and be landed a little nearer, with half the exertion. By this route we shall have sights and smells which the other can't offer us, but whichever we take we shall be sorry."

"Then I say take this," decided Isabel. "I want to be sorry upon the easiest possible terms, this weather."

They hailed the first car that passed, and got into it. Well for them both if she could have exercised this philosophy with regard to the whole day's business, or if she could have given up her plans for it with the same resignation she had practised in regard to the day boat! It seems to me a proof of the small advance our race has made in true wisdom, that we find it so hard to give up doing anything we have meant to do. It matters very little whether the affair is one of enjoyment or of business, we feel the same bitter need of pursuing it to the end. The mere fact of intention gives it a flavor of duty; and dutiolatry, as one may call the devotion, has passed so deeply into our life that we have scarcely a sense any more of the sweetness of even a neglected pleasure. We will not taste the fine, guilty rapture of a deliberate dereliction; the gentle sin of omission is all but blotted from the calendar of our crimes. If I had been Columbus, I should have thought twice before setting sail, when I was quite ready to do so; and as for Plymouth Rock, I should have sternly resisted the blandishments of those twin sirens, Starvation and Cold, who beckoned the Puritans shoreward, and as soon as ever I came into sight of their granite perch should have turned back to England. But it is now too late to repair these errors; and so, on one of the hottest days of last year, behold my obdurate bridal pair, in a Tenth or Twentieth Avenue horse-car, setting forth upon the fulfilment of a series of intentions, any of which had wiselier been left unaccomplished. Isabel had said they would call upon certain people in Fiftieth Street, and then shop slowly down, ice-creaming and staging and variously cooling and calming by the way, until they reached the ticket office on Broadway, whence they could indefinitely betake themselves to the steamboat an hour or two before her departure. She felt that they had yielded sufficiently to circumstances and conditions already on this journey, and she was resolved that the present half-day in New York should be the half-day of her original design.

It was not the most advisable thing, as I have allowed; but it was inevitable, and it afforded them a spectacle which is by no means wanting in sublimity, and which is certainly unique — the spectacle of that great city on a hot day, defiant of the elements and prospering on, with every form of labor and at a terrible cost of life. The man carrying the hod to the top of the walls, that rankly grow and grow as from his life's blood, will only lay down his load when he feels the mortal glare of the sun blaze in upon heart and brain; the plethoric millionaire for whom he toils will plot and plan in his office till he swoons at the desk; the trembling beast must stagger forward while the flame-faced tormentor on the box has strength to lash him on: in all those vast palaces of commerce there are ceaseless sale and purchase, packing and unpacking, lifting up and laying down, arriving and departing loads; in thousands of shops is the unspared and unsparing weariness of selling; in the street, filled by the hurry and suffering of tens of thousands, is the weariness of buying.

Their afternoon's experience was something that Basil and Isabel could, when it was past, look upon only as a kind of vision, magnificent at times, and at other times full of indignity and pain. They seemed to have dreamed of a long horse-car pilgrimage through that squalid street by the riverside; where presently they came to a market, opening upon the view hideous vistas of carnage, and then into a wide avenue, with processions of cars like their own coming and going up and down the center of a foolish and useless breadth, which made even the tall buildings (rising gauntly up among the older houses of one or two stories) on either hand look low, and let in the sun to bake the dust that the hot breaths of wind caught up and sent swirling into the shabby shops. Here they dreamed of the eternal demolition and construction of the city, and farther on of vacant lots full of granite boulders, clambered over by goats. In their dream they had fellow-passengers, whose sufferings made them odious, and whom they were glad to leave behind when they alighted from the car, and running out of the blaze of the avenue quenched themselves in the shade of the cross street. A little strip of shadow lay along the row of brown-stone fronts, but there were intervals where the vacant lots cast no shadow. With great bestowal of thought they studied hopelessly how to avoid these spaces, as if they had been difficult torrents or vast expanses of desert sand; they crept slowly along till they came to such a place, and dashed swiftly across it, and then, fainter than before, moved on. They seemed now and then to stand at doors, and to be told that people were out, and again that they were in; and they had a sense of cool dark parlors, and the airy rustling of light-muslined ladies, of chat and of fans and ice-water, and then they came forth again; and evermore

"The day increased from heat to heat."

At last they were aware of an end of their visits, and of a purpose to go down-town again, and of seeking the nearest car by endless blocks of brown-stone fronts, which with their eternal brown-stone flights of steps, and their handsome, intolerable uniformity, oppressed them like a procession of houses trying to pass a given point and never getting by. Upon these streets there was seldom a soul to be seen; so that when their ringing at a door had evoked answer, it had startled them with vague, sad surprise. In the distance on either hand they could see cars and carts and wagons toiling up and down the avenues, and on the next intersecting pavement sometimes a laborer with his jacket slung across his shoulder, or a dog that had plainly made up his mind to go mad. Up to the time of their getting into one of those phantasmal cars for the return down-townwards they had kept up a show of talk in their wretched dream. They had spoken of other hot days that they had known elsewhere; and they had wondered that the tragical character of heat had been so little recognized. They said that the daily New York murder might even at that moment be somewhere taking place, and that no murder of the whole homicidal year could have such proper circumstance; they morbidly wondered what that day's murder would be, and in what swarming tenement-house, or den of the assassin streets by the riversides — if indeed it did not befall in some such high, close-shuttered, handsome dwelling as those they passed, in whose twilight it would be so easy to strike down the master, and leave him undiscovered and unmourned by the family ignorantly absent at the mountains or the seaside. They conjectured of the horror of midsummer battles, and pictured the anguish of shipwrecked men upon a tropical coast, and the grimy misery of stevedores unloading shiny cargoes of anthracite coal at city docks. But now at last, as they took seats opposite one another in the crowded car, they seemed to have drifted infinite distances and long epochs asunder. They looked hopelessly across the intervening gulf, and mutely questioned when it was and from what far city they or some remote ancestors of theirs had set forth upon a wedding journey. They bade each other a tacit farewell, and with patient, pathetic faces awaited the end of the world.

When they alighted, they took their way up through one of the streets of the great wholesale businesses, to Broadway. On this street was a throng of trucks and wagons lading and unlading; bales and boxes rose and sank by pulleys overhead; the footway was a labyrinth of packages of every shape and size: there was no flagging of the pitiless energy that moved all forward, no sign of how heavy a weight lay on it, save in the reeking faces of its helpless instruments. But when the wedding-journeyers emerged upon Broadway, the other passages and incidents of their dream faded before the superior fantasticality of the spectacle. It was four o'clock, the deadliest hour of the deadly summer day. The spiritless air seemed to have a quality of blackness in it, as if filled with the gloom of low-hovering wings. One half the street lay in shadow, and one half in sun; but the sunshine itself was dim, as if a heat greater than its own had smitten it with languor. Little gusts of sick, warm wind blew across the great avenue at the corners of the intersecting streets. In the upward distance, at which the journeyers looked, the loftier roofs and steeples lifted themselves dim out of the livid atmosphere, and far up and down the length of the street swept a stream of tormented life. All sorts of wheeled things thronged it, conspicuous among which rolled and jarred the gaudily painted stages, with quivering horses driven each by a man who sat in the shade of a branching white umbrella, and suffered with a moody truculence of aspect, and as if he harbored the bitterness of death in his heart for the crowding passengers within, when one of them pulled the strap about his legs and summoned him to halt. Most of the foot passengers kept to the shady side; and to the unaccustomed eyes of the strangers they were not less in number than at any other time, though there were fewer women among them. Indomitably resolute of soul, they held their course with the swift pace of custom, and only here and there they showed the effect of the heat. One man, collarless, with waistcoat unbuttoned and hat set far back from his forehead, waved a fan before his death-white flabby face, and set down one foot after the other with the heaviness of a somnambulist. Another, as they passed him, was saying huskily to the friend at his side, "I can't stand this much longer. My hands tingle as if they had gone to sleep; my heart —" But still the multitude hurried on, passing, repassing, encountering, evading, vanishing into shop-doors and emerging from them, dispersing down the side streets and swarming out of them. It was a scene that possessed the beholder with singular fascination, and in its effect of universal lunacy it might well have seemed the last phase of a world presently to be destroyed. They who were in it but not of it, as they fancied — though there was no reason for this — looked on it amazed; and at last, their own errands being accomplished, and themselves so far cured of the madness of purpose, they cried with one voice that it was a hideous sight, and strove to take refuge from it in the nearest place where the soda fountain sparkled. It was a vain desire. At the front door of the apothecary's hung a thermometer, and as they entered they heard the next comer cry out, with a maniacal pride in the affliction laid upon mankind, "Ninety-seven degrees!" Behind them at the door there poured in a ceaseless stream of people, each pausing at the shrine of heat before he tossed off the hissing draught that two pale, close-clipped boys served them from either side of the fountain. Then in the order of their coming they issued through another door upon the side street; each, as he disappeared, turning his face half round, and casting a casual glance upon a little group near another counter. The group was of a very patient, half frightened, half puzzled looking gentleman who sat perfectly still on a stool, and of a lady who stood beside him, rubbing all over his head a handkerchief full of pounded ice, and easing one hand with the other when the first became tired. Basil drank his soda and paused to look upon this group, which he felt would commend itself to realistic sculpture as eminently characteristic of the local life, and as "The Sunstroke" would sell enormously in the hot season. "Better take a little more of that," the apothecary said, looking up from his prescription, and at the organized sympathy of the seemingly indifferent crowd smiling very kindly at his patient, who thereupon tasted something in the glass he held. "Do you still feel like fainting?" asked the humane authority. "Slightly, now and then," answered the other; "but I'm hanging on hard to the bottom curve of that icicled S on your soda fountain, and I feel that I'm all right as long as I can see that. The people get rather hazy occasionally, and have no features to speak of. But I don't know that I look very impressive myself," he added, in the jesting mood which seems the natural condition of Americans in the face of all embarrassments.

"Oh, you'll do!" the apothecary answered with a laugh; but he said, in answer to an anxious question from the lady, "He mustn't be moved for an hour yet," and gayly pestled away at a prescription, while she resumed her office of grinding the pounded ice round and round upon her husband's skull. Isabel offered her the commiseration of friendly words, and of looks kinder yet; and then, seeing that they could do nothing, she and Basil fell into the endless procession, and passed out of the side door. "What a shocking thing!" she whispered. "Did you see how all the people looked, one after another, so indifferently at that couple, and evidently forgot them the next instant? It was dreadful. I shouldn't like to have you sunstruck in New York."

"That's very considerate of you; but place for place, if any accident must happen to me among strangers, I think I should prefer to have it in New York. The biggest place is always the kindest as well as the cruelest place. Amongst the thousands of spectators the good Samaritan as well as the Levite would be sure to be. As for a sunstroke, it requires peculiar gifts. But if you compel me to a choice in the matter, then I say, give me the busiest part of Broadway for a sunstroke. There is such experience of calamity there that you could hardly fall the first victim to any misfortune. Probably the gentleman at the apothecary's was merely exhausted by the heat, and ran in there for revival. The apothecary has a case of the kind on his hands every blazing afternoon, and knows just what to do. The crowd may be a little *ennuyé* of sunstrokes, and to that degree indifferent; but they most likely know that they can only do harm by an expression of sympathy, and so they delegate their pity as they have delegated their helpfulness, to the proper authority, and go about their business. If a man was overcome in the middle of a village street, the blundering country druggist wouldn't know what to do, and the tender-hearted people would crowd about so that no breath of air could reach the victim."

"Maybe so, dear," said the wife pensively; "but if anything did happen to you in New York, I should like to have the spectators look as if they saw a human being in trouble. Perhaps I'm a little exacting."

"I think you are. Nothing is so hard as to understand that there are human beings in this world besides one's self and one's set. But let us be selfishly thankful that it isn't you and I there in the apothecary's shop, as it might very well be; and let us get to the boat as soon as we can, and end this horrible midsummer-day's dream. We must have a carriage," he added with a tardy wisdom, hailing an empty hack, "as we ought to have had all day; though I'm not sorry, now the worst's over, to have seen the worst."

ARRIVAL AND FIRST DAYS IN VENICE

From 'Venetian Life.' Copyright, 1867 and 1872, by W. D. Howells. Reprinted by permission of the author, and of Houghton Mifflin Company, publishers

I THINK it does not matter just when I first came to Venice. Yesterday and today are the same here. I arrived one winter morning about five o'clock, and was not so full of Soul as I might have been in warmer weather. Yet I was resolved not to go to my hotel in the omnibus (the large, many-seated boat so called), but to have a gondola solely for myself and my luggage. The porter who seized my valise in the station inferred from some very polyglottic Italian of mine the nature of my wish, and ran out and threw that slender piece of luggage into a gondola. I followed, lighted to my seat by a beggar in picturesque and desultory costume. He was one of a class of mendicants whom I came, for my sins, to know better in Venice, and whom I dare say every traveler recollects — the merciless tribe who hold your gondola to shore, and affect to do you a service and not a displeasure, and pretend not to be abandoned swindlers. The Venetians called them *gransieri*, or crab-catchers: but as yet I did not know the name or the purpose of this *poverino* at the station, but merely saw that he had the Venetian eye for color; in the distribution and arrangement of his fragments of dress he had produced some miraculous effects of red, and he was altogether as infamous a figure as any friend of brigands would like to meet in a lonely place. He did not offer to stab me and sink my body in the Grand Canal, as in all Venetian keeping I felt that he ought to have done; but he implored an alms, and I hardly know now whether to exult or regret that I did not understand him, and left him empty-handed. I suppose that he withdrew again the blessings which he had advanced me, as we pushed out into the canal; but I heard nothing, for the wonder of the city was already upon me. All my nether spirit, so to speak, was dulled and jaded by the long, cold railway journey from Vienna, while every surface sense was taken and tangled in the bewildering brilliancy and novelty of Venice. For I think there can be nothing else in the world so full of glittering and exquisite surprise as that first glimpse of Venice which the traveler catches as he issues from the railway station by night, and looks upon her peerless strangeness. There is something in the blessed breath of Italy (how quickly, coming south, you know it, and how bland it is after the harsh transalpine air!) which prepares you for your nocturnal advent into the place; and O you! whoever you are, that journey toward this enchanted city for the first time, let me tell you how happy I count you! There lies before you for your pleasure the spectacle of such singular beauty as no picture can ever show you nor book tell you — beauty which you shall feel perfectly but once, and regret forever.

For my own part, as the gondola slipped away from the blaze and bustle of the station down the gloom and silence of the broad canal, I forgot that I had been freezing two days and nights; that I was at that moment very cold and a little homesick. I could at first feel nothing but that beautiful silence, broken only by the star-silvered dip of the oars. Then on either hand I saw stately palaces rise gray and lofty from the dark waters, holding here and there a lamp against their faces, which brought balconies and columns and carven arches into momentary relief, and threw long streams of crimson into the canal. I could see by that uncertain glimmer how fair was all, but not how sad and old; and so, unhaunted by any pang for the decay that afterward saddened me amid the forlorn beauty of Venice, I glided on. I have no doubt it was a proper time to think all the fantastic things in the world, and I thought them; but they passed vaguely through my mind, without at all interrupting the sensations of sight and sound. Indeed, the past and present mixed there, and the moral and material were blent in the sentiment of utter novelty and surprise. The quick boat slid through old troubles of mine, and unlooked-for events gave it the impulse that carried it beyond and safely around sharp corners of life. And all the while I knew that this was a progress through narrow and crooked canals, and past marble angles of palaces. But I did not know then that this fine confusion of sense and spirit was the first faint impression of the charm of life in Venice.

Dark funereal barges like my own had flitted by, and the gondoliers had warned each other at every turning with hoarse, lugubrious cries; the lines of balconied palaces had never ended; here and there at their doors larger craft were moored, with dim figures of men moving uncertainly about on them. At last we had passed abruptly out of the Grand Canal into one of the smaller channels, and from comparative light into a darkness only remotely affected by some far-streaming corner lamp. But always the pallid, stately palaces; always the dark heaven with its trembling stars above, and the dark water with its trembling stars below: but now innumerable bridges, and an utter lonesomeness, and ceaseless sudden turns and windings. One could not resist a vague feeling of anxiety, in these strait and solitary passages, which was part of the strange enjoyment of the time, and which was referable to the novelty, the hush, the darkness, and the piratical appearance and unaccountable pauses of the gondoliers. Was not this Venice, and is not Venice forever associated with bravoes and unexpected dagger-thrusts? That valise of mine might represent fabulous wealth to the uncultivated imagination. Who, if I made an outcry, could understand the Facts of the Situation (as we say in the journals)? To move on was relief; to pause was regret for past transgressions mingled with good resolutions for the future. But I felt the liveliest mixture of all these emotions when, slipping from the cover of a bridge, the gondola suddenly rested at the foot of a stairway before a closely barred door. The gondoliers rang and rang again, while their passenger

"Divided the swift mind,"

in the wonder whether a door so grimly bolted and austerely barred could possibly open into a hotel, with cheerful overcharges for candles and service. But as soon as the door opened, and he beheld the honest swindling countenance of a hotel *portier,* he felt secure against everything but imposture; and all wild absurdities of doubt and conjecture at once faded from his thought when the *portier* suffered the gondoliers to make him pay a florin too much.

So I had arrived in Venice, and I had felt the influence of that complex spell which she lays upon the stranger. I had caught the most alluring glimpses of the beauty which cannot wholly perish while any fragment of her sculptured walls nods to its shadow in the canal; I had been penetrated by a deep sense of the mystery of the place, and I had been touched already by the anomaly of modern life amid scenes where its presence offers, according to the humor in which it is studied, constant occasion for annoyance or delight, enthusiasm or sadness.

I fancy that the ignorant impressions of the earlier days after my arrival need scarcely be set down even in this perishable record; but I would not wholly forget how, though isolated from all acquaintance and alien to the place, I yet felt curiously at home in Venice from the first. I believe it was because I had after my own fashion loved the beautiful, that I here found the beautiful, where it is supreme, full of society and friendship, speaking a langauge which even in its unfamiliar forms I could partly understand, and at

THE PRINCE AND THE PAUPER

Painting by W. Hatherell in Mark Twain, *The Prince and the Pauper*

once making me citizen of that Venice from which I shall never be exiled. It was not in the presence of the great and famous monuments of art alone that I felt at home: indeed, I could as yet understand their excellence and grandeur only very imperfectly; but wherever I wandered through the quaint and marvelous city I found the good company of

"The fair, the old;"

and to tell the truth, I think it is the best society in Venice, and I learned to turn to it later from other companionship with a kind of relief.

My first rambles, moreover, had a peculiar charm which knowledge of locality has since taken away. They began commonly with some purpose or destination, and ended by losing me in the intricacies of the narrowest, crookedest, and most inconsequent little streets in the world, or left me cast away upon the unfamiliar waters of some canal as far as possible from the point aimed at. Dark and secret little courts lay in wait for my blundering steps, and I was incessantly surprised and brought to surrender by paths that beguiled me up to dead walls or the sudden brinks of canals. The wide and open squares before the innumerable churches of the city were equally victorious, and continually took me prisoner. But all places had something rare and worthy to be seen: if not loveliness of sculpture or architecture, at least interesting squalor and picturesque wretchedness; and I believe I had less delight in proper Objects of Interest than in the dirty neighborhoods that reeked with unwholesome winter damps below, and peered curiously out with frowzy heads and beautiful eyes from the high, heavy-shuttered casements above. Every court had its carven well to show me, in the noisy keeping of the water-carriers and the slatternly, statuesque gossips of the place. The remote and noisome canals were pathetic with empty old palaces peopled by herds of poor, that decorated the sculptured balconies with the tatters of epicene linen, and patched the lofty windows with obsolete hats.

I found the night as full of beauty as the day, when caprice led me from the brilliancy of St. Mark's and the glittering streets of shops that branch away from the Piazza, and lost me in the quaint recesses of the courts, or the tangles of the distant alleys, where the dull little oil lamps vied with the tapers burning before the street-corner shrines of the Virgin in making the way obscure, and deepening the shadows about the doorways and under the frequent arches. I remember distinctly among the beautiful nights of that time, the soft night of late winter which first showed me the scene you may behold from the Public Gardens at the end of the long concave line of the Riva degli Schiavoni. Lounging there upon the southern parapet of the Gardens, I turned from the dim bell-towers of the evanescent islands in the east (a solitary gondola gliding across the calm of the water, and striking its moonlight silver into multitudinous ripples), and glanced athwart the vague shipping in the basin of St. Mark, and saw all the lights from the Piazzetta to the Giudecca, making a crescent of flame in the air, and casting deep into the water under them a crimson glory that sank also down and down in my own heart, and illumined all its memories of beauty and delight. Behind these lamps rose the shadowy masses of church and palace; the moon stood bright and full in the heavens; the gondola drifted away to the northward; the islands of the lagoons seemed to rise and sink with the light palpitations of the waves like pictures on the undulating fields of banners; the stark rigging of a ship showed black against the sky; the Lido sank from sight upon the east, as if the shore had composed itself to sleep by the side of its beloved sea to the music of the surge that gently beat its sands; the yet leafless boughs of the trees above me stirred themselves together, and out of one of those trembling towers in the lagoons one rich full sob burst from the heart of a bell, too deeply stricken with the glory of the scene, and suffused the languid night with the murmur of luxurious, ineffable sadness.

But there is a perfect democracy in the realm of the beautiful, and whatsoever pleases is equal to any other thing there, no matter how low its origin or humble its composition; and the magnificence of that moonlight scene gave me no deeper joy than I won from the fine spectacle of an old man whom I saw burning coffee one night in the little court behind my lodgings, and whom I recollect now as one of the most interesting people I saw in my first days at Venice. All day long the air of that neighborhood had reeked with the odors of the fragrant berry, and all day long this patient old man — sage, let me call him — had turned the sheet-iron cylinder in which it was roasting over an open fire, after the picturesque fashion of roasting coffee in Venice. Now that the night had fallen, and the stars shone down upon him, and the red of the flame luridly illumined him, he showed more grand and venerable than ever. Simple, abstract humanity has its own grandeur in Italy; and it is not hard here for the artist to find the primitive types with which genius loves best to deal. As for this old man, he had the beard of a saint and the dignity of a senator, harmonized with the squalor of a beggar, superior to which shone his abstract, unconscious grandeur of humanity. A vast and calm melancholy, which had nothing to do with burning coffee, dwelt in his aspect and attitude; and if he had been some dread supernatural agency, turning the wheel of fortune, and doing men instead of coffee brown, he could not have looked more sadly and weirdly impressive. When presently he rose from his seat and lifted the cylinder from its place, and the clinging flames leaped after it, and he shook it, and a volume of luminous smoke enveloped him and glorified him — then I felt with secret anguish that he was beyond art, and turned sadly from the spectacle of that sublime and hopeless magnificence.

At other times (but this was in broad daylight) I was troubled by the esthetic perfection of a certain ruffian boy, who sold cakes of baked Indian meal to the soldiers in the military station near the Piazza, and whom I often noted from the windows of the little caffè there, where you get an excellent *caffè bianco* (coffee with milk) for ten soldi and one to the waiter. I have reason to fear that this boy dealt over-shrewdly with the Austrians, for a pitiless war raged between him and one of the sergeants. His hair was dark, his cheek was of a bronze better than olive; and he wore a brave cap of red flannel, drawn down to eyes of lustrous black. For the rest, he gave unity and coherence to a jacket and pantaloons of heterogeneous elements, and, such was the elasticity of his spirit, a buoyant grace to feet incased in wooden shoes. Habitually came a barrel-organist and ground before the barracks, and

"Took the soul
Of that waste place with joy;"

and ever, when this organist came to a certain lively waltz, and threw his whole soul as it were into the crank of his instrument, my beloved ragamuffin failed not to seize another cake-boy in his arms, and thus embraced, to whirl through a wild inspiration of figures, in which there was something grotesquely rhythmic, something of indescribable barbaric magnificence, spiritualized into a grace of movement superior to the energy of the North and the extravagant fervor of the East. It was coffee and not wine that I drank; but I fable all the same that I saw reflected in this superb and artistic superation of the difficulties of dancing in that unfriendly foot-gear, something of the same genius that combated and vanquished the elements, to build its home upon sea-washed sands in marble structures of airy and stately splendor, and gave to architecture new glories full of eternal surprise.

So, I say, I grew early into sympathy and friendship with Venice; and being newly from a land where everything, morally and materially, was in good repair, I rioted sentimentally on the picturesque ruin, the pleasant discomfort and hopelessness of everything about me here. It was not yet the season to behold all the delight of the lazy outdoor life of the place; but nevertheless I could not help seeing that great part of the people, both rich and poor, seemed to have nothing to do, and that nobody seemed to be driven by any inward or outward impulse. When, however, I ceased (as I must in time) to be merely a spectator of this idleness, and learned that I too must assume my share of the common indolence, I found it a grievous burden. Old habits of work, old habits of hope, made my endless leisure irksome to me, and almost intolerable when I ascertained, fairly and finally, that in my desire to fulfil long-cherished but after all merely general designs of literary study, I had forsaken wholesome struggle in the currents where I felt the motion of the age, only to drift into a lifeless eddy of the world, remote from incentive and sensation.

For such is Venice; and the will must be strong and the faith indomitable in him who can long retain, amid the influences of her stagnant quiet, a practical belief in God's purpose of a great moving, anxious, toiling, aspiring world outside. When you have yielded, as after a while I yielded, to these influences, a gentle incredulity possesses you; and if you consent that such a thing is an earnest and useful life, you cannot help wondering why it need be. The charm of the place sweetens your temper, but corrupts you; and I found it a sad condition of my perception of the beauty of Venice and friendship with it, that I came in some unconscious way to regard her fate as my own; and when I began to write the sketches which go to form this book, it was as hard to speak of any ugliness in her, or of the doom written against her in the hieroglyphic seams and fissures of her crumbling masonry, as if the fault and penalty were mine. I do not so greatly blame, therefore, the writers who have committed so many sins of omission concerning her, and made her all light, color, canals, and palaces. One's conscience, more or less uncomfortably vigilant elsewhere, drowses here, and it is difficult to remember that fact is more virtuous than fiction. In other years, when there was life in the city, and this sad ebb of prosperity was full tide in her canals, there might have been some incentive to keep one's thoughts and words from lapsing into habits of luxurious dishonesty, some reason for telling the whole hard truth of things, some policy to serve, some end to gain. But now, what matter?

JOHN HAY

BORN in 1838 at Salem, Indiana, of Scotch ancestry, John Hay passed his early years as does the average intelligent Western boy. When only twenty he was graduated from Brown University, where his work in English composition was thought to indicate literary ability. Studying law at Springfield, Illinois, he began practice there in 1861; but soon after accompanied President Lincoln to Washington as his assistant secretary, and acting as adjutant and aide also, grew into close intimacy with the statesman whose biographer he became. Like most ardent young men of his time, he entered the army, attaining the brevet rank of colonel and assistant adjutant-general. His large opportunities for meeting men, his gift for making friends, and his tactful good sense, especially qualified him for his later diplomatic career.

Soon after the war Colonel Hay went as Secretary of Legation to Paris, where his careful study of French political conditions appears in several of his poems; among them 'Sunrise in the Place de la Concorde,' 'The Sphinx of the Tuileries,' and 'A Triumph of Order.' Sent afterwards to Vienna, he was presently transferred to Madrid as chargé d'affaires. 'Castilian Days' reflects in delightful colors the pleasure he found in the history, the romance, and the beauty of Spain; a pleasure which shows an odd background of American practicality, and a democratic conviction that kings and nobles are as fallible as other men. He greatly admired Castelar, whose acquaintance he made, and translated for American readers his treatise upon 'The Republican Movement in Europe.'

Returning to New York in 1871, Hay joined the staff of the New York Tribune. 'Pike County Ballads,' his second publication, issued in 1871, celebrated in Western dialect the heroism of drinking pilots, swearing engineers, and godless settlers, and caught the fancy of the public by means of its vivid local color and dramatic quality. Some years later these verses were republished in the same volume with his miscellaneous poems, his 'Wanderlieder,' and his translations.

His most important work is the comprehensive history of the life and times of Abraham Lincoln, written in collaboration with John George Nicolay, the great President's private secretary. Appearing first in The Century Magazine, this was published in ten large volumes, which offer a careful historical survey of the whole period of the Civil War, and of the conditions which made it inevitable. Thoroughly understanding the character and motives of Lincoln, and himself a spectator and an actor in the great drama he describes,

Colonel Hay's pages are vividly written, and often touched with personal emotion.

During the administration of Hayes he became first assistant Secretary of State. McKinley later appointed him ambassador at London and on the retirement of Judge Day he became Secretary of State, which position he retained under Roosevelt's administration until his death, July 1, 1905. It is difficult to enumerate briefly Hay's manifold diplomatic successes which made him the idol of his own country and the most conspicuous American in the eyes of all the civilized world. After the Spanish War he handled with remarkable diplomacy the intricate problems which arose in connection with the Philippines, and whether it was with Great Britain over the Alaskan boundary, Samoan negotiations, the question of Chinese trade or the reciprocity treaties for the British West Indies, Secretary Hay's manipulation was always supremely tactful, skilful, and far-sighted. Under his administration of the Department of State American interests in all the world were maintained with a strong hand, while his peaceful and conciliatory spirit strengthened the friendship which existed between the United States and all other nations.

LINCOLN'S DEATH AND FAME

From 'Abraham Lincoln: a History.' Copyright, 1886 and 1890, by John G. Nicolay and John Hay, and reprinted by permission of Mr. Hay and The Century Company, publishers, New York

IN fact, it was among the common people of the entire civilized world that the most genuine and spontaneous manifestations of sorrow and appreciation were produced, and to this fact we attribute the sudden and solid foundation of Lincoln's fame. It requires years, perhaps centuries, to build the structure of a reputation which rests upon the opinion of those distinguished for learning or intelligence; the progress of opinion from the few to the many is slow and painful. But in the case of Lincoln the many imposed their opinion all at once; he was canonized, as he lay on his bier, by the irresistible decree of countless millions. The greater part of the aristocracy of England thought little of him; but the burst of grief from the English people silenced in an instant every discordant voice. It would have been as imprudent to speak slightingly of him in London as it was in New York. Especially among the Dissenters was honor and reverence shown to his name. The humbler people instinctively felt that their order had lost its wisest champion.

Not only among those of Saxon blood was this outburst of emotion seen. In France a national manifestation took place, which the government disliked but did not think it wise to suppress. The students of Paris marched in a body to the American Legation to express their sympathy. A two-cent subscription was started to strike a massive gold medal; the money was soon raised, but the committee was forced to have the work done in Switzerland. A committee of French Liberals brought the medal to the American minister, to be sent to Mrs. Lincoln. "Tell her," said Eugène Pellatan, "the heart of France is in that little box." The inscription had a double sense; while honoring the dead republican, it struck at the Empire: "Lincoln — the Honest Man; abolished Slavery, re-established the Union; Saved the Republic, without veiling the Statue of Liberty."

Everywhere on the Continent the same swift apotheosis of the people's hero was seen. An Austrian deputy said to the writer, "Among my people his memory has already assumed superhuman proportions; he has become a myth, a type of ideal democracy." Almost before the earth closed over him he began to be the subject of fable. The Freemasons of Europe generally regard him as one of them — his portrait in Masonic garb is often displayed; yet he was not one of that brotherhood. The Spiritualists claim him as their most illustrious adept, but he was not a Spiritualist; and there is hardly a sect in the Western world, from the Calvinist to the atheist, but affects to believe he was of their opinion.

A collection of the expressions of sympathy and condolence which came to Washington from foreign governments, associations, and public bodies of all sorts, was made by the State Department, and afterwards published by order of Congress. It forms a large quarto of a thousand pages, and embraces the utterances of grief and regret from every country under the sun in almost every language spoken by man.

But admired and venerated as he was in Europe, he was best understood and appreciated at home. It is not to be denied that in his case, as in that of all heroic personages who occupy a great place in history, a certain element of legend mingles with his righteous fame. He was a man, in fact, especially liable to legend. We have been told by farmers in central Illinois that the brown thrush did not sing for a year after he died. He was gentle and merciful, and therefore he seems in a certain class of annals to have passed all his time in soothing misfortune and pardoning crime. He had more than his share of the shrewd native humor, and therefore the loose jest-books of two centuries have been ransacked for anecdotes to be attributed to him. He was a great and powerful lover of mankind, especially of those not favored by fortune. One night he had a dream, which he repeated the next morning to the writer of these lines, which quaintly illustrates his unpretending and kindly democracy. He was in some great assembly; the people made a lane to let him pass. "He is a common-looking fellow," some one said. Lincoln in his dream turned to his critic and replied in his Quaker phrase, "Friend, the Lord prefers common-looking people; that is why he made so many of them." He that abases himself shall be exalted. Because Lincoln kept himself in such constant sympathy with the common people, whom he respected too highly to flatter or mislead, he was rewarded by a reverence and a love hardly ever given to a human being. Among the humble working people of the South whom he had made free, this veneration and affection easily passed into the supernatural. At a religious meeting among the negroes of the Sea Islands a young man expressed the wish that he might see Lincoln. A gray-headed negro rebuked the rash aspiration: "No man see Linkum. Linkum walk as Jesus walk; no man see Linkum."

But leaving aside these fables, which are a natural enough expression of a popular awe and love, it seems to us that no more just estimate of Lincoln's relation to his time has ever been made, nor perhaps ever will be, than that uttered by one of the wisest and most American of thinkers, Ralph Waldo Emerson, a few days after the assassination. We cannot forbear quoting a few words of this remarkable discourse, which shows how Lincoln seemed to the greatest of his contemporaries: —

"A plain man of the people, an extraordinary fortune attended him. Lord Bacon says, 'Manifest virtues procure reputation; occult ones fortune.' . . . His occupying the chair of State was a triumph of the good sense of mankind and of the public conscience. . . . He grew according to the need; his mind mastered the problem of the day; and as the problem grew, so did his comprehension of it. Rarely was a man so fitted to the event. . . . It cannot be said that there is any exaggeration of his worth. If ever a man was fairly tested, he was. There was no lack of resistance, nor of slander, nor of ridicule. . . . Then what an occasion was the whirlwind of the war! Here was no place for holiday magistrate, nor fair-weather sailor; the new pilot was hurried to the helm in a tornado. In four years — four years of battle days — his endurance, his fertility of resources, his magnanimity, were sorely tried and never found wanting. There by his courage, his justice, his even temper, his fertile counsel, his humanity, he stood a heroic figure in the center of a heroic epoch. He is the true history of the American people in his time; the true representative of this continent — father of his country; the pulse of twenty millions throbbing in his heart, the thought of their minds articulated by his tongue."

The quick instinct by which the world recognized him even at the moment of his death as one of its greatest men, was not deceived. It has been confirmed by the sober thought of a quarter of a century. The writers of each nation compare him with their first popular hero. The French find points of resemblance in him to Henry IV, the Dutch liken him to William of Orange: the cruel stroke of murder and treason by which all three perished in the height of their power naturally suggests the comparison, which is strangely justified in both cases, though the two princes were so widely different in character. Lincoln had the wit, the bonhomie, the keen practical insight into affairs, of the Béarnais; and the tyrannous moral sense, the wide comprehension, the heroic patience of the Dutch patriot, whose motto might have served equally well for the American President — "*Sævis tranquillus in undis.*" European historians speak of him in words reserved for the most illustrious names. Merle d'Aubigné says, "The name of Lincoln will remain one of the greatest that history has to inscribe on its annals." Henri Martin predicts nothing less than a universal apotheosis: "This man will stand out in the traditions of his country and the world as an incarnation of the people, and of modern democracy itself." Emilio Castelar, in an oration against slavery in the Spanish Cortes, called him "humblest of the humble before his conscience, greatest of the great before history."

In this country, where millions still live who were his contemporaries, and thousands who knew him personally; where the envies and jealousies which dog the footsteps of success still linger in the hearts of a few; where journals still exist that loaded his name for four years with daily calumny, and writers of memoirs vainly try to make themselves important by belittling him — his fame has become as universal as the air, as deeply rooted as the hills. The faint discords are not heard in the wide chorus that hails him second to none and equaled by Washington alone. The eulogies of him form a special literature. Preachers, poets, soldiers, and statesmen employ the same phrases of unconditional love and reverence. Men speaking with the authority of fame use unqualified superlatives. Lowell in an immortal ode calls him "new birth of our new soil, the first American." General Sherman says, "Of all the men I ever met, he seemed to possess more of the elements of greatness, combined with goodness, than any other." General Grant, after having met the rulers of almost every civilized country on earth, said Lincoln impressed him as the greatest intellectual force with which he had ever come in contact.

He is spoken of with scarcely less of enthusiasm by the more generous and liberal spirits among those who revolted against his election and were vanquished by his power. General Longstreet calls him "the greatest man of Rebellion times, the one matchless among forty millions for the peculiar difficulties of the period." An eminent Southern orator, referring to our mixed Northern and Southern ancestry, says: "From the union of those colonists, from the straightening of their purposes and the crossing of their blood, slowly perfecting through a century, came he who stands as the first typical American, the first who comprehended within himself all the strength and gentleness, all the majesty and grace of this republic — Abraham Lincoln."

It is not difficult to perceive the basis of this sudden and world-wide fame, nor rash to predict its indefinite duration. There are two classes of men whose names are more enduring than any monument: the great writers, and the men of great achievement — the founders of States, the conquerors. Lincoln has the singular fortune to belong to both these categories; upon these broad and stable foundations his renown is securely built. Nothing would have more amazed him while he lived than to hear himself called a man of letters; but this age has produced few greater writers. We are only recording here the judgment of his peers. Emerson ranks him with Æsop and Pilpay, in his lighter moods, and says: "The weight and penetration of many passages in his letters, messages, and speeches, hidden now by the very closeness of their application to the moment, are destined to a wide fame. What pregnant definitions, what unerring common-sense, what foresight, and on great occasions what lofty, and more than national, what human tone! His brief speech at Gettysburg will not easily be surpassed by words on any recorded occasion."

His style extorted the high praise of French Academicians; Montalembert commended it as a model for the imitation of princes. Many of his phrases form part of the common speech of mankind. It is true that in his writings the range of subjects is not great; he is concerned chiefly with the political problems of the time, and the moral considerations involved in them. But the range of treatment is remarkably wide; it runs from the wit, the gay humor, the florid eloquence of his stump speeches to the marvelous sententiousness and brevity of the letter to Greeley and the address of Gettysburg, and the sustained and lofty grandeur of the Second Inaugural.

The more his writings are studied in connection with the important transactions of his age, the higher will his reputation stand in the opinion of the lettered class. But the men of study and research are never numerous; and it is principally as a man of action that the world at large will regard him. It is the story of his objective life that will forever touch and hold the heart of mankind. His birthright was privation and ignorance — not peculiar to his family, but the universal environment of his place and time; he burst through those enchaining conditions by the force of native genius and will: vice had no temptation for him; his course was as naturally upward as the skylark's; he won, against all conceivable obstacles, a high place in an exacting profession and an honorable position in public and private life; he became the foremost representative of a party founded on an uprising of the national conscience against a secular wrong, and thus came to the awful responsibilities of power in a time of terror and gloom. He met them with incomparable strength and virtue. Caring for nothing but the public good, free from envy or jealous fears, he surrounded himself with the leading men of his party, his most formidable rivals in public esteem, and through four years of stupendous difficulties he was head and shoulders above them all in the vital qualities of wisdom, foresight, knowledge of men, and thorough comprehension of measures. Personally opposed, as the radicals claim, by more than half of his own party in Congress, and bitterly denounced and maligned by his open adversaries, he yet bore himself with such extraordinary discretion and skill that he obtained for the government all the legislation it required, and so impressed himself upon the national mind that without personal effort or solicitation he became the only possible candidate of his party for re-election, and was chosen by an almost unanimous vote of the electoral colleges.

His qualities would have rendered his administration illustrious even in time of peace; but when we consider that, in addition to the ordinary work of the executive office, he was forced to assume the duties of commander-in-chief of the national forces engaged in the most complex and difficult war of modern times, the greatness of spirit as well as the intellectual strength he evinced in that capacity is nothing short of prodigious. Aftertimes will wonder, not at the few and unimportant mistakes he may have committed, but at the intuitive knowledge of his business that he displayed. We would not presume to express a personal opinion in this matter. We use the testimony only of the most authoritative names. General W. T. Sherman has repeatedly expressed the admiration and surprise with which he has read Mr. Lincoln's correspondence with his generals, and his opinion of the remarkable correctness of his military views. General W. F. Smith says: — "I have long held to the opinion that at the close of the war Mr. Lincoln was the superior of his generals in his comprehension of the effect of strategic movements and the proper method of following up victories to their legitimate conclusions." General J. H. Wilson holds the same opinion; and Colonel Robert N. Scott, in whose lamented death the army lost one of its most vigorous and best trained intellects, frequently called Mr. Lincoln "the ablest strategist of the war."

To these qualifications of high literary excellence, and easy practical mastery of affairs of transcendent importance, we must add, as an explanation of his immediate and world-wide fame, his possession of certain moral qualities rarely combined in such high degree in one individual. His heart was so tender that he would dismount from his horse in a forest to replace in their nest young birds which had fallen by the roadside; he could not sleep at night if he knew that a soldier-boy was under sentence of death; he could not, even at the bidding of duty or policy, refuse the prayer of age or helplessness in distress. Children instinctively loved him; they never found his rugged features ugly; his sympathies were quick and seemingly unlimited. He was absolutely without prejudice of class or condition. Frederick Douglass says he was the only man of distinction he ever met who never reminded him, by word or manner, of his color; he was as just and generous to the rich and well-born as to the poor and humble — a thing rare among politicians. He was tolerant even of evil: though no man can ever have lived with a loftier scorn of meanness and selfishness, he yet recognized their existence and counted with them. He said one day, with a flash of cynical wisdom worthy of a La Rochefoucauld, that honest statesmanship was the employment of individual meanness for the public good. He never asked perfection of any one; he did not even insist, for others, upon the high standards he set up for himself. At a time before the word was invented he was the first of opportunists. With the fire of a reformer and a martyr in his heart, he yet proceeded by the ways of cautious and practical statecraft. He always worked with things as they were, while never relinquishing the desire and effort to make them better. To a hope which saw the Delectable Mountains of absolute justice and peace in the future, to a faith that God in his own time would give to all men the things convenient to them, he added a charity which embraced in its deep bosom all the good and the bad, all the virtues and the infirmities of men, and a patience like that of nature, which in its vast and fruitful activity knows neither haste nor rest.

A character like this is among the precious heirlooms of the republic; and by a special good fortune, every part of the country has an equal claim and pride in it. Lincoln's blood came from the veins of New England emigrants, of Middle-State Quakers, of Virginia planters, of Kentucky pioneers; he himself was one of the men who grew up with the earliest growth of the Great West. Every jewel of his mind or his conduct sheds radiance on each portion of the nation. The marvelous symmetry and balance of his intellect and character may have owed something to this varied environment of his race, and they may fitly typify the variety and solidity of the republic. It may not be unreasonable to hope that his name and his renown may be forever a bond of union to the country which he loved with an affection so impartial, and served, in life and in death, with such entire devotion.

[These poems are copyrighted, and are reprinted here by permission of Mr. Hay.]

WHEN PHYLLIS LAUGHS

WHEN Phyllis laughs, in sweet surprise
My heart asks if my dazzling eyes
Or if my ears take more delight
In luscious sound or beauty bright,
When Phyllis laughs.

In crinkled eyelids hid Love lies,
In the soft curving lips I prize
Promise of raptures infinite,
When Phyllis laughs.

Far to the Orient fancy flies.
I see beneath Idalian skies,
Clad only in the golden light,
Calm in perfection's peerless might,
The laughter-loving Venus rise,
When Phyllis laughs.

NIGHT IN VENICE

LOVE, in this summer night, do you recall
Midnight, and Venice, and those skies of June
Thick-sown with stars, when from the still lagoon
We glided noiseless through the dim canal?
A sense of some belated festival
Hung round us, and our own hearts beat in tune
With passionate memories that the young moon
Lit up on dome and tower and palace wall.
We dreamed what ghosts of vanished loves made part
Of that sweet light and trembling, amorous air.
I felt — in those rich beams that kissed your hair,
Those breezes warm with bygone lovers' sighs —
All the dead beauty of Venice in your eyes,
All the old loves of Venice in my heart.

JIM BLUDSO OF THE PRAIRIE BELLE

[Reprinted by permission of Mr. Hay and of Houghton Mifflin Company.]

WALL, no! I can't tell whar he lives,
Becase he don't live, you see;
Leastways, he's got out of the habit
Of livin' like you and me.
Whar have you been for the last three year
That you haven't heard folks tell
How Jimmy Bludso passed in his checks
The night of the Prairie Belle?

He weren't no saint — them engineers
Is all pretty much alike:
One wife in Natchez-under-the-Hill,
And another one here in Pike;
A keerless man in his talk was Jim,
And an awkward hand in a row,
But he never funked, and he never lied —
I reckon he never knowed how.

And this was all the religion he had:
  To treat his engine well;
Never be passed on the river;
  To mind the pilot's bell;
And if ever the Prairie Belle took fire —
  A thousand times he swore
He'd hold her nozzle agin the bank
  Till the last soul got ashore.

All boats has their day on the Mississip,
  And her day come at last —
The Movastar was a better boat,
  But the Belle she *wouldn't* be passed.
And so she come tearin' along, that night —
  The oldest craft on the line —
With a nigger squat on her safety-valve,
  And her furnace crammed, rosin and pine.

The fire bust out as she clared the bar,
  And burnt a hole in the night,
And quick as a flash she turned, and made
  For the willer-bank on the right.
There was runnin' and cursin', but Jim yelled out,
  Over all the infernal roar,
"I'll hold her nozzle agin the bank
  Till the last galoot's ashore."

Through the hot black breath of the burnin' boat
  Jim Bludso's voice was heard,
And they all had trust in his cussedness,
  And knowed he would keep his word.
And sure's you're born, they all got off
  Afore the smoke-stacks fell —
And Bludso's ghost went up alone
  In the smoke of the Prairie Belle.

He weren't no saint — but at judgment
  I'd run my chance with Jim,
'Longside of some pious gentlemen
  That wouldn't shook hands with him.
He seen his duty, a dead-sure thing —
  And went for it thar and then;
And Christ ain't agoing to be too hard
  On a man that died for men.

HENRY ADAMS

THE gifts of expression and literary taste which have always characterized the Adams family were most prominently represented by this historian. He had also its great memory, power of acquisition, intellectual independence, and energy of nature. The latter was tempered in him with inherited self-control, the moderation of judgment bred by wide historical knowledge, and a pervasive atmosphere of literary good-breeding which constantly substituted allusive irony for crude statement, the rapier for the tomahawk.

Henry Adams was the third son of Charles Francis Adams, Sr. — the able Minister to England during the Civil War — and grandson of John Quincy Adams. He was born in Boston, February 16, 1838, graduated from Harvard in 1858, and served as private secretary to his father in England. In 1870 he became editor of the North American Review and Professor of History at Harvard, in which place he won wide repute for originality and power of inspiring enthusiasm for research in his pupils. He wrote several essays and books on historical subjects, and edited others — 'Essays on Anglo-Saxon Law' (1876), 'Documents Relating to New England Federalism' (1877), 'Albert Gallatin' (1879), 'Writings of Albert Gallatin' (1879), 'John Randolph' (1882) in the 'American Statesmen' Series, 'Historical Essays' (1891), 'Mont Saint Michel and Chartres' (1904), 'Life of George Cabot Lodge' (1911); but his great life-work and monument is his nine-volume 'History of the United States, 1801–17' (the Jefferson and Madison administrations), to write which he left his professorship in 1877, and after passing many years in London, in other foreign capitals, in Washington, and elsewhere, in preparation, published the first volume in 1889, and the last in 1891.

The work in its inception (though not in its execution) is a polemic tract — a family vindication, an act of pious duty; its subtitle might be, 'A Justification of John Quincy Adams for Breaking with the Federalist Party.' So taken, the reader who loves historical fights and seriously desires truth should read the chapters on the Hartford Convention and its preliminaries side by side with the corresponding pages in Henry Cabot Lodge's 'Life of George Cabot.' If he cannot judge from the pleadings of these two able advocates with briefs for different sides, it is not for lack of full exposition.

But the 'History' is far more and higher than a piece of special pleading. It is in the main, both as to domestic and international matters, a resolutely cool and impartial presentation of facts and judgments on all sides of a period where passionate partisanship lies almost in the very essence of the questions — a tone contrasting oddly with the political action and feeling of the two Presidents. Even where, as toward the New England Federalists, many readers will consider him unfair in his deductions, he never tampers with or unfairly proportions the facts.

The work is a model of patient study, not alone of what is conventionally accepted as historic material, but of all subsidiary matter necessary to expert discussion of the problems involved. He goes deeply into economic and social facts; he has instructed himself in military science like a West Point student, in army needs like a quartermaster, in naval construction, equipment, and management like a naval officer. Of purely literary qualities, the history presents a high order of constructive art in amassing minute details without obscuring the main outlines; luminous statement; and the results of a very powerful memory which enables him to keep before his vision every incident of the long chronicle with its involved groupings, so that an armory of instructive comparisons, as well as of polemic missiles, is constantly ready to his hand.

The history advances many novel views, and controverts many accepted facts. The relation of Napoleon's warfare against Haiti and Toussaint to the great Continental struggle, and the position he assigns it as the turning point of that greater contest, is perhaps the most important of these. But almost as striking are his views on the impressment problem and the provocations to the War of 1812; wherein he leads to the most unexpected deduction — namely that the grievances on *both* sides were much greater than is generally supposed. He shows that the profit and security of the American merchant service drew thousands of English seamen into it, where they changed their names and passed for American citizens, greatly embarrassing English naval operations. On the other hand he shows that English outrages and insults were so gross that no nation with spirit enough to be entitled to separate existence ought to have endured them. He reverses the severe popular judgment on Madison for consenting to the war — on the assumed ground of coveting another term as President — which every other historian and biographer from Hildreth to Sydney Howard Gay has pronounced, and which has become a stock historical convention; holds Jackson's campaign ending at New Orleans an imbecile undertaking redeemed only by an act of instinctive pugnacity at the end; gives Scott and Jacob Brown the honor they have never before received in fair measure; and in many other points redistributes praise and blame with entire independence, and with curious effect on many popular ideas.

As the fame of Henry Adams among historians was fixed by his historical writings, so his reputation was established among general readers by his autobiography (1906 and 1917), 'The Education of Henry Adams.' It is a brilliant survey of the intellectual and public movements with which he came in contact in his long life, with the reflection upon them of a gifted intellect; an intellect that took more pleasure in speculation than in action.

THE AUSPICES OF THE WAR OF 1812

From 'History of the United States.' Copyright, 1890, by Charles Scribner's Sons

THE American declaration of war against England, July 18, 1812, annoyed those European nations that were gathering their utmost resources for resistance to Napoleon's attack. Russia could not but regard it as an unfriendly act, equally bad for political and commercial interests. Spain and Portugal, whose armies were fed largely if not chiefly on American grain imported by British money under British protection, dreaded to see their supplies cut off. Germany, waiting only for strength to recover her freedom, had to reckon against one more element in Napoleon's vast military resources. England needed to make greater efforts in order to maintain the advantages she had gained in Russia and Spain. Even in America no one doubted the earnestness of England's wish for peace; and if Madison and Monroe insisted on her acquiescence in their terms, they insisted because they believed that their military position entitled them to expect it. The reconquest of Russia and Spain by Napoleon, an event almost certain to happen, could hardly fail to force from England the concessions, not in themselves unreasonable, which the United States required.

This was, as Madison to the end of his life maintained, "a fair calculation"; but it was exasperating to England, who thought that America ought to be equally interested with Europe in overthrowing the military despotism of Napoleon, and should not conspire with him for gain. At first the new war disconcerted the feeble Ministry that remained in office on the death of Spencer Perceval: they counted on preventing it, and did their utmost to stop it after it was begun. The tone of arrogance which had so long characterized government and press disappeared for the moment. Obscure newspapers, like the London Evening Star, still sneered at the idea that Great Britain was to be "driven from the proud pre-eminence which the blood and treasure of her sons have attained for her among the nations, by a piece of striped bunting flying at the mastheads of a few fir-built frigates, manned by a handful of bastards and outlaws" — a phrase which had great success in America — but such defiances expressed a temper studiously held in restraint previous to the moment when the war was seen to be inevitable. . . .

The realization that no escape could be found from an American war was forced on the British public at a moment of much discouragement. Almost simultaneously a series of misfortunes occurred which brought the stoutest and most intelligent Englishmen to the verge of despair. In Spain Wellington, after winning the battle of Salamanca in July, occupied Madrid in August, and obliged Soult to evacuate Andalusia; but his siege of Burgos failed, and as the French generals concentrated their scattered forces, Wellington was obliged to abandon Madrid once more. October 21st he was again in full retreat on Portugal. The apparent failure of his campaign was almost simultaneous with the apparent success of Napoleon's; for the Emperor entered Moscow September 14, and the news of this triumph, probably decisive of Russian submission, reached England about October 3. Three days later arrived intelligence of William Hull's surrender at Detroit; but this success was counterbalanced by simultaneous news of Isaac Hull's startling capture of the Guerrière, and the certainty of a prolonged war.

In the desponding condition of the British people — with a deficient harvest, bad weather, wheat at nearly five dollars a bushel, and the American supply likely to be cut off; consols at 57½, gold at thirty per cent premium; a Ministry without credit or authority, and a general consciousness of blunders, incompetence, and corruption — every new tale of disaster sank the hopes of England and called out wails of despair. In that state of mind the loss of the Guerrière assumed portentous dimensions. The Times was especially loud in lamenting the capture: —

"We witnessed the gloom which that event cast over high and honorable minds. . . . Never before in the history of the world did an English frigate strike to an American; and though we cannot say that Captain Dacres, under all circumstances, is punishable for this act, yet we do say there are commanders in the English navy who would a thousand times rather have gone down with their colors flying, than have set their fellow sailors so fatal an example."

No country newspaper in America, railing at Hull's cowardice and treachery, showed less knowledge or judgment than the London Times, which had written of nothing but war since its name had been known in England. Any American could have assured the English press that British frigates before the Guerrière had struck to American; and even in England men had not forgotten the name of the British frigate Serapis, or that of the American captain Paul Jones. Yet the Times' ignorance was less unreasonable than its requirement that Dacres should have gone down with his ship — a cry of passion the more unjust to Dacres because he fought his ship as long as she could float. Such sensitiveness seemed extravagant in a society which had been hardened by centuries of warfare; yet the Times reflected fairly the feelings of Englishmen. George Canning, speaking in open Parliament not long afterward, said that the loss of the Guerrière and the Macedonian produced a sensation in the country scarcely to be equaled by the most violent convulsions of nature. "Neither can I agree with those who complain of the shock of consternation throughout Great Britain as having been greater than the occasion required. . . . It cannot be too deeply felt that the sacred spell of the invincibility of the British navy was broken by those unfortunate captures."

Of all spells that could be cast on a nation, that of believing itself invincible was perhaps the one most profitably broken; but the process of recovering its senses was agreeable to no nation, and to England, at that moment of distress, it was as painful as Canning described. The matter was not mended by the Courier and Morning Post, who, taking their tone from the Admiralty, complained of the enormous superiority of the American frigates, and called them "line-of-battle ships in disguise." Certainly the American forty-four was a much heavier ship than the British thirty-eight, but the difference had been as well known in the British navy before these actions as it was afterward; and Captain Dacres himself, the Englishman who best knew the relative force of the ships, told his court of inquiry a different story: — "I am so well aware that the success of my opponent was owing to fortune, that it is my earnest wish, and would be the happiest period of my life, to be once more opposed to the Constitution, with them [the old crew] under my command, in a frigate of similar force with the Guerrière." After all had been said, the unpleasant result remained that in future, British frigates, like other frigates, could safely fight only their inferiors in force. What applied to the Guerrière and Macedonian against the Constitution and United States, where the British force was inferior, applied equally to the Frolic against the Wasp, where no inferiority could be shown. The British newspapers thenceforward admitted what America wished to prove, that, ship for ship, British were no more than the equals of Americans.

Society soon learned to take a more sensible view of the subject; but as the first depression passed away, a consciousness of personal wrong took its place. The United States were supposed to have stabbed England in the back at the moment when her hands were tied, when her existence was in the most deadly peril and her anxieties were most heavy. England never could forgive treason so base and cowardice so vile. That Madison had been from the first a tool and accomplice of Bonaparte was thenceforward so fixed an idea in British history that time could not shake it. Indeed, so complicated and so historical had the causes of war become that no one even in America could explain or understand them, while Englishmen could see only that America required England as the price of peace to destroy herself by abandoning her naval power, and that England preferred to die fighting rather than to die by her own hand. The American party in England was extinguished; no further protest was heard against the war; and the British people thought moodily of revenge.

This result was unfortunate for both parties, but was doubly unfortunate for America, because her mode of making the issue told in her enemy's favor. The same impressions which silenced in England open sympathy with America, stimulated in America acute sympathy with England. Argument was useless against people in a passion, convinced of their own injuries. Neither Englishmen nor Federalists were open to reasoning. They found their action easy from the moment they classed the United States as an ally of France, like

Bavaria or Saxony; and they had no scruples of conscience, for the practical alliance was clear, and the fact proved sufficiently the intent. . . .

The loss of two or three thirty-eight-gun frigates on the ocean was a matter of trifling consequence to the British government, which had a force of four ships-of-the-line and six or eight frigates in Chesapeake Bay alone, and which built every year dozens of ships-of-the-line and frigates to replace those lost or worn out; but although American privateers wrought more injury to British interests than was caused or could be caused by the American navy, the pride of England cared little about mercantile losses, and cared immensely for its fighting reputation. The theory that the American was a degenerate Englishman — a theory chiefly due to American teachings — lay at the bottom of British politics. Even the late British minister at Washington, Foster, a man of average intelligence, thought it manifest good taste and good sense to say of the Americans in his speech of February 18, 1813, in Parliament, that "generally speaking, they were not a people we should be proud to acknowledge as our relations." Decatur and Hull were engaged in a social rather than in a political contest, and were aware that the serious work on their hands had little to do with England's power, but much to do with her manners. The mortification of England at the capture of her frigates was the measure of her previous arrogance. . . .

Every country must begin war by asserting that it will never give way; and of all countries England, which had waged innumerable wars, knew best when perseverance cost more than concession. Even at that early moment Parliament was evidently perplexed, and would willingly have yielded had it seen means of escape from its naval fetich, impressment. Perhaps the perplexity was more evident in the Commons than in the Lords; for Castlereagh, while defending his own course with elaborate care, visibly stumbled over the right of impressment. Even while claiming that its abandonment would have been "vitally dangerous if not fatal" to England's security, he added that he "would be the last man in the world to underrate the inconvenience which the Americans sustained in consequence of our assertion of the right of search." The embarrassment became still plainer when he narrowed the question to one of statistics, and showed that the whole contest was waged over the forcible retention of some eight hundred seamen among one hundred and forty-five thousand employed in British service. Granting the number were twice as great, he continued, "would the House believe that there was any man so infatuated, or that the British empire was driven to such straits that for such a paltry consideration as seventeen hundred sailors, his Majesty's government would needlessly irritate the pride of a neutral nation or violate that justice which was due to one country from another?" If Liverpool's argument explained the causes of war, Castlereagh's explained its inevitable result; for since the war must cost England at least 10,000,000 pounds a year, could Parliament be so infatuated as to pay 10,000 pounds a year for each American sailor detained in service, when one-tenth of the amount, if employed in raising the wages of the British sailor, would bring any required number of seamen back to their ships? The whole British navy in 1812 cost 20,000,000 pounds; the pay-roll amounted to only 3,000,000 pounds; the common sailor was paid four pounds bounty and eighteen pounds a year, which might have been trebled at half the cost of an American war.

WHAT THE WAR OF 1812 DEMONSTRATED

From 'History of the United States.' Copyright, 1890, by Charles Scribner's Sons

A PEOPLE whose chief trait was antipathy to war, and to any system organized with military energy, could scarcely develop great results in national administration; yet the Americans prided themselves chiefly on their political capacity. Even the war did not undeceive them, although the incapacity brought into evidence by the war was undisputed, and was most remarkable among the communities which believed themselves to be most gifted with political sagacity. Virginia and Massachusetts by turns admitted failure in dealing with issues so simple that the newest societies, like Tennessee and Ohio, understood them by instinct. That incapacity in national politics should appear as a leading trait in American character was unexpected by Americans, but might naturally result from their conditions. The better test of American character was not political but social, and was to be found not in the government but in the people.

The sixteen years of Jefferson and Madison's rule furnished international tests of popular intelligence upon which Americans could depend. The ocean was the only open field for competition among nations. Americans enjoyed there no natural or artificial advantages over Englishmen, Frenchmen, or Spaniards; indeed, all these countries possessed navies, resources, and experience greater than were to be found in the United States. Yet the Americans developed, in the course of twenty years, a surprising degree of skill in naval affairs. The evidence of their success was to be found nowhere so complete as in the avowals of Englishmen who knew best the history of naval progress. The American invention of the fast-sailing schooner or clipper was the more remarkable because, of all American inventions, this alone sprang from direct competition with Europe. During ten centuries of struggle the nations of Europe had labored to obtain superiority over each other in ship-construction; yet Americans instantly made improvements which gave them superiority, and which Europeans were unable immediately to imitate even after seeing them. Not only were American vessels better in model, faster in sailing, easier and quicker in handling, and more economical in working than the European, but they were also better equipped.

The English complained as a grievance that the Americans adopted new and unwarranted devices in naval warfare; that their vessels were heavier and better constructed, and their missiles of unusual shape and improper use. The Americans resorted to expedients that had not been tried before, and excited a mixture of irritation and respect in the English service, until "Yankee smartness" became a national misdemeanor.

The English admitted themselves to be slow to change their habits, but the French were both quick and scientific; yet Americans did on the ocean what the French, under stronger inducements, failed to do. The French privateer preyed upon British commerce for twenty years without seriously injuring it; but no sooner did the American privateer sail from French ports than the rates of insurance doubled in London, and an outcry for protection arose among English shippers which the Admiralty could not calm. The British newspapers were filled with assertions that the American cruiser was the superior of any vessel of its class, and threatened to overthrow England's supremacy on the ocean.

Another test of relative intelligence was furnished by the battles at sea. Instantly after the loss of the Guerrière the English discovered and complained that American gunnery was superior to their own. They explained their inferiority by the length of time that had elapsed since their navy had found on the ocean an enemy to fight. Every vestige of hostile fleets had been swept away, until, after the battle of Trafalgar, British frigates ceased practice with their guns. Doubtless the British navy had become somewhat careless in the absence of a dangerous enemy, but Englishmen were themselves aware that some other cause must have affected their losses. Nothing showed that Nelson's line-of-battle ships, frigates, or sloops were, as a rule, better fought than the Macedonian and Java, the Avon and Reindeer. Sir Howard Douglas, the chief authority on the subject, attempted in vain to explain British reverses by the deterioration of British gunnery. His analysis showed only that American gunnery was extraordinarily good. Of all vessels, the sloop-of-war — on account of its smallness, its quick motion, and its more accurate armament of thirty-two-pound carronades — offered the best test of relative gunnery, and Sir Howard Douglas in commenting upon the destruction of the Peacock and Avon could only say: — "In these two actions it is clear that the fire of the British vessels was thrown too high, and that the ordnance of their opponents were expressly and carefully aimed at and took effect chiefly in the hull."

The battle of the Hornet and Penguin, as well as those of the Reindeer and Avon, showed that the excellence of American gunnery continued till the close of the war. Whether at point-blank range or at long-distance practice, the Americans used guns as they had never been used at sea before.

None of the reports of former British victories showed that the British fire had been more destructive at any previous time than in 1812, and no report of any commander since the British navy existed showed so much damage inflicted on an opponent in so short a time as was proved to have been inflicted on themselves by the reports of British commanders in the American war. The strongest proof of American superiority was given by the best British officers, like Broke, who strained every nerve to maintain an equality with American gunnery. So instantaneous and energetic was the effort that according to the British historian of the war, " A British forty-six-gun frigate of 1813 was half as effective again as a British forty-six-gun frigate of 1812; " and as he justly said, " the slaughtered crews and the shattered hulks " of the captured British ships proved that no want of their old fighting qualities accounted for their repeated and almost habitual mortifications.

Unwilling as the English were to admit the superior skill of Americans on the ocean, they did not hesitate to admit it, in certain respects, on land. The American rifle in American hands was affirmed to have no equal in the world. This admission could scarcely be withheld after the lists of killed and wounded which followed almost every battle; but the admission served to check a wider inquiry. In truth, the rifle played but a small part in the war. Winchester's men at the river Raisin may have owed their over-confidence, as the British Forty-first owed its losses, to that weapon, and at New Orleans five or six hundred of Coffee's men, who were out of range, were armed with the rifle; but the surprising losses of the British were commonly due to artillery and musketry fire. At New Orleans the artillery was chiefly engaged. The artillery battle of January 1, according to British accounts, amply proved the superiority of American gunnery on that occasion, which was probably the fairest test during the war. The battle of January 8 was also chiefly an artillery battle: the main British column never arrived within fair musket range; Pakenham was killed by a grape-shot, and the main column of his troops halted more than one hundred yards from the parapet.

The best test of British and American military qualities, both for men and weapons, was Scott's battle of Chippewa. Nothing intervened to throw a doubt over the fairness of the trial. Two parallel lines of regular soldiers, practically equal in numbers, armed with similar weapons, moved in close order toward each other across a wide, open plain, without cover or advantage of position, stopping at intervals to load and fire, until one line broke and retired. At the same time two three-gun batteries, the British being the heavier, maintained a steady fire from positions opposite each other. According to the reports, the two infantry lines in the center never came nearer than eighty yards. Major-General Riall reported that then, owing to severe losses, his troops broke and could not be rallied. Comparison of official reports showed that the British lost in killed and wounded four hundred and sixty-nine men; the Americans, two hundred and ninety-six. Some doubts always affect the returns of wounded, because the severity of the wound cannot be known; but dead men tell their own tale. Riall reported one hundred and forty-eight killed; Scott reported sixty-one. The severity of the losses showed that the battle was sharply contested, and proved the personal bravery of both armies. Marksmanship decided the result, and the returns proved that the American fire was superior to that of the British in the proportion of more than fifty per cent. if estimated by the entire loss, and of two hundred and forty-two to one hundred if estimated by the deaths alone.

The conclusion seemed incredible, but it was supported by the results of the naval battles. The Americans showed superiority amounting in some cases to twice the efficiency of their enemies in the use of weapons. The best French critic of the naval war, Jurien de la Gravière, said: — "An enormous superiority in the rapidity and precision of their fire can alone explain the difference in the losses sustained by the combatants." So far from denying this conclusion, the British press constantly alleged it, and the British officers complained of it. The discovery caused great surprise, and in both British services much attention was at once directed to improvement in artillery and musketry. Nothing could exceed the frankness with which Englishmen avowed their inferiority. According to Sir Francis Head, "gunnery was in naval warfare in the extraordinary state of ignorance we have just described, when our lean children, the American people, taught us, rod in hand, our first lesson in the art." The English text-book on Naval Gunnery, written by Major-General Sir Howard Douglas immediately after the peace, devoted more attention to the short American war than to all the battles of Napoleon, and began by admitting that Great Britain had "entered with too great confidence on war with a marine much more expert than that of any of our European enemies." The admission appeared "objectionable" even to the author; but he did not add, what was equally true, that it applied as well to the land as to the sea service.

No one questioned the bravery of the British forces, or the ease with which they often routed larger bodies of militia; but the losses they inflicted were rarely as great as those they suffered. Even at Bladensburg, where they met little resistance, their loss was several times greater than that of the Americans. At Plattsburg, where the intelligence and quickness of Macdonough and his men alone won the victory, his ships were in effect stationary batteries, and enjoyed the same superiority in gunnery. "The Saratoga," said his official report, "had fifty-five round-shot in her hull; the Confiance, one hundred and five. The enemy's shot passed principally just over our heads, as there were not twenty whole hammocks in the nettings at the close of the action."

The greater skill of the Americans was not due to special training; for the British service was better trained in gunnery, as in everything else, than the motley armies and fleets that fought at New Orleans and on the Lakes. Critics constantly said that every American had learned from his childhood

But a question of method remains. How shall we do it?

We should satisfy the law of justice, we should meet all economic requirements, by at one stroke abolishing all private titles, declaring all land public property, and letting it out to the highest bidders in lots to suit, under such conditions as would sacredly guard the private right to improvements.

Thus we should secure, in a more complex state of society, the same equality of rights that in a ruder state were secured by equal partitions of the soil, and by giving the use of the land to whoever could procure the most from it, we should secure the greatest production.

Such a plan, instead of being a wild, impracticable vagary, has (with the exception that he suggests compensation to the present holders of land — undoubtedly a careless concession which he upon reflection would reconsider) been indorsed by no less eminent a thinker than Herbert Spencer, who ('Social Statics,' Chap. ix, Sec. 8) says of it:

"Such a doctrine is consistent with the highest state of civilization; may be carried out without involving a community of goods, and need cause no very serious revolution in existing arrangements. The change required would simply be a change of landlords. Separate ownership would merge into the joint-stock ownership of the public. Instead of being in the possession of individuals, the country would be held by the great corporate body — society. Instead of leasing his acres from an isolated proprietor, the farmer would lease them from the nation. Instead of paying his rent to the agent of Sir John or his Grace, he would pay it to an agent or deputy agent of the community. Stewards would be public officials instead of private ones, and tenancy the only land tenure. A state of things so ordered would be in perfect harmony with the moral law. Under it all men would be equally landlords, all men would be alike free to become tenants. . . . Clearly, therefore, on such a system, the earth might be enclosed, occupied, and cultivated, in entire subordination to the law of equal freedom."

But such a plan, though perfectly feasible, does not seem to me the best. Or rather I propose to accomplish the same thing in a simpler, easier, and quieter way, than that of formally confiscating all the land and formally letting it out to the highest bidders.

To do that would involve a needless shock to present customs and habits of thought — which is to be avoided.

To do that would involve a needless extension of governmental machinery — which is to be avoided.

It is an axiom of statesmanship — which the successful founders of tyranny have understood and acted upon — that great changes can best be brought about under old forms. We, who would free men, should heed the same truth. It is the natural method. When nature would make a higher type, she takes a lower one and develops it. This, also, is the law of social growth. Let us work by it. With the current we may glide fast and far. Against it, it is hard pulling and slow progress.

I do not propose either to purchase or to confiscate private property in land. The first would be unjust; the second, needless. Let the individuals who now hold it still retain, if they want to, possession of what they are pleased to call *their* land. Let them continue to call it *their* land. Let them buy and sell, and bequeath and devise it. We may safely leave them the shell, if we take the kernel. *It is not necessary to confiscate land; it is only necessary to confiscate rent.*

Nor, to take rent for public uses, is it necessary that the state should bother with the letting of lands, and assume the chances of the favoritism, collusion, and corruption this might involve. It is not necessary that any new machinery should be created. The machinery already exists. Instead of extending it, all we have to do is to simplify and reduce it. By leaving to landowners a percentage of rent which would probably be much less than the cost and loss involved in attempting to rent lands through state agency, and by making use of this existing machinery, we may, without jar or shock, assert the common right to land by taking rent for public uses.

We already take some rent in taxation. We have only to make some changes in our modes of taxation to take it all.

What I, therefore, propose, as the simple yet sovereign remedy, which will raise wages, increase the earnings of capital, extirpate pauperism, abolish poverty, give remunerative employment to whoever wishes it, afford free scope to human powers, lessen crime, elevate morals, and taste, and intelligence, purify government and carry civilization to yet nobler heights, is — *to appropriate rent by taxation.*

In this way the state may become the universal landlord without calling herself so, and without assuming a single new function. In form, the ownership of land would remain just as now. No owner of land need be dispossessed, and no restriction need be placed upon the amount of land anyone could hold. For, rent being taken by the state in taxes, land, no matter in whose name it stood, or in what parcels it was held, would be really common property, and every member of the community would participate in the advantages of its ownership.

Now insomuch as the taxation of rent, or land values, must necessarily be increased just as we abolish other taxes, we may put the proposition into practical form by proposing —

To abolish all taxation save that upon land values.

As we have seen, the value of land is at the beginning of society nothing, but as society develops by the increase of population and the advance of the arts, it becomes greater and greater. In every civilized country, even the newest, the value of the land taken as a whole is sufficient to bear the entire expenses of government. In the better developed countries it is much more than sufficient. Hence it will not be enough merely to place all taxes upon the value of land. It will be necessary, where rent exceeds the present governmental revenues, commensurately to increase the amount demanded in taxation, and to continue this increase as society progresses and rent advances. But this is so natural and easy a matter, that it may be considered as involved, or at least understood, in the proposition to put all taxes on the value of land. That is the first step, upon which the practical struggle must be made. When the hare is once caught and killed, cooking him will follow as a matter of course. When the common right to land is so far appreciated that all taxes are abolished save those which fall upon rent, there is no danger of much more than is necessary to induce them to collect the public revenues being left to individual landholders.

Experience has taught me (for I have been for some years endeavoring to popularize this proposition) that wherever the idea of concentrating all taxation upon land values finds lodgment sufficient to induce consideration, it invariably makes way, but that there are few of the classes most to be benefited by it, who at first, or even for a long time afterward, see its full significance and power. It is difficult for workingmen to get over the idea that there is a real antagonism between capital and labor. It is difficult for small farmers and homestead owners to get over the idea that to put all taxes on the value of land would be unduly to tax them. It is difficult for both classes to get over the idea that to exempt capital from taxation would be to make the rich richer, and the poor poorer. These ideas spring from confused thought. But behind ignorance and prejudice there is a powerful interest, which has hitherto dominated literature, education, and opinion. A great wrong always dies hard, and the great wrong which in every civilized country condemns the masses of men to poverty and want will not die without a bitter struggle.

BRET HARTE

FRANCIS BRET HARTE (from whose name, so far as pen purposes are concerned, the Francis was very early dropped) was born in Albany, New York, August 25, 1839. After an ordinary school education he went in 1854 to California — drawn thither, like so many other ambitious youths, by the gold excitement and the prospects of fortune. At first he tried his hand at teaching and mining, and had ample opportunity to study in close contact the wild frontier life which he was afterwards to portray. Unsuccessful in both lines of experiment, he presently entered a printing-office, and in 1857 was in San Francisco as compositor on the Golden Era. Unsigned sketches from his pen soon after this began to attract notice, and he was invited to join the staff of the Californian, to which he contributed a series of clever parodies on the styles and methods of famous contemporary writers of fiction, subsequently published in volume form under the title 'Condensed Novels.' In 1864, Harte had been made secretary of the United States Branch Mint; and during his six-years' tenure of office he produced some of his best known poems — 'John Burns of Gettysburg,' 'The Pliocene Skull,' and 'The Society upon the Stanislaus' among the number. In 1868 the Overland Monthly was started, with Harte as editor. It was now that he began in a systematic way to work up the material furnished by his earlier frontier life. The first result was 'The Luck of Roaring Camp,' which upon its appearance in the second number of the magazine instantly made its mark, and was accepted as heralding the rise of a new star in the literary heavens. No other prose production of its author has enjoyed greater popularity, though as a work of art it will hardly bear comparison with such stories as 'Miggles,' 'Tennessee's Partner,' and 'The Outcasts of Poker Flat,' which followed in rapid succession, and the last-named of which is generally considered the most perfect of his works. In 1871 Bret Harte settled in New York, and became a regular contributor to the Atlantic Monthly. In 1878 he was appointed United States consul in Crefeld, Germany, whence in 1880 he was removed to the more lucrative post in Glasgow, after which time he resided abroad, principally in England, where his books enjoyed wide popularity. His pen still remained active; but despite long absence from the land out of whose life his initial successes were wrought, he continued for the most part to deal with the old California themes, remaining *facile princeps* in a field in which he soon had many imitators. That he ever did anything quite so good as his first group of stories and poems cannot be said, for he undoubtedly paid the penalty of working an exhausted soil, and his later volumes are marked as a whole by the repetition of well-worn motives and by declining spontaneity and power. Hence it is by his earlier writings that he will always be known. Still, the average quality of his output remained unusually high; and when the circumstances of its production are borne in mind, it may perhaps seem remarkable that it should have preserved so many traces of the writer's youthful freshness and vigor.

In estimating Bret Harte's work, allowance has of course to be made for the fact that it was his rare good fortune to break new ground, and to become the first literary interpreter of a life which with its primitive breadth and freedom, its unconventionality and picturesqueness, its striking contrasts of circumstance and character, offered singular opportunities to the novelist. But appreciation of this point must not lead us to underrate the strength and certainty with which the chance of the moment was seized on and turned to use. In the last analysis the secret of Bret Harte's success will be found to inhere not so much in the novelty of the people and incidents described, as in the sterling qualities of his own genius and art.

Among such qualities, those which perhaps most constantly impress the critical reader of his total work are his splendid dramatic instinct, his keen insight into character, his broad sympathy, and his subtle and pervasive humor. In his handling of certain of the more commonplace comic types, he frequently reveals the strong early influence of Dickens, whose familiar method is to be detected for instance in Sal, Mrs. Markle, and even Colonel Starbottle of 'Gabriel Conroy,' and of whom we are often unexpectedly reminded here and there in the author's more distinctive studies. But at his best, and in his own particular field — in such characters as the gamblers Hamlin and Oakhurst, Tennessee's Partner, Kentuck, Miggles, M'liss, Olly, and many others, from his earlier stories especially — Bret Harte is altogether himself. Dealing for the most part with large, strongly marked, elemental types, as these develop and express themselves under conditions which give free play to instinct and passion, he does not indulge in lengthy analyses or detailed descriptions. His men and women are sketched with a few bold firm strokes, and are left to work out their own personalities in speech and deed; and yet, such is the skill with which this is accomplished that they stand out before us as creatures of real flesh and blood, whom we unquestioningly, even if sometimes against our cooler judgment, accept and believe in. Bret Harte does not purposely soften the shadows in his pictures; the baseness and extravagance, the sin and wretchedness, of frontier life are frankly portrayed, as well as its rough chivalry and its crude romance. None the less, there can be little doubt that consciously or unconsciously he contrived to throw an idealizing glamour over the fret and fever, the squalor and misery, of the mine and the camp, and that many of his most lifelike and successful characters are wrought in the imagination, though out of the stuff of fact. His place is emphatically not among the realists, realistic as much of his work undoubtedly is; for the shaping power of dramatic genius molds and fashions the raw material furnished by experience and observation. That — to take a single example — the reprobate Hamlin had no counterpart or original in actual life, is altogether improbable; yet it is certain that in the picture as we have it, much, perhaps very much, is attributable to the cunning and delicacy of the artist's hand. Thus what he gives us is something very different from a photograph. But it is just here that we touch upon what is perhaps one of the finest qualities of his work — a quality not to be separated from his tendency towards idealization. Rarely falling into the didactic, and dwelling habitually upon life's unexplained and inexplicable tragic complexities, he nevertheless suffuses his stories with an atmosphere of charity, eminently clear, sweet, and wholesome. His characteristic men and women, products of rude conditions, are generally rough and often positively vicious; but he succeeds in convincing his readers of their common humanity, and in showing the keen responsiveness to nobler influences still possessed by hearts which, superficially considered, might well seem hopelessly callous and dead. And he does this simply and naturally, without maudlin sentiment or forced rhetoric — without, in a word, playing to the gallery.

The weakness of Bret Harte's writing is closely connected with some of its main elements of strength. A master of condensed and rapid narration, he produced many stories which are too episodical in character and sketchy in method to be completely satisfactory from the artistic point of view; while in his desire to achieve terseness, he occasionally sacrificed clearness of plot. This is particularly the case with his more ambitious efforts, especially with his long novel 'Gabriel Conroy,' an elaborate study of the culture conditions of early California civilization. The book has many admirable points. It abounds in memorable descriptions, vivid and humorous character sketches, and separate scenes of remarkable power. But it lacks wholeness, proportion, lucidity. It is a bundle of episodes, and these episodes do not hang together; its plot is unduly intricate; while the conduct of the story everywhere shows the author's inability to hold in hand and weave into definite pattern the multitudinous threads indispensable to his design. Undoubtedly written under the influence of the huge novels of Dickens, the contrast that it presents on the structural side with such an orderly and well-sustained work as 'Bleak House' is almost painful.

As a writer of verse Bret Harte is unequal. Some of his humorous poetry is too racy and original to be lost; much on the other hand is too temporary and extravagant to find an abiding place in literature. His best verse, artistically considered, is perhaps to be sought in his wonderfully dramatic monologues in dialect. 'Jim' and 'In the Tunnel' are masterpieces of this kind; while 'Plain Language from Truthful James' (currently known as 'The Heathen Chinee') must remain secure of a distinct place in American verse. He died, after a brief illness, at Camberley, England, May 5, 1902.

William Henry Hudson

The following poems are all taken from 'The Poetical Works of Bret Harte,' copyright, 1882, by Houghton Mifflin Company, Boston, and are reprinted by special arrangement with the publishers.

JIM

SAY there! P'r'aps
Some on you chaps
Might know Jim Wild?
Well — no offense:
Thar ain't no sense
In gittin' riled!

Jim was my chum
Up on the Bar:
That's why I come
Down from up yar,
Lookin' for Jim.
Thank ye, sir! *You*
Ain't of that crew —
Blest if you are!

Money? Not much:
That ain't my kind:
I ain't no such.
Rum? — I don't mind,
Seein' it's you.

Well, this yer Jim,
Did you know him? —
Jess 'bout your size;
Same kind of eyes; —
Well, that is strange:
Why, it's two year
Since he came here,
Sick, for a change.

Well, here's to us:
Eh?
The h— you say!
Dead?
That little cuss?

What makes you star',
You over thar?
Can't a man drop
'S glass in yer shop
But you must rar'?
  It wouldn't take
  D— much to break
You and your bar.

        Dead!
Poor — little — Jim!
  Why, thar was me,
  Jones, and Bob Lee,
  Harry and Ben —
  No-account men:
Then to take *him!*

Well, thar, good-by —
No more, sir — I —
        Eh?
What's that you say?
Why, dern it! — sho! —
No? Yes! By Joe!
        Sold!
Sold! Why, you limb,
You ornery,
        Derned old
Long-legged Jim!

THE SOCIETY UPON THE STANISLAUS

I RESIDE at Table Mountain, and my name is Truthful James;
I am not up to small deceit or any sinful games;
And I'll tell in simple language what I know about the row
That broke up our Society upon the Stanislow.

But first I would remark that it is not a proper plan
For any scientific gent to whale his fellow-man,
And if a member don't agree with his peculiar whim,
To lay for that same member for to "put a head" on him.

Now, nothing could be finer or more beautiful to see
Than the first six months' proceedings of that same Society,
Till Brown of Calaveras brought a lot of fossil bones
That he found within a tunnel near the tenement of Jones.

Then Brown he read a paper, and he reconstructed there,
From those same bones, an animal that was extremely rare;
And Jones then asked the Chair for a suspension of the rules,
Till he could prove that those same bones was one of his lost mules.

Then Brown he smiled a bitter smile, and said he was at fault —
It seemed he had been trespassing on Jones's family vault.
He was a most sarcastic man, this quiet Mr. Brown,
And on several occasions he had cleaned out the town.

Now, I hold it is not decent for a scientific gent
To say another is an ass — at least, to all intent;
Nor should the individual who happens to be meant
Reply by heaving rocks at him, to any great extent.

Then Abner Dean of Angel's raised a point of order, when
A chunk of old red sandstone took him in the abdomen,
And he smiled a kind of sickly smile, and curled up on the floor,
And the subsequent proceedings interested him no more.

For in less time than I write it, every member did engage
In a warfare with the remnants of a palæozoic age;
And the way they heaved those fossils in their anger was a sin,
Till the skull of an old mammoth caved the head of Thompson in.

And this is all I have to say of these improper games,
For I live at Table Mountain, and my name is Truthful James;
And I've told in simple language what I knew about the row
That broke up our Society upon the Stanislow.

PLAIN LANGUAGE FROM TRUTHFUL JAMES

TABLE MOUNTAIN

WHICH I wish to remark,
And my language is plain,
That for ways that are dark,
And for tricks that are vain,
The heathen Chinee is peculiar,
Which the same I would rise to explain.

Ah Sin was his name;
  And I shall not deny,
In regard to the same,
  What that name might imply;
But his smile it was pensive and childlike,
  As I frequent remarked to Bill Nye.

It was August the third,
  And quite soft was the skies;
Which it might be inferred
  That Ah Sin was likewise;
Yet he played it that day upon William
  And me in a way I despise.

Which we had a small game,
  And Ah Sin took a hand;
It was euchre: the same
  He did not understand;
But he smiled as he sat by the table
  With a smile that was childlike and bland.

Yet the cards they were stocked
  In a way that I grieve,
And my feelings were shocked
  At the state of Nye's sleeve,
Which was stuffed full of aces and bowers,
  And the same with intent to deceive.

But the hands that were played
  By that heathen Chinee,
And the points that he made,
  Were quite frightful to see —
Till at last he put down a right bower,
  Which the same Nye had dealt unto me.

Then I looked up at Nye,
  And he gazed upon me;
And he rose with a sigh,
  And said, "Can this be?
We are ruined by Chinese cheap labor —"
  And he went for that heathen Chinee.

In the scene that ensued
  I did not take a hand,
But the floor it was strewed
  Like the leaves on the strand
With the cards that Ah Sin had been hiding,
  In the game "he did not understand."

In his sleeves, which were long,
  He had twenty-four packs —
Which was coming it strong,
  Yet I state but the facts;
And we found on his nails, which were taper,
  What is frequent in tapers — that's wax.

Which is why I remark,
  And my language is plain,
That for ways that are dark
  And for tricks that are vain,
The heathen Chinee is peculiar —
  Which the same I am free to maintain.

From the Overland Monthly

DICKENS IN CAMP

ABOVE the pines the moon was slowly drifting,
  The river sang below;
The dim Sierras, far beyond, uplifting
  Their minarets of snow.

The roaring camp-fire, with rude humor, painted
  The ruddy tints of health
On haggard face and form that drooped and fainted
  In the fierce race for wealth;

Till one arose, and from his pack's scant treasure
  A hoarded volume drew,
And cards were dropped from hands of listless leisure
  To hear the tale anew.

And then, while round them shadows gathered faster,
And as the firelight fell,
He read aloud the book wherein the Master
Had writ of "Little Nell."

Perhaps 'twas boyish fancy — for the reader
Was youngest of them all —
But, as he read, from clustering pine and cedar
A silence seemed to fall;

The fire-trees, gathering closer in the shadows,
Listened in every spray,
While the whole camp, with "Nell" on English meadows
Wandered and lost their way.

And so in mountain solitudes, o'ertaken
As by some spell divine,
Their cares dropped from them like the needles shaken
From out the gusty pine.

Lost is that camp and wasted all its fire:
And he who wrought that spell?
Ah! towering pine and stately Kentish spire,
Ye have one tale to tell!

Lost is that camp; but let its fragrant story
Blend with the breath that thrills
With hop-vine's incense all the pensive glory
That fills the Kentish hills.

THE LUCK OF ROARING CAMP

THERE was commotion in Roaring Camp. It could not have been a fight, for in 1850 that was not novel enough to have called together the entire settlement. The ditches and claims were not only deserted, but "Tuttle's grocery" had contributed its gamblers, who, it will be remembered, calmly continued their game the day that French Pete and Kanaka Joe shot each other to death over the bar in the front room. The whole camp was collected before a rude cabin on the outer edge of the clearing. Conversation was carried on in a low tone, but the name of a woman was frequently repeated. It was a name familiar enough in the camp — "Cherokee Sal."

Perhaps the less said of her the better. She was a coarse, and, it was to be feared, a very sinful woman. But at that time she was the only woman in Roaring Camp, and was just then lying in sore extremity, when she most needed the ministration of her own sex. Dissolute, abandoned, and irreclaimable, she was yet suffering a martyrdom hard enough to bear even when veiled by sympathizing womanhood, but now terrible in her loneliness. The primal curse had come to her in that original isolation which must have made the punishment of the first transgression so dreadful. It was, perhaps, part of the expiation of her sin, that, at a moment when she most lacked her sex's intuitive tenderness and care, she met only the half-contemptuous faces of her masculine associates. Yet a few of the spectators were, I think, touched by her sufferings. Sandy Tipton thought it was "rough on Sal," and, in the contemplation of her condition, for a moment rose superior to the fact that he had an ace and two bowers in his sleeve.

It will be seen, also, that the situation was novel. Deaths were by no means uncommon in Roaring Camp, but a birth was a new thing. People had been dismissed the camp effectively, finally, and with no possibility of return; but this was the first time that anybody had been introduced *ab initio*. Hence the excitement.

"You go in there, Stumpy," said a prominent citizen known as "Kentuck," addressing one of the loungers. "Go in there, and see what you kin do. You've had experience in them things."

Perhaps there was a fitness in the selection. Stumpy, in other climes, had been the putative head of two families; in fact, it was owing to some legal informality in these proceedings that Roaring Camp — a city of refuge — was indebted to his company. The crowd approved the choice, and Stumpy was wise enough to bow to the majority. The door closed on the extempore surgeon and midwife, and Roaring Camp sat down outside, smoked its pipe, and awaited the issue.

The assemblage numbered about a hundred men. One or two of these were actual fugitives from justice, some were criminal, and all were reckless. Physically, they exhibited no indication of their past lives and character. The greatest scamp had a Raphael face, with a profusion of blonde hair; Oakhurst, a gambler, had the melancholy air and intellectual abstraction of a Hamlet; the coolest and most courageous man was scarcely over five feet in height, with a soft voice and an embarrassed, timid manner. The term "roughs" applied to them was a distinction rather than a definition. Perhaps in the minor details of fingers, toes, ears, etc., the camp may have been deficient, but these slight omissions did not detract from their aggregate force. The strongest man had but three fingers on his right hand; the best shot had but one eye.

Such was the physical aspect of the men that were dispersed around the cabin. The camp lay in a triangular valley between two hills and a river. The only outlet was a steep trail over the summit of a hill that faced the cabin, now illuminated by the rising moon. The suffering woman might have seen it from the rude bunk whereon she lay — seen it winding like a silver thread until it was lost in the stars above.

A fire of withered pine-boughs added sociability to the gathering. By degrees the natural levity of Roaring Camp returned. Bets were freely offered and taken regarding the result. Three to five that "Sal would get through with it"; even that the child would survive; side bets as to the sex and complexion of the coming stranger. In the midst of an excited discussion an exclamation came from those nearest the door, and the camp stopped to listen. Above the swaying and moaning of the pines, the swift rush of the river, and the crackling of the fire rose a sharp, querulous cry — a cry unlike anything heard before in the camp. The pines stopped moaning, the river ceased to rush, and the fire to crackle. It seemed as if Nature had stopped to listen too.

The camp rose to its feet as one man! It was proposed to explode a barrel of gunpowder, but, in consideration of the situation of the mother, better counsels prevailed, and only a few revolvers were discharged; for, whether owing to the rude surgery of the camp, or some other reason, Cherokee Sal was sinking fast. Within an hour she had climbed, as it were, that rugged road that led to the stars, and so passed out of Roaring Camp, its sin and shame, for ever. I do not think that the announcement disturbed them much, except in speculation as to the fate of the child. "Can he live now?" was asked of Stumpy. The answer was doubtful. The only other being of Cherokee Sal's sex and maternal condition in the settlement was an ass. There was some conjecture as to fitness, but the experiment was tried. It was less problematical than the ancient treatment of Romulus and Remus, and apparently as successful.

When these details were completed, which exhausted another hour, the door was opened, and the anxious crowd of men, who had already formed themselves into a queue, entered in single file. Beside the low bunk or shelf, on which the figure of the mother was starkly outlined below the blankets, stood a pine table. On this a candle-box was placed, and within it, swathed in staring red flannel, lay the last arrival at Roaring Camp. Beside the candle-box was placed a hat. Its use was soon indicated. "Gentlemen," said Stumpy, with a singular mixture of authority and *ex officio* complacency — "Gentlemen will please pass in at the front door, round the table, and out at the back door. Them as wishes to contribute anything toward the orphan will find a hat handy." The first man entered with his hat on; he uncovered, however, as he looked about him, and so unconsciously set an example to the next. In such communities good and bad actions are catching. As the procession filed in comments were audible — criticisms addressed perhaps rather to Stumpy in the character of showman: — "Is that him?" "Mighty small specimen"; "Hasn't mor'n got the color"; "Ain't bigger nor a derringer." The contributions were as characteristic: — A silver tobacco box; a doubloon; a navy revolver, silver mounted; a gold specimen; a very beautifully embroidered lady's handkerchief (from Oakhurst the gambler); a diamond breastpin; a diamond ring (suggested by the pin, with the remark from the giver that he "saw that pin and went two diamonds better"); a slung shot; a Bible (contributor not detected); a golden spur; a silver teaspoon (the initials, I regret to say, were not the giver's); a pair of surgeon's shears; a lancet; a Bank of England note for £5; and about $200 in loose gold and silver coin. During these proceedings Stumpy maintained a silence as impassive as the dead on his left, a gravity as inscrutable as that of the newly-born on his right. Only one incident occurred to break the monotony of the curious procession. As Kentuck bent over the candle-box half curiously, the child turned, and, in a spasm of pain, caught at his groping finger, and held it fast for a moment. Kentuck looked foolish and embarrassed. Something like a blush tried to assert itself in his weather-beaten cheek. "The d—d little cuss!" he said, as he extricated his finger, with perhaps more tenderness and care than he might have been deemed capable of showing. He held that finger a little apart from its fellows as he went out, and examined it curiously. The examination provoked the same original remark in regard to the child. In fact, he seemed to enjoy repeating it. "He rastled with my finger," he remarked to Tipton, holding up the member, "the d—d little cuss!"

It was four o'clock before the camp sought repose. A light burnt in the cabin where the watchers sat, for Stumpy did not go to bed that night. Nor did Kentuck. He drank quite freely, and related with great gusto his experience, invariably ending with his characteristic condemnation of the newcomer. It seemed to relieve him of any unjust implication of sentiment, and Kentuck had the weaknesses of the nobler sex. When everybody else had gone to bed, he walked down to the river and whistled reflectingly. Then he walked up the gulch past the cabin, still whistling with demonstrative unconcern. At a large redwood tree he paused and retraced his steps, and again passed the cabin. Half-way down to the river's bank he again paused, and then turned and knocked at the door. It was opened by Stumpy. "How goes it?" said Kentuck, looking past Stumpy toward the candle-box. "All serene!" replied Stumpy. "Anything up?" "Nothing." There was a pause — an embarrassing one — Stumpy still holding the door. Then Kentuck had recourse to his finger, which he held up to Stumpy. "Rastled with it — the d—d little cuss," he said, and retired.

The next day Cherokee Sal had such rude sepulture as Roaring Camp afforded. After her body had been committed to the hillside, there was a formal meeting of the camp to discuss what should be done with her infant. A resolution to adopt it was unanimous and enthusiastic. But an animated discussion in regard to the manner and feasibility of providing for its wants at once sprang up. It was remarkable that the argument partook of none of those fierce personalities with which discussions were usually conducted at

Roaring Camp. Tipton proposed that they should send the child to Red Dog — a distance of forty miles — where female attention could be procured. But the unlucky suggestion met with fierce and unanimous opposition. It was evident that no plan which entailed parting from their new acquisition would for a moment be entertained. "Besides," said Tom Ryder, "them fellows at Red Dog would swap it, and ring in somebody else on us." A disbelief in the honesty of other camps prevailed at Roaring Camp, as in other places.

The introduction of a female nurse in the camp also met with objection. It was argued that no decent woman could be prevailed upon to accept Roaring Camp as her home, and the speaker urged that "they didn't want any more of the other kind." This unkind allusion to the defunct mother, harsh as it may seem, was the first spasm of propriety — the first symptom of the camp's regeneration. Stumpy advanced nothing. Perhaps he felt a certain delicacy in interfering with the selection of a possible successor in office. But, when questioned, he averred stoutly that he and "Jinny" — the mammal before alluded to — could manage to rear the child. There was something original, independent, and heroic about the plan that pleased the camp. Stumpy was retained. Certain articles were sent for to Sacramento. "Mind," said the treasurer, as he pressed a bag of gold-dust into the expressman's hand, "the best that can be got — lace, you know, and filigree-work and frills — d—n the cost!"

Strange to say, the child thrived. Perhaps the invigorating climate of the mountain camp was compensation for material deficiencies. Nature took the foundling to her broader breast. In that rare atmosphere of the Sierra foot-hills — that air pungent with balsamic odor, that ethereal cordial at once bracing and exhilarating — he may have found food and nourishment, or a subtle chemistry that transmuted ass's milk to lime and phosphorus. Stumpy inclined to the belief that it was the latter and good nursing. "Me and that ass," he would say, "has been father and mother to him! Don't you," he would add, apostrophizing the helpless bundle before him, "never go back on us."

By the time he was a month old the necessity of giving him a name became apparent. He had generally been known as "The Kid," "Stumpy's Boy," "The Coyote" (an allusion to his vocal powers), and even by Kentuck's endearing diminutive of "The d—n little cuss." But these were felt to be vague and unsatisfactory and were at last dismissed under another influence. Gamblers and adventurers are generally superstitious, and Oakhurst one day declared that the baby had brought "the luck" to Roaring Camp. It was certain that of late they had been successful. "Luck" was the name agreed upon, with the prefix of Tommy for greater convenience. No allusion was made to the mother, and the father was unknown. "It's better," said the philosophical Oakhurst, "to take a fresh deal all round. Call him Luck, and start him fair." A day was accordingly set apart for the christening. What was meant by this ceremony the reader may imagine who has already gathered some idea of the reckless irreverence of Roaring Camp. The master of ceremonies was one "Boston," a noted wag, and the occasion seemed to promise the greatest facetiousness. This ingenious satirist had spent two days in preparing a burlesque of the Church service, with pointed local allusions. The choir was properly trained, and Sandy Tipton was to stand godfather. But after the procession had marched to the grove with music and banners, and the child had been deposited before a mock altar, Stumpy stepped before the expectant crowd. "It ain't my style to spoil fun, boys," said the little man, stoutly eyeing the faces around him, "but it strikes me that this thing ain't exactly on the squar. It's playing it pretty low down on this yer baby to ring in fun on him that he ain't goin' to understand. And ef there's goin' to be any godfathers round, I'd like to see who's got any better rights than me." A silence followed Stumpy's speech. To the credit of all humorists be it said that the first man to acknowledge its justice was the satirist thus stopped of his fun. "But," said Stumpy, quickly following up his advantage, "we're here for a christening, and we'll have it. I proclaim you Thomas Luck, according to the laws of the United States and the State of California, so help me God." It was the first time that the name of the Deity had been otherwise uttered than profanely in the camp. The form of christening was perhaps even more ludicrous than the satirist had conceived; but, strangely enough, nobody saw it and nobody laughed. "Tommy" was christened as seriously as he would have been under a Christian roof, and cried and was comforted in as orthodox fashion.

And so the work of regeneration began in Roaring Camp. Almost imperceptibly a change came over the settlement. The cabin assigned to "Tommy Luck" — or "The Luck," as he was more frequently called — first showed signs of improvement. It was kept scrupulously clean and whitewashed. Then it was boarded, clothed, and papered. The rosewood cradle, packed eighty miles by mule, had, in Stumpy's way of putting it, "sorter killed the rest of the furniture." So the rehabilitation of the cabin became a necessity. The men who were in the habit of lounging in at Stumpy's to see "how 'The Luck' got on" seemed to appreciate the change, and, in self-defense, the rival establishment of "Tuttle's grocery" bestirred itself and imported a carpet and mirrors. The reflections of the latter on the appearance of Roaring Camp tended to produce stricter habits of personal cleanliness. Again, Stumpy imposed a kind of quarantine upon those who aspired to the honor and privilege of holding The Luck. It was a cruel mortification to Kentuck — who, in the carelessness of a large nature and the habits of frontier life, had begun to regard all garments as a second cuticle, which, like a snake's, only sloughed off through decay — to be debarred this privilege from certain prudential reasons. Yet such was the subtle influence of innovation that he thereafter appeared regularly every afternoon in a clean shirt and face still shining from his ablutions. Nor were moral and social sanitary laws neglected. "Tommy," who was supposed to spend his whole existence in a persistent attempt to repose, must not be disturbed by noise. The shouting and yelling which had gained the camp its infelicitous title were not permitted within hearing distance of Stumpy's. The men conversed in whispers or smoked with Indian gravity. Profanity was tacitly given up in these sacred precincts and throughout the camp a popular form of expletive known as "D—n the luck!" and "Curse the luck!" was abandoned as having a new personal bearing. Vocal music was not interdicted, being supposed to have a soothing, tranquillizing quality, and one song, sung by "Man-o'-War Jack," an English sailor from her Majesty's Australian colonies, was quite popular as a lullaby. It was a lugubrious recital of the exploits of "the Arethusa, Seventy-four," in a muffled minor, ending with a prolonged dying fall at the burden of each verse, "On b-oo-o-ard of the Arethusa." It was a fine sight to see Jack holding The Luck, rocking from side to side as if with the motion of a ship, and crooning forth this naval ditty. Either through the peculiar rocking of Jack or the length of his song — it contained ninety stanzas, and was continued with conscientious deliberation to the bitter end — the lullaby generally had the desired effect. At such times the men would lie at full length under the trees in the soft summer twilight, smoking their pipes and drinking in the melodious utterances. An indistinct idea that this was pastoral happiness pervaded the camp. "This 'ere kind o' think," said the Cockney Simmons, meditatively reclining on his elbow, "is 'evingly." It reminded him of Greenwich.

On the long summer days The Luck was usually carried to the gulch from whence the golden store of Roaring Camp was taken. There, on a blanket spread over pine-boughs, he would lie while the men were working in the ditches below. Latterly there was a rude attempt to decorate this bower with flowers and sweet-smelling shrubs, and generally some one would bring him a cluster of wild honeysuckles, azaleas, or the painted blossoms of Las Mariposas. The men had suddenly awakened to the fact that there were beauty and significance in these trifles, which they had so long trodden carelessly beneath their feet. A flake of glittering mica, a fragment of variegated quartz, a bright pebble from the bed of the creek, became beautiful to eyes thus cleared and strengthened, and were invariably put aside for The Luck. It was wonderful how many treasures the woods and hillsides yielded that "would do for Tommy." Surrounded by playthings such as never child out of fairyland had before, it is to be hoped that Tommy was content. He appeared to be securely happy, albeit there was an infantine gravity about him, a contemplative light in his round gray eyes, that sometimes worried Stumpy. He was always tractable and quiet, and it is recorded that once, having crept beyond his "corral" — a hedge of tesselated pine-boughs, which surrounded his bed — he dropped over the bank on his head in the soft earth, and remained with his mottled legs in the air in that position for at least five minutes with unflinching gravity. He was extricated without a murmur. I hesitate to record the many other instances of his sagacity, which rest, unfortunately, upon the statements of prejudiced friends. Some of them were not without a tinge of superstition. "I crep' up the bank just now," said Kentuck one day, in a breathless state of excitement, "and dern my skin if he wasn't a talking to a jaybird as was a sittin' on his lap. There they was, just as free and sociable as anything you please, a jawin' at each other just like two cherrybums." Howbeit, whether creeping over the pine-boughs or lying lazily on his back blinking at the leaves above him, to him the birds sang, the squirrels chattered, and the flowers bloomed. Nature was his nurse and playfellow. For him she would let slip between the leaves golden shafts of sunlight that fell just within his grasp; she would send wandering breezes to visit him with the balm of bay and resinous gums; to him the tall redwoods nodded familiarly and sleepily, the bumble-bees buzzed, and the rooks cawed a slumbrous accompaniment.

Such was the golden summer of Roaring Camp. They were "flush times," and the luck was with them. The claims had yielded enormously. The camp was jealous of its privileges and looked suspiciously on strangers. No encouragement was given to immigration, and, to make their seclusion more perfect, the land on either side of the mountain wall that surrounded the camp they duly pre-empted. This, and a reputation for singular proficiency with the revolver, kept the reserve of Roaring Camp inviolate. The expressman — their only connecting link with the surrounding world — sometimes told wonderful stories of the camp. He would say, "They've a street up there in 'Roaring' that would lay over any street in Red Dog. They've got vines and flowers round their houses, and they wash themselves twice a day. But they're mighty rough on strangers, and they worship an Ingin baby."

With the prosperity of the camp came a desire for further improvement. It was proposed to build a hotel in the following spring, and to invite one or two decent families to reside there for the sake of The Luck, who might perhaps profit by female companionship. The sacrifice that this concession to the sex cost these men, who were fiercely sceptical in regard to its general virtue and usefulness, can only be accounted for by their affection for Tommy. A few still held out. But the resolve could not be carried into effect for three months, and the minority meekly yielded in the hope that something might turn up to prevent it. And it did.

The winter of 1851 will long be remembered in the foot-hills. The snow lay deep on the Sierras, and every mountain creek became a river, and every river a lake. Each gorge and gulch was transformed into a tumultuous watercourse that descended the hillsides, tearing down giant trees and scattering its drift and débris along the plain. Red Dog had been twice under water, and Roaring Camp had been forewarned. "Water put the gold into them gulches," said Stumpy. "It's been here once and will be here again!" And that night the North Fork suddenly leaped over its banks and swept up the triangular valley of Roaring Camp.

In the confusion of rushing water, crushing trees, and crackling timber, and the darkness which seemed to flow with the water and blot out the fair valley, but little could be done to collect the scattered camp. When the morning broke, the cabin of Stumpy, nearest the river-bank, was gone. Higher up the gulch they found the body of its unlucky owner; but the pride, the hope, the joy, The Luck, of Roaring Camp had disappeared. They were returning with sad hearts when a shout from the bank recalled them.

It was a relief-boat from down the river. They had picked up, they said, a man and an infant, nearly exhausted, about two miles below. Did anybody know them, and did they belong here?

It needed but a glance to show them Kentuck lying there, cruelly crushed and bruised, but still holding The Luck of Roaring Camp in his arms. As they bent over the strangely assorted pair, they saw that the child was cold and pulseless. "He is dead," said one. Kentuck opened his eyes. "Dead?" he repeated feebly. "Yes, my man, and you are dying too." A smile lit the eyes of the expiring Kentuck. "Dying!" he repeated; "he's a taking me with him. Tell the boys I've got The Luck with me now"; and the strong man, clinging to the frail babe as a drowning man is said to cling to a straw, drifted away into the shadowy river that flows forever to the unknown sea.

EDWARD ROWLAND SILL

THE strain sounded by Edward Rowland Sill has a quality of distinction, and a haunting loveliness of aspiration, such as to endear him to those who rejoice in art which is but the handmaiden to dignity of thought and quiet beauty of form. Life and song with Sill — as with Sidney Lanier, between whom and the New Englander there is spiritual fellowship — were in harmony; and man and writer equally call forth admiration. Sill's life was studious, shy, withdrawn; his work too made no noisy demand on the public. It was not startling in manner. Its appeal was to the inner experience, to the still small voice, which is the soul's monitor. His art showed that unobtrusive obedience to the fundamental technique, which, from the Greek days to our own, has acted as a preservative of the written word.

Sill was born in Windsor, Connecticut, on April 29, 1841, and was graduated from Yale College at the age of twenty. At first he went to California with business plans in mind; but came back to the East, intending to become a minister, and studied for a short time at the Harvard Divinity School. This idea was soon abandoned; and he went to New York City and did editorial work on the New York Evening Mail. Then he went to Ohio to do some teaching, and thence was called to California again in 1871, as principal of the High School at Oakland; and after three years' service there, went to the University of California at Berkeley, to be the professor of English literature — a position he held until 1882, when he returned to Ohio and devoted himself to literary work. He died at Cleveland, February 27, 1887.

But it was the life internal, not the external, which was most significant in the case of Sill. A scholar, an idealist, as a teacher he was very unconventional but intensely inspiring. He fulfilled the grand pedagogic conception that the most fruitful teaching means not so much the imparting of knowledge as the stimulation of a fine personality. In his latest years, when out of health and thrown much upon himself, his broodings were deep and wise, and his choicest lyrics are the precious register of them, another such registration being the remarkable letters he wrote to a few privileged friends. He lived aside from the feverish centers of activity, but kept in the stream of the nobler activities of the human mind and soul. As he wrote in one of the finest of his poems, 'Field-Notes': —

> Life is a game the soul can play
> With fewer pieces than men say.

Again in 'Solitude' he expresses his feeling: —

All alone, alone,
Calm as on a kingly throne,
Take thy place in the crowded land
Self-centered in free self-command.
Far from the chattering tongues of men,
Sitting above their call or ken,
Free from links of manner and form,
Thou shalt learn of the wingèd storm —
God shall speak to thee out of the sky.

All that one knows of Sill's personal side is in consonance with the aspiring note and the intellectual questing that mark his poetry.

Dying comparatively young, at forty-five, there is a sense of incompletion about his literary output. He did not write facilely nor polish much. A book of verse in young manhood, 'The Hermitage and Other Poems' (1867); a mid-manhood volume privately printed, 'The Venus of Milo and Other Poems' (1883); and a well-chosen posthumous selection, 'Poems' (1888), embracing the bulk of his worthiest work — make up the scant list. He produced slowly, and was chary about collecting the pieces which appeared in the Atlantic Monthly and elsewhere; only doing so, indeed, on the urgence of his publishers. But it is quality, not quantity, which defines a writer's place; and the charm, suggestion, and strength of Sill's verse cannot be gainsaid. The dominant trait in him is spirituality, coming out whether he is describing nature — few American poets have been more happy in this — or dealing with the deep heart of man. It is the soul's problem in relation to existence which awakens his warm interest and solicitude. The jocund mood, the touch of humor, were rare with him as a writer, but not entirely wanting, as the very strong satiric piece of verse 'Five Lives' is enough to prove. The playful side of his nature, too, is glimpsed in many of his private letters. Intellectually, and in the matter of diction to a degree, there is an Emersonian flavor to Sill. A lyric like 'Service,' for example, certainly would not have shamed the Concord Sage. Sill's spiritual faith had the same robust optimism as Emerson's, though there was more sensitiveness to the minor chords of life. This strong, affirming belief in the triumph of spirit over flesh makes Sill's verse an ethical tonic, as well as an esthetic delight. 'Field-Notes' is his noblest statement of this helpful philosophy, which, however, crops out continually in his work. This mood and attitude of mind, expressed with sincerity and tenderness, with music and imagination, denote Sill as one whose accomplishment, if slight in extent and unambitious in aim, is of a very high order, and such as could emanate only from a poet truly called to song.

OPPORTUNITY

THIS I beheld, or dreamed it in a dream: —
There spread a cloud of dust along a plain;
And underneath the cloud, or in it, raged
A furious battle, and men yelled, and swords
Shocked upon swords and shields. A prince's banner
Wavered, then staggered backward, hemmed by foes.
A craven hung along the battle's edge,
And thought, "Had I a sword of keener steel —
That blue blade that the King's son bears — but this
Blunt thing — ! " he snapt and flung it from his hand,
And lowering crept away and left the field.
Then came the King's son, wounded, sore bestead,
And weaponless, and saw the broken sword,
Hilt-buried in the dry and trodden sand,
And ran and snatched it; and with battle-shout
Lifted afresh he hewed his enemy down,
And saved a great cause that heroic day.

HOME

THERE lies a little city in the hills;
White are its roofs, dim is each dwelling's door,
And peace with perfect rest its bosom fills.

There the pure mist, the pity of the sea,
Comes as a white, soft hand, and reaches o'er
And touches its still face most tenderly.

Unstirred and calm, amid our shifting years,
Lo! where it lies, far from the clash and roar,
With quiet distance blurred, as if through tears.

O heart, that prayest so for God to send
Some loving messenger to go before
And lead the way to where thy longings end,

Be sure, be very sure, that soon will come
His kindest angel, and through that still door
Into the Infinite love will lead thee home.

THE FOOL'S PRAYER

THE royal feast was done; the King
Sought out some new sport to banish care,
And to his jester cried: "Sir Fool,
Kneel now, and make for us a prayer!"

The jester doffed his cap and bells,
And stood the mocking court before;
They could not see the bitter smile
Behind the painted grin he wore.

He bowed his head, and bent his knee
Upon the monarch's silken stool;
His pleading voice arose: — "O Lord,
Be merciful to me, a fool!

"No pity, Lord, could change the heart
From red with wrong to white as wool:
The rod must heal the sin: but Lord,
Be merciful to me, a fool!

"'Tis not by guilt the onward sweep
Of truth and right, O Lord, we stay;
'Tis by our follies that so long
We hold the earth from heaven away.

"These clumsy feet, still in the mire,
Go crushing blossoms without end;
These hard, well-meaning hands we thrust
Among the heart-strings of a friend.

"The ill-timed truth we might have kept —
Who knows how sharp it pierced and stung?
The word we had not sense to say —
Who knows how grandly it had rung?

"Our faults no tenderness should ask —
The chastening stripes must cleanse them all;
But for our blunders — oh, in shame
Before the eyes of heaven we fall.

"Earth bears no balsam for mistakes;
Men crown the knave and scourge the tool
That did his will: but Thou, O Lord,
Be merciful to me, a fool!"

The room was hushed: in silence rose
The King, and sought his gardens cool;
And walked apart and murmured low,
"Be merciful to me, a fool!"

A MORNING THOUGHT

WHAT if some morning, when the stars were paling,
And the dawn whitened, and the east was clear,
Strange peace and rest fell on me from the presence
Of a benignant spirit standing near;

And I should tell him, as he stood beside me: —
"This is our earth — most friendly earth, and fair;
Daily its sea and shore through sun and shadow
Faithful it turns, robed in its azure air;

"There is blest living here, loving and serving,
And quest of truth, and serene friendships dear:
But stay not, Spirit! Earth has one destroyer —
His name is Death: flee, lest he find thee here!"

And what if then, while the still morning brightened,
And freshened in the elm the summer's breath,
Should gravely smile on me the gentle angel,
And take my hand and say, "My name is Death"?

STRANGE

HE died at night. Next day they came
To weep and praise him; sudden fame
These suddenly warm comrades gave.
They called him pure, they called him brave;
One praised his heart, and one his brain;
All said, "You'd seek his like in vain —
Gentle, and strong, and good": none saw
In all his character a flaw.

At noon he wakened from his trance,
Mended, was well! They looked askance;
Took his hand coldly; loved him not,
Though they had wept him; quite forgot
His virtues; lent an easy ear
To slanderous tongues; professed a fear
He was not what he seemed to be;
Thanked God they were not such as he;
Gave to his hunger stones for bread:
And made him, living, wish him dead.

JOAQUIN MILLER

CINCINNATUS HEINE MILLER, known to literature under the name of "Joaquin Miller," was born November 10, 1841, in the Wabash district of Indiana. In 1854 his parents moved to Oregon, where the poet was brought up amid all the picturesque deprivations of pioneer life. With the next turn of destiny's wheel he became a miner in California, living with his associates a life of adventure, of which he afterwards made good use in his long narrative poems. In 1860 he returned to Oregon and studied law until the next year, when he went as express messenger to the gold-mining districts of Idaho. Returning again to Oregon in 1863, he edited the Democratic Register — a weekly newspaper which was suppressed for disloyalty — after which he began the practice of law in Cañon City.

From 1866 until 1870 Miller held the office of judge of the Grant County court, Oregon; and at the same time made his first serious attempts as a poet. By a strange intuition he felt that his work would meet with more favor abroad than at home; and hence his visit in 1870 to England, where the year following he brought out his 'Songs of the Sierras' simultaneously with their publication in Boston, under the imprint of Roberts Brothers. The name "Joaquin," prefixed to his own on the title-page, the author borrowed from the name of a Mexican brigand, Joaquin Murietta, for whom he had once made a legal defense. The appearance of the 'Songs of the Sierras' made a great stir in England; and Miller was fêted, and lauded with superlative adjectives and epithets, culminating in the illustrious title of the "American Byron." On his return from England, Miller did journalistic work in Washington, D. C., till the autumn of 1887, when he removed to Oakland, California, where he died in 1913.

Besides the volume of poems already mentioned, Miller published in 1873 'Songs of the Sunlands,' in 1875 'Songs of the Desert,' in 1878 'Songs of Italy,' in 1882 his 'Collected Poems,' and in 1887 'Songs of Mexican Seas.' He is also the author of the following prose works: 'The Baroness of New York' (1877), 'The Danites in the Sierras' (1881), 'Shadows of Shasta' (1881), 'Memorie and Rime' (1884), and ''49, or the Gold Seekers of the Sierras' (1884). His 'Songs of the Soul' was published in the summer of 1896, and a revised collected edition of his 'Complete Poetical Works' appeared in San Francisco in 1902.

Miller's chief claim to literary fame rests upon his originality, freshness of style, and vigor of thought and expression. In the sweeping rush of his rhythm there is a suggestion of the roaring streams and swaying forests whose music he heard in his youth. The power to report nature by symbols and pagan metaphors, so that she seems in his poetry to be using her own vernacular, is one of his peculiar gifts. His qualities of style are seen at their best in 'The Isles of the Amazon.' In his shorter lyrical poems there is a gentler cadence, with an undertone of deep melancholy that haunts the reader. This effect is well illustrated in 'The Last Hymn' and 'Down into the Dust.'

In spite of his claim to a high rank among American poets — a claim which England freely granted him — Joaquin Miller worked out more bitterly than most authors the Scriptural sentence concerning a prophet in his own country.

KIT CARSON'S RIDE

From 'Songs of the Sierras'

RUN? Now you bet you; I rather guess so!
But he's blind as a badger. Whoa, Paché boy, whoa!
No, you wouldn't believe it to look at his eyes,
But he is badger-blind, and it happened this wise: —

We lay in the grasses and the sunburnt clover,
That spread on the ground like a great brown cover
Northward and southward, and west and away
To the Brazos, to where our lodges lay,
One broad and unbroken sea of brown,
Awaiting the curtains of night to come down
To cover us over and conceal our flight
With my brown bride, won from an Indian town
That lay in the rear the full ride of a night.

We lounged in the grasses — her eyes were in mine,
And her hands on my knee, and her hair was as wine
In its wealth and its flood, pouring on and all over
Her bosom wine-red, and pressed never by one;
And her touch was as warm as the tinge of the clover
Burnt brown as it reached to the kiss of the sun;
And her words were as low as the lute-throated dove,
And as laden with love as the heart when it beats
In its hot eager answer to earliest love,
Or a bee hurried home by its burthen of sweets.

We lay low in the grass on the broad plain levels,
Old Revels and I, and my stolen brown bride;
And the heavens of blue and the harvest of brown
And beautiful clover were welded as one,
To the right and the left, in the light of the sun.
"Forty full miles if a foot to ride,
Forty full miles if a foot, and the devils
Of red Camanches are hot on the track
When once they strike it. Let the sun go down
Soon, very soon," muttered bearded old Revels
As he peered at the sun, lying low on his back,
Holding fast to his lasso. Then he jerked at his steed,
And he sprang to his feet, and glanced swiftly around,
And then dropped, as if shot, with his ear to the ground,
Then again to his feet, and to me, to my bride,
While his eyes were like fire, his face like a shroud,
His form like a king, and his beard like a cloud,
And his voice loud and shrill, as if blown from a reed: —
"Pull, pull in your lassos, and bridle to steed,
And speed you if ever for life you would speed,
And ride for your lives, for your lives you must ride!
For the plain is aflame, the prairie on fire,
And feet of wild horses hard flying before
I hear like a sea breaking high on the shore;
While the buffalo come like a surge of the sea,
Driven far by the flame, driving fast on us three
As a hurricane comes, crushing palms in his ire."

We drew in the lassos, seized saddle and rein,
Threw them on, cinched them on, cinched them over again,
And again drew the girth, cast aside the macheers,
Cut away tapidaros, loosed the sash from its fold,
Cast aside the catenas red-spangled with gold,
And gold-mounted Colts, the companions of years,
Cast the silken serapes to the wind in a breath,
And so bared to the skin sprang all haste to the horse —
As bare as when born, as when new from the hand
Of God — without word, or one word of command,
Turned head to the Brazos in a red race with death,
Turned head to the Brazos with a breath in the hair
Blowing hot from a king leaving death in his course;
Turned head to the Brazos with a sound in the air
Like the rush of an army, and a flash in the eye

Of a red wall of fire reaching up to the sky,
Stretching fierce in pursuit of a black rolling sea
Rushing fast upon us, as the wind sweeping free
  And afar from the desert blew hollow and hoarse.

  Not a word, not a wail from a lip was let fall;
  Not a kiss from my bride, not a look nor low call
Of love-note or courage: but on o'er the plain
So steady and still, leaning low to the mane,
With the heel to the flank and the hand to the rein,
Rode we on, rode we three, rode we nose and gray nose,
Reaching long, breathing loud, as a creviced wind blows;
Yet we broke not a whisper, we breathed not a prayer;
There was work to be done, there was death in the air,
  And the chance was as one to a thousand for all. .

Gray nose to gray nose, and each steady mustang
Stretched neck and stretched nerve till the arid earth rang,
And the foam from the flank and the croup and the neck
Flew around like the spray on a storm-driven deck.
Twenty miles! — thirty miles! — a dim distant speck —
Then a long reaching line, and the Brazos in sight,
And I rose in my seat with a shout of delight.
I stood in my stirrup and looked to my right —
  But Revels was gone: I glanced by my shoulder
And saw his horse stagger; I saw his head drooping
Hard down on his breast, and his naked breast stooping
  Low down to the mane, as so swifter and bolder
Ran reaching out for us the red-footed fire.
  To right and to left the black buffalo came,
  A terrible surf on a red sea of flame
Rushing on in the rear, reaching high, reaching higher.
And he rode neck to neck to a buffalo bull,
The monarch of millions, with shaggy mane full
  Of smoke and of dust, and it shook with desire
Of battle, with rage and bellowings loud
And unearthly, and up through its lowering cloud
  Came the flash of his eyes like a half-hidden fire,
While his keen crooked horns, through the storm of his mane,
Like black lances lifted and lifted again;
And I looked but this once, for the fire licked through,
And he fell and was lost, as we rode two and two.

I looked to my left then — and nose, neck, and shoulder
  Sank slowly, sank surely, till back to my thighs;
    And up through the black blowing veil of her hair
  Did beam full in mine her two marvelous eyes,
    With a longing and love, yet a look of despair
And of pity for me, as she felt the smoke fold her,
    And flames reaching far for her glorious hair.
Her sinking steed faltered, his eager ears fell
To and fro and unsteady, and all the neck's swell
Did subside and recede, and the nerves fell as dead.
Then she saw sturdy Paché still lorded his head,
  With a look of delight; for nor courage nor bribe,
Nor aught but my bride, could have brought him to me.
For he was her father's, and at South Santafee
Had once won a whole herd, sweeping everything down
In a race where the world came to run for the crown.
And so when I won the true heart of my bride —
    My neighbor's and deadliest enemy's child,
  And child of the kingly war-chief of his tribe —
She brought me this steed to the border the night
She met Revels and me in her perilous flight
From the lodge of the chief to the North Brazos side;
    And said, so half guessing of ill as she smiled,
As if jesting, that I, and I only, should ride
  The fleet-footed Paché, so if kin should pursue
  I should surely escape without other ado
Than to ride, without blood, to the North Brazos side,
And await her — and wait till the next hollow moon
Hung her horns in the palms, when surely and soon
And swift she would join me, and all would be well
Without bloodshed or word. And now as she fell
  From the front, and went down in the ocean of fire,
    The last that I saw was a look of delight
  That I should escape — a love — a desire —
Yet never a word, not one look of appeal,
Lest I should reach hand, should stay hand or stay heel
    One instant for her in my terrible flight.
Then the rushing of fire around me and under,
And the howling of beasts and a sound as of thunder —
Beasts burning and blind and forced onward and over,
As the passionate flame reached around them, and wove her
  Red hands in their hair, and kissed hot till they died —

Till they died with a wild and a desolate moan,
As a sea heart-broken on the hard brown stone; —
And into the Brazos I rode all alone —
All alone, save only a horse long-limbed,
    And blinded and bare and burnt to the skin.
    Then just as the terrible sea came in
  And tumbled its thousands hot into the tide,
Till the tide blocked up and the swift stream brimmed
  In eddies, we struck on the opposite side.

. . . .

Sell Paché — blind Paché? Now, mister, look here:
You have slept in my tent and partook of my cheer
Many days, many days, on this rugged frontier,
For the ways they are rough and Camanches were near;
  But you'd better pack up, sir! That tent is too small
For us two after this! Has an old mountaineer,
  Do you book-men believe, got no tum-tum at all?
Sell Paché! — you buy him! — a bag full of gold! —
You show him! — tell of him the tale I have told!
Why, he bore me through fire, and is blind, and is old! —
Now pack up your papers, and get up and spin
To them cities you tell of — Blast you and your tin!

GOOD AND BAD

From 'Byron'

IN men whom men condemn as ill
I find so much of goodness still,
In men whom men pronounce divine
I find so much of sin and blot,
I do not dare to draw a line
Between the two, where God has not.

SIDNEY LANIER

THE quiet steady widening of the influence of Sidney Lanier since his death is more than a pleasant justification of faith to those who have loved him and believed in him from the first. It suggests the comforting thought that good literature, unconventional in form and original in quality, although for this very reason slower to get a hearing, is sure to receive the eventual recognition it deserves. Many years have elapsed since Lanier's taking-off; and he is now seen more clearly every day to be the most important native singer the Southern United States has produced, and one of the most distinctive and lovely of American singers wherever born. Enthusiastic admirers and followers he has always attracted to him; now the general opinion begins to swing round to what seemed to many, a little time ago, the extravagant encomium of partiality and prejudice.

The circumstances of Sidney Lanier's life furnish a pathetically tragic setting to his pure-souled, beautiful work. A Georgian, he was born at Macon, February 3, 1842; his father was a well-known lawyer of that city. The family on the male side was of Huguenot French descent; on the maternal side the stock was Scotch. Sidney was educated at Oglethorpe College in his native state. The war found him on the Confederate side; and while a prisoner he consoled his spirit with his beloved flute and wrote fugitive verses — early pledges of the twin master passions of Lanier's whole life, literature and music. It was while immured thus that he and Father Tabb, the Maryland poet-priest, struck up the friendship which the latter has commemorated in more than one loving song. Lanier's constitution was delicate; and the exposures and hardships of war developed the seeds of the consumption which he fought heroically through young manhood and into middle life, and finally succumbed to. Some years of experimental occupation followed upon the war experience: he was successively clerk, teacher, and lawyer, taking up the legal profession at the earnest instigation of his father, who could not realize that Lanier's vocation was so different from his own. The letter which the son wrote from Baltimore, taking the decisive step that made him a literary man and musician for better or worse, is impressive and revelatory of his character:

"I have given your last letter the fullest and most careful consideration. After doing so, I feel sure that Macon is not the place for me. If you could taste the delicious crystalline air and the champagne breeze that I've just been rushing about in, I am equally sure that in point of climate you would agree with me that my chance of life is ten times as great here as in Macon. Then as to business. Why should I — nay, how *can* I — settle myself down to be a third-rate struggling lawyer for the balance of my little life, as long as there is a certainty almost absolute that I can do some other thing so much better? . . . My dear father, think how for twenty years, through poverty, through pain, through weariness, through sickness, through the uncongenial atmosphere of a farcical college and of a bare army, and then of an exacting business life — through all of the discouragement of being wholly unacquainted with literary people and literary ways — I say, think how, in spite of all these depressing circumstances and of a thousand more which I could enumerate, these two figures of music and of poetry have kept in my heart so that I could not banish them. Does it not seem to you as to me, that I begin to have the right to enroll myself among the devotees of these two sublime arts, after having followed them so long and so humbly, and through so much bitterness? "

One can well believe that with a man like Lanier, such a choice had in it the solemnity of a consecration. His ideal of Art in the broad sense — whether literary or other — was so lofty that a dedication of himself to the service was the most serious of acts. Nor, through whatever of set-backs, stress, and failure, did he for a moment swerve from that ideal; he held himself as a very priest of Beauty, dignifying at once himself and his calling.

Lanier's literary career began with the publishing of a novel, 'Tiger Lilies' (1867), a book founded on his war experiences, and not a success: fiction was not his natural medium of expression. There is luxuriant unpruned imagination in the story, however, and it is evident that a poet in his first ferment of fancy is hiding there. Meanwhile Lanier was sending his poems to the magazines and getting them back again — the proverbial editor on the lookout for budding genius proving mostly chimerical. Gradually a critic here and there became aware of his worth. 'Corn,' one of his finely representative pieces, appeared in Lippincott's Magazine in 1875, and attracted attention which led to his being employed to write the words for a cantata by Dudley Buck, performed at the Centennial Exhibition in the next year. The Centennial year, too, marks the appearance of the first edition of his poems — a volume containing tentative, immature verse, though promising much to one of critical foresight. The Independent and the Century also opened their doors to the Southern singer. But these chance contributions to periodicals — birds of passage finding a lodgment as it might hap — were grotesquely inadequate for the support of a man with a family — for so far back as 1867, the year his first book was published, he had married Miss Mary H. Day, also of Macon, a woman who in all the gracious ministries of heart and home and spirit was his leal mate. Hence was he forced to do hack-work; a sorry spectacle of Pegasus in harness. He could only use his pen between hemorrhages; and the slender financial resources thus heavily taxed would have utterly failed had it not been for the kind ministries of brother and father. Lanier made a guide-book on Florida, as unlike the customary manual as an

Arabian blood mare is unlike a dray-horse. He edited Froissart for boys — a more congenial task; and did youth the same service with respect to King Arthur, the 'Mabinogion,' and Bishop Percy. Brave, beautiful books they are; for the full-mouthed old words and the bygone deeds of chivalry both appealed to the poet-editor. Then in 1879 came what looked like brighter fortune: he was appointed lecturer on English literature at Johns Hopkins University in Baltimore, to which city he had gone in 1873 to take the position of first flute in the Peabody Orchestra. It must be remembered that to the end music and poetry were the beacon stars in Lanier's overcast, uncertain skies. Now a modest yearly income at least was assured — for the first time in his experience. The alleviation was but brief; for two years later, in the mountains of North Carolina, whither he had wearily gone to make one more struggle for breath, Sidney Lanier's noble soul was loosened from its frail tenement of flesh, and, his wife beside him, he fell on sleep. But that final span of time enabled him to prosecute with diligence and system his favorite studies in the old English literature, and to leave two critical volumes of great value and individuality. 'The Science of English Verse,' published in 1880, is an elaborate and unique analysis of the technical structure and underlying principles of the native metric, developing a new and most interesting theory: that the time quality obtains in English poetry as in music; this thesis being aptly illustrated from the sister art. 'The English Novel and the Principles of its Development,' which appeared three years later, in 1883, is made up of lectures delivered at Johns Hopkins, at a time when Lanier was obliged to sit down while speaking, so weak was he. The book is the most philosophic treatment of the development of our fiction that has been written, seizing upon the central fact of the steady growth of the idea of personality in the novel from Greek days to the present time. It was not until 1884, several years after his death, that his poems were collected finally into a volume, with an admirable introductory essay upon the man and his work by Dr. William Hayes Ward. With this book Lanier came into his own of praise and love.

Lanier's characteristics as a poet — and despite his achievements in prose, it is as a poet he must be considered primarily — are such as to separate him from other American makers of literature. In the first place, his work has the glow and color of the South — an exuberance of imagination and a rhythmic sweep which awaken a kind of exultant delight in the sensitive reader. A consummate artist, Lanier showed himself a pioneer in the handling of words and meters: his richness of rhymes and alliterations, his marvelous feeling for tone-color, fellow him with an English poet like Swinburne. He opened new possibilities of metrical and stanzaic arrangements, and therewith revealed new powers of word-use and combination in modern English poetry; drawing on the treasures of the older word-hoard which his study, taste, and instinct suggested. He certainly broadened in this way the technic of verse, and on this side of his art was truly remarkable. He was too that rare thing, a song-writer. His 'Song of the Chattahoochee,' 'A Song of the Future,' 'A Song of Love,' 'An Evening Song,' and others, are not only to be read but set to music; they are felt to be songs in the full and literal sense. The fact that he was a trained musician, a maker in the neighbor art, qualified him peculiarly in this respect. The musician helped the poet, the poet enriched the maker of music.

Looking to the essential traits that are to technic as the completed structure to the scaffolding that makes it possible, Lanier was a man of fine culture, much read, assimilative, strong of thought, endowed with sane imagination. He did not take petty conceits or stale and attenuated ideas and deck them out in the fine garments of art: he had the modern zest for fact, and was abreast of the times in his conceptions — often an intellectual forerunner. On the problems of state, religion, society, science, art, and literature, his words were deep and wise; and his work reveals him as an advanced thinker on the vital themes of his century. And along with this marked breadth and independency of thought went a profound ethical earnestness, having in it a subtle spirituality that above all else makes this poet distinctive and precious. In his own lovely phrase, reversing the wonted words, he believed in the "holiness of beauty": he perceived that beauty is but one phase of that Triune power, the True, the Good, and the Beautiful, divinely interplaying into each other, never to be dissevered without violence to each and all. Lanier applied the Platonic philosophy to art, and it had for him perfect credence, absolute allegiance.

These gifts and powers, then — technical mastery, original thought, and spiritual perception and fervor — are to be recognized in his best poems. In the shorter, simpler lyrics, notice how the characteristic qualities shine out. How full of the broad spirit of worship is the 'Ballad of Trees and the Master'; how valiantly soul rises above the failing flesh in 'The Stirrup Cup'! What a knightly devotion to womanhood is expressed in 'My Springs,' as high a strain as was ever sung to wife! What a hymning of the ideal relation of word and deed is heard in the melodious measures of 'Life and Song'! And when we turn to the larger, more broadly conceived pieces, what a stanch Americanism blows like a sea-wind through the remarkable 'Psalm of the West'; with what exaltation yet fearless fraternity the Christ is glorified in that noble poem, 'The Crystal'; and what a lesson on the mean, sordid standards of trade is preached in 'The Symphony' — that wonderful creation, which under the allegory of music, is vital with high suggestions for every aspiring soul. Nor must that side of the work in which Nature is limned and worshiped be passed by! for it includes some of the most unforgettable things. Lanier's attitude toward Nature was that of a passionate lover; a pantheist who felt God in everything. 'Clover,' 'From the Flats,' 'Tampa Robins,' 'Corn,' 'The Bee,' 'The Dove,' are poems of this class, and such as have come from no other American singer. They express his loving observation of the picturesque phenomena of his own and other Southern states. They transmute Nature in an ideality which fills the air with voices not of earth, and makes the very grass whisper immortal words.

The culmination of Lanier's art and thought and spiritual force is found in the 'Hymns of the Marshes'; two of which, 'Sunrise' and 'The Marshes of Glynn,' are magnificently imaginative organ-chants of a dying man, never so strong of soul as when his body hung by a tenuous thread to life. The finest of this great series, a majestic swan-song, was written when Lanier lay so weak that he could not lift hand to mouth. And the marvel of it is, that poetry never was made through which pulsed and surged a more puissant vitality. These 'Marsh Hymns' stand among the major productions of modern poetry.

It may be granted that Sidney Lanier in the full tide of plethoric utterance sometimes sacrificed lucidity. His teeming fancy was now and then in surplusage, and ran into the arabesque; though this is not true of his latest work. It is possible, again, that he pushed to an extreme his theory of the close inter-relations of music and verse, claiming for the latter not only lyric but symphonic powers — a view illustrated to a degree in his 'Centennial Ode' with its verbal orchestration. Poetry is a human product, and subject to human limitations. Had Lanier lived longer, had he had a freer opportunity, doubtless his literary bequest would have been richer and more completely expressive of himself. But as it is, in quality and in accomplishment Sidney Lanier takes his place as an American poet of distinction. He is one of those rare illustrations of the union, in a son of genius, of high character and artistic production in harmony therewith; a spectacle feeding the heart with tender thoughts and pure ideals: —

His song was only living aloud,
His work, a singing with his hand.

RICHARD BURTON

SONG OF THE CHATTAHOOCHEE

OUT of the hills of Habersham,
  Down the valleys of Hall,
I hurry amain to reach the plain,
  Run the rapid and leap the fall,
Split at the rock and together again,
  Accept my bed, or narrow or wide,
  And flee from folly on every side,
With a lover's pain to attain the plain
  Far from the hills of Habersham,
  Far from the valleys of Hall.

All down the hills of Habersham,
All through the valleys of Hall,
The rushes cried, *Abide, abide,*
The wilful water-weeds held me thrall,
The laving laurel turned my tide,
The ferns and the fondling grass said *Stay,*
The dewberry dipped for to work delay,
And the little reeds sighed, *Abide, abide,*
Here in the hills of Habersham,
Here in the valleys of Hall.

High o'er the hills of Habersham,
Veiling the valleys of Hall,
The hickory told me manifold
Fair tales of shade; the poplar tall
Wrought me her shadowy self to hold;
The chestnut, the oak, the walnut, the pine,
O'erleaning, with flickering meaning and sign,
Said, *Pass not, so cold, these manifold*
Deep shades of the hills of Habersham,
These glades in the valleys of Hall.

And oft in the hills of Habersham,
And oft in the valleys of Hall,
The white quartz shone, and the smooth brook-stone
Did bar me of passage with friendly brawl;
And many a luminous jewel alone —
Crystal clear or acloud with mist,
Ruby, garnet, and amethyst —
Made lures with the lights of streaming stone
In the clefts of the hills of Habersham,
In the beds of the valleys of Hall.

But oh, not the hills of Habersham,
And oh, not the valley of Hall
Avail: I am fain for to water the plain.
Downward the voices of duty call —
Downward, to toil and be mixed with the main;
The dry fields burn, and the mills are to turn,
And a myriad flowers mortally yearn,
And the lordly main from beyond the plain
Calls o'er the hills of Habersham,
Calls through the valleys of Hall.

TAMPA ROBINS

THE robin laughed in the orange-tree: —
"Ho, windy North, a fig for thee;
While breasts are red and wings are bold
And green trees wave us globes of gold,
Time's scythe shall reap but bliss for me —
Sunlight, song, and the orange-tree.

"Burn, golden globes in leafy sky,
My orange-planets: crimson I
Will shine and shoot among the spheres
(Blithe meteor that no mortal fears),
And thrid the heavenly orange-tree
With orbits bright of minstrelsy.

"If that I hate wild winter's spite —
The gibbet trees, the world in white,
The sky but gray wind over a grave —
Why should I ache, the season's slave?
I'll sing from the top of the orange-tree,
Gramercy, winter's tyranny.

"I'll south with the sun, and keep my clime;
My wing is king of the summer-time;
My breast to the sun his torch shall hold;
And I'll call down through the green and gold,
Time, take thy scythe, reap bliss for me;
Bestir thee under the orange-tree."

EVENING SONG

LOOK off, dear Love, across the sallow sands,
And mark yon meeting of the sun and sea;
How long they kiss in sight of all the lands:
Ah! longer, longer, we.

Now in the sea's red vintage melts the sun,
As Egypt's pearl dissolved in rosy wine,
And Cleopatra night drinks all. 'Tis done:
Love, lay thine hand in mine.

Come forth, sweet stars, and comfort heaven's heart;
  Glimmer, ye waves, round else unlighted sands.
O night! divorce our sun and sky apart —
    Never our lips, our hands.

LIFE AND SONG

IF life were caught by a clarionet,
  And a wild heart, throbbing in the reed,
Should thrill its joy, and trill its fret,
  And utter its heart in every deed,

Then would this breathing clarionet
  Type what the poet fain would be;
For none o' the singers ever yet
  Has wholly lived his minstrelsy,

Or clearly sung his true, true thought,
  Or utterly bodied forth his life,
Or out of life and song has wrought
  The perfect one of man and wife;

Or lived and sung, that Life and Song
  Might each express the other's all,
Careless if life or art were long
  Since both were one, to stand or fall:

So that the wonder struck the crowd,
  Who shouted it about the land: —
His song was only living aloud,
  His work, a singing with his hand!

FROM 'THE MARSHES OF GLYNN'

OH, what is abroad in the marsh and the terminal sea?
  Somehow my soul seems suddenly free
From the weighing of fate and the sad discussion of sin,
By the length and the breadth and the sweep of the marshes of Glynn.

Ye marshes, how candid and simple and nothing-withholding and free
Ye publish yourselves to the sky and offer yourselves to the sea!
Tolerant plains, that suffer the sea and the rains and the sun,
Ye spread and span like the catholic man who hath mightily won
God out of knowledge, and good out of infinite pain,
And sight out of blindness, and purity out of a stain.

As the marsh-hen secretly builds on the watery sod,
Behold I will build me a nest on the greatness of God;
I will fly in the greatness of God as the marsh-hen flies
In the freedom that fills all the space 'twixt the marsh and the skies:
By so many roots as the marsh-grass sends in the sod
I will heartily lay me a-hold on the greatness of God:
Oh, like to the greatness of God is the greatness within
The range of the marshes, the liberal marshes of Glynn.

And the sea lends large, as the marsh; lo, out of his plenty the sea
Pours fast; full soon the time of the flood-tide must be:
Look how the grace of the sea doth go
About and about through the intricate channels that flow
Here and there,
Everywhere,
Till his waters have flooded the uttermost creeks and the low-lying lanes,
And the marsh is meshed with a million veins,
That like as with rosy and silvery essences flow
In the rose-and-silver evening glow.
Farewell, my lord Sun!
The creeks overflow; a thousand rivulets run
'Twixt the roots of the sod; the blades of the marsh-grass stir:
Passeth a hurrying sound of wings that westward whirr;
Passeth, and all is still; and the currents cease to run;
And the sea and the marsh are one.
How still the plains of the waters be!
The tide is in his ecstasy.
The tide is at his highest height;
And it is night.

And now from the Vast of the Lord will the waters of sleep
Roll in on the souls of men;
But who will reveal to our waking ken
The forms that swim and the shapes that creep
Under the waters of sleep?
And I would I could know what swimmeth below when the tide comes in
On the length and the breadth of the marvelous marshes of Glynn.

FROM THE FLATS

WHAT heart-ache — ne'er a hill!
Inexorable, vapid, vague, and chill
The drear sand-levels drain my spirit low.
With one poor word they tell me all they know;
Whereat their stupid tongues, to tease my pain,
Do drawn it o'er again and o'er again.
They hurt my heart with griefs I cannot name:
Always the same, the same.

Nature hath no surprise;
No ambuscade of beauty 'gainst mine eyes
From brake or lurking dell or deep defile;
No humors, frolic forms — this mile, that mile;
No rich reserves or happy-valley hopes
Beyond the bend of roads, the distant slopes.
Her fancy fails, her wild is all run tame:
Ever the same, the same.

Oh, might I through these tears
But glimpse some hill my Georgia high uprears
Where white the quartz and pink the pebble shine,
The hickory heavenward strives, the muscadine
Swings o'er the slope, the oak's far-falling shade
Darkens the dogwood in the bottom glade,
And down the hollow from a ferny nook
Lull sings a little brook!

A BALLAD OF TREES AND THE MASTER

INTO the woods my Master went,
Clean forspent, forspent.
Into the woods my Master came,
Forspent with love and shame.
But the olives they were not blind to him,
The little gray leaves were kind to him;
The thorn-tree had a mind to him
When into the woods he came.

Out of the woods my Master went,
  And he was well content.
Out of the woods my Master came,
Content with death and shame.
When Death and Shame would woo him last,
From under the trees they drew him last;
'Twas on a tree they slew him — last,
  When out of the woods he came.

The preceding poems are all from 'Poems of Sidney Lanier.' Copyright, 1884 and 1891, by Mary D. Lanier, and published by Charles Scribner's Sons.

WILLIAM JAMES

EUROPE knows but one American philosopher. This is William James. And Europe knows him as the American philosopher, because in the most intimate and specific way, he is the philosopher of America. In the history of philosophy, there are always two streams of tendency which cross each other and interpenetrate often but never remain coincident throughout their course. The first and more fundamental is the spontaneous envisagement of the world and of man, the vision of the place of man in nature and of his destiny under the aspect of eternity. The second is largely commentary on the first. The first is composed of theories of life, rooting deep in the experiences and adventures of mankind. The second is essentially a pedantry which elaborates, in the manner of the professor, the implications of the first and carries it to the limit of logical refinement, until it is displaced by a fresh vision at the hands of a fresh thinker. Most philosophy in America has been secondary, professorial, irrelevant to the actual course of life and thought in this country. Its roots lay in a tradition which the circumstances of life rejected and which the adventure of living falsified. This tradition is that of Calvinism. Calvin had a vision which infected great groups of European people. The light of that vision led them to undergo many hardships and to undertake many difficulties. For one it drove a company of them to continental North America. It was the urge within the heart of the Puritan pioneers, of the Pilgrim Fathers. It helped them to fight the wilds in nature and in man, to build their community, and to order their lives. It was an intense thing and it was a learned thing. The wilds of nature, however, rejected the sophistications of learning; they required strength of body and sincerity of soul. The Calvinist tradition hence became mitigated under the stress of the conflict between man and nature which necessitated the belief in neighborly good will, in human initiative, in continual trustworthiness, in responsibility, and in freedom. What the Calvinist brought to America and what he there learned were opposites. The life of America consequently flowed away from Calvinism into other courses. Its rôle was changed from the dynamic organization of an emotion into the skeleton of an idea. It became the preoccupation of the schoolman, thin in utterance, vaguely optimistic in sentiment, and completely irrelevant to the problems of life and living. From Jonathan Edwards to Josiah Royce, it retained this character. Even in Emerson, it failed to come to close grips with the realities with which human life in America was dealing.

That life flowed on, pioneer. It was positive, even in its superstitions and overbeliefs, whether these be Mormonism or Christian Science, or the undiscriminating good-fellowship of Walt Whitman. In its higher reaches it was cheerful, humorous, experimental, with faith in its own power; adventurous without being romantic, pious without ceasing to be essentially humanistic. It was the spirit that trekked across the American continent, that mined the gold, that fought the Civil War, that built the railways, that converted a wilderness into a civilization. It is forward-looking, industrious, democratic. It is the spirit of the industrial democracy of Europe as well, but without the hampering past of mankind in Europe. It is the spirit of the rising masses of Europe, confronting, not a conflict with the repressive machinery of a caste-hardened social order, but virgin Nature, and building a new and freer civilization of her substance. It is this spirit which the philosophy of William James expresses. And it is for this reason that his vogue in Europe is proportional to his articulate visioning of the unconscious guiding forces in the life and hopes of America. His philosophy is a theory of life, not made in the schools but gathered through deep sympathy with the hearts of men whose beating his own responded to, the wide world over.

For, significantly enough, though James was an American thinker, his training was very far from American. The parental household in which he spent his childhood was that of a Swedenborgian clergyman whose concrete spiritism made a lasting modification of James's mind. His youth was spent in schools in French Switzerland, in France itself, and in England. He studied painting with Holman Hunt, and nature with Louis Agassiz. He was in succession a painter, a physician, a physiologist, a psychologist, and a philosopher. After 1872 he was one of the best known members of the Harvard faculty.

His theory of life is technically known as Pragmatism. He got the word from Charles Peirce, and he called it himself a new name for an old way of thinking. But this old way of thinking might as well have been called Americanism, for it is substantially the perception of the nature and destiny of man when human life is apprehended at its fighting weight, and its form and "go" come under direct observation. What then appears is mankind struggling for survival in a world which was not made for it but in which it grew. This world is characterized by a growing diversity and manyness. Not only are man and all living things seeking to win a livelihood at the risk of their lives, but inanimate nature itself is composed of multitudes, each one of which has a character, an idiosyncrasy and selfhood, the destruction of which it resists and the conservation of which seems to be the endeavor of its existence. Each thing in this world is autonomous and self-governed. It exists with other things only in so far as it has succeeded in making an adjustment to them, only in so far as it has succeeded in establishing, in a word, certain habits and forms of interaction, which make the actual unities of the world we live in and know. All these unities are not primary but secondary. They are habits of behaving which things develop toward each other in order that they may be together at all. We call them "laws of nature," but even the most fundamental of the laws of nature are no more. The laws of mechanics, of thermodynamics, of chemistry — they also change, evolve, accommodate. There was a time when they were not, and there will be a time when they shall not be. What in truth characterizes the world as a whole is the fact that all of its parts are constantly undergoing mutations — mutations sometimes compelled from without, and always arising from within. All the items in the world are changing items — novelties keep constantly emerging — and they either succeed in winning a place for themselves in the cosmos or disappear. The cosmos itself is like a team of individuals who have attained to a certain mode of being and acting together. It is a happening, not an eternal form, and its unity is contingent upon the assent, the formed habits of its constituents.

In this cosmos, man has happened, an infinitesimal scrap in an infinite universe. He is no more central to the world than any other thing, not even the gods. For gods there may be, differing in kind and in individuality just as there are men, and having qualities of consciousness with which religious experience suggests men may come into touch and be helped — or frustrated. These gods also may be part of the cosmic team. They also, if they are, must undergo change, must struggle for survival, must work together with men and things for the maintenance of the ordered world, in an environment which is infinitude.

Working, consequently — successful working — is the test. Men and thoughts and things are not born good, they *make* good. It is *becoming*, not being, that counts. All the organs and capacities of man must be strong to maintain themselves and to do their appropriate share in maintaining the organism of which they are parts, if they and it are to survive. Ideas, opinions, hypotheses, arising no matter how, all start really on the same level. Each involves, at the outset, an act of faith, a willingness to believe in the prosperity of its guidance, a willingness, consequently, to take the risk of failure that is likely as not to come by following its guidance. Each has to be set to work to win its way in the control of that aspect of the world or of experience which it intends or designates. Each is true or false, not primarily but eventually, as it succeeds or fails in winning this control. It follows that it is unwise as well as unjust to rule out, *a priori*, any hypothesis, any way of thinking, which as it appears makes a claim to truth. The right, the scientific action is to give it a chance to make good its claim. No matter what an idea may be, it must be tested, so far as possible, experimentally. Whether it be the conception of human survival after death, or of the character of divinity, or the power of the mind to heal, it must not be rejected *a priori*. There is a dogmatism and intolerance of science which can be quite as vicious as the dogmatism and intolerance of religion. The important thing, in this changing world, is the democratic equality of opportunity to make good for ideas as well as for men. That is really the only indispensable assumption of scientific method, and Pragmatism is a theory of scientific method.

James's thinking was impregnated and fertilized through and through by this assumption. His associations of childhood and his youthful training had given him the power of sympathetic insight into the motives and bases for the great variety of human demands, both superstitious and intelligent. Lover of peace and internationalist as he was, he had even sympathy for the instincts which find expression in war, and his proposal of a moral equivalent for it is one of the great documents in the history of the socialization of mankind.

If one were to sum up in a single phrase James's attitude toward the world and toward human life, one might call it that of metaphysical democracy. His sense for individuality in things, his sense for the right of things to their individuality stands out in all his philosophical writing: that is really all that is implied in the metaphysics he has called "radical empiricism"; that is really all that is implied in the method he has named Pragmatism. In ethics, of course, he was a humanist to that degree that nothing human, even the most remote and fanciful of human things, was alien to him. He acknowledged the claim of each and asked for each an opportunity to justify itself by its works. That is the tenor of the collection of essays headed by the famous one on 'The Will to Believe' (1897), and the 'Talks to Teachers, etc.' (1899). That is the assumption underlying his great two-volume 'Psychology' (1892), his 'Pragmatism' (1907), his 'A Pluralistic Universe' (1909), his posthumous 'Some Problems in Philosophy' (1911), the various essays in 'Radical Empiricism' (1912), his study in the 'Varieties of Religious Experience' (1902). In his thinking, what was fundamental and what was best as well as what was most hopeful and most fresh in the life of America and in the life of western civilization as a whole found its first free articulate philosophic expression.

H. M. Kallen

THE MORAL EQUIVALENT OF WAR

Written for the American Association for International Conciliation (1910) and included in 'Memories and Studies' by William James (Longmans, Green & Co.). Reprinted by permission of Mr. Henry James.

THE war against war is going to be no holiday excursion or camping party. The military feelings are too deeply grounded to abdicate their place among our ideals until better substitutes are offered than the glory and shame that come to nations as well as to individuals from the ups and downs of politics and the vicissitudes of trade. There is something highly paradoxical in the modern man's relation to war. Ask all our millions, north and south, whether they would vote now (were such a thing possible) to have our war for the Union expunged from history, and the record of a peaceful transition to the present time substituted for that of its marches and battles, and probably hardly a handful of eccentrics would say yes. Those ancestors, those efforts, those memories and legends, are the most ideal part of what we now own together, a sacred spiritual possession worth more than all the blood poured out. Yet ask those same people whether they would be willing in cold blood to start another civil war now to gain another similar possession, and not one man or woman would vote for the proposition. In modern eyes, precious though wars may be, they must not be waged solely for the sake of the ideal harvest. Only when forced upon one, only when an enemy's injustice leaves us no alternative, is a war now thought permissible.

It was not thus in ancient times. The earlier men were hunting men, and to hunt a neighboring tribe, kill the males, loot the village, and possess the females was the most profitable, as well as the most exciting way of living. Thus were the more martial tribes selected, and in chiefs and peoples a pure pugnacity and love of glory came to mingle with the more fundamental appetite for plunder.

Modern war is so expensive that we feel trade to be a better avenue to plunder; but modern man inherits all the innate pugnacity and all the love of glory of his ancestors. Showing war's irrationality and horror is of no effect upon him. The horrors make the fascination. War is the *strong* life; it is life *in extremis;* war-taxes are the only ones men never hesitate to pay, as the budgets of all nations show us.

History is a bath of blood. The Iliad is one long recital of how Diomedes and Ajax, Sarpedon and Hector *killed*. No detail of the wounds they made is spared us, and the Greek mind fed upon the story. Greek history is a panorama of jingoism and imperialism — war for war's sake, all the citizens being warriors. It is horrible reading, because of the irrationality of it all — save for the purpose of making "history" — and the history is that of the utter ruin of a civilization in intellectual respects perhaps the highest the earth has ever seen.

Those wars were purely piratical. Pride, gold, women, slaves, excitement, were their only motives. In the Peloponnesian War, for example, the Athenians ask the inhabitants of Melos (the island where the 'Venus of Milo' was found), hitherto neutral, to own their lordship. The envoys meet, and hold a debate which Thucydides gives in full, and which, for sweet reasonableness of form, would have satisfied Matthew Arnold. "The powerful exact what they can," said the Athenians, "and the weak grant what they must." When the Meleans say that sooner than be slaves they will appeal to the gods, the Athenians reply: "Of the gods we believe and of men we know that, by a law of their nature, wherever they can rule they will. This law was not made by us, and we are not the first to have acted upon it; we did but inherit it, and we know that you and all mankind, if you were as strong as we are, would do as we do. So much for the gods; we have told you why we expect to stand as high in their good opinion as you." Well, the Meleans still refused, and their town was taken. "The Athenians," Thucydides quietly says, "thereupon put to death all who were of military age and made slaves of the women and children. They then colonized the island, sending thither five hundred settlers of their own."

Alexander's career was piracy pure and simple, nothing but an orgy of power and plunder, made romantic by the character of the hero. There was no rational principle in it, and the moment he died his generals and governors attacked one another. The cruelty of those times is incredible. When Rome finally conquered Greece, Paulus Æmilius was told by the Roman Senate to reward his soldiers for their toil by "giving" them the old kingdom of Epirus. They sacked seventy cities and carried off a hundred and fifty thousand inhabitants as slaves. How many they killed I know not; but in Ætolia they killed all the senators, five hundred and fifty in number. Brutus was "the noblest Roman of them all," but to reanimate his soldiers on the eve of Philippi he similarly promises to give them the cities of Sparta and Thessalonica to ravage, if they win the fight.

Such was the gory nurse that trained societies to cohesiveness. We inherit the warlike type; and for most of the capacities of heroism that the human race is full of we have to thank this cruel history. Dead men tell no tales, and if there were any tribes of other type than this they have left no survivors. Our ancestors have bred pugnacity into our bone and marrow, and thousands of years of peace won't breed it out of us. The popular imagination fairly fattens on the thought of wars. Let public opinion once reach a certain fighting pitch, and no ruler can withstand it. In the Boer War both governments began with bluff, but couldn't stay there, the military tension was too much for them. In 1898 our people had read the word WAR in letters three inches high for three months in every newspaper. The pliant politician McKinley was swept away by their eagerness, and our squalid war with Spain became a necessity.

At the present day, civilized opinion is a curious mental mixture. The military instincts and ideals are as strong as ever, but are confronted by reflective criticisms which sorely curb their ancient freedom. Innumerable writers are showing up the bestial side of military service. Pure loot and mastery seem no longer morally avowable motives, and pretexts must be found for attributing them solely to the enemy. England and we, our army and navy authorities repeat without ceasing, arm solely for "peace," Germany and Japan it is who are bent on loot and glory. "Peace" in military mouths today is a synonym for "war expected." The word has become a pure provocative, and no government wishing peace sincerely should allow it ever to be printed in a newspaper. Every up-to-date Dictionary should say that "peace" and "war" mean the same thing, now *in posse*, now *in actu*. It may even reasonably be said that the intensely sharp competitive *preparation* for war by the nations *is the real war*, permanent, unceasing; and that the battles are only a sort of public verification of the mastery gained during the "peace" interval.

It is plain that on this subject civilized man has developed a sort of double personality. If we take European nations, no legitimate interest of any one of them would seem to justify the tremendous destructions which a war to compass it would necessarily entail. It would seem as though common sense and reason ought to find a way to reach agreement in every conflict of honest interests. I myself think it our bounden duty to believe in such international rationality as possible. But, as things stand, I see how desperately hard it is to bring the peace-party and the war-party together, and I believe that the difficulty is due to certain deficiencies in the program of pacificism which set the militarist imagination strongly, and to a certain extent justifiably, against it. In the whole discussion both sides are on imaginative and sentimental ground. It is but one utopia against another, and everything one says must be abstract and hypothetical. Subject to this criticism and caution, I will try to characterize in abstract strokes the opposite imaginative forces, and point out what to my own very fallible mind seems the best utopian hypothesis, the most promising line of conciliation.

In my remarks, pacificist though I am, I will refuse to speak of the bestial side of the war-régime (already done justice to by many writers) and consider only the higher aspects of militaristic sentiment. Patriotism no one thinks discreditable; nor does anyone deny that war is the romance of history. But inordinate ambitions are the soul of every patriotism, and the possibility of violent death the soul of all romance. The militarily patriotic and romantic-minded everywhere, and especially the professional military class, refuse to admit for a moment that war may be a transitory phenomenon in social evolution. The notion of a sheep's paradise like that revolts, they say, our higher imagination. Where then would be the steeps of life? If war had ever stopped, we should have to reinvent it, on this view, to redeem life from flat degeneration.

Reflective apologists for war at the present day all take it religiously. It is a sort of sacrament. Its profits are to the vanquished as well as to the victor; and quite apart from any questions of profit, it is an absolute good, we are told, for it is human nature at its highest dynamic. Its "horrors" are a cheap price to pay for rescue from the only alternative supposed, of a world of clerks and teachers, of coeducation and zoöphily, of "consumer's leagues" and "associated charities," of industrialism unlimited, and feminism unabashed. No scorn, no hardness, no valor any more! Fie upon such a cattle-yard of a planet!

So far as the central essence of this feeling goes, no healthy-minded person, it seems to me, can help to some degree partaking of it. Militarism is the great preserver of our ideals of hardihood, and human life with no use for hardihood would be contemptible. Without risks or prizes for the darer, history would be insipid indeed; and there is a type of military character which everyone feels that the race should never cease to breed, for everyone is sensitive to its superiority. The duty is incumbent on mankind of keeping military characters in stock — of keeping them, if not for use, then as ends in themselves and as pure pieces of perfection — so that Roosevelt's weaklings and mollycoddles may not end by making everything else disappear from the face of nature.

This natural sort of feeling forms, I think, the innermost soul of army-writings. Without any exception known to me, militarist authors take a highly mystical view of their subject, and regard war as a biological or sociological necessity, uncontrolled by ordinary psychological checks and motives. When the time of development is ripe the war must come, reason or no reason, for the justifications pleaded are invariably fictitious. War is, in short, a permanent human *obligation*. General Homer Lea, in his recent book 'The Valor of Ignorance,' plants himself squarely on this ground. Readiness for war is for him the essence of nationality, and ability in it the supreme measure of the health of nations.

Nations, General Lea says, are never stationary — they must necessarily expand or shrink, according to their vitality or decrepitude. Japan now is culminating; and by the fatal law in question it is impossible that her statesmen should not long since have entered, with extraordinary foresight, upon a vast policy of conquest — the game in which the first moves were her wars with China and Russia and her treaty with England and of which the final objective is the capture of the Philippines, the Hawaiian Islands, Alaska, and the whole of our coast west of the Sierra Passes. This will give Japan what her ineluctable vocation as a state absolutely forces her to claim, the possession of the entire Pacific Ocean; and to oppose these deep designs we Americans have, according to our author, nothing but our conceit, our ignorance, our commercialism, our corruption, and our feminism. General Lea makes a minute technical comparison of the military strength which we at present could oppose to the strength of Japan, and concludes that the islands, Alaska, Oregon, and Southern California would fall almost without resistance, that San Francisco must surrender in a fortnight to a Japanese investment, that in three or four months the war would be over, and our republic, unable to regain what it had heedlessly neglected to protect sufficiently, would then "disintegrate," until perhaps some Cæsar should arise to weld us again into a nation.

A dismal forecast indeed! Yet not unplausible, if the mentality of Japan's statesmen be of the Cæsarian type of which history shows so many examples, and which is all that General Lea seems able to imagine. But there is no reason to think that women can no longer be the mothers of Napoleonic or Alexandrian characters; and if these come in Japan and find their opportunity, just such surprises as 'The Valor of Ignorance' paints may lurk in ambush for us. Ignorant as we still are of the innermost recesses of Japanese mentality, we may be foolhardy to disregard such possibilities.

Other militarists are more complex and more moral in their considerations. The 'Philosophie des Krieges,' by S. R. Steinmetz, is a good example. War, according to this author, is an ordeal instituted by God, who weighs the nations in its balance. It is the essential form of the State, and the only function in which peoples can employ all their powers at once and convergently. No victory is possible save as the resultant of a totality of virtues, no defeat for which some vice or weakness is not responsible. Fidelity, cohesiveness, tenacity, heroism, conscience, education, inventiveness, economy, wealth, physical health, and vigor — there isn't a moral or intellectual point of superiority that doesn't tell, when God holds his assizes and hurls the peoples upon one another. *Die Weltgeschichte ist das Weltgericht;* and Dr. Steinmetz does not believe that in the long run chance and luck play any part in apportioning the issues.

The virtues that prevail, it must be noted, are virtues anyhow, superiorities that count in peaceful as well as in military competition; but the strain on them, being infinitely intenser in the latter case, makes war infinitely more searching as a trial. No ordeal is comparable to its winnowings. Its dread hammer is the welder of men into cohesive states, and nowhere but in such states can human nature adequately develop its capacity. The only alternative is "degeneration."

Dr. Steinmetz is a conscientious thinker, and his book, short as it is, takes much into account. Its upshot can, it seems to me, be summed up in Simon Patten's word, that mankind was nursed in pain and fear, and that the transition to a "pleasure-economy" may be fatal to a being wielding no powers of defense against its disintegrative influences. If we speak of the *fear of emancipation from the fear-régime,* we put the whole situation into a single phrase; fear regarding ourselves now taking the place of the ancient fear of the enemy.

Turn the fear over as I will in my mind, it all seems to lead back to two unwillingnesses of the imagination, one esthetic, and the other moral: unwillingness, first to envisage a future in which army life, with its many elements of charm, shall be forever impossible, and in which the destinies of peoples shall nevermore be decided quickly, thrillingly, and tragically, by force, but only gradually and insipidly by "evolution"; and, secondly, unwillingness to see the supreme theater of human strenuousness closed, and the splendid military aptitudes of men doomed to keep always in a state of latency and never show themselves in action. These insistent unwillingnesses, no less than other esthetic and ethical insistencies, have, it seems to me, to be listened to and respected. One cannot meet them effectively by mere counter-insistency on war's expensiveness and horror. The horror makes the thrill; and when the question is of getting the extremest and supremest out of human nature, talk of expense sounds ignominious. The weakness of so much merely negative criticism is evident — pacificism makes no converts from the military party. The military party denies neither the bestiality nor the horror, nor the expense; it only says that these things tell but half the story. It only says that war is *worth* them; that, taking human nature as a whole, its wars are its best protection against its weaker and more cowardly self, and that mankind cannot *afford* to adopt a peace-economy.

Pacifists ought to enter more deeply into the esthetical and ethical point of view of their opponents. Do that first in any controversy, says J. J. Chapman, *then move the point,* and your opponent will follow. So long as anti-militarists propose no substitute for war's disciplinary function, no *moral equivalent* of war, analogous, as one might say, to the mechanical equivalent of heat, so long they fail to realize the full inwardness of the situation. And as a rule they do fail. The duties, penalties, and sanctions pictured in the utopias they paint are all too weak and tame to touch the military-minded. Tolstoy's pacificism is the only exception to this rule, for it is profoundly pessimistic as regards all this world's values, and makes the fear of the Lord furnish the moral spur provided elsewhere by the fear of the enemy. But our socialistic peace-advocates all believe absolutely in this world's values; and instead of the fear of the Lord and the fear of the enemy, the only fear they reckon with is the fear of poverty if one be lazy. This weakness pervades all the socialistic literature with which I am acquainted. Even in Lowes Dickinson's exquisite dialogue ('Justice and Liberty,' N. Y., 1909), high wages and short hours are the only forces invoked for overcoming man's distaste for repulsive kinds of labor. Meanwhile men at large still live as they always have lived, under a pain-and-fear economy — for those of us who live in an ease-economy are but an island in the stormy ocean — and the whole atmosphere of present-day utopian literature tastes mawkish and dish-watery to people who still keep a sense for life's more bitter flavors. It suggests, in truth, ubiquitous inferiority.

Inferiority is always with us, and merciless scorn of it is the keynote of the military temper. "Dogs, would you live forever?" shouted Frederick the Great. "Yes," say our utopians, "let us live forever, and raise our level gradually." The best thing about our "inferiors" today is that they are as tough as nails, and physically and morally almost as insensitive. Utopianism would see them soft and squeamish, while militarism would keep their callousness, but transfigure it into a meritorious characteristic, needed by "the service," and redeemed by that from the suspicion of inferiority. All the qualities of a man acquire dignity when he knows that the service of the collectivity that owns him needs them. If proud of the collectivity, his own pride rises in proportion. No collectivity is like an army for nourishing such pride; but it has to be confessed that the only sentiment which the image of pacific cosmopolitan industrialism is capable of arousing in countless worthy breasts is shame at the idea of belonging to such a collectivity. It is obvious that the United States of America as they exist today impress a mind like General Lea's as so much human blubber. Where is the sharpness and precipitousness, the contempt for life, whether one's own, or another's? Where is the savage "yes" and "no," the unconditional duty? Where is the conscription? Where is the blood-tax? Where is anything that one feels honored by belonging to?

Having said thus much in preparation, I will now confess my own utopia. I devoutly believe in the reign of peace and in the gradual advent of some sort of a socialistic equilibrium. The fatalistic view of the war-function is to me nonsense, for I know that war-making is due to definite motives and subject to prudential checks and reasonable criticisms, just like any other form of enterprise. And when whole nations are the armies, and the science of destruction vies in intellectual refinement with the sciences of production, I see that war becomes absurd and impossible from its own monstrosity. Extravagant ambitions will have to be replaced by reasonable claims, and nations must make common cause against them. I see no reason why all this should not apply to yellow as well as to white countries, and I look forward to a future when acts of war shall be formally outlawed as between civilized peoples.

All these beliefs of mine put me squarely into the anti-militarist party. But I do not believe that peace either ought to be or will be permanent on this globe, unless the states pacifically organized preserve some of the old elements of army discipline. A permanently successful peace-economy cannot be a simple pleasure-economy. In the more or less socialistic future towards which mankind seems drifting we must still subject ourselves collectively to those severities which answer to our real position upon this only partly hospitable globe. We must make new energies and hardihoods continue the manliness to which the military mind so faithfully clings. Martial virtues must be the enduring cement; intrepidity, contempt of softness, surrender of private interest, obedience to command, must still remain the rock upon which states are built — unless, indeed, we wish for dangerous reactions against commonwealths fit only for contempt, and liable to invite attack whenever a center of crystallization for military-minded enterprise gets formed anywhere in their neighborhood.

The war-party is assuredly right in affirming and reaffirming that the martial virtues, although originally gained by the race through war, are absolute and permanent human goods. Patriotic pride and ambition in their military form are, after all, only specifications of a more general competitive passion. They are its first form, but that is no reason for supposing them to be its last form. Men now are proud of belonging to a conquering nation, and without a murmur they lay down their persons and their wealth, if by so doing they may fend off subjection. But who can be sure that *other aspects of one's country* may not, with time and education and suggestion enough, come to be regarded with similarly effective feelings of pride and shame? Why should men not some day feel that it is worth a blood-tax to belong to a collectivity superior in *any* ideal respect? Why should they not blush with indignant shame if the community that owns them is vile in any way whatsoever? Individuals, daily more numerous, now feel this civic passion. It is only a question of blowing on the spark till the whole population gets incandescent, and on the ruins of the old morals of military honor, a stable system of morals of civic honor builds itself up. What the whole community comes to believe in grasps the individual as in a vise. The war-function has grasped us so far; but constructive interests may some day seem no less imperative, and impose on the individual a hardly lighter burden.

Let me illustrate my idea more concretely. There is nothing to make one indignant in the mere fact that life is hard, that men should toil and suffer pain. The planetary conditions once for all are such, and we can stand it. But that so many men, by mere accidents of birth and opportunity, should have a life of *nothing else* but toil and pain and hardness and inferiority imposed upon them, should have *no* vacation, while others natively no more deserving never get any taste of this campaigning life at all — *this* is capable of arousing indignation in reflective minds. It may end by seeming shameful to all of us that some of us have nothing but campaigning, and others nothing but unmanly ease. If now — and this is my idea — there were, instead of military conscription, a conscription of the whole youthful population to form for a certain number of years a part of the army enlisted against *Nature,* the injustice would tend to be evened out, and numerous other goods to the commonwealth would follow. The military ideals of hardihood and discipline would be wrought into the growing fiber of the people; no one would remain blind, as the luxurious classes now are blind, to man's real relations to the globe he lives on, and to the permanently sour and hard foundations of his higher life. To coal and iron mines, to freight trains, to fishing fleets in December, to dish-washing, clothes-washing, and window-washing, to road-building and tunnel-making, to foundries and stoke-holes, and to the frames of skyscrapers, would our gilded youths be drafted off, according to their choice, to get the childishness knocked out of them, and to come back into society with healthier sympathies and soberer ideas. They would have paid their blood-tax, done their own part in the immemorial human warfare against nature, they would tread the earth more proudly, the women would value them more highly, they would be better fathers and teachers of the following generation.

Such a conscription, with the state of public opinion that would have required it, and with the many moral fruits it would bear, would preserve in the midst of a pacific civilization the manly virtues which the military party is so afraid of seeing disappear in peace. We should get toughness without callousness, authority with as little criminal cruelty as possible, and painful work done cheerily because the duty is temporary, and threatens not, as now, to degrade the whole remainder of one's life. I spoke of the "moral equivalent" of war. So far, war has been the only force that can discipline a whole community, and until an equivalent discipline is organized, I believe that war must have its way. But I have no serious doubt that the ordinary prides and shames of social man, once developed to a certain intensity, are capable of organizing such a moral equivalent as I have sketched, or some other just as effective for preserving manliness of type. It is but a question of time, of skilful propagandism, and of opinion-making men seizing historic opportunities.

The martial type of character can be bred without war. Strenuous honor and disinterestedness abound elsewhere. Priests and medical men are in a fashion educated to it, and we should all feel some degree of it imperative if we were conscious of our work as an obligatory service to the state. We should be *owned*, as soldiers are by the army, and our pride would rise accordingly. We could be poor, then, without humiliation, as army officers now are. The only thing needed henceforward is to inflame the civic temper as past history has inflamed the military temper. H. G. Wells, as usual, sees the center of the situation. "In many ways," he says, "military organization is the most peaceful of activities. When the contemporary man steps from the street, of clamorous insincere advertisement, push, adulteration, underselling, and intermittent employment, into the barrack-yard, he steps on to a higher social place, into an atmosphere of service and co-operation and of infinitely more honorable emulations. Here at least men are not flung out of employment to degenerate because there is no immediate work for them to do. They are fed and drilled and trained for better services. Here at least a man is supposed to win promotion by self-forgetfulness and not by self-seeking. And beside the feeble and irregular endowment of research by commercialism, its little short-sighted snatches at profit by innovation and scientific economy, see how remarkable is the steady and rapid development of method and appliances in naval and military affairs! Nothing is more striking than to compare the progress of civil conveniences which has been left almost entirely to the trader, to the progress in military apparatus during the last few decades. The house-appliances of today, for example, are little better than they were fifty years ago. A house of today is still almost as ill-ventilated, badly heated by wasteful fires, clumsily arranged and furnished as the house of 1858. Houses a couple of hundred years old are still satisfactory places of residence, so little have our standards risen. But the rifle or battleship of fifty years ago was beyond all comparison inferior to those we possess; in power, in speed, in convenience alike. No one has a use now for such superannuated things." ('First and Last Things.')

Wells adds that he thinks that the conceptions of order and discipline, the tradition of service and devotion, of physical fitness, unstinted exertion, and universal responsibility, which universal military duty is now teaching European nations, will remain a permanent acquisition, when the last ammunition has been used in the fireworks that celebrate the final peace. I believe as he does. It would be simply preposterous if the only force that could work ideals of honor and standards of efficiency into English or American natures should be the fear of being killed by the Germans or the Japanese. Great indeed is Fear; but it is not, as our military enthusiasts believe and try to make us believe, the only stimulus known for awakening the higher ranges of men's spiritual energy. The amount of alteration in public opinion which my utopia postulates is vastly less than the difference between the mentality of those black warriors who pursued Stanley's party on the Congo with their cannibal war-cry of "Meat! Meat!" and that of the "general-staff" of any civilized nation. History has seen the latter interval bridged over: the former one can be bridged over much more easily.

HENRY JAMES

"NO one has the faintest conception of what I am trying for," says the celebrated novelist in 'The Death of the Lion,' "and not many have read three pages that I've written; but I must dine with them first — they'll find out when they've time." The words are tinged with Henry James's own disdain of the fashionable world which wears, and wears out, a man of genius like a spangle on its robe. They are tinged too with the mixed regret and satisfaction of an author who knew what it is to grow too fine for one's public. Born in 1843, James established in the seventies and eighties of the last century the kind of reputation that calls for French and German translations. He lived to hear the wits of the late nineties and the following decade calling for the translation of his maturest works into English. Perhaps forty years ago everyone had read, or had attempted to read, a recent novel of his; but there has come up a generation of young people who have been permitted, with the connivance of critics, to concede the excellence of his earlier productions and the "impossibility" of his later ones without looking into either. Shortly before his death in 1916 he emerged for the general public from his obscure memoir-writing, and stood for a moment conspicuous on the sky-line — a dark august figure bowed in devout allegiance beneath the English flag; then with a thunder of ordnance not made for *his* passing he slipped below the horizon. In the hour of trial he had given to England a beautiful gesture, which derived much of its interest from his lifelong refusal to commit himself to any cause but art. Though the adoption of English citizenship by an American would have excited in ordinary circumstances the profane wit of our paragraph-writers, the gravity of this occasion chastened them; and when, a few months later, his death called for comment, many of them clutched at this transference of allegiance as the last, if not the only, intelligible performance of his that was known to them. Some of them, to be sure, remembered, or said they remembered, 'Daisy Miller' as a "perfect little thing of its kind," or professed a not unpleasant acquaintance with 'The Portrait of a Lady,' or even exhibited a vague consciousness that the novelist had treated extensively the "international situation"; but in general they betrayed their "unpreparedness" for defining his talent and valuing his accomplishment.

Criticism should have declared by this time, and should have declared with emphasis and authority, what Henry James was "trying for." It should also have declared whether, when he slipped below the horizon, he sank into the deepening shadows of literary history, or whether he passed on into a widening world of light — the Great Good Place of a grateful and enlightened posterity which will not dine with him but which will read him. May we securely let him pass while we go on to something better; or shall we find, if we go on, that he is the something better to which we come at last? There are wide differences of opinion in the critical jury. Mr. Brownell, who has said a multitude of penetrating things about his mind and his art, and who is, one should suppose, the critic in America best qualified to enjoy and to value him, does not conceal his quiet hope and expectation that among the novelists of the future we shall not meet his like again. Professor Pattee, who is "out" for American local colors and big native American ideas, declares in so many words that Henry James's novels "really accomplish nothing." Recent English criticism strikes up in another key. Ford Madox Ford promises him immortality, if there is any immortality for extraordinarily fine work — a point about which he is doubtful; but he struggles to this handsome conclusion through such fantastic arguments, with such explosions of temper and erratic judgment, through such a stream of "Godforbids" and "Thankgods" and "Godknowses," with such a display of the new literary bad manners, that one wonders how he ever came to occupy himself with an author so dedicated to refinement. The little book of Rebecca West, an acutely positive and intensely glowing young "intellectual," has delightful merits: its adverse criticism is cuttingly phrased if not always precisely keen, its appreciative passages are full of fresh ardor and luminous if not always illuminating imagery; it holds up a candle and swings a censer in the principal niches and chapels of the wide-arching cathedral upon which the builder toiled for half a century; but it rather evades the task of presenting a final and comprehensive view — of explaining, in short, in the honor of what deity the whole edifice was constructed.

I

Let us cut an avenue to the inner shrine by removing from consideration some of the objects for which most of Henry James's American and English compatriots profess a pious veneration. He has insulted all the popular gods of democratic society — for example, the three persons of the French revolutionary trinity and the "sovereign people." Captain Sholto, almost unique among his characters in uttering a political thought, must express pretty nearly his creator's position when he says, "I believe those that are on top the heap are better than those that are under it, that they mean to stay there, and that if they are not a pack of poltroons they will." It would be difficult to name an American author more nearly devoid of emotional interest in the mass of humanity. His attitude towards the "submerged tenth" is chiefly established by his silence with regard to it. In 'The Princess Casamassima,' one of the rare places in which he permits a view of the dark Netherward of society to fall upon the eye of a sensitive observer, this is the reported reaction:

"Some of the women and girls, in particular, were appalling — saturated with alcohol and vice, brutal, bedraggled, obscene. 'What remedy but another deluge, what alchemy but annihilation?' he asked himself as he went his way; and he wondered what fate there could be, in the great scheme of things, for a planet overgrown with such vermin, what redemption but to be hurled against a ball of consuming fire."

The passage is a little deficient — is it not? — in warm fraternal feeling. Let us round out this impression with the reported reaction of a sensitive observer in 'The Madonna of the Future' to a little glimpse of free life in Rome: "Cats and monkeys, monkeys and cats; all human life is there!"

These sensitive observers doubtless had cause for a shudder of revulsion, and dramatic reason as well. Their behavior becomes interesting when one compares it with James's personal account in 'London Notes' of his own attitude towards a very different scene — the preparations for the Victoria Jubilee: "The foremost, the immense impression is of course the constant, the permanent, the ever-supreme — the impression of that greatest glory of our race, its passionate feeling for trade. . . . London has found in this particular chapter of the career of its aged sovereign only an enormous selfish advertisement."

Later he reports that he has been taking refuge from the Jubilee in novel-reading. The great thing to be said for the novelists, he adds, is "that at any given moment they offer us another world, another consciousness, an experience that, *as effective as the dentist's ether, muffles the ache of the actual* and, by helping us to an interval, tides us over and makes us face, in the return to the inevitable, a combination that may at least have changed." Was it a pose to speak of fiction as an ethereal pause in the midst of the perpetual toothache of the actual — and of a great patriotic demonstration as a peculiarly sharp toothache? Or was it "American humor"? The pose, if pose it was, is curiously of a piece with his saying to John Hay, who had been received with an "ovation" on his arrival in Southampton, "What impression does it make in your mind to have these insects creeping about you and saying things to you?"

A partial explanation of this disgust and this detachment from the major interests of the majority of men may be found in a half-dozen familiar facts of his biographical record: the peculiar genius of his Swedenborgian father, his early induction in old New York — his birthplace — into "the religion of foreign things," his foreign language teachers, his early perusal of the London Punch, and his devotion, a little later, to the Revue des Deux Mondes, his glimpses in childhood of London and the Continent, his artistic apprenticeship under John La Farge, his trifling contact with the Harvard Law School, his serious contact as reviewer with the New York Nation and with the Atlantic Monthly, his discovery of a fine vein of fiction, and the permanent settlement of his residence abroad. The leading idea in the elder James's plan for his son's life seems to have been to rescue him from the typical democratic process in order to open to him some finer destiny: to provide him with comfortable means and ample leisure, to save him from every exacting pressure, to preserve him from the stamp of any definite educational system, by perpetual migrations to snap the root of local attachments, to postpone for him as long as possible the choice of a career, so that at last the young man should be whatever he was and do whatever he did by the free impulse of his own spirit. The perfect working of this plan was probably marred by a physical accident at the time of the Civil War, which as Henry James circuitously explains, assigned him to the rôle of an engrossed spectator. Whatever the significance of this incident, the result of the plan of tasting life in New York, Boston, Geneva, London, Paris, Rome, Florence, and Venice was to set up an endless process of observation, comparison, discrimination, selection, and appreciation — a process which for this highly civilized, highly sensitized young spirit, became all absorbing, and made of him a fastidious connoisseur of experience, an artistic celibate to whose finer sense promiscuous mixing in the gross welter of the world was wearisome and unprofitable.

There is no getting round the fact that he was as prodigiously "superior" inside as he was outside the field of art. In his recent much quoted essay on the New Novel he has the air of a conscious old master condescending for the nonce to notice "the rough and tumble 'output'" of the young vulgar democratic herd. A false note in Miss West's treatment of his character is her remark that he lacked "that necessary attribute of the good critic, the power to bid bad authors to go to the devil." Brownell, on the other hand, puts some of his work at the head of American criticism. His 'Hawthorne,' his 'Partial Portraits,' his 'Essays in London and Elsewhere,' his 'Notes on Novelists,' his various "portraits" of cities and "scenes," including 'The American Scene,' and his introductions to his own novels constitute certainly an impressive body of literary and social criticism of unique quality and high interest. As for the "necessary attribute," he sent authors to their appropriate places so civilly and suavely that they probably failed frequently to notice where they were sent; but no critic ever more remorselessly sent to the devil bad authors, mediocre authors, and even very distinguished authors. In his later years, he very blandly, very courteously, sent the whole general public to the devil. He was mortally weary of the general public's obtuseness; he despaired of the general public, and despised it. At the same time he reiterated in his stories, his critical articles, and in the prefaces to the New York edition of his work challenges and entreaties to the critical few to come and find him.

II

In that fascinating work 'The Figure in the Carpet' he depicts, for criticism, what he would have called his own "case." He presents there, amid various intensifications of interest, Hugh Vereker, a master-novelist, head and shoulders above his contemporaries; so that even his devoutest admirers and his most studious critics miss the thing that he has written his books "most *for.*"

"Isn't there," he says to one of them, "for every writer a particular thing of that sort, the thing that most makes him apply himself, the thing without the effort to achieve which he wouldn't write at all, the very passion of his passion, the part of the business in which, for him, the flame of art burns most intensely? . . . There's an idea in my work without which I wouldn't have given a straw for the whole job. . . . It stretches, this little trick of mine, from book to book, and everything else, comparatively, plays over the surface of it. The order, the form, the texture of my books will perhaps constitute for the initiated a complete representation of it. So it is naturally the thing for the critic to look for. It strikes me," Vereker adds, smiling but inscrutable, "even as the thing for the critic to find."

The thing which James hoped chiefly that his critics would some day recognize is not that he is a great stylist, or a learned historian of manners, or the chief of the realists, or a master of psychological analysis. All these things have been noted and asserted by various more or less irreligious strollers through that cathedral-like edifice to which we have likened his works. The thing which he, as the high priest solemnly ministering before the high altar, implored some one to observe and to declare and to explain is that he adored beauty and absolutely nothing else in the world. To the discovery of beauty he dedicates his observation, his analysis, his marvelous and all-too-little-recognized imaginative energy. That is why he sends the rest of the world to the devil, that is his romance, that is his passion, that is why when he discusses his own creations he talks veritably like a soul in bliss. The intimate relation of his fiction to modern realities beguiles the uncritical reader into an erroneous notion that he is a "transcriber," a literal copyist, of life. What in his prefaces he begs us again and again to believe is that his stories originated in mere granules and germs of reality blown by chance breezes to the rich soil of the garden of his imagination, where they took root, and sprang up, and flowered; then they were transplanted with infinite art to the garden of literature. What he offers us, as he repeatedly suggests, is a thousandfold better than life; it is an escape from life. It is an escape from the undesigned into the designed, from chaos into order, from the undiscriminated into the finely assorted, from the languor of the irrelevant to the intensity of the pertinent. It is not reality; he goes so far as to say quite expressly that it is poetry. If that is true, his novels should, in spite of Professor Pattee, "accomplish" something; they should give us on the one hand an ideal and on the other hand a criticism; and they do give us both. Henry James's importance for Anglo-Saxons in general and for Americans in particular is that he is the first novelist writing in English to offer us on a grand scale a purely esthetic criticism of modern society and modern fiction.

His special distinction among writers of prose fiction is in the exclusiveness of his consecration to beauty — a point which in this connection probably requires elucidation. To the religious consciousness all things are ultimately holy or unholy; to the moral consciousness all things are ultimately good or evil; to the scientific consciousness all things are ultimately true or not true; to Henry James all things are ultimately beautiful or ugly. In few men but fanatics and geniuses does any one type of consciousness hold undivided sway, and even among the geniuses and fanatics of the English race the pure esthetic type was till Ruskin's time excessively rare. The normal English consciousness is, for purposes of judgment, a courthouse of several floors and courts to each of which are distributed the cases proper to that jurisdiction. In the criticism of Matthew Arnold, for example, there are distinct courts for the adjudication of spiritual, ecclesiastical, moral, esthetic, political, social, and scientific questions; but Ruskin handles all matters in the esthetic chamber. In Shakespeare's criticism of life, to take the case of a creative artist, the discrimination of experience proceeds on clearly distinguishable levels of consciousness; the exquisite judgment of Sylvia — "holy, fair, and wise is she" — is a certificate of character from three distinct courts. But Henry James, on the contrary, receives and attempts to judge all the kinds of his experience on the single crowded, swarming, humming level of the esthetic consciousness; the apartments above and below are vacant.

It is a much simpler task to indicate his position in literature with reference to the nature of his consciousness than with reference to the forms of his art. Critics attempting to "place" him have said the most bewildering things about his relationship to Richardson, Dickens, George Eliot, Trollope, George Meredith, Stevenson, Turgenev, Balzac, the Goncourts, Flaubert, Maupassant, Zola, and Daudet. To say that he is the disciple of this galaxy is to say everything and nothing. He knew intimately modern literature and many of its producers in England, France, Italy, and Russia, and he is related to them all as we are all related to Adam — and to the sun and the moon and the weather. He doubtless learned something of art from each of them, for he took instruction wherever he could find it — even from "Gyp," as he blushingly confesses in the preface to 'The Awkward Age.' But what different gods were worshiped in this galaxy! Even Meredith, who resembles him in his psychological inquisitiveness, does not in nine-tenths of his novels remotely resemble him in form; moreover, Meredith is a moralist, a sage, a mystic, and a lyrical worshiper of Life, Nature, and other such loose divinities. James called Balzac "the master of us all," he called Turgenev "the beautiful genius," he sympathized intensely with Flaubert's dedication to perfection; but his total representation of life is not much more like that of any of his "masters" than George Eliot's is like Zola's.

It is a curious fact that while American criticism tends to refer him to Europe, English criticism tends to refer him to America. A pretty argument, indeed, could be constructed to prove that he might have been very much what he was, if he had not gone body and soul to Europe, but had simply roved up and down the Atlantic coast comparing the grave conscience of Boston and the open and skyey mind of Concord with the luxurious body and vesture of New York and the antique "gentility" of Richmond — comparing the harvested impressions of these scenes, and weaving into new patterns the finer threads which American tradition had put into his hands; Hawthorne's brooding moral introspection, his penetration of the shadowed quietudes of the heart, his love of still people and quiet places, his golden thread of imagery beaded with brave symbolism, the elaborated euphony of his style; Irving's bland pleasure in the rich surface of things, his delight in manorial dwellings, his sense of the glamour of history, his temperamental and stylistic mellowness and clarity, his worldly well-bred air of being "at ease in Zion"; Poe's artistic exclusiveness, his artistic intelligence, his intensity, his conscious craftsmanship, his zest for discussing the creative process and the technique of literature. As a matter of fact, Henry James does "join on" to the eastern American traditions; he gathers up all these enumerated threads; he assimilates all these forms of consciousness. Hawthorne plays into his hands for depth and inwardness, Irving for outwardness and enrichment, and Poe for vividness and intensity.

The result of this fusion of types is a spacious and richly sophisticated type of the esthetic consciousness of which the closest English analogue is the consciousness of Walter Pater. James is like Pater in his aversion from the world, his dedication to art, his celibacy, his personal decorum and dignity, his high esthetic seriousness, his Epicurean relish in receiving and reporting the multiplicity and intensity of his impressions, and in the exacting closeness of his style. There are distinctions in plenty to be made by anyone curious enough to undertake the comparison; but on the whole there is no better sidelight on James's "philosophy" than Pater's Conclusion to the 'Studies in the Renaissance' and his 'Plato and Platonism'; no better statement of his general literary ideals than Pater's essay on 'Style'; no more interesting "parallel" to his later novels than 'Marius the Epicurean' and 'Imaginary Portraits.' To make the matter a little more specific let the curious inquirer compare the exposure of Pater's consciousness which is ordinarily known as his description of Mona Lisa with the exposure of James's consciousness which is ordinarily known as the description of a telegraph operator ('In the Cage').

III

The reduction of all experience to the esthetic level James himself recognized as a hazardous adventure. At the conclusion of his searching criticism of a fellow-adventurer, Gabriele D'Annunzio, he raises the question whether it can ever hope to be successful. D'Annunzio's adventure he pronounces a dismal failure — that is, of course, an esthetic failure; for in the quest of the beauty of passion the Italian, he declares, has produced the effect of a box of monkeys, or as he periphrastically puts it, "The association rising before us more nearly than any other is that of the manners observable in the most mimetic department of any great menagerie." But, he continues, the question is whether D'Annunzio's case is "the only case of the kind conceivable. May we not suppose another with the elements differently mixed? May we not in imagination alter the proportions within or the influences without, and look with cheerfulness for a different issue? *Need* the esthetic adventure, in a word, organized for real discovery, give us no more comforting news of success? . . . To which probably the sole answer is that no man can say."

The last sentence is modest but cannot have been wholly sincere; for James must have known that his own works answer all these questions in the affirmative. His own case is an altogether different variety of the species; his "news" is infinitely more comforting than D'Annunzio's. The particular ugliness, the morbid erotic obsession, on which D'Annunzio foundered, James like Pater sailed serenely by. His esthetic vision had a far wider range and a far higher level of observation than that of almost any of the Latin votaries of "art for art"—Gautier or Flaubert, for example. And yet, let us admit it frankly once for all, his representation of life offends the whole-souled critical sense intensely in some particulars and on what is fundamentally the same ground as that on which these others offend it. His representation of life is an esthetic flat; it sins against the diversity, the thick rotundity, the integrity of life. Its exquisitely arranged scenes and situations and atmospheres are not infrequently "ugly," as he would say, with the absence of moral energy and action. In 'The Awkward Age,' for example, in that society which lives for "the finer things," which perceives, and compares, and consults, and so perfectly masters its instincts, the situation fairly shouts for the presence of at least one young man conceivably capable of bursting like Lochinvar through the circle of intriguing petticoats to carry off the heroine. The atmosphere of 'The Golden Bowl' is ineffable—"There had been," says the author, "beauty day after day, and there had been for the spiritual lips something of the pervasive taste of it." The atmosphere is ineffably rich, still, golden, and, in the long run, stifling; the perceptive Mr. Verver, who is in it, gives a superb image of its effect:

"That's all I mean at any rate—that it's 'sort of' soothing: as if we were sitting about on divans, with pigtails, smoking opium and seeing visions. 'Let us then be up and doing'—what is it Longfellow says? That seems sometimes to ring out; like the police breaking in—into our opium den—to give us a shake."

One may properly stress the point of his sin against the integrity of life because it is of the essence of the esthetic case. It explains the vague but profound resentment which some readers who do not balk at James's difficulty feel when they have got "inside." Critics like Brownell, Ford, and Miss West all point towards but do not, I think, quite touch the heart of the matter when they say that James lacks "the historic sense." A part of the historic sense he indubitably has, and far more historical learning is implied in his work than is explicit in it; he loves the color and form of the past, he feels the "beauties" of history. But history to him, even the history of his own life, is a kind of magnificent picture gallery through which he strolls, delightedly commenting on the styles of different schools and periods, and pausing now and then for special expression of rapture before a masterpiece. Miss West beautifully flames with indignation at his "jocular" references to the Franco-Prussian War and at his unsympathetic treatment of the French Revolution till she hits upon the explanation that he was out of Europe while the Franco-Prussian War raged, and that he was not born at the time of the French Revolution, so that he could no more speak well of it "than he could propose for his club a person whom he had never met." The explanation doesn't fit all the facts. He was not out of England when, in his introduction to Rupert Brooke's letters, he expressed his satisfaction that the English tradition "should have flowered *in a specimen so beautifully producible*." The appreciation of Brooke is one of the most beautifully passionate tributes ever written; but the passion is purely esthetic; the inveterate air of the connoisseur viewing a new picture in the gallery of masterpieces he cannot shake off. He was not speaking of events that took place before he was born when he said of the assassination of Lincoln in his 'Notes of a Son and Brother':

"The collective sense of what had occurred was of a sadness too noble not somehow to inspire, and it was truly in the air that, whatever we had as a nation failed to produce, *we could at least gather round this perfection of classic woe*. True enough, as we were to see, the immediate harvest of our loss was almost too ugly to be borne — for nothing more sharply comes back to me than the tune to which the esthetic sense, if one glanced from *that* high window, recoiled in dismay from the sight of Mr. Andrew Johnson perched on the stricken scene."

Any good American will flame with indignation when he reads that passage; it so fails to present the subject; it is so horribly inadequate; it so affronts what Lord Morley would call "the high moralities" of life. With its stricken "scene," its esthetic rapture, its esthetic dismay, it insults the moral sense as a man would insult it who should ask one to note the exquisite slope of a woman's neck at the funeral of her husband. It makes one burn to break the glass in the high esthetic window. It sins against the integrity of life as, to take some distinguished examples, Renan's 'Vie de Jésus' and Pater's 'Plato and Platonism' sin against it. To present the Spartan boy as a nineteenth-century esthete or to present the life of Jesus as essentially "delicious" is to miss in the quest of distinction the most vital and obvious of distinctions. It is a blunder into which simple, gross, whole-souled men like Fielding or Smollett or Dickens could never have fallen. It is a crudity of which only the most exquisite esthete is capable; and he perching exclusively in his high esthetic window absolutely cannot avoid it. It is of the pure esthetic consciousness, not the intellect, that Emerson should have written his terse little couplet:

> Gravely it broods apart on joy
> And, truth to tell, amused by pain.

IV

When all these discriminations against the usurpations and blindnesses of the esthetic sense have been made it remains to be said that the infinitely seductive, and endlessly stimulating virtue of Henry James is the quintessential refinement, the intriguing complexity, the white-hot ardor of his passion for beauty. One feels the sacred flame most keenly, perhaps, in novels and tales like 'The Figure in the Carpet,' 'The Next Time,' 'The Death of the Lion,' 'The Lesson of the Master,' 'Roderick Hudson,' and 'The Tragic Muse,' in all of which he is interpreting the spirit of the artist or treating the conflict between the world and art. One feels it in the words of the young man in 'The Tragic Muse' who abandons the prospect of a brilliant political career to become a portrait painter: "The cleanness and quietness of it, the independent effort to do something, to leave something which shall give joy to man long after that howling has died away to the last ghost of an echo — such a vision solicits me in the watches of the night with an almost irresistible force."

One feels it in the words of the young diplomat in the same novel, who is infatuated with a fine piece of acting: "He floated in the felicity of it, in the general encouragement of a sense of the perfectly *done*." One feels it in the words of the novelist in 'The Lesson of the Master,' who says he has missed "the great things" — namely, "the sense which is the real life of the artist and the absence of which is his death, of having drawn from his intellectual instrument the finest music that nature had hidden in it, of having played it as it should be played."

For a born man of letters the first effect of this passion for perfection is an immense solicitude for style, that is to say, for an exact verbal and rhythmical correspondence between his conception of beauty and his representation of it. Judgment upon style, then, involves two distinct points: first, the question whether the conception is beautiful, and, secondly, the question whether the representation is exact. In the case of Henry James there should not be much dispute about the exactness and completeness of the representation; no man ever strove more remorselessly or on the whole more successfully to reproduce the shape and color and movement of his esthetic experience. The open question is whether his conceptions were beautiful; and on this point the majority of his critics have agreed that his earlier conceptions were beautiful but that his later conceptions were not. To that, in the last analysis, one must reduce the famous discussion of his two, or three, or half-a-dozen "styles."

Anyone who reads the works through in chronological order can explode to his own satisfaction the notion that James in any book or year or decade deliberately changed his sentence structure. What changed was his conception of beauty, and that changed by an entirely gradual multiplication of distinctions through the enrichment of his consciousness and the intensification of his vision. To his youthful eye beauty appeared in clear light, clear color, sharp outline, solid substance; accordingly the work of his earlier period abounds in figures distinct as in an etching of the eighteenth century, grouping themselves as on a canvas of Gainsborough's, and conversing and interacting with the brilliant lucidity and directness of persons in a comedy of Congreve's. To his maturer vision beauty has less of body and more of soul; it is not so much in things as in the illimitable effluence and indefinable *aura* of things; it reveals itself less to eye and ear and hand — though these are its avenues of approach — than to some mysterious inner organ which it moves to a divine abstraction from sense, to an ecstasy of pure contemplation; accordingly, late works like 'The Sacred Fount' and 'The Golden Bowl' present rather presences than persons, dim Maeterlinckian presences gliding through the shadow and shimmer of Turneresque landscapes and Maeterlinckian country-houses, and rarely saying or doing anything whatever of significance to vulgar ear or eye. The evolution of his artistic interest may be summed up in this way: he begins with an interest in the seen, the said, the enacted; and he ends by regarding all that as an obstruction in the way of his latest interest, namely, the presentation of the unseen, the unsaid, the unacted — the vast quantity of mental life in highly civilized beings which makes no outward sign, the invisible drama upon which most of his predecessors had hardly raised the curtain.

The difficulty in the later works is not primarily in the sentence structure but in the point of view. The sentences in the most difficult of the novels, 'The Sacred Fount,' are generally as neat, terse, and alert as the sentences in 'The Europeans,' which is within the comprehension of an intelligent child. When they are long and intricate they usually imprison and precisely render some intricate and rewarding beauty of a moment of consciousness luxuriously full: for example, this moment of Strether's in 'The Ambassadors':

"How could he wish it to be lucid for others, for anyone, that he, for the hour, saw reasons enough in the mere way the bright, clean, ordered water-side life came in at the open window? — the mere way Mme. de Vionnet, opposite him over their intensely white table-linen, their *omelette aux tomates*, their bottle of straw-colored chablis, thanked him for everything almost with the smile of a child, while her gray eyes moved in and out of their talk, back to the quarter of the warm spring air, in which early summer had already begun to throb, and then back to his face and their human questions."

Only attend till the beauty of that crowded moment reproduces itself in your consciousness, and you will not complain much of the difficult magic of its evocation.

Beyond almost all the English novelists of his time Henry James has applied his passion for beauty to the total form and composition of his stories. He cares little for the "slice of life," the loose episodic novel, the baggy autobiographical novel, so much in vogue of late, into which the author attempts to pitch the whole of contemporary life and to tell annually all that he knows and feels up to the date of publication, without other visible principle of selection. With extremely few exceptions his subjects present themselves to him either as "pictures" to be kept rigorously within the limits of a frame, or as "dramas" to be kept within the limits of a stage, or as alternations of "drama" with "picture." How he imposes upon himself the laws of painter and playwright, how he chooses his "center of composition," handles his "perspective," accumulates his "values," turns on the "lights" — all this he has told with extraordinary gusto in those prefaces which more illuminate the fine art of fiction than anything else — one is tempted to say, than everything else — on the subject. The point for us here is that he strives to make the chosen form and the intended effect govern with an "exquisite economy" every admitted detail. The ideal is to express everything that belongs in the "picture," everything that is *in* the relations of the persons of the drama, but nothing else.

V

His exacting esthetic sense determines the field no less than the form of his fiction. A quite definite social ideal conceived in the esthetic consciousness is implicit in his representation of a really *idle* leisure class — an ideal ultimately traceable to his own upbringing and to his early contact with the Emersonian rather than the Carlylean form of transcendentalism. He has a positive distaste for our contemporary hero — "the man who does things"; the *summum bonum* for him is not an action but a state of being — an untroubled awareness of beauty. Hence his manifested predilection for "highly civilized young Americans, born to an easy fortune and a tranquil destiny"; for artists who amateurishly sketch and loiter through lovely Italian springs, though conscious of "social duties" that await them beyond the Alps; for diplomats devoted to the theater and members of Parliament who dabble in paint; for Italian princesses and princes free from the cares of state; for French counts and countesses who have nothing to keep up but the traditions of their "race"; for English lords with no occupation but the quest of a lady; for American millionaires who have left "trade" three thousand miles behind them to collect impressions, curios, and sons-in-law in Europe. Objectors may justly complain that he seems unable to conceive of a really fine lady or a really fine gentleman or a really decent marriage without a more or less huge fortune in the background or in the foreground of the picture; and it may be added that to the sense of a truly "Emersonian" mind the clink and consideration of gold in most of his crucial instances is a harsh and profound note of vulgarity vibrating through his noble society. He is entirely sincere when he says, in speaking of Balzac, that the object of money is to enable one to forget it. Yet fine ladies, fine gentlemen, and fine society as he understands these matters are, to tell the hard truth, impossible except in the conditions created by affluence and leisure. In comparative poverty one may be good; but one cannot, in the Jamesian sense, be beautiful!

Society cannot in the Jamesian sense be beautiful till the pressures of untoward physical circumstances, of physical needs, and of engagements with " active life " are removed, and men and women are free to live " from within outward," subjecting themselves only to the environment and entering only the relationships dictated by the esthetic sense. Let us not undervalue the significance of this ideal, either with reference to life or with reference to literature. It is inadequate; but it has the high merit of being finely human. It had the precious virtue of utterly delivering Henry James from the riotous and unclean hands of the " naturalists." To it he owes the splendid distinction that when half the novelists of Europe, carried off their feet by the naturalistic drift of the age, began to go a-slumming in the muck and mire of civilization, to explore man's simian relationships, to exploit *la bête humaine* and *l'homme moyen sensuel,* to prove the ineluctability of flesh and fate and instinct and environment — he, with aristocratic contempt of them and their formulas and their works, withdrew farther and farther from them, drew proudly out of the drift of the age, and set his imagination the task of presenting the fairest specimens of humanity in a choice, sifted society tremendously disciplined by its own ideals but generally liberated from all other compelling forces. Precisely because he keeps mere carnality out of his picture, holds passion rigorously under stress, presents the interior of a refined consciousness — precisely for these reasons he can produce a more intense pleasure in the reader by the representation of a momentary gush of tears or a single swift embrace than most of our contemporaries can produce with chapter after chapter of storms and seductions.

The controlling principle in Henry James's imaginary world is neither religion nor morality nor physical necessity nor physical instinct. The controlling principle is a sense of style, under which vice, to adapt Burke's words, loses half its evil by losing all its grossness. In the noble society *noblesse,* and nothing else, obliges. Even in the early " international " novels we witness the transformation of Puritan morality, of which the sanction was religious, into a kind of chivalry, of which the sanctions are individual taste and class loyalty. Madame de Mauve, the lovely American married to a naughty French husband in that charming little masterpiece which bears her name, is not exhibited as preserving her " virtue " when she rejects her lover; she is exhibited as preserving her *fineness.* Her American lover acquiesces in his dismissal not from any sudden pang of conscience but from a sudden recognition that if he persists in his suit he will be doing precisely what the vulgar French world and one vulgar spectator in particular expect him to do. In the earlier novels such as 'Madame de Mauve,' 'Daisy Miller,' and 'The American,' the straightness, the innocence, the firmness of the American conscience are rather played up as beauties against the European background. Yet as early as 1878 he had begun, with the delightfully vivacious and witty 'Europeans,' his criticism of the intellectual dullness and emotional poverty of the New England sense of "righteousness" — a criticism wonderfully culminating in 'The Ambassadors' (1903), in which the highly perceptive Strether, sent to France to reclaim an erring son of New England, is himself converted to the European point of view.

Noblesse in the later novels inspires beauties of behavior beyond the reaches of the Puritan imagination. It is astonishing to observe how many heroes and heroines of the later period are called upon to attest their fineness by a firm clear-eyed mendacity. 'The Wings of a Dove,' for example, is a vast conspiracy of silence to keep a girl who knows she is dying from knowing that her friends know that she knows. To lie with a wry face is a blemish on one's character. "*I* lie well, thank God," says Mrs. Lowder, "when, as sometimes will happen, there's nothing else so good." In the same novel poor Densher, who rather hates lying, rises to it: "The single thing that was clear in complications was that, whatever happened, one was to behave as a gentleman — to which was added indeed the perhaps slightly less shining truth that complications might sometimes have their tedium beguiled by a study of the question of how a gentleman would behave."

When he is tempted to throw up his adventure in noble mendacity he is held to it in this way: as soon as he steps into the Palazzo Leporelli in Venice where the dying lady resides he sees "all the elements of the business compose, as painters called it, differently" — he sees himself as a figure in a Veronese picture and he lives up to the grand style of the picture. He actively fosters the "suppressions" which are "in the direct interest of everyone's good manners, everyone's really quite generous ideal."

The most elaborate and subtle of all James' tributes to the esthetic ideal in conduct is 'The Golden Bowl' — a picture in eight hundred pages of the relations existing between Maggie Verver and her husband the Prince, between Maggie's father Adam Verver and his second wife Charlotte, and between each one of the quadrangle and all the rest. Before the pair of marriages took place we are made to understand that an undefinedly intimate relation had existed between the Prince and Charlotte, of which Maggie and her father were unaware; and after the marriages we are made to understand that the undefinedly intimate relation was resumed. All four of the parties to this complex relationship are thoroughly civilized; they are persons fit for the highest society: that is to say, they have wealth, beauty, exquisite taste, and ability to tell a lie with a straight face. What will be the outcome? The outcome is that, without overt act, or plain speech, or displayed temper on any hand, each one by psychic tact divines "everything," and Mr. and Mrs. Verver quietly return to America. Why is the *liaison* dissolved with such celestial decorum? It is dissolved, because the "principals" in it perceive the esthetic "impossibility" of continuing their relations in that atmosphere of silent but lucid "awareness"; and it is dissolved with decorum because all the persons concerned are infinitely superior to the vulgarity of rows, ruptures, and public proceedings. The "criticism of life" implicit in the entire novel becomes superbly explicit in Maggie's vision of the ugliness and barbarousness of the behavior of ordinary mortals in like circumstances:

"She might fairly, as she watched them, have missed it [hot angry jealousy] as a lost thing; have yearned for it, for the straight vindictive view, the rights of resentment, the rages of jealousy, the protests of passion, as for something she had been cheated of not least: a range of feelings which for many women would have meant so much, but which for *her* husband's wife, for her father's daughter, figured nothing nearer to experience than a wild eastern caravan, looming into view with crude colors in the sun, fierce pipes in the air, high spears against the sky, all a thrill, a natural joy to mingle with, but turning off short before it reached her and plunging into other defiles."

Does not that description of Maggie's vision throb with a fine passion of its own — throb with the excitement of James' imaginative insight into the possible amenity of human intercourse in a society esthetically disciplined and controlled?

James's works throb with that fine passion from the beginning to the end — just as Pater's do. Criticism's favorite epithets for him hitherto have been "cold," "analytical," "scientific," "passionless," "pitiless" historian of the manners of a futile society. That view of him is doomed to disappear before the closer scrutiny which he demanded and which he deserves. He is not an historian of manners; he is a trenchant idealistic critic of life from the esthetic point of view.

He is not pitiless except in the exposure of the "ugly," which to his sense includes all forms of evil; in that task he is remorseless whether he is exposing the ugliness of American journalism as in 'The Reverberator,' or the ugliness of a thin nervous hysterical intellectualism and feminism as in 'The Bostonians,' or the ugliness of murder as in 'The Other House,' or the ugliness of irregular sexual relations as in 'What Maisie Knew,' or the ugliness of corrupted childhood as in 'The Turn of the Screw.' The deep-going uglinesses in the last three cases are presented with a superlative intenseness of artistic passion. If the effect is not thrilling in the first case and heartrending in the last two, it is because Anglo-Saxons are quite unaccustomed to having their deeps of terror and pity, their moral centers, touched through the esthetic nerves. Granting the fact, there is no reason why they should deny the presence of a passion of antipathy in a man to whose singular consciousness the objectionable inveterately takes the shape of the ugly.

What, however, is more incomprehensible is the general failure of criticism to recognize the ardor of his quite unscientific attachment to the beautiful. His alleged deficiency in charm, it is asserted, is due to the fact that he does not sympathize with or love any of his characters. The alleged fact is not a fact. He sympathizes intensely with all his artists and novelists, with all his connoisseurs of life, with all his multitude of miraculously perceptive persons, from the American homesick for England in the 'Passionate Pilgrim' through the young woman aware of the fineness of old furniture in 'The Spoils of Poynton' to Maggie and Mr. Verver in 'The Golden Bowl.' And he dotes, devoutly dotes, dotes in idolatry upon the enriched consciousness, the general awareness, and the physical loveliness of his women. He cannot "abide" a plain heroine, even if she is to be a criminal. Of Rose, the murderess in 'The Other House,' he says the most exquisite things — "She carries the years almost as you do, and her head better than any young woman I've ever seen. *Life is somehow becoming to her.*" In almost every novel that he wrote he touched some woman or other with the soft breath of pure esthetic adoration — a refining and exalting emotion which is the note of Sherringham's relation to Miriam in 'The Tragic Muse':

"Beauty was the principle of everything she did. . . . He could but call it a felicity and an importance incalculable, and but know that it connected itself with universal values. To see this force in operation, to sit within its radius and feel it shift and revolve and change and never fail, was a corrective to the depression, the humiliation, the bewilderment of life. It transported our troubled friend from the vulgar hour and the ugly fact; drew him to something that had no warrant but its sweetness, no name nor place save as the pure, the remote, the antique."

This is the "very ecstasy of love"; and for this virtue, in the years to come, one adept after another reading the thirty or forty volumes of James which anyone can read with ease and the fifteen or twenty richer volumes which demand closer application — for this virtue one adept after another, till a brave company gathers, is certain to say, "I discriminate; but I adore him!"

STUART P. SHERMAN

THE MADONNA OF THE FUTURE

From 'A Passionate Pilgrim, and Other Tales.' Copyright, 1875, by James R. Osgood & Co. Reprinted by permission of Houghton Mifflin Company, publishers, Boston

WE had been talking about the masters who had achieved but a single masterpiece — the artists and poets who but once in their lives had known the divine afflatus, and touched the high level of the best. Our host had been showing us a charming little cabinet picture by a painter whose name we had never heard, and who after this one spasmodic bid for fame had apparently relapsed into fatal mediocrity. There was some discussion as to the frequency of this phenomenon; during which I observed H—— sat silent, finishing his cigar with a meditative air, and looking at the picture which was being handed round the table. "I don't know how common a case it is," he said at last, "but I've seen it. I've known a poor fellow who painted his one masterpiece — and," he added with a smile, "he didn't even paint that. He made his bid for fame and missed it." We all knew H—— for a clever man who had seen much of men and manners, and had a great stock of reminiscences. Some one immediately questioned him further; and while I was engrossed with the raptures of my neighbor over the little picture, he was induced to tell his tale. If I were to doubt whether it would bear repeating, I should only have to remember how that charming woman our hostess, who had left the table, ventured back in rustling rose color to pronounce our lingering a want of gallantry, and finding us a listening circle had sunk into her chair in spite of our cigars, and heard the story out so graciously that when the catastrophe was reached, she glanced across at me and showed me a tender tear in each of her beautiful eyes.

It relates to my youth, and to Italy: two fine things! (H—— began). I had arrived late in the evening at Florence, and while I finished my bottle of wine at supper, had fancied that, tired traveler though I was, I might pay the city a finer compliment than by going vulgarly to bed. A narrow passage wandered darkly away out of the little square before my hotel, and looked as if it bored into the heart of Florence. I followed it, and at the end of ten minutes emerged upon a great piazza, filled only with the mild autumn moonlight. Opposite rose the Palazzo Vecchio like some huge civic fortress, with the great bell-tower springing from its embattled verge like a mountain pine from the edge of a cliff. At its base in its protected shadow gleamed certain dim sculptures which I wonderingly approached. One of the images on the left of the palace door was a magnificent colossus, shining through the dusky air like some embodied Defiance. In a moment I recognized him as Michael

Angelo's David. I turned with a certain relief from his sinister strength to a slender figure in bronze, stationed beneath the high, light loggia which opposes the free and elegant span of its arches to the dead masonry of the palace: a figure supremely shapely and graceful; gentle almost, in spite of his holding out with his light nervous arm the snaky head of the slaughtered Gorgon. His name is Perseus, and you may read his story, not in Greek mythology, but in the memoirs of Benvenuto Cellini. Glancing from one of these fine fellows to the other, I probably uttered some irrepressible commonplace of praise; for as if provoked by my voice, a man rose from the steps of the loggia where he had been sitting in the shadow, and addressed me in good English — a small slim personage, clad in a sort of black-velvet tunic (as it seemed), and with a mass of auburn hair, which gleamed in the moonlight, escaping from a little medieval berreta. In a tone of the most insinuating deference he asked me for my "impressions." He seemed picturesque, fantastic, slightly unreal. Hovering there in this consecrated neighborhood, he might have passed for the genius of esthetic hospitality — if the genius of esthetic hospitality were not commonly some shabby little custode, flourishing a calico pocket-handkerchief, and openly resentful of the divided franc. This fantasy was made none the less plausible by the brilliant tirade with which he greeted my embarrassed silence.

"I've known Florence long, sir, but I've never known her so lovely as tonight. It's as if the ghosts of her past were abroad in the empty streets. The present is sleeping; the past hovers about us like a dream made visible. Fancy the old Florentines strolling up in couples to pass judgment on the last performance of Michael, of Benvenuto! We should come in for a precious lesson if we might overhear what they say. The plainest burgher of them in his cap and gown had a taste in the matter! That was the prime of art, sir. The sun stood high in heaven, and his broad and equal blaze made the darkest places bright and the dullest eyes clear. We live in the evening of time! We grope in the gray dusk, carrying each our poor little taper of selfish and painful wisdom, holding it up to the great models and to the dim idea, and seeing nothing but overwhelming greatness and dimness. The days of illumination are gone! But do you know I fancy — I fancy" — and he grew suddenly almost familiar in this visionary fervor — "I fancy the light of that time rests upon us here for an hour! I have never seen the David so grand, the Perseus so fair! Even the inferior productions of John of Bologna and of Baccio Bandinelli seem to realize the artist's dream. I feel as if the moonlit air were charged with the secrets of the masters, and as if, standing here in religious contemplation, we might — we might witness a revelation!" Perceiving at this moment, I suppose, my halting comprehension reflected in my puzzled face, this interesting rhapsodist paused and blushed. Then with a melancholy smile, "You think me a moonstruck charlatan, I suppose. It's not my habit to hang about the piazza and pounce upon innocent tourists. But tonight I confess I'm under the charm. And then somehow I fancied you too were an artist!"

"I'm not an artist, I'm sorry to say, as you must understand the term. But pray make no apologies. I am also under the charm: your eloquent reflections have only deepened it."

"If you're not an artist, you're worthy to be one!" he rejoined with a bow. "A young man who arrives at Florence late in the evening, and instead of going prosaically to bed, or hanging over the travelers' book at his hotel, walks forth without loss of time to pay his devoirs to the beautiful, is a young man after my own heart!"

The mystery was suddenly solved: my friend was an American! He must have been, to take the picturesque so prodigiously to heart. "None the less so, I trust," I answered, "if the young man is a sordid New Yorker."

"New Yorkers," he solemnly proclaimed, "have been munificent patrons of art!"

For a moment I was alarmed. Was this midnight reverie mere Yankee enterprise, and was he simply a desperate brother of the brush who had posted himself here to extort an "order" from a sauntering tourist? But I was not called to defend myself. A great brazen note broke suddenly from the far-off summit of the bell-tower above us, and sounded the first stroke of midnight. My companion started, apologized for detaining me, and prepared to retire. But he seemed to offer so lively a promise of further entertainment that I was indisposed to part with him, and suggested that we should stroll homeward together. He cordially assented, so we turned out of the Piazza, passed down before the statued arcade of the Uffizi, and came out upon the Arno.

What course we took I hardly remember; but we roamed slowly about for an hour, my companion delivering by snatches a sort of moon-touched esthetic lecture. I listened in puzzled fascination, and wondered who the deuce he was. He confessed with a melancholy but all-respectful head-shake to his American origin. "We are the disinherited of Art!" he cried. "We are condemned to be superficial! We are excluded from the magic circle. The soil of American perception is a poor little barren artificial deposit. Yes! we are wedded to imperfection. An American, to excel, has just ten times as much to learn as a European. We lack the deeper sense. We have neither taste nor tact nor force. How should we have them? Our crude and garish climate, our silent past, our deafening present, the constant pressure about us of unlovely circumstance, are as void of all that nourishes and prompts and inspires the artist as my sad heart is void of bitterness in saying so! We poor aspirants must live in perpetual exile."

"You seem fairly at home in exile," I answered, "and Florence seems to me a very pretty Siberia. But do you know my own thought? Nothing is so idle as to talk about our want of a nutritive soil, of opportunity, or inspiration, and all the rest of it. The worthy part is to do something fine! There's no law in our glorious Constitution against that. Invent, create, achieve! No matter if you've to study fifty times as much as one of these! What else are you an artist for? Be you our Moses," I added, laughing and laying my hand on his shoulder, "and lead us out of the house of bondage!"

"Golden words — golden words, young man!" he cried with a tender smile. "'Invent, create, achieve!' Yes, that's our business: I know it well. Don't take me in Heaven's name for one of your barren complainers — querulous cynics who have neither talent nor faith! I'm at work!" — and he glanced about him and lowered his voice as if this were a quite peculiar secret — "I'm at work night and day. I've undertaken a *creation!* I'm no Moses; I'm only a poor, patient artist: but it would be a fine thing if I were to cause some slender stream of beauty to flow in our thirsty land! Don't think me a monster of conceit," he went on, as he saw me smile at the avidity with which he adopted my fantasy: "I confess that I'm in one of those moods when great things seem possible! This is one of my nervous nights — I dream waking! When the south wind blows over Florence at midnight, it seems to coax the soul from all the fair things locked away in her churches and galleries; it comes into my own little studio with the moonlight, and sets my heart beating too deeply for rest. You see I am always adding a thought to my conception! This evening I felt that I couldn't sleep unless I had communed with the genius of Michael!"

He seemed deeply versed in local history and tradition, and he expatiated *con amore* on the charms of Florence. I gathered that he was an old resident, and that he had taken the lovely city into his heart. "I owe her everything," he declared. "It's only since I came here that I have really lived, intellectually. One by one all profane desires, all mere worldly aims, have dropped away from me, and left me nothing but my pencil, my little note-book" (and he tapped his breast pocket), "and the worship of the pure masters — those who were pure because they were innocent, and those who were pure because they were strong!"

"And have you been very productive all this time?" I asked with amenity.

He was silent awhile before replying. "Not in the vulgar sense!" he said at last. "I have chosen never to manifest myself by imperfection. The good in every performance I have reabsorbed into the generative force of new creations; the bad — there's always plenty of that — I have religiously destroyed. I may say, with some satisfaction, that I have not added a mite to the rubbish of the world. As a proof of my conscientiousness" — and he stopped short and eyed me with extraordinary candor, as if the proof were to be overwhelming — "I've never sold a picture! 'At least no merchant traffics in my heart!' Do you remember the line in Browning? My little studio has never been profaned by superficial, feverish, mercenary work. It's a temple of labor, but of leisure! Art is long. If we work for ourselves, of course we must hurry. If we work for her, we must often pause. She can wait!"

This had brought us to my hotel door; somewhat to my relief, I confess, for I had begun to feel unequal to the society of a genius of this heroic strain. I left him, however, not without expressing a friendly hope that we should meet again. The next morning my curiosity had not abated: I was anxious to see him by common daylight. I counted upon meeting him in one of the many esthetic haunts of Florence, and I was gratified without delay. I found him in the course of the morning in the Tribune of the Uffizi — that little treasure chamber of perfect works. He had turned his back on the Venus de Medici, and with his arms resting on the railing which protects the pictures, and his head buried in his hands, he was lost in the contemplation of that superb triptych of Andrea Mantegna — a work which has neither the material splendor nor the commanding force of some of its neighbors, but which, glowing there with the loveliness of patient labor, suits possibly a more constant need of the soul. I looked at the picture for some time over his shoulder; at last, with a heavy sigh, he turned away and our eyes met. As he recognized me a deep blush rose to his face; he fancied perhaps that he had made a fool of himself overnight. But I offered him my hand with a frankness which assured him I was not a scoffer.

I knew him by his ardent *chevelure;* otherwise he was much altered. His midnight mood was over, and he looked as haggard as an actor by daylight. He was far older than I had supposed, and he had less bravery of costume and gesture. He seemed quite the poor, patient artist he had proclaimed himself, and the fact that he had never sold a picture was more obvious than glorious. His velvet coat was threadbare; and his short slouched hat, of an antique pattern, revealed a rustiness which marked it an "original," and not one of the picturesque reproductions which brethren of his craft affect. His eye was mild and heavy, and his expression singularly gentle and acquiescent; the more so for a certain pallid leanness of visage which I hardly knew whether to refer to the consuming fire of genius or to a meager diet. A very little talk, however, cleared his brow and brought back his eloquence.

"And this is your first visit to these enchanted halls?" he cried. "Happy, thrice happy youth!" And taking me by the arm, he prepared to lead me to each of the pre-eminent works in turn and show me the cream of the gallery. But before we left the Mantegna, he pressed my arm and gave it a loving look. "*He* was not in a hurry," he murmured. "He knew nothing of 'raw Haste, half-sister to Delay'!" How sound a critic my friend was, I am unable to say; but he was an extremely amusing one — overflowing with opinions, theories, and sympathies, with disquisition and gossip and anecdote. He was a shade too sentimental for my own sympathies, and I fancied he was rather too fond of superfine discriminations and of discovering subtle intentions in the shallow felicities of chance. At moments too he plunged into the sea of metaphysics, and floundered awhile in waters too deep for intellectual security. But his abounding knowledge and happy judgment told a touching story of long attentive hours in this worshipful company; there was a reproach to my wasteful saunterings in so devoted a culture of opportunity. "There are two moods," I remember his saying, "in which we may walk through galleries — the critical and the ideal. They seize us at their pleasure, and we can never tell which is to take its turn. The critical mood, oddly, is the genial one, the friendly, the condescending. It relishes the pretty trivialities of art, its vulgar clevernesses, its conscious graces. It has a kindly greeting for anything which looks as if, according to his light, the painter had enjoyed doing it — for the little Dutch cabbages and kettles, for the taper fingers and breezy mantles of late-coming Madonnas, for the little blue-hilled, pastoral, sceptical Italian landscapes. Then there are the days of fierce, fastidious longing — solemn feasts of the intellect — when all vulgar effort and all petty success is a weariness, and everything but the best — the best of the best — disgusts. In these hours we are relentless aristocrats of taste. We'll not take Michael for granted, we'll not swallow Raphael whole!"

The gallery of the Uffizi is not only rich in its possessions, but peculiarly fortunate in that fine architectural accident, as one may call it, which unites it — with the breadth of river and city between them — to those princely chambers of the Pitti Palace. The Louvre and the Vatican hardly give you such a sense of sustained inclosure as those long passages projected over street and stream to establish a sort of inviolate transition between the two palaces of art. We passed along the gallery in which those precious drawings by eminent hands hang chaste and gray above the swirl and murmur of the yellow Arno, and reached the ducal saloons of the Pitti. Ducal as they are, it must be confessed that they are imperfect as show-rooms, and that with their deep-set windows and their massive moldings it is rather a broken light that reaches the pictured walls. But here the masterpieces hang thick, and you seem to see them in a luminous atmosphere of their own. And the great saloons, with their superb dim ceilings, their outer wall in splendid shadow, and the somber opposite glow of mellow canvas and dusky gilding, make, themselves, almost as fine a picture as the Titians and Raphaels they imperfectly reveal. We lingered briefly before many a Raphael and Titian; but I saw my friend was impatient, and I suffered him at last to lead me directly to the goal of our journey — the most tenderly fair of Raphael's Virgins, the Madonna in the Chair. Of all the fine pictures of the world, it seemed to me this is the one with which criticism has least to do. None betrays less effort; less of the mechanism of effect and of the irrepressible discord between conception and result, which shows dimly in so many consummate works. Graceful, human, near to our sympathies as it is, it has nothing of manner, of method, nothing almost of style; it blooms there in rounded softness, as instinct with harmony as if it were an immediate exhalation of genius. The figure melts away the spectator's mind into a sort of passionate tenderness, which he knows not whether he has given to heavenly purity or to earthly charm. He is intoxicated with the fragrance of the tenderest blossom of maternity that ever bloomed on earth.

"That's what I call a fine picture," said my companion, after we had gazed awhile in silence. "I have a right to say so, for I've copied it so often and so carefully that I could repeat it now with my eyes shut. Other works are of Raphael: this *is* Raphael himself. Others you can praise, you can qualify, you can measure, explain, account for: this you can only love and admire. I don't know in what seeming he walked among men while this divine mood was upon him; but after it, surely, he could do nothing but die: this world had nothing more to teach him. Think of it awhile, my friend, and you'll admit that I'm not raving. Think of his seeing that spotless image not for a moment, for a day, in a happy dream, as a restless fever-fit — not as a poet in a five-minutes' frenzy, time to snatch his phrase and scribble his immortal stanza — but for days together, while the slow labor of the brush went on, while the foul vapors of life interposed, and the fancy ached with tension, fixed, radiant, distinct, as we see it now! What a master, certainly! But ah, what a seer!"

"Don't you imagine," I answered, "that he had a model, and that some pretty young woman —"

"As pretty a young woman as you please — it doesn't diminish the miracle! He took his hint, of course, and the young woman possibly sat smiling before his canvas. But meanwhile the painter's idea had taken wings. No lovely human outline could charm it to vulgar fact. He saw the fair form made perfect; he rose to the vision without tremor, without effort of wing; he communed with it face to face, and resolved into finer and lovelier truth the purity which completes it as the perfume completes the rose. That's what they call idealism: the word's vastly abused, but the thing is good. It's my own creed, at any rate. Lovely Madonna, model at once and muse, I call you to witness that I too am an idealist!"

"An idealist, then," I said half jocosely, wishing to provoke him to further utterance, "is a gentleman who says to Nature in the person of a beautiful girl, 'Go to, you're all wrong! Your fine is coarse, your bright is dim, your grace is *gaucherie*. This is the way you should have done it!' Isn't the chance against him?"

He turned upon me almost angrily, but perceiving the genial flavor of my sarcasm, he smiled gravely. "Look at that picture," he said, "and cease your irreverent mockery! Idealism is *that!* There's no explaining it; one must feel the flame! It says nothing to Nature, or to any beautiful girl, that they'll not both forgive! It says to the fair woman, 'Accept me as your artist-friend, lend me your beautiful face, trust me, help me, and your eyes shall be half my masterpiece!' No one so loves and respects the rich realities of nature as the artist whose imagination caresses and flatters them. He knows what a fact may hold (whether Raphael knew, you may judge by his portrait behind us there, of Tommaso Inghirami); but his fancy hovers about it as Ariel above the sleeping prince. There is only one Raphael, but an artist may still be an artist. As I said last night, the days of illumination are gone: visions are rare; we have to look long to see them. But in meditation we may still woo the ideal; round it, smooth it, perfect it. The result — the result — " here his voice faltered suddenly, and he fixed his eyes for a moment on the picture; when they met my own again they were full of tears — " the result may be less than this; but still it may be good, it may be *great!* " he cried with vehemence. " It may hang somewhere, in after years, in goodly company, and keep the artist's memory warm. Think of being known to mankind after some such fashion as this! of hanging here through the slow centuries in the gaze of an altered world, living on and on in the cunning of an eye and hand that are part of the dust of ages, a delight and a law to remote generations; making beauty a force, and purity an example! "

" Heaven forbid," I said smiling, " that I should take the wind out of your sails: but doesn't it occur to you that beside being strong in his genius, Raphael was happy in a certain good faith of which we have lost the trick? There are people, I know, who deny that his spotless Madonnas are anything more than pretty blondes of that period, enhanced by the Raphaelesque touch, which they declare is a profane touch. Be that as it may, people's religious and esthetic needs went hand in hand; and there was, as I may say, a demand for the Blessed Virgin, visible and adorable, which must have given firmness to the artist's hand. I'm afraid there is no demand now."

My companion seemed painfully puzzled; he shivered, as it were, in this chilling blast of scepticism. Then shaking his head with sublime confidence, " There is always a demand! " he cried: " that ineffable type is one of the eternal needs of man's heart; but pious souls long for it in silence, almost in shame. Let it appear, and this faith grows brave. How *should* it appear in this corrupt generation? It can't be made to order. It could indeed when the order came, trumpet-toned, from the lips of the Church herself, and was addressed to genius panting with inspiration. But it can spring now only from the soil of passionate labor and culture. Do you really fancy that while from time to time a man of complete artistic vision is born into the world, that image can perish? The man who paints it has painted everything. The subject admits of every perfection — form, color, expression, composition. It can be as simple as you please, and yet as rich; as broad and pure, and yet as full of delicate detail. Think of the chance for flesh in the little naked, nestling child, irradiating divinity; of the chance for drapery in the chaste and ample garment of the mother! Think of the great story you compress into that simple theme! Think, above all, of the mother's face and its ineffable suggestiveness; of the mingled burden of joy and trouble, the tenderness turned to worship, and the worship turned to far-seeing pity! Then look at it all in perfect line and lovely color, breathing truth and beauty and mastery! "

"'*Anch' io son pittore!*'"[1] I cried. "Unless I'm mistaken, you've a masterpiece on the stocks. If you put all that in, you'll do more than Raphael himself did. Let me know when your picture is finished, and wherever in the wide world I may be I'll post back to Florence and make my bow to — the *Madonna of the future!*"

He blushed vividly and gave a heavy sigh, half of protest, half of resignation. "I don't often mention my picture, in so many words. I detest this modern custom of premature publicity. A great work needs silence, privacy, mystery even. And then, do you know, people are so cruel, so frivolous, so unable to imagine a man's wishing to paint a Madonna at this time of day, that I've been laughed at — laughed at, sir!" And his blush deepened to crimson. "I don't know what has prompted me to be so frank and trustful with you. You look as if you wouldn't laugh at me. My dear young man," — and he laid his hand on my arm — "I'm worthy of respect. Whatever my talents may be, I'm honest. There's nothing grotesque in a pure ambition, or in a life devoted to it!"

There was something so sternly sincere in his look and tone that further questions seemed impertinent. I had repeated opportunity to ask them, however; for after this we spent much time together. Daily, for a fortnight, we met by appointment, to see the sights. He knew the city so well, he had strolled and lounged so often through its streets and churches and galleries, he was so deeply versed in its greater and lesser memories, so imbued with the local genius, that he was an altogether ideal *valet de place;* and I was glad enough to leave my Murray at home, and gather facts and opinions alike from his gossiping commentary. He talked of Florence like a lover, and admitted that it was a very old affair; he had lost his heart to her at first sight. "It's the fashion to talk of all cities as feminine," he said; "but as a rule, it's a monstrous mistake. Is Florence of the same sex as New York, as Chicago? She's the sole true woman of them all; one feels towards her as a lad in his teens feels to some beautiful older woman with a 'history.' It's a sort of aspiring gallantry she creates." This disinterested passion seemed to stand my friend in stead of the common social ties; he led a lonely life, apparently, and cared for nothing but his work. I was duly flattered by his having taken my frivolous self into his favor, and by his generous sacrifice of precious hours, as they must have been, to my society. We spent many of these hours among those early paintings in which Florence is so rich, returning ever and anon with restless sympathies to wonder whether these tender blossoms of art had not a vital fragrance and savor more precious than the full-fruited knowledge of the later works. We lingered often in the sepulchral chapel of San Lorenzo, and watched Michael Angelo's dim-visaged warrior sitting there like some awful Genius of Doubt and brooding behind his eternal mask upon the

[1] "I am a painter also" — Correggio's famous remark on inspecting a collection of paintings.

mysteries of life. We stood more than once in the little convent chambers where Fra Angelico wrought as if an angel indeed had held his hand, and gathered that sense of scattered dews and early bird-notes which makes an hour among his relics seem like a morning stroll in some monkish garden. We did all this and much more — wandered into dark chapels, damp courts, and dusty palace-rooms, in quest of lingering hints of fresco and lurking treasures of carving.

I was more and more impressed with my companion's prodigious singleness of purpose. Everything was a pretext for some wildly idealistic rhapsody or reverie. Nothing could be seen or said that did not end sooner or later in a glowing discourse on the true, the beautiful, and the good. If my friend was not a genius, he was certainly a monomaniac; and I found as great a fascination in watching the odd lights and shades of his character as if he had been a creature from another planet. He seemed indeed to know very little of this one, and lived and moved altogether in his own little province of art. A creature more unsullied by the world it is impossible to conceive; and I often thought it a flaw in his artistic character that he hadn't a harmless vice or two. It amused me vastly at times to think that he was of our shrewd Yankee race; but after all, there could be no better token of his American origin than this high esthetic fever. The very heat of his devotion was a sign of conversion: those born to European opportunity manage better to reconcile enthusiasm with comfort. He had, moreover, all our native mistrust for intellectual discretion and our native relish for sonorous superlatives. As a critic he was vastly more generous than just; and his mildest terms of approbation were "stupendous," "transcendent," and "incomparable." The small-change of admiration seemed to him no coin for a gentleman to handle; and yet, frank as he was intellectually, he was personally altogether a mystery. His professions somehow were all half-professions; and his allusions to his work and circumstances left something dimly ambiguous in the background. He was modest and proud, and never spoke of his domestic matters. He was evidently poor; yet he must have had some slender independence, since he could afford to make so merry over the fact that his culture of ideal beauty had never brought him a penny. His poverty, I suppose, was his motive for neither inviting me to his lodging nor mentioning its whereabouts. We met either in some public place or at my hotel, where I entertained him as freely as I might without appearing to be prompted by charity. He seemed always hungry, which was his nearest approach to a "redeeming vice." I made a point of asking no impertinent questions; but each time we met I ventured to make some respectful allusion to the *magnum opus* — to inquire, as it were, as to its health and progress. "We're getting on, with the Lord's help," he would say with a grave smile. "We're doing well. You see I have the grand advantage that I lose no time. These hours I spend with you are pure profit. They're *suggestive!* Just as the truly religious soul is always at worship, the genuine artist is always in labor. He takes his property wherever he finds it, and learns some precious secret from every object that stands up in the light. If you but knew the rapture of observation! I gather with every glance some hint for light, for color or relief! When I get home, I pour out my treasures into the lap of my Madonna. Oh, I'm not idle! *Nulla dies sine linea.*"

I was introduced in Florence to an American lady whose drawing-room had long formed an attractive place of reunion for the foreign residents. She lived on a fourth floor, and she was not rich; but she offered her visitors very good tea, little cakes at option, and conversation not quite to match. Her conversation had mainly an esthetic flavor, for Mrs. Coventry was famously "artistic." Her apartment was a sort of Pitti Palace *au petit pied*. She possessed "early masters" by the dozen — a cluster of Peruginos in her dining-room, a Giotto in her boudoir, an Andrea del Sarto over her parlor chimney-piece. Backed by these treasures, and by innumerable bronzes, mosaics, majolica dishes, and little worm-eaten diptychs showing angular saints on gilded panels, our hostess enjoyed the dignity of a sort of high-priestess of the arts. She always wore on her bosom a huge miniature copy of the Madonna della Seggiola. Gaining her ear quietly one evening, I asked her whether she knew that remarkable man Mr. Theobald.

"Know him!" she exclaimed; "know poor Theobald! All Florence knows him — his flame-colored locks, his black-velvet coat, his interminable harangues on the beautiful, and his wondrous Madonna that mortal eye has never seen, and that mortal patience has quite given up expecting."

"Really," I cried, "you don't believe in his Madonna?"

"My dear ingenuous youth," rejoined my shrewd friend, "has he made a convert of you? Well, we all believed in him once: he came down upon Florence and took the town by storm. Another Raphael, at the very least, had been born among men, and poor dear America was to have the credit of him. Hadn't he the very hair of Raphael flowing down on his shoulders? The hair, alas, but not the head! We swallowed him whole, however; we hung upon his lips and proclaimed his genius on the house-tops. The women were all dying to sit to him for their portraits and be made immortal, like Leonardo's Joconde. We decided that his manner was a good deal like Leonardo's — mysterious and inscrutable and fascinating. Mysterious it certainly was; mystery was the beginning and the end of it. The months passed by, and the miracle hung fire; our master never produced his masterpiece. He passed hours in the galleries and churches, posturing, musing, and gazing; he talked more than ever about the beautiful — but he never put brush to canvas. We had all subscribed, as it were, to the great performance; but as it never came off, people began to ask for their money again. I was one of the last of the faithful; I carried devotion so far as to sit to him for my head. If you could have seen the horrible creature he made of me, you would admit that even a woman with no more vanity than will tie her bonnet straight must have cooled off then. The man didn't know the very alphabet of drawing! His strong point, he intimated, was his sentiment; but is it a consolation, when one has been painted a fright, to know it has been done with peculiar gusto? One by one, I confess, we fell away from the faith; and Mr. Theobald didn't lift his little finger to preserve us. At the first hint that we were tired of waiting and that we should like the show to begin, he was off in a huff. 'Great work requires time, contemplation, privacy, mystery! O ye of little faith!' We answered that we didn't insist on a great work; that the five-act tragedy might come at his convenience; that we merely asked for something to keep us from yawning, some inexpensive little *lever de rideau*. Hereupon the poor man took his stand as a genius misconceived and persecuted, an *âme méconnue,* and washed his hands of us from that hour! Now, I believe he does me the honor to consider me the head and front of the conspiracy formed to nip his glory in the bud — a bud that has taken twenty years to blossom. Ask him if he knows me, and he'll tell you I'm a horribly ugly old woman who has vowed his destruction because he wouldn't paint her portrait as a pendant to Titian's Flora. I fancy that since then he has had none but chance followers: innocent strangers like yourself, who have taken him at his word. The mountain's still in labor; I've not heard that the mouse has been born. I pass him once in a while in the galleries, and he fixes his great dark eyes on me with a sublimity of indifference, as if I were a bad copy of a Sassoferrato! It is a long time ago now that I heard that he was making studies for a Madonna who was to be a *résumé* of all the other Madonnas of the Italian school — like that antique Venus who borrowed a nose from one great image and an ankle from another. It's certainly a masterly idea. The parts may be fine, but when I think of my unhappy portrait I tremble for the whole. He has communicated this striking idea under the pledge of solemn secrecy to fifty chosen spirits — to every one he has ever been able to buttonhole for five minutes. I suppose he wants to get an order for it, and he's not to blame; for Heaven knows how he lives. — I see by your blush," my hostess frankly continued, "that you have been honored with his confidence. You needn't be ashamed, my dear young man: a man of your age is none the worse for a certain generous credulity. Only allow me to give you a word of advice: keep your credulity out of your pockets! Don't pay for the picture till it's delivered. You've not been treated to a peep at it, I imagine. No more have your fifty predecessors in the faith. There are people who doubt whether there is any picture to be seen. I fancy, myself, that if one were to get into his studio, one would find something very like the picture in that tale of Balzac's — a mere mass of incoherent scratches and daubs, a jumble of dead paint!"

I listened to this pungent recital in silent wonder. It had a painfully plausible sound, and was not inconsistent with certain shy suspicions of my own. My hostess was a clever woman, and presumably a generous one. I determined to let my judgment wait upon events. Possibly she was right; but if she was wrong, she was cruelly wrong! Her version of my friend's eccentricities made me impatient to see him again and examine him in the light of public opinion. On our next meeting, I immediately asked him if he knew Mrs. Coventry. He laid his hand on my arm and gave me a sad smile. "Has she taxed *your* gallantry at last?" he asked. "She's a foolish woman. She's frivolous and heartless, and she pretends to be serious and kind. She prattles about Giotto's second manner and Vittoria Colonna's liaison with 'Michael' — one would think that Michael lived across the way and was expected in to take a hand at whist — but she knows as little about art, and about the conditions of production, as I know about Buddhism. — She profanes sacred words," he added more vehemently, after a pause. "She cares for you only as some one to hand teacups in that horrible mendacious little parlor of hers, with its trumpery Peruginos! If you can't dash off a new picture every three days, and let her hand it round among her guests, she tells them in plain English you're an impostor!"

This attempt of mine to test Mrs. Coventry's accuracy was made in the course of a late afternoon walk to the quiet old church of San Miniato, on one of the hilltops which directly overlook the city, from whose gate you are guided to it by a stony and cypress-bordered walk, which seems a most fitting avenue to a shrine. No spot is more propitious to lingering repose [2] than the broad terrace in front of the church; where, lounging against the parapet, you may glance in slow alternation from the black and yellow marbles of the church façade, seamed and cracked with time and wind-sown with a tender flora of its own, down to the full domes and slender towers of Florence, and over to the blue sweep of the wide-mouthed cup of mountains into whose hollow the little treasure-city has been dropped. I had proposed, as a diversion from the painful memories evoked by Mrs. Coventry's name, that Theobald should go with me the next evening to the opera, where some rarely played work was to be given. He declined, as I had half expected; for I had observed that he regularly kept his evenings in reserve, and never alluded to his manner of passing them. "You have reminded me before," I said smiling, "of that charming speech of the Florentine painter in Alfred de Musset's 'Lorenzaccio': — 'I do no harm to any one. I pass my days in my studio. On Sunday I go to the Annunziata, or to Santa Maria: the monks think I have a voice; they dress me in a white gown and a red cap, and I take a share in the choruses; sometimes I do a little solo: these are the only times I go into public. In the evening I visit my sweetheart; when the night is fine, we pass it on her balcony.' I don't know whether you have a sweetheart, or whether she has a balcony. But if you're so happy, it's certainly better than trying to find a charm in a third-rate *prima donna*."

He made no immediate response, but at last he turned to me solemnly. "Can you look upon a beautiful woman with reverent eyes?"

[2] 1869.

"Really," I said, "I don't pretend to be sheepish, but I should be sorry to think I was impudent." And I asked him what in the world he meant. When at last I had assured him that I could undertake to temper admiration with respect, he informed me, with an air of religious mystery, that it was in his power to introduce me to the most beautiful woman in Italy. "A beauty with a soul!"

"Upon my word," I cried, "you're extremely fortunate. I shall rejoice to witness the conjunction."

"This woman's beauty," he answered, "is a lesson, a morality, a poem! It's my daily study."

Of course, after this, I lost no time in reminding him of what, before we parted, had taken the shape of a promise. "I feel somehow," he had said, "as if it were a sort of violation of that privacy in which I have always contemplated her beauty. This is friendship, my friend. No hint of her existence has ever fallen from my lips. But with too great a familiarity we are apt to lose a sense of the real value of things, and you perhaps will throw some new light upon it and offer a fresher interpretation." We went accordingly by appointment to a certain ancient house in the heart of Florence — the precinct of the Mercato Vecchio — and climbed a dark steep staircase to the very summit of the edifice. Theobald's beauty seemed as jealously exalted above the line of common vision as the Belle aux Cheveux d'Or in her tower-top. He passed without knocking into the dark vestibule of a small apartment, and flinging open an inner door, ushered me into a small saloon. The room seemed mean and somber, though I caught a glimpse of white curtains swaying gently at an open window. At a table, near a lamp, sat a woman dressed in black, working at a piece of embroidery. As Theobald entered, she looked up calmly, with a smile; but seeing me, she made a movement of surprise, and rose with a kind of stately grace. Theobald stepped forward, took her hand and kissed it, with an indescribable air of immemorial usage. As he bent his head, she looked at me askance, and I thought she blushed.

"Behold the Serafina!" said Theobald frankly, waving me forward. "This is a friend, and a lover of the arts," he added, introducing me. I received a smile, a courtesy, and a request to be seated.

The most beautiful woman in Italy was a person of a generous Italian type, and of a great simplicity of demeanor. Seated again at her lamp, with her embroidery, she seemed to have nothing whatever to say. Theobald, bending towards her in a sort of Platonic ecstasy, asked her a dozen paternally tender questions as to her health, her state of mind, her occupations, and the progress of her embroidery, which he examined minutely and summoned me to admire. It was some portion of an ecclesiastical vestment — yellow satin wrought with an elaborate design of silver and gold. She made answer in a full, rich voice, but with a brevity which I hesitated whether to attribute to native reserve or to the profane constraint of my presence. She had been that morning to confession; she had also been to market, and had bought a chicken for dinner. She felt very happy; she had nothing to complain of, except that the people for whom she was making her vestment, and who furnished her materials, should be willing to put such rotten silver thread into the garment, as one might say, of the Lord. From time to time, as she took her slow stitches, she raised her eyes and covered me with a glance which seemed at first to denote a placid curiosity; but in which, as I saw it repeated, I thought I perceived the dim glimmer of an attempt to establish an understanding with me at the expense of our companion. Meanwhile, as mindful as possible of Theobald's injunction of reverence, I considered the lady's personal claims to the fine compliment he had paid her.

That she was indeed a beautiful woman I perceived, after recovering from the surprise of finding her without the freshness of youth. Her beauty was of a sort which in losing youth loses little of its essential charm, expressed for the most part as it was in form and structure, and as Theobald would have said, in "composition." She was broad and ample, low-browed and large-eyed, dark and pale. Her thick brown hair hung low beside her cheek and ear, and seemed to drape her head with a covering as chaste and formal as the veil of a nun. The poise and carriage of her head was admirably free and noble, and the more effective that their freedom was at moments discreetly corrected by a little sanctimonious droop, which harmonized admirably with the level gaze of her dark and quiet eye. A strong, serene physical nature, and the placid temper which comes of no nerves and no troubles, seemed this lady's comfortable portion. She was dressed in plain dull black, save for a sort of dark-blue kerchief which was folded across her bosom and exposed a glimpse of her massive throat. Over this kerchief was suspended a little silver cross. I admired her greatly, and yet with a large reserve. A certain mild intellectual apathy belonged properly to her type of beauty, and had always seemed to round and enrich it; but this *bourgeoise* Egeria, if I viewed her right, betrayed a rather vulgar stagnation of mind. There might have been once a dim spiritual light in her face; but it had long since begun to wane. And furthermore, in plain prose, she was growing stout. My disappointment amounted very nearly to complete disenchantment when Theobald, as if to facilitate my covert inspection, declaring that the lamp was very dim and that she would ruin her eyes without more light, rose and fetched a couple of candles from the mantelpiece, which he placed lighted on the table. In this brighter illumination I perceived that our hostess was decidedly an elderly woman. She was neither haggard nor worn nor gray: she was simply coarse. The "soul" which Theobald had promised seemed scarcely worth making such a point of; it was no deeper mystery than a sort of matronly mildness of lip and brow. I would have been ready even to declare that that sanctified bend of the head was nothing more than the trick of a person constantly working at embroidery. It occurred to me even that it was a trick of a less innocent sort; for in spite of the mellow quietude of her wits, this stately needlewoman dropped a hint that she took the situation rather less *au sérieux* than her friend. When he rose to light the candles, she looked across at me with a quick, intelligent smile, and tapped her forehead with her forefinger; then, as from a sudden feeling of compassionate loyalty to poor Theobald I preserved a blank face, she gave a little shrug and resumed her work.

What was the relation of this singular couple? Was he the most ardent of friends, or the most reverent of lovers? Did she regard him as an eccentric youth whose benevolent admiration of her beauty she was not ill pleased to humor, at this small cost of having him climb into her little parlor and gossip of summer nights? With her decent and somber dress, her simple gravity, and that fine piece of priestly needlework, she looked like some pious lay member of a sisterhood, living by special permission outside her convent walls. Or was she maintained here aloft by her friend in comfortable leisure, so that he might have before him the perfect eternal type, uncorrupted and untarnished by the struggle for existence? Her shapely hands, I observed, were very fair and white; they lacked the traces of what is called "honest toil."

"And the pictures, how do they come on?" she asked of Theobald after a long pause.

"Finely, finely! I have here a friend whose sympathy and encouragement give me new faith and ardor."

Our hostess turned to me; gazed at me a moment rather inscrutably; and then, tapping her forehead with the gesture she had used a minute before, "He has a magnificent genius!" she said with perfect gravity.

"I am inclined to think so," I answered with a smile.

"Eh, why do you smile?" she cried. "If you doubt it, you must see the *bambino!*" And she took the lamp and conducted me to the other side of the room, where on the wall, in a plain black frame, hung a large drawing in red chalk. Beneath it was festooned a little bowl for holy water. The drawing represented a very young child, entirely naked, half nestling back against his mother's gown, but with his two little arms outstretched, as if in the act of benediction. It was executed with singular freedom and power, and yet seemed vivid with the sacred bloom of infancy. A sort of dimpled elegance and grace, mingled with its boldness, recalled the touch of Correggio. "That's what he can do!" said my hostess. "It's the blessed little boy whom I lost. It's his very image, and the Signor Teobaldo gave it me as a gift. He has given me many things beside!"

I looked at the picture for some time, and admired it vastly. Turning back to Theobald, I assured him that if it were hung among the drawings in the Uffizi and labeled with a glorious name, it would hold its own. My praise seemed to give him extreme pleasure; he pressed my hands, and his eyes filled with tears. It moved him apparently with the desire to expatiate on the history of the drawing; for he rose and made his adieux to our companion, kissing her hand with the same mild ardor as before. It occurred to me that the offer of a similar piece of gallantry on my own part might help me to know what manner of woman she was. When she perceived my intention, she withdrew her hand, dropped her eyes solemnly, and made me a severe courtesy. Theobald took my arm and led me rapidly into the street.

"And what do you think of the divine Serafina?" he cried with fervor.

"It's certainly good solid beauty!" I answered.

He eyed me an instant askance, and then seemed hurried along by the current of remembrance. "You should have seen the mother and the child together, seen them as I first saw them — the mother with her head draped in a shawl, a divine trouble in her face, and the *bambino* pressed to her bosom. You would have said, I think, that Raphael had found his match in common chance. I was coming in, one summer night, from a long walk in the country, when I met this apparition at the city gate. The woman held out her hand. I hardly knew whether to say, 'What do you want?' or to fall down and worship. She asked for a little money. I saw that she was beautiful and pale. She might have stepped out of the stable of Bethlehem! I gave her money and helped her on her way into the town. I had guessed her story. She too was a maiden mother, and she had been turned out into the world in her shame. I felt in all my pulses that here was my subject marvelously realized. I felt like one of the old convent artists who had had a vision. I rescued the poor creatures, cherished them, watched them as I would have done some precious work of art, some lovely fragment of fresco discovered in a moldering cloister. In a month — as if to deepen and consecrate the pathos of it all — the poor little child died. When she felt that he was going, she held him up to me for ten minutes, and I made that sketch. You saw a feverish haste in it, I suppose: I wanted to spare the poor little mortal the pain of his position. After that, I doubly valued the mother. She is the simplest, sweetest, most natural creature that ever bloomed in this brave old land of Italy. She lives in the memory of her child, in her gratitude for the scanty kindness I have been able to show her, and in her simple religion! She's not even conscious of her beauty; my admiration has never made her vain. Heaven knows I've made no secret of it. You must have observed the singular transparency of her expression, the lovely modesty of her glance. And was there ever such a truly virginal brow, such a natural classic elegance in the wave of the hair and the arch of the forehead? I've studied her; I may say I know her. I've absorbed her little by little; my mind is stamped and imbued, and I have determined now to clinch the impression: I shall at last invite her to sit for me!"

"'At last' — 'at last'?" I repeated in much amazement. "Do you mean that she has never done so yet?"

"I've not really had — a — a sitting," said Theobald, speaking very slowly. "I've taken notes, you know; I've got my grand fundamental impression. That's the great thing! But I've not actually had her as a model, posed and draped and lighted, before my easel."

What had become for the moment of my perception and my tact, I am at a loss to say; in their absence I was unable to repress headlong exclamation. I was destined to regret it. We had stopped at a turning, beneath a lamp. "My poor friend," I exclaimed, laying my hand on his shoulder, "you've *dawdled!* She's an old, old woman — for a Madonna!"

It was as if I had brutally struck him; I shall never forget the long, slow, almost ghastly look of pain with which he answered me. "Dawdled — old, old!" he stammered. "Are you joking?"

"Why, my dear fellow, I suppose you don't take the woman for twenty?"

He drew a long breath and leaned against a house, looking at me with questioning, protesting, reproachful eyes; at last, starting forward and grasping my arm — "Answer me solemnly: does she seem to you truly old? Is she wrinkled, is she faded, am I blind?"

Then at last I understood the immensity of his illusion; how one by one the noiseless years had ebbed away, and left him brooding in charmed inaction, forever preparing for a work forever deferred. It seemed to me almost a kindness now to tell him the plain truth. "I should be sorry to say you're blind," I answered, "but I think you're deceived. You've lost time in effortless contemplation. Your friend was once young and fresh and virginal; but I protest that was some years ago. Still, she has *de beaux restes!* By all means make her sit for you!" I broke down: his face was too horribly reproachful.

He took off his hat and stood passing his handkerchief mechanically over his forehead. "*De beaux restes?* I thank you for sparing me the plain English. I must make up my Madonna out of *de beaux restes!* What a masterpiece she'll be! Old — old! Old — old!" he murmured.

"Never mind her age," I cried, revolted at what I had done, "never mind my impression of her! You have your memory, your notes, your genius. Finish your picture in a month. I proclaim it beforehand a masterpiece, and I hereby offer you for it any sum you may choose to ask."

He stared, but he seemed scarcely to understand me. "Old — old!" he kept stupidly repeating. "If she is old, what am I? If her beauty has faded, where — where is my strength? Has life been a dream? Have I worshiped too long — have I loved too well?" The charm, in truth, was broken. That the chord of illusion should have snapped at my light, accidental touch showed how it had been weakened by excessive tension. The poor fellow's sense of wasted time, of vanished opportunity, seemed to roll in upon his soul in waves of darkness. He suddenly dropped his head and burst into tears.

I led him homeward with all possible tenderness; but I attempted neither to check his grief, to restore his equanimity, nor to unsay the hard truth. When we reached my hotel I tried to induce him to come in. "We'll drink a glass of wine," I said, smiling, "to the completion of the Madonna."

With a violent effort he held up his head, mused for a moment with a formidably somber frown, and then giving me his hand, "I'll finish it," he cried, "in a month! No, in a fortnight! After all, I have it *here!*" and he tapped his forehead. "Of course she's old! She can afford to have it said of her — a woman who has made twenty years pass like a twelvemonth! Old — old! Why, sir, she shall be eternal!"

I wished to see him safely to his own door; but he waved me back and walked away with an air of resolution, whistling and swinging his cane. I waited a moment, and then followed him at a distance, and saw him proceed to cross the Santa Trinità Bridge. When he reached the middle he suddenly paused, as if his strength had deserted him, and leaned upon the parapet gazing over into the river. I was careful to keep him in sight; I confess that I passed ten very nervous minutes. He recovered himself at last, and went his way, slowly and with hanging head.

That I should have really startled poor Theobald into a bolder use of his long-garnered stores of knowledge and taste, into the vulgar effort and hazard of production, seemed at first reason enough for his continued silence and absence; but as day followed day without his either calling or sending me a line, and without my meeting him in his customary haunts — in the galleries, in the chapel at San Lorenzo, or strolling between the Arno-side and the great hedge screen of verdure which, along the drive of the Cascine, throws the fair occupants of barouche and phaeton into such becoming relief — as for more than a week I got neither tidings nor sight of him, I began to fear that I had fatally offended him; and that instead of giving wholesome impetus to his talent, I had brutally paralyzed it. I had a wretched suspicion that I had made him ill. My stay at Florence was drawing to a close; and it was important that before resuming my journey I should assure myself of the truth. Theobald to the last had kept his lodging a mystery, and I was altogether at a loss where to look for him. The simplest course was to make inquiry of the beauty of the Mercato Vecchio; and I confess that unsatisfied curiosity as to the lady herself counseled it as well. Perhaps I had done her injustice, and she was as immortally fresh and fair as he conceived her. I was at any rate anxious to behold once more the ripe enchantress who had made twenty years pass as a twelvemonth. I repaired accordingly one morning to her abode, climbed the interminable staircase, and reached her door. It stood ajar; and as I hesitated whether to enter, a little serving-maid came clattering out with an empty kettle, as if she had just performed some savory errand. The inner door too was open; so I crossed the little vestibule and entered the room in which I had formerly been received. It had not its evening aspect. The table, or one end of it, was spread for a late breakfast; and before it sat a gentleman — an individual at least of the male sex — dealing justice upon a beefsteak and onions and a bottle of wine. At his elbow, in friendly proximity, was placed the lady of the house. Her attitude as I entered was not that of an enchantress. With one hand she held in her lap a plate of smoking macaroni; with the other she had lifted high in air one of the pendulous filaments of this succulent compound, and was in the act of slipping it gently down her throat. On the uncovered end of the table, facing her companion, were ranged half a dozen small statuettes, of some snuff-colored substance resembling terra-cotta. He, brandishing his knife with ardor, was apparently descanting on their merits.

Evidently I darkened the door. My hostess dropped her macaroni — into her mouth, and rose hastily with a harsh exclamation and a flushed face. I immediately perceived that the Signora Serafina's secret was even better worth knowing than I had supposed, and that the way to learn it was to take it for granted. I summoned my best Italian, I smiled and bowed and apologized for my intrusion; and in a moment, whether or no I had dispelled the lady's irritation, I had at least stimulated her prudence. I was welcome, she said; I must take a seat. This was another friend of hers — also an artist, she declared with a smile which was almost amiable. Her companion wiped his mustache and bowed with great civility. I saw at a glance that he was equal to the situation. He was presumably the author of the statuettes on the table, and he knew a money-spending *forestiere* when he saw one. He was a small, wiry man, with a clever, impudent, tossed-up nose, a sharp little black eye, and waxed ends to his mustache. On the side of his head he wore jauntily a little crimson velvet smoking-cap, and I observed that his feet were incased in brilliant slippers. On Serafina's remarking with dignity that I was the friend of Mr. Theobald, he broke out into that fantastic French of which Italians are so insistently lavish, and declared with fervor that Mr. Theobald was a magnificent genius.

"I'm sure I don't know," I answered with a shrug. "If you're in a position to affirm it, you have the advantage of me. I've seen nothing from his hand but the *bambino* yonder, which certainly is fine."

He declared that the *bambino* was a masterpiece, a pure Correggio. It was only a pity, he added with a knowing laugh, that the sketch had not been made on some good bit of honeycombed old panel. The stately Serafina hereupon protested that Mr. Theobald was the soul of honor, and that he would never lend himself to a deceit. "I'm not a judge of genius," she said, "and I know nothing of pictures. I'm but a poor simple widow; but I know that the Signor Teobaldo has the heart of an angel and the virtue of a saint. — He's my benefactor," she added sententiously. The afterglow of the somewhat sinister flush with which she had greeted me still lingered in her cheek, and perhaps did not favor her beauty: I could not but fancy it a wise custom of Theobald's to visit her only by candlelight. She was coarse, and her poor adorer was a poet.

"I have the greatest esteem for him," I said: "it is for this reason that I have been uneasy at not seeing him for ten days. Have you seen him? Is he perhaps ill?"

"Ill! Heaven forbid!" cried Serafina, with genuine vehemence.

Her companion uttered a rapid expletive, and reproached her with not having been to see him. She hesitated a moment; then she simpered the least bit and bridled. "He comes to see me — without reproach! But it would not be the same for me to go to him, though indeed you may almost call him a man of holy life."

"He has the greatest admiration for you," I said. "He would have been honored by your visit."

She looked at me a moment sharply. "More admiration than you. Admit that!" Of course I protested with all the eloquence at my command; and my mysterious hostess then confessed that she had taken no fancy to me on my former visit, and that, Theobald not having returned, she believed I had poisoned his mind against her. "It would be no kindness to the poor gentleman, I can tell you that," she said. "He has come to see me every evening for years. It's a long friendship! No one knows him as well as I."

"I don't pretend to know him, or to understand him," I said. "He's a mystery! Nevertheless, he seems to me a little —" And I touched my forehead and waved my hand in the air.

Serafina glanced at her companion a moment, as if for inspiration. He contented himself with shrugging his shoulders, as he filled his glass again. The *padrona* hereupon gave me a more softly insinuating smile than would have seemed likely to bloom on so candid a brow. "It's for that that I love him!" she said. "The world has so little kindness for such persons. It laughs at them, and despises them, and cheats them. He is too good for this wicked life! It's his fancy that he finds a little Paradise up here in my poor apartment. If he thinks so, how can I help it? He has a strange belief — really, I ought to be ashamed to tell you — that I resemble the Blessed Virgin: Heaven forgive me! I let him think what he pleases, so long as it makes him happy. He was very kind to me once, and I am not one that forgets a favor. So I receive him every evening civilly, and ask after his health, and let him look at me on this side and that! For that matter, I may say it without vanity, I was worth looking at once! And he's not always amusing, poor man! He sits sometimes for an hour without speaking a word, or else he talks away, without stopping, on art and nature, and beauty and duty, and fifty fine things that are all so much Latin to me. I beg you to understand that he has never said a word to me that I mightn't decently listen to. He may be a little cracked, but he's one of the saints."

"Eh!" cried the man, "the saints were all a little cracked!"

Serafina, I fancied, left part of her story untold; but she told enough of it to make poor Theobald's own statement seem intensely pathetic in its exalted simplicity. "It's a strange fortune, certainly," she went on, "to have such a friend as this dear man — a friend who's less than a lover and more than a friend." I glanced at her companion, who preserved an impenetrable smile, twisted the end of his mustache, and disposed of a copious mouthful. Was *he* less than a lover? "But what will you have?" Serafina pursued. "In this hard world one mustn't ask too many questions; one must take what comes and keep what one gets. I've kept my good friend for twenty years, and I do hope that at this time of day, signore, you've not come to turn him against me!"

I assured her that I had no such design, and that I should vastly regret disturbing Mr. Theobald's habits or convictions. On the contrary, I was alarmed about him, and I should immediately go in search of him. She gave me his address, and a florid account of her sufferings at his non-appearance. She had not been to him, for various reasons; chiefly because she was afraid of displeasing him, as he had always made such a mystery of his home.

"You might have sent this gentleman!" I ventured to suggest.

"Ah," cried the gentleman, "he admires the Signora Serafina, but he wouldn't admire me." And then, confidentially, with his finger on his nose, "He's a purist!"

I was about to withdraw, on the promise that I would inform the Signora Serafina of my friend's condition, when her companion, who had risen from table and girded his loins apparently for the onset, grasped me gently by the arm, and led me before the row of statuettes. "I perceive by your conversation, signore, that you are a patron of the arts. Allow me to request your honorable attention for these modest products of my own ingenuity. They are brand-new, fresh from my atelier, and have never been exhibited in public. I have brought them here to receive the verdict of this dear lady, who is a good critic, for all she may pretend to the contrary. I am the inventor of this peculiar style of statuette — of subject, manner, material, everything. Touch them, I pray you; handle them: you needn't fear. Delicate as they look, it is impossible they should break! My various creations have met with great success. They are especially admired by Americans. I have sent them all over Europe — to London, Paris, Vienna! You may have observed some little specimens in Paris, on the Boulevard, in a shop of which they constitute the specialty. There is always a crowd about the window. They form a very pleasing ornament for the mantel-shelf of a gay young bachelor, for the boudoir of a pretty woman. You couldn't make a prettier present to a person with whom you wished to exchange a harmless joke. It is not classic art, signore, of course; but between ourselves, isn't classic art sometimes rather a bore? Caricature, burlesque — *la charge,* as the French say — has hitherto been confined to paper, to the pen and pencil. Now, it has been my inspiration to introduce it into statuary. For this purpose I have invented a peculiar plastic compound which you will permit me not to divulge. That's my secret, signore! It's as light, you perceive, as cork, and yet as firm as alabaster! I frankly confess that I really pride myself as much on this little stroke of chemical ingenuity as upon the other element of novelty in my creations — my types. What do you say to my types, signore? The idea is bold: does it strike you as happy? Cats and monkeys, monkeys and cats — all human life is there! Human life, of course I mean, viewed with the eye of the satirist! To combine sculpture and satire, signore, has been my unprecedented ambition. I flatter myself that I have not egregiously failed."

As this jaunty Juvenal of the chimneypiece delivered himself of his persuasive allocution, he took up his little groups successively from the table, held them aloft, turned them about, rapped them with his knuckles, and gazed at them lovingly with his head on one side. They consisted each of a cat and a monkey, fantastically draped, in some preposterously sentimental conjunction. They exhibited a certain sameness of motive, and illustrated chiefly the different phases of what, in delicate terms, may be called gallantry and coquetry; but they were strikingly clever and expressive, and were at once very perfect cats and monkeys and very natural men and women. I confess, however, that they failed to amuse me. I was doubtless not in a mood to enjoy them, for they seemed to me peculiarly cynical and vulgar. Their imitative felicity was revolting. As I looked askance at the complacent little artist, brandishing them between finger and thumb, and caressing them with an amorous eye, he seemed to me himself little more than an exceptionally intelligent ape. I mustered an admiring grin, however, and he blew another blast. "My figures are studied from life! I have a little menagerie of monkeys whose frolics I contemplate by the hour. As for the cats, one has only to look out of one's back window! Since I have begun to examine these expressive little brutes, I have made many profound observations. Speaking, signore, to a man of imagination, I may say that my little designs are not without a philosophy of their own. Truly, I don't know whether the cats and monkeys imitate us, or whether it's we who imitate them." I congratulated him on his philosophy, and he resumed. "You will do me the honor to admit that I have handled my subjects with delicacy. Eh, it was needed, signore! I have been free, but not too free — eh? Just a hint, you know! You may see as much or as little as you please. These little groups, however, are no measure of my invention. If you will favor me with a call at my studio, I think that you will admit that my combinations are really infinite. I likewise execute figures to command. You have perhaps some little motive — the fruit of your philosophy of life, signore — which you would like to have interpreted. I can promise to work it up to your satisfaction; it shall be as malicious as you please! Allow me to present you with my card, and to remind you that my prices are moderate. Only sixty francs for a little group like that. My statuettes are as durable as bronze — *ære perennius*, signore — and between ourselves, I think they are more amusing!"

As I pocketed his card I glanced at Madonna Serafina, wondering whether she had an eye for contrasts. She had picked up one of the little couples and was tenderly dusting it with a feather broom.

What I had just seen and heard had so deepened my compassionate interest in my deluded friend, that I took a summary leave, and made my way directly to the house designated by this remarkable woman. It was in an obscure corner of the opposite side of the town, and presented a somber and squalid appearance. An old woman in the doorway, on my inquiring for Theobald, ushered me in with a mumbled blessing and an expression of relief at the poor gentleman having a friend. His lodging seemed to consist of a single room at the top of the house. On getting no answer to my knock, I opened the door, supposing that he was absent; so that it gave me a certain shock to find him sitting there helpless and dumb. He was seated near the single window, facing an easel which supported a large canvas. On my entering, he looked up at me blankly, without changing his position, which was that of absolute lassitude and dejection, his arms loosely folded, his legs stretched before him, his head hanging on his breast. Advancing into the room, I perceived that his face vividly corresponded with his attitude. He was pale, haggard, and unshaven, and his dull and sunken eye gazed at me without a spark of recognition. I had been afraid that he would greet me with fierce reproaches, as the cruelly officious patron who had turned his peace to bitterness; and I was relieved to find that my appearance awakened no visible resentment. "Don't you know me?" I asked as I put out my hand. "Have you already forgotten me?"

He made no response, kept his position stupidly, and left me staring about the room. It spoke most plaintively for itself. Shabby, sordid, naked, it contained, beyond the wretched bed, but the scantiest provision for personal comfort. It was bedroom at once and studio — a grim ghost of a studio. A few dusty casts and prints on the walls, three or four old canvases turned face inward, and a rusty-looking color-box, formed, with the easel at the window, the sum of its appurtenances. The place savored horribly of poverty. Its only wealth was the picture on the easel, presumably the famous Madonna. Averted as this was from the door, I was unable to see its face; but at last, sickened by the vacant misery of the spot, I passed behind Theobald, eagerly and tenderly. I can hardly say that I was surprised at what I found: a canvas that was a mere dead blank, cracked and discolored by time. This was his immortal work! Though not surprised I confess I was powerfully moved, and I think that for five minutes I could not have trusted myself to speak. At last my silent nearness affected him; he stirred and turned, and then rose and looked at me with a slowly kindling eye. I murmured some kind, ineffective nothings about his being ill and needing advice and care; but he seemed absorbed in the effort to recall distinctly what had last passed between us. "You were right," he said with a pitiful smile, "I'm a dawdler! I'm a failure! I shall do nothing more in this world. You opened my eyes; and though the truth is bitter, I bear you no grudge. Amen! I've been sitting here for a week, face to face with the truth, with the past, with my weakness and poverty and nullity. I shall never touch a brush! I believe I've neither eaten nor slept. Look at that canvas! " he went on, as I relieved my emotion in the urgent request that he would come home with me and dine. "That was to have contained my masterpiece! Isn't it a promising foundation? The elements of it are all *here*." And he tapped his forehead with that mystic confidence which had marked the gesture before. "If I could only transpose them into some brain that had the hand, the will! Since I've been sitting here taking stock of my intellects, I've come to believe that I have the material for a hundred masterpieces. But my hand is paralyzed now, and they'll never be painted. I never began! I waited and waited to be worthier to begin, and wasted my life in preparation. While I fancied my creation was growing, it was dying. I've taken it all too hard! Michael Angelo didn't when he went at the Lorenzo! He did his best at a venture, and his venture is immortal. *That's* mine! " And he pointed, with a gesture I shall never forget, at the empty canvas. "I suppose we're a genus by ourselves in the providential scheme — we talents that can't act, that can't do nor dare! We take it out in talk, in plans and promises, in study, in visions! But our visions, let me tell you," he cried with a toss of his head, "have a way of being brilliant, and a man hasn't lived in vain who has seen the things I have! Of course you'll not believe in them when that bit of worm-eaten cloth is all I have to show for them; but to convince you, to enchant and astound the world, I need only the hand of Raphael. I have his brain. A pity, you'll say, I haven't his modesty! Ah, let me babble now: it's all I have left! I'm the half of a genius! Where in the wide world is my other half? Lodged perhaps in the vulgar soul, the cunning, ready fingers of some dull copyist, or some trivial artisan who turns out by the dozen his easy prodigies of touch! But it's not for me to sneer at him: he at least does something. He's not a dawdler! Well for me if I had been vulgar and clever and reckless — if I could have shut my eyes and dealt my stroke! "

What to say to the poor fellow, what to do for him, seemed hard to determine; I chiefly felt that I must break the spell of his present inaction, and remove him from the haunted atmosphere of the little room it seemed such cruel irony to call a studio. I cannot say I persuaded him to come out with me; he simply suffered himself to be led, and when we began to walk in the open air I was able to measure his pitifully weakened condition. Nevertheless he seemed in a certain way to revive, and murmured at last that he would like to go to the Pitti Gallery. I shall never forget our melancholy stroll through those gorgeous halls, every picture on whose walls seemed, even to my own sympathetic vision, to glow with a sort of insolent renewal of strength and luster. The eyes and lips of the great portraits seemed to smile in ineffable scorn of the dejected pretender who had dreamed of competing with their triumphant authors; the celestial candor, even, of the Madonna in the Chair, as we paused in perfect silence before her, was tinged with the sinister irony of the women of Leonardo. Perfect silence indeed marked our whole progress — the silence of a deep farewell; for I felt in all my pulses, as Theobald, leaning on my arm, dragged one heavy foot after the other, that he was looking his last. When we came out, he was so exhausted that instead of taking him to my hotel to dine, I called a carriage and drove him straight to his own poor lodging. He had sunk into an extraordinary lethargy; he lay back in the carriage with his eyes closed, as pale as death, his faint breathing interrupted at intervals by a sudden gasp, like a smothered sob or a vain attempt to speak. With the help of the old woman who had admitted me before, and who emerged from a dark back court, I contrived to lead him up the long steep staircase and lay him on his wretched bed. To her I gave him in charge, while I prepared in all haste to seek a physician. But she followed me out of the room with a pitiful clasping of her hands.

"Poor, dear, blessed gentleman," she murmured: "is he dying?"

"Possibly. How long has he been thus?"

"Since a night he passed ten days ago. I came up in the morning to make his poor bed, and found him sitting up in his clothes before that great canvas he keeps there. Poor, dear, strange man, he says his prayers to it! He had not been to bed, nor since then properly! What has happened to him? Has he found out about the Serafina?" she whispered with a glittering eye and a toothless grin.

"Prove at least that one old woman can be faithful," I said, "and watch him well till I come back."

My return was delayed through the absence of the English physician on a round of visits, and my vainly pursuing him from house to house before I overtook him. I brought him to Theobald's bedside none too soon. A violent fever had seized our patient, and the case was evidently grave. A couple of hours later I knew that he had brain fever. From this moment I was with him constantly; but I am far from wishing to describe his illness. Excessively painful to witness, it was happily brief. Life burned out in delirium. A certain night that I passed at his pillow, listening to his wild snatches of regret, of aspiration, of rapture and awe at the phantasmal pictures with which his brain seemed to swarm, recurs to my memory now like some stray page from a lost masterpiece of tragedy.

Before a week was over we had buried him in the little Protestant cemetery on the way to Fiesole. The Signora Serafina, whom I had caused to be informed of his illness, had come in person, I was told, to inquire about its progress; but she was absent from his funeral, which was attended by but a scanty concourse of mourners. Half a dozen old Florentine sojourners, in spite of the prolonged estrangement which had preceded his death, had felt the kindly impulse to honor his grave. Among them was my friend Mrs.

Coventry, whom I found on my departure waiting at her carriage door at the gate of the cemetery.

"Well," she said, relieving at last with a significant smile the solemnity of our immediate greeting, "and the great Madonna? Have you seen her after all?"

"I've seen her," I said; "she's mine — by bequest. But I shall never show her to you."

"And why not, pray?"

"My dear Mrs. Coventry, you'd not understand her!"

"Upon my word, you're polite."

"Excuse me: I'm sad and vexed and bitter." And with reprehensible rudeness I marched away. I was excessively impatient to leave Florence: my friend's dark spirit seemed diffused through all things. I had packed my trunk to start for Rome that night; and meanwhile, to beguile my unrest, I aimlessly paced the streets. Chance led me at last to the church of San Lorenzo. Remembering poor Theobald's phrase about Michael Angelo — "He did his best at a venture" — I went in and turned my steps to the chapel of the tombs. Viewing in sadness the sadness of its immortal treasures, I fancied, while I stood there, that the scene demanded no ampler commentary. As I passed through the church again to depart, a woman, turning away from one of the side altars, met me face to face. The black shawl depending from her head draped picturesquely the handsome visage of Madonna Serafina. She stopped as she recognized me, and I saw that she wished to speak. Her eye was bright, and her ample bosom heaved in a way that seemed to portend a certain sharpness of reproach. But the expression of my own face apparently drew the sting from her resentment, and she addressed me in a tone in which bitterness was tempered by a sort of dogged resignation. "I know it was you, now, that separated us," she said. "It was a pity he ever brought you to see me! Of course you couldn't think of me as he did. Well, the Lord gave him, the Lord has taken him. I've just paid for a nine-days' mass for his soul. And I can tell you this, signore — I never deceived him. Who put it into his head that I was made to live on holy thoughts and fine phrases? It was his own fancy, and it pleased him to think so. Did he suffer much?" she added more softly, after a pause.

"His sufferings were great, but they were short."

"And did he speak of me?" She had hesitated, and dropped her eyes; she raised them with her question, and revealed in their somber stillness a gleam of feminine confidence, which for the moment revived and illumined her beauty. Poor Theobald! Whatever name he had given his passion, it was still her fine eyes that had charmed him.

"Be contented, madam," I answered, gravely.

She dropped her eyes again, and was silent. Then exhaling a full, rich sigh, as she gathered her shawl together: "He was a magnificent genius!"

I bowed, and we separated.

Passing through a narrow side street on my way back to my hotel, I perceived above a doorway a sign which it seemed to me I had read before. I suddenly remembered that it was identical with the superscription of a card that I had carried for an hour in my waistcoat pocket. On the threshold stood the ingenious artist whose claims to public favor were thus distinctly signalized, smoking a pipe in the evening air, and giving the finishing polish with a bit of rag to one of his inimitable "combinations." I caught the expressive curl of a couple of tails. He recognized me, removed his little red cap with a most obsequious bow, and motioned me to enter his studio. I returned his bow and passed on, vexed with the apparition. For a week afterwards, whenever I was seized among the ruins of triumphant Rome with some peculiarly poignant memory of Theobald's transcendent illusions and deplorable failure, I seemed to hear a fantastic, impertinent murmur, "Cats and monkeys, monkeys and cats — all human life is there!"

GEORGE W. CABLE

PERHAPS the first intimation given to the world of a literary and artistic awakening in the Southern States of America after the Civil War, was the appearance in Scribner's Magazine of a series of short stories, written by an unknown and hitherto untried hand, and afterwards collected and republished in 'Old Creole Days.' This was long before the vogue of the short story; and that the publication of these tales was regarded as a literary event in those days is sufficient testimony to their power.

They were fresh, full of color and poetic feeling — romantic with the romance that abounds in the life they portrayed, redolent of indigenous perfumes — magnolia, lemon, orange, and myrtle, mingled with French exotics of the boudoir — interpretative in these qualities, through a fine perception, of a social condition resulting from the transplanting to a semi-tropical soil of a conservative, wealthy, and aristocratic French community. Herein lay much of their most inviting charm; but more than this, they were racy with twinkling humor, tender with a melting pathos, and intensely dramatic.

An intermixture of races with strong caste prejudices, and a time of revolution and change, present eminently the condition and the moment for the romance. When, in addition, the artist finds at hand an almost tropical setting, and so picturesque a confusion of liquid tongues as exists in the old Franco-Spanish-Afro-Italian-American city of New Orleans, there would seem to be nothing left to be desired as "material." George W. Cable, the artist who seized instinctively this opportunity, was born at New Orleans on October 12, 1844, of colonial Virginia stock on the one side, and New England on the other. His early life was full of vicissitudes, and he was over thirty before he discovered story-telling to be his true vocation. From that time on he diligently followed it, publishing four novels, 'The Grandissimes,' 'Dr. Sevier,' 'Bonaventure,' and 'John March, Southerner,' besides another volume of short stories.

That, having received his impressions in the period of transition and ferment following the upheaval of 1861–1865, with the resulting exaggerations and distortions of a normal social condition, he chose to lay his scenes a half-century earlier, proclaims him still more the artist; who would thus gain a freer play of fancy and a surer perspective, and who, saturated with his subject, was not afraid to trust his imagination to interpret it.

That he saw with open sympathetic eyes and a loving heart, he who runs may read in any chance page that a casual opening of his books will reveal. That the people whom he has so affectionately depicted have not loved him in return, is perhaps only a corroboration of his own words when he wrote, in his charming tale 'Belles Demoiselles Plantation,' "The Creoles never forgive a public mention." That they are tender of heart, sympathetic, and generous in their own social and domestic relations, Cable's readers cannot fail to know. But the caste line has ever been a dangerous boundary — a live wire charged with a deadly if invisible fluid — and he is a brave man who dares lay his hand upon it.

More than this, the old-time Creole was an aristocrat who chose to live behind a battened door, as does his descendant today. His privacy, so long undisturbed, has come to be his prerogative. Witness this spirit in the protest of the inimitable Jean-ah Poquelin — the hero giving his name to one of the most dramatic stories ever penned — when he presents himself before the American governor of Louisiana to declare that he will not have his privacy invaded by a proposed street to pass his door: — "I want you tell Monsieur le President, *strit — can't — pass — at — me — 'ouse.*" The Creoles of Cable's generation were as jealous of their retirement as was the brave old man Poquelin; and to have it invaded by a young American who not only threw their pictures upon his canvas, but standing behind it, reproduced their eccentricities of speech for applauding Northern audiences, was a crime unforgivable in their moral code.

Added to this, Cable stands accused of giving the impression that the Louisiana Creole is a person of African taint; but are there not many refutations of this charge in the internal evidence of his work? As for instance where in 'The Grandissimes' he writes, "His whole appearance was a dazzling contradiction of the notion that a Creole is a person of mixed blood"; and again when he alludes to "the slave dialect," is the implication not unequivocal that this differed from the speech of the drawing-room? It is true that he found many of his studies in the Quadroon population, who spoke a patois that was partly French; but such was the "slave dialect" of the man of color who came into his English through a French strain, or perhaps only through a generation of close French environment.

A civilization that is as protective in its conservatism as are the ten-foot walls of brick with which its people surround their luxurious dwellings may be counted on to resent portrayal at short range, even though it were unequivocally eulogistic. That Cable is a most conscientious artist, and that he has been absolutely true to the letter as he saw it, there can be no question; but whether his technical excellences are always broadly representative or not is not so certain. That the writer who has so amply proven his own joy in the wealth of his material, should have been beguiled by its picturesqueness into a partisanship for the class making a special appeal, is not surprising. But truth in art is largely a matter of selection; and if Cable has sinned in the gleaning, it was undoubtedly because of visual limitation, rather than a conscious discrimination.

In 'The Grandissimes,' his most ambitious work, we have an important contribution to representative literature. In the pleasant guise of his fascinating fiction he has essayed the history of a civilization, and in many respects the result is a great book. That such a work should attain its highest merit in impartial truth when taken as a whole, goes without saying.

The dramatic story of Bras Coupé is true as belonging to the time and the situation. So is that of Palmyre the Octoroon, or of Honoré Grandissime's "f. m. c." the half-brother, or of the pitiful voodoo woman Clemence, the wretched old *marchande de calas*. Had he produced nothing more than his first small volume of seven tales, he would have made for himself an honored place in literature.

From 1886 to his death in 1925 Cable resided in Northampton, Mass. His later publications include 'The Cavalier' (1901); 'Bylow Hill' (1902); 'Kincaid's Battery' (1908); '"Posson Jone'" and Père Raphael' (1909); 'Gideon's Band' (1914); and 'The Amateur Garden' (1914).

"POSSON JONE'"

From 'Old Creole Days.' Copyright, 1879, 1881, 1883, by Charles Scribner's Sons

TO Jules St.-Ange — elegant little heathen — there yet remained at manhood a remembrance of having been to school, and of having been taught by a stony-headed Capuchin that the world is round — for example, like a cheese. This round world is a cheese to be eaten through, and Jules had nibbled quite into his cheese-world already at twenty-two.

He realized this, as he idled about one Sunday morning where the intersection of Royal and Conti Streets some seventy years ago formed a central corner of New Orleans. Yes, yes, the trouble was he had been wasteful and honest. He discussed the matter with that faithful friend and confidant, Baptiste, his yellow body-servant. They concluded that, papa's patience and *tante's* pin-money having been gnawed away quite to the rind, there were left open only these few easily enumerated resorts: — to go to work — they shuddered; to join Major Innerarity's filibustering expedition; or else — why not? — to try some games of confidence. At twenty-two one must begin to be something. Nothing else tempted; could that avail? One could but try. It is noble to try; and besides, they were hungry. If one could "make the friendship" of some person from the country, for instance, with money — not expert at cards or dice, but as one would say, willing to learn — one might find cause to say some "Hail Marys."

The sun broke through a clearing sky and Baptiste pronounced it good for luck. There had been a hurricane in the night. The weed-grown tile-roofs were still dripping, and from lofty brick and low adobe walls a rising steam responded to the summer sunlight. Up-street, and across the Rue du Canal, one could get glimpses of the gardens in Faubourg Ste.-Marie standing in silent wretchedness, so many tearful Lucretias, tattered victims of the storm. Short remnants of the wind now and then came down the narrow street in erratic puffs, heavily laden with odors of broken boughs and torn flowers, skimmed the little pools of rain-water in the deep ruts of the unpaved street, and suddenly went away to nothing, like a juggler's butterflies or a young man's money.

It was very picturesque, the Rue Royale. The rich and poor met together. The locksmith's swinging key creaked next door to the bank; across the way, crouching mendicant-like in the shadow of a great importing house, was the mud laboratory of the mender of broken combs. Light balconies overhung the rows of showy shops and stores open for trade this Sunday morning and pretty Latin faces of the higher class glanced over their savagely pronged railings upon the passers below. At some windows hung lace curtains, flannel duds at some, and at others only the scraping and sighing one-hinged shutter groaning toward Paris after its neglectful master.

M. St.-Ange stood looking up and down the street for nearly an hour. But few ladies, only the inveterate mass-goers, were out. About the entrance of the frequent *cafés* the masculine gentility stood leaning on canes, with which now one and now another beckoned to Jules, some even adding pantomimic hints of the social cup.

M. St.-Ange remarked to his servant without turning his head that somehow he felt sure he should soon return those *bons* that the mulatto had lent him.

"What will you do with them?"

"Me!" said Baptiste, quickly; "I will go and see the bull-fight in the Place Congo."

"There is to be a bull-fight? But where is M. Cayetano?"

"Ah, got all his affairs wet in the tornado. Instead of his circus, they are to have a bull-fight — not an ordinary bull-fight with sick horses, but a buffalo-and-tiger fight. I would not miss it — "

Two or three persons ran to the opposite corner, and commenced striking at something with their canes. Others followed. Can M. St.-Ange and servant, who hasten forward — can the Creoles, Cubans, Spaniards, San Domingo refugees, and other loungers — can they hope it is a fight? They hurry forward. Is a man in a fit? The crowd pours in from the side-streets. Have they killed a so-long snake? Bareheaded shopmen leave their wives, who stand upon chairs. The crowd huddles and packs. Those on the outside make little leaps into the air, trying to be tall.

"What is the matter?"

"Have they caught a real live rat?"

"Who is hurt?" asks someone in English.

"*Personne,*" replies a shopkeeper; "a man's hat blow' in the gutter; but he has it now. Jules pick' it. See, that is the man, head and shoulders on top the res'."

"He in the homespun?" asks a second shopkeeper. "Humph! an *Américain* — a West Floridian; bah!"

"But wait; 'st! he is speaking; listen!"

"To who is he speak — ?"

"Sh-sh-sh! to Jules."

"Jules who?"

"Silence, you! To Jules St.-Ange, what howe me a bill since long time. Sh-sh-sh!"

Then the voice was heard.

Its owner was a man of giant stature, with a slight stoop in his shoulders, as if he was making a constant good-natured attempt to accommodate himself to ordinary doors and ceilings. His bones were those of an ox. His face was marked more by weather than age, and his narrow brow was bald and smooth. He had instantaneously formed an opinion of Jules St. Ange, and the multitude of words, most of them lingual curiosities, with which he was rasping the wide-open ears of his listeners, signified, in short, that as sure as his name was Parson Jones, the little Creole was a "plum gentleman."

M. St.-Ange bowed and smiled, and was about to call attention, by both gesture and speech, to a singular object on top of the still uncovered head, when the nervous motion of the *Américain* anticipated him, as, throwing up an immense hand, he drew down a large roll of bank-notes. The crowd laughed, the West-Floridian joining, and began to disperse.

"Why, that money belongs to Smyrny Church," said the giant.

"You are very dengerous to make your money expose like that, Misty Posson Jone'," said St.-Ange, counting it with his eyes.

The countryman gave a start and smile of surprise.

"How d'dyou know my name was Jones?" he asked; but, without pausing for the Creole's answer, furnished in his reckless way some further specimens of West-Floridian English; and the conciseness with which he presented full intelligence of his home, family, calling, lodging-house, and present and future plans, might have passed for consummate art, had it not been the most run-wild nature. "And I've done been to Mobile, you know, on busi*ness* for Bethesdy Church. It's the on'yest time I ever been from home; now you wouldn't of believed that, would you? But I admire to have saw you, that's so. You've got to come and eat with me. Me and my boy ain't been fed yit. What might one call yo' name? Jools? Come on, Jools. Come on, Colossus. That's my niggah — his name's Colossus of Rhodes. Is that yo' yallah boy, Jools? Fetch him along, Colossus. It seems like a special provi*dence.*— Jools, do you believe in a special provi*dence?* "

Jules said he did.

The new-made friends moved briskly off, followed by Baptiste and a short square old negro, very black and grotesque, who had introduced himself to the mulatto with many glittering and cavernous smiles as "d'body-servant of d'Rev'n' Mr. Jones."

Both pairs enlivened their walk with conversation. Parson Jones descanted upon the doctrine he had mentioned, as illustrated in the perplexities of cotton-growing, and concluded that there would always be "a special provi*dence* again' cotton untell folks quits a-pressin' of it and haulin of it on Sundays!"

"*Je dis,*" said St.-Ange, in response, "I thing you is juz right. I believe, me, strong-strong in the improvidence, yes. You know my papa he hown a sugah-plantation, you know. 'Jules, me son,' he say one time to me, 'I goin' to make one baril sugah to fedge the moze high price in New Orleans.' Well, he take his bez baril sugah — I nevah see a so careful man like me papa always to make a so beautiful sugah *et sirop*. 'Jules, go at Father Pierre an' ged this lill pitcher fill with holy-water, an' tell him sen' his tin bucket, and I will make it fill with *quitte*.' I ged the holy-water; my papa sprinkle it over the baril, an' make one cross on the 'ead of the baril."

"Why, Jules," said Parson Jones, "that didn't do no good."

"Din do no good! Id broughd the so great value! You can strike me dead if thad baril sugah din fedge the more high cost than any other in the city. *Parceque,* the man what buy that baril sugah he make a mistake of one hundred pound" — falling back — "*mais* certainlee!"

"And you think that was growin' out of the holy-water?" asked the parson.

"*Mais,* what could make it else? Id could not be the *quitte,* because my papa keep the bucket, an' forget to sen' the *quitte* to Father Pierre."

Parson Jones was disappointed.

"Well, now, Jools, you know, I don't think that was right. I reckon you must be a plum Catholic."

M. St.-Ange shrugged. He would not deny his faith.

"I am a *Catholique, mais*" — brightening as he hoped to recommend himself anew — "not a good one."

"Well, you know," said Jones — "where's Colossus? Oh! all right. Colossus strayed off a minute in Mobile, and I plum lost him for two days. Here's the place; come in. Colossus and this boy can go to the kitchen. — Now, Colossus, what *air* you a-beckonin' at me faw?"

He let his servant draw him aside and address him in a whisper.

"Oh, go 'way!" said the parson with a jerk. "Who's goin' to throw me? What? Speak louder. Why, Colossus, you shayn't talk so, saw. 'Pon my soul, you're the mightiest fool I ever taken up with. Jest you go down that alley-way with this yalla boy, and don't show yo' face untell yo' called!"

The negro begged; the master wrathily insisted.

"Colossus, will you do ez I tell you, or shell I hev' to strike you, saw?"

"Oh Mahs Jimmy, I — I's gwine; but —" he ventured nearer — "don't on no account drink nothin', Mahs Jimmy."

Such was the negro's earnestness that he put one foot in the gutter, and fell heavily against his master. The parson threw him off angrily.

"Thar, now! Why, Colossus, you must of been dosted with sumthin'; yo' plum crazy. — Humph, come on, Jools, let's eat! Humph! to tell me that, when I never taken a drop, exceptin' for chills, in my life — which he knows so as well as me!"

The two masters began to ascend a stair.

"*Mais,* he is a sassy; I would sell him, me," said the young Creole.

"No, I wouldn't do that," replied the parson; "though there is people in Bethesdy who says he is a rascal. He's a powerful smart fool. Why, that boy's got money, Jools; more money than religion, I reckon. I'm shore he fallen into mighty bad company —" they passed beyond earshot.

Baptiste and Colossus, instead of going to the tavern kitchen, passed to the next door and entered the dark rear corner of a low grocery, where, the law notwithstanding, liquor was covertly sold to slaves. There, in the quiet company of Baptiste and the grocer, the colloquial powers of Colossus, which were simply prodigious, began very soon to show themselves.

"For whilst," said he, "Mahs Jimmy has eddication, you know — whilst he has eddication, I has 'scretion. He has eddication and I has 'scretion, an' so we gits along."

He drew a black bottle down the counter, and, laying half his length upon the damp board, continued: —

"As a p'inciple I discredits de imbimin' of awjus liquors. De imbimin' of awjus liquors, de wiolution of de Sabbaf, de playin' of de fiddle, and de usin' of bywords, dey is de fo' sins of de conscience, an' if any man sin de fo' sins of de conscience, de debble done sharp his fork fo' dat man. — Ain't dat so, boss?"

The grocer was sure it was so.

"Neberdeless, mind you —" here the orator brimmed his glass from the bottle and swallowed the contents with a dry eye — "mind you, a roytious man, sech as ministers of de gospel and dere body-sarvants, can take a *leetle* for de weak stomach."

But the fascinations of Colossus' eloquence must not mislead us; this is the story of a true Christian; to wit, Parson Jones.

The parson and his new friend ate. But the coffee M. St.-Ange declared he could not touch: it was too wretchedly bad. At the French Market, near by, there was some noble coffee. This, however, would have to be bought, and Parson Jones had scruples.

"You see, Jools, every man has his conscience to guide him, which it does so in —"

"Oh, yes!" cried St.-Ange, "conscien'; thad is the bez, Posson Jone'. Certainlee! I am a *Catholique,* you is a *schismatique:* you thing it is wrong to dring some coffee — well, then, it *is* wrong; you thing it is wrong to make the sugah to ged the so large price — well, then, it *is* wrong; I thing it is right — well, then, it *is* right: it is all 'abit; *c'est tout.* What a man thing is right, *is right;* 'tis all 'abit. A man muz nod go again' his conscien'. My faith! do you thing I would go again' my conscien'? *Mais allons,* led us go and ged some coffee."

"Jools."

"W'at?"

"Jools, it ain't the drinkin' of coffee, but the buyin' of it on a Sabbath. You must really excuse me, Jools, it's again' conscience, you know."

"Ah!" said St.-Ange, "*c'est* very true. For you it would be a sin, *mais* for me it is only 'abit. Rilligion is a very strange; I know a man one time, he thing it was wrong to go to cock-fight Sunday evening. I thing it is all 'abit. *Mais,* come, Posson Jone'; I have got one friend, Miguel; led us go at his house and ged some coffee. Come; Miguel have no familie; only him and Joe — always like to see friend; *allons,* led us come yonder."

"Why, Jools, my dear friend, you know," said the shamefaced parson, "I never visit on Sundays."

"Never w'at?" asked the astounded Creole.

"No," said Jones smiling awkwardly.

"Never visite?"

"Exceptin' sometimes amongst church-members," said Parson Jones.

"*Mais,*" said the seductive St.-Ange, "Miguel and Joe is church-member' — certainlee! They love to talk about rilligion. Come at Miguel and talk about some rilligion. I am nearly expire for me coffee."

Parson Jones took his hat from beneath his chair and rose up.

"Jools," said the weak giant, "I ought to be in church right now."

"*Mais,* the church is right yonder at Miguel', yes. Ah!" continued St.-Ange, as they descended the stairs, "I thing every man muz have the rilligion he like the bez — me, I like the *Catholique* rilligion the bez — for me it *is* the bez. Every man will sure go to heaven if he like his rilligion the bez."

"Jools," said the West-Floridian, laying his great hand tenderly upon the Creole's shoulder, as they stepped out upon the *banquette,* "do you think you have any shore hopes of heaven?"

"Yass!" replied St.-Ange; "I am sure-sure. I thing everybody will go to heaven. I thing you will go, *et* I thing Miguel will go, *et* Joe — everybody, I thing — *mais,* hof course, not if they not have been christen'. Even I thing some niggers will go."

"Jools," said the parson, stopping in his walk — "Jools, I *don't* want to lose my niggah."

"You will not lose him. With Baptiste he *cannot* ged loose."

But Colossus' master was not reassured. "Now," said he, still tarrying, "this is jest the way; had I of gône to church — "

"Posson Jone' — " said Jules.

"What?"

"I tell you. We goin' to church!"

"Will you?" asked Jones, joyously.

"*Allons* come along," said Jules, taking his elbow.

They walked down the Rue Chartres, passed several corners, and by-and-by turned into a cross-street. The parson stopped an instant as they were turning, and looked back up the street.

"W'at you lookin'?" asked his companion.

"I thought I saw Cólossus," answered the parson, with an anxious face; "I reckon 'twa'nt him, though." And they went on.

The street they now entered was a very quiet one. The eye of any chance passer would have been at once drawn to a broad, heavy, white brick edifice on the lower side of the way, with a flag-pole standing out like a bowsprit from one of its great windows, and a pair of lamps hanging before a large closed entrance. It was a theater, honeycombed with gambling-dens. At this morning hour all was still, and the only sign of life was a knot of little barefoot girls gathered within its narrow shade, and each carrying an infant relative. Into this place the parson and M. St.-Ange entered, the little nurses jumping up from the sills to let them pass in.

A half-hour may have passed. At the end of that time the whole juvenile company were laying alternate eyes and ears to the chinks, to gather what they could of an interesting quarrel going on within.

"I did not, saw! I given you no cause of offense, saw! It's not so, saw! Mister Jools simply mistaken the house — thinkin' it was a Sabbath-school! No such thing, saw; I *ain't* bound to bet! Yes, I kin git out! Yes, without bettin'! I hev a right to my opinion; I reckon I'm a *white man,* saw! No, saw! I on'y said I didn't think you could get the game on them cards. 'Sno such thing, saw! I do *not* know how to play! I wouldn't hev a rascal's money ef I should win it! Shoot ef you dare! You can kill me, but you cayn't scare me! No, I shayn't bet! I'll die first! Yes, saw; Mr. Jools can bet for me if he admires to; I ain't his mostah."

Here the speaker seemed to direct his words to St.-Ange.

"Saw, I don't understand you, saw. I never said I'd loan you money to bet for me. I didn't suspicion this from you, saw. No, I won't take any more lemonade; it's the most notorious stuff I ever drank, saw!"

M. St.-Ange's replies were in *falsetto* and not without effect; for presently the parson's indignation and anger began to melt. "Don't ask me, Jools, I can't help you. It's no use; it's a matter of conscience with me, Jools."

"*Mais oui!* 'tis a matt' of conscien' wid me, the same."

"But, Jools, the money's none o' mine, nohow; it belongs to Smyrny, you know."

"If I could make jus' *one* bet," said the persuasive St.-Ange, "I would leave this place, fas'-fas', yes. If I had thing — *mais* I did not soupspicion this from you. Posson Jone' — "

"Don't, Jools, don't!"

"No, Posson Jone'!"

"You're bound to win?" said the parson, wavering.

"*Mais certainement!* But it is not to win that I want; 'tis me conscien' — me honor!"

"Well, Jools, I hope I'm not a-doin' no wrong. I'll loan you some of this money if you say you'll come right out 'thout takin' your winnin's."

All was still. The peeping children could see the parson as he lifted his hand to his breast-pocket. There it paused a moment in bewilderment, then plunged to the bottom. It came back empty, and fell lifelessly at his side. His head dropped upon his breast, his eyes were for a moment closed, his broad palms were lifted and pressed against his forehead, a tremor seized him, and he fell all in a lump to the floor. The children ran off with their infant-loads, leaving Jules St.-Ange swearing by all his deceased relatives, first to Miguel and Joe, and then to the lifted parson, that he did not know what had become of the money "except if" the black man had got it.

In the rear of ancient New Orleans, beyond the sites of the old rampart, a trio of Spanish forts, where the town has since sprung up and grown old, green with all the luxuriance of the wild Creole summer, lay the Congo Plains. Here stretched the canvas of the historic Cayetano, who Sunday after Sunday sowed the sawdust for his circus-ring.

But today the great showman had fallen short of his printed promise. The hurricane had come by night, and with one fell swash had made an irretrievable sop of everything. The circus trailed away its bedraggled magnificence, and the ring was cleared for the bull.

Then the sun seemed to come out and work for the people. "See," said the Spaniards, looking up at the glorious sky with its great white fleets drawn off upon the horizon, "see — heaven smiles upon the bull-fight!"

In the high upper seats of the rude amphitheater sat the gayly decked wives and daughters of the Gascons, from the *métairies* along the Ridge, and the chattering Spanish women of the Market, their shining hair unbonneted to the sun. Next below were their husbands and lovers in Sunday blouses, milkmen, butchers, bakers, black-bearded fishermen, Sicilian fruiterers, swarthy Portuguese sailors in little woolen caps, and strangers of the graver sort: mariners of England, Germany, and Holland. The lowest seats were full of trappers, smugglers, Canadian *voyageurs,* drinking and singing; *Américains,* too — more's the shame — from the upper rivers — who will not keep their seats — who ply the bottle, and who will get home by and by and tell how wicked Sodom is; broad-brimmed, silver-braided Mexicans too, with their copper cheeks and bat's eyes, and their tinkling spurred heels. Yonder in that quieter section are the quadroon women in their black lace shawls — and there is Baptiste; and below them are the turbaned black women, and there is — but he vanishes — Colossus.

The afternoon is advancing, yet the sport, though loudly demanded, does not begin. The *Américains* grow derisive and find pastime in gibes and raillery. They mock the various Latins with their national inflections, and answer their scowls with laughter. Some of the more aggressive shout pretty French greetings to the women of Gascony and one bargeman, amid peals of applause, stands on a seat and hurls a kiss to the quadroons. The marines of England, Germany, and Holland, as spectators, like the fun, while the Spaniards look black and cast defiant imprecations upon their persecutors. Some Gascons, with timely caution, pick their women out and depart, running a terrible fire of gallantries.

In hope of truce, a new call is raised for the bull: "The bull! the bull! — hush!"

In a tier near the ground a man is standing and calling — standing head and shoulders above the rest — calling in the *Américaine* tongue. Another man, big and red, named Joe, and a handsome little Creole in elegant dress and full of laughter, wish to stop him, but the flatboatmen, ha-ha-ing and cheering, will not suffer it. Ah, through some shameful knavery of the men into whose hands he has fallen, he is drunk! Even the women can see that; and now he throws his arms wildly and raises his voice until the whole great circle hears it. He is preaching!

Ah! kind Lord, for a special providence now! The men of his own nation — men from the land of the open English Bible and temperance cup and song — are cheering him on to mad disgrace. And now another call for the appointed sport is drowned by the flatboatmen singing the ancient tune of 'Mear.' You can hear the words —

"Old Grimes is dead, that good old soul —"

from ribald lips and throats turned brazen with laughter, from singers who toss their hats aloft and roll in their seats; the chorus swells to the accompaniment of a thousand brogans —

"He used to wear an old gray coat
All buttoned down before."

A ribboned man in the arena is trying to be heard and the Latins raise one mighty cry for silence. The big red man gets a hand over the parson's mouth, and the ribboned man seizes his moment.

Uncle Remus stood looking suspiciously at the telephone after his Miss Sally had turned away.

"Miss Sally," he said presently, "wuz you talkin' ter Mars John?"

"Certainly. Who did you suppose it was?"

"Wharbouts wuz Mars John?"

"At his office."

"Way down yan on Yallerbamer street?"

"Yes."

At this piece of information Uncle Remus emitted a groan that was full of doubt and pity, and went into the dining-room. His Miss Sally laughed, and then an idea seemed to strike her. She called him back, and wen again to the telephone.

"Is that you, Central? . . . Please connect eleven-forty with fourteen-sixty." There was a fluttering sound in the instrument, and then the lady said: "Yes, it's me! . . . Here's Remus. . . . Yes, but he wants to talk to you."

"Here, Remus, take this and put it to your ear. Here, simpleton! it won't hurt you."

Uncle Remus took the ear-piece and handled it as though it had been a loaded pistol. He tried to look in at both ends, and then he placed it to his ear and grinned sheepishly. He heard a thin, sepulchral, but familiar voice calling out, "Hello, Remus!" and his sheepish grin gave place to an expression of uneasy astonishment.

"Hello, Remus! Hello-ello-ello-ello-o-o!"

"Is dat you, Mars John?"

"Of course it is, you bandy-legged old villain. I have no time to be standing here. What do you want?"

"How in de name er God you git in dar, Mars John?"

"In where?"

"In dish yer — in dish yer appleratus."

"Oh, you be fiddlestick! What do you want?"

"Mars John, kin you see me — er is she all dark in dar?"

"Are you crazy? Where is your Miss Sally?"

"She in yer, hollun en laughin'. Mars John, how you gwine git out'n dar?"

"Dry up! Good-night!"

"Yer 'tis, Miss Sally," said Uncle Remus, after listening a moment. "Dey's a mighty zoonin' gwine on in dar, en I dunner whe'er Mars John tryin' ter scramble out, er whe'er he des tryin' fer ter make hisse'f comfertuble in dar."

"What did he say, Remus?"

"He up en 'low'd dat one un us wuz a vilyun, but dey wuz such a buzzin' gwine on in dar dat I couldn't 'zactly ketch de rights un it."

Uncle Remus went back to his place by the dining-room fire, and after a while began to mutter and talk to himself.

"What's the matter now?" his Miss Sally asked.

"I 'uz des a-sayin' dat I know Mars John mus' be suffun some'rs."

"Why?"

"Oh, I des knows it; kaze' ef he ain't w'at make he talk so weak? He bleedz ter be in trouble. I'm a-tellin' you de Lord's trufe: dat w'ite man talk like he ain't bigger den one er deze yer little teenchy chany dolls. I boun' you," he continued, "ef I 'uz a w'ite 'oman en Mars John wuz my ole man, I'd snatch up my bonnet en I'd natally sail 'roun' dish yer town twel I fine out w'at de matter wid 'im. I would dat."

The old man's Miss Sally laughed until the tears came in her eyes, and then she said: —

"There's a piece of pie on the sideboard. Do get it, and hush so much talking."

"Thanky, mistiss, thanky!" exclaimed Uncle Remus, shuffling across the room. He got the pie and returned to his chair. "Dish yer pie," he continued, holding it up between his eyes and the fire, "dish yer pie come in good time, kaze Mars John talk so weak en fur off it make me feel right empty. I speck he be well time he git home, en ef he 'uz ter git holt er dish yer pie, hit mought make 'im have bad dreams."

In a few moments the pie had disappeared, and when his Miss Sally looked at him a little later he was fast asleep.

SARAH ORNE JEWETT

NO part of the United States has been treated in literature more frequently than New England. Yet Miss Jewett found in its familiar scenes a beauty that no one else had been able to express. Many writers have since paid her art the tribute of imitation.

Sarah Orne Jewett was born in South Berwick, Maine, in 1849; a product of the best New England birth and breeding. Besides the usual school training, she received a deeper culture from her father, a physician and a man of wide attainments and keen observation. A country doctor, he had to make excursions inland and alongshore to visit his scattered patients; and the young girl sitting beside him learned to know the characters she was to immortalize in literature, as she knew the landscape and the sky. She was a girl not past her youth when her first book, 'Deephaven,' was published in 1877. This was a story of New England life, told in the form of an autobiography; and slight as it was in incident, betrayed a breadth and a refinement which seemed to come from careful training, but which were really the unerring product of a genuine gift for literature, kindled by the observation of a fresh mind and an affectionate sympathy.

The effect upon her many readers was like the gift of sight to the blind. Frequenters of the town — for 'Deephaven' stands for any fisher village on the Maine coast — recollected having seen "Mrs. Bonny" searching for a tumbler, the meek widow with the appearance of a black beetle and the wail of a banshee, the funeral procession on its sad journey, the Captains, the interesting ladies "Mrs. Kew" and "Mrs. Dockum." 'Deephaven' was followed by a series of stories, all breathing forth an air of calm leisure that in its avoidance of hurry or catastrophe suggests the almost forgotten note of Goldsmith and Irving.

Miss Jewett's portrayal of character, habits, traits, speech, was all perfectly true, although drawn from that very rural and village New England life which other writers, clever and merciless, had convinced the world to be wholly sordid and melancholy. With wider comprehension, she showed that there are differing points of view of any given conditions, and that a life in these pinched and narrow surroundings may be as complex an affair as one passed in the heart of London. Her patriotic and kindly part was to portray it with a good deal of horizon, a clear sky, and vital human interest.

Her rare gift was exercised, for the most part, in the field in which America has only France as her rival, that of the short story. Although she produced several successful novels, her 'Deephaven' is a series of figures, landscapes, and interiors, rather than a woven scheme. Perhaps the rare intuition which taught her the secrets of her shy reserved characters, revealed to her that her strength did not lie in the constructive power which holds in its grasp varied and complex interests, terminating in an inevitable conclusion.

A simple incident sufficed for her machinery; her local color was a part of the substance of her creation, not imposed upon it, and no more than Hawthorne did she seem to be conscious of the necessity of making it a setting for her figures. She wrote of that into which she was born; and her creations — even when they were in such foreign settings as Irish-American life, in the inimitable stories 'The Brogans,' 'Between Mass and Vespers,' and 'The Little Captive Maid' — glowed with that internal personality which is never counterfeited, as has been said of Hawthorne's 'Marble Faun.'

The emotion of love as a passion, the essential of a novel, is almost absent from her sketches; or, treated as one of many other emotions and principles, has a certain originality due to its abstemiousness. Life indeed, as portrayed by her, proceeds so exactly as it would naturally proceed, that when the incident has been told, and the quiet, veracious talk has been retailed, the story comes to an end because it could not go on without being a different story. This method would not do for a novel: and yet, little composition as there seems to be about them, Miss Jewett's stories are as delicately constructed, with as true a method and as perfect a knowledge of technique, as Guy de Maupassant's; and they are permeated with a humor all their own. "It is not only the delightful mood in which these little masterpieces are written," says Howells of 'The King of Folly Island,' "but the perfect artistic restraint, the truly Greek temperance without one touch too much, which render them exquisite, make them perfect in their way."

Her lovely spirit, sweet and compassionate, is a tacit appeal for the characters at which her humor bids us smile. Her people are introduced sitting in their quiet New England homes, going about their small affairs: housewives, captains unseaworthy through time or stress of weather, the village schoolmistress or seamstress, the old soldier, the heroine with blue eyes and rosy cheeks, walking through the scene without one fluttering ribbon of coquetry — all these appear with as little grouping as if we had walked into "Deephaven" or "Winby" itself. With perfect sympathy she takes under her protection all those whom irreverence or thoughtlessness has flouted, or whom personal peculiarities have made ridiculous. With her we are amused by their quaintness; but human nature, even forlorn and fallen human nature, is dignified into its true likeness under her serene and compassionate touch. Nowhere, in our large body of local-color fiction, can be found more insight, sympathy, and beauty than in the little group of sketches, 'The Country of the Pointed Firs.'

Her charm is the charm which Richard Dole found in 'A Marsh Island,' where he was so willingly a prisoner; and is that which comes from the view of a landscape, broad, unaccented, lying under a summer sky, breathing the fragrance of grass and wild flowers. It does not invite criticism any more than it deprecates close scrutiny.

If artist may be compared with artist, Miss Jewett might be described as a water-colorist; her sketches resting for their value not upon dramatic qualities or strong color, but upon their pure tone and singleness of effort. And she was not sensibly in her story, any more than a painter is in his picture. It was in this that her engaging modesty and admirable self-restraint lay.

Miss Jewett was the author of a dozen volumes of fiction, among the more important of which are—'A Marsh Island' (1885); 'A White Heron and Other Stories' (1886); 'The King of Folly Island, and Other People' (1888); 'Strangers and Wayfarers' (1890); 'A Native of Winby and Other Tales' (1893); 'The Life of Nancy' (1895); 'The Country of the Pointed Firs' (1896); and 'The Tory Lover' (1901). She died in 1909.

MISS TEMPY'S WATCHERS

From 'The King of Folly Island, and Other People.' Copyright, 1888, by Sarah O. Jewett. Reprinted by permission of Houghton Mifflin Company, publishers, Boston

THE time of year was April; the place was a small farming town in New Hampshire, remote from any railroad. One by one the lights had been blown out in the scattered houses near Miss Tempy Dent's; but as her neighbors took a last look out of doors, their eyes turned with instinctive curiosity toward the old house, where a lamp burned steadily. They gave a little sigh. "Poor Miss Tempy!" said more than one bereft acquaintance; for the good woman lay dead in her north chamber, and the light was a watchers' light. The funeral was set for the next day at one o'clock.

The watchers were two of the oldest friends, Mrs. Crowe and Sarah Ann Binson. They were sitting in the kitchen, because it seemed less awesome than the unused best room; and they beguiled the long hours by steady conversation. One would think that neither topics nor opinions would hold out, at that rate, all through the long spring night; but there was a certain degree of excitement just then, and the two women had risen to an unusual level of expressiveness and confidence. Each had already told the other more than one fact that she had determined to keep secret; they were again and again tempted into statements that either would have found impossible by daylight. Mrs. Crowe was knitting a blue yarn stocking for her husband; the foot was already so long that it seemed as if she must have forgotten to narrow it at the proper time. Mrs. Crowe knew exactly what she was about, however; she was of a much cooler disposition than Sister Binson, who made futile attempts at some sewing, only to drop her work into her lap whenever the talk was most engaging.

Their faces were interesting — of the dry, shrewd, quick-witted New England type, with thin hair twisted neatly back out of the way. Mrs. Crowe could look vague and benignant, and Miss Binson was, to quote her neighbors, a little too sharp-set; but the world knew that she had need to be, with the load she must carry of supporting an inefficient widowed sister and six unpromising and unwilling nieces and nephews. The eldest boy was at last placed with a good man to learn the mason's trade. Sarah Ann Binson, for all her sharp, anxious aspect, never defended herself when her sister whined and fretted. She was told every week of her life that the poor children never would have had to lift a finger if their father had lived; and yet she had kept her steadfast way with the little farm, and patiently taught the young people many useful things, for which, as everybody said, they would live to thank her. However pleasureless her life appeared to outward view, it was brimful of pleasure to herself.

Mrs. Crowe, on the contrary, was well-to-do; her husband being a rich farmer and an easy-going man. She was a stingy woman, but for all that she looked kindly; and when she gave away anything, or lifted a finger to help anybody, it was thought a great piece of beneficence, and a compliment indeed, which the recipient accepted with twice as much gratitude as double the gift that came from a poorer and more generous acquaintance. Everybody liked to be on good terms with Mrs. Crowe. Socially she stood much higher than Sarah Ann Binson. They were both old schoolmates and friends of Temperance Dent, who had asked them one day, not long before she died, if they would not come together and look after the house, and manage everything when she was gone. She may have had some hope that they might become closer friends in this period of intimate partnership, and that the richer woman might better understand the burdens of the poorer. They had not kept the house the night before; they were too weary with the care of their old friend, whom they had not left until all was over.

There was a brook which ran down the hillside very near the house, and the sound of it was much louder than usual. When there was silence in the kitchen, the busy stream had a strange insistence in its wild voice, as if it tried to make the watchers understand something that related to the past.

"I declare, I can't begin to sorrow for Tempy yet. I am so glad to have her at rest," whispered Mrs. Crowe. "It is strange to set here without her, but I can't make it clear that she has gone. I feel as if she had got easy and dropped off to sleep, and I'm more scared about waking her up than knowing any other feeling."

"Yes," said Sarah Ann, "it's just like that, ain't it? But I tell you we are goin' to miss her worse than we expect. She's helped me through with many a trial, has Temperance. I ain't the only one who says the same neither."

These words were spoken as if there were a third person listening; somebody beside Mrs. Crowe. The watchers could not rid their minds of the feeling that they were being watched themselves. The spring wind whistled in the window crack now and then, and buffeted the little house in a gusty way that had a sort of companionable effect. Yet on the whole it was a very still night, and the watchers spoke in a half-whisper.

"She was the freest-handed woman that ever I knew," said Mrs. Crowe decidedly. "According to her means, she gave away more than anybody. I used to tell her 'twa'n't right. I used really to be afraid that she went without too much — for we have a duty to ourselves."

Sister Binson looked up in a half-amused, unconscious way, and then recollected herself.

Mrs. Crowe met her look with a serious face. "It ain't so easy for me to give as it is for some," she said simply, but with an effort which was made possible only by the occasion. "I should like to say, while Tempy is laying here yet in her own house, that she has been a constant lesson to me. Folks are too kind, and shame me with thanks for what I do. I ain't such a generous woman as poor Tempy was, for all she had nothin' to do with, as one may say."

Sarah Binson was much moved at this confession, and was even pained and touched by the unexpected humility. "You have a good many calls on you," she began, and then left her kind little compliment half finished.

"Yes, yes; but I've got means enough. My disposition's more of a cross to me as I grow older, and I made up my mind this morning that Tempy's example should be my pattern henceforth." She began to knit faster than ever.

"'Tain't no use to get morbid; that's what Tempy used to say herself," said Sarah Ann, after a minute's silence. "Ain't it strange to say 'used to say'?" and her voice choked a little. "She never did like to hear folks git goin' about themselves."

"'Twas only because they're apt to do it so as other folks will say 'twasn't so, an' praise 'em up," humbly replied Mrs. Crowe, "and that ain't my object. There wa'n't a child but what Tempy set herself to work to see what she could do to please it. One time my brother's folks had been stopping here in the summer, from Massachusetts. The children was all little, and they broke up a sight of toys, and left 'em when they were going away. Tempy come right up after they rode by, to see if she couldn't help me set the house to rights, and she caught me just as I was going to fling some of the clutter into the stove. I was kind of tired out, starting 'em off in season. 'Oh, give me them!' says she, real pleading; and she wropped 'em up and took 'em home with her when she went, and she mended 'em up and stuck 'em together, and made some young one or other happy with every blessed one.

You'd thought I'd done her the biggest favor. 'No thanks to me. I should ha' burnt 'em, Tempy,' says I."

"Some of 'em came to our house, I know," said Miss Binson. "She'd take a lot o' trouble to please a child, 'stead o' shoving of it out o' the way, like the rest of us when we're drove."

"I can tell you the biggest thing she ever gave, and I don't know's there's anybody left but me to tell it. I don't want it forgot," Sarah Binson went on, looking up at the clock to see how the night was going. "It was that pretty-looking Trevor girl, who taught the Corners school, and married so well afterwards, out in New York State. You remember her, I daresay?"

"Certain," said Mrs. Crowe, with an air of interest.

"She was a splendid scholar, folks said, and give the school a great start; but she'd overdone herself getting her education, and working to pay for it, and she all broke down one spring, and Tempy made her come and stop with her awhile — you remember that? Well, she had an uncle, her mother's brother out in Chicago, who was well off and friendly, and used to write to Lizzie Trevor, and I daresay make her some presents; but he was a lively, driving man, and didn't take time to stop and think about his folks. He hadn't seen her since she was a little girl. Poor Lizzie was so pale and weakly that she just got through the term o' school. She looked as if she was just going straight off in a decline. Tempy she cosseted her up awhile, and then, next thing folks knew, she was tellin' round how Miss Trevor had gone to see her uncle, and meant to visit Niagary Falls on the way and stop over night. Now I happened to know, in ways I won't dwell on to explain, that the poor girl was in debt for her schoolin' when she come here, and her last quarter's pay had just squared it off at last, and left her without a cent ahead hardly: but it had fretted her thinking of it, so she paid it all; they might have dunned her that she owed it to. An' I taxed Tempy about the girl's goin' off on such a journey, till she owned up, rather'n have Lizzie blamed, that she'd given her sixty dollars, same's if she was rolling in riches, and sent her off to have a good rest and vacation."

"Sixty dollars!" exclaimed Mrs. Crowe. "Tempy only had ninety dollars a year that came in to her; rest of her livin' she got by helpin' about, with what she raised off this little piece o' ground, sand one side an' clay the other. An' how often I've heard her tell, years ago, that she'd rather see Niagary than any other sight in the world!"

The women looked at each other in silence; the magnitude of the generous sacrifice was almost too great for their comprehension.

"She was just poor enough to do that!" declared Mrs. Crowe at last, in an abandonment of feeling. "Say what you may, I feel humbled to the dust"; and her companion ventured to say nothing. She never had given away sixty dollars at once, but it was simply because she never had it to give. It came to her very lips to say in explanation, "Tempy was so situated"; but she checked herself in time, for she would not break in upon her own loyal guarding of her dependent household.

"Folks say a great deal of generosity, and this one's being public-sperited, and that one free-handed about giving," said Mrs. Crowe, who was a little nervous in the silence. "I suppose we can't tell the sorrow it would be to some folks not to give, same's 'twould be to me not to save. I seem kind of made for that, as if 'twas what I'd got to do. I should feel sights better about it if I could make it evident what I was savin' for. If I had a child, now, Sarah Ann," and her voice was a little husky — "if I had a child, I should think I was heapin' of it up because he was the one trained by the Lord to scatter it again for good. But here's Crowe and me, we can't do anything with money, and both of us like to keep things same's they've always been. Now Priscilla Dance was talking away like a mill-clapper, week before last. She'd think I would go right off and get one o' them new-fashioned gilt-and-white papers for the best room, and some new furniture, an' a marble-top table. And I looked at her, all struck up. 'Why,' says I, 'Priscilla, that nice old velvet paper ain't hurt a mite. I shouldn't feel 'twas my best room without it. Dan'el says 'tis the first thing he can remember rubbin' his little baby fingers on to it, and how splendid he thought them red roses was.' I maintain," continued Mrs. Crowe stoutly, "that folks wastes sights o' good money doin' just such foolish things. Tearin' out the insides o' meetin'-houses, and fixin' the pews different; 'twas good enough as 'twas, with mendin': then hard times come, an' they want to put it all back same's 'twas before."

This touched upon an exciting subject to active members of that parish. Miss Binson and Mrs. Crowe belonged to opposite parties, and had at one time come as near hard feelings as they could and yet escape them. Each hastened to speak of other things and to show her untouched friendliness.

"I do agree with you," said Sister Binson, "that few of us know what use to make of money beyond everyday necessities. You've seen more o' the world than I have, and know what's expected. When it comes to taste and judgment about such things, I ought to defer to others"; and with this modest avowal the critical moment passed when there might have been an improper discussion.

In the silence that followed, the fact of their presence in a house of death grew more clear than before. There was something disturbing in the noise of a mouse gnawing at the dry boards of a closet wall near by. Both the watchers looked up anxiously at the clock; it was almost the middle of the night, and the whole world seemed to have left them alone with their solemn duty. Only the brook was awake.

"Perhaps we might give a look upstairs now," whispered Mrs. Crowe, as if she hoped to hear some reason against their going just then to the chamber of death; but Sister Binson rose, with a serious and yet satisfied countenance, and lifted the small lamp from the table. She was much more used to watching than Mrs. Crowe, and much less affected by it. They opened the door into a small entry with a steep stairway; they climbed the creaking stairs, and entered the cold upper room on tiptoe. Mrs. Crowe's heart began to beat very fast as the lamp was put on a high bureau, and made long fixed shadows about the walls. She went hesitatingly toward the solemn shape under its white drapery, and felt a sense of remonstrance as Sarah Ann gently, but in a business-like way, turned back the thin sheet.

"Seems to me she looks pleasanter and pleasanter," whispered Sarah Ann Binson impulsively, as they gazed at the white face with its wonderful smile. "Tomorrow 'twill all have faded out. I do believe they kind of wake up a day or two after they die, and it's then they go." She replaced the light covering, and they both turned quickly away; there was a chill in this upper room.

"'Tis a great thing for anybody to have got through, ain't it?" said Mrs. Crowe softly, as she began to go down the stairs on tiptoe. The warm air from the kitchen beneath met them with a sense of welcome and shelter.

"I don't know why it is, but I feel as near again to Tempy down here as I do up there," replied Sister Binson. "I feel as if the air was full of her, kind of. I can sense things now and then that she seems to say. Now I never was one to take up with no nonsense of sperits and such, but I declare I felt as if she told me just now to put some more wood into the stove."

Mrs. Crowe preserved a gloomy silence. She had suspected before this that her companion was of a weaker and more credulous disposition than herself. "'Tis a great thing to have got through," she repeated, ignoring definitely all that had last been said. "I suppose you know as well as I that Tempy was one that always feared death. Well, it's all put behind her now; she knows what 'tis." Mrs. Crowe gave a little sigh, and Sister Binson's quick sympathies were stirred toward this other old friend, who also dreaded the great change.

"I'd never like to forgit almost those last words Tempy spoke plain to me," she said gently, like the comforter she truly was. "She looked up at me once or twice, that last afternoon after I come to set by her and let Mis' Owen go home; and I says, 'Can I do anything to ease you, Tempy?' and the tears come into my eyes so I couldn't see what kind of a nod she give me. 'No, Sarah Ann, you can't, dear,' says she; and then she got her breath again, and says she, looking at me real meanin', 'I'm only a-gettin' sleepier and sleepier; that's all there is,' says she, and smiled up at me kind of wishful, and shut her eyes. I knew well enough all she meant. She'd been lookin' out for a chance to tell me, and I don't know's she ever said much afterwards."

Mrs. Crowe was not knitting; she had been listening too eagerly. "Yes, 'twill be a comfort to think of that sometimes," she said in acknowledgment.

"I know that old Dr. Prince said once in evenin' meetin' that he'd watched by many a dyin' bed, as we well knew, and enough o' his sick folks had been scared o' dyin' their whole lives through; but when they come to the last, he'd never seen one but was willin', and most were glad to go. ''Tis as natural as bein' born or livin' on,' he said. I don't know what had moved him to speak that night. You know he wa'n't in the habit of it, and 'twas the monthly concert of prayer for foreign missions anyways," said Sarah Ann; "but 'twas a great stay to the mind to listen to his words of experience."

"There never was a better man," responded Mrs. Crowe in a really cheerful tone. She had recovered from her feeling of nervous dread, the kitchen was so comfortable with lamplight and firelight; and just then the old clock began to tell the hour of twelve with leisurely whirring strokes.

Sister Binson laid aside her work, and rose quickly and went to the cupboard. "We'd better take a little to eat," she explained. "The night will go fast after this. I want to know if you went and made some o' your nice cupcake, while you was home today?" she asked in a pleased tone; and Mrs. Crowe acknowledged such a gratifying piece of thoughtfulness for this humble friend who denied herself all luxuries. Sarah Ann brewed a generous cup of tea, and the watchers drew their chairs up to the table presently, and quelled their hunger with good country appetites. Sister Binson put a spoon into a small old-fashioned glass of preserved quince, and passed it to her friend. She was most familiar with the house, and played the part of hostess. "Spread some o' this on your bread and butter," she said to Mrs. Crowe. "Tempy wanted me to use some three or four times, but I never felt to. I know she'd like to have us comfortable now, and would urge us to make a good supper, poor dear."

"What excellent preserves she did make!" mourned Mrs. Crowe. "None of us has got her light hand at doin' things tasty. She made the most of everything, too. Now, she only had that one old quince-tree down in the far corner of the piece; but she'd go out in the spring and tend to it, and look at it so pleasant, and kind of expect the old thorny thing into bloomin'."

"She was just the same with folks," said Sarah Ann. "And she'd never git more'n a little apernful o' quinces, but she'd have every mite o' goodness out o' those, and set the glasses up onto her best-room closet shelf, *so* pleased. 'Twa'nt but a week ago tomorrow mornin' I fetched her a little taste o' jelly in a teaspoon; and she says 'Thank ye,' and took it; an' the minute she tasted it she looked up at me as worried as could be. 'Oh, I don't want to eat that,' says she. 'I always keep that in case o' sickness.' 'You're goin' to have the good o' one tumbler yourself,' says I. 'I'd just like to know who's sick now, if you ain't!' An' she couldn't help laughin', I spoke up so smart. Oh dear me, how I shall miss talkin' over things with her! She always sensed things, and got just the p'int you meant."

"She didn't begin to age until two or three years ago, did she?" asked Mrs. Crowe. "I never saw anybody keep her looks as Tempy did. She looked young long after I begun to feel like an old woman. The doctor used to say 'twas her young heart, and I don't know but what he was right. How she did do for other folks! There was one spell she wasn't at home a day for a fortnight. She got most of her livin' so, and that made her own potatoes and things last her through. None o' the young folks could get married without her, and all the old ones was disappointed if she wa'n't round when they was down with sickness and had to go. An' cleanin', or tailorin' for boys, or rug-hookin' — there was nothin' but what she could do as handy as most. 'I do love to work!' — 'a'n't you heard her say that twenty times a week?"

Sarah Ann Binson nodded, and began to clear away the empty plates. "We may want a taste o' somethin' more towards mornin'," she said. "There's plenty in the closet here; and in case some comes from a distance to the funeral, we'll have a little table spread after we get back to the house."

"Yes, I was busy all the mornin'. I've cooked up a sight o' things to bring over," said Mrs. Crowe. "I felt 'twas the last I could do for her."

They drew their chairs near the stove again, and took up their work. Sister Binson's rocking-chair creaked as she rocked; the brook sounded louder than ever. It was more lonely when nobody spoke, and presently Mrs. Crowe returned to her thoughts of growing old.

"Yes, Tempy aged all of a sudden. I remember I asked her if she felt as well as common, one day, and she laughed at me good. There: when Dan'el begun to look old, I couldn't help feeling as if somethin' ailed him, and like as not 'twas somethin' he was goin' to git right over, and I dosed him for it stiddy, half of one summer."

"How many things we shall be wanting to ask Tempy!" exclaimed Sarah Ann Binson after a long pause. "I can't make up my mind to doin' without her. I wish folks could come back just once, and tell us how 'tis where they've gone. Seems then we could do without 'em better."

The brook hurried on, the wind blew about the house now and then; the house itself was a silent place, and the supper, the warm fire, and an absence of any new topics for conversation made the watchers drowsy. Sister Binson closed her eyes first, to rest them for a minute; and Mrs. Crowe glanced at her compassionately, with a new sympathy for the hard-worked little woman. She made up her mind to let Sarah Ann have a good rest, while she kept watch alone; but in a few minutes her own knitting was dropped, and she too fell asleep. Overhead, the pale shape of Tempy Dent, the outworn body of that generous, loving-hearted, simple soul, slept on also in its white raiment. Perhaps Tempy herself stood near, and saw her own life and its surroundings with new understanding. Perhaps she herself was the only watcher.

Later, by some hours, Sarah Ann Binson woke with a start. There was a pale light of dawn outside the small windows. Inside the kitchen the lamp burned dim. Mrs. Crowe awoke too.

"I think Tempy'd be the first to say 'twas just as well we both had some rest," she said, not without a guilty feeling.

Her companion went to the outer door, and opened it wide. The fresh air was none too cold, and the brook's voice was not nearly so loud as it had been in the midnight darkness. She could see the shapes of the hills, and the great shadows that lay across the lower country. The east was fast growing bright.

"'Twill be a beautiful day for the funeral," she said, and turned again, with a sigh, to follow Mrs. Crowe up the stairs. The world seemed more and more empty without the kind face and helpful hands of Tempy Dent.

THE BRANDON HOUSE

From 'Deephaven.' Copyright, 1877, by James R. Osgood & Co.

I DO not know that the Brandon House is really very remarkable, but I never have been in one that interested me in the same way. Kate used to recount to select audiences at school some of her experiences with her Aunt Katharine; and it was popularly believed that she once carried down some indestructible picture-books when they were first in fashion, and the old lady basted them for her to hem round the edges at the rate of two a day. It may have been fabulous. It was impossible to imagine any children in the old place; everything was for grown people; even the stair railing was too high to slide down on. The chairs looked as if they had been put, at the furnishing of the house, in their places, and there they meant to remain. The carpets were particularly interesting; and I remember Kate's pointing out to me one day a great square figure in one, and telling me she used to keep house there with her dolls for lack of a better play-house, and if one of them chanced to fall outside the boundary stripe, it was immediately put to bed with a cold. It is a house with great possibilities; it might easily be made charming. There are four very large rooms on the lower floor, and six above, a wide hall in each story, and a fascinating garret over the whole, where were many mysterious old chests and boxes, in one of which we found Kate's grandmother's love-letters; and you may be sure the vista of rummages which Mr. Lancaster had laughed about was explored to its very end. . . . Facing each other are two old secretaries, and one of them we ascertained to be the hiding-place of secret drawers, in which may be found valuable records deposited by ourselves one rainy day when we first explored it. We wrote, between us, a tragic "journal" on some yellow old letter-paper we found in the desk. We put it in the most hidden drawer by itself, and flatter ourselves that it will be regarded with great interest some time or other. Of one of the front rooms, "the best chamber," we stood rather in dread. It is very remarkable that there seem to be no ghost stories connected with any part of the house, particularly this. We are neither of us nervous; but there is certainly something dismal about the room. The huge curtained bed and immense easy-chairs, windows and everything, were draped in some old-fashioned kind of white cloth which always seemed to be waving and moving about of itself. The carpet was most singularly colored with dark reds and indescribable grays and browns; and the pattern, after a whole summer's study, could never be followed with one's eye. The paper was captured in a French prize somewhere sometime in the last century; and part of the figure was shaggy, and therein little spiders found habitation, and went visiting their acquaintances across the shiny places. The color was an unearthly pink and a forbidding maroon, with dim white spots, which gave it the appearance of having molded. It made you low-spirited to look long in the mirror; and the great lounge one could not have cheerful associations with, after hearing that Miss Brandon herself did not like it, having seen so many of her relatives lie there dead. There were fantastic china ornaments from Bible subjects on the mantel; and the only picture was one of the Maid of Orleans, tied with an unnecessarily strong rope to a very stout stake. The best parlor we also rarely used, because all the portraits which hung there had for some unaccountable reason taken a violent dislike to us, and followed us suspiciously with their eyes. The furniture was stately and very uncomfortable, and there was something about the room which suggested an invisible funeral.

JAMES WHITCOMB RILEY

JAMES WHITCOMB RILEY was born in Greenfield, Indiana, in 1849. His father, Reuben A. Riley, a native of Pennsylvania, was a lawyer of ability and was considered one of the most effective political speakers of his community. In the Civil War he became captain of cavalry and then achieved distinction as a citizen in the little county-seat during the years following the war. Young Riley seems to have been exceptionally fortunate in his earliest education. The schools of his town were notably good, his teacher was, as he says, "a little old woman rosy and roly-poly who looked as though she might have come tumbling out of a fairy story, so lovable was she and so jolly and so amiable." Then later he came under the direction of Lee O. Harris, himself a poet who "had ever the sweet spirit of a companion rather than the manner of an instructor." Harris introduced him to some of the best poetry and encouraged him to commit to memory and to recite pieces that he liked. Most of the work at school was irksome to him: "There was but one book at school in which I found the slightest interest — McGuffey's old leather-bound reader. It was the tallest book known, and to the boys of my size it was a matter of eternal wonder how I could belong to the big class in that reader." One of the first books which he bought was 'The Divine Emblems' by Quarles.

The regular curriculum of the schools of those days, even when adapted by such a sympathetic teacher as Harris, and of the colleges not far from Greenfield, was not for him, so in his sixteenth year he gave it up altogether and went out into the world to see with his own eyes and to find out what it all meant. He began to write verses not because he wished to be a poet or because he desired to live in a literary atmosphere, but bcause that was the way he must express himself about what he saw and felt. Regarding his facility in versifying he wrote afterwards: "After long labor at verse, you will find there comes a time when everything you see or hear, touch, taste, or smell, resolves itself into rhyme, and rattles away till you can't rest. I mean this literally. The people you meet upon the streets are so many disarranged rhymes, and only need proper coupling. The boulders in the side-walks are jangled words. The crowd of corner loungers is a mangled sonnet with a few lines lacking; the farmer and his teams an idyl of the road, perfected and complete when he stops at the picture of a grocery and hitches to an exclamation point."

Everywhere he saw the interesting panorama of life, at the court-house whither he went with his father to sessions of the county court, in the print shop, the political meetings, besides the adjoining towns and counties which he invaded in the rôle of a traveling sign painter, musician, and story-teller. The people of a typical Indiana county seat on the great thoroughfare, The National Road, were the originals for all his subsequent efforts in verse and nourished his imagination and memory throughout his life.

Riley's first verses to be printed appeared in the Indianapolis Mirror, The Danbury News, Hearth and Home, and the Indianapolis Herald. Later he found employment on the Anderson Democrat and finally on the Indianapolis Journal from 1877 to 1885. While he was associated with the Anderson Democrat he wrote 'Leonainie' and passed it off as a recently discovered poem by Poe. The hoax was so successful that it deceived some of the best American critics, much to the discomfort of the author. Recognition which was not local followed the publication of a series of letters which appeared in the Journal signed Benj. F. Johnson of Boone, consisting of dialect verses introduced with the editorial comment of a Boone County farmer and printed as the old farmer is supposed to have written them. Although these verses were well received and newspapers everywhere copied them, young Riley had his days of gloom. At the instigation of his former teacher, Lee Harris, he sent some of his recent poems to Longfellow who, as Riley afterwards wrote, "replied in his kind and gentle manner with the substantial encouragement for which I had long thirsted." A few of these early poems were put together and published in 1883 under the title, 'The Old Swimmin' Hole and 'Leven More Poems' by Benj. F. Johnson of Boone. This was the first of a number of volumes, the best known of which are the following, besides many selections of his poems and several large editions:

'Afterwhiles' (1888); 'Pipes o' Pan at Zekesbury' (1889); 'Old-Fashioned Roses' (1888); 'Rhymes of Childhood' (1891); 'Green Fields and Running Brooks' (1893); 'Poems at Home' (1893); 'Armazindy' (1894); 'Rubaiyat of Doc Sifers' (1897); 'Home Folks' (1900).

Fame came to him quickly and while he was yet young. In 1887 he was invited to New York to take part in an authors' reading and was introduced by James Russell Lowell as "the voice of a true poet." Then came an urgent call for him to read from his own poems, so insistent that his natural shyness yielded and quickly he became one of the most successful popular readers in America. The discomfort of going about over the country, which annoyed him, was in part relieved by association with such men as Mark Twain, Robert J. Burdette, George Cable, Eugene Field, and "Bill Nye." The years after 1883 brought him continuous applause so that at the time of his death he was probably the most popular poet of his time, widely read in this country and in England. In his own state he was the most beloved citizen, idolized by men of all classes and children of all ages. He received honorary degrees from Yale, Wabash, and the Universities of Pennsylvania and Indiana, and in 1912 the gold medal for poetry by the Academy of

WRITERS OF MODERN AMERICA

THE COLUMBIA UNIVERSITY COURSE IN LITERATURE

BASED ON

THE WORLD'S BEST LITERATURE

The Columbia University Course in Literature

WRITERS OF MODERN AMERICA

VOLUME 2

COSMO PUBLICATIONS

2010 New Delhi

WRITERS OF MODERN AMERICA

THIS VOLUME IS A PART OF THE SERIES
THE COLUMBIA UNIVERSITY COURSE IN LITERATURE

INDIVIDUAL VOLUMES BEING RELEASED TO FULFILL CONSTANT DEMAND FROM THE READERS

First published by COSMO 2010

ISBN 978-81-307-0934-5 (Set)
ISBN 978-81-307-0848-5 (Volume 2)

Published by
COSMO PUBLICATIONS
for
GENESIS PUBLISHING PVT. LTD.
24-B, Ansari Road, Darya Ganj,
New Delhi-110 002,
INDIA

Printed in India

JAMES LANE ALLEN

THE literary work of James Lane Allen was begun with maturer powers and wider culture than most writers exhibit in their first publications. His mastery of English was acquired with difficulty, and his knowledge of Latin he obtained through years of instruction as well as of study. The wholesome open-air atmosphere which pervades his stories, their pastoral character and love of nature, come from the tastes bequeathed to him by three generations of paternal ancestors, easy-going gentleman-farmers of the blue-grass region of Kentucky. On a farm near Lexington, in this beautiful country of stately homes, fine herds, and great flocks, the author was born, in 1849; and there he spent his childhood and youth.

About 1885 he came to New York to devote himself to literature; for though he had contributed poems, essays, and criticisms to leading periodicals, his first important work was a series of articles descriptive of the Blue-Grass Region, published in Harper's Magazine. The field was new, the work was fresh, and the author's ability was at once recognized. Inevitably he chose Kentucky for the scene of his stories, knowing and loving, as he did, her characteristics and her history. While preparing his articles on 'The Blue-Grass Region,' he had studied the Trappist Monastery and the Convent of Loretto, as well as the records of the Catholic Church in Kentucky; and his first stories, 'The White Cowl' and 'Sister Dolorosa,' which appeared in The Century Magazine, were the first fruits of this labor. A controversy arose as to the fairness of these portraitures; but however opinions may differ as to his characterization, there can be no question of the truthfulness of the exposition of the medieval spirit of those retreats.

This tendency to use a historic background marks most of Allen's stories. In 'The Choir Invisible' pioneer Kentucky once more exists. The old clergyman of 'Flute and Violin' lived and died in Lexington, and had been long forgotten when his story "touched the vanishing halo of a hard and saintly life." The old negro preacher, with texts embroidered on his coat-tails, was another figure of reality, unnoticed until he became one of the 'Two Gentlemen of Kentucky.' In Lexington lived and died "King Solomon," who had almost faded from memory when his historian found the record of the poor vagabond's heroism during the plague, and made it memorable in a story that touches the heart and fills the eyes. 'A Kentucky Cardinal,' with 'Aftermath,' its second part, is full of history, and of historic personages. 'Summer in Arcady: A Tale of Nature,' the next of Allen's stories, is no less based on local history and no less full of local color than his other tales, notwithstanding its general unlikeness.

This book sounds a deeper note which grows louder in the later tales. If the realism still has a poetic aspect, the poetry is less pastoral and the realities of city and of sex appear less veiled. The transference from local to more general themes is marked in 'The Reign of Law' and 'The Mettle of the Pasture,' volumes which provoked wide discussion, as well as in what may be called a new series of novels that began with 'The Bride of the Mistletoe' (1909). Allen died in 1925.

A COURTSHIP

From 'Summer in Arcady'

THE sunlight grew pale the following morning; a shadow crept rapidly over the blue; bolts darted about the skies like maddened redbirds; the thunder, ploughing its way down the dome as along zigzag cracks in the stony street, filled the caverns of the horizon with reverberations that shook the earth; and the rain was whirled across the landscape in long, white, wavering sheets. Then all day quiet and silence throughout Nature except for the drops, tapping high and low the twinkling leaves; except for the new melody of woodland and meadow brooks, late silvery and with a voice only for their pebbles and moss and mint, but now yellow and brawling and leaping back into the grassy channels that were their old-time beds; except for the indoor music of dripping eaves and rushing gutters and overflowing rain-barrels. And when at last in the gold of the cool west the sun broke from the edge of the gray, over what a green, soaked, fragrant world he reared the arch of Nature's peace!

Not a little blade of corn in the fields but holds in an emerald vase its treasures of white gems. The hemp-stalks bend so low under the weight of their plumes, that were a vesper sparrow to alight on one for his evening hymn, it would go with him to the ground. The leaning barley and rye and wheat flash in the last rays their jeweled beards. Under the old apple-trees, golden-brown mushrooms are already pushing upward through the leaf-loam, rank with many an autumn's dropping. About the yards the peonies fall with faces earthward. In the stable-lots the larded porkers, with bristles as clean as frost, and flesh of pinky whiteness, are hunting with nervous nostrils for the lush purslain. The fowls are driving their bills up and down their wet breasts. And the farmers who have been shelling corn for the mill come out of their barns, with their coats over their shoulders, on the way to supper, look about for the plow-horses, and glance at the western sky, from which the last drops are falling.

But soon only a more passionate heat shoots from the sun into the planet. The plumes of the hemp are so dry again, that by the pollen shaken from their tops you can trace the young rabbits making their way out to the dusty paths. The shadows of white clouds sail over purple stretches of blue-grass, hiding the sun from the steady eye of the turkey, whose brood is spread out before her like a fan on the earth. At early morning the neighing of the stallions is heard around the horizon; at noon the bull makes the deep, hot pastures echo with his majestic summons; out in the blazing meadows the butterflies strike the afternoon air with more impatient wings; under the moon all night the play of ducks and drakes goes on along the margins of the ponds. Young people are running away and marrying; middle-aged farmers surprise their wives by looking in on them at their butter-making in the sweet dairies; and Nature is lashing everything — grass, fruit, insects, cattle, human creatures — more fiercely onward to the fulfilment of her ends. She is the great heartless haymaker, wasting not a ray of sunshine on a clod, but caring naught for the light that beats upon a throne, and holding man and woman, with their longing for immortality, and their capacities for joy and pain, as of no more account than a couple of fertilizing nasturtiums.

The storm kept Daphne at home. On the next day the earth was yellow with sunlight, but there were puddles along the path, and a branch rushing swollen across the green valley in the fields. On the third, her mother took the children to town to be fitted with hats and shoes, and Daphne also, to be freshened up with various moderate adornments, in view of a protracted meeting soon to begin. On the fourth, some ladies dropped in to spend the day, bearing in mind the episode at the dinner, and having grown curious to watch events accordingly. On the fifth her father carried out the idea of cutting down some cedar-trees in the front yard for fence posts; and whenever he was working about the house, he kept her near to wait on him in unnecessary ways. On the sixth, he rode away with two hands and an empty wagon-bed for some work on the farm; her mother drove off to another dinner — dinners never cease in Kentucky, and the wife of an elder is not free to decline invitations; and at last she was left alone in the front porch, her face turned with burning eagerness toward the fields. In a little while she had slipped away.

All these days Hilary had been eager to see her. He was carrying a good many girls in his mind that summer; none in his heart; but his plans concerning these latter were for the time forgotten. He hung about that part of his farm from which he could have descried her in the distance. Each forenoon and afternoon, at the usual hour of her going to her uncle's, he rode over and watched for her. Other people passed to and fro — children and servants — but not Daphne; and repeated disappointments fanned his desire to see her.

When she came into sight at last, he was soon walking beside her, leading his horse by the reins.

"I have been waiting to see you, Daphne," he said, with a smile, but general air of seriousness. "I have been waiting a long time for a chance to talk to you."

"And I have wanted to see you," said Daphne, her face turned away and her voice hardly to be heard. "I have been waiting for a chance to talk to you."

The change in her was so great, so unexpected, it contained an appeal to him so touching, that he glanced quickly at her. Then he stopped short and looked searchingly around the meadow.

The thorn tree is often the only one that can survive on these pasture lands. Its spikes, even when it is no higher than the grass, keep off the mouths of grazing stock. As it grows higher, birds see it standing solitary in the distance and fly to it, as a resting-place in passing. Some autumn day a seed of the wild grape is thus dropped near its root; and in time the thorn tree and the grapevine come to thrive together.

As Hilary now looked for some shade to which they could retreat from the blinding, burning sunlight, he saw one of these standing off at a distance of a few hundred yards. He slipped the bridle-reins through the head-stall, and giving his mare a soft slap on the shoulder, turned her loose to graze.

"Come over here and sit down out of the sun," he said, starting off in his authoritative way. "I want to talk to you."

Daphne followed in his wake, through the deep grass.

When they reached the tree, they sat down under the rayless boughs. Some sheep lying there ran round to the other side and stood watching them, with a frightened look in their clear, peaceful eyes.

"What's the matter?" he said, fanning his face, and tugging with his fore-finger to loosen his shirt collar from his moist neck. He had the manner of a powerful comrade who means to succor a weaker one.

"Nothing," said Daphne, like a true woman.

"Yes, but there is," he insisted. "I got you into trouble. I didn't think of that when I asked you to dance."

"You had nothing to do with it," retorted Daphne, with a flash. "I danced for spite."

He threw back his head with a peal of laughter. All at once this was broken off. He sat up, with his eyes fixed on the lower edge of the meadow.

"Here comes your father," he said gravely.

Daphne turned. Her father was riding slowly through the bars. A wagon-bed loaded with rails crept slowly after him.

In an instant the things that had cost her so much toil and so many tears to arrange — her explanations, her justifications, and her parting — all the reserve and the coldness that she had laid up in her heart, as one fills high a little ice-house with fear of far-off summer heat — all were quite gone, melted away. And everything that he had planned to tell her was forgotten also at the sight of that stern figure on horseback bearing unconsciously down upon them.

"If I had only kept my mouth shut about his old fences," he said to himself. "Confound my bull!" and he looked anxiously at Daphne, who sat with her eyes riveted on her father. The next moment she had turned, and they were laughing in each other's faces.

"What shall I do?" she cried, leaning over and burying her face in her hands, and lifting it again, scarlet with excitement.

"Don't do anything," he said calmly.

"But Hilary, if he sees us, we are lost."

"If he sees us, we are found."

"But he mustn't see me here!" she cried, with something like real terror. "I believe I'll lie down in the grass. Maybe he'll think I am a friend of yours."

"My friends all sit up in the grass," said Hilary.

But Daphne had already hidden.

Many a time, when a little girl, she had amused herself by screaming like a hawk at the young guineas, and seeing them cuddle invisible under small tufts and weeds. Out in the stable lot, where the grass was grazed so close that the geese could barely nip it, she would sometimes get one of the negro men to scare the little pigs, for the delight of seeing them squat as though hidden, when they were no more hidden than if they had spread themselves out upon so many dinner dishes. All of us reveal traces of this primitive instinct upon occasion. Daphne was doing her best to hide now.

When Hilary realized it he moved in front of her, screening her as well as possible.

"Hadn't you better lie down, too?" she asked.

"No," he replied quickly.

"But if he sees you, he might take a notion to ride over this way!"

"Then he'll have to ride."

"But, Hilary, suppose he were to find me lying down here behind you, hiding?"

"Then he'll have to find you."

"You get me into trouble, and then you won't help me out!" exclaimed Daphne with considerable heat.

"It might not make matters any better for me to hide," he answered quietly. "But if he comes over here and tries to get us into trouble, I'll see then what I can do."

Daphne lay silent for a moment, thinking. Then she nestled more closely down, and said with gay, unconscious archness: "I'm not hiding because I'm afraid of him. I'm doing it just because I want to."

She did not know that the fresh happiness flushing her at that moment came from the fact of having Hilary between herself and her father as a protector; that she was drinking in the delight a woman feels in getting playfully behind the man she loves in the face of danger: but her action bound her to him and brought her more under his influence.

His words showed that he also felt his position — the position of the male who stalks forth from the herd and stands the silent challenger. He was young, and vain of his manhood in the usual innocent way that led him to carry the chip on his shoulder for the world to knock off; and he placed himself before Daphne with the understanding that if they were discovered, there would be trouble. Her father was a violent man, and the circumstances were not such that any Kentucky father would overlook them. But with his inward seriousness, his face wore its usual look of reckless unconcern.

"Is he coming this way?" asked Daphne, after an interval of impatient waiting.

"Straight ahead. Are you hid?"

"I can't see whether I'm hid or not. Where is he now?"

"Right on us."

"Does he see you?"

"Yes."

"Do you think he sees me?"

"I'm sure of it."

"Then I might as well get up," said Daphne, with the courage of despair, and up she got. Her father was riding along the path in front of them, but not looking. She was down again like a partridge.

"How could you fool me, Hilary? Suppose he *had* been looking!"

"I wonder what he thinks I'm doing, sitting over here in the grass like a stump," said Hilary. "If he takes me for one, he must think I've got an awful lot of roots."

"Tell me when it's time to get up."

"I will."

He turned softly toward her. She was lying on her side, with her burning cheek in one hand. The other hand rested high on the curve of her hip. Her braids had fallen forward, and lay in a heavy loop about her lovely shoulders. Her eyes were closed, her scarlet lips parted in a smile. The edges of her snow-white petticoats showed beneath her blue dress, and beyond these one of her feet and ankles. Nothing more fragrant with innocence ever lay on the grass.

"Is it time to get up now?"

"Not yet," and he sat bending over her.

"Now?"

"Not yet," he repeated more softly.

"Now, then?"

"Not for a long time."

His voice thrilled her, and she glanced up at him. His laughing eyes were glowing down upon her under his heavy mat of hair. She sat up and looked toward the wagon crawling away in the distance; her father was no longer in sight.

One of the ewes, dissatisfied with a back view, stamped her forefoot impatiently, and ran round in front, and out into the sun. Her lambs followed, and the three, ranging themselves abreast, stared at Daphne, with a look of helpless inquiry.

"Sh-pp-pp!" she cried, throwing up her hands at them, irritated. "Go away!"

They turned and ran; the others followed; and the whole number, falling into line, took a path meekly homeward. They left a greater sense of privacy under the tree. Several yards off was a small stock pond. Around the edge of this the water stood hot and green in tracks of the cattle and the sheep, and about these pools the yellow butterflies were thick, alighting daintily on the promontories of the mud, or rising two by two through the dazzling atmosphere in columns of enamored flight.

Daphne leaned over to the blue grass where it swayed unbroken in the breeze, and drew out of their sockets several stalks of it, bearing on their tops the purplish seed-vessels. With them she began to braid a ring about one of her fingers in the old simple fashion of the country.

As they talked, he lay propped on his elbow, watching her fingers, the soft slow movements of which little by little wove a spell over his eyes. And once again the power of her beauty began to draw him beyond control. He felt a desire to seize her hands, to crush them in his. His eyes passed upward along her tapering wrists, the skin of which was like mother-of-pearl; upward along the arm to the shoulder — to her neck — to her deeply crimsoned cheeks — to the purity of her brow — to the purity of her eyes, the downcast lashes of which hid them like conscious fringes.

An awkward silence began to fall between them. Daphne felt that the time had come for her to speak. But, powerless to begin, she feigned to busy herself all the more devotedly with braiding the deep-green circlet. Suddenly he drew himself through the grass to her side.

"Let *me!*"

"No!" she cried, lifting her arm above his reach and looking at him with a gay threat. "You don't know how."

"I do know how," he said, with his white teeth on his red underlip, and his eyes sparkling; and reaching upward, he laid his hand in the hollow of her elbow and pulled her arm down.

"No! No!" she cried again, putting her hands behind her back. "You will spoil it!"

"I will not spoil it," he said, moving so close to her that his breath was on her face, and reaching round to unclasp her hands.

"No! No! No!" she cried, bending away from him. "I don't want any ring!" and she tore it from her finger and threw it out on the grass. Then she got up, and, brushing the grass seed off her lap, put on her hat.

He sat cross-legged on the grass before her. He had put on his hat, and the brim hid his eyes.

"And you are not going to stay and talk to me?" he said in a tone of reproachfulness, without looking up.

She was excited and weak and trembling, and so she put out her hand and took hold of a strong loop of the grape-vine hanging from a branch of the thorn, and laid her cheek against her hand and looked away from him.

"I thought you were better than the others," he continued, with the bitter wisdom of twenty years. "But you women are all alike. When a man gets into trouble, you desert him. You hurry him on to the devil. I have been turned out of the church, and now you are down on me. Oh, well! But you know how much I have always liked you, Daphne."

It was not the first time he had acted this character. It had been a favorite rôle. But Daphne had never seen the like. She was overwhelmed with happiness that he cared so much for her; and to have him reproach her for indifference, and see him suffering with the idea that she had turned against him — that instantly changed the whole situation. He had not heard then what had taken place at the dinner. Under the circumstances, feeling certain that the secret of her love had not been discovered, she grew emboldened to risk a little more.

So she turned toward him smiling, and swayed gently as she clung to the vine.

"Yes; I have my orders not even to speak to you! Never again!" she said, with the air of tantalizing.

"Then stay with me a while now," he said, and lifted slowly to her his appealing face. She sat down, and screened herself with a little feminine transparency.

"I can't stay long: it's going to rain!"

He cast a wicked glance at the sky from under his hat; there were a few clouds on the horizon.

"And so you are never going to speak to me again?" he said mournfully.

"Never!" How delicious her laughter was.

"I'll put a ring on your finger to remember me by."

He lay over in the grass and pulled several stalks. Then he lifted his eyes beseechingly to hers.

"Will you let me?"

Daphne hid her hands. He drew himself to her side and took one of them forcibly from her lap.

With a slow, caressing movement he began to braid the grass ring around her finger — in and out, around and around, his fingers laced with her fingers, his palm lying close upon her palm, his blood tingling through the skin upon her blood. He made the braiding go wrong, and took it off and began over again. Two or three times she drew a deep breath, and stole a bewildered look at his face, which was so close to hers that his hair brushed it — so close that she heard the quiver of his own breath. Then all at once he folded his hands about hers with a quick, fierce tenderness, and looked up at her. She turned her face aside and tried to draw her hand away. His clasp tightened. She snatched it away, and got up with a nervous laugh.

"Look at the butterflies! Aren't they pretty?"

He sprang up and tried to seize her hand again.

"You shan't go home yet!" he said, in an undertone.

"Shan't I?" she said, backing away from him. "Who's going to keep me?"

"*I am,*" he said, laughing excitedly and following her closely.

"My father's coming!" she cried out as a warning.

He turned and looked: there was no one in sight.

"He *is* coming — sooner or later!" she called.

She had retreated several yards off into the sunlight of the meadow.

The remembrance of the risk that he was causing her to run checked him. He went over to her.

"When can I see you again — soon?"

He had never spoken so seriously to her before. He had never before been so serious. But within the last hour Nature had been doing her work, and its effect was immediate. His sincerity instantly conquered her. Her eyes fell.

"No one has any right to keep us from seeing each other!" he insisted. "We must settle that for ourselves."

Daphne made no reply.

"But we can't meet here any more — with people passing backward and forward!" he continued rapidly and decisively. "What has happened today mustn't happen again."

"No!" she replied, in a voice barely to be heard. "It must never happen again. We can't meet here."

They were walking side by side now toward the meadow path. As they reached it he paused.

"Come to the back of the pasture — tomorrow! — at four o'clock!" he said, tentatively, recklessly.

Daphne did not answer as she moved away from him along the path homeward.

"Will you come?" he called out to her.

She turned and shook her head. Whatever her own new plans may have become, she was once more happy and laughing.

"Come, Daphne!"

She walked several paces further and turned and shook her head again.

"Come!" he pleaded.

She laughed at him.

He wheeled round to his mare grazing near. As he put his foot into the stirrup, he looked again: she was standing in the same place, laughing still.

"*You* go," she cried, waving him good-by. "There'll not be a soul to disturb you! Tomorrow — at four o'clock!"

"Will you be there?" he said.

"Will you?" she answered.

"I'll be there tomorrow," he said, "and every other day till you come."

By permission of the Macmillan Company, Publishers

BRANDER MATTHEWS

BORN at New Orleans, February 21, 1852, Brander Matthews was educated in New York, where he was graduated from Columbia College in 1871 and from the Columbia Law School two years later. He was admitted to the bar, but a fortunate choice soon turned him to the profession of letters. His first book was published in 1879, and since that date he has contributed uninterruptedly to literature, in drama, fiction, biography, and perhaps most signally, in criticism. In recognition of the distinction of his books he was called to Columbia as lecturer in English in 1891, and in the following year was appointed professor of literature. In 1899 he became the professor of dramatic literature, and in this professorate he has been, since 1903, until his retirement in 1924, the senior member of the Department of English in the university.

He has been a prolific author in several fields. Beginning with a volume on 'The Theaters of Paris' in 1880, he continued his studies of the French stage with 'French Dramatists of the Nineteenth Century' in 1881. Without taking leave of the field of criticism, he then devoted himself principally for more than ten years to the drama, the novel, and the short story. His comedy of 'Margery's Lovers,' produced in 1884, was followed by 'This Picture and That' in 1887 and 'The Decision of the Court' in 1893; and he also collaborated with George H. Jessop in 'A Gold Mine' (1887) and 'On Probation' (1889), and with Bronson Howard in 'Peter Stuyvesant' (1898). In fiction he was more productive; the titles of the novels and short stories in his seventeen volumes of narrative are too numerous for full citation here. They include 'Tom Paulding' (1892), 'His Father's Son' (1895), 'Tales of Fantasy and Fact' (1896), 'Outlines in Local Color' (1897), 'A Confident Tomorrow' (1899), and 'Vistas of New York' (1912). Without delivering himself to the rigors of realistic theory, Professor Matthews consistently wrote of the life that passed before his eyes; and if one type of his fiction should be selected more than another for especial mention, it should probably be such stories as the 'Vignettes of Manhattan' (1894), in which, over and above the tale that is told, he has given us faithful etchings of certain characters and certain modes of living which the hurried growth of the metropolis has all but obliterated and which now endure dimly in the memories of men turned gray.

During the years devoted largely to drama and to fiction, Professor Matthews was also steadily producing in the essay form, using it principally for literary and dramatic criticism, and in the last twenty years the bulk of his work has been done in this field. In the total product of his pen his criticisms form the major part, and probably will prove his most valuable work. 'Pen and Ink,' from 1888, is a sheaf of essays on various subjects, grave and gay. 'Americanisms and Briticisms' (1892) presents, among other things, an unbiased study of variant diction in which information is seasoned with amusement. 'Studies of the Stage' (1894) treats various aspects of the art to which the author has given most thought and devotion. 'Bookbindings, Old and New' (1895) betrays by its title another interest of the author which is reflected here and there in others of his works. The 'Introduction to the Study of American Literature' (1896) has been a companion to thousands of students through school and college courses. 'Aspects of Fiction' (1896) contains, beside much else, studies in the technic of the novel and the short story, an art to which, incidentally, the author has contributed in criticism a body of doctrine comparable with the more extended doctrine of the drama of which he has been a leading formulator. Criticism of this and other kinds he carries on into 'The Historical Novel and Other Essays' in 1901. In 'Parts of Speech,' from the same year, he returns to a study somewhat similar to that of the title-essay in 'Americanisms and Briticisms.' In 'The Development of the Drama' (1903) he traces the history of dramatic art from its beginnings among barbarian tribes to its full development in modern society. Then, after two volumes of essays on various subjects in 'Inquiries and Opinions' (1907) and 'The American of the Future, and Other Essays' (1909), he returns to the art of play-making in 'A Study of the Drama' in 1910. 'A Study of Versification' followed this in the next year. Miscellaneous treatises on literary topics were combined in 'Gateways to Literature' in 1913. 'A Book About the Theater,' in 1916, is the author's latest volume of studies in his favorite art; and his autobiography, 'These Many Years' (1917) is a delightful and interesting record of his experiences and his memories.

Within the limits of this article it is not possible to mention, even by name, all the works of Professor Matthews. A list that should include, besides those already mentioned and others similar in kind, his various pamphlets and booklets, his numerous prefaces and extensive editorial work, and the chapters he has contributed to volumes written in collaboration, would be impressive for its length; and it is superfluous to say that the exceptionally sustained quality of work so varied has long since assured him a position in the front rank of contemporary authors in America. But two at least of his later volumes call for especial notice. In more than one sense his biography of 'Molière,' from 1910, and his 'Shakespeare as a Playwright,' from 1913, are the work of a lifetime. The one he had actually planned in youth; and the other voices with equal emphasis a lifelong interest. But more than this, the matured critical gifts of the author, which had always been devoted most willingly and most valuably to the drama, find here their amplest opportunity in the two leading dramatists of modern times; and the principles of the dramatic art, which the author has derived from the study of its entire history and which he has formulated in a score of other works, are here given their fullest application and illustration. To Professor Matthews the drama has always been much more than a literary art. It is the picture of an action shown not merely in words, but in the flesh, in the persons of certain actors before a certain audience in a certain kind of theater. It is a plastic as well as a literary art. For the kind of criticism that recognizes it as such, Professor Matthews has been one of the leading spokesmen in America, and possibly his success in this endeavor has been his main achievement as a critic. It is therefore natural that the most original chapters of his 'Molière' and of his 'Shakespeare' should be those that attempt to show — what had been too often neglected — how the plays of these dramatists were molded, in accordance with the cardinal laws of all drama, with an eye upon the actors who were to produce them, upon the audiences who were to witness them, and upon the theaters which aided and limited the presentation of them.

The work of Professor Matthews has not failed of recognition. Since the days when he used to write for the Saturday Review his reputation has been international. He is a member of many clubs and societies in America and abroad. Of several of these he was a founder, among them the Authors and the Players in New York, and the Kinsmen in New York and London. He was also an organizer of the American Copyright League, of the Columbia University Press, of the Dunlap Society, of the National Institute of Arts and Letters, and of the Simplified Spelling Board. The last three of these he has served as president or chairman. He bears the honorary doctorate from several universities, wears the ribbon of the Legion of Honor, and sits in the American Academy of Arts and Letters. His friends form a host; the list of them is like a roll-call of the great men of three nations in the last half-century. It is not necessary to add that he knows himself how to be a friend. In conversation he is one of the foremost of American wits. In his work he has been at once a scholar and a man of letters — one of the few men of his time who has given to scholarship the voice of literature. That voice, above all else, has been one of clarity. They say in France that if a sentence is not clear it is not French. Certainly we of the English tongue can boast no such distinction. But the author whose work we have here been reviewing has been a lifelong reader of French prose, and whether this be part of the reason or not, there is no exaggeration in the statement that if a sentence fails of clarity it was not written by Brander Matthews. And clarity in diction, here as usually, is the token of lucidity of mind and sincerity of purpose.

ERNEST HUNTER WRIGHT

AMERICAN CHARACTER

From 'The American of the Future and Other Essays.' Copyright by Charles Scribner's Sons, and reprinted by their permission

I

IN a volume recording a series of talks with Tolstoi, published by a French writer in the final months of 1904, we are told that the Russian novelist thought the Dukhobors had attained to a perfected life, in that they were simple, free from envy, wrath, and ambition, detesting violence, refraining from theft and murder, and seeking ever to do good. Then the Parisian interviewer asked which of the peoples of the world seemed most remote from the perfection to which the Dukhobors had elevated themselves; and when Tolstoi returned that he had given no thought to this question, the French correspondent suggested that we Americans deserved to be held up to scorn as the least worthy of nations.

The tolerant Tolstoi asked his visitor why he thought so ill of us; and the journalist of Paris then put forth the opinion that we Americans are "a people terribly practical, avid of pleasure, systematically hostile to all idealism. The ambition of the American's heart, the passion of his life, is money; and it is rather a delight in the conquest and possession of money than in the use of it. The Americans ignore the arts; they despise disinterested beauty. And now, moreover, they are imperialists. They could have remained peaceful without danger to their national existence; but they had to have a fleet and an army. They set out after Spain, and attacked her; and now they begin to defy Europe. Is there not something scandalous in this revelation of the conquering appetite in a new people with no hereditary predisposition toward war?"

It is to the credit of the French correspondent that after setting down this fervid arraignment, he was honest enough to record Tolstoi's dissent. But although he dissented, the great Russian expressed little surprise at the virulence of this diatribe. No doubt it voiced an opinion familiarized to him of late by many a newspaper of France and of Germany. Fortunately for us, the assertion that foreign nations are a contemporaneous posterity is not quite true. Yet the opinion of foreigners, even when most at fault, must have its value for us as a useful corrective of conceit. We ought to be proud of our country; but we need not be vain about it. Indeed, it would be difficult for the most patriotic of us to find any satisfaction in the figure of the typical American which apparently exists in the mind of most Europeans, and which seems to be a composite photograph of the backwoodsman of Cooper, the negro of Mrs. Stowe, and the Mississippi river folk of Mark Twain, modified perhaps by more vivid memories of Buffalo Bill's Wild West. Surely this is a strange monster; and we need not wonder that foreigners feel towards it as Voltaire felt toward the prophet Habakkuk — whom he declared to be "capable of anything."

It has seemed advisable to quote here what the Parisian journalist said of us, not because he himself is a person of consequence, indeed, he is so obscure that there is no need even to mention his name, but because he has had the courage to attempt what Burke declared to be impossible — to draw an indictment against a whole nation. It would be easy to retort on him in kind, for, unfortunately — and to the grief of all her friends — France has laid herself open to accusations as sweeping and as violent. It would be easy to dismiss the man himself as one whose outlook on the world is so narrow that it seems to be little more than what he can get through a chance slit in the wall of his own self-sufficiency. It would be easy to answer him in either of these fashions, but what is easy is rarely worth while; and it is wiser to weigh what he said and to see if we cannot find our profit in it.

Sifting the essential charges from out the mass of his malevolent accusation, we find this Frenchman alleging first, that we Americans care chiefly for making money; second, that we are hostile to art and to all forms of beauty; and thirdly, that we are devoid of ideals. These three allegations may well be considered, one by one, beginning with the assertion that we are mere money-makers.

II

Now, in so far as this Frenchman's belief is but an exaggeration of the saying of Napoleon's, that the English were a nation of shopkeepers, we need not wince, for the Emperor of the French found to his cost that those same English shopkeepers had a stout stomach for fighting. Nor need we regret that we can keep shop profitably, in these days when the doors of the bankers' vaults are the real gates of the Temple of Janus, war being impossible until they open. There is no reason for alarm or for apology so long as our shopkeeping does not cramp our muscle or curb our spirit, for, as Bacon declared three centuries ago, "walled towns, stored arsenals and armories, goodly races of horse, chariots of war, elephants, ordnance, artillery, and the like, all this is but a sheep in a lion's skin, except the breed and disposition of the people be stout and warlike."

Even the hostile French traveler did not accuse us of any flabbiness of fiber; indeed, he declaimed especially against our "conquering appetite," which seemed to him scandalous "in a new people with no hereditary predisposition toward war." But here he fell into a common blunder; the United States may be a new nation — although as a fact the stars-and-stripes is now older than the tricolor of France, the union jack of Great Britain, and the standards of those newcomers among the nations, Italy and Germany — the United

States may be a new nation, but the people here have had as many ancestors as the population of any other country. The people here, moreover, have "a hereditary predisposition toward war," or at least toward adventure, since they are, every man of them, descended from some European more venturesome than his fellows, readier to risk the perils of the Western Ocean and bolder to front the unknown dangers of an unknown land. The warlike temper, the aggressiveness, the imperialistic sentiment — these are in us no new development of unexpected ambition; and they ought not to surprise anyone familiar with the way in which our forefathers grasped this Atlantic coast first, then thrust themselves across the Alleghenies, spread abroad to the Mississippi, and reached out at last to the Rockies and to the Pacific. The lust of adventure may be dangerous, but it is no new thing; it is in our blood, and we must reckon with it.

Perhaps it is because "the breed and disposition of the people" is "stout and warlike" that our shopkeeping has been successful enough to awaken envious admiration among other races whose energy may have been relaxed of late. After all, the arts of war and the arts of peace are not so unlike; and in either a triumph can be won only by an imagination strong enough to foresee and to divine what is hidden from the weakling. We are a trading community, after all and above all, even if we come of fighting stock. We are a trading community, just as Athens was, and Venice and Florence. And like the men of these earlier commonwealths, the men of the United States are trying to make money. They are striving to make money not solely to amass riches, but partly because having money is the outward and visible sign of success — because it is the most obvious measure of accomplishment.

In his talk with Tolstoi our French critic revealed an unexpected insight when he asserted that the passion of American life was not so much the use of money as a delight in the conquest of it. Many an American man of affairs would admit without hesitation that he would rather make half a million dollars than inherit a million. It is the process he enjoys, rather than the result; it is the tough tussle in the open market which gives him the keenest pleasure, and not the idle contemplation of wealth safely stored away. He girds himself for battle and fights for his own hand; he is the son and the grandson of the stalwart adventurers who came from the Old World to face the chances of the new. This is why he is unwilling to retire as men are wont to do in Europe when their fortunes are made. Merely to have money does not greatly delight him — although he would regret not having it; but what does delight him unceasingly is the fun of making it.

The money itself often he does not know what to do with; and he can find no more selfish use for it than to give it away. He seems to recognize that his making it was in some measure due to the unconscious assistance of the community as a whole; and he feels it his duty to do something for the people among whom he lives. It must be noted that the people themselves also expect this from him; they expect him sooner or later to pay his footing. As a result of this pressure of public opinion and of his own lack of interest in money itself, he gives freely. In time he comes to find pleasure in this as well; and he applies his business sagacity to his benefactions. Nothing is more characteristic of modern American life than this pouring out of private wealth for public service. Nothing remotely resembling it is to be seen now in any country of the Old World; and not even in Athens in its noblest days was there a larger-handed lavishness of the individual for the benefit of the community.

Again, in no country of the Old World is the prestige of wealth less powerful than it is here. This, of course, the foreigner fails to perceive; he does not discover that it is not the man who happens to possess money that we regard with admiration but the man who is making money, and thereby proving his efficiency and indirectly benefiting the community. To many it may sound like an insufferable paradox to assert that nowhere in the civilized world today is money itself of less weight than here in the United States; but the broader his opportunity the more likely is an honest observer to come to this unexpected conclusion. Fortunes are made in a day almost, and they may fade away in a night; as the Yankee proverb put it pithily, "it's only three generations from shirt-sleeves to shirt-sleeves." Wealth is likely to lack something of its glamour in a land where well-being is widely diffused and where a large proportion of the population have either had a fortune and lost it, or else expect to gain one in the immediate future.

Probably also there is no country which now contains more men who do not greatly care for large gains and who have gladly given up money-making for some other occupation they found more profitable for themselves. These are the men like Thoreau — in whose 'Walden,' now half a century old, we can find an emphatic declaration of all the latest doctrines of the simple life. We have all heard of Agassiz — the best of Americans, even though he was born in another republic — how he repelled the proffer of large terms for a series of lectures, with the answer that he had no time to make money. Closely akin was the reply of a famous machinist in response to an inquiry as to what he had been doing — to the effect that he had accomplished nothing of late — "we have just been building engines and making money, and I'm about tired of it." There are not a few men today in these toiling United States who hold with Ben Jonson that "money never made any man rich — but his mind."

But while this is true, while there are some men among us who care little for money, and while there are many who care chiefly for the making of it, ready to share it when made with their fellow-citizens, candor compels the admission that there are also not a few who are greedy and grasping, selfish and shameless, and who stand forward, conspicuous and unscrupulous, as if to justify to the full the aspersions which foreigners cast upon us. Although these men manage for the most part to keep within the letter of the law, their morality is that of the wrecker and of the pirate. It is a symptom of health in the body politic that the proposal has been made to inflict social ostracism upon the criminal rich. We need to stiffen our conscience and to set up a loftier standard of social intercourse, refusing to fellowship with the men who make their money by overriding the law or by undermining it — just as we should have declined the friendship of Captain Kidd laden down with stolen treasure.

In the immediate future these men will be made to feel that they are under the ban of public opinion. One sign of an acuter sensitiveness is the recent outcry against the acceptance of "tainted money" for the support of good works. Although it is wise always to give a good deed the credit of a good motive, yet it is impossible sometimes not to suspect that certain large gifts have an aspect of "conscience money." Some of them seem to be the result of a desire to divert public attention from the evil way in which the money was made to the nobler manner in which it is spent. They appear to be the attempt of a social outlaw to buy his peace with the community. Apparently there are rich men among us, who, having sold their honor for a price, would now gladly give up the half of their fortunes to get it back.

Candor compels the admission also that by the side of the criminal rich there exists the less noxious but more offensive class of the idle rich, who lead lives of wasteful luxury and of empty excitement. When the French reporter who talked with Tolstoi called us Americans "avid of pleasure" it was this little group he had in mind, as he may have seen the members of it splurging about in Paris, squandering and self-advertising. Although these idle rich now exhibit themselves most openly and to least advantage in Paris and in London, their foolish doings are recorded superabundantly in our own newspapers; and their demoralizing influence is spread abroad. The snobbish report of their misguided attempts at amusement may even be a source of danger in that it seems to recognize a false standard of social success or in that it may excite a miserable ambition to emulate these pitiful frivolities. But there is no need of delaying longer over the idle rich; they are only a few, and they have doomed themselves to destruction, since it is an inexorable fact that those who break the laws of nature can have no hope of executive clemency.

"Patience a little; learn to wait,
Years are long on the clock of fate."

III

The second charge which the wandering Parisian journalist brought against us was that we ignore the arts and that we despise disinterested beauty. Here again the answer that is easiest is not altogether satisfactory. There is no difficulty in declaring that there are American artists, both painters and sculptors, who have gained the most cordial appreciation in Paris itself, or in drawing attention to the fact that certain of the minor arts — that of the silversmith, for one, and for another, that of the glass-blower, and the glass-cutter — flourish in the United States at least as freely as they do anywhere else, while the art of designing in stained glass has had a new birth here, which has given it a vigorous vitality lacking in Europe since the Middle Ages. It would not be hard to show that our American architects are now undertaking to solve new problems wholly unknown to the builders of Europe, and that they are often succeeding in this grapple with unprecedented difficulty. Nor would it take long to draw up a list of the concerted efforts of certain of our cities to make themselves more worthy and more sightly with parks well planned and with public buildings well-proportioned and appropriately decorated. We might even invoke the memory of the evanescent loveliness of the White City that graced the shores of Lake Michigan a few years ago; and we might draw attention again to the Library of Congress, a later effort of the allied arts of the architect, the sculptor, and the painter.

But however full of high hope for the future we may esteem these several instances of our reaching out for beauty, we must admit — if we are honest with ourselves — that they are all more or less exceptional, and that to offset this list of artistic achievements the Devil's Advocate could bring forward a damning catalogue of crimes against good taste which would go far to prove that the feeling for beauty is dead here in America and also the desire for it. The Devil's Advocate would bid us consider the flaring and often vulgar advertisements that disfigure our highways, the barbaric ineptness of many of our public buildings, the squalor of the outskirts of our towns and villages, the hideousness and horror of the slums in most of our cities, the negligent toleration of dirt and disorder in our public conveyances, and many another pitiable deficiency of our civilization present in the minds of all of us.

The sole retort possible is a plea of confession and avoidance, coupled with a promise of reformation. These evils are evident and they cannot be denied. But they are less evident today than they were yesterday; and we may honestly hope that they will be less evident tomorrow. The bare fact that they have been observed warrants the belief that unceasing effort will be made to do away with them. Once aroused, public opinion will work its will in due season. And here occasion serves to deny boldly the justice of a part of the accusation which the French reporter brought against us. It may be true that we "ignore the arts" — although this is an obvious overstatement of the case; but it is not true that we "despise beauty." However ignorant the American people may be as a whole, they are in no sense hostile toward art — as certain other peoples seem to be. On the contrary, they welcome it; with all their ignorance, they are anxious to understand it; they are pathetically eager for it. They are so desirous of it that they want it in a hurry, only too often to find themselves put off with an empty imitation. But the desire itself is indisputable; and its accomplishment is likely to be helped along by the constant commingling here of peoples from various other stocks than the Anglo-Saxon, since the mixture of races tends always to a swifter artistic development.

It is well to probe deeper into the question and to face the fact that not only in the arts but also in the sciences we are not doing all that may fairly be expected of us. Athens was a trading city as New York is, but New York has had no Sophocles and no Phidias. Florence and Venice were towns whose merchants were princes, but no American city has yet brought forth a Giotto, a Dante, a Titian. It is now nearly threescore years and ten since Emerson delivered his address on the 'American Scholar,' which has well been styled our intellectual Declaration of Independence, and in which he expressed the hope that "perhaps the time is already come . . . when the sluggard intellect of this continent will look from under its iron lids and fulfil the postponed expectation of the world with something better than the exertions of a mechanical skill." Nearly seventy years ago was this prophecy uttered which still echoes unaccomplished.

In the nineteenth century, in which we came to maturity as a nation, no one of the chief leaders of art, even including literature in its broadest aspects, and no one of the chief leaders in science, was native to our country. Perhaps we might claim that Webster was one of the world's greatest orators and that Parkman was one of the world's greatest historians; but probably the experts outside of the United States would be found unprepared and unwilling to admit either claim, however likely it may be to win acceptance in the future. Lincoln is indisputably one of the world's greatest statesmen; and his fame is now firmly established throughout the whole of civilization. But this is all we can assert; and we cannot deny that we have given birth to very few indeed of the foremost poets, dramatists, novelists, painters, sculptors, architects, or scientific discoverers of the last hundred years.

Alfred Russell Wallace, whose renown is linked with Darwin's and whose competence as a critic of scientific advance is beyond dispute, has declared that the nineteenth century was the most wonderful of all since the world began. He asserts that the scientific achievements of the last hundred years, both in the discovery of general principles and in their practical application, exceed in number the sum total of the scientific achievements to be credited to all the centuries that went before. He considers, first of all, the practical applications, which made the aspect of civilization in 1900 differ in a thousand ways from what it had been in 1801. He names a dozen of these practical applications: railways, steam navigation, the electric telegraph, the telephone, friction-matches, gas-lighting, electric lighting, the photograph, the Roentgen rays, spectrum analysis, anæsthetics, and antiseptics. It is with pride that an American can check off not a few of these utilities as being due wholly or in large part to the ingenuity of one or another of his countrymen.

But his pride has a fall when Wallace draws up a second list not of mere inventions but of those fundamental discoveries, of those fecundating theories underlying all practical applications and making them possible, of those principles "which have extended our knowledge or widened our conceptions of the universe." Of these he catalogs twelve; and we are pained to find that no American has had an important share in the establishment of any of these broad generalizations. He may have added a little here and there; but no single one of all the twelve discoveries is mainly to be credited to any American. It seems as if our French critic was not so far out when he asserted that we were "terribly practical." In the application of principles, in the devising of new methods, our share was larger than that of any other nation. In the working out of the stimulating principles themselves, our share was less than "a younger brother's portion."

It is only fair to say, however, that even though we may not have brought forth a chief leader of art or of science to adorn the wonderful century, there are other evidences of our practical sagacity than those set down by Wallace, evidences more favorable and of better augury for our future. We derived our language and our laws, our public justice and our representative government from our English ancestors, as we derived from the Dutch our religious toleration and perhaps also our large freedom of educational opportunity. In our time we have set an example to others and helped along the progress of the world. President Eliot holds that we have made five important contributions to the advancement of civilization. First of all, we have done more than any other people to further peace-keeping, and to substitute legal arbitration for the brute conflict of war. Second, we have set a splendid example of the broadest religious toleration — even though Holland had first shown us how. Thirdly, we have made evident the wisdom of universal manhood suffrage. Fourthly, by our welcoming of newcomers from all parts of the earth, we have proved that men belonging to a great variety of races are fit for political freedom. Finally, we have succeeded in diffusing material well-being among the whole population to an extent without parallel in any other country in the world.

These five American contributions to civilization are all of them the result of the practical side of the American character. They may even seem commonplace as compared with the conquering exploits of some other races. But they are more than merely practical; they are all essentially moral. As President Eliot insists, they are "triumphs of reason, enterprise, courage, faith, and justice over passion, selfishness, inertness, timidity, and distrust. Beneath each of these developments there lies a strong ethical sentiment, a strenuous moral and social purpose. It is for such work that multitudinous democracies are fit."

IV

A "strong ethical sentiment," and a "strenuous moral purpose" cannot flourish unless they are deeply rooted to idealism. And here we find an adequate answer to the third assertion of Tolstoi's visitor, who maintained that we are "hostile to all idealism." Our idealism may be of a practical sort, but it is idealism none the less. Emerson was an idealist, although he was also a thrifty Yankee. Lincoln was an idealist, even if he was also a practical politician, an opportunist, knowing where he wanted to go, but never crossing a bridge before he came to it. Emerson and Lincoln had ever a firm grip on the facts of life; each of them kept his gaze fixed on the stars — and he also kept his feet firm on the soil.

There is a sham idealism, boastful and shabby, which stares at the moon and stumbles in the mud, as Shelley and Poe stumbled. But the basis of the highest genius is always a broad common sense. Shakespeare and Molière were held in esteem by their comrades for their understanding of affairs; and they each of them had money out at interest. Sophocles was entrusted with command in battle; and Goethe was the shrewdest of the Grand Duke's counselors. The idealism of Shakespeare and of Molière, of Sophocles and of Goethe, is like that of Emerson and of Lincoln; it is unfailingly practical. And thereby it is sharply set apart from the aristocratic idealism of Plato and of Renan, of Ruskin and of Nietzsche, which is founded on obvious self-esteem and which is sustained by arrogant and inexhaustible egotism. True idealism is not only practical, it is also liberal and tolerant.

Perhaps it might seem to be claiming too much to insist on certain points of similarity between us and the Greeks of old. The points of dissimilarity are only too evident to most of us; and yet there is a likeness as well as an unlikeness. Professor Butcher has recently asserted that "no people was ever less detached from the practical affairs of life" than the Greeks, "less insensible to outward utility; yet they regarded prosperity as a means, never as an end. The unquiet spirit of gain did not take possession of their souls. Shrewd traders and merchants, they were yet idealists. They did not lose sight of the higher and distinctively human aims which give life its significance." It will be well for us if this can be said of our civilization two thousand years after its day is done; and it is for us to make sure that "the unquiet spirit of gain" shall not take possession of our souls. It is for us also to rise to the attitude of the Greeks, among whom, as Professor Butcher points out, "money lavished on personal enjoyment was counted vulgar, oriental, inhuman."

There is comfort in the memory of Lincoln and of those whose death on the field of Gettysburg he commemorated. The men who there gave up their lives that the country might live, had answered to the call of patriotism, which is one of the sublimest images of idealism. There is comfort also in the recollection of Emerson, and in the fact that for many of the middle years of the nineteenth century he was the most popular of lecturers, with an unfading attractiveness to the plain people, perhaps, because, in Lowell's fine phrase, he "kept constantly burning the beacon of an ideal life above the lower region of turmoil." There is comfort again in the knowledge that idealism is one manifestation of imagination, and that imagination itself is but an intenser form of energy. That we have energy and to spare, no one denies; and we may reckon him a nearsighted observer who does not see also that we have our full share of imagination, even though it has not yet expressed itself in the loftiest regions of art and of science. The outlook is hopeful, and it is not true that

> "We, like sentries, are obliged to stand
> In starless nights and wait the appointed hour."

The foundations of our commonwealth were laid by the sturdy Elizabethans who bore across the ocean with them their portion of that imagination which in England flamed up in rugged prose and in superb and soaring verse. In two centuries and a half the sons of these stalwart Englishmen have lost nothing of their ability to see visions and to dream dreams, and to put solid foundations under their castles in the air. The flame may seem to die down for a season, but it springs again from the embers most unexpectedly, as it broke forth furiously in 1861. There was imagination at the core of the little war for the freeing of Cuba — the very attack on Spain, which the Parisian journalist cited to Tolstoi as the proof of our predatory aggressiveness. We said that we were going to war for the sake of the ill-used people in the suffering island close to our shores; we said that we would not annex Cuba; we did the fighting that was needful — and we kept our word. It is hard to see how even the most bitter critics can discover in this anything selfish.

There was imagination also in the sudden stopping of all the steamcraft, of all the railroads, of all the street-cars, of all the incessant traffic of the whole nation, at the moment when the body of a murdered chief magistrate was lowered into the grave. This pause in the work of the world was not only touching, it had a large significance to anyone seeking to understand the people of these United States. It was a testimony that the Greeks would have appreciated; it had the bold simplicity of an Attic inscription. And we would thrill again in sympathetic response if it was in the pages of Plutarch that we read the record of another instance. When the time arrived for Admiral Sampson to surrender the command of the fleet he had brought back to Hampton Roads, he came on deck to meet there only those officers whose prescribed duty required them to take part in the farewell ceremonies as set forth in the regulations. But when he went over the side of the flagship he found that the boat which was to bear him ashore was manned by the rest of the officers, ready to row him themselves and eager to render this last personal service; and then from every other ship of the fleet there put out a boat also manned by officers, to escort for the last time the commander whom they loved and honored.

V

As another illustration of our regard for the finer and loftier aspects of life, consider our parks, set apart for the use of the people by the city, the state, and the nation. In the cities of this new country the public playgrounds have had to be made, the most of them, and at high cost — whereas the towns of the Old World have come into possession of theirs for nothing, more often than not inheriting the private recreation-grounds of their rulers. And Europe has little or nothing to show similar either to the reservations of certain states, like the steadily enlarging preserves in the Catskills and the Adirondacks, or to the ampler national parks, the Yellowstone, the Yosemite, and the Grand Canyon of the Colorado, some of them far larger in area than one at least of the original thirteen states. Overcoming the pressure of private greed, the people have ordained the preservation of this natural beauty and its protection for all time under the safe guardianship of the nation and with free access to all who may claim admission to enjoy it.

In like manner many of the battlefields, whereon the nation spent its blood that it might be what it is and what it hopes to be — these have been taken over by the nation itself and set apart and kept as holy places of pilgrimage. They are free from the despoiling hand of any individual owner. They are adorned with monuments recording the brave deeds of the men who fought there. They serve as constant reminders of the duty we owe to our country and of the debt we owe to those who made it and who saved it for us. And the loyal veneration with which these fields of blood have been cherished here in the United States finds no counterpart in any country in Europe, no matter how glorious may be its annals of military prowess. Even Waterloo is in private hands; and its broad acres, enriched by the bones of thousands, are tilled every year by the industrious Belgian farmers. Yet it was a Frenchman, Renan, who told us that what welds men into a nation is "the memory of great deeds done in common and the will to accomplish yet more."

According to the theory of the conservation of energy, there ought to be about as much virtue in the world at one time as at another. According to the theory of the survival of the fittest, there ought to be a little more now than there was a century ago. We Americans today have our faults, and they are abundant enough and blatant enough, and foreigners take care that we shall not overlook them; but our ethical standard — however imperfectly we may attain to it — is higher than that of the Greeks under Pericles, of the Romans under Cæsar, of the English under Elizabeth. It is higher even than that of our forefathers who established our freedom, as those know best who have most carefully inquired into the inner history of the American Revolution. In nothing was our advance more striking than in the different treatment meted out to the vanquished after the Revolution and after the Civil War. When we made our peace with the British the native Tories were proscribed, and thousands of loyalists left the United States to carry into Canada the indurated hatred of the exiled. But after Lee's surrender at Appomattox, no body of men, no single man indeed, was driven forth to live an alien for the rest of his days; even though a few might choose to go, none were compelled.

This change of conduct on the part of those who were victors in the struggle was evidence of an increasing sympathy. Not only is sectionalism disappearing, but with it is departing the feeling that really underlies it — the distrust of those who dwell elsewhere than where we do. This distrust is common all over Europe today. Here in America it has yielded to a friendly neighborliness which makes the family from Portland, Maine, soon find itself at home in Portland, Oregon. It is getting hard for us to hate anybody — especially since we have disestablished the devil. We are good-natured and easy-going; Herbert Spencer even denounced this as our immediate danger, maintaining that we were too good-natured, too easy-going, too tolerant of evil; and he insisted that we needed to strengthen our wills to protest against wrong, to wrestle with it resolutely, and to overcome it before it is firmly rooted.

VI

We are kindly and we are helpful; and we are fixed in the belief that somehow everything will work out all right in the long run. But nothing will work out all right unless we so make it work; and excessive optimism may be as corrupting to the fiber of the people as "the Sabbathless pursuit of fortune," as Bacon termed it. When Mr. John Morley was last in this country he seized swiftly upon a chance allusion of mine to this ingrained hopefulness of ours. "Ah, what you call optimism," he cried, "I call fatalism." But an optimism which is solidly based on a survey of the facts cannot fairly be termed fatalism; and another British student of political science, Mr. James Bryce, has recently pointed out that the intelligent native American has — and by experience is justified in having — a firm conviction that the majority of qualified voters are pretty sure to be right.

Then he suggested a reason for the faith that is in us, when he declared that no such feeling exists in Europe, since in Germany the governing class dreads the spread of socialism, in France the republicans know that it is not impossible that Monarchism and Clericalism may succeed in upsetting the Republic, while in Great Britain each party believes that the other party, when it succeeds, succeeds by misleading the people, and neither party supposes that the majority are any more likely to be right than to be wrong.

Mr. Morley and Mr. Bryce were both here in the United States in the fall of 1904, when we were in the midst of a presidential election, one of those prolonged national debates, creating incessant commotion, but invaluable agents of our political education, in so far as they force us all to take thought about the underlying principles of policy, by which we wish to see the government guided. It was while this political campaign was at its height that the French visitor to the Russian novelist was setting his notes in order and copying out his assertion that we Americans were mere money-grubbers, "systematically hostile to all idealism." If this unthinking Parisian journalist had only taken the trouble to consider the addresses which the chief speakers of the two parties here in the United States were then making to their fellow-citizens in the hope of winning votes, he would have discovered that these practical politicians, trained to perceive the subtler shades of popular feeling, were founding all their arguments on the assumption that the American people as a whole wanted to do right. He would have seen that the appeal of these stalwart partisans was rarely to prejudice or to race-hatred — evil spirits that various orators have sought to arouse and to intensify in the more recent political discussions of the French themselves.

An examination of the platforms, of the letters of the candidates, and of the speeches of the more important leaders on both sides revealed to an American observer the significant fact that "each party tried to demonstrate that it was more peaceable, more equitable, more sincerely devoted to lawful and righteous behavior than the other"; and "the voter was instinctively credited with loving peace and righteousness, and with being stirred by sentiments of good-will toward men." This seems to show that the heart of the people is sound, and that it does not throb in response to ignoble appeals. It seems to show that there is here the desire ever to do right and to see right done, even if the will is weakened a little by easy-going good-nature, and even if the will fails at times to stiffen itself resolutely to make sure that the right shall prevail.

"Liberty hath a sharp and double edge fit only to be handled by just and virtuous men," so Milton asserted long ago, adding that "to the bad and dissolute, it becomes a mischief unwieldy in their own hands." Even if we Americans can clear ourselves of being "bad and dissolute," we have much to do before we may claim to be "just and virtuous." Justice and virtue are not to be had for the asking; they are the rewards of a manful contest with selfishness and with sloth. They are the results of an honest effort to think straight, and to apply eternal principles to present needs. Merely to feel is only the beginning; what remains is to think and to act.

A British historian, Mr. Frederic Harrison, who came here to spy out the land three or four years before Mr. Morley and Mr. Bryce last visited us, was struck by the fact — and by the many consequences of the fact — that "America is the only land on earth where caste has never had a footing, nor has left a trace." It seemed to him that "vast numbers and the passion of equality tend to low averages in thought, in manners, and in public opinion, which the zeal of the devoted minority tends gradually to raise to higher planes of thought and conduct." He believed that we should solve our problems one by one because "the zeal for learning, justice, and humanity" lies deep in the American heart. Mr. Harrison did not say it in so many words, but it is implied in what he did say, that the absence of caste and the presence of low averages in thought, in manners, and in public opinion, impose a heavier task on the devoted minority, whose duty it is to keep alive the zeal for learning, justice, and humanity.

Which of us, if haply the spirit moves him, may not elect himself to this devoted minority? Why should not we also, each in our own way, without pretense, without boastfulness, without bullying, do whatsoever in us lies for the attainment of justice and of virtue? It is well to be a gentleman and a scholar; but after all it is best to be a man, ready to do a man's work in the world. And indeed there is no reason why a gentleman and a scholar should not also be a man. He will need to cherish what Huxley called "that enthusiasm for truth, that fanaticism for veracity, which is a greater possession than much learning, a nobler gift than the power of increasing knowledge." He will need also to remember that

> Kings have their dynasties — but not the mind;
> Cæsar leaves other Cæsars to succeed,
> But Wisdom, dying, leaves no heir behind.

HENRY CUYLER BUNNER

THE position which Henry Cuyler Bunner has come to occupy in the literary annals of our time strengthens as the days pass. If the stream of his genius flowed in gentle rivulets, it traveled as far and spread its fruitful influence as wide as many a statelier river. He was above all things a poet. In his prose as in his verse he has revealed the essential qualities of a poet's nature: he dealt with the life which he saw about him in a spirit of broad humanity and with genial sympathy. When he fashioned the tender triolet on the pitcher of mignonette, or sang of the 'little red box at Vesey Street, he wrote of what he knew; and his stories, even when embroidered with quaint fancies, tread firmly the American soil of the nineteenth century. But Bunner's realism never concerned itself with the record of trivialities for their own sake. When he portrayed the lower phases of city life, it was the humor of that life he caught, and not its sordidness; its kindliness, and not its brutality. His mind was healthy, and since it was a poet's mind, the point upon which it was so nicely balanced was love: love of the trees and flowers, love of his little brothers in wood and field, love of his country home, love of the vast city in its innumerable aspects; above all, love of his wife, his family, and his friends; and all these outgoings of his heart have found touching expression in his verse. Indeed, this attitude of affectionate kinship with the world has colored all his work; it has made his satire sweet-tempered, given his tales their winning grace, and lent to his poetry its abiding power.

The work upon which Bunner's fame must rest was all produced within a period of less than fifteen years. He was born in 1855 at Oswego, New York. He went to the city of New York when very young, and received his education there. A brief experience of business life sufficed to make his true vocation clear, and at the age of eighteen he began his literary apprenticeship on the Arcadian. When that periodical passed away, Puck was just struggling into existence, and for the English edition, which was started in 1877, Bunner's services were secured. Half his short life was spent in editorial connection with that paper. To his wisdom and literary abilities is due in large measure the success which for years attended the enterprise. Bunner had an intimate knowledge of American character and understood the foibles of his countrymen; but he was never cynical, and his satire was without hostility. He despised opportunist journalism. His editorials were clear and vigorous; free not from partisanship, but from partisan rancor, and they made for honesty and independence. His firm stand against political corruption, socialistic vagaries, the misguided and often criminal efforts of labor agitators, and all the visionary schemes of diseased minds, has contributed to the stability of sound and self-respecting American citizenship.

Bunner's first decided success in story-telling was 'The Midge,' which appeared in 1886. It is a tale of New York life in the interesting old French quarter of South Fifth Avenue. Again, in 'The Story of a New York House,' he displayed the same quick feeling for the spirit of the place. This tale first appeared in the newly founded Scribner's Magazine, to which he was later a constant contributor. Here some of his best short stories have been published, including the excellent 'Zadoc Pine,' with its healthy presentation of independent manhood in contest with the oppressive exactions of labor organizations. But Bunner was no believer in stories with a tendency; the conditions which lie at the root of great sociological questions he used as artistic material, never as texts. His stories are distinguished by simplicity of motive; each is related with fine unobtrusive humor and with an underlying pathos, never unduly emphasized. The most popular of his collections of tales is that entitled 'Short Sixes,' which, having first appeared in Puck, were published in book form in 1891. A second volume came out three years later. When the shadow of death had already fallen upon Bunner, a new collection of his sketches was in process of publication: 'Jersey Street and Jersey Lane.' In these, as in the still later 'Suburban Sage,' is revealed the same fineness of sympathetic observation in town and country that we have come to associate with Bunner's name. Among his prose writings there remains to be mentioned the series from Puck entitled 'Made in France.' These are an application of the methods of Maupassant to American subjects; they display that wonderful facility in reproducing the flavor of another's style which is exhibited in Bunner's verse in a still more eminent degree. His prose style never attained the perfection of literary finish, but it is easy and direct, free from sentimentality and rhetoric; in the simplicity of his conceptions and the delicacy of his treatment lies its chief charm.

Bunner's verse, on the other hand, shows a complete mastery of form. He was a close student of Horace; he tried successfully the most exacting of exotic verse-forms, and enjoyed the distinction of having written the only English example of the difficult Chant-Royal. Graceful *vers de société* and bits of witty epigram flowed from him without effort. But it was not to this often dangerous facility that Bunner owed his poetic fame. His tenderness, his quick sympathy with nature, his insight into the human heart, above all, the love and longing that filled his soul, have infused into his perfected rhythms the spirit of universal brotherhood that underlies all genuine poetry. His 'Airs from Arcady' (1884) achieved a success unusual for a volume of poems; and the love lyrics and patriotic songs of his later volume, 'Rowen,' maintain the high level of the earlier book. A few of his poems, as the lovely 'One, Two, Three,' have become popular favorites and have found their way into the anthologies and school readers. If his place is not among the greatest, he has at least produced a sufficient body of fine verse to rescue his name from oblivion and render his memory dear to all who value the legacy of a sincere and genuine poet. He died on May 11, 1896, at the age of forty-one.

TRIOLET

From 'Airs from Arcady.' Copyright by Charles Scribner's Sons

A PITCHER of mignonette,
In a tenement's highest casement:
Queer sort of flower-pot — yet
That pitcher of mignonette
Is a garden in heaven set,
To the little sick child in the basement —
The pitcher of mignonette,
In the tenement's highest casement.

THE LOVE-LETTERS OF SMITH

From 'Short Sixes.' Copyright by Keppler and Schwarzmann

WHEN the little seamstress had climbed to her room in the story over the top story of the great brick tenement house in which she lived, she was quite tired out. If you do not understand what a story over a top story is, you must remember that there are no limits to human greed, and hardly any to the height of tenement houses. When the man who owned that seven-story tenement found that he could rent another floor, he found no difficulty in persuading the guardians of our building laws to let him clap another story on the roof, like a cabin on the deck of a ship; and in the southeasterly of the four apartments on this floor the little seamstress lived. You could just see the top of her window from the street — the huge cornice that had capped the original front, and that served as her window-sill now, quite hid all the lower part of the story on top of the top story.

The little seamstress was scarcely thirty years old, but she was such an old-fashioned little body in so many of her looks and ways that I had almost spelled her "sempstress," after the fashion of our grandmothers. She had been a comely body, too; and would have been still, if she had not been thin and pale and anxious-eyed.

She was tired out tonight, because she had been working hard all day for a lady who lived far up in the "New Wards" beyond Harlem River, and after the long journey home she had to climb seven flights of tenement-house stairs. She was too tired, both in body and in mind, to cook the two little chops she had brought home. She would save them for breakfast, she thought. So she made herself a cup of tea on the miniature stove, and ate a slice of dry bread with it. It was too much trouble to make toast.

But after dinner she watered her flowers. She was never too tired for that, and the six pots of geraniums that caught the south sun on the top of the cornice did their best to repay her. Then she sat down in her rocking-chair by the window and looked out. Her eyry was high above all the other buildings, and she could look across some low roofs opposite and see the further end of Tompkins Square, with its sparse spring green showing faintly through the dusk. The eternal roar of the city floated up to her and vaguely troubled her. She was a country girl; and although she had lived for ten years in New York, she had never grown used to that ceaseless murmur. Tonight she felt the languor of the new season, as well as the heaviness of physical exhaustion. She was almost too tired to go to bed.

She thought of the hard day done and the hard day to be begun after the night spent on the hard little bed. She thought of the peaceful days in the country, when she taught school in the Massachusetts village where she was born. She thought of a hundred small slights that she had to bear from people better fed than bred. She thought of the sweet green fields that she rarely saw nowadays. She thought of the long journey forth and back that must begin and end her morrow's work, and she wondered if her employer would think to offer to pay her fare. Then she pulled herself together. She must think of more agreeable things or she could not sleep. And as the only agreeable things she had to think about were her flowers, she looked at the garden on top of the cornice.

A peculiar gritting noise made her look down, and she saw a cylindrical object that glittered in the twilight, advancing in an irregular and uncertain manner toward her flower-pots. Looking closer, she saw that it was a pewter beer-mug, which somebody in the next apartment was pushing with a two-foot rule. On top of the beer-mug was a piece of paper, and on this paper was written, in a sprawling, half-formed hand:

porter
pleas excuse the libberty And
drink it

The seamstress started up in terror and shut the window. She remembered that there was a man in the next apartment. She had seen him on the stairs on Sundays. He seemed a grave, decent person; but — he must be drunk. She sat down on her bed all a-tremble. Then she reasoned with herself. The man was drunk, that was all. He probably would not annoy her further. And if he did, she had only to retreat to Mrs. Mulvaney's apartment in the rear; and Mr. Mulvaney, who was a highly respectable man and worked in a boiler-shop, would protect her. So, being a poor woman who had already had occasion to excuse — and refuse — two or three "libberties" of like sort, she made up her mind to go to bed like a reasonable seamstress, and she did. She was rewarded, for when her light was out, she could see in the moonlight that the two-foot rule appeared again with one joint bent back, hitched itself into the mug-handle, and withdrew the mug.

The next day was a hard one for the little seamstress, and she hardly thought of the affair of the night before until the same hour had come around again, and she sat once more by her window. Then she smiled at the remembrance. "Poor fellow," she said in her charitable heart. "I've no doubt he's *awfully* ashamed of it now. Perhaps he was never tipsy before. Perhaps he didn't know there was a lone woman in here to be frightened."

Just then she heard a gritting sound. She looked down. The pewter pot was in front of her, and the two-foot rule was slowly retiring. On the pot was a piece of paper, and on the paper was

porter
good for the helth
it makes meet

This time the little seamstress shut her window with a bang of indignation. The color rose to her pale cheeks. She thought that she would go down to see the janitor at once. Then she remembered the seven flights of stairs; and she resolved to see the janitor in the morning. Then she went to bed, and saw the mug drawn back just as it had been drawn back the night before.

The morning came, but somehow the seamstress did not care to complain to the janitor. She hated to make trouble — and the janitor might think — and — and — well, if the wretch did it again she would speak to him herself, and that would settle it. And so on the next night, which was a Thursday, the little seamstress sat down by her window, resolved to settle the matter. And she had not sat there long, rocking in the creaking little rocking-chair which she had brought with her from her old home, when the pewter pot hove in sight, with a piece of paper on the top. This time the legend read:

Perhaps you are afrade i. will
adress you
i am not that kind

The seamstress did not quite know whether to laugh or to cry. But she felt that the time had come for speech. She leaned out of her window and addressed the twilight heaven.

"Mr. — Mr. — sir — I — will you *please* put your head out of the window so that I can speak to you?"

The silence of the other room was undisturbed. The seamstress drew back, blushing. But before she could nerve herself for another attack, a piece of paper appeared on the end of the two-foot rule.

when i Say a thing i
mene it
i have Sed i would not
Adress you and i
Will not

What was the little seamstress to do? She stood by the window and thought hard about it. Should she complain to the janitor? But the creature was perfectly respectful. No doubt he meant to be kind. He certainly was kind, to waste these pots of porter on her. She remembered the last time — and the first — that she had drunk porter. It was at home, when she was a young girl, after she had the diphtheria. She remembered how good it was, and how it had given her back her strength. And without one thought of what she was doing, she lifted the pot of porter and took one little reminiscent sip — two little reminiscent sips — and became aware of her utter fall and defeat. She blushed now as she had never blushed before, put the pot down, closed the window, and fled to her bed like a deer to the woods.

And when the porter arrived the next night, bearing the simple appeal —

Don't be afrade of it
drink it all

the little seamstress arose and grasped the pot firmly by the handle, and poured its contents over the earth around her largest geranium. She poured the contents out to the last drop, and then she dropped the pot, and ran back and sat on her bed and cried, with her face hid in her hands.

"Now," she said to herself, "you've done it! And you're just as nasty and hard-hearted and suspicious and mean as — as pusley!" And she wept to think of her hardness of heart. "He will never give me a chance to say 'I am sorry,'" she thought. And really, she might have spoken kindly to the poor man, and told him that she was much obliged to him, but that he really must not ask her to drink porter with him.

"But it's all over and done now," she said to herself as she sat at her window on Saturday night. And then she looked at the cornice, and saw the faithful little pewter pot traveling slowly toward her.

She was conquered. This act of Christian forbearance was too much for her kindly spirit. She read the inscription on the paper —

porter is good for Flours
but better for Fokes

and she lifted the pot to her lips, which were not half so red as her cheeks, and took a good, hearty, grateful draught.

She sipped in thoughtful silence after this first plunge, and presently she was surprised to find the bottom of the pot in full view. On the table at her side a few pearl buttons were screwed up in a bit of white paper. She untwisted the paper and smoothed it out, and wrote in a tremulous hand — she *could* write a very neat hand:

Thanks.

This she laid on the top of the pot, and in a moment the bent two-foot rule appeared and drew the mail-carriage home. Then she sat still, enjoying the warm glow of the porter, which seemed to have permeated her entire being with a heat that was not at all like the unpleasant and oppressive heat of the atmosphere, an atmosphere heavy with the spring damp. A gritting on the tin aroused her. A piece of paper lay under her eyes:

fine groing weather
Smith

Now it is unlikely that in the whole round and range of conversational commonplaces there was one other greeting that could have induced the seamstress to continue the exchange of communications. But this simple and homely phrase touched her country heart. What did "groing weather" matter to the toilers in this waste of brick and mortar? This stranger must be, like herself, a country-bred soul, longing for the new green and the upturned brown mold of the country fields. She took up the paper, and wrote under the first message:

Fine

But that seemed curt: "for —" she added; "for" what? She did not know. At last in desperation she put down "potatoes." The piece of paper was withdrawn, and came back with an addition:

Too mist for potatos

And when the little seamstress had read this, and grasped the fact that "m-i-s-t" represented the writer's pronunciation of "moist," she laughed softly to herself. A man whose mind at such a time was seriously bent upon potatoes was not a man to be feared. She found a half-sheet of note-paper, and wrote:

I lived in a small village before I came to New York, but I am afraid I do not know much about farming. Are you a farmer?

The answer came:

have ben most Every thing
farmed a Spel in Maine
Smith

As she read this, the seamstress heard the church clock strike nine.

"Bless me, is it so late?" she cried, and she hurriedly penciled *Good Night,* thrust the paper out, and closed the window. But a few minutes later, passing by, she saw yet another bit of paper on the cornice, fluttering in the evening breeze. It said only *good nite,* and after a moment's hesitation, the little seamstress took it in and gave it shelter.

After this they were the best of friends. Every evening the pot appeared, and while the seamstress drank from it at her window, Mr. Smith drank from its twin at his; and notes were exchanged as rapidly as Mr. Smith's early education permitted. They told each other their histories, and Mr. Smith's was one of travel and variety, which he seemed to consider quite a matter of course. He had followed the sea, he had farmed, he had been a logger and a hunter in the Maine woods. Now he was foreman of an East River lumber-yard, and he was prospering. In a year or two he would have enough laid by to go home to Bucksport and buy a share in a ship-building business. All this dribbled out in the course of a jerky but variegated correspondence, in which autobiographic details were mixed with reflections moral and philosophical.

A few samples will give an idea of Mr. Smith's style:

i was one trip to van demens
land

To which the seamstress replied:

It must have been very interesting.

But Mr. Smith disposed of this subject very briefly:

it wornt

Further he vouchsafed:

i seen a chinese cook in
hong kong could cook flapjacks
like your mother

a mishnery that sells Rum
is the menest of Gods crechers

a bulfite is not what it is
cract up to Be

the dagos are wussen the
brutes

i am 6 1¾
but my Father was 6 foot 4

The seamstress had taught school one winter, and she could not refrain from making an attempt to reform Mr. Smith's orthography. One evening, in answer to this communication —

i killd a Bare in Maine 600
lbs waight

she wrote:

Isn't it generally spelled Bear?

but she gave up the attempt when he responded:

a bare is a mene animle any
way you spel him

The spring wore on, and the summer came, and still the evening drink and the evening correspondence brightened the close of each day for the little seamstress. And the draught of porter put her to sleep each night, giving her a calmer rest than she had ever known during her stay in the noisy city; and it began, moreover, to make a little "meet" for her. And then the thought that she was going to have an hour of pleasant companionship somehow gave her courage to cook and eat her little dinner, however tired she was. The seamstress's cheeks began to blossom with the June roses.

And all this time Mr. Smith kept his vow of silence unbroken, though the seamstress sometimes tempted him with little ejaculations and exclamations to which he might have responded. He was silent and invisible. Only the smoke of his pipe, and the clink of his mug as he set it down on the cornice, told her that a living, material Smith was her correspondent. They never met on the stairs, for their hours of coming and going did not coincide. Once or twice they passed each other in the street — but Mr. Smith looked straight ahead of him about a foot over her head. The little seamstress thought he was a very fine-looking man, with his six feet one and three quarters and his thick brown beard. Most people would have called him plain.

Once she spoke to him. She was coming home one summer evening, and a [illegible] of corner-loafers stopped her and demanded money to buy beer, as is their custom. Before she had time to be frightened, Mr. Smith appeared — whence, she knew not — scattered the gang like chaff, and collaring two of the human hyenas, kicked them, with deliberate, ponderous, alternate kicks, until they writhed in ineffable agony. When he let them crawl away, she turned to him and thanked him warmly, looking very pretty now, with the color in her cheeks. But Mr. Smith answered no word. He stared over her head, grew red in the face, fidgeted nervously, but held his peace until his eyes fell on a rotund Teuton passing by.

"Say, Dutchy" he roared. The German stood aghast. "I ain't got nothing to write with!" thundered Mr. Smith, looking him in the eye. And then the man of his word passed on his way.

And so the summer went on, and the two correspondents chatted silently from window to window, hid from sight of all the world below by the friendly cornice. And they looked out over the roof and saw the green of Tompkins Square grow darker and dustier as the months went on.

Mr. Smith was given to Sunday trips into the suburbs, and he never came back without a bunch of daisies or black-eyed Susans or, later, asters or golden-rod for the little seamstress. Sometimes, with a sagacity rare in his sex, he brought her a whole plant, with fresh loam for potting.

He gave her also a reel in a bottle, which, he wrote, he had "maid" himself, and some coral, and a dried flying-fish that was something fearful to look upon, with its sword-like fins and its hollow eyes. At first she could not go to sleep with that flying-fish hanging on the wall.

But he surprised the little seamstress very much one cool September evening, when he shoved this letter along the cornice:

Respected and Honored Madam:

Having long and vainly sought an opportunity to convey to you the expression of my sentiments, I now avail myself of the privilege of epistolary communication to acquaint you with the fact that the Emotions, which you have raised in my breast, are those which should point to Connubial Love and Affection rather than to simple Friendship. In short, Madam, I have the Honor to approach you with a Proposal, the acceptance of which will fill me with ecstatic Gratitude, and enable me to extend to you those Protecting Cares, which the Matrimonial Bond makes at once the Duty and the Privilege of him, who would, at no distant date, lead to the Hymeneal Altar one whose charms and virtues should suffice to kindle its Flames, without extraneous Aid

I remain, Dear Madam,

Your Humble Servant and
Ardent Adorer, J. Smith

The little seamstress gazed at this letter a long time. Perhaps she was wondering in what Ready Letter-Writer of the last century Mr. Smith had found his form. Perhaps she was amused at the results of his first attempt at punctuation. Perhaps she was thinking of something else, for there were tears in her eyes and a smile on her small mouth.

But it must have been a long time, and Mr. Smith must have grown nervous, for presently another communication came along the line where the top of the cornice was worn smooth. It read:

If not understood will you
mary me

The little seamstress seized a piece of paper and wrote: —

If I say Yes, will you speak to me?

Then she rose and passed it out to him, leaning out of the window, and their faces met.

GEORGE EDWARD WOODBERRY

THE reputation of Professor Woodberry began with the appearance of 'The North Shore Watch, and Other Poems,' in 1883. Though he later won fame as a scholar and critic, and as a singularly gifted teacher of literature, he is essentially a poet, and all his work carries the atmosphere of poetic ideals and of song. His first book of poems might be used to illustrate most of the points of view and many of the moods which appeared more fully developed in his later verse, in his criticism, and in his teaching — the love of the Greek tradition, for example, the note of tragedy, and, curiously blended, the notes of optimism and sometimes of disillusion. Few Americans have written of life with more thoughtfulness or with keener criticism; yet the effect of his writing, as of his teaching, has been to encourage the noblest ideals in his many devoted readers, especially in young men. It is hard to appraise his poetry without speaking chiefly of this influence of his, one of the most extraordinary in our literary history, exerted always toward idealistic ends, inspiring not so much a philosophy as an elevation of life.

This emotional appeal of his verse counts with his readers for rather more than his technique, yet he is among the most gifted and the most skilful lyric poets now living in the United States. Whether the illustrations be sought in the beautiful elegy which gave the name to his first book, or in the still finer 'Agathon,' in the same volume — perhaps his best poem — or in 'Wild Eden,' (1899), or in a later book, the remarkable sonnet sequence called 'Ideal Passion' (1917), he is always a singer, a master of language for musical rather than for epigrammatic purposes. Some of the songs in 'Wild Eden' excel for pure charm anything else that American literature has produced in this kind.

Professor Woodberry's repute as a scholar rests chiefly on the masterly life of Poe (1897), revised and enlarged to two volumes in 1909; on the life of Hawthorne (1902), a less famous but more sympathetic work; and on the life of Emerson (1907). Though the soundness of his scholarship is most easily recognized in his biographies, it is felt in all his criticism — in his 'Heart of Man' (1899), in 'The Torch' (1903), and in 'Great Writers' (1907); and through his most scholarly passages the glamour of his poetic prose is undiminished. His readers usually differ, according to their temperaments, as to whether 'Taormina' or 'The Defense of Poetry,' in 'The Heart of Man,' or the essay on Vergil, in 'Great Writers,' is his finest writing in prose, but it is safe to say that the quality of these pieces — their magnificent sweep of thought, their loftiness of mood, and their loveliness of phrase — can be matched in no other American writer. The essay on Vergil, or the little handbook on 'The Appreciation of Literature,' gives some idea of his remarkable insight into poetry. But there can be no written record of the spell which he cast during his teaching years over hundreds of young men, who testify in innumerable ways to his inspiration for good.

George Edward Woodberry was born at Beverly, Massachusetts, May 12, 1855; and was educated at Phillips Exeter, and at Harvard, where he was graduated in 1877. After several years' teaching in the Nebraska State University, he was from 1891 to 1903 professor first of English, then of Comparative Literature in Columbia. Since 1903 most of his time has been devoted to writing, chiefly at his birthplace or in Italy.

JOHN ERSKINE

The following poems are all copyrighted by George Edward Woodberry, and are reprinted by permission of the author, and of Houghton Mifflin Company, publishers

AT GIBRALTAR

I

ENGLAND, I stand on thy imperial ground,
 Not at all a stranger: as thy bugles blow,
 I feel within my blood old battles flow —
The blood whose ancient founts in thee are found.
Still surging dark against the Christian bound
 Wide Islam presses; well its peoples know
 Thy heights that watch them wandering below;
I think how Lucknow heard their gathering sound.

I turn, and meet the cruel, turbaned face.
 England, 'tis sweet to be so much thy son!
I feel the conqueror in my blood and race:
 Last night Trafalgar awed me, and today
Gibraltar wakened; hark, thy evening gun
 Startles the desert over Africa!

II

Thou art the rock of empire, set mid-seas
 Between the East and West, that God has built;
 Advance thy Roman borders where thou wilt,
While run thy armies true with his decrees.

Law, justice, liberty — great gifts are these;
  Watch that they spread where English blood is spilt,
  Lest, mixed and sullied with his country's guilt,
The soldier's life-stream flow, and Heaven displease!

Two swords there are: one naked, apt to smite —
  Thy blade of war; and, battle-storied, one
Rejoices in the sheath, and hides from light.
  American I am: would wars were done!
Now westward, look, my country bids good-night —
  Peace to the world from ports without a gun!

LINES

NOW snowy Apennines shining
  Should breathe my spirit bare;
My heart should cease repining
  In the rainbow-haunted air:
But cureless sorrow carries
  My heart beyond the sea,
Nor comfort in it tarries
  Save thoughts of thee.

The branch of olive shaken
  Silvers the azure sea;
Winds in the ilex weaken:
  Oh, wert thou here with me,
Gray olive, dark ilex, bright ocean,
  The radiant mountains round,
Never for love's devotion
  Were sweeter lodging found!

SODOMA'S 'CHRIST SCOURGED'

I SAW in Siena pictures,
  Wandering wearily;
I sought not the names of the masters
  Nor the works men care to see;

But once in a low-ceiled passage
  I came on a place of gloom,
Lit here and there with halos
  Like saints within the room.
The pure, serene, mild colors
  The early artists used
Had made my heart grow softer,
  And still on peace I mused.
Sudden I saw the Sufferer,
  And my frame was clenched with pain;
Perchance no throe so noble
  Visits my soul again.
Mine were the stripes of the scourging;
  On my thorn-pierced brow blood ran;
In my breast the deep compassion
  Breaking the heart for man.
I drooped with heavy eyelids,
  Till evil should have its will;
On my lips was silence gathered;
  My waiting soul stood still.
I gazed, nor knew I was gazing;
  I trembled, and woke to know
Him whom they worship in heaven
  Still walking on earth below.
Once have I borne his sorrows
  Beneath the flail of fate!
Once, in the woe of his passion,
  I felt the soul grow great!
I turned from my dead Leader!
  I passed the silent door;
The gray-walled street received me:
  On peace I mused no more.

SONG

From 'Agathon'

WHEN love in the faint heart trembles,
  And the eyes with tears are wet,
Oh, tell me what resembles
  Thee, young Regret?

Violets with dewdrops drooping,
  Lilies o'erfull of gold,
Roses in June rains stooping,
  That weep for the cold,
    Are like thee, young Regret.

Bloom, violets, lilies, and roses!
  But what, young Desire,
Like thee, when love discloses
    Thy heart of fire?
The wild swan unreturning,
  The eagle alone with the sun,
The long-winged storm-gulls burning
  Seaward when day is done,
    Are like thee, young Desire.

WOODROW WILSON

HIGH political station in America rarely comes to the pure publicist. Conditions do not favor the recognition and advancement in the official world of men whose claim to leadership is based primarily on an intellectual mastery of statecraft unaccompanied by a long practical apprenticeship in politics. A Guizot, a Macaulay, or a Morley, finds here no open road to power. In recent years he has been finding a less open road in England and France, owing to the development there of the same cause that has operated here — the highly organized party, recruiting its leaders from those who successfully manage the machinery and woo the electorate of local constituencies. Such an organization can commonly offer only a political excursion to the scholar, give him a term or two in Congress where it considers him an amateur, or honor itself by placing him in a distinguished but unstrategic office. The United States has not been lacking at any time in statesmen who were also eminent as scholars and men of letters. But scholarship and letters were not their sanction in politics. The springs of their power, if they had real power, lay elsewhere in the early cultivation of politics as an art, not as a science. Woodrow Wilson was the conspicuous exception to this rule. Alone among American Presidents, almost alone among American statesmen of high rank, he was first drawn in mature years into practical political life in recognition of eminence in scientific political thought. He was fifty-four years old when, on the strength of a reputation entirely academic and literary, he was taken from the head of Princeton University to the Governorship of New Jersey with the well-understood prospect of becoming President of the United States.

Yet, however academic may have been Woodrow Wilson's relations to public affairs through all his formative years, there was nothing abstract about those relations. If he was not in practical politics, his work was of practical politics, concerned with the concrete realities rather than the theories of government, with its vital functioning, which is often obscured in the operation of its conventional and traditional forms. Even in his student days this trait clearly marked him. It gave distinction to his work as a teacher. It fitted him as few men have been fitted outside the rough and tumble of affairs to adapt the working structure of his political theories to the changing material and human factors of public problems.

Woodrow Wilson inherited from his Scotch-Irish ancestors a strenuously logical mind and a rugged fixity of purpose. They combined habits of intellectual abstraction with extreme practicality. His grandfather, James Wilson, came to America in 1807 and became a printer in Pennsylvania. Later in Ohio he founded and edited two newspapers. Woodrow's father, Joseph Ruggles Wilson, was a Presbyterian clergyman. After preaching and teaching in Ohio he became a professor in Hampden Sidney College, Virginia, and in 1855 settled as pastor of a church in Staunton, Va., where on December 28, 1856, Thomas Woodrow Wilson, named after his maternal grandfather, was born. Two years later the family removed to Augusta, Ga., then to Columbia, S. C., and again just before Woodrow entered college, to Wilmington, N. C. The elder Wilson had studied at Princeton Theological Seminary and the son naturally went to the New Jersey college, where James McCosh was then at the height of his fame.

Woodrow Wilson was a good but not an extraordinary student, a normal youth who made friends and loved companionship and entered into the usual activities of college life. He developed a taste for reading and debate. More important, he developed a perfectly clear vision of his aim in life and a pertinacity in pursuing it. He would be a leader in public affairs. The avenues through which he sought influence were changed by circumstances, but never his singleness of purpose, or his intelligent self-direction. "This choice of the best thing for his purpose," said his classmate, Robert Bridges, "was the marked quality of Wilson in his student days." At that time, before sociology had become a popular subject for post-graduate study, the law was the natural approach to politics. Moreover, it was a desirable part of preparation for serious study of government. Accordingly, in the autumn after his graduation in 1879, Wilson matriculated in the law school of the University of Virginia. There he gave much attention to public speaking as a necessary training for his chosen work. Though a Southerner only by accident of birth, environment and association turned him toward the South for his professional career, and on his admission to the bar in 1882 he opened an office in Atlanta, which because of its rapid growth seemed a promising field for a young attorney. Clients were slow in coming and the work for those who did come soon convinced him that the routine of trivial legal business did not lead to that field of public law where his interest lay. So he abandoned practice and, drawn by the post-graduate courses with which Johns Hopkins was just setting a new standard for American universities, he determined to fit himself to be a teacher of politics. He spent two years at Baltimore, receiving the degree of Ph.D. in 1886. In 1885 he went to Bryn Mawr College as associate in history. The next year he became associate professor of history and political science. In 1888 he took the chair of history and political economy at Wesleyan University, and two years later he was called to the chair of jurisprudence at Princeton. His brilliant work as a teacher and writer on history and politics gave him a wide reputation, and when President Paton retired in 1902 he was elected President of Princeton. His administration was characterized by the attempt, through the introduction of a preceptorial system, to bring to the great mass of the students the larger intellectual life which is too often the possession of only the more ambitious. He also sought a more democratic organization of the student body. Outside of the University he was particularly active in the Short Ballot movement, which aimed to secure a more intelligent choice of officials by simplifying the task of the electorate and at the same time to make those officials more clearly responsible for administrative results.

Meantime, Democrats, searching for new leaders who could take advantage of the opening opportunities for their party as none of their old commanders associated with discarded doctrines and methods could hope to do, fixed upon him as a figure of promise. In 1910 he was elected Governor of New Jersey. His early estrangement from the political leaders who had brought him into office and his measures to control corporations added to his popular prestige. In the contest for the Democratic presidential nomination of 1912 his leading rival was Speaker Champ Clark. Though Wilson had been an opponent of free silver and in a much quoted letter had asked somebody to knock William Jennings Bryan "into a cocked hat," Bryan turned from Clark, whom he had favored, on the ground that Tammany had come to his support. This paved the way for Wilson's nomination, which took place after a protracted struggle on the forty-sixth ballot. He triumphed over the divided opposition of Roosevelt and Taft and, despite the reunion of the Republicans and Progressives four years later in support of Charles E. Hughes, he was re-elected.

Although the campaign had been largely influenced by the cry, "He kept us out of war," Germany's revival of its indiscriminate destruction by submarines at the beginning of 1917 frustrated his hopes of peace, and in April of that year forced the United States into the struggle. Once in the war, he acted with great energy and an unyielding will. His gift for crystallizing popular thought added greatly to his world-wide prestige, which reached its height with the conclusion of the armistice and his sailing for Europe on December 4, 1918, personally to conduct the peace negotiations. There he exercised a dominating influence, especially in the formation of the League of Nations. Returning home, he entered on an unsuccessful speaking campaign to bring about America's adhesion to the League and force the Senate to ratify the treaty without amendment. On September 26, 1919, while on this trip, he was prostrated and was for many weeks completely disabled. He recovered sufficiently to resume the direction of his office to the end of his term in 1921, and then lived in retirement at Washington until his death on February 3, 1924.

The stirring events of Woodrow Wilson's administration are too recent and too much in controversy to permit detached judgment of his statesmanship. Neither does the review of his political struggles nor the appraisal of his policies belong in the presentation of Wilson as a thinker and a man of letters.

Throughout his career he was a voluminous writer. His first book was 'Congressional Government: A Study in American Politics' (1885). 'The State: Elements of Historical and Practical Politics' (1889) is a manual on the organization of government in the United States and European countries. 'The State and Federal Government of the United States' followed in 1891. 'Division and Reunion, 1829–1889' (1893) is the last volume of the series 'Epochs of American History.' 'An Old Master and Other Political Essays' (1893) takes its title from a tribute to Adam Smith. 'Mere Literature and Other Essays' (1896) contains studies of Burke and Bagehot, the essay on the writing of history, and his 'Calendar of Great Americans.' 'George Washington,' a spirited biography, appeared in 1896; 'A History of the American People,' in 1902; and 'Constitutional Government in the United States,' in 1908. He wrote the chapter 'State Rights, 1850–1860' in the 'Cambridge Modern History.' 'The New Freedom: A Call for the Emancipation of the Generous Energies of a People' (1913) was the definition of his own attitude toward industrial questions at the time of his election to the Presidency. It was a plea for nineteenth-century *laissez-faire* liberalism robbed of its *laissez faire* and buttressed with the guarantees of state regulation.

Woodrow Wilson's first significant publication was the product of his undergraduate days and was in a peculiar sense prophetic. Its analysis of the executive power in the United States laid the foundation of his conception of the place that the President should fill as a leader of national thought and an influence on legislation, which so avowedly inspired his own administration. This essay on 'Cabinet Government in the United States,' published in the International Review for August, 1879, was an inquiry into the realities of American government working underneath its forms. It was written in the spirit of Bagehot, who influenced him greatly and to whom he later paid a glowing tribute in the essay, 'A Literary Politician.' It is significant, however, that, with all his admiration for Bagehot and his desire to be like him "a man with an imagination which, though it stands aloof, is yet quick to conceive the very things in the thick of which the politician struggles," Wilson felt the deepest lack in Bagehot to be a want of sympathy "with the voiceless body of the people, with the 'mass of unknown men.'" Wilson in his first review summed up his analysis of our administrative machinery with the statement: "Our government is practically carried on by irresponsible committees." He noted that this was due to the lack of anybody in Congress to speak for the nation as a whole. The executive had no means of proposing and explaining measures directly to Congress. A binding link was needed in a responsible cabinet to secure intelligently articulated legislation and vigorous execution. This idea he steadily held and adapted to practical conditions. In 1884 he returned to it in an essay on 'Committee or Cabinet Government,' published in the Overland Monthly, and he used both articles as preliminary studies for his doctor's thesis at Johns Hopkins, which was published in book form under the title 'Congressional Government.' Like its forerunners, instead of deducing our government from its constitutional preconception, it sought in the actual methods of business to discover what our constitution was as a working instrument. Thirteen years later in his 'Constitutional Government in the United States,' made up of lectures delivered at Columbia University, he expressed his political ideas most completely and again dwelt on the fact that the President was much more than the forms of law made him. He was "the leader of his party and the guide of the nation in political purpose, and therefore in legal action." After his election to the Presidency, Wilson in a letter against a single-term amendment, showed how steadily he had been looking to the evolution of the ministerial system. He pointed out that the Presidency was passing through a transitional stage, and that the President "must be Prime Minister, as much concerned with the guidance of legislation as with the just and orderly execution of law," the "spokesman of the nation in everything." As President he acted on that theory, perhaps not more effectively than any of his predecessors, but certainly more frankly and more consciously as a molder of institutions. To establish leadership he substituted the Presidential speech for the traditional message and used it with an increasing tone of confident authority, which reached its highest expression in his address calling for the recognition of war with Germany and formulating the American policy in the struggle. For its elevation of spirit, largeness of conception, and felicity of phrase that address is likely to hold an enduring place among great state papers. It is the best example of President Wilson's style and method when he undertook at once to direct and to express popular opinion.

The writing of history was with Wilson an avocation incidental to the development of his philosophy of politics. His chief work in that field, 'A History of the American People,' is concerned less with events than with their significance in forming the character and institutions of the United States. He broke sharply away from the tendency to exaggerate the importance of "original research" and present the accumulation of facts as the supreme duty of the historian. He sought like Macaulay to arouse the imagination with vivid pictures and bold generalizations, without, like Macaulay, becoming a special pleader. He brought a national vision to the study of American life. He had an instinct for the things that meant the spirit of America in the tangled web of Old World conceptions and New World provincialisms. This is even more apparent in some of his shorter essays than in the popular narrative of the history. In an address before the New Jersey Historical Society in 1895 he dwelt on the Westerner as "the type and master of our American life." 'A Calendar of Great Americans' pays warm and discriminating tribute to Hamilton, whose "English talent for conservation gave to our fiber the stiffness of maturity" and without whom "our national life would have miscarried at the very first"; to Madison as "a type of the slow and thoughtful

English genius for affairs"; to Jefferson, un-American in his philosophical radicalism and sentimental abstractions; to John Quincy Adams and Calhoun as great provincials; but it is in Franklin, Washington, Marshall, Webster, Clay, Grant, and Lee that he found the essence of America, and, above all, in Lincoln. In 'The States and the Federal Government,' a review article of 1908, this son of Virginia sought the pragmatic solution of the old controversy and pointed out that the actual distribution of authority was not a question of sovereignty, but of vitality, and that the bounds of federal power were only those set by the conservative temper of the country — an evolutionary view, which in office led him freely to approve measures that he deemed opportune, even though they involved new demarcations in his own constitutional law. In the same spirit he met the Southerner's view of a government by contract with the doctrine that union had a validity in 1859 that it did not possess in 1789. This feeling for government as an organism, for law and institutions as something living and self-growing, permeated all his political and historical writing and made his teaching dynamic. It gave to opportunism the sanction of principle. It lent flexibility to the most crystallized political conceptions.

An instinct for the interesting marked all of Wilson's work. Dealing almost entirely with historical facts and political theories, he saw them with imagination. His style is literary. It unmistakably reflects the scholar and his genial poise; but at the same time it is vivid and swift moving. He avoids the conventional expression, is given to epigrams and loves the synthetic catchword that becomes the symbol for a whole train of ideas. "The new freedom," "watchful waiting," "too proud to fight," "peace without victory," "the world must be made safe for democracy" — all testify to his aptitude for the striking phrase; some, to the danger of its incautious indulgence. Owing to this habit the apparent clearness of his style is sometimes deceptive. He often uses a concise and vivid phrase that seems to involve a definiteness of thought or commitment, which does not survive analysis; because what he really does is not to formulate a concrete meaning, but to use a concrete expression as a token for general ideas subject to interpretation in many different ways. He did this more in his later political addresses than in his earlier writings; doubtless because it rallied sentiment in support of policies on the details of which agreement was not at the moment possible. But the method was the natural evolution of his literary style, of his gift for seeing things in the large and for applying imagination to the interpretation of facts.

ROSCOE C. E. BROWN

ADDRESS OF THE PRESIDENT OF THE UNITED STATES

Delivered at a Joint Session of the Two Houses of Congress, April 2, 1917

GENTLEMEN OF THE CONGRESS:

I have called the Congress into extraordinary session because there are serious, very serious, choices of policy to be made, and made immediately, which it was neither right nor constitutionally permissible that I should assume the responsibility of making.

On the third of February last I officially laid before you the extraordinary announcement of the Imperial German Government that on and after the first day of February it was its purpose to put aside all restraints of law or of humanity and use its submarines to sink every vessel that sought to approach either the ports of Great Britain and Ireland or the western coasts of Europe or any of the ports controlled by the enemies of Germany within the Mediterranean. That had seemed to be the object of the German submarine warfare earlier in the war, but since April of last year the Imperial Government had somewhat restrained the commanders of its undersea craft in conformity with its promise then given to us that passenger boats should not be sunk and that due warning would be given to all other vessels which its submarines might seek to destroy, when no resistance was offered or escape attempted, and care taken that their crews were given at least a fair chance to save their lives in their open boats. The precautions taken were meager and haphazard enough, as was proved in distressing instance after instance in the progress of the cruel and unmanly business, but a certain degree of restraint was observed. The new policy has swept every restriction aside. Vessels of every kind, whatever their flag, their character, their cargo, their destination, their errand, have been ruthlessly sent to the bottom without warning and without thought of help or mercy for those on board, the vessels of friendly neutrals along with those of belligerents. Even hospital ships and ships carrying relief to the sorely bereaved and stricken people of Belgium, though the latter were provided with safe conduct through the proscribed areas by the German Government itself and were distinguished by unmistakable marks of identity, have been sunk with the same reckless lack of compassion or of principle.

I was for a little while unable to believe that such things would in fact be done by any government that had hitherto subscribed to the humane practices of civilized nations. International law had its origin in the attempt to set up some law which would be respected and observed upon the seas, where no nation had right of dominion and where lay the free highways of the world. By painful stage after stage has that law been built up, with meager enough results, indeed, after all was accomplished that could be accomplished, but always with a clear view, at least, of what the heart and conscience of mankind demanded. This minimum of right the German Government has swept aside under the plea of retaliation and necessity and because it had no weapons which it could use at sea except these which it is impossible to employ as it is employing them without throwing to the winds all scruples of humanity or of respect for the understandings that were supposed to underlie the intercourse of the world. I am not now thinking of the loss of property involved, immense and serious as that is, but only of the wanton and wholesale destruction of the lives of noncombatants, men, women, and children, engaged in pursuits which have always, even in the darkest periods of modern history, been deemed innocent and legitimate. Property can be paid for; the lives of peaceful and innocent people cannot be. The present German submarine warfare against commerce is a warfare against mankind.

It is a war against all nations. American ships have been sunk, American lives taken, in ways which it has stirred us very deeply to learn of, but the ships and people of other neutral and friendly nations have been sunk and overwhelmed in the waters in the same way. There has been no discrimination. The challenge is to all mankind. Each nation must decide for itself how it will meet it. The choice we make for ourselves must be made with a moderation of counsel and a temperateness of judgment befitting our character and our motives as a nation. We must put excited feeling away. Our motive will not be revenge or the victorious assertion of the physical might of the nation, but only the vindication of right, of human right, of which we are only a single champion.

When I addressed the Congress on the twenty-sixth of February last I thought that it would suffice to assert our neutral rights with arms, our right to use the seas against unlawful interference, our right to keep our people safe against unlawful violence. But armed neutrality, it now appears, is impracticable. Because submarines are in effect outlaws when used as the German submarines have been used against merchant shipping, it is impossible to defend ships against their attacks as the law of nations has assumed that merchantmen would defend themselves against privateers or cruisers, visible craft giving chase upon the open sea. It is common prudence in such circumstances, grim necessity indeed, to endeavor to destroy them before they have shown their own intention. They must be dealt with upon sight, if dealt with at all. The German Government denies the right of neutrals to use arms at all within the areas of the sea which it has proscribed, even in the defense of rights which no modern publicist has ever before questioned their right to defend. The intimation is conveyed that the armed guards which we have placed on our merchant ships will be treated as beyond the pale of law and subject to be dealt with as pirates would be. Armed neutrality is ineffectual enough at best; in such circumstances and in the face of such pretensions it is worse than ineffectual: it is likely only to produce what it was meant to prevent; it is practically certain to draw us into the war without either the rights or the effectiveness of belligerents. There is one choice we cannot make, we are incapable of making: we will not choose the path of submission and suffer the most sacred rights of our nation and our people to be ignored or violated. The wrongs against which we now array ourselves are no common wrongs; they cut to the very roots of human life.

With a profound sense of the solemn and even tragical character of the step I am taking and of the grave responsibilities which it involves, but in unhesitating obedience to what I deem my constitutional duty, I advise that the Congress declare the recent course of the Imperial German Government to be in fact nothing less than war against the Government and people of the United States; that it formally accept the status of belligerent which has thus been thrust upon it; and that it take immediate steps not only to put the country in a more thorough state of defense but also to exert all its power and employ all its resources to bring the Government of the German Empire to terms and end the war.

What this will involve is clear. It will involve the utmost practicable co-operation in counsel and action with the governments now at war with Germany, and, as incident to that, the extension to those governments of the most liberal financial credits, in order that our resources may so far as possible be added to theirs. It will involve the organization and mobilization of all the material resources of the country to supply the materials of war and serve the incidental needs of the nation in the most abundant and yet the most economical and efficient way possible. It will involve the immediate full equipment of the navy in all respects but particularly in supplying it with the best means of dealing with the enemy's submarines. It will involve the immediate addition to the armed forces of the United States already provided for by law in case of war at least five hundred thousand men, who should, in my opinion, be chosen upon the principle of universal liability to service, and also the authorization of subsequent additional increments of equal force so soon as they may be needed and can be handled in training. It will involve also, of course, the granting of adequate credits to the Government, sustained, I hope, so far as they can equitably be sustained by the present generation, by well conceived taxation.

I say sustained so far as may be equitable by taxation because it seems to me that it would be most unwise to base the credits which will now be necessary entirely on money borrowed. It is our duty, I most respectfully urge, to protect our people so far as we may against the very serious hardships and evils which would be likely to arise out of the inflation which would be produced by vast loans.

In carrying out the measures by which these things are to be accomplished we should keep constantly in mind the wisdom of interfering as little as possible in our own preparation and in the equipment of our own military forces with the duty — for it will be a very practical duty — of supplying the nations already at war with Germany with the materials which they can obtain only from us or by our assistance. They are in the field and we should help them in every way to be effective there.

I shall take the liberty of suggesting, through the several executive departments of the Government, for the consideration of your committees, measures for the accomplishment of the several objects I have mentioned. I hope that it will be your pleasure to deal with them as having been framed after very careful thought by the branch of the Government upon which the responsibility of conducting the war and safeguarding the nation will most directly fall.

While we do these things, these deeply momentous things, let us be very clear, and make very clear to all the world what our motives and our objects are. My own thought has not been driven from its habitual and normal course by the unhappy events of the last two months, and I do not believe that the thought of the nation has been altered or clouded by them. I have exactly the same things in mind now that I had in mind when I addressed the Senate on the twenty-second of January last; the same that I had in mind when I addressed the Congress on the third of February and on the twenty-sixth of February. Our object now, as then, is to vindicate the principles of peace and justice in the life of the world as against selfish and autocratic power and to set up amongst the really free and self-governed peoples of the world such a concert of purpose and of action as will henceforth ensure the observance of those principles. Neutrality is no longer feasible or desirable where the peace of the world is involved and the freedom of its peoples, and the menace to that peace and freedom lies in the existence of autocratic governments backed by organized force which is controlled wholly by their will, not by the will of the people. We have seen the last of neutrality in such circumstances. We are at the beginning of an age in which it will be insisted that the same standards of conduct and of responsibility for wrong done shall be observed among nations and their governments that are observed among the individual citizens of civilized states.

We have no quarrel with the German people. We have no feeling towards them but one of sympathy and friendship. It was not upon their impulse that their government acted in entering this war. It was not with their previous knowledge or approval. It was a war determined upon as wars used to be determined upon in the old, unhappy days when peoples were nowhere consulted by their rulers and wars were provoked and waged in the interest of dynasties or of little groups of ambitious men who were accustomed to use their fellow-men as pawns and tools. Self-governed nations do not fill their neighbor states with spies or set the course of intrigue to bring about some critical posture of affairs which will give them an opportunity to strike and make conquest. Such designs can be successfully worked out only under cover and where no one has the right to ask questions. Cunningly contrived plans of deception or aggression, carried, it may be, from generation to generation, can be worked out and kept from the light only within the privacy of courts or behind the carefully guarded confidences of a narrow and privileged class. They are happily impossible where public opinion commands and insists upon full information concerning all the nation's affairs.

A steadfast concert for peace can never be maintained except by a partnership of democratic nations. No autocratic government could be trusted to keep faith within it or observe its covenants. It must be a league of honor, a partnership of opinion. Intrigue would eat its vitals away; the plottings of inner circles who could plan what they would and render account to no one would be a corruption seated at its very heart. Only free peoples can hold their purpose and their honor steady to a common end and prefer the interests of mankind to any narrow interest of their own.

Does not every American feel that assurance has been added to our hope for the future peace of the world by the wonderful and heartening things that have been happening within the last few weeks in Russia? Russia was known by those who knew it best to have been always in fact democratic at heart, in all the vital habits of her thought, in all the intimate relationships of her people that spoke their natural instinct, their habitual attitude towards life. The autocracy that crowned the summit of her political structure, long as it had stood and terrible as was the reality of its power, was not in fact Russian in origin, character, or purpose; and now it has been shaken off and the great, generous Russian people have been added in all their naïve majesty and might to the forces that are fighting for freedom in the world, for justice, and for peace. Here is a fit partner for a League of Honor.

One of the things that has served to convince us that the Prussian autocracy was not and could never be our friend is that from the very outset of the present war it has filled our unsuspecting communities and even our offices of government with spies and set criminal intrigues everywhere afoot against our national unity of counsel, our peace within and without, our industries and our commerce. Indeed it is now evident that its spies were here even before the war began; and it is unhappily not a matter of conjecture but a fact proved in our courts of justice that the intrigues which have more than once come perilously near to disturbing the peace and dislocating the industries of the country have been carried on at the instigation, with the support, and even under the personal direction of official agents of the Imperial Government accredited to the Government of the United States. Even in checking these things and trying to extirpate them we have sought to put the most generous interpretation possible upon them because we knew that their source lay, not in any hostile feeling or purpose of the German people towards us (who were, no doubt as ignorant of them as we ourselves were), but only in the selfish designs of a Government that did what it pleased and told its people nothing. But they have played their part in serving to convince us at last that that Government entertains no real friendship for us and means to act against our peace and security at its convenience. That it means to stir up enemies against us at our very doors the intercepted note to the German Minister at Mexico City is eloquent evidence.

We are accepting this challenge of hostile purpose because we know that in such a government, following such methods, we can never have a friend; and that in the presence of its organized power, always lying in wait to accomplish we know not what purpose, there can be no assured security for the democratic governments of the world. We are now about to accept gage of battle with this natural foe to liberty and shall, if necessary, spend the whole force of the nation to check and nullify its pretensions and its power. We are glad, now that we see the facts with no veil of false pretense about them, to fight thus for the ultimate peace of the world and for the liberation of its peoples, the German peoples included: for the rights of nations great and small and the privilege of men everywhere to choose their way of life and of obedience. The world must be made safe for democracy. Its peace must be planted upon the tested foundations of political liberty. We have no selfish ends to serve. We desire no conquest, no dominion. We seek no indemnities for ourselves, no material compensation for the sacrifices we shall freely make. We are but one of the champions of the rights of mankind. We shall be satisfied when those rights have been made as secure as the faith and the freedom of nations can make them.

Just because we fight without rancor and without selfish object, seeking nothing for ourselves but what we shall wish to share with all free peoples, we shall, I feel confident, conduct our operations as belligerents without passion and ourselves observe with proud punctilio the principles of right and of fair play we profess to be fighting for.

I have said nothing of the governments allied with the Imperial Government of Germany because they have not made war upon us or challenged us to defend our right and our honor. The Austro-Hungarian Government has, indeed, avowed its unqualified endorsement and acceptance of the reckless and lawless submarine warfare adopted now without disguise by the Imperial German Government, and it has therefore not been possible for this Government to receive Count Tarnowski, the Ambassador recently accredited to this Government by the Imperial and Royal Government of Austria-Hungary; but that Government has not actually engaged in warfare against citizens of the United States on the seas, and I take the liberty, for the present at least, of postponing a discussion of our relations with the authorities at Vienna. We enter this war only where we are clearly forced into it because there are no other means of defending our rights.

It will be all the easier for us to conduct ourselves as belligerents in a high spirit of right and fairness because we act without animus, not in enmity towards a people or with the desire to bring any injury or disadvantage upon them, but only in armed opposition to an irresponsible government which has thrown aside all considerations of humanity and of right and is running amuck. We are, let me say again, the sincere friends of the German people, and shall desire nothing so much as the early re-establishment of intimate relations of mutual advantage between us — however hard it may be for them, for the time being, to believe that this is spoken from our hearts. We have borne with their present Government through all these bitter months because of that friendship — exercising a patience and forbearance which would otherwise have been impossible. We shall, happily, still have an opportunity to prove that friendship in our daily attitude and actions towards the millions of men and women of German birth and native sympathy who live amongst us and share our life, and we shall be proud to prove it towards all who are in fact loyal to their neighbors and to the Government in the hour of test. They are, most of them, as true and loyal Americans as if they had never known any other fealty or allegiance. They will be prompt to stand with us in rebuking and restraining the few who may be of a different mind and purpose. If there should be disloyalty, it will be dealt with with a firm hand of stern repression; but, if it lifts its head at all, it will lift it only here and there and without countenance except from a lawless and malignant few.

It is a distressing and oppressive duty, Gentlemen of the Congress, which I have performed in thus addressing you. There are, it may be, many months of fiery trial and sacrifice ahead of us. It is a fearful thing to lead this great peaceful people into war, into the most terrible and disastrous of all wars, civilization itself seeming to be in the balance. But the right is more precious than peace, and we shall fight for the things which we have always carried nearest our hearts — for democracy, for the right of those who submit to authority to have a voice in their own governments, for the rights and liberties of small nations, for a universal dominion of right by such a concert of free peoples as shall bring peace and safety to all nations and make the world itself at last free. To such a task we can dedicate our lives and our fortunes, everything that we are and everything that we have, with the pride of those who know that the day has come when America is privileged to spend her blood and her might for the principles that gave her birth and happiness and the peace which she has treasured. God helping her, she can do no other.

THEODORE ROOSEVELT

MORE than one American statesman has also challenged consideration as a man of letters. No one could deny an honorable place in the history of American literature to the authors of the Declaration of Independence, of the two Bunker Hill Orations, and of the Gettysburg Address. The many-sidedness of Franklin, even more obvious than that of Jefferson, Webster, or Lincoln, has been made manifest by the fact that he has demanded parallel lives in the 'American Statesmen' series and in the series of 'American Men of Letters' — pending a third biography whenever there is a series of 'American Men of Science.' Yet Franklin was an author only casually and as it were by accident, since he never published a book; and the contributions which Jefferson, Webster, and Lincoln made to literature were strictly incidental to their political activities.

Theodore Roosevelt is a statesman who made himself known as a man of letters before he attained to prominence in public life and who attained to the highest position in the nation without relaxing his interest in letters and without ceasing to write copiously upon a variety of topics wholly apart from politics. Born in 1858 and graduated from Harvard in 1880, he had begun a 'Naval History of the War of 1812' while still a student in college. This first book was completed and published in 1882. As a result of two or three years' residence in Dakota, he was able to write a record of the 'Hunting Trips of a Ranchman,' which appeared in 1885, to be followed in 1888 by a kindred volume, 'Ranch Life and the Hunting Trail,' and in 1893 by a third book entitled 'The Wilderness Hunter.' The writing of this series of out-of-door books did not interfere with the young author's serious study of American political history. He contributed to the 'American Statesman' series a biography of Thomas H. Benton (1886) and a biography of Gouverneur Morris (1887); and for the series of 'Historic Towns' he prepared the volume on New York (1890).

His most important book, the work which gave him his solid standing as a historian and which led to his election to the presidency of the American Historical Association, is 'The Winning of the West.' The first volume appeared in 1889 and the fourth in 1896. It may be described as a continuation of Parkman's series of books describing the struggle of France and England for the control of North America. Parkman ended his labors with his account of the victory of Wolfe over Montcalm, which decided the conflict, and at the moment of this decision the English colonists were already beginning to thrust themselves across the Alleghenies and to possess themselves of unexplored territory remote from the fringe of settlements along the Atlantic coast, within which they had been content to confine themselves for the century and a half that followed the earliest permanent settlements in Virginia and Massachusetts. The sweep toward the West, continuing even during the dark days of the Revolutionary War, became irresistible in the years following the recognition of the independence of the United States. This steady expansion of the young American nation caused the frontier to be pushed further and further away from the ocean as decade followed decade. And it afforded a superb theme for a young historian who, although born in the East, had made himself intimate with the West in the course of his residence and of his travels beyond the Mississippi.

It was this western experience and this familiarity with the men of the frontier which — at the outbreak of the Spanish War — instigated the raising of a regiment composed of men used to outdoor life and hardened by its vicissitudes. At the conclusion of this brief war, Colonel Roosevelt wrote a history of this organization, a history which was necessarily more or less autobiographical — 'The Rough Riders' published in 1898. Two years later he sent forth his sympathetic study of the career of the masterful Oliver Cromwell. In 1897 he had collected into a volume a group of his essays and addresses, and in 1900 he made a second similar collection, each of them taking its title from that of the opening paper; the earlier was called 'American Ideals,' and the latter, 'The Strenuous Life.' This last was immediately translated into the leading European languages.

The 'Outdoor Pastimes of an American Hunter,' issued in 1902, may be regarded as a fourth volume in the series begun nearly a score of years earlier with 'Hunting Trips.' And closely akin to these are the two ampler tomes describing the author's explorations and investigations as a formal naturalist, 'African Game Trails' (1910), and 'Through the Brazilian Wilderness' (1914). Between the journeys of which accounts are given in these two books, there had been published in 1913 a volume of 'Passages from a Possible Autobiography,' and a volume of addresses and essays, 'History as Literature.' Later selections from his occasional writings are 'A Booklover's Holiday in the Open' (1916), 'Fear God and Take Your Own Part' (1916), and 'The Great Adventure' (1918).

When the list of Roosevelt's books is surveyed as a whole, this two-sidedness discloses itself as multifariousness. There are half a dozen volumes of adventure in different quarters of the globe. There are three biographies and at least two volumes which are autobiographical. There are three historical works of which one is in four volumes and is not complete. And there are several collections of addresses and essays with a remarkably wide range of topics, political and sociological, historical and biographical, critical and literary. These many volumes vary in value as they differ in theme; but they are all of them interesting, each in its own kind; they are none of them perfunctory or careless or casual; they always represent the keen effort and the full energy of the writer; and they unfailingly disclose the flavor of his intense personality. In whatever department of literature he may have chosen to express himself it is always himself that he expresses. He does his own thinking in his own fashion; and he says what he has to say in his own way, with due regard to the traditions but with no effort to suppress his own individuality. Rather is it that individuality which vitalizes the various books and fills them with tingling life. And they are as sincere in workmanship as they are honest in intent.

Roosevelt's writing is nourished by omnivorous reading, in all literatures, ancient and modern. These incessant adventures among books have been undertaken for the sheer enjoyment they have given, for delight in the craftsmanship of the many writers, and for pleasure in the information they may supply about nature and about human nature. As a result, his outlook on literature is as broad as his outlook on life; and his retentive memory has been stored with knowledge ever alive because it has been acquired by active interest, not merely accumulated by arid labor for a set purpose.

Roosevelt's vocabulary is as varied as it is vivacious. It is perhaps to the poets rather than to the prose masters that he owes the picturesqueness of his own style — the certainty of the noun, the propriety of the adjective, the vigor of the verb. He possessed the faculty of inventing felicitous phrases, which exactly express his thought and which are so picturesque and so useful that they immediately passed into current speech, used by thousands who ignore or are ignorant of their authorship. No one can mistake the meaning of Roosevelt's advocacy of the "strenuous life" or his insistence on the "square deal"; and when he denounced certain "malefactors of great wealth" as "undesirable citizens" those thus designated made haste to don the cap that fitted them.

Yet it is not by his miscellaneous writings, by his essays and addresses, his biographies and autobiographies that Colonel Roosevelt may best claim a prominent position among men of letters. These miscellaneous writings are characteristic and they are interesting, each in its own way and in its own degree; but they are not so important nor so likely to be enduring as the boldly built and solidly constructed history of 'The Winning of the West,' quite as characteristic as its author's lesser efforts and quite as interesting, but having a larger scope and a deeper purpose. To describe what he has accomplished in these four successive volumes it may be well to borrow from his own 'History as Literature,' his presidential address to the American Historical Association, in which he set forth the qualities of a true historian. 'The Winning of the West' is a historical work which possesses literary quality and which is therefore "a permanent contribution to the sum of man's wisdom, enjoyment, and inspiration," because its writer has added "wisdom to knowledge and the gift of expression to the gift of imagination."

'The Winning of the West' was dedicated to Francis Parkman; and probably its author would have been proud to be counted the loyal follower of that great writer. John Fiske declared that of all American historians, Parkman "is the most deeply and peculiarly American, yet he is at the same time the broadest and most cosmopolitan," and his vivid account of "the struggle between the machine-like socialistic despotism of New France and the free and spontaneous political vitality of New England" is to be placed "among the world's few masterpieces of the highest rank, along with the works of Herodotus, Thucydides, and Gibbon."

In a cordial appreciation, written in 1892 while Parkman was yet alive, the author of 'The Winning of the West' asserted that the author of 'France and England in North America' had "shown all the qualities of the historian, capacity for wide and deep research, accuracy in details combined with power to subordinate these details to the general effect, a keen perception of the essential underlying causes and results, and the mastery of a singularly clear, pure, and strong style." Parkman had a great subject and he "treated it with knowledge, with impartiality, and with enthusiasm." All these qualities, justly ascribed to Parkman, are in large measure to be ascribed also to his eulogist, whose main subject, less important than Parkman's, he treats with equal knowledge, impartiality, and enthusiasm.

Elsewhere in this same criticism the younger author praised the elder for having acquainted himself by hard experience with the life and character of the men of the border, white and red; Parkman knew "the Indian character and the character of the white frontiersman by personal observation as well as by books; neither knowledge by itself being of much value to the historian." This double equipment was as necessary for the chronicler of the spread of the English-speaking stock westward across the continent as it was for the narrator of the preceding struggle which had resulted in the possibility of this expansion. In the preface to the first volume of 'The Winning of the West,' the author explains that for a number of years he had spent most of his time on the frontier, "and had lived and worked like any other frontiersman." And the points of resemblance between his life and that led by the men on the earlier frontier, further east, a century before, were "numerous and striking."

The historian needs two qualifications; neither of them is frequent; and they are very rarely found united. He must be, first of all, a man of scientific integrity, indefatigably conscientious in the search for the facts, and austerely honest in his dealing with these facts. Then, secondly, he must be a man of letters, an artist in structure and in style, with keen zest and untiring joy in the proper presentation of the results of his research. And thirdly he ought to be a moralist able to disclose the ethical value of the events he has been elucidating. The author of 'The Winning of the West' emphatically withstands the application of this simple test.

He has gone to the sources, sparing no toil which could increase his store of documents; but he is never content to be a mere analyst, a collector of facts, willing to weigh evidence carefully but unwilling to draw the inferences by which only can these facts be illuminated. He has the artist's delight in the selection of the fact of real importance and in the suppression of the non-essential. He does not neglect the details, but he makes these contribute to the larger portrayal of the whole; and he never lets the single trees prevent us from seeing the forest. With an intimate understanding of the frontier as a place and of its inhabitants as conditioned by it, he has the more abidingly needful sympathy with the frontier as a state of mind. He has a fine feeling for the relative values of the several parts of his work and he is able to relate them in due proportion and to bind them together harmoniously. He is a born story-teller with a swift eye for the salient episode and for the outstanding character.

He has the unerring vision which pierces behind the event and spies out its significance, unimportant as it might seem. And while he is vivid and picturesque, while he is setting forth strange happenings and portraying highly colored specimens of humanity, it is with the finer meaning of his history that he is ever preoccupied, with its value to us now, a century after these stalwart adventurers have faded from the memory of men. He writes history for its own sake, no doubt; but he has also the alert moral sense and the interpreting imagination which enable him at the same time to write history for our sakes also.

BRANDER MATTHEWS

BIOGRAPHICAL NOTE. — In addition to his prominence in American oratory and literature, Theodore Roosevelt had a long record of public service and of political distinction. From 1882 to 1884 he was a member of the New York State Legislature, and then a delegate to the Republican National Convention. After being a candidate for Mayor of New York City in 1886, he acted as United States Civil Service Commissioner from 1889 to 1895, after which he served for two years as president of the New York Board of Police Commissioners.

After this service to the state and to the city of New York, Roosevelt became Assistant-Secretary of the Navy, but, on the outbreak of the Spanish-American war in 1898, he resigned his position and, with Surgeon (afterwards Major-General) Leonard Wood, organized the first United States Cavalry, since known as "Roosevelt's Rough Riders," with whom he rendered distinguished service in Cuba, notably at Las Guasimas.

On his return his political career began again. For one year he was Governor of New York; on November 4, 1900, he was elected Vice-President of the United States, and on the death of William McKinley on September 14, 1901, succeeded to the Presidency, to which he was subsequently elected on November 8, 1904. In 1912 as candidate of the Progressive Party he ran against Woodrow Wilson. In 1909–10 he traveled through Africa, shooting big game and making political addresses in Egypt. He returned by way of Europe; he was royally received everywhere, although he announced he was traveling as a "private citizen with no claim to precedence." After the political campaign of 1912, and in response to cordial invitations, he visited several countries in South America, particularly Brazil and Argentina, where he again combined speech-making with exploration. During the World War he wrote and spoke indefatigably; his death on January 6, 1919, cut short his activity. J. B. Bishop edited 'Theodore Roosevelt's Letters to His Children' (1919), and in 1925 'Selections from the Correspondence of Theodore Roosevelt and Henry Cabot Lodge' appeared. A complete Memorial Edition of his works, edited by H. Hagedorn, was prepared in 1923–25.

CITIZENSHIP IN A REPUBLIC

An Address delivered at the Sorbonne, Paris, April 23, 1910. Published along with other essays by Theodore Roosevelt in a volume entitled 'History as Literature.' Copyright by Charles Scribner's Sons and reprinted by their permission

STRANGE and impressive associations rise in the mind of a man from the New World who speaks before this august body in this ancient institution of learning. Before his eyes pass the shadows of mighty kings and warlike nobles, of great masters of law and theology; through the shining dust of the dead centuries he sees crowded figures that tell of the power and learning and splendor of times gone by; and he sees also the innumerable host of humble students to whom clerkship meant emancipation, to whom it was well-nigh the only outlet from the dark thraldom of the Middle Ages.

This was the most famous university of medieval Europe at a time when no one dreamed that there was a New World to discover. Its services to the cause of human knowledge already stretched far back into the remote past at a time when my forefathers, three centuries ago, were among the sparse bands of traders, plowmen, wood-choppers, and fisherfolk, who, in hard struggle with the iron unfriendliness of the Indian-haunted land, were laying the foundations of what has now become the giant republic of the West. To conquer a continent, to tame the shaggy roughness of wild nature, means grim warfare; and the generations engaged in it cannot keep, still less add to, the stores of garnered wisdom which once were theirs, and which are still in the hands of their brethren who dwell in the old land. To conquer the wilderness means to wrest victory from the same hostile forces with which mankind struggled in the immemorial infancy of our race. The primeval conditions must be met by primeval qualities which are incompatible with the retention of much that has been painfully acquired by humanity as through the ages it has striven upward toward civilization. In conditions so primitive there can be but a primitive culture. At first only the rudest schools can be established, for no others would meet the needs of the hard-driven, sinewy folk who thrust forward the frontier in the teeth of savage man and savage nature; and many years elapse before any of these schools can develop into seats of higher learning and broader culture.

The pioneer days pass; the stump-dotted clearings expand into vast stretches of fertile farmland; the stockaded clusters of log cabins change into towns; the hunters of game, the fellers of trees, the rude frontier traders and tillers of the soil, the men who wander all their lives long through the wilderness as the heralds and harbingers of an oncoming civilization, themselves vanish before the civilization for which they have prepared the way. The children of their successors and supplanters, and then their children and children's children, change and develop with extraordinary rapidity. The conditions accentuate vices and virtues, energy and ruthlessness, all the good qualities and all the defects of an intense individualism, self-reliant, self-centered, far more conscious of its rights than of its duties, and blind to its own shortcomings. To the hard materialism of the frontier days succeeds the hard materialism of an industrialism even more intense and absorbing than that of the older nations; although these themselves have likewise already entered on the age of a complex and predominantly industrial civilization.

As the country grows, its people, who have won success in so many lines, turn back to try to recover the possessions of the mind and the spirit, which perforce their fathers threw aside in order better to wage the first rough battles for the continent their children inherit. The leaders of thought and of action grope their way forward to a new life, realizing, sometimes dimly, sometimes clear-sightedly, that the life of material gain, whether for a nation or an individual, is of value only as a foundation, only as there is added to it the uplift that comes from devotion to loftier ideals. The new life thus sought can in part be developed afresh from what is round about in the New World; but it can be developed in full only by freely drawing upon the treasure-houses of the Old World, upon the treasures stored in the ancient abodes of wisdom and learning, such as this where I speak today. It is a mistake for any nation merely to copy another; but it is an even greater mistake, it is a proof of weakness in any nation, not to be anxious to learn from another, and willing and able to adapt that learning to the new national conditions and make it fruitful and productive therein. It is for us of the New World to sit at the feet of the Gamaliel of the Old; then, if we have the right stuff in us, we can show that Paul in his turn can become a teacher as well as a scholar.

Today I shall speak to you on the subject of individual citizenship, the one subject of vital importance to you, my hearers, and to me and my countrymen, because you and we are citizens of great democratic republics. A democratic republic such as each of ours—an effort to realize in its full sense government by, of, and for the people—represents the most gigantic of all possible social experiments, the one fraught with greatest possibilities alike for good and evil. The success of republics like yours and like ours means the glory, and our failure the despair, of mankind; and for you and for us the question of the quality of the individual citizen is supreme. Under other forms of government, under the rule of one man or of a very few men, the quality of the rulers is all-important. If, under such governments, the quality of the rulers is high enough, then the nation may for generations lead a brilliant career, and add substantially to the sum of world achievement, no matter how low the quality of the average citizen; because the average citizen is an almost negligible quantity in working out the final results of that type of national greatness.

But with you and with us the case is different. With you here, and with us in my own home, in the long run, success or failure will be conditioned upon the way in which the average man, the average woman, does his or her duty, first in the ordinary, everyday affairs of life, and next in those great occasional crises which call for the heroic virtues. The average citizen must be a good citizen if our republics are to succeed. The stream will not permanently rise higher than the main source; and the main source of national power and national greatness is found in the average citizenship of the nation. Therefore it behooves us to do our best to see that the standard of the average citizen is kept high; and the average cannot be kept high unless the standard of the leaders is very much higher.

It is well if a large proportion of the leaders in any republic, in any democracy, are, as a matter of course, drawn from the classes represented in this audience today; but only provided that those classes possess the gifts of sympathy with plain people and of devotion to great ideals. You and those like you have received special advantages; you have all of you had the opportunity for mental training; many of you have had leisure; most of you have had a chance for the enjoyment of life far greater than comes to the majority of your fellows. To you and your kind much has been given, and from you much should be expected. Yet there are certain failings against which it is especially incumbent that both men of trained and cultivated intellect, and men of inherited wealth and position, should especially guard themselves, because to these failings they are especially liable; and if yielded to, their—your—chances of useful service are at an end.

Let the man of learning, the man of lettered leisure, beware of that queer and cheap temptation to pose to himself and to others as the cynic, as the man who has outgrown emotions and beliefs, the man to whom good and evil are as one. The poorest way to face life is to face it with a sneer. There are many men who feel a kind of twisted pride in cynicism; there are many who confine themselves to criticism of the way others do what they themselves dare not even attempt. There is no more unhealthy being, no man less worthy of respect, than he who either really holds, or feigns to hold, an attitude of sneering disbelief toward all that is great and lofty, whether in achievement or in that noble effort which, even if it fails, comes second to achievement. A cynical habit of thought and speech, a readiness to criticize work which the critic himself never tries to perform, an intellectual aloofness which will not accept contact with life's realities — all these are marks, not, as the possessor would fain think, of superiority, but of weakness. They mark the men unfit to bear their part manfully in the stern strife of living, who seek, in the affectation of contempt for the achievements of others, to hide from others and from themselves their own weakness. The rôle is easy; there is none easier, save only the rôle of the man who sneers alike at both criticism and performance.

It is not the critic who counts; not the man who points out how the strong man stumbles, or where the doer of deeds could have done them better. The credit belongs to the man who is actually in the arena, whose face is marred by dust and sweat and blood; who strives valiantly; who errs, and comes short again and again, because there is no effort without error and shortcoming; but who does actually strive to do the deeds; who knows the great enthusiasms, the great devotions; who spends himself in a worthy cause; who at the best knows in the end of the triumph of high achievement, and who at the worst, if he fails, at least fails while daring greatly, so that his place shall never be with those cold and timid souls who know neither victory nor defeat. Shame on the man of cultivated taste who permits refinement to develop into a fastidiousness that unfits him for doing the rough work of a workaday world! Among the free peoples who govern themselves there is but a small field of usefulness open for the men of cloistered life who shrink from contact with their fellows. Still less room is there for those who deride or slight what is done by those who actually bear the brunt of the day; nor yet for those others who always profess that they would like to take action, if only the conditions of life were not what they actually are. The man who does nothing cuts the same sordid figure in the pages of history, whether he be cynic, or fop, or voluptuary. There is little use for the being whose tepid soul knows nothing of the great and generous emotion, of the high pride, the stern belief, the lofty enthusiasm, of the men who quell the storm and ride the thunder. Well for these men if they succeed; well also, though not so well, if they fail, given only that they have nobly ventured, and have put forth all their heart and strength. It is war-worn Hotspur, spent with hard fighting, he of the many errors and the valiant end, over whose memory we love to linger, not over the memory of the young lord who "but for the vile guns would have been a soldier."

France has taught many lessons to other nations; surely one of the most important is the lesson her whole history teaches, that a high artistic and literary development is compatible with notable leadership in arms and statecraft. The brilliant gallantry of the French soldier has for many centuries been proverbial; and during these same centuries at every court in Europe the "freemasons of fashion" have treated the French tongue as their common speech; while every artist and man of letters, and every man of science able to appreciate that marvelous instrument of precision, French prose, has turned toward France for aid and inspiration. How long the leadership in arms and letters has lasted is curiously illustrated by the fact that the earliest masterpiece in a modern tongue is the splendid French epic which tells of Roland's doom and the vengeance of Charlemagne when the lords of the Frankish host were stricken at Roncesvalles.

Let those who have, keep, let those who have not, strive to attain, a high standard of cultivation and scholarship. Yet let us remember that these stand second to certain other things. There is need of a sound body, and even more need of a sound mind. But above mind and above body stands character — the sum of those qualities which we mean when we speak of a man's force and courage, of his good faith and sense and honor. I believe in exercise for the body, always provided that we keep in mind that physical development is a means and not an end. I believe, of course, in giving to all the people a good education. But the education must contain much besides book learning in order to be really good. We must ever remember that no keenness and subtleness of intellect, no polish, no cleverness, in any way make up for the lack of the great solid qualities. Self-restraint, self-mastery, common sense, the power of accepting individual responsibility and yet of acting in conjunction with others, courage, and resolution — these are the qualities which mark a masterful people. Without them no people can control itself, or save itself from being controlled from the outside. I speak to a brilliant assemblage; I speak in a great university which represents the flower of the highest intellectual development; I pay all homage to intellect, and to elaborate and specialized training of the intellect; and yet I know I shall have the assent of all of you present when I add that more important still are the commonplace, everyday qualities and virtues.

Such ordinary, everyday qualities include the will and the power to work, to fight at need, and to have plenty of healthy children. The need that the average man shall work is so obvious as hardly to warrant insistence. There are a few people in every country so born that they can lead lives of leisure. These fill a useful function if they make it evident that leisure does not mean idleness; for some of the most valuable work needed by civilization is essentially non-remunerative in its character, and of course the people who do this work should in large part be drawn from those to whom remuneration is an object of indifference. But the average man must earn his own livelihood. He should be trained to do so, and he should be trained to feel that he occupies a contemptible position if he does not do so; that he is not an object of envy if he is idle, at whichever end of the social scale he stands, but an object of contempt, an object of derision.

In the next place the good man should be both a strong and a brave man; that is, he should be able to fight, he should be able to serve his country as a soldier, if the need arises. There are well-meaning philosophers who declaim against the unrighteousness of war. They are right only if they lay all their emphasis upon the unrighteousness. War is a dreadful thing, and unjust war is a crime against humanity. But it is such a crime because it is unjust, not because it is war. The choice must ever be in favor of righteousness, and this whether the alternative be peace or whether the alternative be war. The question must not be merely, Is there to be peace or war? The question must be, Is the right to prevail? Are the great laws of righteousness once more to be fulfilled? And the answer from a strong and virile people must be, "Yes," whatever the cost. Every honorable effort should always be made to avoid war, just as every honorable effort should always be made by the individual in private life to keep out of brawl, to keep out of trouble; but no self-respecting individual, no self-respecting nation, can or ought to submit to wrong.

Finally, even more important than ability to work, even more important than ability to fight at need, is it to remember that the chief of blessings for any nation is that it shall leave its seed to inherit the land. It was the crown of blessings in Biblical times; and it is the crown of blessings now. The greatest of all curses is the curse of sterility, and the severest of all condemnations should be that visited upon wilful sterility. The first essential in any civilization is that the man and the woman shall be father and mother of healthy children, so that the race shall increase and not decrease. If this is not so, if through no fault of the society there is failure to increase, it is a great misfortune. If the failure is due to deliberate and wilful fault, then it is not merely a misfortune, it is one of those crimes of ease and self-indulgence, of shrinking from pain and effort and risk, which in the long run Nature punishes more heavily than any other. If we of the great republics, if we, the free people who claim to have emancipated ourselves from the thraldom of wrong and error, bring down on our heads the curse that comes upon the wilfully barren, then it will be an idle waste of breath to prattle of our achievements, to boast of all that we have done. No refinement of life, no delicacy of taste, no material progress, no sordid heaping up of riches, no sensuous development of art and literature, can in any way compensate for the loss of the great fundamental virtues; and of these great fundamental virtues the greatest is the race's power to perpetuate the race.

Character must show itself in the man's performance both of the duty he owes himself and of the duty he owes the state. The man's foremost duty is owed to himself and his family; and he can do this duty only by earning money, by providing what is essential to material well-being; it is only after this has been done that he can hope to build a higher superstructure on the solid material foundation; it is only after this has been done that he can help in movements for the general well-being. He must pull his own weight first, and only after this can his surplus strength be of use to the general public. It is not good to excite that bitter laughter which expresses contempt; and contempt is what we feel for the being whose enthusiasm to benefit mankind is such that he is a burden to those nearest him; who wishes to do great things for humanity in the abstract, but who cannot keep his wife in comfort or educate his children.

Nevertheless, while laying all stress on this point, while not merely acknowledging but insisting upon the fact that there must be a basis of material well-being for the individual as for the nation, let us with equal emphasis insist that this material well-being represents nothing but the foundation, and that the foundation, though indispensable, is worthless unless upon it is raised the superstructure of a higher life. That is why I decline to recognize the mere multimillionaire, the man of mere wealth, as an asset of value to any country; and especially as not an asset to my own country. If he has earned or uses his wealth in a way that makes him of real benefit, of real use — and such is often the case — why, then he does become an asset of worth. But it is the way in which it has been earned or used, and not the mere fact of wealth, that entitles him to the credit. There is need in business, as in most other forms of human activity, of the great guiding intelligence. Their places cannot be supplied by any number of lesser intelligences. It is a good thing that they should have ample recognition, ample reward. But we must not transfer our admiration to the reward instead of to the deed rewarded; and if what should be the reward exists without the service having been rendered, then admiration will come only from those who are mean of soul. The truth is that, after a certain measure of tangible material success or reward has been achieved, the question of increasing it becomes of constantly less importance compared to other things that can be done in life. It is a bad thing for a nation to raise and to admire a false standard of success; and there can be no falser standard than that set by the deification of material well-being in and for itself. The man who, for any cause for which he himself is accountable, has failed to support himself and those for whom he is responsible, ought to feel that he has fallen lamentably short in his prime duty. But the man who, having far surpassed the limit of providing for the wants, both of body and mind, of himself and of those depending upon him, then piles up a great fortune, for the acquisition or retention of which he returns no corresponding benefit to the nation as a whole, should himself be made to feel that, so far from being a desirable, he is an unworthy, citizen of the community; that he is to be neither admired nor envied; that his right-thinking fellow countrymen put him low in the scale of citizenship, and leave him to be consoled by the admiration of those whose level of purpose is even lower than his own.

My position as regards the moneyed interests can be put in a few words. In every civilized society property rights must be carefully safeguarded; ordinarily, and in the great majority of cases, human rights and property rights are fundamentally and in the long run identical; but when it clearly appears that there is a real conflict between them, human rights must have the upper hand, for property belongs to man and not man to property.

In fact, it is essential to good citizenship clearly to understand that there are certain qualities which we in a democracy are prone to admire in and of themselves, which ought by rights to be judged admirable or the reverse solely from the standpoint of the use made of them. Foremost among these I should include two very distinct gifts — the gift of money-making, and the gift of oratory. Money-making, the money touch, I have spoken of above. It is a quality which in a moderate degree is essential. It may be useful when developed to a very great degree, but only if accompanied and controlled by other qualities; and without such control the possessor tends to develop into one of the least attractive types produced by a modern industrial democracy. So it is with the orator. It is highly desirable that a leader of opinion in a democracy should be able to state his views clearly and convincingly. But all that the oratory can do of value to the community is to enable the man thus to explain himself; if it enables the orator to persuade his hearers to put false values on things, it merely makes him a power for mischief. Some excellent public servants have not the gift at all, and must rely upon their deeds to speak for them; and unless the oratory does represent genuine conviction based on good common sense and able to be translated into efficient performance, then the better the oratory the greater the damage to the public it deceives. Indeed, it is a sign of marked political weakness in any commonwealth if the people tend to be carried away by mere oratory, if they tend to value words in and for themselves, as divorced from the deeds for which they are supposed to stand. The phrase-maker, the phrase-monger, the ready talker, however great his power, whose speech does not make for courage, sobriety, and right understanding, is simply a noxious element in the body politic, and it speaks ill for the public if he has influence over them. To admire the gift of oratory without regard to the moral quality behind the gift is to do wrong to the republic.

Of course all that I say of the orator applies with even greater force to the orator's latter-day and more influential brother, the journalist. The power of the journalist is great, but he is entitled neither to respect nor admiration because of that power unless it is used aright. He can do, and he often does, great good. He can do, and he often does, infinite mischief. All journalists, all writers, for the very reason that they appreciate the vast possibilities of their profession, should bear testimony against those who deeply discredit it. Offenses against taste and morals, which are bad enough in a private citizen, are infinitely worse if made into instruments for debauching the community through a newspaper. Mendacity, slander, sensationalism, inanity, vapid triviality, all are potent factors for the debauchery of the public mind and conscience. The excuse advanced for vicious writing, that the public demands it and that the demand must be supplied, can no more be admitted than if it were advanced by the purveyors of food who sell poisonous adulterations.

In short, the good citizen in a republic must realize that he ought to possess two sets of qualities, and that neither avails without the other. He must have those qualities which make for efficiency; and he must also have those qualities which direct the efficiency into channels for the public good. He is useless if he is inefficient. There is nothing to be done with that type of citizen of whom all that can be said is that he is harmless. Virtue which is dependent upon a sluggish circulation is not impressive. There is little place in active life for the timid good man. The man who is saved by weakness from robust wickedness is likewise rendered immune from the robuster virtues. The good citizen in a republic must first of all be able to hold his own. He is no good citizen unless he has the ability which will make him work hard and which at need will make him fight hard. The good citizen is not a good citizen unless he is an efficient citizen.

But if a man's efficiency is not guided and regulated by a moral sense, then the more efficient he is the worse he is, the more dangerous to the body politic. Courage, intellect, all the masterful qualities, serve but to make a man more evil if they are used merely for that man's own advancement, with brutal indifference to the rights of others. It speaks ill for the community if the community worships these qualities and treats their possessors as heroes regardless of whether the qualities are used rightly or wrongly. It makes no difference as to the precise way in which this sinister efficiency is shown. It makes no difference whether such a man's force and ability betray themselves in the career of money-maker or politician, soldier or orator, journalist or popular leader. If the man works for evil, then the more successful he is the more he should be despised and condemned by all upright and far-seeing men. To judge a man merely by success is an abhorrent wrong; and if the people at large habitually so judge men, if they grow to condone wickedness because the wicked man triumphs, they show their inability to understand that in the last analysis free institutions rest upon the character of citizenship, and that by such admiration of evil they prove themselves unfit for liberty.

The homely virtues of the household, the ordinary workaday virtues which make the woman a good housewife and housemother, which make the man a hard worker, a good husband and father, a good soldier at need, stand at the bottom of character. But of course many others must be added thereto if a state is to be not only free but great. Good citizenship is not good citizenship if exhibited only in the home. There remain the duties of the individual in relation to the state, and these duties are none too easy under the conditions which exist where the effort is made to carry on free government in a complex, industrial civilization. Perhaps the most important thing the ordinary citizen, and, above all, the leader of ordinary citizens, has to remember in political life is that he must not be a sheer doctrinaire. The closet philosopher, the refined and cultured individual who from his library tells how men ought to be governed under ideal conditions, is of no use in actual governmental work; and the one-sided fanatic, and still more the mob-leader, and the insincere man who to achieve power promises what by no possibility can be performed, are not merely useless but noxious.

The citizen must have high ideals, and yet he must be able to achieve them in practical fashion. No permanent good comes from aspirations so lofty that they have grown fantastic and have become impossible and indeed undesirable to realize. The impracticable visionary is far less often the guide and precursor than he is the embittered foe of the real reformer, of the man who, with stumblings and shortcomings, yet does in some shape, in practical fashion, give effect to the hopes and desires of those who strive for better things. Woe to the empty phrase-maker, to the empty idealist, who instead of making ready the ground for the man of action, turns against him when he appears and hampers him as he does the work! Moreover, the preacher of ideals must remember how sorry and contemptible is the figure which he will cut, how great the damage that he will do, if he does not himself, in his own life, strive measurably to realize the ideals that he preaches for others. Let him remember also that the worth of the ideal must be largely determined by the success with which it can in practice be realized. We should abhor the so-called "practical" men whose practicality assumes the shape of that peculiar baseness which finds its expression in disbelief in morality and decency, in disregard of high standards of living and conduct. Such a creature is the worst enemy of the body politic. But only less desirable as a citizen is his nominal opponent and real ally, the man of fantastic vision who makes the impossible better forever the enemy of the possible good.

We can just as little afford to follow the doctrinaires of an extreme individualism as the doctrinaires of an extreme socialism. Individual initiative, so far from being discouraged, should be stimulated; and yet we should remember that, as society develops and grows more complex, we continually find that things which once it was desirable to leave to individual initiative can, under the changed conditions, be performed with better results by common effort. It is quite impossible, and equally undesirable, to draw in theory a hard-and-fast line which shall always divide the two sets of cases. This everyone who is not cursed with the pride of the closet philosopher will see, if he will only take the trouble to think about some of our commonest phenomena. For instance, when people live on isolated farms or in little hamlets, each house can be left to attend to its own drainage and water supply; but the mere multiplication of families in a given area produces new problems which, because they differ in size, are found to differ not only in degree but in kind from the old; and the questions of drainage and water supply have to be considered from the common standpoint. It is not a matter for abstract dogmatizing to decide when this point is reached; it is a matter to be tested by practical experiment. Much of the discussion about socialism and individualism is entirely pointless, because of failure to agree on terminology. It is not good to be the slave of names. I am a strong individualist by personal habit, inheritance, and conviction; but it is a mere matter of common sense to recognize that the state, the community, the citizens acting together, can do a number of things better than if they were left to individual action. The individualism which finds its expression in the abuse of physical force is checked very early in the growth of civilization, and we of today should in our turn strive to shackle or destroy that individualism which triumphs by greed and cunning, which exploits the weak by craft instead of ruling them by brutality. We ought to go with any man in the effort to bring about justice and the equality of opportunity, to turn the tool-user more and more into the tool-owner, to shift burdens so that they can be more equitably borne. The deadening effect on any race of the adoption of a logical and extreme socialistic system could not be overstated; it would spell sheer destruction; it would produce grosser wrong and outrage, fouler immorality, than any existing system. But this does not mean that we may not with great advantage adopt certain of the principles professed by some given set of men who happen to call themselves Socialists; to be afraid to do so would be a mark of weakness on our part.

But we should not take part in acting a lie any more than in telling a lie. We should not say that men are equal where they are not equal, nor proceed upon the assumption that there is an equality where it does not exist; but we should strive to bring about a measurable equality, at least to the extent of preventing the inequality which is due to force or fraud. Abraham Lincoln, a man of the plain people, blood of their blood and bone of their bone, who all his life toiled and wrought and suffered for them and at the end died for them, who always strove to represent them, who would never tell an untruth to or for them, spoke of the doctrine of equality with his usual mixture of idealism and sound common sense. He said (I omit what was of merely local significance):

"I think the authors of the Declaration of Independence intended to include all men, but that they did not mean to declare all men equal *in all respects*. They did not mean to say all men were equal in color, size, intellect, moral development, or social capacity. They defined with tolerable distinctness in what they did consider all men created equal — equal in certain inalienable rights, among which are life, liberty, and the pursuit of happiness. This they said, and this they meant. They did not mean to assert the obvious untruth that all were then actually enjoying that equality, or yet that they were about to confer it immediately upon them. They meant to set up a standard maxim for free society which should be familiar to all — constantly looked to, constantly labored for, and even though never perfectly attained, constantly approximated, and thereby constantly spreading and deepening its influence, and augmenting the happiness and value of life to all people, everywhere."

We are bound in honor to refuse to listen to those men who would make us desist from the effort to do away with the inequality which means injustice; the inequality of right, of opportunity, of privilege. We are bound in honor to strive to bring ever nearer the day when, as far as is humanly possible, we shall be able to realize the ideal that each man shall have an equal opportunity to show the stuff that is in him by the way in which he renders service. There should, so far as possible, be equality of opportunity to render service; but just so long as there is inequality of service there should and must be inequality of reward. We may be sorry for the general, the painter, the artist, the worker in any profession or of any kind, whose misfortune rather than whose fault it is that he does his work ill. But the reward must go to the man who does his work well; for any other course is to create a new kind of privilege, the privilege of folly and weakness; and special privilege is injustice, whatever form it takes.

To say that the thriftless, the lazy, the vicious, the incapable, ought to have the reward given to those who are far-sighted, capable, and upright, is to say what is not true and cannot be true. Let us try to level up, but let us beware of the evil of leveling down. If a man stumbles, it is a good thing to help him to his feet. Every one of us needs a helping hand now and then. But if a man lies down, it is a waste of time to try to carry him; and it is a very bad thing for everyone if we make men feel that the same reward will come to those who shirk their work and to those who do it.

Let us, then, take into account the actual facts of life, and not be misled into following any proposal for achieving the millennium, for re-creating the golden age, until we have subjected it to hard-headed examination. On the other hand, it is foolish to reject a proposal merely because it is advanced by visionaries. If a given scheme is proposed, look at it on its merits, and, in considering it, disregard formulas. It does not matter in the least who proposes it, or why. If it seems good, try it. If it proves good, accept it; otherwise reject it. There are plenty of men calling themselves Socialists with whom, up to a certain point, it is quite possible to work. If the next step is one which both we and they wish to take, why of course take it, without any regard to the fact that our views as to the tenth step may differ. But, on the other hand, keep clearly in mind that, though it has been worth while to take one step, this does not in the least mean that it may not be highly disadvantageous to take the next. It is just as foolish to refuse all progress because people demanding it desire at some points to go to absurd extremes, as it would be to go to these absurd extremes simply because some of the measures advocated by the extremists were wise.

The good citizen will demand liberty for himself, and as a matter of pride he will see to it that others receive the liberty which he thus claims as his own. Probably the test of true love of liberty in any country is the way in which minorities are treated in that country. Not only should there be complete liberty in matters of religion and opinion, but complete liberty for each man to lead his life as he desires, provided only that in so doing he does not wrong his neighbor. Persecution is bad because it is persecution, and without reference to which side happens at the moment to be the persecutor and which the persecuted. Class hatred is bad in just the same way, and without any regard to the individual who, at a given time, substitutes loyalty to a class for loyalty to the nation, or substitutes hatred of men because they happen to come in a certain social category, for judgment awarded them according to their conduct. Remember always that the same measure of condemnation should be extended to the arrogance which would look down upon or crush any man because he is poor and to the envy and hatred which would destroy a man because he is wealthy. The overbearing brutality of the man of wealth or power, and the envious and hateful malice directed against wealth or power, are really at root merely different manifestations of the same quality, merely the two sides of the same shield. The man who, if born to wealth and power, exploits and ruins his less fortunate brethren is at heart the same as the greedy and violent demagogue who excites those who have not property to plunder those who have. The gravest wrong upon his country is inflicted by that man, whatever his station, who seeks to make his countrymen divide primarily on the line that separates class from class, occupation from occupation, men of more wealth from men of less wealth, instead of remembering that the only safe standard is that which judges each man on his worth as a man, whether he be rich or poor, without regard to his profession or to his station in life. Such is the only true democratic test, the only test that can with propriety be applied in a republic. There have been many republics in the past, both in what we call antiquity and in what we call the Middle Ages. They fell, and the prime factor in their fall was the fact that the parties tended to divide along the line that separates wealth from poverty. It made no difference which side was successful; it made no difference whether the republic fell under the rule of an oligarchy or the rule of a mob. In either case, when once loyalty to a class had been substituted for loyalty to the republic, the end of the republic was at hand. There is no greater need today than the need to keep ever in mind the fact that the cleavage between right and wrong, between good citizenship and bad citizenship, runs at right angles to, and not parallel with, the lines of cleavage between class and class, between occupation and occupation. Ruin looks us in the face if we judge a man by his position instead of judging him by his conduct in that position.

In a republic, to be successful we must learn to combine intensity of conviction with a broad tolerance of difference of conviction. Wide differences of opinion in matters of religious, political, and social belief must exist if conscience and intellect alike are not to be stunted, if there is to be room for healthy growth. Bitter internecine hatreds, based on such differences, are signs, not of earnestness of belief, but of that fanaticism which, whether religious or anti-religious, democratic or anti-democratic, is itself but a manifestation of the gloomy bigotry which has been the chief factor in the downfall of so many, many nations.

Of one man in especial, beyond anyone else, the citizens of a republic should beware, and that is of the man who appeals to them to support him on the ground that he is hostile to other citizens of the republic, that he will secure for those who elect him, in one shape or another, profit at the expense of other citizens of the republic. It makes no difference whether he appeals to class hatred or class interest, to religious or anti-religious prejudice. The man who makes such an appeal should always be presumed to make it for the sake of furthering his own interest. The very last thing that an intelligent and self-respecting member of a democratic community should do is to reward any public man because that public man says he will get the private citizen something to which this private citizen is not entitled, or will gratify some emotion or animosity which this private citizen ought not to possess. Let me illustrate this by one anecdote from my own experience. A number of years ago I was engaged in cattle-ranching on the great plains of the western United States. There were no fences. The cattle wandered free, the ownership of each being determined by the brand; the calves were branded with the brand of the cows they followed. If on the round-up an animal was passed by, the following year it would appear as an unbranded yearling, and was then called a maverick. By the custom of the country these mavericks were branded with the brand of the man on whose range they were found. One day I was riding the range with a newly hired cowboy, and we came upon a maverick. We roped and threw it; then we built a little fire, took out a cinch-ring, heated it at the fire; and the cowboy started to put on the brand. I said to him, "It is So-and-so's brand," naming the man on whose range we happened to be. He answered: "That's all right, boss; I know my business." In another moment I said to him: "Hold on, you are putting on my brand!" To which he answered: "That's all right; I always put on the boss's brand." I answered: "Oh, very well. Now you go straight back to the ranch and get what is owing to you; I don't need you any longer." He jumped up and said: "Why, what's the matter? I was putting on your brand." And I answered: "Yes, my friend, and if you will steal *for* me you will steal *from* me."

Now, the same principle which applies in private life applies also in public life. If a public man tries to get your vote by saying that he will do something wrong *in* your interest, you can be absolutely certain that if ever it becomes worth his while he will do something wrong *against* your interest.

So much for the citizenship of the individual in his relations to his family, to his neighbor, to the state. There remain duties of citizenship which the state, the aggregation of all the individuals, owes in connection with other states, with other nations. Let me say at once that I am no advocate of a foolish cosmopolitanism. I believe that a man must be a good patriot before he can be, and as the only possible way of being, a good citizen of the world. Experience teaches us that the average man who protests that his international feeling swamps his national feeling, that he does not care for his country because he cares so much for mankind, in actual practice proves himself the foe of mankind; that the man who says that he does not care to be a citizen of any one country, because he is a citizen of the world, is in very fact usually an exceedingly undesirable citizen of whatever corner of the world he happens at the moment to be in. In the dim future all moral needs and moral standards may change; but at present, if a man can view his own country and all other countries from the same level with tepid indifference, it is wise to distrust him, just as it is wise to distrust the man who can take the same dispassionate view of his wife and his mother. However broad and deep a man's sympathies, however intense his activities, he need have no fear that they will be cramped by love of his native land.

Now, this does not mean in the least that a man should not wish to do good outside of his native land. On the contrary, just as I think that the man who loves his family is more apt to be a good neighbor than the man who does not, so I think that the most useful member of the family of nations is normally a strongly patriotic nation. So far from patriotism being inconsistent with a proper regard for the rights of other nations, I hold that the true patriot, who is as jealous of the national honor as a gentleman is of his own honor, will be careful to see that the nation neither inflicts nor suffers wrong, just as a gentleman scorns equally to wrong others or to suffer others to wrong him. I do not for one moment admit that political morality is different from private morality, that a promise made on the stump differs from a promise made in private life. I do not for one moment admit that a man should act deceitfully as a public servant in his dealings with other nations, any more than that he should act deceitfully in his dealings as a private citizen with other private citizens. I do not for one moment admit that a nation should treat other nations in a different spirit from that in which an honorable man would treat other men.

In practically applying this principle to the two sets of cases there is, of course, a great practical difference to be taken into account. We speak of international law; but international law is something wholly different from private or municipal law, and the capital difference is that there is a sanction for the one and no sanction for the other; that there is an outside force which compels individuals to obey the one, while there is no such outside force to compel obedience as regards the other. International law will, I believe, as the generations pass, grow stronger and stronger until in some way or other there develops the power to make it respected. But as yet it is only in the first formative period. As yet, as a rule, each nation is of necessity obliged to judge for itself in matters of vital importance between it and its neighbors, and actions must of necessity, where this is the case, be different from what they are where, as among private citizens, there is an outside force whose action is all powerful and must be invoked in any crisis of importance. It is the duty of wise statesmen, gifted with the power of looking ahead, to try to encourage and build up every movement which will substitute or tend to substitute some other agency for force in the settlement of international disputes. It is the duty of every honest statesman to try to guide the nation so that it shall not wrong any other nation. But as yet the great civilized peoples, if they are to be true to themselves and to the cause of humanity and civilization, must keep ever in mind that in the last resort they must possess both the will and the power to resent wrong-doing from others. The men who sanely believe in a lofty morality preach righteousness; but they do not preach weakness, whether among private citizens or among nations. We believe that our ideals should be high, but not so high as to make it impossible measurably to realize them. We sincerely and earnestly believe in peace; but if peace and justice conflict, we scorn the man who would not stand for justice though the whole world came in arms against him.

And now, my hosts, a word in parting. You and I belong to the only two republics among the great powers of the world. The ancient friendship between France and the United States has been, on the whole, a sincere and disinterested friendship. A calamity to you would be a sorrow to us. But it would be more than that. In the seething turmoil of the history of humanity certain nations stand out as possessing a peculiar power or charm, some special gift of beauty or wisdom or strength, which puts them among the immortals, which makes them rank forever with the leaders of mankind. France is one of these nations. For her to sink would be a loss to all the world. There are certain lessons of brilliance and of generous gallantry that she can teach better than any of her sister nations. When the French peasantry sang of Malbrook, it was to tell how the soul of this warrior-foe took flight upward through the laurels he had won. Nearly seven centuries ago, Froissart, writing of a time of dire disaster, said that the realm of France was never so stricken that there were not left men who would valiantly fight for it. You have had a great past. I believe that you will have a great future. Long may you carry yourselves proudly as citizens of a nation which bears a leading part in the teaching and uplifting of mankind.

OWEN WISTER

THE fiction of Owen Wister has delightfully saved from oblivion a picturesque period of frontier life in America. Wister was born in Philadelphia in 1860. Three years of his boyhood were spent abroad. At Harvard he became interested in music as well as in literature, and after his graduation he went to Paris to study composition. Family affairs soon brought him home. He was then compelled to seek health in Wyoming and Arizona. There he found, to use his own words, "Saturday eternal, where you slept out-of-doors, rode a horse, roped steers, and wore deadly weapons." With recovered health, he entered the Harvard Law School, and after completing his work there, settled down to the practice of law in Philadelphia. But frontier life had laid its spell upon him and year after year he returned to its mountains and its plains. It was not until 1891, however, after the final push to authorship had been given by Mérimée's 'Carmen,' that his saturation ran over in the form of fiction. From that time law began to yield to literature.

In 1896 eight magazine stories were collected in 'Red Men and White.' This was followed by 'Lin McLean,' 'The Jimmyjohn Boss and Other Stories,' and, in 1902, 'The Virginian, a Horseman of the Plains,' Owen Wister's finest single achievement. In 1911 appeared 'Members of the Family,' another collection of frontier stories, as the title suggests. The illuminating preface to this volume tells us that much of the material in the author's carefully kept diaries has not yet been used. Besides this homogeneous group, Wister's most important fiction is to be found in 'Philosophy 4,' a swift and delightful tale of undergraduate life at Harvard, and 'Lady Baltimore,' the true heroine of which is not the girl, not even the cake that gives the novel its name, but Charleston, "the most lovely, the most wistful town in America." In the realm of satire, 'How Doth the Simple Spelling Bee' deals severely with those who would interfere with the habits of the English language. In 'The Seven Ages of Washington' and 'U. S. Grant' Owen Wister has turned his enthusiastic patriotism into the channels of national biography. 'The Pentecost of Calamity' (1915) is an attack upon Prussianism, which found a host of responsive readers. He has also contributed much, both of prose and verse, to the magazines.

But Owen Wister's golden gift to American literature is his handling of frontier life between 1874 and 1890. To this splendid indigenous material he brought not only an open mind and an unusual sense of humor but also a broad culture and a restrained artistry. He is himself one of the characters, an outsider, a tenderfoot, who uses the first person and who can openly love his

Lin McLean and his nameless Virginian. Though his range covers most of the country west of the Missouri, Wyoming and Arizona are his chosen field, and Wyoming more than Arizona, and most of all, the cattle country and the cattle people. The outdoor life that he depicts is bathed in an enormous sunlight, a virgin air, and is fragrant with the wild clean odor of the sage-brush. The scenery embraces unfooted mountains, vast plains blanketed with tawny alkali dust, and crowded with antelope. Besides cowboys, there are soldiers, Indians, a few women, hard or gentle, a bishop who is first a man, nomads whose home is the saddle-blanket. The rude life tests manhood in unusual ways. The gentle Virginian must help lynch his one-time friend in order to maintain such justice as can exist in territorial Wyoming. The weak go under, and therefore, beneath the laughter and the daring deeds, the ground-swell of tragedy is often felt. Those who survive earn hard, squander hard, drink and swear hard; they are careless of morals and of life; they are childlike, democratic, yet not easy of approach. Owen Wister has made these men live for us — their courage, their comradeship, their male reticence and their male gossip, and their faithfulness to the given word. He has reproduced their humorous exaggeration of speech and their sinister jokes that can "raise both a laugh and a silence."

MARY LELAND HUNT

SPECIMEN JONES

From 'Red Men and White.' Copyright, 1895, by Harper & Brothers

EPHRAIM, the proprietor of Twenty Mile, had wasted his day in burying a man. He did not know the man. He had found him, or what the Apaches had left of him, sprawled among some charred sticks just outside the Cañon del Oro. It was a useful discovery in its way; for otherwise Ephraim might have gone on hunting his strayed horses near the cañon, and ended among charred sticks himself. Very likely the Indians were far away by this time; but he returned to Twenty Mile with the man tied to his saddle, and his pony nervously snorting. And now the day was done, and the man lay in the earth, and they had even built a fence round him; for the hole was pretty shallow, and coyotes have a way of smelling this sort of thing a long way off when they are hungry, and the man was not in a coffin. They were always short of coffins in Arizona.

Day was done at Twenty Mile, and the customary activity prevailed inside that flat-roofed cube of mud. Sounds of singing, shooting, dancing, and Mexican tunes on the concertina came out of the windows hand in hand, to widen and die among the hills. A limber, pretty boy, who might be nineteen, was dancing energetically; while a grave old gentleman, with tobacco running down his beard, pointed a pistol at the boy's heels, and shot a hole in the earth now and then to show that the weapon was really loaded. Everybody was quite used to all of this — excepting the boy. He was an Eastern new-comer, passing his first evening at a place of entertainment.

Night in and night out every guest at Twenty Mile was either happy and full of whisky, or else his friends were making arrangements for his funeral. There was water at Twenty Mile — the only water for twoscore of miles. Consequently it was an important station on the road between the southern country and Old Camp Grant, and the new mines north of the Mescal Range. The stunt, liquor-perfumed adobe cabin lay on the gray floor of the desert like an isolated slab of chocolate. A corral, two desolate stable sheds, and the slowly turning windmill, were all else. Here Ephraim and one or two helpers abode, armed against Indians and selling whisky. Variety in their vocation of drinking and killing was brought them by the travelers. These passed and passed through the glaring vacant months: some days only one ragged fortune-hunter, riding a pony; again by twos and threes, with high-loaded burros; and sometimes they came in companies, walking beside their clanking freight wagons. Some were young, and some were old; and all drank whisky, and wore knives and guns to keep each other civil. Most of them were bound for the mines, and some of them sometimes returned. No man trusted the next man; and their names, when they had any, would be O'Rafferty, Angus, Schwartzmeyer, José Maria, and Smith. All stopped for one night; some longer — remaining drunk and profitable to Ephraim; now and then one stayed permanently, and had a fence built round him. Whoever came, and whatever befell them, Twenty Mile was chronically hilarious after sundown — a dot of riot in the dumb Arizona night.

On this particular evening they had a tenderfoot. The boy, being new in Arizona, still trusted his neighbor. Such people turned up occasionally. This one had paid for everybody's drink several times, because he felt friendly, and never noticed that nobody ever paid for his. They had played cards with him, stolen his spurs, and now they were making him dance. It was an ancient pastime; yet two or three were glad to stand round and watch it, because it was some time since they had been to the opera. Now the tenderfoot had misunderstood these friends at the beginning, supposing himself to be among good fellows; and they naturally set him down as a fool. But even while dancing you may learn much, and suddenly. The boy, besides being limber, had good tough black hair; and it was not in fear, but with a cold blue eye, that he looked at the old gentleman. The trouble had been that his own revolver had somehow hitched, so he could not pull it from the holster at the necessary moment.

"Tried to draw on me, did yer?" said the old gentleman. "Step higher! Step now, or I'll crack open yer kneepans, ye robin's-egg."

"Thinks he's having a bad time," remarked Ephraim. "Wonder how he'd like to have been that man the Injuns had sport with?"

"Weren't his ear funny?" said one who had helped bury the man.

"Ear?" said Ephraim. "You boys ought to have been along when I found him, and seen the way they'd fixed up his mouth." Ephraim explained the details simply, and the listeners shivered. But Ephraim was a humorist. "Wonder how it feels," he continued, "to have —"

Here the boy sickened at his comments and the loud laughter. Yet a few hours earlier these same half-drunken jesters had laid the man to rest with decent humanity. The boy was taking his first dose of Arizona. By no means was everybody looking at his jig. They had seen tenderfeet so often. There was a Mexican game of cards; there was the concertina; and over in the corner sat Specimen Jones, with his back to the company, singing to himself. Nothing had been said or done that entertained him in the least. He had seen everything quite often.

"Higher! skip higher, you elegant calf," remarked the old gentleman to the tenderfoot. "High-yer!" And he placidly fired a fourth shot that scraped the boy's boot at the ankle and threw earth over the clock, so that you could not tell the minute from the hour hand.

"'Drink to me only with thine eyes,'" sang Specimen Jones softly. They did not care much for his songs in Arizona. These lyrics were all, or nearly all, that he retained of the days when he was twenty — although he was but twenty-six now.

The boy was cutting pigeon-wings, the concertina played 'Matamoras,' Jones continued his lyric, when two Mexicans leaped at each other, and the concertina stopped with a quack.

"Quit it!" said Ephraim from behind the bar, covering the two with his weapon. "I don't want any greasers scrapping round here tonight. We've just got cleaned up."

It had been cards; but the Mexicans made peace, to the regret of Specimen Jones. He had looked round with some hopes of a crisis, and now for the first time he noticed the boy.

"Blamed if he ain't neat," he said. But interest faded from his eye, and he turned again to the wall. "Lieb Vaterland magst ruhig sein,'" he melodiously observed. His repertory was wide and refined. When he sang he was always grammatical.

"Ye kin stop, kid," said the old gentleman, not unkindly; and he shoved his pistol into his belt.

The boy ceased. He had been thinking matters over. Being lithe and strong, he was not tired nor much out of breath; but he was trembling with the plan and the prospect he had laid out for himself. "Set 'em up," he said to Ephraim. "Set 'em up again all round."

His voice caused Specimen Jones to turn and look once more; while the old gentleman, still benevolent, said, "Yer langwidge means pleasanter than it sounds, kid." He glanced at the boy's holster, and knew he need not keep a very sharp watch as to that. Its owner had bungled over it once already. All the old gentleman did was to place himself next the boy on the off side from the holster; any move the tenderfoot's hand might make for it would be green and unskilful, and easily anticipated. The company lined up along the bar, and the bottle slid from glass to glass. The boy and his tormentor stood together in the middle of the line; and the tormentor, always with half a thought for the holster, handled his drink on the wet counter, waiting till all should be filled and ready to swallow simultaneously, as befits good manners.

"Well, my regards," he said, seeing the boy raise his glass; and as the old gentleman's arm lifted in unison, exposing his waist, the boy reached down a lightning hand, caught the old gentleman's own pistol, and jammed it in his face.

"Now you'll dance," said he.

"Whoop!" exclaimed Specimen Jones, delighted. "*Blamed* if he ain't neat!" And Jones's handsome face lighted keenly.

"Hold on!" the boy sang out, for the amazed old gentleman was mechanically drinking his whisky out of sheer fright. The rest had forgotten their drinks. "Not one swallow," the boy continued. "No, you'll not put it down either. You'll keep hold of it, and you'll dance all round this place. Around and around. And don't you spill any. And I'll be thinking what you'll do after that."

Specimen Jones eyed the boy with growing esteem. "Why, he ain't bigger than a pint of cider," said he.

"Prance away!" commanded the tenderfoot, and fired a shot between the old gentleman's not widely straddled legs.

"You hev the floor, Mr. Adams," Jones observed respectfully, at the old gentleman's agile leap. "I'll let no man here interrupt you." So the capering began, and the company stood back to make room. "I've saw juicy things in this Territory," continued Specimen Jones, aloud to himself, "but this combination fills my bill."

He shook his head sagely, following the black-haired boy with his eye. That youth was steering Mr. Adams round the room with the pistol, proud as a ring-master. Yet not altogether. He was only nineteen; and though his heart beat stoutly, it was beating alone in a strange country. He had come straight to this from hunting squirrels along the Susquehanna, with his mother keeping supper warm for him in the stone farm-house among the trees. He had read books in which hardy heroes saw life, and always triumphed with precision on the last page; but he remembered no receipt for this particular situation. Being good game American blood, he did not think now about the Susquehanna; but he did long with all his might to know what he ought to do next to prove himself a man. His buoyant rage, being glutted with the old gentleman's fervent skipping, had cooled; and a stress of reaction was falling hard on his brave young nerves. He imagined everybody against him. He had no notion that there was another American wanderer there, whose reserved and whimsical nature he had touched to the heart.

The fickle audience was with him, of course, for the moment — since he was upper dog and it was a good show; but one in that room was distinctly against him. The old gentleman was dancing with an ugly eye; he had glanced down to see just where his knife hung at his side, and he had made some calculations. He had fired four shots; the boy had fired one. "Four and one hez always made five," the old gentleman told himself with much secret pleasure, and pretended that he was going to stop his double-shuffle. It was an excellent trap, and the boy fell straight into it. He squandered his last precious bullet on the spittoon near which Mr. Adams happened to be at the moment, and the next moment Mr. Adams had him by the throat. They swayed and gulped for breath, rutting the earth with sharp heels; they rolled to the floor and floundered with legs tight tangled, the boy blindly striking at Mr. Adams with the pistol-butt, and the audience drawing closer to lose nothing, when the bright knife flashed suddenly. It poised — and flew across the room, harmless; for a foot had driven into Mr. Adams's arm, and he felt a cold ring grooving his temple. It was the smooth, chilly muzzle of Specimen Jones's six-shooter.

"That's enough," said Jones. "More than enough."

Mr. Adams, being mature in judgment, rose instantly, like a good old sheep, and put his knife back obedient to orders. But in the brain of the overstrained, bewildered boy, universal destruction was whirling. With a face stricken lean with ferocity, he staggered to his feet, plucking at his obstinate holster, and glaring for a foe. His eye fell first on his deliverer, leaning easily against the bar watching him, while the more and more curious audience scattered, and held themselves ready to murder the boy if he should point his pistol their way. He was dragging at it clumsily, and at last it came. Specimen Jones sprang like a cat, and held the barrel vertical, and gripped the boy's wrist.

"Go easy, son," said he. "I know how you're feelin'."

The boy had been wrenching to get a shot at Jones; and now the quietness of the man's voice reached his brain, and he looked at Specimen Jones. He felt a potent brotherhood in the eyes that were considering him, and he began to fear he had been a fool. There was his dwarf Eastern revolver, slack in his inefficient fist, and the singular person still holding its barrel and tapping one derisive finger over the end, careless of the risk to his first joint.

"Why, you little —— ——," said Specimen Jones, caressingly, to the hypnotized youth, "if you was to pop that squirt off at me, I'd turn you up and spank you. Set 'em up, Ephraim."

But the commercial Ephraim hesitated, and Jones remembered. His last cent was gone. It was his third day at Ephraim's. He had stopped, having a little money, on his way to Tucson, where a friend had a job for him, and was waiting. He was far too experienced a character ever to sell his horse or his saddle on these occasions, and go on drinking. He looked as if he might, but he never did; and this was what disappointed business men like Ephraim in Specimen Jones.

But now, here was this tenderfoot he had undertaken to see through, and Ephraim reminding him that he had no more of the wherewithal. "Why, so I haven't," he said with a short laugh, and his face flushed. "I guess," he continued hastily, "this is worth a dollar or two." He drew a chain up from below his flannel shirt-collar and over his head. He drew it a little slowly. It had not been taken off for a number of years — not, indeed, since it had been placed there originally. "It ain't brass," he added lightly, and strewed it along the counter without looking at it. Ephraim did look at it; and being satisfied, began to uncork a new bottle while the punctual audience came up for its drink.

"Won't you please let me treat?" said the boy unsteadily. "I ain't likely to meet you again, sir." Reaction was giving him trouble inside.

"Where are you bound, kid?"

"Oh, just a ways up the country," answered the boy, keeping a grip on his voice.

"Well, you *may* get there. Where did you pick up that — that thing? Your pistol, I mean."

"It's a present from a friend," replied the tenderfoot with dignity.

"Farewell gift, wasn't it, kid? Yes; I thought so. Now I'd hate to get an affair like that from a friend. It would start me wondering if he liked me as well as I'd always thought he did. Put up that money, kid. You're drinking with me. Say, what's yer name?"

"Cumnor — J. Cumnor."

"Well, J. Cumnor, I'm glad to know you. Ephraim, let me make you acquainted with Mr. Cumnor. Mr. Adams, if you're rested from your quadrille, you can shake hands with my friend. Step around, you Miguels and Serapios and Cristobals, whatever you claim your names are. This is Mr. J. Cumnor."

The Mexicans did not understand either the letter or the spirit of these American words; but they drank their drink, and the concertina resumed its acrid melody. The boy had taken himself off without being noticed.

"Say, Speç," said Ephraim to Jones: "I'm no hog. Here's yer chain. You'll be along again."

"Keep it till I'm along again," said the owner.

"Just as you say, Speç," answered Ephraim smoothly, and he hung the pledge over an advertisement chromo of a nude cream-colored lady with bright straw hair, holding out a bottle of somebody's champagne. Specimen Jones sang no more songs, but smoked and leaned in silence on the bar. The company were talking of bed, and Ephraim plunged his glasses into a bucket to clean them for the morrow.

"Know anything about that kid?" inquired Jones abruptly.

Ephraim shook his head as he washed.

"Traveling alone, ain't he?"

Ephraim nodded.

"Where did you say you found that fellow layin,' the Injuns got?"

"Mile this side the cañon. 'Mong them sand-humps."

"How long had he been there, do you figure?"

"Three days, anyway."

Jones watched Ephraim finish his cleansing. "Your clock needs wiping," he remarked. "A man might suppose it was nine, to see that thing, the way the dirt hides the hands. Look again in half an hour and it'll say three. That's the kind of clock gives a man the jams. Sends him crazy."

"Well, that ain't a bad thing to be in this country," said Ephraim, rubbing the glass case and restoring identity to the hands. "If that man had been crazy he'd been livin' right now. Injuns 'll never touch lunatics."

"That band have passed here and gone north," Jones said. "I saw a smoke among the foot-hills as I come along day before yesterday. I guess they're aiming to cross the Santa Catalina. Most likely they're that band from round the San Carlos that were reported as raiding down in Sonora."

"I seen well enough," said Ephraim, "when I found him, that they wasn't going to trouble us any, or they'd have been around by then."

He was quite right; but Specimen Jones was thinking of something else. He went out to the corral, feeling disturbed and doubtful. He saw the tall white freight-wagon of the Mexicans, looming and silent; and a little way off, the new fence where the man lay. An odd sound startled him, though he knew it was no Indians at this hour; and he looked down into a little dry ditch. It was the boy, hidden away flat on his stomach among the stones, sobbing.

"Oh, snakes!" whispered Specimen Jones, and stepped back. The Latin races embrace and weep, and all goes well; but among Saxons, tears are a horrid event. Jones never knew what to do when it was a woman; but this was truly disgusting. He was well seasoned by the frontier—had tried a little of anything: town and country, ranches, saloons, stage-driving, marriage occasionally, and latterly mines. He had sundry claims staked out, and always carried pieces of stone in his pockets, discoursing upon their mineral-bearing capacity, which was apt to be very slight. That is why he was called Specimen Jones. He had exhausted all the important sensations, and did not care much for anything more. Perfect health and strength kept him from discovering that he was a saddened, drifting man. He wished to kick the boy for his baby performance; and yet he stepped carefully away from the ditch so the boy should not suspect his presence. He found himself standing still, looking at the dim, broken desert.

"Why, hell," complained Specimen Jones, "he played the little man to start with. He did so. He scared that old horse-thief Adams just about dead. Then he went to kill me, that kep him from bein' buried early tomorrow. I've been wild that way myself, and wantin' to shoot up the whole outfit." Jones looked at the place where his middle finger used to be, before a certain evening in Tombstone. "But I never —" He glanced towards the ditch, perplexed. "What's that mean? Why in the world does he git to cryin' for *now*, do you suppose?" Jones took to singing without knowing it. "'Ye shepherds, tell me, have you seen my Flora pass this way?'" he murmured. Then a thought struck him. "Hello, kid!" he called out. There was no answer.

"Of course," said Jones. "Now he's ashamed to hev me see him come out of there." He walked with elaborate slowness round the corral and behind a shed. "Hello, you kid!" he called again.

"I was thinking of going to sleep," said the boy, appearing quite suddenly. "I — I'm not used to riding all day. I'll get used to it, you know," he hastened to add.

"'Ha-ve you seen my Flo —' Say, kid, where you bound, anyway?"

"San Carlos."

"San Carlos! Oh. Ah. '— Flo-ra pass this way?'"

"Is it far, sir?"

"Awful far, sometimes. It's always liable to be far through the Arivaypa Cañon."

"I didn't expect to make it between meals," remarked Cumnor.

"No. Sure. What made you come this route?"

"A man told me."

"A man? Oh. Well, it *is* kind o' difficult, I admit, for an Arizonan not to lie to a stranger. But I think I'd have told you to go by Tres Alamos and Point of Mountain. It's the road the man that told you would choose himself every time. Do you like Injuns, kid?"

Cumnor snapped eagerly.

"Of course you do. And you've never saw one in the whole minute and a half you've been alive. I know all about it."

"I'm not afraid," said the boy.

"Not afraid? Of course you ain't. What's your idea in going to Carlos? Got town lots there?"

"No," said the literal youth, to the huge internal diversion of Jones. "There's a man there I used to know back home. He's in the cavalry. What sort of a town is it for sport?" asked Cumnor, in a gay-Lothario tone.

"*Town?*" Specimen Jones caught hold of the top rail of the corral. "*Sport?* Now I'll tell you what sort of a town it is. There ain't no streets. There ain't no houses. There ain't any land and water in the usual meaning of them words. There's Mount Turnbull. It's pretty near a usual mountain, but you don't want to go there. The Creator didn't make San Carlos. It's a heap older than him. When he got around to it after slickin' up Paradise and them fruit-trees, he just left it to be as he found it, as a sample of the way they done business before he come along. He 'a'n't done any work around that spot at all, he 'a'n't. Mix up a barrel of sand and ashes and thorns, and jam scorpions and rattlesnakes along in, and dump the outfit on stones, and heat yer stones red-hot, and set the United States army loose over the place chasin' Apaches, and you've got San Carlos."

Cumnor was silent for a moment. "I don't care," he said. "I want to chase Apaches."

"Did you see that man Ephraim found by the cañon?" Jones inquired.

"Didn't get here in time."

"Well, there was a hole in his chest made by an arrow. But there's no harm in that if you die at wunst. That chap didn't, you see. You heard Ephraim tell about it. They'd done a number of things to the man before he could die. Roastin' was only one of 'em. Now your road takes you through the mountains where these Injuns hev gone. Kid, come along to Tucson with me," urged Jones suddenly.

Again Cumnor was silent. "Is my road different from other people's?" he said, finally.

"Not to Grant, it ain't. These Mexicans are hauling freight to Grant. But what's the matter with your coming to Tucson with me?"

"I started to go to San Carlos, and I'm going," said Cumnor.

"You're a poor chuckle-headed fool!" burst out Jones in a rage. "And you can go for all I care — you and your Christmas-tree pistol. Like as not you won't find your cavalry friend at San Carlos. They've killed a lot of them soldiers huntin' Injuns this season. Good night."

Specimen Jones was gone. Cumnor walked to his blanket-roll, where his saddle was slung under the shed. The various doings of the evening had bruised his nerves. He spread his blankets among the dry cattle-dung, and sat down, taking off a few clothes slowly. He lumped his coat and overalls under his head for a pillow, and putting the despised pistol alongside, lay between the blankets. No object showed in the night but the tall freight-wagon. The tenderfoot thought he had made altogether a fool of himself upon the first trial trip of his manhood, alone on the open sea of Arizona. No man, not even Jones now, was his friend. A stranger, who could have had nothing against him but his inexperience, had taken the trouble to direct him on the wrong road. He did not mind definite enemies — he had punched the heads of those in Pennsylvania, and would not object to shooting them here: but this impersonal, surrounding hostility of the unknown was new and bitter; the cruel, assassinating, cowardly Southwest, where prospered those jailbirds whom the vigilantes had driven from California. He thought of the nameless human carcass that lay near, buried that day, and of the jokes about its mutilations. Cumnor was not an innocent boy, either in principles or in practice; but this laughter about a dead body had burned into his young, unhardened soul. He lay watching with hot, dogged eyes the brilliant stars. A passing wind turned the windmill, which creaked a forlorn minute, and ceased. He must have gone to sleep and slept soundly; for the next he knew, it was the cold air of dawn that made him open his eyes. A numb silence lay over all things, and the tenderfoot had that moment of curiosity as to where he was now which comes to those who have journeyed for many days. The Mexicans had already departed with their freight-wagon. It was not entirely light, and the embers, where these early starters had cooked their breakfast, lay glowing in the sand across the road. The boy remembered seeing a wagon where now he saw only chill, distant peaks; and while he lay quiet and warm, shunning full consciousness, there was a stir in the cabin, and at Ephraim's voice reality broke upon his drowsiness, and he recollected Arizona and the keen stress of shifting for himself. He noted the gray paling round the grave. Indians? He would catch up with the Mexicans, and travel in their company to Grant. Freighters made but fifteen miles in the day, and he could start after breakfast and be with them before they stopped to noon. Six men need not worry about Apaches, Cumnor thought. The voice of Specimen Jones came from the cabin, and sounds of lighting the stove, and the growling conversation of men getting up. Cumnor, lying in his blankets, tried to overhear what Jones was saying, for no better reason than that this was the only man he had met lately who had seemed to care whether he were alive or dead. There was the clink of Ephraim's whisky-bottles, and the cheerful tones of old Mr. Adams saying, "It's better'n brushin' yer teeth"; and then further clinking, and an inquiry from Specimen Jones.

"Whose spurs?" said he.

"Mine." This from Mr. Adams.

"How long have they been yourn?"

"Since I got 'em, I guess."

"Well, you've enjoyed them spurs long enough." The voice of Specimen Jones now altered in quality. "And you'll give 'em back to that kid."

Muttering followed that the boy could not catch. "You'll give 'em back," repeated Jones. "I seen you lift 'em from under that chair when I was in the corner."

"That's straight, Mr. Adams," said Ephraim. "I noticed it myself, though I had no objections, of course. But Mr. Jones has pointed out — "

"Since when have you growed so honest, Jones?" cackled Mr. Adams, seeing that he must lose his little booty. "And why didn't you raise yer objections when you seen me do it?"

"I didn't know the kid," Jones explained. "And if it don't strike you that game blood deserves respect, why it does strike me."

Hearing this, the tenderfoot, outside in his shed, thought better of mankind and life in general, arose from his nest, and began preening himself. He had all the correct trappings for the frontier, and his toilet in the shed gave him pleasure. The sun came up, and with a stroke struck the world to crystal. The near sand-hills went into rose; the crabbed yucca and the mesquite turned transparent, with lances and pale films of green, like drapery graciously veiling the desert's face; and distant violet peaks and edges framed the vast enchantment beneath the liquid exhalations of the sky. The smell of bacon and coffee from open windows filled the heart with bravery and yearning; and Ephraim, putting his head round the corner, called to Cumnor that he had better come in and eat. Jones, already at table, gave him the briefest nod; but the spurs were there, replaced as Cumnor had left them under a chair in the corner. In Arizona they do not say much at any meal, and at breakfast nothing at all; and as Cumnor swallowed and meditated, he noticed the cream-colored lady and the chain, and he made up his mind he should assert his identity with regard to that business, though how and when was not clear to him. He was in no great haste to take up his journey. The society of the Mexicans whom he must sooner or later overtake did not tempt him. When breakfast was done he idled in the cabin, like the other guests, while Ephraim and his assistant busied about the premises. But the morning grew on; and the guests, after a season of smoking and tilted silence against the wall, shook themselves and their effects together, saddled, and were lost among the waste thorny hills. Twenty Mile became hot and torpid. Jones lay on three consecutive chairs, occasionally singing; and old Mr. Adams had not gone away either, but watched him, with more tobacco running down his beard.

"Well," said Cumnor, "I'll be going."

"Nobody's stopping you," remarked Jones.

"You're going to Tucson?" the boy said, with the chain problem still unsolved in his mind. "Good-by, Mr. Jones. I hope I'll — we'll —"

"That'll do," said Jones; and the tenderfoot, thrown back by his severity, went to get his saddle-horse and his burro.

Presently Jones remarked to Mr. Adams that he wondered what Ephraim was doing, and went out. The old gentleman was left alone in the room, and he swiftly noticed that the belt and pistol of Specimen Jones were left alone with him. The accoutrement lay by the chair its owner had been lounging in. It is an easy thing to remove cartridges from the chambers of a revolver, and replace the weapon in its holster so that everything looks quite natural. The old gentleman was entertained with the notion that somewhere in Tucson, Specimen Jones might have a surprise; and he did not take a minute to prepare this, drop the belt as it lay before, and saunter innocently out of the saloon. Ephraim and Jones were criticizing the tenderfoot's property as he packed his burro.

"Do you make it a rule to travel with ice-cream?" Jones was inquiring.

"They're for water," Cumnor said. "They told me at Tucson I'd need to carry water for three days on some trails."

It was two good-sized milk-cans that he had; and they bounced about on the little burro's pack, giving him as much amazement as a jackass can feel. Jones and Ephraim were hilarious.

"Don't go without your spurs, Mr. Cumnor," said the voice of old Mr. Adams, as he approached the group. His tone was particularly civil.

The tenderfoot had indeed forgotten his spurs; and he ran back to get them. The cream-colored lady still had the chain hanging upon her, and Cumnor's problem was suddenly solved. He put the chain in his pocket, and laid the price of one round of drinks for last night's company on the shelf below the chromo. He returned with his spurs on, and went to his saddle that lay beside that of Specimen Jones under the shed. After a moment he came with his saddle to where the men stood talking by his pony, slung it on, and tightened the cinches; but the chain was now in the saddle-bag of Specimen Jones, mixed up with some tobacco, stale bread, a box of matches, and a hunk of fat bacon. The men at Twenty Mile said good day to the tenderfoot, with monosyllables and indifference, and watched him depart into the heated desert. Wishing for a last look at Jones, he turned once, and saw the three standing, and the chocolate brick of the cabin, and the windmill white and idle in the sun.

"He'll be gutted by night," remarked Mr. Adams.

"I ain't buryin' him, then," said Ephraim.

"Nor I," said Specimen Jones. "Well, it's time I was getting to Tucson."

He went to the saloon, strapped on his pistol, saddled, and rode away. Ephraim and Mr. Adams returned to the cabin; and here is the final conclusion they came to, after three hours of discussion as to who took the chain and who had it just then: —

Ephraim. Jones, he hadn't no cash.

Mr. Adams. The kid, he hadn't no sense.

Ephraim. The kid, he lent the cash to Jones.

Mr. Adams. Jones, he goes off with his chain.

Both. What damn fools everybody is, anyway!

And they went to dinner. But Mr. Adams did not mention his relations with Jones's pistol. Let it be said in extenuation of that performance, that Mr. Adams supposed Jones was going to Tucson, where he said he was going, and where a job and a salary were awaiting him. In Tucson an unloaded pistol, in the holster of so handy a man on the drop as was Specimen, would keep people civil, because they would not know, any more than the owner, that it was unloaded; and the mere possession of it would be sufficient in nine chances out of ten — though it was undoubtedly for the tenth that Mr. Adams had a sneaking hope. But Specimen Jones was not going to Tucson. A contention in his mind as to whether he would do what was good for himself, or what was good for another, had kept him sullen ever since he got up. Now it was settled, and Jones in serene humor again. Of course he had started on the Tucson road, for the benefit of Ephraim and Mr. Adams.

The tenderfoot rode along. The Arizona sun beat down upon the deadly silence; and the world was no longer of crystal, but a mesa, dull and gray and hot. The pony's hoofs grated in the gravel; and after a time the road dived down and up among lumpy hills of stone and cactus, always nearer the fierce glaring Sierra Santa Catalina. It dipped so abruptly in and out of the shallow sudden ravines, that on coming up from one of these into the sight of the country again, the tenderfoot's heart jumped at the close apparition of another rider quickly bearing in upon him from gullies where he had been moving unseen. But it was only Specimen Jones.

"Hello!" said he, joining Cumnor. "Hot, ain't it?"

"Where are you going?" inquired Cumnor.

"Up here a ways." And Jones jerked his finger generally towards the Sierra, where they were heading.

"Thought you had a job in Tucson."

"That's what I have."

Specimen Jones had no more to say; and they rode for a while, their ponies' hoofs always grating in the gravel, and the milk-cans lightly clanking on the burro's pack. The bunched blades of the yuccas bristled steel-stiff; and as far as you could see, it was a gray waste of mounds and ridges sharp and blunt, up to the forbidding boundary walls of the Tortilita one way and the Santa Catalina the other. Cumnor wondered if Jones had found the chain. Jones was capable of not finding it for several weeks, or of finding it at once and saying nothing.

"You'll excuse my meddling with your business?" the boy hazarded.

Jones looked inquiring.

"Something's wrong with your saddle-pocket."

Specimen saw nothing apparently wrong with it; but perceiving Cumnor was grinning, unbuckled the pouch. He looked at the boy rapidly, and looked away again; and as he rode, still in silence, he put the chain back round his neck below the flannel shirt-collar.

"Say, kid," he remarked after some time, "what does J. stand for?"

"J.? Oh, my name! Jock."

"Well, Jock, will you explain to me as a friend how you ever come to be such a fool as to leave yer home — wherever and whatever it was — in exchange for this here God-forsaken and iniquitous hole?"

"If you'll explain to me," said the boy, greatly heartened, "how you come to be ridin' in the company of a fool, instead of goin' to your job at Tucson."

The explanation was furnished before Specimen Jones had framed his reply. A burning freight-wagon and five dismembered human stumps lay in the road. This was what had happened to the Miguels and Serapios and the concertina. Jones and Cumnor, in their dodging and struggles to exclude all expressions of growing mutual esteem from their speech, had forgotten their journey; and a sudden bend among the rocks where the road had now brought them revealed the blood and fire staring them in the face. The plundered wagon was three parts empty; its splintered, blazing boards slid down as they burned, into the fiery heap on the ground; packages of soda and groceries and medicines slid with them, bursting into chemical spots of green and crimson flame; a wheel crushed in and sank, spilling more packages that flickered and hissed; the garbage of combat and murder littered the earth; and in the air hung an odor that Cumnor knew, though he had never smelled it before. Morsels of dropped booty up among the rocks showed where the Indians had gone; and one horse remained, groaning, with an accidental arrow in his belly.

"We'll just kill him," said Jones; and his pistol snapped idly, and snapped again, as his eye caught a motion — a something — two hundred yards up among the boulders on the hill. He whirled round. The enemy was behind them also. There was no retreat. "Yourn's no good!" yelled Jones fiercely, for Cumnor was getting out his little foolish revolver. "Oh, what a trick to play on a man! Drop off yer horse, kid; drop, and do like me. Shootin's no good here, even if I was loaded. *They* shot, and look at them now. God bless them ice-cream freezers of yourn, kid! Did you ever see a crazy man? If you 'ain't, *make it up as you go along!*"

More objects moved up among the boulders. Specimen Jones ripped off the burro's pack, and the milk-cans rolled on the ground. The burro began grazing quietly, with now and then a step towards new patches of grass. The horses stood where their riders had left them, their reins over their heads, hanging and dragging. From two hundred yards on the hill the ambushed Apaches showed, their dark, scattered figures appearing cautiously one by one, watching with suspicion. Specimen Jones seized up one milk-can, and Cumnor obediently did the same.

"You kin dance, kid, and I kin sing, and we'll go to it," said Jones. He rambled in a wavering loop, and diving eccentrically at Cumnor, clashed the milk-cans together. "'Es schallt ein Ruf wie Donnerhall,'" he bawled, beginning the song of 'Die Wacht am Rhein.' "Why don't you dance?" he shouted sternly. The boy saw the terrible earnestness of his face, and clashing his milk-cans in turn, he shuffled a sort of jig. The two went over the sand in loops, toe and heel; the donkey continued his quiet grazing, and the flames rose hot and yellow from the freight-wagon. And all the while the stately German hymn pealed among the rocks, and the Apaches crept down nearer the bowing, scraping men. The sun shone bright, and their bodies poured with sweat. Jones flung off his shirt; his damp, matted hair was half in ridges and half glued to his forehead, and the delicate gold chain swung and struck his broad, naked breast. The Apaches drew nearer again, their bows and arrows held uncertainly. They came down the hill, fifteen or twenty, taking a long time, and stopping every few yards. The milk-cans clashed, and Jones thought he felt the boy's strokes weakening. 'Die Wacht am Rhein' was finished, and now it was 'Ha-ve you seen my Flora pass this way?' "You mustn't play out, kid," said Jones, very gently — "indeed you mustn't"; and he at once resumed his song.

The silent Apaches had now reached the bottom of the hill. They stood some twenty yards away, and Cumnor had a good chance to see his first Indians. He saw them move, and the color and slim shape of their bodies, their thin arms, and their long, black hair. It went through his mind that if he had no more clothes on than that, dancing would come easier. His boots were growing heavy to lift, and his overalls seemed to wrap his sinews in wet, strangling thongs. He wondered how long he had been keeping this up. The legs of the Apaches were free, with light moccasins only half-way to the thigh, slenderly held up by strings from the waist. Cumnor envied their unencumbered steps as he saw them again walk nearer to where he was dancing. It was long since he had eaten, and he noticed a singing dullness in his brain, and became frightened at his thoughts, which were running and melting into one fixed idea. This idea was to take off his boots, and offer to trade them for a pair of moccasins. It terrified him — this endless, molten rush of thoughts; he could see them coming in different shapes from different places in his head, but they all joined immediately, and always formed the same fixed idea. He ground his teeth to master this encroaching inebriation of his will and judgment. He clashed his can more loudly to wake him to reality, which he still could recognize and appreciate. For a time he found it a good plan to listen to what Specimen Jones was singing, and tell himself the name of the song, if he knew it. At present it was 'Yankee Doodle,' to which Jones was fitting words of his own. These ran, " Now I'm going to try a bluff, And mind you do what I do "; and then again, over and over. Cumnor waited for the word " bluff "; for it was hard and heavy, and fell into his thoughts, and stopped them for a moment. The dance was so long now he had forgotten about that. A numbness had been spreading through his legs, and he was glad to feel a sharp pain in the sole of his foot. It was a piece of gravel that had somehow worked its way in, and was rubbing through the skin into the flesh. " That's good," he said aloud. The pebble was eating the numbness away, and Cumnor drove it hard against the raw spot, and relished the tonic of its burning friction.

The Apaches had drawn into a circle. Standing at some interval apart, they entirely surrounded the arena. Shrewd, half convinced, and yet with awe, they watched the dancers, who clashed their cans slowly now in rhythm to Jones's hoarse, parched singing. He was quite master of himself, and led the jig round the still blazing wreck of the wagon, and circled in figures of eight between the corpses of the Mexicans, clashing the milk-cans above each one. Then, knowing his strength was coming to an end, he approached an Indian whose splendid fillet and trappings denoted him of consequence; and Jones was near shouting with relief when the Indian shrank backward. Suddenly he saw Cumnor let his can drop; and without stopping to see why, he caught it up, and slowly rattling both, approached each Indian in turn with tortuous steps. The circle that had never uttered a sound till now, receded, chanting almost in a whisper some exorcising song which the man with the fillet had begun. They gathered round him, retreating always; and the strain, with its rapid muttered words, rose and fell softly among them. Jones had supposed the boy was overcome by faintness, and looked to see where he lay. But it was not faintness. Cumnor, with his boots off, came by and walked after the Indians in a trance. They saw him, and quickened their pace, often turning to be sure he was not overtaking them. He called to them unintelligibly, stumbling up the sharp hill, and pointing to the boots. Finally he sat down. They continued ascending the mountain, herding close round the man with the feathers, until the rocks and the filmy tangles screened them from sight; and like a wind that hums uncertainly in grass, their chanting died away.

The sun was half behind the western range when Jones next moved. He called, and getting no answer, he crawled painfully to where the boy lay on the hill. Cumnor was sleeping heavily; his head was hot, and he moaned. So Jones crawled down, and fetched blankets and the canteen of water. He spread the blankets over the boy, wet a handkerchief and laid it on his forehead; then he lay down himself.

The earth was again magically smitten to crystal. Again the sharp cactus and the sand turned beautiful, and violet floated among the mountains, and rose-colored orange in the sky above them.

"Jock," said Specimen at length.

The boy opened his eyes.

"Your foot is awful, Jock. Can you eat?"

"Not with my foot."

"Ah, God bless you, Jock! You ain't turruble sick. But *can* you eat?"

Cumnor shook his head.

"Eatin's what you need, though. Well, here." Specimen poured a judicious mixture of whisky and water down the boy's throat, and wrapped the awful foot in his own flannel shirt. "They'll fix you over to Grant. It's maybe twelve miles through the cañon. It ain't a town any more than Carlos is, but the soldiers 'll be good to us. As soon as night comes, you and me must somehow git out of this."

Somehow they did — Jones walking and leading his horse and the imperturbable little burro, and also holding Cumnor in the saddle. And when Cumnor was getting well in the military hospital at Grant, he listened to Jones recounting to all that chose to hear how useful a weapon an ice-cream freezer can be, and how if you'll only chase Apaches in your stocking feet they are sure to run away. And then Jones and Cumnor both enlisted; and I suppose Jones's friend is still expecting him in Tucson.

WILLIAM SYDNEY PORTER (O. HENRY)

WILLIAM SYDNEY PORTER, whom it is simpler to designate by his chosen name of O. Henry, was born at Greensboro in North Carolina on September 11, 1862. His father, Dr. Algernon Porter, a man sprung of New England stock, was a practising physician, with a queer absorption in mechanical invention and a dreamer's interest in the problem of perpetual motion. His mother, whom he lost when three years old, seems to have been a woman of a certain talent and with a sweetness of disposition which endeared her to all about her. But the biographers of O. Henry may seek in vain to find any special significance in the environment or circumstances of his youth. His education was merely that of Charles Dickens and William Shakespeare, with even smaller Latin and of Greek nothing. Such instruction as he ever had was imparted by his aunt, a Miss Evelina Porter, who carried on a sort of " dame's school " — a little class taught in her own home. Here O. Henry was a "scholar" till he was fifteen years old, but a pupil apparently of no especial promise. A certain crude ability for drawing pictures of " Miss Lina " and her scholars on his slate may be dignified, if one will, to the rank of an artistic gift. Had it been cultivated with diligence, it might have made of O. Henry a black-and-white cartoonist of the third rank. His fondness for reading " dime novels " and tales of adventure, his instinctive appreciation of the 'Arabian Nights,' and his absorption in the novels of Scott, Hugo, and Dickens, is a heritage that he shared with ninety-nine of every hundred boys of his time and country. Of higher education, of colleges and of culture, in its professional sense, O. Henry seems to have known nothing and cared nothing from first to last. Yet while his education was of the humblest and his reading only of the usual range, he seems to have possessed in an unusual degree the art of seizing the light and color of what he read, and making it, in a peculiar way, his own. But when all is said and done there was nothing in the first twenty years of O. Henry's life that could have marked him out for eminence.

After leaving school O. Henry worked for five years in the drug store of his uncle in his native town, a dull drudgery which he afterwards referred to as " a grind that was agony to him." It brought him nothing but a slender livelihood, a local reputation as a pleasant fellow of genial humor, and with that a certain acquaintance with drugs which supplied him with touches of local color for numberless stories, and which was to stand him in good stead in the darkest hours of his life.

Release from his drudgery came in the form of an invitation from the Hall family of Greensboro to go out with them to their ranch in La Salle County, Texas. There O. Henry passed two years, leading the glorious open-air life of an amateur cowboy and bronco buster. In his leisure hours on the ranch he made his first beginnings in literature — little stories written to please himself, for art's sake alone, and, with the instinct of the artist, committed to the flames.

From the ranch O. Henry "drifted" — it was to become his regular method of locomotion — to the city of Austin. Here he worked for two years as the bookkeeper of a real estate firm. Later on (it was in January 1887) he obtained, through political influence, a situation in the General Land Office at Austin. The four years which O. Henry passed in the employment of the State of Texas may well have been the happiest in his life. They were signalized by his somewhat romantic marriage with Miss Athol Estes, then only seventeen years old. It was a love match in every way, involving an elopement in a borrowed buggy, a midnight invasion of the house of a Presbyterian minister, with the easy forgiveness of an affectionate mother as a happy ending to the episode. With marriage came responsibility and effort. O. Henry turned instinctively to literary work. We hear of him as a writer of "items" for the Houston Daily Post, and of little sketches for the Detroit Free Press and Truth of New York. The birth of his daughter, Margaret Worth Porter, seemed to complete the promise of his opening happiness.

Then the shadows began to darken. O. Henry's political position vanished as it had come. In an ill-omened hour he secured, (January 1894) a position as paying and receiving teller of the First National Bank of Austin. The institution, it would appear, was a marvel of mismanagement. Its funds were borrowed — and, it would seem, were even misappropriated — in the most free and easy fashion. As O. Henry worked at his teller's counter, temptation beckoned him on one side and domestic need on the other. He was tempted and he fell. That, at least, was the judgment of the courts of law.

For the time being, O. Henry's sin, if sin there was, did not find him out. He left the service of the bank (December 1894), turned to his natural bent, and started in Austin a queer little journal of the comic sort called The Rolling Stone. It rolled for about a year. After its demise, O. Henry joined the staff of the Houston Daily Post, writing little sketches and "postscripts," as he called them, with illustrations of his own.

Then the blow fell. A warrant was issued for him and he fled. He sheltered himself first in New Orleans, then plunged into exile as a wanderer in Central and South America. His fate was made doubly bitter by the need of leaving behind his young wife, now smitten with a fatal illness. Of his wanderings in the republics of the south we have, save as the inspiration and background of his literary work, but little trace. But there is no doubt that Latin America, and the sad fate that brought him there and gave him eyes to see, first called forth the real genius of the man. Latin America fascinated O. Henry. The languor of the tropics; the sunlit seas with their open bays and broad sanded beaches, with green palms nodding on the slopes above — white-painted steamers lazily at anchor — quaint Spanish towns, with adobe houses and wide squares, sunk in their noonday sleep — beautiful Señoritas drowsing away the afternoon in hammocks; the tinkling of the mule bells on the mountain track above the town — the cries of unknown birds issuing from the dense green of the unbroken jungle — and at night in the soft darkness, the low murmur of the guitar, soft thrumming with the voice of love — these are the sights and sounds of O. Henry's Central and South America. Here live and move his tattered revolutionists, his gaudy generals of the mimic army of the existing republic; hither ply his white-painted steamers of the fruit trade; here the American consul, with a shadowed past and $600 a year, drinks away the remembrance of his northern energy and his college education in the land of forgetfulness. Hither the absconding banker from the States is dropped from the passing steamer, clutching tight in his shaking hand his valise of stolen dollars; him the disguised detective, lounging beside the little drinking shop, watches with a furtive eye. And here in this land of enchantment the broken lives, the wasted hopes, the ambition that was never reached, the frailty that was never conquered, are somehow pieced together and illuminated into what they might have been — and even the reckless crime and the open sin, viewed in the softened haze of such an atmosphere, are half forgiven.

News reached O. Henry that his wife was dying. He returned to Texas, to stand beside her death-bed (July 25, 1897), and then to surrender himself to the law. He was tried, after many delays, and sentenced (February 17, 1898) to five years in the penitentiary at Columbus, Ohio. There is no need to dwell on the long misery of his prison life. Whatever his fault, he atoned it by his sufferings and the courage with which they were borne. The extent of his fault itself has been questioned. That he was technically guilty is probably beyond a doubt. But there is ground for believing that he was at the worst merely the instrument of the wrong of others, a victim to his own easy and careless nature. "I want to state solemnly to you," he wrote, after his sentence, to the mother of his dead wife, "that I am absolutely innocent of wrong doing." Those who have learned to know and to love O. Henry through his books may take this comfort from his written word.

For a part of O. Henry's time in the penitentiary his lot was mitigated by his being allowed to serve as night drug clerk in the prison dispensary. Here he found the spare time, and the courage, to continue his literary work; writing no longer little sketches and anecdotes, but completed stories, imprinted with the marvelous blending of humor and pathos and that wide sympathy with human frailty and suffering which is the crown of all his work.

"In the silent watches of the night," writes Professor Alphonso Smith, in his 'O. Henry Biography,' "when the only sound heard was the occasional sigh or groan from the beds which were stretched before him in the hospital ward, or the tramp of the passing guard, O. Henry came into his own."

About a dozen of O. Henry's stories (he wrote in all over two hundred) were written in his prison.

Good conduct shortened his sentence. He left the penitentiary on July 24, 1901. He joined his little daughter and her grandmother in Pittsburgh, and there set himself to work regularly as a writer of short stories, the occupation that filled the rest of his life. He moved to New York in 1902. His matchless stories found a ready acceptance in the columns of the magazines. He might have acquired, had he so wished it, the noisy fame of a successful author. But his was a bruised life. He carried his shame and his genius into a deliberate obscurity. His pen name of "O. Henry," he seems to have adopted early in his career; but so greatly did he dread notoriety that he varied it with others.

In New York, O. Henry lived for eight years, practically unknown to the hurrying world about him. But such a light — even in humble quarters, in an apartment house on Twenty-Third Street — could not remain altogether under a bushel. Editors began to clamor for his work. A great New York journal contracted for a story a week, at a price of a hundred dollars, an engagement which O. Henry maintained for over a year. Publishers began to gather up his work and issue it in book form. 'Cabbages and Kings,' a group of Latin-American stories, pieced together into something like a continuous tale, appeared in 1904. It was followed by 'The Four Million' in 1906, 'The Trimmed Lamp' and 'The Heart of the West' in 1907, 'The Voice of the City' and 'The Gentle Grafter' in 1908, 'Roads of Destiny' and 'Options' in 1909, and 'Strictly Business' and 'Whirligigs' in 1910. The volumes called 'Sixes and Sevens' and 'Rolling Stones' appeared after his death. Each of his books is a collection of short stories, about twenty to a volume. A novel — unless one so designates 'Cabbages and Kings' — he never wrote. A play he often meditated yet never achieved. But it is an error of the grossest kind to say that O. Henry's work is not sustained. In reality his field is vast. His New York stories, like those of Central America or of the West, form one great picture as gloriously comprehensive in its scope as the novels of Dickens or the canvas of a Da Vinci.

The stories that deal with the lights and shadows of the city of 'The Four Million' may perhaps be considered as his best work. What O. Henry did for Central America he does again for New York. It is transformed by the magic of his imagination. He waves a wand over it and it becomes a city of mystery and romance. It is no longer the roaring, surging metropolis that we thought we knew, with its clattering "elevated," its unending crowds, and on every side the repellent selfishness of the rich, the grim struggle of the poor, and the listless despair of the outcast. It has become, as O. Henry loves to call it, Bagdad upon the Subway. The glare has gone. There is a soft light suffusing the city. Its corner drug stores are turned into enchanted bazaars. From the open doors of its restaurants and palm rooms, there issues such a melody of softened music that we feel we have but to cross the threshold and there is Bagdad waiting for us beyond. A transformed waiter hands us to a chair at a little table — Arabian, one will swear it — beside an enchanted rubber tree. There is red wine such as Omar Khayyam drank, here on Sixth Avenue. At the tables about us are a strange and interesting crew — dervishes in the disguise of American business men, caliphs masquerading as tourists, bedouins from Syria and fierce fantassins from the desert turned into western visitors from Texas, and among them — can we believe our eyes? — houris from the inner harems of Ispahan and Candahar, whom we mistook but yesterday for the ladies of a Shubert chorus! As we pass out we pay our money to an enchanted cashier with golden hair — sitting behind glass — under the spell of some magician without a doubt — and then taking O. Henry's hand we wander forth among the ever changing scenes of night adventure, the mingled tragedy and humor of 'The Four Million' that his pen alone can depict. Now did ever Haroun al Raschid and his viziers, wandering at will in the narrow streets of their Arabian city, meet such varied adventure as lies before us, strolling hand in hand with O. Henry in the new Bagdad that he reveals?

Late in his life (in 1907) O. Henry married again. His second wife was a Miss Coleman, a companion of his childhood days in his native town. But even in the years after his marriage he seems to have lived as quietly, and with the same aversion to general society as before. His real life was in his work, and the inspiration for it was found in his solitary wanderings in the city of 'The Four Million.' Unique indeed it was. For O. Henry — in his real work — could write only by the light within. There was no elaborate scheme of preparation to take the place of the inspired word. He read nothing, or next to it. He investigated nothing. He saw nobody. He had no propaganda, no views to expound, no lesson, in the meaner sense, to teach. His was not the dull industry that investigates, note-book in hand, the slum, the factory, and the market-place, and turns the mass of accumulated fact into the vast Contemporary Novel that pours its slow current through the channel of a thousand pages.

Ignorant — undoubtedly — except of life itself — gloriously ignorant he was. No college — not even a theological school — could have matriculated him. Even of New York — so they now tell us — he knew practically nothing. But of little threads and patches, a vision of a haggard face seen for a moment in a crowd — a fallen word, the chance glance of an eye — of such as this, interwoven with the cross thread of his marvelous imagination, he did his matchless work.

In what should have been the midday of O. Henry's achievement, there fell upon him the hand of a wasting and mortal disease which brought him slowly to his end, his courage and his gentle kindliness unbroken to the last. The end came at the Polyclinic Hospital, New York, on June 5, 1910. O. Henry died as he had lived, a smile upon his lips. "Don't turn down the light," he is reported to have said to those beside his bed, and then, as the words of a popular song flickered across his mind, he added, "I'm afraid to go home in the dark."

STEPHEN LEACOCK

THE COP AND THE ANTHEM

From 'The Four Million.' Copyright by Doubleday, Page & Co., and reprinted by their permission

ON his bench in Madison Square, Soapy moved uneasily. When wild geese honk high of nights, and when women without sealskin coats grow kind to their husbands, and when Soapy moves uneasily on his bench in the park, you may know that winter is near at hand.

A dead leaf fell in Soapy's lap. That was Jack Frost's card. Jack is kind to the regular denizens of Madison Square, and gives fair warning of his annual call. At the corners of four streets he hands his pasteboard to the North Wind, footman of the mansion of All Outdoors, so that the inhabitants thereof may make ready.

Soapy's mind became cognizant of the fact that the time had come for him to resolve himself into a singular Committee of Ways and Means to provide against the coming rigor. And therefore he moved uneasily on his bench.

The hibernatorial ambitions of Soapy were not of the highest. In them there were no considerations of Mediterranean cruises, of soporific southern skies or drifting in the Vesuvian Bay. Three months on the Island was what his soul craved. Three months of assured board and bed and congenial company, safe from Boreas and blue coats, seemed to Soapy the essence of things desirable.

For years the hospitable Blackwell's had been his winter quarters. Just as his more fortunate fellow New Yorkers had bought their tickets to Palm Beach and the Riviera each winter, so Soapy had made his humbler arrangements for his annual hegira to the Island. And now the time was come. On the previous night three Sabbath newspapers, distributed beneath his coat, bout his ankles and over his lap, had failed to repulse the cold as he slept o. his bench near the spurting fountain in the ancient square. So the Island loomed big and timely in Soapy's mind. He scorned the provisions made in the name of charity for the city's dependents. In Soapy's opinion the Law was more benign than Philanthropy. There was an endless round of institutions, municipal and eleemosynary, on which he might set out and receive lodging and food accordant with the simple life. But to one of Soapy's proud spirit the gifts of charity are encumbered. If not in coin you must pay in humiliation of spirit for every benefit received at the hands of philanthropy. As Cæsar had his Brutus, every bed of charity must have its toll of a bath, every loaf of bread its compensation of a private and personal inquisition. Wherefore it is better to be a guest of the law, which though conducted by rules, does not meddle unduly with a gentleman's private affairs.

Soapy having decided to go to the Island, at once set about accomplishing his desire. There were many easy ways of doing this. The pleasantest was to dine luxuriously at some expensive restaurant; and then, after declaring insolvency, be handed over quietly and without uproar to a policeman. An accommodating magistrate would do the rest.

Soapy left his bench and strolled out of the square and across the level sea of asphalt, where Broadway and Fifth Avenue flow together. Up Broadway he turned, and halted at a glittering café where are gathered together nightly the choicest products of the grape, the silkworm, and the protoplasm.

Soapy had confidence in himself from the lowest button of his vest upward. He was shaven, and his coat was decent and his neat black, ready-tied four-in-hand had been presented to him by a lady missionary on Thanksgiving Day. If he could reach a table in the restaurant unsuspected, success would be his. The portion of him that would show above the table would raise no doubt in the waiter's mind. A roasted mallard duck, thought Soapy, would be about the thing — with a bottle of Chablis, and then Camembert, a demitasse, and a cigar. One dollar for the cigar would be enough. The total would not be so high as to call forth any supreme manifestation of revenge from the café management; and yet the meat would leave him filled and happy for the journey to his winter refuge.

But as Soapy set foot inside the restaurant door the headwaiter's eye fell upon his frayed trousers and decadent shoes. Strong and ready hands turned him about and conveyed him in silence and haste to the sidewalk and averted the ignoble fate of the menaced mallard.

Soapy turned off Broadway. It seemed that his route to the coveted island was not to be an epicurean one. Some other way of entering limbo must be thought of.

At a corner of Sixth Avenue electric lights and cunningly displayed wares behind plate-glass made a shop window conspicuous. Soapy took a cobblestone and dashed it through the glass. People came running round the corner, a policeman in the lead. Soapy stood still, his hands in his pockets, and smiled at the sight of brass buttons.

"Where's the man that done that?" inquired the officer excitedly.

"Don't you figure out that I might have had something to do with it?" said Soapy, not without sarcasm, but friendly, as one greets good fortune.

The policeman's mind refused to accept Soapy even as a clue. Men who smash windows do not remain to parley with the law's minions. They take to their heels. The policeman saw a man half way down the block running to catch a car. With a drawn club he joined in the pursuit. Soapy, with disgust in his heart, loafed along, twice unsuccessful.

On the opposite side of the street was a restaurant of no great pretensions. It catered to large appetites and modest purses. Its crockery and atmosphere were thick; its soup and napery thin. Into this place Soapy took his accusive shoes and telltale trousers without challenge. At a table he sat and consumed beefsteak, flapjacks, doughnuts, and pie. And then to the waiter he betrayed the fact that the minutest coin and himself were strangers.

"Now, get busy and call a cop," said Soapy. "And don't keep a gentleman waiting."

"No cop for youse," said the waiter, with a voice like butter cakes and an eye like the cherry in a Manhattan cocktail. "Hey, Con!"

Neatly upon his left ear on the callous pavement two waiters pitched Soapy. He arose, joint by joint, as a carpenter's rule opens, and beat the dust from his clothes. Arrest seemed but a rosy dream. The Island seemed very far away. A policeman who stood before a drug store two doors away laughed and walked down the street.

Five blocks Soapy traveled before his courage permitted him to woo capture again. This time the opportunity presented what he fatuously termed to himself a "cinch." A young woman of a modest and pleasing guise was standing before a show window gazing with sprightly interest at its display of shaving mugs and inkstands, and two yards from the window a large policeman of severe demeanor leaned against a water plug.

It was Soapy's design to assume the rôle of the despicable and execrated "masher." The refined and elegant appearance of his victim and the contiguity of the conscientious cop encouraged him to believe that he would soon feel the pleasant official clutch upon his arm that would insure his winter quarters on the right little, tight little isle.

Soapy straightened the lady missionary's ready-made tie, dragged his shrinking cuffs into the open, set his hat at a killing cant and sidled toward the young woman. He made eyes at her, was taken with sudden coughs and "hems," smiled, smirked, and went brazenly through the impudent and contemptible litany of the "masher." With half an eye Soapy saw that the policeman was watching him fixedly. The young woman moved away a few steps, and again bestowed her absorbed attention upon the shaving mugs. Soapy followed, boldly stepping to her side, raised his hat and said:

"Ah there, Bedelia! Don't you want to come and play in my yard?"

The policeman was still looking. The persecuted young woman had but to beckon a finger and Soapy would be practically en route for his insular haven. Already he imagined he could feel the cozy warmth of the station-house. The young woman faced him and, stretching out a hand, caught Soapy's coat sleeve.

"Sure, Mike," she said joyfully, "if you'll blow me to a pail of suds. I'd have spoken to you sooner, but the cop was watching."

With the young woman playing the clinging ivy to his oak Soapy walked past the policeman overcome with gloom. He seemed doomed to liberty.

At the next corner he shook off his companion and ran. He halted in the district where by night are found the lightest streets, hearts, vows, and librettos. Women in furs and men in great coats moved gaily in the winter air. A sudden fear seized Soapy that some dreadful enchantment had rendered him immune to arrest. The thought brought a little of panic upon it, and when he came upon another policeman lounging grandly in front of a transplendent theater he caught at the immediate straw of "disorderly conduct."

On the sidewalk Soapy began to yell drunken gibberish at the top of his harsh voice. He danced, howled, raved, and otherwise disturbed the welkin.

The policeman twirled his club, turned his back to Soapy and remarked to a citizen.

"'Tis one of them Yale lads celebratin' the goose egg they give to the Hartford College. Noisy; but no harm. We've instructions to lave them be."

Disconsolate, Soapy ceased his unavailing racket. Would never a policeman lay hands on him? In his fancy the Island seemed an unattainable Arcadia. He buttoned his thin coat against the chilling wind.

In a cigar store he saw a well-dressed man lighting a cigar at a swinging light. His silk umbrella he had set by the door on entering. Soapy stepped inside, secured the umbrella and sauntered off with it slowly. The man at the cigar light followed hastily.

"My umbrella," he said sternly.

"Oh, is it?" sneered Soapy, adding insult to petit larceny. "Well, why don't you call a policeman? I took it. Your umbrella! Why don't you call a cop. There stands one on the corner."

The umbrella owner slowed his steps. Soapy did likewise, with a presentiment that luck would again run against him. The policeman looked at the two curiously.

"Of course," said the umbrella man, "that is — well, you know how these mistakes occur — I — if that's your umbrella I hope you'll excuse me — I picked it up this morning in a restaurant — if you recognize it as yours, why — I hope you'll — "

"Of course it's mine," said Soapy viciously.

The ex-umbrella man retreated. The policeman hurried to assist a tall blond in an opera cloak across the street in front of a street car that was approaching two blocks away.

Soapy walked eastward through a street damaged by improvements. He hurled the umbrella wrathfully into an excavation. He muttered against the men who wear helmets and carry clubs. Because he wanted to fall into their clutches, they seemed to regard him as a king who could do no wrong.

At length Soapy reached one of the avenues to the east where the glitter and turmoil was but faint. He set his face down this toward Madison Square, for the homing instinct survives even when the home is a park bench.

But on an unusually quiet corner Soapy came to a standstill. Here was an old church, quaint and rambling and gabled. Through one violet-stained window a soft light glowed, where, no doubt, the organist loitered over the keys, making sure of his mastery of the coming Sabbath anthem. For there drifted out to Soapy's ears sweet music that caught and held him transfixed against the convolutions of the iron fence.

The moon was above, lustrous and serene; vehicles and pedestrians were few; sparrows twittered sleepily in the eaves — for a little while the scene might have been a country churchyard. And the anthem that the organist played cemented Soapy to the iron fence, for he had known it well in the days when his life contained such things as mothers and roses and ambitions and friends and immaculate thoughts and collars.

The conjunction of Soapy's receptive state of mind and the influences about the old church wrought a sudden and wonderful change in his soul. He viewed with swift horror the pit into which he had tumbled, the degraded days, unworthy desires, dead hopes, wrecked faculties, and base motives that made up his existence.

And also in a moment his heart responded thrillingly to this novel mood. An instantaneous and strong impulse moved him to battle with his desperate fate. He would pull himself out of the mire; he would make a man of himself again; he would conquer the evil that had taken possession of him. There was time; he was comparatively young yet; he would resurrect his old eager ambitions and pursue them without faltering. Those solemn but sweet organ notes had set up a revolution in him. Tomorrow he would go into the roaring downtown district and find work. A fur importer had once offered him a place as driver. He would find him tomorrow and ask for the position. He would be somebody in the world. He would —

Soapy felt a hand laid on his arm. He looked quickly around into the broad face of a policeman.

"What are you doin' here?" asked the officer.

"Nothin'," said Soapy.

"Then come along," said the policeman.

"Three months on the Island," said the Magistrate in the Police Court the next morning.

MARY WILKINS FREEMAN

IN the neighborhood of 1890 certain short stories of rural life in New England began to attract attention in English-speaking countries. They were written by Mary Eleanor Wilkins, a woman of Puritan descent, one of whose ancestors, John Holbrook, served as selectman, magistrate, and captain in King Philip's War. Mary Wilkins was born in Randolph, a village near Boston, but her parents early removed to Vermont, which, as she writes, seems more like her native state. She studied for a time at Mount Holyoke Seminary, but one may guess that the most important part of her education was derived from reading and observation. For many years Randolph was her home. In 1902 she married Dr. Charles A. Freeman of Metuchen, New Jersey. Since many unfounded stories about her life have somehow got into print, it should be added that she has never been occupied with any business or profession except that of writing.

Her first volume was 'The Adventures of Ann' (1886), a handful of stories that had appeared in the magazines. This was followed by the collections entitled 'A Humble Romance' (1887), 'A New England Nun' (1891), and 'Young Lucretia' (1892). Miss Wilkins then sought a wider field in the novel, composing between 1892 and 1897 'Jane Field,' 'Pembroke,' 'Madelon,' an historical romance, and 'Jerome,' besides 'Giles Corey, Yeoman,' a play of colonial times. This group comprises the author's most important work in the larger form. The best examples are 'Jane Field' and 'Pembroke,' which in material and method closely resemble the short stories that preceded them. In her voluminous later work she has at times forsaken New England for New Jersey and has sought interest in somewhat spectacular effects, or, as in 'The Portion of Labor,' in contemporary matters.

In spite of the damage wrought by over-production and work in alien fields, Mrs. Freeman's fame seems secure. It rests upon her short stories, seen at their best in the collections called 'A Humble Romance' and 'A New England Nun.' Many other writers, notably Sarah Orne Jewett, have drawn fine and faithful pictures of country life in New England, but not one has written with such poignant yet unobtrusive sympathy, such delicate humor, such a wealth of concrete detail, or with a technique that at times so nearly approaches perfection. The life that she knew so truly by heart was that of the village and the farm-house. In many ways it was unlovely. Poverty, narrowness, and the New England dialect prevail. There is much yielding to primitive impulses of temper, curiosity, and household tyranny, and there are stubborn dislikes and stupidities. It was a life that would be intolerable if its gnarly characters were not often mellowed by humor and homely good sense, or elevated by pride, by fierce integrity, by unselfish heartaches and costly generosities. Everywhere may be felt the tense moral fiber that makes New England the conscience of the nation. Repentance for venial sin bulks large, and many a plot turns on the need of the soul for expiation or open confession of wrong-doing.

Though death and failure enter into the stories, nearly all close in some mood of reconciliation, the satisfaction of some hidden hunger, the emergence of some unsuspected nobility, some proud or pathetic renunciation. Rarely are the events as romantic as in that tale of lowly chivalry called 'A Humble Romance'; but Mrs. Freeman is too good an artist to neglect the story, and she has the power to select the culminating moment in a drama that has lasted long and to give absorbing interest to events that are outwardly petty. Women predominate. Many a tale of spinster or widow permits no intrusion of the male, and he is not missed. The most memorable characters are the old, the elderly, and those just leaving youth behind. In the love stories the fragile girls who fade or bloom according to the ebb or flow of their romance are less individual than those of more stalwart mind who, jilted or forced to jilt, become easily fixed, to use Mrs. Freeman's phrase, "in the peace and pride of old maidenhood," or than the elderly lovers whose tardy steps turn towards the altar with a kind of awkward grace. More tragical are the meek wives of tyrannical husbands, whether roused to rebellion late in life, as in 'The Revolt of "Mother"' or to unselfish deception, as in the tenderly humorous 'Gentian.' But these tyrants have hearts that may be wrought upon, and we are made to feel the humor and the pathos in the lot of the men, young or old, who cannot slacken their own rein upon their wills.

It is not merely Mrs. Freeman's sympathy, humor, and sensitiveness to moral beauty that keep her dramas of humble life from leaving a sordid impression. She possesses, also, a delicate sensuousness, that, without deviating from the truth, distils every element of charm from commonplace objects — the color and fragrance of ordinary flowers, the sanctities of order and cleanliness, the good savor of homely fare suggesting comfort, shelter, and coziness, the fugitive dignities and the ameliorating graces that may go along with poverty and a degree of narrowness. And at her best she attains a technique that seems inborn rather than acquired. There is little comment or analysis. Her men and women reveal their inner selves in the face, the figure, the dress; in their gestures, actions, or talk. Concrete and vivid details crowd her short sentences and short paragraphs. There is no word too much. Nothing, for example, could be more delicately finished than the quiet little masterpiece in psychology entitled 'A New England Nun.'

THE REVOLT OF "MOTHER"

From 'A New England Nun, and Other Stories.' Copyright, 1891, by Harper & Brothers

"FATHER!"

"What is it?"

"What are them men diggin' over there in the field for?"

There was a sudden dropping and enlarging of the lower part of the old man's face, as if some heavy weight had settled therein; he shut his mouth tight, and went on harnessing the great bay mare. He hustled the collar on to her neck with a jerk.

"Father!"

The old man slapped the saddle upon the mare's back.

"Look here, father, I want to know what them men are diggin' over in the field for, an' I'm goin' to know."

"I wish you'd go into the house, mother, an' 'tend to your own affairs," the old man said then. He ran his words together, and his speech was almost as inarticulate as a growl.

But the woman understood: it was her most native tongue. "I ain't goin' into the house till you tell me what them men are doin' over there in the field," said she.

Then she stood waiting. She was a small woman, short and straight-waisted like a child in her brown cotton gown. Her forehead was mild and benevolent between the smooth curves of gray hair; there were meek downward lines about her nose and mouth: but her eyes, fixed upon the old man, looked as if the meekness had been the result of her own will, never of the will of another.

They were in the barn, standing before the wide open doors. The spring air, full of the smell of growing grass and unseen blossoms, came in their faces. The deep yard in front was littered with farm wagons and piles of wood; on the edges, close to the fence and the house, the grass was a vivid green, and there were some dandelions.

The old man glanced doggedly at his wife as he tightened the last buckles on the harness. She looked as immovable to him as one of the rocks in his pasture-land, bound to the earth with generations of blackberry vines. He slapped the reins over the horse and started forth from the barn.

"*Father!*" said she.

The old man pulled up. "What is it?"

"I want to know what them men are diggin' over there in that field for."

"They're diggin' a cellar, I s'pose, if you've got to know."

"A cellar for what?"

"A barn."

"A barn! You ain't goin' to build a barn over there where we was goin' to have a house, father?"

The old man said not another word. He hurried the horse into the farm wagon, and clattered out of the yard, jouncing as sturdily on his seat as a boy.

The woman stood a moment looking after him; then she went out of the barn across a corner of the yard to the house. The house, standing at right angles with the great barn and a long reach of sheds and out-buildings, was infinitesimal compared with them. It was scarcely as commodious for people as the little boxes under the barn eaves were for doves.

A pretty girl's face, pink and delicate as a flower, was looking out of one of the house windows. She was watching three men who were digging over in the field which bounded the yard near the road line. She turned quietly when the woman entered.

"What are they digging for, mother?" said she. "Did he tell you?"

"They're diggin' for — a cellar for a new barn."

"O mother, he ain't goin' to build another barn?"

"That's what he says."

A boy stood before the kitchen glass combing his hair. He combed slowly and painstakingly, arranging his brown hair in a smooth hillock over his forehead. He did not seem to pay any attention to the conversation.

"Sammy, did you know father was going to build a new barn?" asked the girl.

The boy combed assiduously.

"Sammy!"

He turned, and showed a face like his father's under his smooth crest of hair. "Yes, I s'pose I did," he said reluctantly.

"How long have you known it?" asked his mother.

"'Bout three months, I guess."

"Why didn't you tell of it?"

"Didn't think 'twould do no good."

"I don't see what father wants another barn for," said the girl in her sweet, slow voice. She turned again to the window, and stared out at the digging men in the field. Her tender, sweet face was full of a gentle distress. Her forehead was as bald and innocent as a baby's, with the light hair strained back from it in a row of curl-papers.

She was quite large, but her soft curves did not look as if they covered muscles.

Her mother looked sternly at the boy. "Is he goin' to buy more cows?" said she. The boy did not reply: he was tying his shoes.

"Sammy, I want you to tell me if he's goin' to buy more cows."

"I s'pose he is."

"How many?"

"Four, I guess."

His mother said nothing more. She went into the pantry, and there was a clatter of dishes. The boy got his cap from a nail behind the door, took an old arithmetic from the shelf, and started for school. He was lightly built, but clumsy. He went out of the yard with a curious spring in the hips, that made his loose home-made jacket tilt up in the rear.

The girl went to the sink, and began to wash the dishes that were piled up there. Her mother came promptly out of the pantry, and shoved her aside. "You wipe 'em," said she; "I'll wash. There's a good many this mornin'."

The mother plunged her hands vigorously into the water; the girl wiped the plates slowly and dreamily. "Mother," said she, "don't you think it's too bad father's going to build that new barn, much as we need a decent house to live in?"

Her mother scrubbed a dish fiercely. "You a'n't found out yet we're women-folks, Nanny Penn," said she. "You a'n't seen enough of men-folks yet to. One of these days you'll find it out; an' then you'll know that we know only what men-folks think we do, so far as any use of it goes, an' how we'd ought to reckon men-folks in with Providence, an' not complain of what they do any more than we do of the weather."

"I don't care: I don't believe George is anything like that, anyhow," said Nanny. Her delicate face flushed pink, her lips pouted softly, as if she were going to cry.

"You wait an' see. I guess George Eastman ain't no better than other men. You hadn't ought to judge father, though. He can't help it, 'cause he don't look at things jest the way we do. An' we've been pretty comfortable here, after all. The roof don't leak — 'a'n't never but once — that's one thing. Father's kept it shingled right up."

"I do wish we had a parlor."

"I guess it won't hurt George Eastman any to come to see you in a nice clean kitchen. I guess a good many girls don't have as good a place as this. Nobody's ever heard me complain."

"I 'a'n't complained either, mother."

"Well, I don't think you'd better — a good father an' a good home as you've got. S'pose your father made you go out an' work for your livin'? Lots of girls have to that ain't no stronger an' better able to than you be."

Sarah Penn washed the frying-pan with a conclusive air. She scrubbed the outside of it as faithfully as the inside. She was a masterly keeper of her box of a house. Her one living-room never seemed to have in it any of the dust which the friction of life with inanimate matter produces. She swept, and there seemed to be no dirt to go before the broom; she cleaned, and one could see no difference. She was like an artist so perfect that he has apparently no art. Today she got out a mixing-bowl and a board, and rolled some pies, and there was no more flour upon her than upon her daughter, who was doing finer work. Nanny was to be married in the fall, and she was sewing on some white cambric and embroidery. She sewed industriously while her mother cooked; her soft, milk-white hands showed whiter than her delicate work.

"We must have the stove moved out in the shed before long," said Mrs. Penn. "Talk about not havin' things! it's been a real blessin' to be able to put a stove up in that shed in hot weather. Father did one good thing when he fixed that stovepipe out there."

Sarah Penn's face as she rolled her pies had that expression of meek vigor which might have characterized one of the New Testament saints. She was making mince-pies. Her husband, Adoniram Penn, liked them better than any other kind. She baked twice a week. Adoniram often liked a piece of pie between meals. She hurried this morning. It had been later than usual when she began, and she wanted to have a pie baked for dinner. However deep a resentment she might be forced to hold against her husband, she would never fail in sedulous attention to his wants.

Nobility of character manifests itself at loop-holes when it is not provided with large doors. Sarah Penn's showed itself today in flaky dishes of pastry. So she made the pies faithfully, while across the table she could see, when she glanced up from her work, the sight that rankled in her patient and steadfast soul — the digging of the cellar of the new barn where Adoniram, forty years ago, had promised her their new house should stand.

The pies were done for dinner. Adoniram and Sammy were home a few minutes after twelve o'clock. The dinner was eaten with serious haste. There was never much conversation at the table in the Penn family. Adoniram asked a blessing, and they ate promptly; then rose up and went about their work.

Sammy went back to school, taking soft sly lopes out of the yard like a rabbit. He wanted a game of marbles before school, and feared his father would give him some chores to do. Adoniram hastened to the door and called after him, but he was out of sight.

"I don't see what you let him go for, mother," said he. "I wanted him to help me unload that wood."

Adoniram went to work out in the yard unloading wood from the wagon. Sarah put away the dinner dishes, while Nanny took down her curl-papers and changed her dress. She was going down to the store to buy some more embroidery and thread.

When Nanny was gone Mrs. Penn went to the door. "Father!" she called.

"Well, what is it?"

"I want to see you jest a minute, father."

"I can't leave this wood nohow. I've got to git it unloaded an' go for a load of gravel afore two o'clock. Sammy had ought to helped me. You hadn't ought to let him go to school so early."

"I want to see you jest a minute."

"I tell ye I can't, nohow, mother."

"Father, you come here." Sarah Penn stood in the door like a queen; she held her head as if it bore a crown; there was that patience which makes authority royal in her voice. Adoniram went.

Mrs. Penn led the way into the kitchen, and pointed to a chair. "Sit down, father," said she: "I've got somethin' I want to say to you."

He sat down heavily; his face was quite stolid, but he looked at her with restive eyes. "Well, what is it, mother?"

"I wanted to know what you're buildin' that new barn for, father?"

"I 'a'n't got nothin' to say about it."

"It can't be you think you need another barn?"

"I tell ye, I 'a'n't got nothin 'to say about it, mother; an' I ain't goin' to say nothin'."

"Be you goin' to buy more cows?"

Adoniram did not reply; he shut his mouth tight.

"I know you be, as well as I want to. Now, father, look here" — Sarah Penn had not sat down; she stood before her husband in the humble fashion of a Scripture woman — "I'm goin' to talk real plain to you; I never have sence I married you, but I'm goin' to now. I 'a'n't never complained, an' I ain't goin' to complain now, but I'm goin' to talk plain. You see this room here, father: you look at it well. You see there ain't no carpet on the floor, an' you see the paper is all dirty, an' droppin' off the walls. We 'a'n't had no new paper on it for ten year, an' then I put it on myself, an' it didn't cost but ninepence a roll. You see this room, father: it's all the one I've had to work in an' eat in an' sit in sence we was married. There ain't another woman in the whole town whose husband 'a'n't got half the means you have, but what's got better. It's all the room Nanny's got to have her company in; an' there ain't one of her mates but what's got better, an' their fathers not so able as hers is. It's all the room she'll have to be married in. What would you have thought, father, if we had had our weddin' in a room no better than this? I was married in my mother's parlor, with a carpet on the floor, an' stuffed furniture, an' a mahogany card table. An' this is all the room my daughter will have to be married in. Look here, father!"

Sarah Penn went across the room as though it were a tragic stage. She flung open a door and disclosed a tiny bedroom, only large enough for a bed and bureau, with a path between. "There, father," said she — "there's all the room I've had to sleep in, forty year. All my children were born there — the two that died, an' the two that's livin'. I was sick with a fever there."

She stepped to another door and opened it. It led into the small, ill-lighted pantry. "Here," said she, "is all the buttery I've got — every place I've got for my dishes, to set away my victuals in, an' to keep my milk-pans in. Father, I've been takin' care of the milk of six cows in this place, an' now you're goin' to build a new barn, an' keep more cows, an' give me more to do in it."

She threw open another door. A narrow crooked flight of stairs wound upward from it. "There, father," said she, "I want you to look at the stairs that go up to them two unfinished chambers, that are all the places our son an' daughter have had to sleep in, all their lives. There ain't a prettier girl in town nor a more ladylike one than Nanny, an' that's the place she has to sleep in. It ain't so good as your horse's stall; it ain't so warm and tight."

Sarah Penn went back and stood before her husband. "Now, father," said she, "I want to know if you think you're doin' right an' accordin' to what you profess. Here, when we was married, forty year ago, you promised me faithful that we should have a new house built in that lot over in the field before the year was out. You said you had money enough, an' you wouldn't ask me to live in no such place as this. It is forty year now, an' you've been makin' more money, an' I've been savin' of it for you ever since, an' you ain't built no house yet. You've built sheds an' cow-houses an' one new barn, an' now you're goin' to build another. Father, I want to know if you think it's right. You're lodgin' your dumb beasts better than you are your own flesh an' blood. I want to know if you think it's right."

"I 'a'n't got nothin' to say."

"You can't say nothin' without ownin' it ain't right, father. An' there's another thing — I 'a'n't complained; I've got along forty year, an' I s'pose I should forty more, if it wa'n't for that: if we don't have another house, Nanny she can't live with us after she's married. She'll have to go somewhere's else to live away from us; an' it don't seem as if I could have it so, noways, father. She wa'n't ever strong. She's got considerable color, but there wa'n't never any backbone to her. I've always took the heft of everything off her, an' she ain't fit to keep house an' do everything herself. She'll be all worn out inside of a year. Think of her doin' all the washin' an' ironin' an' bakin' with them soft white hands an' arms, an' sweepin'! I can't have it so, noways, father."

Mrs. Penn's face was burning, her mild eyes gleamed. She had pleaded her little cause like a Webster; she had ranged from severity to pathos: but her opponent employed that obstinate silence which makes eloquence futile with mocking echoes. Adoniram arose clumsily.

"Father, 'a'n't you got nothin' to say?" said Mrs. Penn.

"I've got to go off after that load of gravel. I can't stan' here talkin' all day."

"Father, won't you think it over, an' have a house built there instead of a barn?"

"I 'a'n't got nothin' to say."

Adoniram shuffled out. Mrs. Penn went into her bedroom. When she came out her eyes were red. She had a roll of unbleached cotton cloth. She spread

EDITH WHARTON

FINLEY PETER DUNNE

Courtesy of *Vanity Fair*, New York

BOOTH TARKINGTON

Photograph by Underwood & Underwood, New York

EDGAR A. ROBINSON

Courtesy of The Macmillan Company, New York

it out on the kitchen table, and began cutting out some shirts for her husband. The men over in the field had a team to help them this afternoon; she could hear their halloos. She had a scanty pattern for the shirts: she had to plan and piece the sleeves.

Nanny came home with her embroidery, and sat down with her needlework. She had taken down her curl-papers, and there was a soft roll of fair hair like an aureole over her forehead; her face was as delicately fine and clear as porcelain. Suddenly she looked up, and the tender red flamed all over her face and neck. "Mother," said she.

"What say?"

"I've been thinking — I don't see how we're goin' to have any — wedding in this room. I'd be ashamed to have his folks come, if we didn't have anybody else."

"Mebbe we can have some new paper before then; I can put it on. I guess you won't have no call to be ashamed of your belongin's."

"We might have the wedding in the new barn," said Nanny with gentle pettishness. "Why, mother, what makes you look so?"

Mrs. Penn had started, and was staring at her with a curious expression. She turned again to her work and spread out a pattern carefully on the cloth. "Nothin'," said she.

Presently Adoniram clattered out of the yard in his two-wheeled dump-cart, standing as proudly upright as a Roman charioteer. Mrs. Penn opened the door and stood there a minute looking out; the halloos of the men sounded louder.

It seemed to her all through the spring months that she heard nothing but the halloos, and the noises of saws and hammers. The new barn grew fast. It was a fine edifice for this little village. Men came on pleasant Sundays, in their meeting suits and clean shirt-bosoms, and stood around it admiringly. Mrs. Penn did not speak of it, and Adoniram did not mention it to her; although sometimes, upon a return from inspecting it, he bore himself with injured dignity.

"It's a strange thing how your mother feels about the new barn," he said confidentially to Sammy one day.

Sammy only grunted, after an odd fashion for a boy: he had learned it from his father.

The barn was all completed ready for use by the third week in July. Adoniram had planned to move his stock in on Wednesday; on Tuesday he received a letter which changed his plans. He came in with it early in the morning. "Sammy's been to the post-office," said he, "an' I've got a letter from Hiram." Hiram was Mrs. Penn's brother, who lived in Vermont.

"Well," said Mrs. Penn, "what does he say about the folks?"

"I guess they're all right. He says he thinks if I come up country right off, there's a chance to buy jest the kind of a horse I want." He stared reflectively out of the window at the new barn.

Mrs. Penn was making pies. She went on clapping the rolling-pin into the crust, although she was very pale, and her heart beat loudly.

"I dun' know but what I'd better go," said Adoniram. "I hate to go off jest now, right in the midst of hayin'; but the ten-acre lot's cut, an' I guess Rufus an' the others can git along without me three or four days. I can't get a horse round here to suit me, nohow; an' I've got to have another for all that wood-haulin' in the fall. I told Hiram to watch out, an' if he got wind of a good horse to let me know. I guess I'd better go."

"I'll get out your clean shirt an' collar," said Mrs. Penn calmly.

She laid out Adoniram's Sunday suit and his clean clothes, on the bed in the little bedroom. She got his shaving-water and razor ready. At last she buttoned on his collar and fastened his black cravat.

Adoniram never wore his collar and cravat except on extra occasions. He held his head high, with a rasped dignity. When he was all ready, with his coat and hat brushed, and a lunch of pie and cheese in a paper bag, he hesitated on the threshold of the door. He looked at his wife, and his manner was defiantly apologetic. "*If* them cows come today, Sammy can drive 'em into the new barn," said he; "an' when they bring the hay up, they can pitch it in there."

"Well," replied Mrs. Penn.

Adoniram set his shaven face ahead and started. When he had cleared the door-step, he turned and looked back with a kind of nervous solemnity. "I shall be back by Saturday if nothin' happens," said he.

"Do be careful, father," returned his wife.

She stood in the door with Nanny at her elbow and watched him out of sight. Her eyes had a strange, doubtful expression in them; her peaceful forehead was contracted. She went in, and about her baking again. Nanny sat sewing. Her wedding-day was drawing nearer, and she was getting pale and thin with her steady sewing. Her mother kept glancing at her.

"Have you got that pain in your side this mornin'?" she asked.

"A little."

Mrs. Penn's face, as she worked, changed, her perplexed forehead smoothed, her eyes were steady, her lips firmly set. She formed a maxim for herself, although incoherently with her unlettered thoughts. "Unsolicited opportunities are the guide-posts of the Lord to the new roads of life," she repeated in effect, and she made up her mind to her course of action.

"S'posin' I *had* wrote to Hiram," she muttered once, when she was in the pantry — "s'posin' I had wrote, an' asked him if he knew of any horse? But I didn't, an' father's goin' wa'n't none of my doin'. It looks like a providence." Her voice rang out quite loud at the last.

"What you talkin' about, mother?" called Nanny.

"Nothin'."

Mrs. Penn hurried her baking; at eleven o'clock it was all done. The load of hay from the west field came slowly down the cart track, and drew up at the new barn. Mrs. Penn ran out. "Stop!" she screamed — "stop!"

The men stopped and looked; Sammy upreared from the top of the load, and stared at his mother.

"Stop!" she cried out again. "Don't you put the hay in that barn: put it in the old one."

"Why, he said to put it in here," returned one of the haymakers wonderingly. He was a young man, a neighbor's son, whom Adoniram hired by the year to help on the farm.

"Don't you put the hay in the new barn: there's room enough in the old one, ain't there?" said Mrs. Penn.

"Room enough," returned the hired man, in his thick, rustic tones. "Didn't need the new barn, nohow, far as room's concerned. Well, I s'pose he changed his mind." He took hold of the horses' bridles.

Mrs. Penn went back to the house. Soon the kitchen windows were darkened, and a fragrance like warm honey came into the room.

Nanny laid down her work. "I thought father wanted them to put the hay into the new barn?" she said wonderingly.

"It's all right," replied her mother.

Sammy slid down from the load of hay, and came in to see if dinner was ready.

"I ain't goin' to get a regular dinner today, as long as father's gone," said his mother. "I've let the fire go out. You can have some bread-an'-milk an' pie. I thought we could get along." She set out some bowls of milk, some bread, and a pie on the kitchen table. "You'd better eat your dinner now," said she. "You might jest as well get through with it. I want you to help me afterward."

Nanny and Sammy stared at each other. There was something strange in their mother's manner. Mrs. Penn did not eat anything herself. She went into the pantry, and they heard her moving dishes while they ate. Presently she came out with a pile of plates. She got the clothes-basket out of the shed, and packed them in it. Nanny and Sammy watched. She brought out cups and saucers, and put them in with the plates.

"What are you goin' to do, mother?" inquired Nanny in a timid voice. A sense of something unusual made her tremble, as if it were a ghost. Sammy rolled his eyes over his pie.

"You'll see what I' m going to do," replied Mrs. Penn. "If you're through, Nanny, I want you to go upstairs an' pack up your things; an' I want you, Sammy, to help me take down the bed in the bedroom."

"O mother, what for?" gasped Nanny.

"You'll see."

During the next few hours a feat was performed by this simple, pious New England mother, which was equal in its way to Wolfe's storming of the Heights of Abraham. It took no more genius and audacity of bravery for Wolfe to cheer his wondering soldiers up those steep precipices, under the sleeping eyes of the enemy, than for Sarah Penn, at the head of her children, to move all their household goods into the new barn while her husband was away.

Nanny and Sammy followed their mother's instructions without a murmur; indeed, they were overawed. There is a certain uncanny and superhuman quality about all such purely original undertakings as their mother's was to them. Nanny went back and forth with her light loads, and Sammy tugged with sober energy.

At five o'clock in the afternoon the little house in which the Penns had lived for forty years had emptied itself into the new barn.

Every builder builds somewhat for unknown purposes, and is in a measure a prophet. The architect of Adoniram Penn's barn, while he designed it for the comfort of four-footed animals, had planned better than he knew for the comfort of humans. Sarah Penn saw at a glance its possibilities. Those great box stalls, with quilts hung before them, would make better bedrooms than the one she had occupied for forty years; and there was a tight carriage-room. The harness-room, with its chimney and shelves, would make a kitchen of her dreams. The great middle space would make a parlor, by-and-by, fit for a palace. Upstairs there was as much room as down. With partitions and windows, what a house would there be! Sarah looked at the row of stanchions before the allotted space for cows, and reflected that she would have her front entry there.

At six o'clock the stove was up in the harness-room, the kettle was boiling, and the table set for tea. It looked almost as home-like as the abandoned house across the yard had ever done. The young hired man milked, and Sarah directed him calmly to bring the milk to the new barn. He came gaping, dropping little blots of foam from the brimming pails on the grass. Before the next morning he had spread the story of Adoniram Penn's wife moving into the new barn, all over the little village. Men assembled in the store and talked it over; women with shawls over their heads scuttled into each other's houses before their work was done. Any deviation from the ordinary course of life in this quiet town was enough to stop all progress in it. Everybody paused to look at the staid, independent figure on the side track. There was a difference of opinion with regard to her. Some held her to be insane; some, of a lawless and rebellious spirit.

Friday the minister went to see her. It was in the forenoon, and she was at the barn door shelling peas for dinner. She looked up and returned his salutation with dignity, then she went on with her work. She did not invite him in. The saintly expression of her face remained fixed, but there was an angry flush over it.

The minister stood awkwardly before her, and talked. She handled the peas as if they were bullets. At last she looked up, and her eyes showed the spirit that her meek front had covered for a lifetime.

"There ain't no use talkin', Mr. Hersey," said she. "I've thought it all over an' over, an' I believe I'm doin' what's right. I've made it the subject of prayer, an' it's betwixt me an' the Lord an' Adoniram. There ain't no call for nobody else to worry about it."

"Well, of course, if you have brought it to the Lord in prayer, and feel satisfied that you are doing right, Mrs. Penn," said the minister, helplessly. His thin gray-bearded face was pathetic. He was a sickly man; his youthful confidence had cooled: he had to scourge himself up to some of his pastoral duties as relentlessly as a Catholic ascetic, and then he was prostrated by the smart.

"I think it's right jest as much as I think it was right for our forefathers to come over from the old country, 'cause they didn't have what belonged to 'em," said Mrs. Penn. She arose. The barn threshold might have been Plymouth Rock from her bearing. "I don't doubt you mean well, Mr. Hersey," said she, "but there are things people hadn't ought to interfere with. I've been a member of the church for over forty year. I've got my own mind an' my own feet, an' I'm goin' to think my own thoughts an' go my own ways; an' nobody but the Lord is goin' to dictate to me unless I've a mind to have him. Won't you come in an' set down? How is Mis' Hersey?"

"She is well, I thank you," replied the minister. He added some more perplexed apologetic remarks; then he retreated.

He could expound the intricacies of every character study in the Scriptures, he was competent to grasp the Pilgrim Fathers and all historical innovators; but Sarah Penn was beyond him. He could deal with primal cases, but parallel ones worsted him. But after all, although it was aside from his province, he wondered more how Adoniram Penn would deal with his wife than how the Lord would. Everybody shared the wonder. When Adoniram's four new cows arrived, Sarah ordered three to be put in the old barn, the other in the house shed where the cooking-stove had stood. That added to the excitement. It was whispered that all four cows were domiciled in the house.

Towards sunset on Saturday, when Adoniram was expected home, there was a knot of men in the road near the new barn. The hired man had milked, but he still hung around the premises. Sarah Penn had supper all ready. There were brown bread and baked beans and a custard pie; it was the supper that Adoniram loved on a Saturday night. She had on a clean calico, and she bore herself imperturbably. Nanny and Sammy kept close at her heels. Their eyes were large, and Nanny was full of nervous tremors. Still there was to them more pleasant excitement than anything else. An inborn confidence in their mother over their father asserted itself.

Sammy looked out of the harness-room window. "There he is," he announced in an awed whisper. He and Nanny peeped around the casing. Mrs.

Penn kept on about her work. The children watched Adoniram leave the new horse standing in the drive while he went to the house door. It was fastened. Then he went around to the shed. That door was seldom locked, even when the family was away. The thought how her father would be confronted by the cow flashed upon Nanny. There was a hysterical sob in her throat. Adoniram emerged from the shed, and stood looking about in a dazed fashion. His lips moved; he was saying something, but they could not hear what it was. The hired man was peeping around a corner of the old barn, but nobody saw him.

Adoniram took the new horse by the bridle and led him across the yard to the new barn. Nanny and Sammy slunk close to their mother. The barn doors rolled back, and there stood Adoniram, with the long mild face of the great Canadian farm horse looking over his shoulder.

Nanny kept behind her mother, but Sammy stepped suddenly forward, and stood in front of her.

Adoniram stared at the group. "What on airth you all down here for?" said he. "What's the matter over to the house?"

"We've come here to live, father," said Sammy. His shrill voice quavered out bravely.

"What" — Adoniram sniffed — "what is it smells like cookin'?" said he. He stepped forward and looked in the open door of the harness-room. Then he turned to his wife. His old bristling face was pale and frightened. "What on airth does this mean, mother?" he gasped.

"You come in here, father," said Sarah. She led the way into the harness-room and shut the door. "Now, father," said she, "you needn't be scared. I ain't crazy. There ain't nothin' to be upset over. But we've come here to live, an' we're goin' to live here. We've got jest as good a right here as new horses an' cows. The house wa'n't fit for us to live in any longer, an' I made up my mind I wa'n't goin' to stay there. I've done my duty by you forty year, an' I'm goin' to do it now; but I'm goin' to live here. You've got to put in some windows and partitions; an' you'll have to buy some furniture."

"Why, mother!" the old man gasped.

"You'd better take your coat off an' get washed — there's the wash-basin — an' then we'll have supper."

"Why, mother!"

Sammy went past the window, leading the new horse to the old barn. The old man saw him, and shook his head speechlessly. He tried to take off his coat, but his arms seemed to lack the power. His wife helped him. She poured some water into the tin basin, and put in a piece of soap. She got the comb and brush, and smoothed his thin gray hair after he had washed. Then she put the beans, hot bread, and tea on the table. Sammy came in, and the family drew up. Adoniram sat looking dazedly at his plate, and they waited.

"Ain't you goin' to ask a blessin', father?" said Sarah.

And the old man bent his head and mumbled.

All through the meal he stopped eating at intervals, and stared furtively at his wife; but he ate well. The home food tasted good to him, and his old frame was too sturdily healthy to be affected by his mind. But after supper he went out, and sat down on the step of the smaller door at the right of the barn, through which he had meant his Jerseys to pass in stately file, but which Sarah designed for her front house door; and he leaned his head on his hands.

After the supper dishes were cleared away and the milk-pans washed, Sarah went out to him. The twilight was deepening. There was a clear green glow in the sky. Before them stretched the smooth level of field; in the distance was a cluster of haystacks like the huts of a village; the air was very cool and calm and sweet. The landscape might have been an ideal one of peace.

Sarah bent over and touched her husband on one of his thin, sinewy shoulders. "Father!"

The old man's shoulders heaved: he was weeping.

"Why, don't do so, father," said Sarah.

"I'll — put up the — partitions, an' — everything you — want, mother."

Sarah put her apron up to her face; she was overcome by her own triumph.

Adoniram was like a fortress whose walls had no active resistance, and went down the instant the right besieging tools were used. "Why, mother," he said hoarsely, "I hadn't no idee you was so set on 't as all this comes to."

EDITH WHARTON

EDITH WHARTON is one of the foremost writers producing English fiction today. She was born in New York, January 24, 1862. Her mother was a granddaughter of General Ebenezer Stevens of Revolutionary fame. Her father, George Frederic Jones, had no profession but lived on his income. Edith Newbold Jones was taught at home by governesses and tutors. At least half her youth was spent abroad, so that she received an unusual training in French, Italian, and German. In 1885 she married Edward Wharton of Boston. For years she has made Paris her home. During the Great War she devoted mind and heart to war charities. In 1916, in recognition of her services, the French Government bestowed upon her the Cross of the Legion of Honor. Her wide knowledge of art, history, and literature are reflected in 'Italian Villas,' 'Italian Backgrounds,' and 'A Motor-Flight through France,' as well as in much of her fiction. In 1915 she planned and edited 'The Book of the Homeless,' compiled to aid Belgian refugees, and she has put her personal impressions of the war into 'Fighting France,' which closes with an admirable chapter on 'The Tone of France.' A slim volume of polished verse, 'Actæon to Diana' (1909), is the most personal of her writings. The sonnet entitled 'The One Grief' may perhaps be singled out for its poignant simplicity.

Mrs. Wharton has given to the public no hasty or immature work. Her first volume, a collection of stories entitled 'The Greater Inclination,' was published in 1899 and was followed in 1900 by 'The Touchstone' and in 1901 by 'Crucial Instances,' another collection of stories. These early volumes attracted wide attention, not only for their range — the tragic, the humorous, the ironical — but also for their extraordinary technique and a style always lucid and at will brilliant with epigram or touched with poetical suggestion. In both material and manner, the critics were prompt to see a discipleship to Henry James. The essential likeness is perhaps grounded upon a common instinct for logic, for psychology, a preoccupation with motive and the analysis of character. Mrs. Wharton has continued to write short stories of unusual merit and wide range of subject-matter, but her highest excellence is to be sought in the prolonged short story and the novel, which offer opportunity for the unfolding of character and for large social backgrounds. In 'The Touchstone' and 'Sanctuary,' which belong to the former class, she tells, with a fine commingling of passion, restraint, and tenderness, stories of spiritual regeneration. In 'Madame de Treymes' two ideals clash, and the hero, in following abstract truth, as he must, sacrifices the woman he loves as well as himself. In 'Ethan Frome' (1911) a moment of idyllic and unlawful love moves swiftly to a tragedy more terrible than death. The background is the icy isolation of a New England farm-house in the winters of long ago.

Mrs. Wharton's first novel was 'The Valley of Decision' (1902). This romance of eighteenth-century Italy has atmosphere and charm, but its two volumes remain upon the shelves of public libraries when her later books are commonly lost, stolen, or out. In 1905 appeared the novel ironically called 'The House of Mirth.' Its theme is the conflict between a New York woman's frivolous heredity, education, and environment and her intermittent and belated gropings for what is right and fine. 'The House of Mirth' has all the vitality and directness wanting in 'The Valley of Decision,' and although the story closes in external failure, there is at the end a moment of spiritual triumph and a mystical union of the lovers whom all the conditions of life had conspired to keep apart. The very readable but less effective 'Fruit of the Tree' was followed by 'The Reef,' which gives us the loveliest of Mrs. Wharton's heroines, seen with her child and a winning stepson on the background of French country life. Before her readers had a chance to praise the sympathy of 'The Reef,' its author took their breath away with 'The Custom of the Country,' whose very title is an indictment of one product of American society. The central figure ends her social adventures on two continents with no more soul than when she began them. This unsparing satire is softened by charming glimpses of older New York, for Mrs. Wharton, like Mrs. Ward, is always able to draw aside the curtain and show us restful places where "gentilesse" has long held sway. 'Summer' (1917) reverts to rural life in New England.

Some of Mrs. Wharton's work — whole groups, in fact, of the short stories — have brought upon her the reproach of being an apostle of culture. It has been complained that the surfaces are too brilliant, the points at issue too esoteric, the irony too frequent, the feeling for the ridiculous and the incongruous too strong. She has indeed little pity for sentimentality, complacency, or any variety of "educated mispronunciation," and though quite aware of the "intuitive felicities" of the heart, she is sometimes as severe as life itself upon the feeble, the ineffective, the negatively good. We should be sorry to lose her salt and stinging reminders of our shabby souls or manners, but her work does not end there. Her views are in part expressed in 'The Fruit of the Tree': "Life is not a matter of abstract principles, but a succession of pitiful compromises with fate, of concessions to old tradition, old beliefs, old charities, and frailties." She is often concerned, then, with the invisible chains of our past, our environment, our education, or of our goodness or badness or dullness; with our failure to seize the one chance of happiness or helpfulness, with the irony of life that brings the cup to our lips too late, or with chance that dashes it away untasted. Truth is Mrs. Wharton's favorite virtue. She cannot save her reader's feelings by the easy lie of an averted tragedy and her solutions are seldom simple. Her most dreadful tragedy is that whose end is an incapacity to learn, a deadness to ideals, a paralysis of the mind or heart. But Mrs. Wharton's vision of life is not all ironical or tragical. She feels "those dear contradictions and irrelevancies that will always make flesh and blood prevail against a syllogism," and she delights in bringing out from their shy retreat the soul's subtle delicacies, hesitations, reticences. A beautiful illustration of her ability to throw a white light upon such matters is 'The Daunt Diana,' which tells what an almost human appeal a loved and long-sought object can make to the heart of man.

During the Great War Mrs. Wharton lived face to face with the most terrible suffering. For that reason it might be unsafe to regard as significant the fact that in a later volume of short stories, 'Xingu' (1916), every number is a tragedy except the entertaining farce that furnishes the title. Without losing her powers of analysis, Mrs. Wharton's style has been steadily growing more direct and dramatic, and her flexible art shows no sign of having reached a limit. Such of her later books as 'Ethan Frome,' 'The Age of Innocence,' 'Glimpses of the Moon' (in which she takes up the same problem as in 'The House of Mirth' and gives a different outcome), 'Twilight Sleep,' and 'The Children,' confirm this judgment.

MARY LELAND HUNT

FROM 'THE REEF'

THE light of the October afternoon lay on an old high-roofed house which enclosed in its long expanse of brick and yellowish stone the breadth of a grassy court filled with the shadow and sound of limes. From the escutcheoned piers at the entrance of the court a level drive, also shaded by limes, extended to a white-barred gate beyond which an equally level avenue of grass, cut through a wood, dwindled to a blue-green blur against a sky banked with still white slopes of cloud.

In the court, half-way between house and drive, a lady stood. She held a parasol above her head, and looked now at the house-front, with its double flight of steps meeting before a glazed door under sculptured trophies, now down the drive toward the grassy cutting through the wood. Her air was less of expectancy than of contemplation: she seemed not so much to be watching for any one, or listening for an approaching sound, as letting the whole aspect of the place sink into her while she held herself open to its influence. Yet it was no less apparent that the scent was not new to her. There was no eagerness of investigation in her survey: she seemed rather to be looking about her with eyes to which, for some intimate inward reason, details long since familiar had suddenly acquired an unwonted freshness.

This was in fact the exact sensation of which Mrs. Leath was conscious as she came forth from the house and descended into the sunlit court. She had come to meet her stepson, who was likely to be returning at that hour from an afternoon's shooting in one of the more distant plantations, and she carried in her hand the letter which had sent her in search of him; but with her first step out of the house all thought of him had been effaced by another series of impressions.

The scene about her was known to satiety. She had seen Givré at all seasons of the year, and for the greater part of every year, since the far-off day of her marriage; the day when, ostensibly driving through its gates at her husband's side, she had actually been carried there on a cloud of iris-winged visions.

The possibilities which the place had then represented were still vividly present to her. The mere phrase "a French chateau" had called up to her youthful fancy a throng of romantic associations, poetic, pictorial, and emotional; and the serene face of the old house, seated in its park among the poplar-bordered meadows of middle France, had seemed, on her first sight of it, to hold out to her a fate as noble and dignified as its own mien.

Though she could still call up that phase of feeling it had long since passed, and the house had for a time become to her the very symbol of narrowness and monotony. Then, with the passing of years, it had gradually acquired a less inimical character, had become, not again a castle of dreams, evoker of fair images and romantic legend, but the shell of a life slowly adjusted to its dwelling: the place one came back to, the place where one had one's duties, one's habits, and one's books, the place one would naturally live in till one died: a dull house, an inconvenient house, of which one knew all the defects, the shabbinesses, the discomforts, but to which one was so used that one could hardly, after so long a time, think one's self away from it without suffering a certain loss of identity.

Now, as it lay before her in the autumn mildness, its mistress was surprised at her own insensibility. She had been trying to see the house through the eyes of an old friend who, the next morning, would be driving up to it for the first time; and in so doing she seemed to be opening her own eyes upon it after a long interval of blindness.

The court was very still, yet full of latent life: the wheeling and rustling of pigeons about the rectangular yews and across the sunny gravel; the sweep of rooks above the lustrous grayish-purple slates of the roof, and the stir of the tree-tops as they met the breeze which every day, at that hour, came punctually up from the river.

Just such a latent animation glowed in Anna Leath. In every nerve and vein she was conscious of that equipoise of bliss which the fearful human heart scarce dares acknowledge. She was not used to strong or full emotions; but she had always known that she should not be fraid of them. She was not afraid now; but she felt a deep inward stillness.

The immediate effect of the feeling had been to send her forth in quest of her stepson. She wanted to stroll back with him and have a quiet talk before they re-entered the house. It was always easy to talk to him, and at this moment he was the one person to whom she could have spoken without fear of disturbing her inner stillness. She was glad, for all sorts of reasons, that Madame de Chantelle and Effie were still at Ouchy with the governess, and that she and Owen had the house to themselves. And she was glad that even he was not yet in sight. She wanted to be alone a little longer; not to think but to let the long slow waves of joy break over her one by one.

She walked out of the court and sat down on one of the benches that bordered the drive. From her seat she had a diagonal view of the long house-front and of the domed chapel terminating one of the wings. Beyond a gate in the courtyard wall the flower-garden drew its dark-green squares and raised its statues against the yellowing background of the park. In the borders only a few late pinks and crimsons smoldered, but a peacock strutting in the sun seemed to have gathered into his outspread fan all the summer glories of the place.

In Mrs. Leath's hand was the letter which had opened her eyes to these things, and a smile rose to her lips at the mere feeling of the paper between her fingers. The thrill it sent through her gave a keener edge to every sense. She felt, saw, breathed the shining world as though a thin impenetrable veil had suddenly been removed from it.

Just such a veil, she now perceived, had always hung between herself and life. It had been like the stage gauze which gives an illusive air of reality to the painted scene behind it, yet proves it, after all, to be no more than a painted scene.

She had been hardly aware, in her girlhood, of differing from others in this respect. In the well-regulated well-fed Summers world the unusual was regarded as either immoral or ill-bred, and people with emotions were not visited. Sometimes, with a sense of groping in a topsy-turvy universe, Anna had wondered why everybody about her seemed to ignore all the passions and sensations which formed the stuff of great poetry and memorable action. In a community composed entirely of people like her parents and her parents' friends she did not see how the magnificent things one read about could ever have happened. She was sure that if anything of the kind had occurred in her immediate circle her mother would have consulted the family clergyman, and her father perhaps even have rung up the police; and her sense of humor compelled her to own that, in the given conditions, these precautions might not have been unjustified.

Little by little the conditions conquered her, and she learned to regard the substance of life as a mere canvas for the embroideries of poet and painter, and its little swept and fenced and tended surface as its actual substance. It was in the visioned region of action and emotion that her fullest hours were spent; but it hardly occurred to her that they might be translated into experience, or connected with anything likely to happen to a young lady living in West Fifty-fifth Street.

She perceived, indeed, that other girls, leading outwardly the same life as herself, and seemingly unaware of her world of hidden beauty, were yet possessed of some vital secret which escaped her. There seemed to be a kind of freemasonry between them; they were wider awake than she, more alert, and surer of their wants if not of their opinions. She supposed they were "cleverer," and accepted her inferiority good-humoredly, half aware, within herself, of a reserve of unused power which the others gave no sign of possessing.

This partly consoled her for missing so much of what made their "good time"; but the resulting sense of exclusion, of being somehow laughingly but firmly debarred from a share of their privileges, threw her back on herself and deepened the reserve which made envious mothers cite her as a model of lady-like repression.

Love, she told herself, would one day release her from this spell of unreality. She was persuaded that the sublime passion was the key to the enigma; but it was difficult to relate her conception of love to the forms it wore in her experience. Two or three of the girls she had envied for their superior acquaintance with the arts of life had contracted, in the course of time, what were variously described as "romantic" or "foolish" marriages; one even made a runaway match, and languished for a while under a cloud of social reprobation. Here, then, was passion in action, romance converted to reality; yet the heroines of these exploits returned from them untransfigured, and their husbands were as dull as ever when one had to sit next to them at dinner.

Her own case, of course, would be different. Some day she would find the magic bridge between West Fifty-fifth Street and life; once or twice she had even fancied that the clue was in her hand. The first time was when she had met young Darrow. She recalled even now the stir of the encounter. But his passion swept over her like a wind that shakes the roof of the forest without reaching its still glades or rippling its hidden pools. He was extraordinarily intelligent and agreeable, and her heart beat faster when he was with her. He had a tall fair easy presence and a mind in which the lights of irony played pleasantly through the shades of feeling. She liked to hear his voice almost as much as to listen to what he was saying, and to listen to what he was saying almost as much as to feel that he was looking at her; but he wanted to kiss her, and she wanted to talk to him about books and pictures, and have him insinuate the eternal theme of their love into every subject they discussed.

Whenever they were apart a reaction set in. She wondered how she could have been so cold, called herself a prude and an idiot, questioned if any man could really care for her, and got up in the dead of night to try new ways of doing her hair. But as soon as he reappeared her head straightened itself on her slim neck and she sped her little shafts of irony, or flew her little kites of erudition, while hot and cold waves swept over her, and the things she really wanted to say choked in her throat and burned the palms of her hands.

Often she told herself that any silly girl who had waltzed through a season would know better than she how to attract a man and hold him; but when she said " a man " she did not really mean George Darrow.

Then one day, at a dinner, she saw him sitting next to one of the silly girls in question: the heroine of the elopement which had shaken West Fifty-fifth Street to its base. The young lady had come back from her adventure no less silly than when she went; and across the table the partner of her flight, a fat young man with eye-glasses, sat stolidly eating terrapin and talking about polo and investments.

The young woman was undoubtedly as silly as ever; yet after watching her for a few minutes Miss Summers perceived that she had somehow grown luminous, perilous, obscurely menacing to nice girls and the young men they intended eventually to accept. Suddenly, at the sight, a rage of possessorship awoke in her. She must save Darrow, assert her right to him at any price. Pride and reticence went down in a hurricane of jealousy. She heard him laugh, and there was something new in his laugh. . . . She watched him talking, talking. . . . He sat slightly sideways, a faint smile beneath his lids, lowering his voice as he lowered it when he talked to her. She caught the same inflections, but his eyes were different. It would have offended her once if he had looked at her like that. Now her one thought was that none but she had a right to be so looked at. And that girl of all others! What illusions could he have about a girl who, hardly a year ago, had made a fool of herself over the fat young man stolidly eating terrapin across the table? If that was where romance and passion ended, it was better to take to district visiting or algebra!

All night she lay awake and wondered: " What was she saying to him? How shall I learn to say such things? " and she decided that her heart would tell her — that the next time they were alone together the irresistible word would spring to her lips. He came the next day, and they were alone, and all she found was: " I didn't know that you and Kitty Mayne were such friends."

He answered with indifference that he didn't know it either, and in the reaction of relief she declared: " She's certainly ever so much prettier than she was. . . ."

" She's rather good fun," he admitted, as though he had not noticed her other advantages; and suddenly Anna saw in his eyes the look she had seen there the previous evening.

She felt as if he were leagues and leagues away from her. All her hopes dissolved, and she was conscious of sitting rigidly, with high head and straight lips, while the irresistible word fled with a last wing-beat into the golden mist of her illusions. . . .

She was still quivering with the pain and bewilderment of this adventure when Fraser Leath appeared. She met him first in Italy, where she was travelling with her parents; and the following winter he came to New York. In Italy he had seemed interesting: in New York he became remarkable. He seldom spoke of his life in Europe, and let drop but the most incidental allusions to the friends, the tastes, the pursuits which filled his cosmopolitan days; but in the atmosphere of West Fifty-fifth Street he seemed the embodiment of a storied past. He presented Miss Summers with a prettily-bound anthology of the old French poets and, when she showed a discriminating pleasure in the gift, observed with his grave smile: "I didn't suppose I should find any one here who would feel about these things as I do." On another occasion he asked her acceptance of a half-effaced eighteenth-century pastel which he had surprisingly picked up in a New York auction-room. "I know no one but you who would really appreciate it," he explained.

He permitted himself no other comments, but these conveyed with sufficient directness that he thought her worthy of a different setting. That she should be so regarded by a man living in an atmosphere of art and beauty, and esteeming them the vital elements of life, made her feel for the first time that she was understood. Here was some one whose scale of values was the same as hers, and who thought her opinion worth hearing on the very matters which they both considered of supreme importance. The discovery restored her self-confidence, and she revealed herself to Mr. Leath as she had never known how to reveal herself to Darrow.

As the courtship progressed, and they grew more confidential, her suitor surprised and delighted her by little explosions of revolutionary sentiment. He said: "Shall you mind, I wonder, if I tell you that you live in a dreadfully conventional atmosphere?" and, seeing that she manifestly did not mind: "Of course I shall say things now and then that will horrify your dear delightful parents — I shall shock them awfully, I warn you."

In confirmation of this warning he permitted himself an occasional playful fling at the regular church-going of Mr. and Mrs. Summers, at the innocuous character of the literature in their library, and at their guileless appreciations in art. He even ventured to banter Mrs. Summers on her refusal to receive the irrepressible Kitty Mayne, who, after a rapid passage with George Darrow, was now involved in another and more flagrant adventure.

"In Europe, you know, the husband is regarded as the only judge in such matters. As long as he accepts the situation — " Mr. Leath explained to Anna, who took his view the more emphatically in order to convince herself that, personally, she had none but the most tolerant sentiments toward the lady.

The subversiveness of Mr. Leath's opinions was enhanced by the distinction of his appearance and the reserve of his manners. He was like the anarchist with a gardenia in his buttonhole who figures in the higher melodrama. Every word, every allusion, every note of his agreeably-modulated voice, gave Anna a glimpse of a society at once freer and finer, which observed the traditional forms but had discarded the underlying prejudices; whereas the world she knew had discarded many of the forms and kept almost all the prejudices.

In such an atmosphere as his an eager young woman, curious as to all the manifestations of life, yet instinctively desiring that they should come to her in terms of beauty and fine feeling, must surely find the largest scope for self-expression. Study, travel, the contact of the world, the comradeship of a polished and enlightened mind, would combine to enrich her days and form her character; and it was only in the rare moments when Mr. Leath's symmetrical blond mask bent over hers, and his kiss dropped on her like a cold smooth pebble, that she questioned the completeness of the joys he offered.

There had been a time when the walls on which her gaze now rested had shed a glare of irony on these early dreams. In the first years of her marriage the sober symmetry of Givré had suggested only her husband's neatly-balanced mind. It was a mind, she soon learned, contentedly absorbed in formulating the conventions of the unconventional. West Fifty-fifth Street was no more conscientiously concerned than Givré with the momentous question of "what people did"; it was only the type of deed investigated that was different. Mr. Leath collected his social instances with the same seriousness and patience as his snuff-boxes. He exacted a rigid conformity to his rules of non-conformity and his scepticism had the absolute accent of a dogma. He even cherished certain exceptions to his rules as the book-collector prizes a "defective" first edition. The Protestant church-going of Anna's parents had provoked his gentle sarcasm; but he prided himself on his mother's devoutness, because Madame de Chantelle, in embracing her second husband's creed, had become part of a society which still observes the outward rites of piety.

Anna, in fact, had discovered in her amiable and elegant mother-in-law an unexpected embodiment of the West Fifty-fifth Street ideal. Mrs. Summers and Madame de Chantelle, however strongly they would have disagreed as to the authorized source of Christian dogma, would have found themselves completely in accord on all the momentous minutiæ of drawing-room conduct; yet Mr. Leath treated his mother's foibles with a respect which Anna's experience of him forbade her to attribute wholly to filial affection.

In the early days, when she was still questioning the Sphinx instead of trying to find an answer to it, she ventured to tax her husband with his inconsistency.

"You say your mother won't like it if I call on that amusing little woman who came here the other day, and was let in by mistake; but Madame de Chantelle tells me she lives with her husband, and when mother refused to visit Kitty Mayne you said —"

Mr. Leath's smile arrested her. "My dear child, I don't pretend to apply the principles of logic to my poor mother's prejudices — !"

"But if you admit that they *are* prejudices — ?"

"There are prejudices and prejudices. My mother, of course, got hers from Monsieur de Chantelle, and they seem to me as much in their place in this house as the potpourri in your hawthorn jar. They preserve a social tradition of which I should be sorry to lose the least perfume. Of course I don't expect you, just at first, to feel the difference, to see the *nuance*. In the case of little Madame de Vireville, for instance: you point out that she's still under her husband's roof. Very true; and if she were merely a Paris acquaintance — especially if you had met her, as one still might, in the *right kind* of house in Paris — I should be the last to object to your visiting her. But in the country it's different. Even the best provincial society is what you would call narrow: I don't deny it; and if some of our friends met Madame de Vireville at Givré — well, it would produce a bad impression. You're inclined to ridicule such considerations, but gradually you'll come to see their importance; and meanwhile, do trust me when I ask you to be guided by my mother. It is always well for a stranger in an old society to err a little on the side of what you call its prejudices but I should rather describe as its traditions."

After that she no longer tried to laugh or argue her husband out of his convictions. They *were* convictions, and therefore unassailable. Nor was any insincerity implied in the fact that they sometimes seemed to coincide with hers. There were occasions when he really did look at things as she did; but for reasons so different as to make the distance between them all the greater. Life to Mr. Leath was like a walk through a carefully classified museum, where, in moments of doubt, one had only to look at the number and refer to one's catalogue; to his wife it was like groping about in a huge dark lumber-room where the exploring ray of curiosity lit up now some shape of breathing beauty and now a mummy's grin.

In the first bewilderment of her new state these discoveries had had the effect of dropping another layer of gauze between herself and reality. She seemed farther than ever removed from the strong joys and pangs for which she felt herself made. She did not adopt her husband's view, but insensibly she began to live his life. She tried to throw a compensating ardor into the secret excursions of her spirit, and thus the old vicious distinction between romance and reality was re-established for her, and she resigned herself again to the belief that "real life" was neither real nor alive.

The birth of her little girl swept away this delusion. At last she felt herself in contact with the actual business of living: but even this impression was not enduring. Everything but the irreducible crude fact of child-bearing assumed, in the Leath household, the same ghostly tinge of unreality. Her husband, at the time, was all that his own ideal of a husband required. He was attentive, and even suitably moved; but as he sat by her bedside, and thoughtfully proffered to her the list of people who had "called to inquire," she looked first at him, and then at the child between them, and wondered at the blundering alchemy of Nature. . . .

With the exception of the little girl herself, everything connected with that time had grown curiously remote and unimportant. The days that had moved so slowly as they passed seemed now to have plunged down headlong steeps of time; and as she sat in the autumn sun, with Darrow's letter in her hand, the history of Anna Leath appeared to its heroine like some gray shadowy tale that she might have read in an old book, one night as she was falling asleep. . . .

Two brown blurs emerging from the farther end of the wood-vista gradually defined themselves as her stepson and an attendant gamekeeper. They grew slowly upon the bluish background, with occasional delays and re-effacements, and she sat still, waiting till they should reach the gate at the end of the drive, where the keeper would turn off to his cottage and Owen continue on to the house.

She watched his approach with a smile. From the first days of her marriage she had been drawn to the boy, but it was not until after Effie's birth that she had really begun to know him. The eager observation of her own child had shown her how much she had still to learn about the slight fair boy whom the holidays periodically restored to Givré. Owen, even then, both physically and morally, furnished her with the oddest of commentaries on his father's mien and mind. He would never, the family sighingly recognized, be nearly as handsome as Mr. Leath; but his rather charmingly unbalanced face, with its brooding forehead and petulant boyish smile, suggested to Anna what his father's countenance might have been could one have pictured its neat features disordered by a rattling breeze. She even pushed the analogy farther, and descried in her stepson's mind a quaintly-twisted reflection of her husband's. With his bursts of door-slamming activity, his fits of bookish indolence, his crude revolutionary dogmatizing, and his flashes of precocious irony, the boy was not unlike a boisterous embodiment of his father's theories. It was as though Fraser Leath's ideas, accustomed to hang like marionettes on their pegs, should suddenly come down and walk. There were moments, indeed, when Owen's humors must have suggested to his progenitor the gambols of an infant Frankenstein; but to Anna they were the voice of her secret rebellions, and her tenderness to her stepson was partly based on her severity toward herself. As he had the courage she had lacked, so she meant him to have the chances she had missed; and every effort she made for him helped to keep her own hopes alive.

Her interest in Owen led her to think more often of his mother and sometimes she would slip away and stand alone before her predecessor's portrait. Since her arrival at Givré the picture — a "full length" by a once fashionable artist — had undergone the successive displacements of an exiled consort removed farther and farther from the throne; and Anna could not help noting that these stages coincided with the gradual decline of the artist's fame. She had a fancy that if his credit had been in the ascendant the first Mrs. Leath might have continued to throne over the drawing-room mantelpiece, even to the exclusion of her successor's effigy. Instead of this, her peregrinations had finally landed her in the shrouded solitude of the billiard-room, an apartment which no one ever entered, but where it was understood that "the light was better," or might have been if the shutters had not been always closed.

Here the poor lady, elegantly dressed, and seated in the middle of a large lonely canvas, in the blank contemplation of a gilt console, had always seemed to Anna to be waiting for visitors who never came.

"Of course they never came, you poor thing! I wonder how long it took you to find out that they never would?" Anna had more than once apostrophized her, with a derision addressed rather to herself than to the dead; but it was only after Effie's birth that it occurred to her to study more closely the face in the picture, and speculate on the kind of visitors that Owen's mother might have hoped for.

"She certainly doesn't look as if they would have been the same kind as mine: but there's no telling, from a portrait that was so obviously done 'to please the family,' and that leaves Owen so unaccounted for. Well, they never came, the visitors; they never came; and she died of it. She died of it long before they buried her: I'm certain of that. Those are stone-dead eyes in the picture. . . . The loneliness must have been awful, if even Owen couldn't keep her from dying of it. And to feel it so she must have *had* feelings — real live ones, the kind that twitch and tug. And all she had to look at all her life was a gilt console — yes, that's it, a gilt console screwed to the wall! That's exactly and absolutely what he is!"

She did not mean, if she could help it, that either Effie or Owen should know that loneliness, or let her know it again. They were three, now, to keep each other warm, and she embraced both children in the same passion of motherhood, as though one were not enough to shield her from her predecessor's fate.

Sometimes she fancied that Owen Leath's response was warmer than that of her own child. But then Effie was still hardly more than a baby, and Owen, from the first, had been almost "old enough to understand"; certainly *did* understand now, in a tacit way that yet perpetually spoke to her. This sense of his understanding was the deepest element in their feeling for each other. There were so many things between them that were never spoken of, or even indirectly alluded to, yet that, even in their occasional discussions and differences, formed the unadduced arguments making for final agreement. . . .

Musing on this, she continued to watch his approach; and her heart began to beat a little faster at the thought of what she had to say to him. But when he reached the gate she saw him pause, and after a moment he turned aside as if to gain a cross-road through the park.

She started up and waved her sunshade, but he did not see her. No doubt he meant to go back with the gamekeeper, perhaps to the kennels, to see a retriever who had hurt his leg. Suddenly she was seized by the whim to overtake him. She threw down the parasol, thrust her letter into her bodice, and catching up her skirts began to run.

She was slight and light, with a natural ease and quickness of gait, but she could not recall having run a yard since she had romped with Owen in his school-days; nor did she know what impulse moved her now. She only knew that run she must, that no other motion, short of flight, would have been buoyant enough for her humor. She seemed to be keeping pace with some inward rhythm, seeking to give bodily expression to the lyric rush of her thoughts. The earth always felt elastic under her, and she had a conscious joy in treading it; but never had it been as soft and springy as today. It seemed actually to rise and meet her as she went, so that she had the feeling, which sometimes came to her in dreams, of skimming miraculously over short bright waves. The air, too, seemed to break in waves against her, sweeping by on its current all the slanted lights and moist sharp perfumes of the failing day. She panted to herself: "This is nonsense!" her blood hummed back: "But it's glorious!" and she sped on till she saw that Owen had caught sight of her and was striding back in her direction. Then she stopped and waited, flushed and laughing, her hands clasped against the letter in her breast.

"No, I'm not mad," she called out; "but there's something in the air today — don't you feel it? — And I wanted to have a little talk with you," she added as he came up to her, smiling at him and linking her arm in his.

He smiled back, but above the smile she saw the shade of anxiety which, for the last two months, had kept its fixed line between his handsome eyes.

"Owen, don't look like that! I don't want you to!" she said imperiously.

He laughed. "You said that exactly like Effie. What do you want me to do? To race with you as I do Effie? But I shouldn't have a show!" he protested, still with the little frown between his eyes.

"Where are you going?" she asked.

"To the kennels. But there's not the least need. The vet has seen Garry and he's all right. If there's anything you wanted to tell me — "

"Did I say there was? I just came out to meet you — I wanted to know if you'd had good sport."

The shadow dropped on him again. "None at all. The fact is I didn't try. Jean and I have just been knocking about in the woods. I wasn't in a sanguinary mood."

They walked on with the same light gait, so nearly of a height that keeping step came as naturally to them as breathing. Anna stole another look at the young face on a level with her own.

"You *did* say there was something you wanted to tell me," her stepson began after a pause.

" Well, there is." She slackened her pace involuntarily, and they came to a pause and stood facing each other under the limes.

" Is Darrow coming? " he asked.

She seldom blushed, but at the question a sudden heat suffused her. She held her head high.

" Yes: he's coming. I just heard. He arrives tomorrow. But that's not — " She saw her blunder and tried to rectify it. " Or rather, yes, in a way it is my reason for wanting to speak to you — "

" Because he's coming? "

" Because he's not yet here."

" It's about him, then? "

He looked at her kindly, half-humorously, an almost fraternal wisdom in his smile.

" About — ? No, no: I meant that I wanted to speak today because it's our last day alone together."

" Oh, I see." He had slipped his hands into the pockets of his tweed shooting jacket and lounged along at her side, his eyes bent on the moist ruts of the drive, as though the matter had lost all interest for him.

" Owen — "

He stopped again and faced her. " Look here, my dear, it's no sort of use."

" What's no use? "

" Anything on earth you can any of you say."

She challenged him: " Am *I* one of ' any of you '? "

He did not yield. " Well, then — anything on earth that even *you* can say."

" You don't in the least know what I can say — or what I mean to."

" Don't I, generally? "

She gave him this point, but only to make another. " Yes; but this is particularly. I want to say . . . Owen, you've been admirable all through."

He broke into a laugh in which the odd elder-brotherly note was once more perceptible.

" Admirable," she emphasized. " And so has *she*."

" Oh, and so have you to *her!* " His voice broke down to boyishness. " I've never lost sight of that for a minute, It's been altogether easier for her, though," he threw off presently.

" On the whole, I suppose it has. Well — " she summed up with a laugh, " aren't you all the better pleased to be told you've behaved as well as she? "

" Oh, you know, I've not done it for *you*," he tossed back at her, without the least note of hostility in the affected lightness of his tone.

" Haven't you, though, perhaps — the least bit? Because, after all, you knew I understood? "

" You've been awfully kind about pretending to."

She laughed. " You don't believe me? You must remember I had your grandmother to consider."

"Yes: and my father — and Effie, I suppose — and the outraged shades of Givré!" He paused, as if to lay more stress on the boyish sneer: "Do you likewise include the late Monsieur de Chantelle?"

His stepmother did not appear to resent the thrust. She went on, in the same tone of affectionate persuasion: "Yes: I must have seemed to you too subject to Givré. Perhaps I have been. But you know that was not my real object in asking you to wait, to say nothing to your grandmother before her return."

He considered. "Your real object, of course, was to gain time."

"Yes — but for whom? Why not for *you?*"

"For me?" He flushed up quickly. "You don't mean — ?"

She laid her hand on his arm and looked gravely into his handsome eyes.

"I mean that when your grandmother gets back from Ouchy I shall speak to her — "

"You'll speak to her . . . ?"

"Yes; if only you'll promise to give me time — "

"Time for her to send for Adelaide Painter?"

"Oh, she'll undoubtedly send for Adelaide Painter!"

The allusion touched a spring of mirth in both their minds, and they exchanged a laughing look.

"Only you must promise not to rush things. You must give me time to prepare Adelaide too," Mrs. Leath went on.

"Prepare her too?" He drew away for a better look at her. "Prepare her for what?"

"Why, to prepare your grandmother! For your marriage. Yes, that's what I mean. I'm going to see you through, you know — "

His feint of indifference broke down and he caught her hand. "Oh, you dear divine thing! I didn't dream — "

"I know you didn't." She dropped her gaze and began to walk on slowly. "I can't say you've convinced me of the wisdom of the step. Only I seem to see that other things matter more — and that not missing things matters most. Perhaps I've changed — or *your* not changing has convinced me. I'm certain now that you won't budge. And that was really all I ever cared about."

"Oh, as to not budging — I told you so months ago: you might have been sure of that! And how can you be any surer today than yesterday?"

"I don't know. I suppose one learns something every day — "

"Not at Givré!" he laughed, and shot a half-ironic look at her. "But you haven't really *been* at Givré lately — not for months! Don't you suppose I've noticed that, my dear?"

She echoed his laugh to merge it in an undenying sigh. "Poor Givré. . . ."

"Poor empty Givré! With so many rooms full and yet not a soul in it — except of course my grandmother, who *is* its soul!"

They had reached the gateway of the court and stood looking with a common accord at the long soft-hued façade on which the autumn light was dying. " It looks so made to be happy in — " she murmured.

" Yes — today, today! " He pressed her arm a little. " Oh, you darling — to have given it that look for me! " He paused, and then went on in a lower voice: " Don't you feel we owe it to the poor old place to do what we can to give it that look? You, too, I mean? Come, let's make it grin from wing to wing! I've such a mad desire to say outrageous things to it — haven't you? After all, in old times there must have been living people here! "

Loosening her arm from his she continued to gaze up at the house-front, which seemed, in the plaintive decline of light, to send her back the mute appeal of something doomed.

" It *is* beautiful," she said.

" A beautiful memory! Quite perfect to take out and turn over when I'm grinding at the law in New York, and you're — " He broke off and looked at her with a questioning smile. " Come! Tell me. You and I don't have to say things to talk to each other. When you turn suddenly absent-minded and mysterious I always feel like saying: 'Come back. All is discovered.' "

She returned his smile. " You know as much as I know. I promise you that."

He wavered, as if for the first time uncertain how far he might go. " I don't know Darrow as much as you know him," he presently risked.

She frowned a little. " You said just now we didn't need to say things — "

" Was *I* speaking? I thought it was your eyes — " He caught her by both elbows and spun her halfway round, so that the late sun shed a betraying gleam on her face. " They're such awfully conversational eyes! Don't you suppose they told me long ago why it's just today you've made up your mind that people have got to live their own lives — even at Givré? "

FINLEY PETER DUNNE

FINLEY PETER DUNNE was born of Irish parentage in Chicago on July 10, 1867. Educated in the public schools, he entered newspaper life as a reporter in 1885. Between 1892 and 1900 he served on the editorial staff of several Chicago papers. Later, in New York, he was for several years an editor of the American Magazine, and had charge of the Department called 'In the Interpreter's House.' He is a member of the National Institute of Arts and Letters.

Although Dunne's literary activities have been many-sided, he lives for the American people principally if not solely as Mr. Dooley.

The conversations between Mr. Martin Dooley and his rather subservient crony Mr. Hennessy were suggested by real experience with real people. Dunne gives a pleasant glimpse of the facts in the preface to his first collection of Dooley papers, 'Mr. Dooley in War and Peace' (1898). One need not distinguish too nicely between fact and fiction, but one must insist upon the human reality, the "indigeneity" — to use Howells' formidable but expressive word — of this Middle Western Irish-American philosopher-"barkeep." Mr. Dooley's saloon stood on the outer edge of Chicago on "Archey Road," "forninst th' gas-house and beyant Healey's slough and not far from the polis station." He was born in Ireland, but he has a long life of sound Americanism behind him. His has been rather an observant and reflective life than an active one. He is somewhat sedentary of habit. As Mr. Hennessy reminded him on one occasion: "All this time ye've been standin' behind this bar ladlin' out disturbance to th' Sixth Wa-ard, an' ye haven't been as far east as Mitchigan Avnoo in twinty years."

The young journalist wrote up the sage saloon-keeper as a "local character" likely to amuse passingly some readers of the paper to which he was attached. The sketch attracted enough attention to justify repetition. Finally, it became an institution in the Chicago Journal and Evening Post. But it was the national topic of the Spanish War that brought Mr. Dooley out of his local obscurity. Even then, since Dunne's first volume was published anonymously, it was rather Mr. Dooley who became famous overnight than Mr. Dunne. Indeed, Dunne had so merged his literary personality with Mr. Dooley that for the larger public he existed only as Mr. Dooley. From time to time Dunne has essayed other literary rôles, other modes of expression. His papers 'In the Interpreter's House' in the American Magazine were a seriously intended effort. They proved their author's versatility; the character of Mr. Worldly Wiseman gave promise of satirical possibilities; one of them — on the bravery or cowardice exhibited in the disaster of the Titanic — tapped a new vein in Dunne's talent of earnestness and eloquence; but they made no stir. People wanted more of Mr. Dooley, and would have nothing else from his creator.

So for nearly a decade nothing of importance — indeed, little of unimportance — happened without Mr. Dooley making remarks about it to Mr. Hennessy. Mr. Dooley thus became more than a household name; he was a national institution. He commented good-humoredly but incisively on the brag and blundering of our Spanish War as of Britain's Boer War, the egomania and attitudinizings of the Kaiser — merely absurd they seemed then — the solemn anachronisms of King George's Coronation, the hilarities of Hobson, the donativeness of Carnegie, on Booker Washington in the White House, on "Teddy Rosenfelt" in all aspects, on Woman's Suffrage, on political conventions and other conventions, on Golf. The mood of his comment varied from slightly disguised serious reflection on life to passing quirks of wit like this from the skit on golf. Said Mr. Dooley: "'Th' best players is called scratch-men.' 'What's that f'r?' Mr. Hennessy asked. 'It's a Scotch game,' said Mr. Dooley, with a wave of his hand."

Mr. Hennessy is the one interlocutor. A certain Mr. Hogan is often referred to, a Mr. Cassidy occasionally, and a Teutonic rival in the business, Schwartzmeister, but they never appear. Indeed, Hennessy himself only serves to keep Mr. Dooley talking. He is merely the foil to a monologue, yet he is an appreciable character — honest, positive enough when his mind is really made up, but easily overawed by his more dominant friend and not quick enough to catch on. There is virtually no action. Mr. Dooley picks up or lays down a newspaper, or wipes off his bar.

Mr. Dooley's brogue is itself an interesting achievement. It is not "stage" Irish. I cannot say whether it is dialectically accurate — as Synge's dialects may be, for instance. Dunne is no philologian, but he has taken down Mr. Dooley from dictation, as it were. It is *his* Irish-American as he spoke it in Chicago at the turning of the twentieth century. It is first-hand reality — that which gives distinction generally to the Dooley dialogues. They are glorified "interviews" by a reporter of talent.

The dialogues appeared first in a Chicago newspaper. They in a way belong to the newspaper. A number were written for the American Magazine while Dunne was an editor, but they seemed out of place. They suggest — and have most fittingly appeared as comment of the day — "hot fuit fra the press." From time to time they have been collected into little volumes, the most important of which are 'Mr. Dooley in Peace and War' (1898); 'Mr. Dooley in the Hearts of his Countrymen' (1898); 'Mr. Dooley's Philosophy' (1900); 'Mr. Dooley's Opinions' (1901); 'Observations by Mr. Dooley' (1902); 'Dissertations by Mr. Dooley' (1906); 'Mr. Dooley Says' (1910). Obviously, these collections are not for continuous reading.

It is too soon to hazard a guess as to the permanence of Mr. Dooley in

American literature. But one may confidently affirm that he exercised a happy influence on his own time morally and *pour rire*. If Mark Twain still may claim the supremacy of American humor, Mr. Dooley at least has earned that of Irish-American humor — a title perhaps in principle even more truly representative of the great Melting Pot.

JEFFERSON BUTLER FLETCHER

These selections are taken from 'Mr. Dooley in Peace and War.' Copyright by Small, Maynard, & Company, and reprinted by their permission

OUR CUBAN ALLIES

"WELL, sir," said Mr. Dooley, "dam thim Cubians! If I was Gin'ral Shafter, I'd back up th' wagon in front iv th' dure an' I'd say to Gin'ral Garshy, I'd say, 'I want you'; an' I'd have thim all down at th' station an' dacently booked be th' desk sergeant befure th' fall iv night. Th' impydince iv thim!"

"What have they been doin'?" Mr. Hennessy asked.

"Failin' to undherstand our civilization," said Mr. Dooley. "Ye see, it was this way. This is th' way it was: Gin'ral Garshy with wan hundherd thousan' men's been fightin' bravely f'r two years f'r to liberyate Cubia. F'r two years he's been marchin' his sivinty-five thousan' men up an' down th' island, desthroyin' th' haughty Spanyard be th' millyons. Whin war was declared, he offered his own sarvice an' th' sarvices iv his ar-rmy iv fifty thousan' men to th' United States; an' while waitin' f'r ships to arrive, he marched at th' head iv his tin thousan' men down to Sandago de Cuba an' captured a cigar facthry, which they soon rayjooced to smokin' ruins. They was holdin' this position — Gin'ral Garshy an' his gallant wan thousan' men — whin Gin'ral Shafter arrived. Gin'ral Garshy immedjitly offered th' sarvices iv himsilf an' his two hundherd men f'r the capture iv Sandago; an', when Gin'ral Shafter arrived, there was Gin'ral Garshy with his gallant band iv fifty Cubians, r-ready to eat at a minyit's notice.

"Gin'ral Shafter is a big, coorse, two-fisted man fr'm Mitchigan, an', whin he see Gin'ral Garshy an' his twinty-five gallant followers, 'Fr-ront,' says he. 'This way,' he says, 'step lively,' he says, 'an' move some iv these things,' he says. 'Sir,' says Gin'ral Garshy, 'd'ye take me f'r a dhray?' he says. 'I'm a sojer,' he says, 'not a baggage car,' he says. 'I'm a Cubian pathrite, an' I'd lay down me life an' the lives iv ivry wan iv th' eighteen brave men iv me devoted ar-rmy,' he says; 'but I'll be dam'd if I carry a thrunk,' he says. 'I'll fight whiniver 'tis cool,' he says, 'an' they ain't wan iv these twelve men here that wudden't follow me to hell if they was awake at th' time,' he says; 'but,' he says, 'if 'twas wurruk we were lookin' f'r, we cud have found it long ago,' he says. 'They'se a lot iv it in this counthry that nobody's usin',' he says. 'What we want,' he says, 'is freedom,' he says; 'an' if ye think we have been in th' woods dodgin' th' savage corryspondint f'r two year,' he says, 'f'r th' sake iv r-rushin' yer laundhry home,' he says, ''tis no wondher,' he says, 'that th' r-roads fr'm Marinette to Kalamazoo is paved with goold bricks bought be th' people iv ye'er native State,' he says.

"So Shafter had to carry his own thrunk; an' well it was f'r him that it wasn't Gin'ral Miles', the weather bein' hot. An' Shafter was mad clear thorugh; an', whin he took hold iv Sandago, an' was sendin' out invitations, he scratched Garshy. Garshy took his gallant band iv six back to th' woods; an' there th' three iv thim ar-re now, ar-rmed with forty r-rounds iv canned lobster, an' ready to raysist to th' death. Him an' th' other man has written to Gin'ral Shafter to tell him what they think iv him, an' it don't take long."

"Well," said Mr. Hennessy, "I think Shafter done wrong. He might've asked Garshy in f'r to see th' show, seein' that he's been hangin' ar-round f'r a long time, doin' th' best he cud."

"It isn't that," explained Mr. Dooley. "The throuble is th' Cubians don't undherstand our civilization. Over here freedom means hard wurruk. What is th' ambition iv all iv us, Hinnissy? 'Tis ayether to hold our job or to get wan. We want wurruk. We must have it. D'ye raymimber th' sign th' mob carrid in th' procession las' year? 'Give us wurruk, or we perish,' it said. They had their heads bate in be polismen because no philan-thropist'd come along an' make thim shovel coal. Now, in Cubia, whin th' mobs turns out, they carry a banner with the wurruds, 'Give us nawthin' to do, or we perish.' Whin a Cubian comes home at night with a happy smile on his face, he don't say to his wife an' childher, 'Thank Gawd, I've got wurruk at last!' He says, 'Thank Gawd, I've been fired.' An' th' childher go out, and they say, 'Pah-pah has lost his job.' And Mrs. Cubian buys hersilf a new bonnet; and where wanst they was sorrow an' despair all is happiness an' a cottage organ.

"Ye can't make people here undherstand that, an' ye can't make a Cubian undherstand that freedom means th' same thing as a pinitinchry sintince. Whin we thry to get him to wurruk, he'll say: 'Why shud I? I haven't committed anny crime.' That's goin' to be th' throuble. Th' first thing we know we'll have another war in Cubia whin we begin disthributin' good jobs, twelve hours a day, wan sivinty-five. Th' Cubians ain't civilized in our own way. I sometimes think I've got a touch iv Cubian blood in me own veins."

ON THE DREYFUS CASE

"I SEE be th' pa-apers," said Mr. Dooley, "that Col. Hinnery, th' man that sint me frind Cap Dhry-fuss to th' cage, has moved on. I suppose they'll give th' Cap a new thrile now."

"I hope they won't," said Mr. Hennessy. "I don't know annything about it, but I think he's guilty. He's a Jew."

"Well," said Mr. Dooley, "ye'er thoughts on this subject is inthrestin', but not conclusive, as Dorsey said to th' Pollack that thought he cud lick him. Ye have a r-right to ye'er opinyon, an' ye'll hold it annyhow, whether ye have a r-right to it or not. Like most iv ye'er fellow-citizens, ye start impartial. Ye don't know annything about th' case. If ye knew annything, ye'd not have an opinyon wan way or th' other. They'se niver been a matther come up in my time that th' American people was so sure about as they ar're about th' Dhry-fuss case. Th' Frinch ar-re not so sure, but they'se not a polisman in this counthry that can't tell ye jus' where Dhry-fuss was whin th' remains iv th' poor girl was found. That's because th' thrile was secret. If 'twas an open thrile, an' ye heerd th' tisti-mony, an' knew th' language, an' saw th' safe afther 'twas blown open, ye'd be puzzled, an' not care a rush whether Dhry-fuss was naked in a cage or takin' tay with his uncle at th' Benny Brith Club.

"I haven't made up me mind whether th' Cap done th' shootin' or not. He was certainly in th' neighborhood whin th' fire started, an' th' polis dug up quite a lot iv lead pipe in his back yard. But it's wan thing to sus-pect a man iv doin' a job an' another thing to prove that he didn't. Me frind Zola thinks he's innocint, an' he raised th' divvle at th' thrile. Whin th' judge come up on th' bench an' opined th' coort, Zola was settin' down below with th' lawyers. 'Let us pro-ceed,' says th' impartial an' fair-minded judge, 'to th' thrile iv th' haynious monsther Cap Dhry-fuss,' he says. Up jumps Zola, an' he says in Frinch: 'Jackuse,' he says, which is a hell of a mane thing to say to anny man. An' they thrun him out. 'Judge,' says th' attorney f'r th' difinse, 'an' gintlemen iv th' jury,' he says. 'Ye're a liar,' says th' judge. 'Cap, ye're guilty, an' ye know it,' he says. 'Th' decision iv th' coort is that ye be put in a cage, an' sint to th' Divvle's own island f'r th' r-rest iv ye'er life,' he says. 'Let us proceed to hearin' th' tisti-mony,' he says. 'Call all th' witnesses at wanst,' he says, 'an' lave thim have it out on th' flure,' he says. Be this time Zola has come back; an' he jumps up, an', says he, 'Jackuse,' he says. An' they thrun him out.

"'Before we go anny farther,' says th' lawyer f'r th' difinse, 'I wish to sarve notice that, whin this thrile is over, I intind,' he says, 'to wait outside,' he says, 'an' hammer th' hon'rable coort into an omelet,' he says. 'With these few remarks I will close,' he says. 'Th' coort,' says th' judge, 'is always r-ready to defind th' honor iv France,' he says; 'an', if th' larned counsel will con-sint,' he says, 'to step up here f'r a minyit,' he says, 'th' coort'll put a sthrangle hold on him that'll not do him a bit iv good,' he says. 'Ah!' he says. 'Here's me ol' frind Pat th' Clam,' he says. 'Pat, what d'ye know about this case?' he says. 'None iv ye'er business,' says Pat. 'Answered like a man an' a sojer,' says th' coort. 'Jackuse,' says Zola fr'm the dureway. An' they thrun him out. 'Call Col. Hinnery,' says th' coort. 'He ray-fuses to answer.' 'Good. Th' case is clear. Cap forged th' will. Th' coort will now adjourn f'r dools, an' all ladin' officers iv th' ar-rmy not in disgrace already will assimble in jail, an' com-mit suicide,' he says. 'Jackuse,' says Zola, an' started f'r th' woods, pursued by his fellow-editors. He's off somewhere in a three now hollerin' 'Jackuse' at ivry wan that passes, sufferin' martyrdom f'r his coun-thry an' writin' now an' thin about it all.

"That's all I know about Cap Dhry-fuss' case, an' that's all anny man knows. Ye didn't know as much, Hinnissy, till I told ye. I don't know whether Cap stole th' dog or not."

"What's he charged with?" Mr. Hennessy asked, in bewilderment.

"I'll niver tell ye," said Mr. Dooley. "It's too much to ask."

"Well, annyhow," said Mr. Hennessy, "he's guilty, ye can bet on that."

JACK LONDON

A GREAT deal of Jack London's writing is autobiographical. It will come as no surprise to one who has read him that the author was himself a poor boy, that he spent years among rough strong men, who had to fight against both nature and man to keep alive, and that the working of the law of the survival of the fittest remained for him the most glorious and the most interesting spectacle the world has to offer. He had great sympathy with the poor, with whom he had lived; but the socialism which he preached was never convincing, for most of his work is a reduction of all human issues to the test of sheer brute strength, of primal values which have little to do with society.

If he is not convincing in the process of this reduction, once he has brought all down to the arena he can stage a thrilling show. There is some variety: primitive man, dogs and wolves, fair-skinned prize-fighters, and sea captains who could have put Samson to shame. There are always terrific poundings, violent smells, roars and groans of fury, and blood flowing from a hundred wounds and staining the ground red. Though one may get very quickly a surfeit of this brutality, the spectacle goes on day and night, never relaxed, always terrific, always surprising. Jack London has inexhaustible power and vitality.

Thanks to these qualities 'The Call of the Wild' (1903) roused the attention of the reading public over a great part of the world. In this story of a dog who, snatched from peaceful domestic surroundings and set down in the frigid wilderness of Alaska, becomes once again the splendid primal beast from which his race had sprung, Jack London is at his best. It was written early in his career as an author. In the novels and stories which rapidly followed he attained here and there a similar excellence; but he never surpassed it, nor was he ever again so successful in the handling of a novel as a whole. One wonders why, and the reason is not far to seek.

So long as he dealt with life in the open and with the struggles of men among men, his power and vitality stood him in good stead. The conduct of life which he has recorded in 'The Call of the Wild' and in the first parts of 'The Sea Wolf' and of 'Burning Daylight' is reducible to the test of brute strength. But the social intercourse and the influence of sensibilities responsive to what we call beauty cannot be measured by such a test. Perhaps these things are not worth cherishing. Well and good: to be true to the primal in us let us give them over. But this is what Jack London was unwilling to do. The result is an unpleasant mixture. While on the one hand he purposely bent his energies to make the refinements of life seem puny and not a little contemptible, on the other he showed more and more towards these very refinements a sort of subservience which is not the more congruous for being patronizing.

Perhaps he never grasped the full significance of these amenities. At any rate he was at his worst in the analysis of character, especially of women, and in the sentimental preaching of a romantic socialism. But he was invariably powerful when he wrote of the primal in man and beast. Though one suspects a deliberate too much laying on of realism, there is none the less something hearty and bracing in most of what he has written of life in the open amidst fierce elements, with all that it entails of titanic struggle. He knew this side of life at first hand. And he was always a master of spirited narration. That mastery was born in him, a precious and, in these days, a rare gift. He was at his best in all ways when his story carried him along. Then his characters sprang out of the page in action, his descriptions became vivid, and his style ran along strong and free. At such moments, one recognizes in him some of the elements of greatness. Always something, perhaps much, of what his work lacks in discrimination is made up for in sheer vitality and exuberance.

A few facts of his life may be mentioned. He was born in San Francisco in January 1876. As a boy he was oftener at work on the ranches of California or round the water front than in school. Later he fitted himself for the university, but was able to study there less than a year. In 1897 he joined the rush of gold seekers to the Klondike. He had always wanted to write, and on his return from Alaska he turned his experience there into literary copy. Two volumes of short stories and 'The Call of the Wild' brought him into prominence. Thereafter he wrote steadily, up to the time of his death (November 22, 1916). He was war correspondent during the Russo-Japanese war; and few years went by that he did not give rein in some way to his ever adventurous spirit. In addition to the novels already mentioned, some of the best known are: 'Before Adam,' 'Martin Eden,' 'Smoke Bellew,' and 'White Fang.' He wrote many volumes of short stories, some of which are excellently done, and some essays of mediocre character.

LELAND HALL

FROM 'THE SEA WOLF'

[The narrator, Humphrey Van Weyden of San Francisco, has been rescued from a collision at sea, and finds himself on a sealing schooner outward bound. The captain is in a fit of anger because of the death of the mate.]

WOLF LARSEN ceased swearing as suddenly as he had begun. He relighted his cigar and glanced around. His eyes chanced upon the cook.

"Well, Cooky?" he began, with a suaveness that was cold and of the temper of steel.

"Yes, sir," the cook eagerly interpolated, with appeasing and apologetic servility.

"Don't you think you've stretched that neck of yours just about enough? It's unhealthy, you know. The mate's gone, so I can't afford to lose you too. You must be very, very careful of your health, Cooky. Understand?"

His last word, in striking contrast with the smoothness of his previous utterance, snapped like the lash of a whip. The cook quailed under it.

"Yes, sir," was the meek reply, as the offending head disappeared into the galley.

At this sweeping rebuke, which the cook had only pointed, the rest of the crew became uninterested and fell to work at one task or another. A number of men, however, who were lounging about a companionway between the galley and the hatch, and who did not seem to be sailors, continued talking in low tones with one another. These, I afterward learned, were the hunters, the men who shot the seals, and a very superior breed to common sailor-folk.

"Johansen!" Wolf Larsen called out. A sailor stepped forward obediently. "Get your palm and needle and sew the beggar up. You'll find some old canvas in the sail-locker. Make it do."

"What'll I put on his feet, sir?" the man asked, after the customary "Ay, ay, sir."

"We'll see to that," Wolf Larsen answered, and elevated his voice in a call of "Cooky."

Thomas Mugridge popped out of his galley like a jack-in-the-box.

"Go below and fill a sack with coal."

"Any of you fellows got a Bible or prayer-book?" was the captain's next demand, this time of the hunters lounging about the companionway.

They shook their heads, and some one made a jocular remark which I did not catch, but which raised a general laugh.

Wolf Larsen made the same demand of the sailors. Bibles and prayer-books seemed scarce articles, but one of the men volunteered to pursue the quest amongst the watch below, returning in a minute with the information that there was none.

The captain shrugged his shoulders. "Then we'll drop him over without any palavering, unless our clerical-looking castaway has the burial service at sea by heart."

By this time he had swung fully around and was facing me.

"You're a preacher, aren't you?" he asked.

The hunters — there were six of them — to a man, turned and regarded me. I was painfully aware of my likeness to a scarecrow. A laugh went up at my appearance — a laugh that was not lessened or softened by the dead man stretched and grinning on the deck before us; a laugh that was as rough and harsh and frank as the sea itself; that arose out of coarse feelings and blunted sensibilities, from natures that knew neither courtesy nor gentleness.

Wolf Larsen did not laugh, though his gray eyes lighted with a slight glint of amusement; and in that moment, having stepped forward quite close to him, I received my first impression of the man himself, of the man as apart from his body and from the torrent of blasphemy I had heard him spew forth. The face, with large features and strong lines, of the square order, yet well filled out, was apparently massive at first sight; but again, as with the body, the massiveness seemed to vanish and a conviction to grow of a tremendous and excessive mental or spiritual strength that lay behind, sleeping in the deeps of his being. The jaw, the chin, the brow rising to a goodly height and swelling heavily above the eyes — these, while strong in themselves, unusually strong, seemed to speak an immense vigor or virility of spirit that lay behind and beyond and out of sight. There was no sounding such a spirit, no measuring, no determining of metes and bounds, nor neatly classifying in some pigeonhole with others of similar type.

The eyes — and it was my destiny to know them well — were large and handsome, wide apart as the true artist's are wide, sheltering under a heavy brow and arched over by thick black eyebrows. The eyes themselves were of that baffling protean gray which is never twice the same; which runs through many shades and colorings like intershot silk in sunshine; which is gray, dark and light, and greenish gray, and sometimes of the clear azure of the deep sea. They were eyes that masked the soul with a thousand guises, and that sometimes opened, at rare moments, and allowed it to rush up as though it were about to fare forth nakedly into the world on some wonderful adventure — eyes that could brood with the hopeless somberness of leaden skies; that could snap and crackle points of fire like those which sparkle from a whirling sword; that could grow chill as an arctic landscape, and yet again, that could warm and soften and be all a-dance with love-lights, intense and masculine, luring and compelling, which at the same time fascinate and dominate women till they surrender in a gladness of joy and of relief and sacrifice.

But to return. I told him that, unhappily for the burial service, I was not a preacher, when he sharply demanded:

"What do you do for a living?"

I confess I had never had such a question asked me before, nor had I ever canvassed it. I was quite taken aback, and before I could find myself had sillily stammered, "I — I am a gentleman."

His lip curled in a swift sneer.

"I have worked, I do work," I cried impetuously, as though he were my judge and I required vindication, and at the same time very much aware of my arrant idiocy in discussing the subject at all.

"For your living?"

There was something so imperative and masterful about him that I was quite beside myself — "rattled," as Furuseth would have termed it, like a quaking child before a stern schoolmaster.

"Who feeds you?" was his next question.

"I have an income," I answered stoutly, and could have bitten my tongue the next instant. "All of which, you will pardon my observing, has nothing whatsoever to do with what I wish to see you about."

But he disregarded my protest.

"Who earned it? Eh? I thought so. Your father. You stand on dead men's legs. You've never had any of your own. You couldn't walk alone between two sunrises and hustle the meat for your belly for three meals. Let me see your hand."

His tremendous, dormant strength must have stirred, swiftly and accurately, or I must have slept a moment, for before I knew it he had stepped two paces forward, gripped my right hand in his, and held it up for inspection. I tried to withdraw it, but his fingers tightened, without visible effort, till I thought mine would be crushed. It is hard to maintain one's dignity under such circumstances. I could not squirm or struggle like a schoolboy. Nor could I attack such a creature who had but to twist my arm to break it. Nothing remained but to stand still and accept the indignity. I had time to notice that the pockets of the dead man had been emptied on the deck, and that his body and his grin had been wrapped from view in canvas, the folds of which the sailor, Johansen, was sewing together with coarse white twine, shoving the needle through with a leather contrivance fitted on the palm of his hand.

Wolf Larsen dropped my hand with a flirt of disdain.

"Dead men's hands have kept it soft. Good for little else than dish-washing and scullion work."

"I wish to be put ashore," I said firmly, for I now had myself in control. "I shall pay you whatever you judge your delay and trouble to be worth."

He looked at me curiously. Mockery shone in his eyes.

"I have a counter proposition to make, and for the good of your soul. My mate's gone, and there'll be a lot of promotion. A sailor comes aft to take mate's place, cabin-boy goes for'ard to take sailor's place, and you take the cabin-boy's place, sign the articles for the cruise, twenty dollars per month and found. Now what do you say? And mind you, it's for your own soul's sake. It will be the making of you. You might learn in time to stand on your own legs and perhaps to toddle along a bit."

But I took no notice. The sails of the vessel I had seen off to the southwest had grown larger and plainer. They were of the same schooner-rig as the Ghost, though the hull itself, I could see, was smaller. She was a pretty sight, leaping and flying toward us, and evidently bound to pass at close range. The wind had been momentarily increasing, and the sun, after a few angry gleams, had disappeared. The sea had turned a dull leaden gray and grown rougher, and was now tossing foaming white caps to the sky. We were traveling faster and heeled farther over. Once, in a gust, the rail dipped under the sea, and the decks on that side were for the moment awash with water that made a couple of the hunters hastily lift their feet.

"That vessel will soon be passing us," I said, after a moment's pause. "As she is going in the opposite direction, she is very probably bound for San Francisco."

"Very probably," was Wolf Larsen's answer, as he turned partly away from me and cried out, "Cooky! Oh, Cooky!"

The Cockney popped out of the galley.

"Where's that boy? Tell him I want him."

"Yes, sir"; and Thomas Mugridge fled swiftly aft and disappeared down another companionway near the wheel. A moment later he emerged, a heavy-set young fellow of eighteen or nineteen, with a glowering, villainous countenance, trailing at his heels.

"'Ere 'e is sir," the cook said.

But Wolf Larsen ignored that worthy, turning at once to the cabin-boy.

"What's your name, boy?"

"George Leach, sir," came the sullen answer, and the boy's bearing showed clearly that he divined the reason for which he had been summoned.

"Not an Irish name," the captain snapped sharply. "O'Toole or McCarthy would suit your mug a damn sight better. Unless, very likely, there's an Irishman in your mother's woodpile."

I saw the young fellow's hands clench at the insult, and the blood crawl scarlet up his neck.

"But let that go," Wolf Larsen continued. "You may have very good reasons for forgetting your name, and I'll like you none the worse for it as long as you toe the mark. Telegraph Hill, of course, is your port of entry. It sticks out all over your mug. Tough as they make them and twice as nasty. I know the kind. Well, you can make up your mind to have it taken out of you on this craft. Understand? Who shipped you, anyway?"

"McCready and Swanson."

"Sir!" Wolf Larsen thundered.

"McCready and Swanson, sir," the boy corrected, his eyes burning with a bitter light.

"Who got the advance money?"

"They did, sir."

"I thought as much. And damned glad you were to let them have it. Couldn't make yourself scarce too quick, with several gentlemen you may have heard of looking for you."

The boy metamorphosed into a savage on the instant. His body bunched together as though for a spring, and his face became as an infuriated beast's as he snarled, "It's a —"

"A what?" Wolf Larsen asked, a peculiar softness in his voice, as though he were overwhelmingly curious to hear the unspoken word.

The boy hesitated, then mastered his temper. "Nothin', sir. I take it back."

"And you have shown me I was right." This with a gratified smile. "How old are you?"

"Just turned sixteen, sir."

"A lie. You'll never see eighteen again. Big for your age at that, with muscles like a horse. Pack up your kit and go for'ard into the fo'c'sle. You're a boat-puller now. You're promoted; see?"

Without waiting for the boy's acceptance, the captain turned to the sailor who had just finished the gruesome task of sewing up the corpse. "Johansen, do you know anything about navigation?"

"No, sir."

"Well, never mind; you're mate just the same. Get your traps aft into the mate's berth."

"Ay, ay, sir," was the cheery response, as Johansen started forward.

In the meantime the erstwhile cabin-boy had not moved.

"What are you waiting for?" Wolf Larsen demanded.

"I didn't sign for boat-puller, sir," was the reply. "I signed for cabin-boy. An' I don't want no boat-pullin' in mine."

"Pack up and go for'ard."

The boy glowered sullenly, but refused to move.

Then came another stirring of Wolf Larsen's tremendous strength. It was utterly unexpected, and it was over and done with between the ticks of two seconds. He had sprung fully six feet across the deck and driven his fist into the other's stomach. At the same moment, as though I had been struck myself, I felt a sickening shock in the pit of my stomach. I instance this to show the sensitiveness of my nervous organization at the time, and how unused

I was to spectacles of brutality. The cabin-boy — and he weighed one hundred and sixty-five at the very least — crumpled up. His body wrapped limply about the fist like a wet rag about a stick. He lifted into the air, described a short curve, and struck the deck alongside the corpse on his head and shoulders, where he lay and writhed in agony.

"Well?" Larsen asked of me. "Have you made up your mind?"

I had glanced occasionally at the approaching schooner, and it was now almost abreast of us and not more than a couple of hundred yards away. It was a very trim and neat little craft. I could see a large, black number on one of its sails, and I had seen pictures of pilot-boats.

"What vessel is that?" I asked.

"The pilot-boat Lady Mine," Wolf Larsen answered grimly. "Got rid of her pilots and running into San Francisco. She'll be there in five or six hours with this wind."

"Will you please signal it, then, so that I may be put ashore?"

"Sorry, but I've lost the signal book overboard," he remarked, and the group of hunters grinned.

I debated a moment, looking him squarely in the eyes. I had seen the frightful treatment of the cabin-boy, and knew that I should very probably receive the same, if not worse. As I say, I debated with myself, and then I did what I consider the bravest act of my life. I ran to the side, waving my arms and shouting:

"Lady Mine ahoy! Take me ashore! A thousand dollars if you take me ashore!"

I waited, watching two men who stood by the wheel, one of them steering. The other was lifting a megaphone to his lips. I did not turn my head, though I expected every moment a killing blow from the human brute behind me. At last, after what seemed centuries, unable longer to stand the strain, I looked around. He had not moved. He was standing in the same position, swaying easily to the roll of the ship and lighting a fresh cigar.

"What is the matter? Anything wrong?"

This was the cry from the Lady Mine.

"Yes!" I shouted, at the top of my lungs. "Life or death! One thousand dollars if you take me ashore!"

"Too much 'Frisco tanglefoot for the health of my crew!" Wolf Larsen shouted after. "This one" — indicating me with his thumb — "fancies sea-serpents and monkeys just now!"

The man on the Lady Mine laughed back through the megaphone. The pilot-boat plunged past.

"Give him hell for me!" came a final cry, and the two men waved their arms in farewell.

I leaned despairingly over the rail, watching the trim little schooner swiftly increasing the bleak sweep of ocean between us. And she would probably be in San Francisco in five or six hours! My head seemed bursting. There was an ache in my throat as though my heart were up in it. A curling wave struck the side and splashed salt spray on my lips. The wind puffed strongly, and the Ghost heeled far over, burying her lee rail. I could hear the water rushing down upon the deck.

When I turned around, a moment later, I saw the cabin-boy staggering to his feet. His face was ghastly white, twitching with suppressed pain. He looked very sick.

"Well, Leach, are you going for'ard?" Wolf Larsen asked.

"Yes, sir," came the answer of a spirit cowed.

"And you?" I was asked.

"I'll give you a thousand —" I began, but was interrupted.

"Stow that! Are you going to take up your duties as cabin-boy? Or do I have to take you in hand?"

What was I to do? To be brutally beaten, to be killed perhaps, would not help my case. I looked steadily into the cruel gray eyes. They might have been granite for all the light and warmth of a human soul they contained. One may see the soul stir in some men's eyes, but his were bleak, and cold, and gray as the sea itself.

"Well?"

"Yes," I said.

"Say 'yes, sir.'"

"Yes, sir," I corrected.

"What is your name?"

"Van Weyden, sir."

"First name?"

"Humphrey, sir; Humphrey Van Weyden."

"Age?"

"Thirty-five, sir."

"That'll do. Go to the cook and learn your duties."

And thus it was that I passed into a state of involuntary servitude to Wolf Larsen. He was stronger than I, that was all. But it was very unreal at the time. It is no less unreal now that I look back upon it. It will always be to me a monstrous, inconceivable thing, a horrible nightmare.

"Hold on, don't go yet."

I stopped obediently in my walk toward the galley.

"Johansen, call all hands. Now that we've everything cleaned up, we'll have the funeral and get the decks cleared of useless lumber."

While Johansen was summoning the watch below, a couple of sailors, under the captain's direction, laid the canvas-swathed corpse upon a hatch-cover. On either side the deck, against the rail and bottoms up, were lashed a number of small boats. Several men picked up the hatch-cover with its ghastly freight, carried it to the lee side, and rested it on the boats, the feet pointing overboard. To the feet was attached the sack of coal which the cook had fetched.

I had always conceived a burial at sea to be a very solemn and awe-inspiring event, but I was quickly disillusioned, by this burial at any rate. One of the hunters, a little dark-eyed man whom his mates called "Smoke," was telling stories, liberally intersprinkled with oaths and obscenities; and every minute or so the group of hunters gave mouth to a laughter that sounded to me like a wolf-chorus or the barking of hell-hounds. The sailors trooped noisily aft, some of the watch below rubbing the sleep from their eyes, and talked in low tones together. There was an ominous and worried expression on their faces. It was evident that they did not like the outlook of a voyage under such a captain and begun so inauspiciously. From time to time they stole glances at Wolf Larsen, and I could see that they were apprehensive of the man.

He stepped up to the hatch-cover, and all caps came off. I ran my eyes over them — twenty men all told, twenty-two including the man at the wheel and myself. I was pardonably curious in my survey, for it appeared my fate to be pent up with them on this miniature floating world for I knew not how many weeks or months. The sailors, in the main, were English and Scandinavian, and their faces seemed of the heavy, stolid order. The hunters, on the other hand, had stronger and more diversified faces with hard lines and the marks of the free play of passions. Strange to say, and I noted it at once, Wolf Larsen's features showed no such evil stamp. There seemed nothing vicious in them. True, there were lines, but they were the lines of decision and firmness. It seemed, rather, a frank and open countenance, which frankness or openness was enhanced by the fact that he was smooth-shaven. I could hardly believe — until the next incident occurred — that it was the face of a man who could behave as he had behaved to the cabin-boy.

At this moment, as he opened his mouth to speak, puff after puff struck the schooner and pressed her side under. The wind shrieked a wild song through the rigging. Some of the hunters glanced anxiously aloft. The lee rail, where the dead man lay, was buried in the sea, and as the schooner lifted and righted the water swept across the deck, wetting us above our shoe-tops. A shower of rain drove down upon us, each drop stinging like a hailstone. As it passed, Wolf Larsen began to speak, the bareheaded men swaying in unison to the heave and lunge of the deck.

"I only remember one part of the service," he said, "and that is, 'And the body shall be cast into the sea.' So cast it in."

He ceased speaking. The men holding the hatch-cover seemed perplexed, puzzled no doubt by the briefness of the ceremony. He burst upon them in a fury.

"Lift up that end there, damn you! What the hell's the matter with you?"

They elevated the end of the hatch-cover with pitiful haste, and, like a dog flung overside, the dead man slid feet first into the sea. The coal at his feet dragged him down. He was gone.

"Johansen," Wolf Larsen said briskly to the new mate, "keep all hands on deck now they're here. Get in the topsails and jibs and make a good job of it. We're in for a sou'easter. Better reef the jib and mainsail, too, while you're about it."

In a moment the decks were in commotion, Johansen bellowing orders and the men pulling or letting go ropes of various sorts — all naturally confusing to a landsman such as myself. But it was the heartlessness of it that especially struck me. The dead man was an episode that was past, an incident that was dropped, in a canvas covering with a sack of coal, while the ship sped along and her work went on. Nobody had been affected. The hunters were laughing at a fresh story of Smoke's; the men pulling and hauling, and two of them climbing aloft; Wolf Larsen was studying the clouding sky to windward; and the dead man, dying obscenely, buried sordidly, and sinking, down, down —

Then it was that the cruelty of the sea, its relentlessness and awfulness, rushed upon me. Life had become cheap and tawdry, a beastly and inarticulate thing, a soulless stirring of the ooze and slime. I held onto the weather rail, close by the shrouds, and gazed out across the desolate foaming waves to the low-lying fog-banks that hid San Francisco and the California coast. Rain-squalls were driving in between, and I could scarcely see the fog. And this strange vessel, with its terrible men, pressed under by wind and sea and ever leaping up and out, was heading away into the southwest, into the great and lonely Pacific expanse.

FRANK NORRIS

THE career of Frank Norris opened with so much promise and was cut off so prematurely that his fame has from the first been colored by expectations of what he might have become had he lived to realize them. He seemed, indeed, as the new century opened, to be a singularly authentic and prophetic voice. Of the three great American novelists then living, Mark Twain by most readers was hardly thought of as a novelist at all, William Dean Howells had already come to his subdued later manner, and Henry James had long been separated from his own country by persistent foreign residence and from the world at large by the intricacy of his language and the subtlety of his concerns. American fiction in general had been devoted for thirty years to the recording of sectional singularities and had been gradually worn down to a low tone from which the very recent rage for historical romance had not quite lifted it. Into this staid tradition Frank Norris, barely preceded by Harold Frederic and Stephen Crane, broke with a disturbing voice.

He was one of the least sectional of American novelists. Born in Chicago, where he passed his boyhood, in 1870, a student of art in Paris for two years, ıdent for four years at the University of California and for one graduate ır at Harvard, newspaper correspondent in South Africa at the time of the neson raid and in Cuba during the Santiago campaign, and journalist in ı Francisco, Norris had a vision of his native land which set him with the vement, already feebly under way, to "continentalize" American literature. was not a victim of that movement, which led some good men to an arid mopolitanism, but Zola, his chief teacher, and Kipling had taught Norris ' much the strength of realism depends upon facts observed in their native :es. And though one of his earliest passions was Froissart, and his first book, vernelle' (1892), was a verse romance upon a medieval French theme, his ture plots were laid almost entirely in settings with which he was familiar. ıat so many of them are Californian must be ascribed to his early death; l. meant later to turn to other regions.

What gave Norris this large "continental" view of his materials was a certain epic disposition which he had. He tended to vast plans and conceived trilogies. His "Epic of the Wheat"—'The Octopus' (1901), which deals with the production of wheat in California, 'The Pit' (1903), which deals with the distribution of wheat in the Chicago Board of Trade, and 'The Wolf,' which was to have dealt with the relieving of a famine in Europe by American wheat—he thought of as three distinct novels, bound together only by the cosmic spirit of the wheat which comes up from the abundant earth and moves irresistibly to its appointed purpose, guided, of course, by men, and fought and played over by them, but always mightier than they and actually their master. Another trilogy to which he meant to give years of work would have centered about the battle of Gettysburg, one part for each day, and would have sought to present what Norris considered the American spirit as his "Epic of the Wheat" sought to present an impersonal force of nature. Such conceptions explain the grandiose manner which Norris never lost, and they serve to explain the passion of his realism.

This passion, a kind of fiery zeal for the truth, was the quality which marked Norris and his kind off from the older realists. Zola had had it, and Norris, who called Zola "the very head of the Romanticists," was even willing to name his own form of realism romantic if he could thus argue for the use in fiction of deeper truths than the minute and surface matters which, in his judgment, were the chief stock of realism. Perhaps the most obvious instance in his work of this romantic tendency is the story of Vanamee, the sheep-herder in 'The Octopus,' who has mystical communings with the spirit of his dead mistress. But equally romantic, in fact, was Norris's constant preoccupation with "elemental" emotions. His heroes are nearly all violent men, wilful, passionate, combative; his heroines — thick-haired, large-armed women, almost all of a single physical type — are endowed with a rich and deep, if slow, vitality. Love, in Norris's world, is the mating of vikings and valkyries. A plain case of such heroic passions may be found in 'Moran of the Lady Letty' (1898), the story of Ross Wilbur, a civilized young S Franciscan who is shanghaied upon a Pacific fishing boat and, among ma adventures, meets and loves Moran Sternersen, a splendid Norse sava whom he wins with the valor bred in him by a primitive life. Condy Riv and Travis Bessemer in 'Blix' (1899), Ward Bennett and Lloyd Sear in 'A Man's Woman' (1900), Annixter and Hilma Tree in 'The Octop Curtis Jadwin and Laura Dearborn in 'The Pit,' are actually the same p of lovers repeated, though Rivers is a novelist, Bennett an arctic explc Annixter a ranchman, Jadwin a grain speculator, and the women may daughters of leisure, like Travis, or dairy girls, like Hilma. In 'McTeag (1899), the protagonist, married to a woman who is not his match, fina murders her. Love, however, is by no means the chief concern of these nov , which are full of ardently detailed phases of life which had not yet ap-peared, or at least had not yet become common, in fiction: shark-fishing and beach-combing off the California coast; the minute doings of vulgar people in San Francisco, and the city's Bohemian aspects; the deadly perils of arctic exploration; the plowing, planting, harvesting, sheep-herding, merry-making, rabbit-killing of California ranchmen; their struggle with the railroad — the octopus — for the possession of the land they have tilled; the enormous conflicts of trading in the Chicago wheat pit and its effect upon all who come within its reach; the sordid dissipations of undergraduates, as presented in the posthumous but early 'Vandover and the Brute' (1914). In all these Norris sought to find the basic elements of human nature and to present them with ruthless accuracy. His eagerness to be truthful gave him a large energy, particularly in scenes of action, which not many novelists have equaled, but the same eagerness, along with a journalist's speed and a journalist's vividness, gave him also too often a journalist's lack of body and meaning. That Norris's opinions were never very important is made plain by his volume of essays, 'The Responsibilities of the Novelist' (1903). And as he died at thirty-two he must remain notable not for the depth which age might have brought but for the fire and strength which he had from his youth.

CARL VAN DOREN

FROM 'THE OCTOPUS'

As Presley and Harran trotted on along the county road they continually passed or overtook other horsemen, or buggies, carryalls, buckboards, or even farm wagons, going in the same direction. These were full of the farming people from all the country round about Bonneville, on their way to the rabbit drive — the same people seen at the barn dance — in their Sunday finery, the girls in muslin frocks and garden hats, the men with linen dusters over their black clothes; the older women in prints and dotted calicoes. Many of these latter had already taken off their bonnets — the day was very hot — and pinning them in newspapers, stowed them under the seats. They tucked their handkerchiefs into the collars of their dresses, or knotted them about their fat necks, to keep out the dust. From the axletrees of the vehicles swung carefully covered buckets of galvanized iron, in which the lunch was packed. The younger children, the boys with great frilled collars, the girls with ill-fitting shoes cramping their feet, leaned from the sides of buggy and carryall, eating bananas and "macaroons," staring about with ox-like stolidity. Tied to the axles the dogs followed the horses' hoofs with lolling tongues coated with dust.

The California summer lay blanketwise and smothering over all the land. The hills, bone-dry, were browned and parched. The grasses and wild-oats, sear and yellow, snapped like glass filaments under foot. The roads, the bordering fences, even the lower leaves and branches of the trees, were thick and gray with dust. All color had been burned from the landscape, except in the irrigated patches, that in the waste of brown and dull yellow glowed like oases.

The wheat, now close to its maturity, had turned from pale yellow to golden yellow, and from that to brown. Like a gigantic carpet, it spread itself over all the land. There was nothing else to be seen but the limitless sea of wheat as far as the eye could reach, dry, rustling, crisp, and harsh in the rare breaths of hot wind out of the southeast.

As Harran and Presley went along the county road, the number of vehicles and riders increased. They overtook and passed Hooven and his family in the former's farm wagon, a saddled horse tied to the back board. The little Dutchman, wearing the old frock coat of Magnus Derrick, and a new broad-brimmed straw hat, sat on the front seat with Mrs. Hooven. The little girl Hilda, and the older daughter Minna, were behind them on a board laid across the sides of the wagon. Presley and Harran stopped to shake hands.

"Say," cried Hooven, exhibiting an old, but extremely well kept rifle, "say, bei Gott, me, I tek some schatz at dose rebbit, you bedt. Ven he hef shtop to run and sit oop soh, bei der hind laigs on, I oop mit der guhn und bing! I cetch um."

"The marshals won't allow you to shoot, Bismarck," observed Presley, looking at Minna.

Hooven doubled up with merriment.

"Ho! dot's hell of some fine joak. Me, *I'm one oaf dose mairschell mine-selluf,*" he roared with delight, beating his knee. To his notion, the joke was irresistible. All day long, he could be heard repeating it. "Und Mist'r Praicelie, he say, 'Dose mairschell woand led you schoot, Bismarck,' und *me,* ach Gott, *me,* aindt I mine-selluf one oaf dose mairschell?"

As the two friends rode on, Presley had in his mind the image of Minna Hooven, very pretty in a clean gown of pink gingham, a cheap straw sailor hat from a Bonneville store on her blue black hair. He remembered her very pale face, very red lips, and eyes of greenish blue — a pretty girl certainly, always trailing a group of men behind her. Her love affairs were the talk of all Los Muertos.

"I hope that Hooven girl won't go to the bad," Presley said to Harran.

"Oh, she's all right," the other answered. "There's nothing vicious about Minna, and I guess she'll marry that foreman on the ditch gang, right enough."

"Well, as a matter of course, she's a good girl," Presley hastened to reply, "only she's too pretty for a poor girl, and too sure of her prettiness besides. That's the kind," he continued, "who would find it pretty easy to go wrong if they lived in a city."

Around Caraher's was a veritable throng. Saddle horses and buggies by the score were clustered underneath the shed or hitched to the railings in front of the watering trough. Three of Broderson's Portuguese tenants and a couple of workmen from the Railroad shops in Bonneville were on the porch, already very drunk.

Continually, young men, singly or in groups, came from the doorway, wiping their lips with sidelong gestures of the hand. The whole place exhaled the febrile bustle of the saloon on a holiday morning.

The procession of teams streamed on through Bonneville, reinforced at every street corner. Along the Upper Road from Quien Sabe and Guadalajara came fresh auxiliaries, Spanish-Mexicans from the town itself — swarthy young men on capering horses, dark-eyed girls and matrons, in red and black and yellow, more Portuguese in brand-new overalls, smoking long thin cigars. Even Father Sarria appeared.

"Look," said Presley, "there goes Annixter and Hilma. He's got his buckskin back." The master of Quien Sabe, in top laced boots and campaign hat, a cigar in his teeth, followed along beside the carryall. Hilma and Mrs. Derrick were on the back seat, young Vacca driving. Harran and Presley bowed, taking off their hats.

"Hello, hello, Pres," cried Annixter, over the heads of the intervening crowd, standing up in his stirrups and waving a hand. "Great day! What a mob, hey? Say, when this thing is over and everybody starts to walk into the barbecue, come and have lunch with us. I'll look for you, you and Harran. Hello, Harran, where's the Governor?"

"He didn't come today," Harran shouted back, as the crowd carried him farther away from Annixter. "Left him and old Broderson at Los Muertos."

The throng emerged into the open country again, spreading out upon the Osterman ranch. From all directions could be seen horses and buggies driving across the stubble, converging upon the rendezvous. Osterman's Ranch house was left to the eastward; the army of the guests hurrying forward — for it began to be late — to where around a flagpole, flying a red flag, a vast crowd of buggies and horses was already forming. The marshals began to appear. Hooven, descending from the farm wagon, pinned his white badge to his hat brim and mounted his horse. Osterman, in marvelous riding clothes of English pattern, galloped up and down upon his best thoroughbred, cracking jokes with everybody, chaffing, joshing, his great mouth distended in a perpetual grin of amiability.

"Stop here, stop here," he vociferated, dashing along in front of Presley and Harran, waving his crop. The procession came to a halt, the horses' heads pointing eastward. The line began to be formed. The marshals, perspiring, shouting, fretting, galloping about, urging this one forward, ordering this one back, ranged the thousands of conveyances and cavaliers in a long line, shaped like a wide open crescent. Its wings, under the command of lieutenants, were slightly advanced. Far out before its center Osterman took his place, delighted beyond expression at his conspicuousness, posing for the gallery, making his horse dance.

"Wail, aindt dey gowun to gommence den bretty soohn," exclaimed Mrs.

Hooven, who had taken her husband's place on the forward seat of the wagon.

"I never was so warm," murmured Minna, fanning herself with her hat. All seemed in readiness. For miles over the flat expanse of stubble, curved the interminable lines of horses and vehicles. At a guess, nearly five thousand people were present. The drive was one of the largest ever held. But no start was made; immobilized, the vast crescent stuck motionless under the blazing sun. Here and there could be heard voices uplifted in jocular remonstrance.

"Oh, I say, get a move on, somebody."

"*All* aboard."

"Say, I'll take root here pretty soon."

Some took malicious pleasure in starting false alarms.

"Ah, *here* we go."

"Off, at last."

"We're off."

Invariably these jokes fooled some one in the line. An old man, or some old woman, nervous, hard of hearing, always gathered up the reins and started off, only to be hustled and ordered back into the line by the nearest marshal. This manœuver never failed to produce its effect of hilarity upon those near at hand. Everybody laughed at the blunderer, the joker jeering audibly.

"Hey, come back here."

"Oh, he's easy."

"Don't be in a hurry, Grandpa."

"Say, you want to drive all the rabbits yourself."

Later on, a certain group of these fellows started a huge "josh."

"Say, that's what we're waiting for, the 'do-funny.'"

"The do-funny?"

"Sure, you can't drive rabbits without the 'do-funny.'"

"What's the do-funny?"

"Oh, say, she don't know what the do-funny is. We can't start without it, sure. Pete went back to get it."

"Oh, you're joking me, there's no such thing."

"Well, aren't we *waiting* for it?"

"Oh, look, look," cried some women in a covered rig. "See, they are starting already 'way over there."

In fact, it did appear as if the far extremity of the line was in motion. Dust rose in the air above it.

"They *are* starting. Why don't we start?"

"No, they've stopped. False alarm."

"They've not, either. Why don't we move?"

But as one or two began to move off, the nearest marshal shouted wrathfully:

"Get back there, get back there."

"Well, they've started over there."

"Get back, I tell you."

"Where's the 'do-funny'?"

"Say, we're going to miss it all. They've all started over there."

A lieutenant came galloping along in front of the line, shouting:

"Here, what's the matter here? Why don't you start?"

There was a great shout. Everybody simultaneously uttered a prolonged "Oh-h."

"We're off."

"Here we go for sure this time."

"Remember to keep the alignment," roared the lieutenant. "Don't go too fast."

And the marshals, rushing here and there on their sweating horses to points where the line bulged forward, shouted, waving their arms: "Not too fast, not too fast. . . . Keep back here. . . . Here, keep closer together here. Do you want to let all the rabbits run back between you?"

A great confused sound rose into the air — the creaking of axles, the jolt of iron tires over the dry clods, the click of brittle stubble under the horses' hoofs, the barking of dogs, the shouts of conversation and laughter.

The entire line, horses, buggies, wagons, gigs, dogs, men and boys on foot and armed with clubs moved slowly across the fields, sending up a cloud of white dust, that hung above the scene like smoke. A brisk gaiety was in the air. Everyone was in the best of humor, calling from team to team, laughing, skylarking, joshing. Garnett, of the Ruby Rancho, and Gethings, of the San Pablo, both on horseback, found themselves side by side. Ignoring the drive and the spirit of the occasion, they kept up a prolonged and serious conversation on an expected rise in the price of wheat. Dabney, also on horseback, followed them, listening attentively to every word, but hazarding no remark.

Mrs. Derrick and Hilma sat in the back seat of the carryall, behind young Vacca. Mrs. Derrick, a little disturbed by such a concourse of people, frightened at the idea of the killing of so many rabbits, drew back in her place, her young-girl eyes troubled and filled with a vague distress. Hilma, very much excited, leaned from the carryall, anxious to see everything, watching for rabbits, asking innumerable questions of Annixter, who rode at her side.

The change that had been progressing in Hilma, ever since the night of the famous barn-dance, now seemed to be approaching its climax; first the girl, then the woman, last of all the Mother. Conscious dignity, a new element in her character, developed. The shrinking, the timidity of the girl just awakening to the consciousness of sex, passed away from her. The confusion, the troublous complexity of the woman, a mystery even to herself, disappeared. Motherhood dawned, the old simplicity of her maiden days came back to her. It was no longer a simplicity of ignorance, but of supreme knowledge, the simplicity of the perfect, the simplicity of greatness. She looked the world fearlessly in the eyes. At last, the confusion of her ideas, like frightened birds, re-settling, adjusted itself, and she emerged from the trouble calm, serene, entering into her divine right, like a queen into the rule of a realm of perpetual peace.

And with this, with the knowledge that the crown hung poised above her head, there came upon Hilma a gentleness infinitely beautiful, infinitely pathetic; a sweetness that touched all who came near her with the softness of a caress. She moved surrounded by an invisible atmosphere of Love. Love was in her wide-opened brown eyes, Love — the dim reflection of that descending crown poised over her head — radiated in a faint luster from her dark, thick hair. Around her beautiful neck, sloping to her shoulders with full, graceful curves, Love lay encircled like a necklace — Love that was beyond words, sweet, breathed from her parted lips. From her white, large arms downward to her pink finger-tips — Love, an invisible electric fluid, disengaged itself, subtle, alluring. In the velvety huskiness of her voice, Love vibrated like a note of unknown music.

Annixter, her uncouth, rugged husband, living in this influence of a wife, who was also a mother, at all hours touched to the quick by this sense of nobility, of gentleness, and of love, the instincts of a father already clutching and tugging at his heart, was trembling on the verge of a mighty transformation. The hardness and inhumanity of the man was fast breaking up. One night, returning late to the Ranch house, after a compulsory visit to the city, he had come upon Hilma asleep. He had never forgotten that night. A realization of his boundless happiness in this love he gave and received, the thought that Hilma *trusted* him, a knowledge of his own unworthiness, a vast and humble thankfulness that his God had chosen him of all men for this great joy, had brought him to his knees for the first time in all his troubled, restless life of combat and aggression. He prayed, he knew not what — vague words, wordless thoughts, resolving fiercely to do right, to make some return for God's gift thus placed within his hands.

Where once Annixter had thought only of himself, he now thought only of Hilma. The time when this thought of another should broaden and widen into thought of *Others*, was yet to come; but already, as in the case of Mrs. Dyke, it had broadened to enfold another child and another mother bound to him by no ties other than those of humanity and pity. In time, starting from this point, it would reach out more and more till it should take in all men and all women, and the intolerant selfish man, while retaining all of his native strength, should become tolerant and generous, kind and forgiving.

For the moment, however, the two natures struggled within him. A fight was to be fought, one more, the last, the fiercest, the attack of the enemy who menaced his very home and hearth, was to be resisted. Then, peace attained, arrested development would once more proceed.

Hilma looked from the carryall, scanning the open plain in front of the advancing line of the drive.

"Where are the rabbits?" she asked of Annixter. "I don't see any at all."

"They are way ahead of us yet," he said. "Here, take the glasses."

He passed her his field glasses, and she adjusted them.

"Oh, yes," she cried, "I see. I can see five or six, but oh, so far off."

"The beggars run 'way ahead, at first."

"I should say so. See them run — little specks. Every now and then they sit up, their ears straight up in the air."

"Here, look, Hilma, there goes one close by."

From out of the ground apparently, some twenty yards distant, a great jack sprang into view, bounding away with tremendous leaps, his black-tipped ears erect. He disappeared, his gray body losing itself against the gray of the ground.

"Oh, a big fellow."

"Hi, yonder's another."

"Yes, yes, oh, look at him run."

From off the surface of the ground, at first apparently empty of all life, and seemingly unable to afford hiding place for so much as a field-mouse, jack-rabbits started up at every moment as the line went forward. At first, they appeared singly and at long intervals; then in twos and threes, as the drive continued to advance. They leaped across the plain, and stopped in the distance, sitting up with straight ears, then ran on again, were joined by others; sank down flush to the soil — their ears flattened; started up again, ran to the side, turned back once more, darted away with incredible swiftness, and were lost to view only to be replaced by a score of others.

Gradually, the number of jacks to be seen over the expanse of stubble in front of the line of teams increased. Their antics were infinite. No two acted precisely alike. Some lay stubbornly close in a little depression between two clods, till the horses' hoofs were all but upon them, then sprang out from their hiding-place at the last second. Others ran forward but a few yards at a time, refusing to take flight, scenting a greater danger before them than behind. Still others, forced up at the last moment, doubled with lightning alacrity in their tracks, turning back to scuttle between the teams, taking desperate chances. As often as this occurred, it was the signal for a great uproar.

"Don't let him get through; don't let him get through."

"Look out for him, there he goes."

Horns were blown, bells rung, tin pans clamorously beaten. Either the jack escaped, or confused by the noise, darted back again, fleeing away as if his life depended on the issue of the instant. Once even, a bewildered rabbit jumped fair into Mrs. Derrick's lap as she sat in the carryall, and was out again like a flash.

"Poor frightened thing," she exclaimed; and for a long time afterward, she retained upon her knees the sensation of the four little paws quivering with excitement, and the feel of the trembling furry body, with its wildly beating heart, pressed against her own.

By noon the number of rabbits discernible by Annixter's field glasses on ahead was far into the thousands. What seemed to be ground resolved itself, when seen through the glasses, into a maze of small moving bodies, leaping, ducking, doubling, running back and forth — a wilderness of agitated ears, white tails, and twinkling legs. The outside wings of the curved line of vehicles began to draw in a little; Osterman's ranch was left behind, the drive continued on over Quien Sabe.

As the day advanced, the rabbits, singularly enough, became less wild. When flushed, they no longer ran so far nor so fast, limping off instead a fe feet at a time, and crouching down, their ears close upon their backs. Thus it was that by degrees the teams began to close up on the main herd. At every instant the numbers increased. It was no longer thousands, it was tens of thousands. The earth was alive with rabbits.

Denser and denser grew the throng. In all directions nothing was to be seen but the loose mass of the moving jacks. The horns of the crescent of teams began to contract. Far off the corral came into sight. The disintegrated mass of rabbits commenced, as it were, to solidify, to coagulate. At first, each jack was some three feet distant from his nearest neighbor, but this space diminished to two feet, then to one, then to but a few inches. The rabbits began leaping over one another.

Then the strange scene defined itself. It was no longer a herd covering the earth. It was a sea, whipped into confusion, tossing incessantly, leaping, falling, agitated by unseen forces. At times the unexpected tameness of the rabbits all at once vanished. Throughout certain portions of the herd eddies of terror abruptly burst forth. A panic spread; then there would ensue a blind wild rushing together of thousands of crowded bodies, and a furious scrambling over backs, till the scuffing thud of innumerable feet over the earth rose to a reverberating murmur as of distant thunder, here and there pierced by the strange, wild cry of the rabbit in distress.

The line of vehicles was halted. To go forward now meant to trample the rabbits under foot. The drive came to a standstill while the herd entered the corral. This took time, for the rabbits were by now too crowded to run. However, like an opened sluice-gate, the extending flanks of the entrance of the corral slowly engulfed the herd. The mass, packed tight as ever, by degrees diminished, precisely as a pool of water when a dam is opened. The last stragglers went in with a rush, and the gate was dropped.

"Come, just have a look in here," called Annixter.

Hilma, descending from the carryall, and joined by Presley and Harran, approached and looked over the high board fence.

"Oh, did you ever see anything like that?" she exclaimed.

The corral, a really large enclosure, had proved all too small for the number of rabbits collected by the drive. Inside it was a living, moving, leaping, breathing, twisting mass. The rabbits were packed two, three, and four feet deep. They were in constant movement; those beneath struggling to the top, those on top sinking and disappearing below their fellows. All wildness, all fear of man, seemed to have entirely disappeared. Men and boys reaching over the sides of the corral, picked up a jack in each hand, holding them by the ears, while two reporters from San Francisco papers took photographs of the scene. The noise made by the tens of thousands of moving bodies was as the noise of wind in a forest, while from the hot and sweating mass there rose a strange odor, penetrating, ammoniacal, savoring of wild life.

On signal, the killing began. Dogs that had been brought there for that purpose when let into the corral refused, as had been half expected, to do the work. They snuffed curiously at the pile, then backed off, disturbed, perplexed. But the men and boys — Portuguese for the most part — were more eager. Annixter drew Hilma away, and, indeed, most of the people set about the barbecue at once.

In the corral, however, the killing went forward. Armed with a club in each hand, the young fellows from Guadalajara and Bonneville, and the farm boys from the ranches, leaped over the rails of the corral. They walked unsteadily upon the myriad of crowding bodies underfoot, or, as space was cleared, sank almost waist deep into the mass that leaped and squirmed about them. Blindly, furiously, they struck and struck. The Anglo-Saxon spectators round about drew back in disgust, but the hot, degenerated blood of Portuguese, Mexican, and mixed Spaniard boiled up in excitement at this wholesale slaughter.

But only a few of the participants of the drive cared to look on. All the guests betook themselves some quarter of a mile farther on into the hills.

The picnic and barbecue were to be held around the spring where Broderson Creek took its rise. Already two entire beeves were roasting there; teams were hitched, saddles removed, and men, women, and children, a great throng, spread out under the shade of the live oaks. A vast confused clamor rose in the air, a babel of talk, a clatter of tin plates, of knives and forks. Bottles were uncorked, napkins and oilcloths spread over the ground. The men lit pipes and cigars, the women seized the occasion to nurse their babies.

Osterman, ubiquitous as ever, resplendent in his boots and English riding breeches, moved about between the groups, keeping up an endless flow of talk, cracking jokes, winking, nudging, gesturing, putting his tongue in his cheek, never at a loss for a reply, playing the goat.

"That josher, Osterman, always at his monkey-shines, but a good fellow for all that; brainy too. Nothing stuck up about him either, like Magnus Derrick."

"Everything all right, Buck?" inquired Osterman, coming up to where Annixter, Hilma, and Mrs. Derrick were sitting down to their lunch.

"Yes, yes, everything right. But we've no corkscrew."

"No screw-cork — no scare-crow? Here you are," and he drew from his pocket a silver-plated jack-knife with a corkscrew attachment.

Harran and Presley came up, bearing between them a great smoking, roasted portion of beef just off the fire. Hilma hastened to put forward a huge china platter.

Osterman had a joke to crack with the two boys, a joke that was rather broad, but as he turned about, the words almost on his lips, his glance fell upon Hilma herself, whom he had not seen for more than two months. She had handed Presley the platter, and was now sitting with her back against the tree, between two boles of the roots. The position was a little elevated and the supporting roots on either side of her were like the arms of a great chair — a chair of state. She sat thus, as on a throne, raised above the rest, the radiance of the unseen crown of motherhood glowing from her forehead, the beauty of the perfect woman surrounding her like a glory.

And the josh died away on Osterman's lips, and unconsciously and swiftly he bared his head. Something was passing there in the air about him that he did not understand, something, however, that imposed reverence and profound respect. For the first time in his life, embarrassment seized upon him, upon this joker, this wearer of clothes, this teller of funny stories, with his large, red ears, bald head, and comic actor's face. He stammered confusedly and took himself away, for the moment abstracted, serious, lost in thought.

By now everyone was eating. It was the feeding of the People, elemental, gross, a great appeasing of appetite, an enormous quenching of thirst. Quarters of beef, roasts, ribs, shoulder, haunches were consumed, loaves of bread by the thousands disappeared, whole barrels of wine went down the dry and dusty throats of the multitude. Conversation lagged while the People ate, while hunger was appeased. Everybody had their fill. One ate for the sake of eating, resolved that there should be nothing left, considering it a matter of pride to exhibit a clean plate.

After dinner, preparations were made for games. On a flat plateau at the top of one of the hills the contestants were to strive. There was to be a foot-race of young girls under seventeen, a fat men's race, the younger fellows were to put the shot, to compete in the running broad jump and the standing high jump, in the hop, skip, and step, and in wrestling.

Presley was delighted with it all. It was Homeric, this feasting, this vast consuming of meat and bread and wine, followed now by games of strength. An epic simplicity and directness, an honest Anglo-Saxon mirth and innocence, commended it. Crude it was; coarse it was, but no taint of viciousness was here. These people were good people, kindly, benignant even, always readier to give than to receive, always more willing to help than to be helped. They were good stock. Of such was the backbone of the nation — sturdy Americans every one of them. Where else in the world round were such strong, honest men, such strong, beautiful women?

BOOTH TARKINGTON

IN what has come to be known as the "Indiana Group" of contemporary authors, Booth Tarkington has a prominent place. His reputation is probably second only to that of James Whitcomb Riley. His stories include pure romance, as in 'Monsieur Beaucaire'; the localized novel, describing life in Indiana, as in 'The Conquest of Canaan'; the American abroad, as in 'His Own People'; and studies of boy life, as in 'Penrod.'

'Monsieur Beaucaire' is a conventional romance of the type that has descended from Dumas, with less swashbuckling and more gentleness. Its swift movement, fine spirit of chivalry, and cleverness of phrase suggest the stage; and, indeed, when dramatized it made a pleasing and successful play.

In both 'The Gentleman from Indiana' and 'The Conquest of Canaan' Tarkington has made skilful use of local color. Like others of the Indiana group he has seen the literary possibilities of the small town, with its sharply marked characters, its limited outlook, and stubbornly maintained conventions. The esthetic barrenness, the religious and moral Pharisaism of our American middle classes, are to us a familiar accusation. But Tarkington finds here aspiration also, and spirit and courage. After reading these descriptions of western life one has a feeling of something forcefully positive about these people. He gives also the physical atmosphere of the town: the level mediocrity of its streets, the wilting heat of its long summer days, the piercing winter storms, and the flat expanse of monotonous country beyond.

'The Turmoil,' in breadth of conception and strength of treatment, is a distinctly impressive book. The scene is a growing, pushing, forceful, ugly industrial city, proud of its bigness and its wealth, and quite unconscious of its ugliness. It is making money and is self-complacent. The spirit of the town is typified in Mr. Sheridan, its richest and most energetic citizen. His ideals are militantly materialistic. Naturally he is puzzled by his poet son, Bibbs, who is neither vigorous nor interested in money. The father, the mother, the son, and the heroine are all clearly drawn, and are all of different types. In the contest between father and son and in their final understanding the author displays both psychological insight and skill of invention. The story is not a denunciation of material interest. In the end one feels satisfied with the author's adjustment of values.

Quite the most distinctive thing Tarkington has yet written is 'Penrod.' These sketches of the doings of a twelve-year-old boy in a small town seem new by reason of their very vividness and truth to life. They are, in a sense, a culmination of a long series of books about children. But no one has caught so well that real world of the boy, so vivid to him and so apart from his elders. Penrod's pranks are seldom intended to make trouble; trouble comes of them because the boy's purposes and interests do not run parallel with those of adults. His standards, his values, are different; hence the apparent capriciousness of praise or punishment. Penrod and his friends typify the perpetual boy, quite as well as do Tom Sawyer and Huckleberry Finn. They are of one family. Transfer Tom and Huck to a small Indiana town, put them under the dominion of conventional middle-class parents with social standards to maintain, confine them in school five days a week, and they would react just as Penrod and Sam do.

In 'Seventeen,' we have the boy, adolescent and in love, ineffably silly and defiantly conceited. The book is excellent comedy. Like Meredith's 'Egoist,' it provokes the male reader's denial. Perhaps this is one evidence of its truth.

With 'Alice Adams' Tarkington showed a new type of strength. In a theme such as Howells used in 'Silas Lapham,' that is, the effort to rise in the social scale, he gives a keen analysis of a young girl's mind, against a somber background of frustration and failure.

In 'The Magnificent Ambersons' and 'The Midlander' he returned to the same theme as in 'The Turmoil,' and shows the effect of the industrial development upon certain types of Middle Westerners. In 'The Plutocrat' he sends one of these industrial kings to Africa, with amusing and striking effects. Finally, in 'Women' and 'Claire Ambler' he has centered upon the psychology of women, young and middle-aged, with subtle keenness and understanding sympathy.

A BOY AND HIS DOG

From 'Penrod.' Copyright by Doubleday, Page & Co., and reprinted by their permission

PENROD sat morosely upon the back fence and gazed with envy at Duke, his wistful dog.

A bitter soul dominated the various curved and angular surfaces known by a careless world as the face of Penrod Schofield. Except in solitude, that face was almost always cryptic and emotionless; for Penrod had come into his twelfth year wearing an expression carefully trained to be inscrutable. Since the world was sure to misunderstand everything, mere defensive instinct prompted him to give it as little as possible to lay hold upon. Nothing is more impenetrable than the face of a boy who has learned this, and Penrod's was habitually as fathomless as the depth of his hatred this morning for the literary activities of Mrs. Lora Rewbush — an almost universally respected fellow-citizen, a lady of charitable and poetic inclinations, and one of his own mother's most intimate friends.

Mrs. Lora Rewbush had written something which she called 'The Children's Pageant of the Table Round'; and it was to be performed in public that very afternoon at the Women's Arts and Guild Hall, for the benefit of the Colored Infants' Betterment Society. And if any flavor of sweetness remained in the nature of Penrod Schofield after the dismal trials of the school-week just past, that problematic, infinitesimal remnant was made pungent acid by the imminence of his destiny to form a prominent feature of the spectacle, and to declaim the loathsome sentiments of a character named upon the program the Child Sir Lancelot.

After each rehearsal he had plotted escape, and only ten days earlier there had been a glimmer of light: Mrs. Lora Rewbush caught a very bad cold, and it was hoped it might develop into pneumonia; but she recovered so quickly that not even a rehearsal of the Children's Pageant was postponed. Darkness closed in. Penrod had rather vaguely debated plans for a self-mutilation such as would make his appearance as the Child Sir Lancelot inexpedient on public grounds; it was a heroic and attractive thought, but the results of some extremely sketchy preliminary experiments caused him to abandon it.

There was no escape; and at last his hour was hard upon him. Therefore he brooded on the fence and gazed with envy at his wistful Duke.

The dog's name was undescriptive of his person, which was obviously the result of a singular series of mésalliances. He wore a grizzled mustache and indefinite whiskers; he was small and shabby, and looked like an old postman. Penrod envied Duke because he was sure Duke would never be compelled to be a Child Sir Lancelot. He thought a dog free and unshackled to go or come as the wind listeth. Penrod forgot the life he led Duke.

There was a long soliloquy upon the fence, a plaintive monologue without words; the boy's thoughts were adjectives, but they were expressed by a running film of pictures in his mind's eye, morbidly prophetic of the hideosities before him. Finally he spoke aloud, with such spleen that Duke rose from his haunches and lifted one ear in keen anxiety.

"'I hight Sir Lancelot du Lake, the Child,
Gentul-hearted, meek, and mild.
What though I'm *but* a littul child,
Gentul-hearted, meek and —' *Oof!*"

All of this except "oof" was a quotation from the Child Sir Lancelot, as conceived by Mrs. Lora Rewbush. Choking upon it, Penrod slid down from the fence, and with slow and thoughtful steps entered a one-storied wing of the stable, consisting of a single apartment, floored with cement and used as a storeroom for broken bric-à-brac, old paint-buckets, decayed garden-hose, worn-out carpets, dead furniture, and other condemned odds and ends not yet considered hopeless enough to be given away.

In one corner stood a large box, a part of the building itself: it was eight feet high and open at the top, and it had been constructed as a sawdust magazine from which was drawn material for the horse's bed in a stall on the other side of the partition. The big box, so high and towerlike, so commodious, so suggestive, had ceased to fulfil its legitimate function; though, providentially, it had been at least half full of sawdust when the horse died. Two years had gone by since that passing; an interregnum in transportation during which Penrod's father was "thinking" (he explained sometimes) of an automobile. Meanwhile, the gifted and generous sawdust-box had served brilliantly in war and peace. It was Penrod's stronghold.

There was a partially defaced sign upon the front wall of the box; the donjon-keep had known mercantile impulses:

The O. K. RaBiT Co.
PENROD ScHoFiELD AND CO.
iNQuiRE FOR PRicEs

This was a venture of the preceding vacation, and had netted, at one time, an accrued and owed profit of $1.38. Prospects had been brightest on the very eve of cataclysm. The storeroom was locked and guarded, but twenty-seven rabbits and Belgian hares, old and young, had perished here on a single night — through no human agency, but in a foray of cats, the besiegers treacherously tunneling up through the sawdust from the small aperture which opened into the stall beyond the partition. Commerce has its martyrs.

Penrod climbed upon a barrel, stood on tiptoe, grasped the rim of the box; then, using a knot-hole as a stirrup, threw one leg over the top, drew himself up, and dropped within. Standing upon the packed sawdust, he was just tall enough to see over the top.

Duke had not followed him into the storeroom, but remained near the open doorway in a concave and pessimistic attitude. Penrod felt in a dark corner of the box and laid hands upon a simple apparatus consisting of an old bushel-basket with a few yards of clothes-line tied to each of its handles. He passed the ends of the lines over a big spool, which revolved upon an axle of wire suspended from a beam overhead, and, with the aid of this improvised pulley, lowered the empty basket until it came to rest in an upright position upon the floor of the storeroom at the foot of the sawdust-box.

"Eleva-ter!" shouted Penrod. "Ting-ting!"

Duke, old and intelligently apprehensive, approached slowly, in a semi-circular manner, deprecatingly, but with courtesy. He pawed the basket delicately; then, as if that were all his master had expected of him, uttered one bright bark, sat down, and looked up triumphantly. His hypocrisy was shallow: many a horrible quarter of an hour had taught him his duty in this matter.

"El-e-*vay*-ter!" shouted Penrod sternly. "You want me to come down there *to* you?"

Duke looked suddenly haggard. He pawed the basket feebly again and, upon another outburst from on high, prostrated himself flat. Again threatened, he gave a superb impersonation of a worm.

"You get in that el-e-VAY-ter!"

Reckless with despair, Duke jumped into the basket, landing in a disheveled posture, which he did not alter until he had been drawn up and poured out upon the floor of sawdust within the box. There shuddering, he lay in dough-nut shape and presently slumbered.

It was dark in the box, a condition that might have been remedied by sliding back a small wooden panel on runners, which would have let in ample light from the alley; but Penrod Schofield had more interesting means of illumination. He knelt, and from a former soap-box, in a corner, took a lantern without a chimney, and a large oil-can, the leak in the latter being so nearly inperceptible that its banishment from household use had seemed to Penrod as inexplicable as it was providential.

He shook the lantern near his ear: nothing splashed; there was no sound but a dry clinking. But there was plenty of kerosene in the can; and he filled the lantern, striking a match to illumine the operation. Then he lit the lantern and hung it upon a nail against the wall. The sawdust floor was slightly impregnated with oil, and the open flame quivered in suggestive proximity to the side of the box; however, some rather deep charrings of the plank against which the lantern hung offered evidence that the arrangement was by no means a new one, and indicated at least a possibility of no fatality occurring this time.

Next Penrod turned up the surface of the sawdust in another corner of the floor, and drew forth a cigar-box in which were half a dozen cigarettes, made of hayseed and thick brown wrapping paper, a lead pencil, an eraser, and a small note-book the cover of which was labeled in his own handwriting:

"English Grammar. Penrod Schofield. Room 6, Ward School Nomber Seventh."

The first page of this book was purely academic; but the study of English undefiled terminated with a slight jar at the top of the second: "Nor must an adverb be used to modif —"

Immediately followed:

"HARoLD RAMoREZ THE RoADAGENT
OR WiLD LiFE AMoNG THE
ROCKY MTS."

And the subsequent entries in the book appeared to have little concern with Room 6, Ward School Nomber Seventh.

FROM 'THE TURMOIL'

THERE is a midland city in the heart of fair, open country, a dirty and wonderful city nestling dingily in the fog of its own smoke. The stranger must feel the dirt before he feels the wonder, for the dirt will be upon him instantly. It will be upon him and within him, since he must breathe it, and he may care for no further proof that wealth is here better loved than cleanliness; but whether he cares or not, the negligently tended streets incessantly press home the point, and so do the flecked and grimy citizens. At a breeze he must smother in whirlpools of dust, and if he should decline at any time to inhale the smoke he has the meager alternative of suicide.

The smoke is like the bad breath of a giant panting for more and more riches. He gets them and pants the fiercer, smelling and swelling prodigiously. He has a voice, a hoarse voice, hot and rapacious, trained to one tune: "Wealth! I will get Wealth! I will make Wealth! I will sell Wealth for more Wealth! My house shall be dirty, my garment shall be dirty, and I will foul my neighbor so that he cannot be clean — but I will get Wealth! There shall be no clean thing about me: my wife shall be dirty and my child shall be dirty, but I will get Wealth!" And yet it is not wealth that he is so greedy for: what the giant really wants is hasty riches. To get these he squanders wealth upon the four winds, for wealth is in the smoke.

Not quite so long ago as a generation, there was no panting giant here, no heaving, grimy city; there was but a pleasant big town of neighborly people who had understanding of one another, being, on the whole, much of the same type. It was a leisurely and kindly place — "homelike," it was called — and when the visitor had been taken through the State Asylum for the Insane and made to appreciate the view of the cemetery from a little hill, his host's duty as Baedeker was done. The good burghers were given to jogging comfortably about in phaetons or in surreys for a family drive on Sunday. No one was very rich; few were poor; the air was clean, and there was time to live.

But there was a spirit abroad in the land, and it was strong here as elsewhere — a spirit that had moved in the depths of the American soil and labored there, sweating, till it stirred the surface, rove the mountains, and emerged, tangible and monstrous, the god of all good American hearts — Bigness. And that god wrought the panting giant.

In the souls of the burghers there had always been the profound longing for size. Year by year the longing increased until it became an accumulated force: We must Grow! We must be Big! We must be Bigger! Bigness means Money! And the thing began to happen; their longing became a mighty Will. We must be Bigger! Bigger! Bigger! Get people here! Coax them here! Bribe them! Swindle them into coming if you must, but get them! Shout them into coming! Deafen them into coming! Any kind of people; all kinds of people! We must be Bigger! Blow! Boost! Brag! Kill the fault-finder! Scream and bellow to the Most High: Bigness is patriotism and honor! Bigness is love and life and happiness! Bigness is Money! We want Bigness!

They got it. From all the states the people came; thinly at first, and slowly, but faster and faster in thicker and thicker swarms as the quick years went by. White people came, and black people and brown people and yellow people; the negroes came from the South by the thousands and thousands, multiplying by other thousands and thousands faster than they could die. From the four quarters of the earth the people came, the broken and the unbroken, the tame and the wild — Germans, Irish, Italians, Hungarians, Scotch, Welsh, English, French, Swiss, Swedes, Norwegians, Greeks, Poles, Russian Jews, Dalmatians, Armenians, Roumanians, Bulgarians, Servians, Persians, Syrians, Japanese, Chinese, Turks, and every hybrid that these could propagate. And if there were no Eskimos nor Patagonians, what other human strain that earth might furnish failed to swim and bubble in this crucible?

With Bigness came the new machinery and the rush; the streets began to roar and rattle, the houses to tremble; the pavements were worn under the tread of hurrying multitudes. The old, leisurely, quizzical look of the faces was lost in something harder and warier; and a cockney type began to emerge discernibly — a cynical young mongrel, barbaric of feature, muscular and cunning; dressed in good fabrics fashioned apparently in imitation of the sketches drawn by newspaper comedians. The female of his kind came with him — a pale girl, shoddy and a little rouged; and they communicated in a nasal argot, mainly insolences and elisions. Nay, the common speech of the people showed change: in place of the old midland vernacular, irregular but clean, and not unwholesomely drawling, a jerky dialect of coined metaphors began to be heard, held together by *gunnas* and *gottas* and much fostered by the public journals.

The city piled itself high in the center, tower on tower for a nucleus, and spread itself out over the plain, mile after mile; and in its vitals, like benevolent bacilli contending with malevolent in the body of a man, missions and refuges offered what resistance they might to the saloons and all the hells that cities house and shelter. Temptation and ruin were ready commodities on the market for purchase by the venturesome; highwaymen walked the streets at night and sometimes killed; snatching thieves were busy everywhere in the dusk; while housebreakers were a common apprehension and frequent reality. Life itself was somewhat safer from intentional destruction than it was in medieval Rome during a faction war — though the Roman murderer was more like to pay for his deed — but death or mutilation beneath the wheels lay in ambush at every crossing.

The politicians let the people make all the laws they liked; it did not matter much, and the taxes went up, which is good for politicians. Law-making was a pastime of the people; nothing pleased them more. Singular fermentation of their humor, they even had laws forbidding dangerous speed. More marvelous still, they had a law forbidding smoke! They forbade chimneys to smoke and they forbade cigarettes to smoke. They made laws for all things and forgot them immediately; though sometimes they would remember after a while, and hurry to make new laws that the old laws should be enforced — and then forget both new and old. Wherever enforcement threatened Money or Votes — or wherever it was too much bother — it became a joke. Influence was the law.

So the place grew. And it grew strong.

Straightway when he came, each man fell to the same worship:

Give me of thyself, O Bigness:
Power to get more power!
Riches to get more riches!
Give me of thy sweat that I may sweat more!
Give me Bigness to get more Bigness to myself,
O Bigness, for Thine is the Power and the Glory! And there is no end but
Bigness, ever and for ever!

The Sheridan Building was the biggest skyscraper; the Sheridan Trust Company was the biggest of its kind, and Sheridan himself had been the biggest builder and breaker and truster and buster under the smoke. He had come from a country cross-roads, at the beginning of the growth, and he had gone up and down in the booms and relapses of that period; but each time he went down he rebounded a little higher, until finally, after a year of overwork and anxiety — the latter not decreased by a chance, remote but possible, of recuperation from the former in the penitentiary — he found himself on top, with solid substance under his feet; and thereafter "played it safe." But his hunger to get was unabated, for it was in the very bones of him and grew fiercer.

He was the city incarnate. He loved it, calling it God's country, as he called the smoke Prosperity, breathing the dingy cloud with relish. And when soot fell upon his cuff he chuckled; he could have kissed it. "It's good! It's good!" he said, and smacked his lips in gusto. "Good, clean soot; it's our life blood, God bless it!" The smoke was one of his great enthusiasms; he laughed at a committee of plaintive housewives who called to beg his aid against it. "Smoke's what brings your husbands' money home on Saturday night," he told them, jovially. "Smoke may hurt your little shrubberies in the front yard some, but it's the catarrhal climate and the adenoids that starts your chuldern coughing. Smoke makes the climate better. Smoke means good health: it makes the people wash more. They have to wash so much they wash off the microbes.

You go home and ask your husbands what smoke puts in their pockets out o' the pay-roll — and you'll come around next time to get me to turn out more smoke instead o' chokin' it off!"

It was Narcissism in him to love the city so well; he saw his reflection in it; and, like it, he was grimy, big, careless, rich, strong, and unquenchably optimistic. From the deepest of his inside all the way out he believed it was the finest city in the world. "Finest" was his word. He thought of it as his city as he thought of his family as his family; and just as he profoundly believed his city to be the finest city in the world, so did he believe his family to be — in spite of his son Bibbs — the finest family in the world. As a matter of fact, he knew nothing worth knowing about either.

Bibbs Sheridan was a musing sort of boy, poor in health, and considered the failure — the "odd one" — of the family. Born during that most dangerous and anxious of the early years, when the mother fretted and the father took his chance, he was an ill-nourished baby, and grew meagerly, only lengthwise, through a feeble childhood. At his christening he was committed for life to "Bibbs," mainly through lack of imagination on his mother's part, for though it was her maiden name, she had no strong affection for it; but it was "her turn" to name the baby, and, as she explained later, she "couldn't think of anything else she liked *at all!*" She offered this explanation one day when the sickly boy was nine and after a long fit of brooding had demanded some reason for his name's being Bibbs. He requested then with unwonted vehemence to be allowed to exchange names with his older brother, Roscoe Conkling Sheridan, or with the oldest, James Sheridan, Junior, and upon being refused went down into the cellar and remained there the rest of that day. And the cook, descending toward dusk, reported that he had vanished; but a search revealed that he was in the coal-pile, completely covered and still burrowing. Removed by force and carried upstairs, he maintained a cryptic demeanor, refusing to utter a syllable of explanation, even under the lash. This obvious thing was wholly a mystery to both parents; the mother was nonplussed, failed to trace and connect; and the father regarded his son as a stubborn and mysterious fool, an impression not effaced as the years went by.

At twenty-two Bibbs was physically no more than the outer scaffolding of a man, waiting for the building to begin inside — a long-shanked, long-faced, rickety youth, sallow and hollow and haggard, dark-haired and dark-eyed, with a peculiar expression of countenance; indeed, at first sight of Bibbs Sheridan a stranger might well be solicitous, for he seemed upon the point of tears. But to a slightly longer gaze, not grief, but mirth, was revealed as his emotion; while a more searching scrutiny was proportionately more puzzling — he seemed about to burst out crying or to burst out laughing, one or the other, inevitably, but it was impossible to decide which. And Bibbs never, on any occasion of his life, either laughed aloud or wept.

He was a "disappointment" to his father. At least that was the parent's word — a confirmed and established word after his first attempt to make a "business man" of the boy. He sent Bibbs to "begin at the bottom and learn from the ground up" in the machine-shop of the Sheridan Automatic Pump Works, and at the end of six months the family physician sent Bibbs to begir at the bottom and learn from the ground up in a sanitarium.

"You needn't worry, mamma," Sheridan told his wife. "There's nothin'. the matter with Bibbs except he hates work so much it makes him sick. *I* put him in the machine-shop, and I guess I know what I'm doin' about as well as the next man. Ole Doc Gurney always was one o' them nutty alarmists. Does he think I'd do anything 'd be bad for my own flesh and blood? He makes me tired!"

Anything except perfectly definite health or perfectly definite disease was incomprehensible to Sheridan. He had a genuine conviction that lack of physical persistence in any task involving money must be due to some subtle weakness of character itself, to some profound shiftlessness or slyness. He understood typhoid fever, pneumonia, and appendicitis — one had them, and either died or got over them and went back to work — but when the word "nervous" appeared in a diagnosis he became honestly suspicious: he had the feeling that there was something contemptible about it, that there was a nigger in the wood-pile somewhere.

"Look at me," he said. "Look at what *I* did at his age! Why, when I was twenty years old, wasn't I up every morning at four o'clock choppin' wood — yes! and out in the dark and the snow — to build a fire in a country grocery store? And here Bibbs has to go and have a *doctor* because he can't — Pho! it makes me tired! If he'd gone at it like a man he wouldn't be sick."

He paced the bedroom — the usual setting for such parental discussions — in his nightgown, shaking his big, grizzled head and gesticulating to his bedded spouse. "My Lord!" he said. "If a little, teeny bit o' work like this is too much for him, why, he ain't fit for anything! It's nine tenths imagination, and the rest of it — well, I won't say it's deliberate, but I *would* like to know just how much of it's put on!"

"Bibbs didn't want the doctor," said Mrs. Sheridan. "It was when he was here to dinner that night, and noticed how he couldn't eat anything. Honey, you better come to bed."

"Eat!" he snorted. "Eat! It's work that makes men eat! And it's imagination that keeps people from eatin'. Busy men don't get time for that kind of imagination; and there's another thing you'll notice about good health, if you'll take the trouble to look around you, Mrs. Sheridan: busy men haven't got time to be sick and they don't *get* sick. You just think it over and you'll find that ninety-nine per cent of the sick people you know are either women loafers. Yes, ma'am!"

"Honey," she said again, drowsily, "you better come to bed."

"Look at the other boys," her husband bade her. "Look at Jim and Roscoe.

Look at how *they* work! There isn't a shiftless bone in their bodies. Work never made Jim or Roscoe sick. Jim takes half the load off my shoulders already. Right now there isn't a harder-workin', brighter business man in this city than Jim. I've pushed him, but he give me something to push *against*. You can't push 'nervous dyspepsia'! And look at Roscoe; just *look* at what that boy's done for himself, and barely twenty-seven years old — married, got a fine wife, and ready to build for himself with his own money, when I put up the New House for you and Edie."

"Papa, you'll catch cold in your bare feet," she murmured. "You better come to bed."

"And I'm just as proud of Edie, for a girl," he continued, emphatically, "as I am of Jim and Roscoe for boys. She'll make some man a mighty good wife when the time comes. She's the prettiest and talentedest girl in the United States! Look at that poem she wrote when she was in school and took the prize with; it's the best poem I ever read in my life, and she'd never even tried to write one before. It's the finest thing I ever read, and R. T. Bloss said so, too; and I guess he's a good enough literary judge for me — turns out more advertisin' liter'cher than any man in this city. I tell you she's smart. Look at the way she worked me to get me to promise the New House — and I guess you had your finger in that, too, mamma! This old shack's good enough for me, but you and little Edie 'll have to have your way. I'll get behind her and push her same as I will Jim and Roscoe. I tell you I'm mighty proud o' them three chuldern! But Bibbs — " He paused, shaking his head. "Honest, mamma, when I talk to men that got *all* their boys doin' well and worth their salt, why, I have to keep my mind on Jim and Roscoe and forget about Bibbs."

Mrs. Sheridan tossed her head fretfully upon the pillow. "You did the best you could, papa," she said, impatiently, "so come to bed and quit reproachin' yourself for it."

He glared at her indignantly. "Reproachin' myself!" he snorted. "I ain't doin' anything of the kind! What in the name o' goodness would I want to reproach myself for? And it wasn't the 'best *I* could,' either. It was the best *anybody* could! I was givin' him a chance to show what was in him and make a man of himself — and here he goes and gets 'nervous dyspepsia' on me!"

He went to the old-fashioned gas-fixture, turned out the light, and muttered his way morosely into bed.

"What?" said his wife, crossly, bothered by a subsequent mumbling.

"More like hook-worm, I said," he explained, speaking louder. "*I don't* know what to do with him!"

RICHARD WATSON GILDER

RICHARD WATSON GILDER was the son of a clergyman, the Rev. William H. Gilder, who published two literary reviews in Philadelphia. He was born in Bordentown, New Jersey, February 8, 1844, and with such ancestry and home influence came easily to journalism and literary work. He got his schooling in the Bellevue Seminary, which was founded by his father. As with so many young Americans of the time, the war came to interrupt his studies; and in 1863 he served in the "Emergency Corps," in the defense of Carlisle, Pennsylvania. Gilder was one of the American writers who most successfully combined journalism and literature. He began by doing newspaper work, and then by a natural transition became in 1869 editor of Hours at Home, and shortly thereafter associate editor of Scribner's Monthly with Dr. J. G. Holland. This representative monthly was changed in name to The Century, and upon the death of Dr. Holland in 1881 Gilder became its editor-in-chief. His influence in this conspicuous position was truly wholesome and helpful in the encouraging of literature, and in the discussion of current questions of importance through a popular medium which reaches great numbers of the American people. The Century under his direction was ever receptive to young writers and artists of ability, and many since known to fame made their maiden appearance in its pages.

In addition to his influence on the literary movement, Mr. Gilder was very active in philanthropic and political work. He helped secure legislation for the improvement of tenements in cities; he took much interest in the formation of public kindergartens; and gave of his time and strength to further other reforms. His influence in New York City, too, was a strong factor in developing the social aspects of literary and art life there. From Dickinson College he received the degree of LL.D., and from Princeton that of L.H.D.

Gilder's reputation as a writer is based upon his verse: only very occasionally did he publish an essay, though thoughtful, strongly written editorials from his pen in his magazine were frequent. But it was his verse-writing that gave him his place — a distinct and honorable one — in American letters. The fine quality and promise of his work was recognized upon the publication of 'The New Day' in 1875, a first volume which was warmly received. It showed the influence of Italian studies, and contained lyric work of much imaginative beauty. The musicalness of it and the delicately ideal treatment of the love passion were noticeable characteristics. In his subsequent books — 'The Celestial Passion' (1887), 'Lyrics' (1885 and 1887), 'Two Worlds, and Other Poems' (1891), 'The Great Remembrance, and Other Poems' (1893):

the contents of these being gathered finally into the one volume 'Five Books of Song' (1894) — he gave still further proof of his genuine lyric gift, his work in later years having a wider range of themes, a broadening vision and deepening purpose. He remained nevertheless essentially a lyrist, a maker of songs; a thorough artist who had seriousness, dignity, and charm. His was an earnest nature, sensitive alike to vital contemporaneous problems and to the honeysweet voice of the Ideal. He died on November 18, 1909.

TWO SONGS FROM 'THE NEW DAY'

I

NOT from the whole wide world I chose thee,
Sweetheart, light of the land and the sea!
The wide, wide world could not inclose thee —
For thou art the whole wide world to me.

II

Years have flown since I knew thee first,
And I know thee as water is known of thirst;
Yet I knew thee of old at the first sweet sight,
And thou art strange to me, Love, tonight.

"ROSE-DARK THE SOLEMN SUNSET"

ROSE-DARK the solemn sunset
That holds my thought of thee;
With one star in the heavens
And one star in the sea.

On high no lamp is lighted,
Nor where the long waves flow,
Save the one star of evening
And the shadow star below.

Light of my life, the darkness
Comes with the twilight dream;
Thou art the bright star shining,
And I but the shadowy gleam.

THE SONNET

WHAT is a sonnet? 'Tis the pearly shell
  That murmurs of the far-off murmuring sea;
  A precious jewel carved most curiously;
It is a little picture painted well.
What is a sonnet? 'Tis the tear that fell
  From a great poet's hidden ecstasy;
  A two-edged sword, a star, a song — ah me!
Sometimes a heavy-tolling funeral bell.
  This was the flame that shook with Dante's breath;
    The solemn organ whereon Milton played,
And the clear glass where Shakespeare's shadow falls:
  A sea this is — beware who ventureth!
    For like a fiord the narrow floor is laid
Mid-ocean to the sheer mountain walls.

AMERICA

From 'The Great Remembrance'

LAND that we love! Thou Future of the World!
  Thou refuge of the noble heart oppressed!
  Oh, never be thy shining image hurled
    From its high place in the adoring breast
Of him who worships thee with jealous love!
Keep thou thy starry forehead as the dove
  All white, and to the eternal Dawn inclined!
  Thou art not for thyself, but for mankind,
And to despair of thee were to despair
  Of man, of man's high destiny, of God!
  Of thee should man despair, the journey trod
Upward, through unknown eons, stair on stair,
  By this our race, with bleeding feet and slow,
  Were but the pathway to a darker woe
Than yet was visioned by the heavy heart
  Of prophet. To despair of thee! Ah no!
For thou thyself art Hope; Hope of the World thou art!

ON THE LIFE-MASK OF ABRAHAM LINCOLN

THIS bronze doth keep the very form and mold
Of our great martyr's face. Yes, this is he:
That brow all wisdom, all benignity;
That human, humorous mouth; those cheeks that hold
Like some harsh landscape all the summer's gold;
That spirit fit for sorrow, as the sea
For storms to beat on; the lone agony
Those silent, patient lips too well foretold.
Yes, this is he who ruled a world of men
As might some prophet of the elder day —
Brooding above the tempest and the fray
With deep-eyed thought and more than mortal ken.
A power was his beyond the touch of art
Or armèd strength — his pure and mighty heart.

"CALL ME NOT DEAD"

CALL me not dead when I, indeed, have gone
Into the company of the ever-living
High and most glorious poets! Let thanksgiving
Rather be made. Say: — "He at last hath won
Rest and release, converse supreme and wise,
Music and song and light of immortal faces;
Today, perhaps, wandering in starry places,
He hath met Keats, and known him by his eyes.
Tomorrow (who can say?) Shakespeare may pass,
And our lost friend just catch one syllable
Of that three-centuried wit that kept so well;
Or Milton; or Dante, looking on the grass
Thinking of Beatrice, and listening still
To chanted hymns that sound from the heavenly hill."

AFTER-SONG

From 'The New Day'

THROUGH love to light! Oh, wonderful the way
That leads from darkness to the perfect day!
From darkness and from sorrow of the night
To morning that comes singing o'er the sea.
Through love to light! Through light, O God, to thee,
Who art the love of love, the eternal light of light!

FROM 'NON SINE DOLORE'

NO passing burden is our earthly sorrow,
That shall depart in some mysterious morrow.
'Tis His one universe where'er we are —
One changeless law from sun to viewless star.
Were sorrow evil here, evil it were forever,
Beyond the scope and help of our most keen endeavor
God doth not dote,
His everlasting purpose shall not fail.
Here where our ears are weary with the wail
And weeping of the sufferers; there where the Pleiads float —
Here, there, forever, pain most dread and dire
Doth bring the intensest bliss, the dearest and most sure.
'Tis not from Life aside, it doth endure
Deep in the secret heart of all existence.
It is the inward fire,
The heavenly urge, and the divine insistence.
Uplift thine eyes, O Questioner, from the sod!
It were no longer Life,
If ended were the strife;
Man were not man, God were not truly God.

EUGENE FIELD

EUGENE FIELD was born in St. Louis, Missouri, September 2 or 3, 1850. He was of New England ancestry, and spent his early years in Massachusetts. "While he gloried in the West," wrote one of his biographers, "and remained loyal to the section which gave him birth and in which he chose to cast his lot, he was not less proud of his New England blood, and not the less conscious of his New England training." He studied at Williams and Knox Colleges, and at the University of Michigan, and after his graduation in 1871 he traveled in Europe.

Returning to St. Louis he became engaged in journalism, and was connected with various newspapers in St. Louis, St. Joseph, Kansas City, and Denver, until he finally settled in Chicago. Through his tales and poems he acquired popularity, and in addition to his labors as a journalist and poet he became a favorite lecturer. Of his love of curios his brother says:

"For years he had been an indefatigable collector, and he took a boyish pleasure not only in his souvenirs of long journeys and distinguished men and women, but in the queer toys and trinkets of children, which seemed to give him inspiration for much that was effective in childhood verse. To the careless observer the immense array of weird dolls and absurd toys in his working-room meant little more than an idiosyncratic passion for the anomalous, but those who were near to him knew what a connecting link they were between him and little children, of whom he wrote, and how each trumpet and drum, each 'spinster doll,' each little toy-dog, each little tin soldier, played its part in the poems he sent out into the world."

He was extremely fond of children, and some of his best poetry was written on themes that interest childhood. His numerous lullabies have been set to music by several American composers. He was a devoted student of Horace, from whom he made many translations. Some of these are included in 'Echoes from a Sabine Farm,' which he wrote with his brother, Roswell Martin Field, and which was published soon after his death, which took place in Chicago, November 4, 1895. His last books were 'My House' and 'The Love Affairs of a Bibliomaniac,' a series of essays on literary subjects, interspersed with short poems. His other publications include: 'A Little Book of Western Verse'; 'A Little Book of Profitable Tales'; 'Love Songs of Childhood'; 'A Second Book of Verse'; and 'The Holy Cross and Other Tales,' the initial story of which has for its theme the death of the Wandering Jew upon the mountain of the Holy Cross. A complete edition of Field's works (10 vols., New York, 1896) is enriched with critical and personal estimates of the man and the writer by Joel Chandler Harris, Julian Hawthorne, E. E. Hale, Francis Wilson, and Edmund Clarence Stedman. Stedman says:

"Of all moderns, then, here or in the old world, Eugene Field seems to be most like the survival or revival of the ideal jester of knightly times; as if Yorick himself were incarnated, or as if a superior bearer of the bauble at the court of Italy, or France, or of the English King Hal, had come to life again — as much out of time as Twain's Yankee at the court of King Arthur; but not out of place, for he fitted himself as aptly to his folk and region as Puck to the fays and mortals of a wood near Athens. . . . To come to the jesters of history — which is so much less real than fiction — what laurels are greener than those of Triboulet, and Will Somers, and John Heywood, dramatist and master of the King's merry interludes? Their shafts were feathered with mirth and song but pointed with wisdom; and well might old John Trussell say: — 'It often happens that wise counsel is more sweetly followed when it is tempered with folly, and earnest is the less offensive if it be delivered in jest.' Yes, Field 'caught on' to his time — a complex American, with the obstreperous *bizarrerie* of the frontier and the artistic delicacy of our oldest culture always at odds with him; but he was above all a child of nature, a frolic incarnate, and just as he would have been in any time or country. Fortune had given him that unforgettable mummer's face, that clean-cut, mobile visage, that animated natural mask. No one else had so deep and rich a voice for the reading of the music and pathos of a poet's lines; and no actor ever managed both face and voice better than he in delivering his own verses, merry or sad."

RICHARD BURTON

TO THE PASSING SAINT

CHRISTMAS

From 'A Second Book of Verse.' Copyright, 1892, by Julia Sutherland Field. Reprinted by permission of Charles Scribner's Sons, publishers, New York

AS tonight you came your way,
Bearing earthward heavenly joy,
Tell me, O dear saint, I pray,
Did you see my little boy?

By some fairer voice beguiled,
Once he wandered from my sight;
He is such a little child,
He should have my love this night.

It has been so many a year —
  Oh, so many a year since then!
Yet he was so very dear;
  Surely he will come again.

If upon your way you see
  One whose beauty is divine,
Will you send him back to me?
  He is lost, and he is mine.

Tell him that his little chair
  Nestles where the sunbeams meet;
That the shoes he used to wear
  Yearn to kiss his dimpled feet;

Tell him of each pretty toy
  That was wont to share his glee;
Maybe that will bring my boy
  Back to them, and back to me.

O dear saint, as on you go
  Through the glad and sparkling frost,
Bid those bells ring high and low
  For a little child that's lost!

O dear saint, that blessest men
  With the grace of Christmas joy,
Soothe this heart with love again —
  Give me back my little boy!

DUTCH LULLABY

From 'A Little Book of Western Verse.' Copyright, 1889, by E. Field. Reprinted by permission of Charles Scribner's Sons, publishers, New York

WYNKEN, Blynken, and Nod one night
  Sailed off in a wooden shoe —
Sailed on a river of misty light
  Into a sea of dew.
"Where are you going, and what do you wish?"
The old moon asked the three.

"We have come to fish for the herring-fish
That live in this beautiful sea;
Nets of silver and gold have we,"
Said Wynken,
Blynken,
And Nod.

The old moon laughed, and sung a song,
As they rocked in the wooden shoe;
And the wind that sped them all night long
Ruffled the waves of dew;
The little stars were the herring-fish
That lived in the beautiful sea.
"Now cast your nets wherever you wish,
But never afraid are we!"
So cried the stars to the fishermen three,
Wynken,
Blynken,
And Nod.

All night long their nets they threw
For the fish in the twinkling foam,
Then down from the sky came the wooden shoe,
Bringing the fishermen home;
'Twas all so pretty a sail, it seemed
As if it could not be;
And some folks thought 'twas a dream they'd dreamed
Of sailing that beautiful sea.
But I shall name you the fishermen three,
Wynken,
Blynken,
And Nod.

Wynken and Blynken are two little eyes,
And Nod is a little head,
And the wooden shoe that sailed the skies
Is a wee one's trundle-bed;
So shut your eyes while mother sings
Of wonderful sights that be,
And you shall see the beautiful things
As you rock on the misty sea,
Where the old shoe rocked the fishermen three,
Wynken,
Blynken,
And Nod.

IPSWICH

From 'A Second Book of Verse.' Copyright, 1892, by Julia Sutherland Field. Reprinted by permission of Charles Scribner's Sons, publishers, New York

IN Ipswich, nights are cool and fair,
  And the voice that comes from the yonder sea
Sings to the quaint old mansions there
  Of "the time, the time that used to be";
And the quaint old mansions rock and groan,
And they seem to say in an undertone,
With half a sigh and with half a moan: —
  "It was, but it never again will be."

In Ipswich, witches weave at night
  Their magic spells with impish glee,
They shriek and laugh in their demon flight
  From the old Main House to the frightened sea,
And ghosts of eld come out to weep
Over the town that is fast asleep;
And they sob and they wail, as on they creep: —
  "It was, but it never again will be."

In Ipswich riseth Heart-Break Hill,
  Over against the calling sea;
And through the nights so deep and chill
  Watcheth a maiden constantly —
Watcheth alone, nor seems to hear
Over the roar of the waves anear
The pitiful cry of a far-off year: —
  "It was, but it never again will be."

In Ipswich once a witch I knew —
  An artless Saxon witch was she;
By that flaxen hair and those eyes of blue,
  Sweet was the spell she cast on me.
Alas! but the years have wrought me ill,
And the heart that is old and battered and chill
Seeketh again on Heart-Break Hill
  What was, but never again can be.

Dear Anna, I would not conjure down
  The ghost that cometh to solace me;
I love to think of old Ipswich town,
  Where somewhat better than friends were we:
For with every thought of the dear old place
Cometh again the tender grace
Of a Saxon witch's pretty face,
  As it was, and is, and ever shall be.

AMERICAN POETRY SINCE 1900

THE last decade of the nineteenth century closed a long and remarkably uniform epoch in American poetry. With the death of Lowell in 1891, Whittier and Whitman in 1892, and Holmes in 1894, there passed a tradition that had not only dominated poetry for the better part of a century, but had defined it. The bearded and benignant faces of these poets, with those of Bryant and Longfellow, dead a few years earlier, were known in every schoolroom; and their poems,

> Not too bright and good
> For human nature's daily food,

were in all hearts. Even the rebel Whitman had become " the good gray poet." And although some of the younger choir were beginning to sing, no poet either at the time or in the succeeding third of a century has so surely commanded the love of the great mass of Americans.

The dominance of the established tradition was shown by the slight regard paid to Emily Dickinson, who had died in 1886, but whose poems, beginning to be published in the nineties, had to wait a generation for full recognition. Strikingly individual in imagery, careless of syntax and rhyme, daring in thought, they appeared at that time wilfully perverse. It remained for the second decade of the twentieth century to place her, with Poe and Whitman, in the first rank of American poets. She could condense a whole picture in a single phrase:

> The reticent volcano keeps
> His never slumbering plan;

The sea,

> An everywhere of silver
> With ropes of sand
> To keep it from effacing
> The track called land.

Bells, that

> Leap upon their silver feet
> In frantic melody.

The snake, that " narrow fellow in the grass ":

> Yet when a child, and barefoot,
> I more than once, at morn,

Have passed, I thought, a whip-lash
Unbraiding in the sun,
When, stooping to secure it,
It wrinkled, and was gone.

More than that, the arrows of her slender songs pierced the depths of human experience and the heights of philosophic thought. In one poem, she tells the secret of her peculiar power of condensation:

To make a prairie it takes clover
        and one bee —
One clover and a bee
And reverie.
The reverie alone will do
If bees are few.

With "one clover and a bee and reverie" Miss Dickinson made a microscopic universe large enough to contain the major issues of life and love, of sorrow and death, of nature and God. Her century, however, preferred its prairies fuller of clovers and bees, and not so full of reverie.

The immediate poetic hope of the times seemed to lie in the youthful revolt to nature, exhilarating in the nineties though somewhat mild in retrospect, of Richard Hovey and Bliss Carman, in 'Songs from Vagabondia' (1894) and successive volumes in 1896 and 1900. Hovey, who died in 1900 in the first flush of power, is still remembered for the 'Stein Song' dear to college glee clubs. Carman, a Canadian poet of deserved repute, has since published many volumes celebrating with lyric grace and vigor the simple delights of out-of-door life; his singing quality and vividness of image may be illustrated by the lines

The scarlet of the maples can shake me like a cry
Of bugles going by,
And my lonely spirit thrills
To see the frosty asters like a smoke upon the hills.

Revolt of another sort, that had wide recognition at the time, was voiced in Edwin Markham's 'The Man with the Hoe' (1899), which took the stooped figure of Millet's painting as symbolic of the laboring classes crushed and dehumanized by toil, and demanding to be restored to "the upward looking and the light." Two years later, Markham wrote 'Lincoln, the Man of the People,' continuing with fresh vigor the poetic tradition by which, from Whitman and Lowell to Fletcher and Benét, the figure of Lincoln has become a sort of American King Arthur, whom each poet molds into the likeness of his own ideals.

By the turn of the century, there had emerged the important figure of William Vaughn Moody. Taking upon himself the rôle of poet as prophet, he turned a mind well stored with the major classics, from Æschylus down, upon the problems of the new day. In 'Gloucester Moors' he imaged the world a gallant ship steering through space but not knowing her port, commanded by a "ruthless few," while the rest lay battened in the slaver's pen. In 'The Menagerie' he gave a spiritual and moral interpretation to evolution, the age-long strife of nature to achieve man —

> but, mind you, perfect Man,
> The radiant and the loving, yet to be —

and pictured the satiric laughter of the menagerie animals, nature's botchwork, at her finished job,

> A little man in trousers, slightly jagged.

The untamed and destructive dominance of machinery is his theme in 'The Brute.' Public affairs also inspired him; 'The Quarry' is a protest against the threatened partition of China; 'An Ode in Time of Hesitation' and 'To a Soldier Fallen in the Philippines' give passionate expression to his belief that annexation of the Islands was a betrayal of national honor. Woman triumphing in revolt is the theme of 'The Death of Eve'; aged Eve, about to die, returns to the Garden and dances about the Tree, chanting to God,

> "Behold, against thy will, against thy word,
> Against the wrath and warning of thy sword,
> Eve has been Eve, O Lord."

In the dramatic trilogy left unfinished at Moody's death, which was to sum up his philosophy, Eve was the figure chosen to achieve the final reconciliation between Man and God, disrupted by the revolt of Prometheus and the Judgment necessitated by the logic of the universe.

These themes, often so modern, were embodied in a style of high seriousness, richer and loftier, at times, than anything in our earlier poetry, though clearly in the established poetic tradition. It was a style removed from the common speech sometimes to a degree that now seems artificial:

> to my listening heart
> The still earth doth empart
> Assurance of her jubilant emprise.

In many passages, it rose to a high dignity, as in the long crescendo of the spread of springtime over the continent, in the 'Ode in Time of Hesitation':

And on to where the Pictured Rocks are hung,
And yonder where, gigantic, wilful, young,
Chicago sitteth at the northwest gates,
With restless violent hands and casual tongue
Molding her mighty fates,
The Lakes shall robe them in ethereal sheen;
And like a larger sea, the vital green
Of springing wheat shall vastly be outflung
Over Dakota and the prairie states.

Great lyric beauty there is, too, as in the stanzas of 'Gloucester Moors' describing the earth sailing through space:

This earth is not the steadfast place
We landsmen build upon;
From deep to deep she varies pace,
And while she comes, is gone.
Beneath my feet I feel
Her smooth bulk heave and dip;
With velvet plunge and soft upreel
She swings and steadies to her keel
Like a gallant, gallant ship.

Memorable, too, are Pandora's songs in 'The Fire Bringer,'

Of wounds and sore defeat
I made my battle stay,

and the exquisite 'I Saw the Spring and Summer Pass,' with its concluding lines that have a mystical simplicity suggestive of Blake.

Moody's poems, which had appeared at intervals from 1900, were collected in 1912, two years after his death. During these twelve years, poetry had kept, in the main, to conservative, even to academic, channels, and within these channels had not flowed with great profusion. George Santayana, philosopher and mystic, published in 1910 his collected sonnets, inspired (as he says in the edition of 1923) not "by exactly an English Muse, but the same, or the ghost of the same, that visited Boëthius or Alfred de Musset or Leopardi." George E. Woodberry, John Erskine, William Ellery Leonard were, like Moody, university poets of distinction, though of less range. Percy MacKaye and Josephine Preston Peabody, recognized lyric poets, attempted the revival of romantic drama in verse; Miss Peabody's 'The Piper' was probably the most successful of these plays, though MacKaye's 'Fenris the Wolf' has more intensity. Edith Thomas wrote a number of competent, graceful lyrics, the best known of which, with its note of proud finality, is 'Frost Tonight.' Lizette Woodworth Reese had long been writing simply phrased short poems rich in controlled emotion, that remain fresh when much verse of greater pretensions has faded; her sonnet 'Tears' is rightly in all the anthologies. Anna Hempstead Branch sang with sincere note the spiritual meanings of commonplace toil. More widely read, perhaps, were the conventionally pleasant verses of Henry Van Dyke, and the conventionally raucous 'Yukon Ballads' of Robert W. Service. George Sterling and Madison Cawein carried on, through numerous volumes, the romantic tradition without quite the romantic fire. Among these poets were a few reaching out towards the newer day, but with very little recognition; on the whole, there appeared to be nothing very new or significant to sing, and no way to sing it except to tunes that were getting too familiar.

Then, in the years 1912 to 1915, under the leadership of a few outstanding poets, occurred what amounted to a revolution in both the substance and the form of poetry. In substance, it was a revolution to realism; a recognition of the truth about both the outer and the inner life of modern times, followed by a revivified and more sincere idealism. In form, it was a discarding of the highly wrought verse technique of romanticism, and a substitution for it of the vocabulary and sentence form of colloquial speech, put into all sorts of experimental rhythms. Many of these were based on the natural rhythms of spoken prose, literal, or heightened by emotion. Many sought new and artificial patterns, either in more varied groupings of syllable and stress, or in rhythms taken from the Orient or from primitive races, or merely in artifices of printing and spacing on the type-page. The new movement was encouraged by a sudden development of poetry societies, poetry magazines, anthologies, annual prizes, and especially by the active championship and provocative criticism of Harriet Monroe, William Marion Reedy, Amy Lowell, and others. Like the Elizabethan and the Romantic movements, it rested upon a very widespread production, in the spirit of free experimentation, and with the concomitant "lunatic fringe." Its ultimate success, however, rests mainly upon the contributions of certain outstanding men and women whose work has by this time won such general recognition that it seems likely to endure.

Of these, Edwin Arlington Robinson has generally been accorded a first place, because of his sustained integrity both of thought and of style. Exactly contemporary by birth with Moody, and like him making his first appeal to the public in the nineties, he belongs to a later generation not only in popular recognition, but in the form and substance of his thought. A severe literalness, stripped both of romantic image and of lyric emphasis, and a corresponding restraint and even understatement of emotion, give his poems the superficial appearance of a cold intellectuality. Below the surface, however, glows an intense and passionate realization of the comic and tragic ironies of life. Graver and less buoyant than Browning, Robinson is like him in his absorption in the problems of human character. His people are defined with dramatic clearness: the romanticist, Miniver Cheevy, born too late; Aunt Imogen, who

> Could make stars out where once had palled
> A future's emptiness;

and that unnamed Poor Relation, whose " memories go foraging for bits of childhood song they treasure "; old Isaac and Archibald, tapping the cider barrels or playing seven-up in heaven; Uncle Ananias,

> Wearing upon his forehead, with no fear,
> The laurel of approved iniquity;

Eben Flood, friendless and old, with his jug, convivially welcoming himself home in the moonlight. Robinson is interested in the world's failures. He takes Captain Craig —

> . . . old and hungry, but the worst of it
> Was a forlorn familiar consciousness
> That he had failed again —

and makes him the exponent of a philosophy of cosmic humor:

> You quiver and you clutch
> For something larger, something unfulfilled,
> Some wiser kind of joy that you shall have
> Never, until you learn to laugh with God.

In his rendering of the Arthurian romances ('Merlin,' 'Lancelot,' and 'Tristram') Robinson follows the external details of the old legends much more closely than did Tennyson. But his tales are even further than Tennyson's 'Idylls' from the medieval; he invests the characters with modern minds, self-critical and self-torturing, and the lists they fight in are those of the spirit. Love and hate alike, coming against the inexorable law of life and fate, resolve themselves, in defeat, into compassionate understanding, or into compassion without understanding. Even King Mark, the villain of the piece in old story, finally condemns neither the guilty lovers nor Andred who slew them:

> " I am not sure that you have not done well.
> God knows what you have done. I do not know.
> There was no more for them — and this is peace."

Arthur, as he waits in the dawn for news of the execution by fire to which he has condemned Guinevere, undergoes a mental torture that consumes both his personal anger and his sense of the obligation to punish guilt, and leaves only a flame of pity for her amid the flame. Lancelot's surrender of her to the king, the scene of Gawaine's death and that of the final parting of Lancelot and Guinevere at Almesbury, reveal a depth of tragic suffering and of grave beauty in their acceptance of a fate that transcends human passion.

Robert Frost's first widely popular book, 'North of Boston' (1914) was called by himself "this book of people." Tragedies of the isolated hill farms of New England, like 'The Death of the Hired Man,' 'Home Burial' (the barrier between the man who must dig his child's grave, and the wife who thinks him callous), 'A Servant to Servants' (the lone and overworked woman on the brink of insanity) are quietly told in an unstressed blank verse that never departs from the simple patterns of daily speech, and that by characteristic New England restraint keeps the emotion wholly sincere and utterly poignant. 'The Code' reveals with grim humor the explosive sensitiveness of the silent farm-hand, who explains to the city employer that

> The hand that knows his business won't be told
> To do work better or faster — those two things,

and tells a story of how he had taken offense at a boss for trying to hurry him in the hayfield, and had buried him under a whole rackful of hay.

> "Weren't you relieved to find he wasn't dead?"
> "No! yet I don't know — it's hard to say.
> I went about to kill him fair enough."
> "You took an awkward way. Did he discharge you?"
> "Discharge me? No! He knew I did just right."

In the same volume are several poems, 'Mending Wall,' 'After Apple Picking,' 'The Woodpile,' of a quality peculiarly Frost's own. The familiar aspects of farm and hill are given with, apparently, the utmost simplicity and literalness, yet with unspoken implications of wider meaning. While neither explicitly didactic like Wordsworth, nor patently symbolic, like Blake, Frost constantly suggests, like these, meanings below the fact he so objectively gives. In 'The Runaway' (from 'New Hampshire,' 1923), one may read a comment on all youthful inexperience and terror into the literal picture of the little Morgan colt running away in fright, at his first sight of snow; and the lovely 'Spring Pools' (from 'West Running Brook,' 1928) hints at more than actual pools or actual trees

> that have it in their pent up buds
> To darken nature and be summer woods —
> Let them think twice before they use their powers
> To blot out and drink up and sweep away
> These flowery waters and these watery flowers
> From snow that melted only yesterday.

Frost's later poems show a ripening and sweetening like that of celery or winter apples in the sharp air of the north; with no loss of his sense of reality, he has gained in a humorous tolerance of the universe.

Edgar Lee Masters, in 'The Spoon River Anthology' (1915), drew a realistic picture of the sinister aspects of village life, through the imaginative device of making the tombstones reveal the hidden secrets of the dead. In compact little vignettes, with the hardness of steel engravings, the inner stories of more than two hundred men and women are laid bare; stories of misshapen lives, of hidden lusts and cruelties, of unrealized hopes, of brutal deaths. There is an attempt to include also more idealistic figures; but except for a few, like Anne Rutledge, Father Malloy the priest, and ninety-six-year-old Lucinda Matlock, the last of the pioneers, these are less alive than the thwarted or unfulfilled characters of the earlier pages. The village photographer Rutherford McDowell sums up the essential thought of the book:

> And these grandchildren and great-grandchildren
> Of the pioneers! —
> Truly did my camera record their faces, too,
> With so much of the old strength gone,
> And the old faith gone,
> And the old mastery of life gone,
> And the old courage gone,
> Which labors and loves and suffers and sings
> Under the sun!

Masters has published other volumes, including a 'New Spoon River' (1924), but the original 'Spoon River Anthology' remains his most significant work, and claims an important place in the literature of the exposure of village life, so widely developed in the novels of the period.

Carl Sandburg, in 'Chicago Poems' (1916) and successive books to 'Good Morning, America' (1928), assuming the mantle of Whitman, speaks for continental America. The change of idiom, since Moody wrote, may be shown by contrasting his lines

> Chicago sitteth at the northwest gates . . .
> Molding her mighty fates

with Sandburg's

> Hog Butcher for the World,
> Tool maker, Stacker of Wheat,
> Player with Railroads and the Nation's Freight Handler;
> Stormy, husky, brawling,
> City of the Big Shoulders.

The highly imaginative titles of these volumes ('Chicago Poems,' 'Smoke and Steel,' 'Slabs of the Sunburnt West,' 'Good Morning, America') show the range of his subjects — the skyscraper, the slaughter-house, the steel mills, the harvest fields, the stretches of prairie and desert; he presents America as a sort of uncouth democratic giant, working amid much turmoil and crudity but greeting the future with confident good cheer. And he is a visionary, this giant of the new America:

The skyscrapers fasten their perpendicular alphabets far across the changing
 silver triangles of stars and streets.
And who made 'em? Who made the skyscrapers?
Man made 'em, the little two-legged joker, Man.
Out of his head, out of his dreaming, scheming sky piece,
Out of proud little diagrams that danced softly in his head —
 Man made the skyscrapers.

It seems curious that from the vast breadth of Sandburg's work, the most quoted of his poems should be that whimsical bit of imagery,

The fog comes
On little cat feet.

Yet scattered through his volumes are many fresh and colorful little glimpses of natural beauty for which he tempers his voice to a lyric delicacy. Such is the 'Nocturne in a Deserted Brickyard,' in which in the moonlight

Fluxions of yellow and dusk on the waters
Make a wide dreaming pansy of an old pond in the night,

and 'Night Stuff,' with the moon "a lovely woman, a lonely woman, lost in a silver dress, a circus rider's dress."

Sandburg, more than any American poet, was able to express the vast and tragic disaster of the World War. In 'Statistics,' Napoleon, roused in the old sarcophagus by the sound of twenty-one million men, turns back to his long sleep:

It is not my world answering;
It is some dreamer who knows not
The world I marched in
From Calais to Moscow.

'Killers' gives relentlessly the horror of millions of men

Fixed in the drag of the world's heartbreak,
Eating and drinking, toiling on a long job of killing.

'Grass,' in its restraint, its finality, is the best:

Pile the bodies high at Austerlitz and Waterloo.
Shovel them under and let me work:
I am the grass; I cover all.

And pile them high at Gettysburg,
And pile them high at Ypres and Verdun.
Shovel them under and let me work.
Two years, ten years, and passengers will ask the conductor:
What place is this?
Where are we now?

I am the grass.
Let me work.

The democratization of poetry which Sandburg sought in irregular rhythms, in colloquial diction and slang, and in themes from industrial life, Vachel Lindsay sought in heavily stressed brass-band rhythms and in themes based on crowd emotions, particularly those of the primitive minded. His most characteristic poems are of the type he has named the "Higher Vaudeville," intended for platform chanting, and full of the echoes of banjos and tambourines, bass drums and automobile horns. In some, he tries to revive primitive choral effects in which the leader is answered by a chanting crowd on the refrain. His most imaginative poem is 'The Congo,' in which drunken negroes in a saloon, gay negroes dancing the juba, or pious ones going into a trance under the preacher's spell, call up visions of the African jungle:

Then I saw the Congo, creeping through the black,
Cutting through the jungle with a golden track —

and of the terror inspired by the witch-men and "Mumbo Jumbo, god of the Congo."

With these attempts to take poetry out of the books and the colleges and restore it to the common people may be placed the very active collecting of folk-poetry in the southern Appalachians, of songs and ballads of cowboys and frontiersmen, of sailors' chanteys, of the lore of that cosmic lumberman Paul Bunyan, as well as that great mass of songs of the people assembled by Carl Sandburg under the title 'The American Songbag.'

Not all experimentation was in the direction of the language or the emotions of the people. There were very active groups of literary and esthetic theorists, drawing from the history of poetics or from foreign literatures authority for new techniques. The "Imagists" formulated a creed based, essentially, on the connotative power of exact images freshly seen and phrased with precision; they used a variety of rhythmic forms, from free verse to a sort of medley of prose and doggerel called polyphonic prose. Among this group, "H. D." (Mrs. Richard Aldington) achieved a severe beauty in her carefully engraved cameos on Greek themes; John Gould Fletcher, whose poems are full of the splendor of light and color, painted Venetian canvases of the Mississippi, the deserts, and the far West; Amy Lowell, influential as much for her ardent championship of the newer forms as for her own experiments with them, produced some poems sparkling with sunlight. The opening lines of her 'City of Falling Leaves'; the bright and delicate 'Venus Transiens'; the startling 'Night Clouds,' in which

> The white mares of the moon are all standing on their hind legs
> Pawing at the green porcelain doors of the remote heavens,

all show her delight in movement and color. 'Patterns' seems likely to survive as a beautiful expression of the frustrated passion of a woman whose lover has been killed in war.

Experimental in a different direction is the early work of Alfred Kreymborg, leader of a group of radical poets called "Others." His first volume, 'Mushrooms' (1916), was full of oddities, kept from being altogether freakish by humor and imagination. A number of poets were, like him, striving for a new idiom in verse which should be very brief, compact, and suggestive. Adelaide Crapsey, a scholar in the field of metrics, invented a five-line form which she named "Cinquains":

> There be
> Three silent things:
> The falling snow . . . the hour
> Before the dawn . . . the mouth of one
> Just dead.

Emily Dickinson would have liked this form. Several poets, including Miss Lowell and Mr. Fletcher, sought similar effects in Chinese and Japanese verse patterns.

In the more conventionally lyric forms, a number of poets wrote with intensity of feeling and with well developed command of a varied technique. Sarah Teasdale's brief songs of personal emotion, classical in their restraint and finished art, reveal a nature deeply sensitive to beauty. Edna St. Vincent Millay's verse has a rare lyric quality. While some of it has a pose of either sensual sentimentalism or flippancy, it more frequently sounds depths of beauty, either mystical, as in her first poem, 'Renascence,' or austere, as in her later sonnet, 'Euclid Alone Has Looked on Beauty Bare.' In 'The Buck in the Snow' (1928) is a group of tragic poems inspired by the execution of Sacco and Vanzetti:

Wine from these grapes I shall be treading surely
Morning and noon and night until I die.
Stained with these grapes I shall lie down and die.

Intimately personal as much of her poetry is, the deeper impersonal note is often heard as an undertone; and one divines something like a pledge in one of her later sonnets:

Have done with blossoms for a time, be bare;
Split rock; plunge downward; take heroic soil;
Deeper than bones — no pasture for you there;
Deeper than water, deeper than gold and oil:
Earth's fiery core alone can feed the bough
That blooms between Orion and the Plough.

Of other lyrists there is not room to speak. There are many — Braithwaite's Year Book for 1926 lists over seventeen hundred writers whose poems were accepted in magazines of the preceding year. Not all, of course, have any real pretensions; but a considerable number of them have long been esteemed, and many others have yet to show whether they are real stars or fireflies, who, to quote Frost,

Though they never equal stars in size
(And they were never really stars at heart)
Achieve at times a very star-like start.
Only of course they can't sustain the part.

The new movement in poetry has been almost wholly concerned with lyric and short narrative forms. Sustained narrative on a limited scale was attempted by Miss Lowell in 'Can Grande's Castle' (1918) and 'Legends' (1921), short tales in highly colorful verse. John G. Neidhardt has been working for years on an historical narrative of epic proportions on pioneering in the West; three sections already published ('The Song of Hugh Glass,' 1915, 'The Song of the Three Friends,' 1919, 'The Song of the Indian Wars,' 1925) show power to sustain a story of serious interest, and to portray character. William Ellery Leonard, in 'Two Lives' (published 1925), sublimates an agonizing domestic tragedy to poetry of great beauty and idealism. Stephen Vincent Benét, in 'John Brown's Body' (1928), spreads a vast panorama of the Civil War, with something of the motion-picture structure; against a background of marching and counter-marching and the confusion of victory and defeat, typical characters appear and reappear in vividly drawn episodes, driven by forces that none of them understand, least of all John Brown himself, who becomes a symbolic figure of the new civilization.

In retrospect, one may ask what is the present outcome of the poetic turmoil of the past fifteen years. It is clear that we have gained much wider interest in poetry of many kinds, based on a belief in its vital importance. In technique, verse forms are handled with much greater flexibility and subtlety, and poetic diction is fresher, more vivid, and nearer to the spoken language of today. In substance, poetry is wider in range of subjects, more a part of contemporary life, more outspoken, and through the tonic effect of the realistic movement, committed to a more soundly based idealism.

Contemporary criticism of the new movement in poetry has been relatively abundant. Amy Lowell, in 'Tendencies in Modern American Poetry' (1917) presented with enthusiasm and analyzed with discernment the essentially new realism of Robinson, Frost, and Masters, the lyric idealism and cosmopolitanism of Sandburg, and the Imagist techniques of "H. D." and Fletcher. In 'A Critical Fable' (published anonymously in 1922) she turned against the shade of her distinguished relative the weapon of his own satiric couplets of 'A Fable for Critics' in an attempt to convince him of the superiority of modern verse. Louis Untermeyer, in 'The New Era in American Poetry' (1919) and Marguerite Wilkinson, in 'New Voices' (1919, 1921) stressed the discarding of outworn literary conventions and the intense interest shown by new poets in their own world. Conrad Aiken, in 'Scepticisms' (1919), acknowledging the richness of invention of many of the new poets, maintained that they were poor in art, in real distinction, and urged higher critical standards. John Livingston Lowes, in 'Convention and Revolt in Poetry' (1919) developed a general theory of the establishment of conventions and of recurrent reactions from them, and applied it specifically to the revolt then at its height. Various collections, such as Monroe and Henderson's 'The New Poetry' (1913; enlarged 1923), W. S. Braithwaite's 'Anthology of Magazine Verse and Yearbook of American Poetry' (annually since 1913), Jessie B. Rittenhouse's three 'Books of Modern Verse,' and Louis Untermeyer's 'Modern American Poetry' (1913, 1921, 1925) have also tended to shape and develop the poetry of today.

In general, it may be said that special pleading for the various extreme types of revolutionary poetry and heated attacks upon them, common in critical discussion ten years ago, have given way to a broader appraisal of the values inherent in the various experimental forms and new themes.

ALLAN ABBOTT

MODERN FICTION

FOR the purposes of this sketch modern American fiction signifies creative writing between 1900 and the present, a period of twenty-eight years divided into approximately equal parts by the Great War. Divergence between the fiction preceding 1914 and that following, not amazingly apparent a decade after peace, will increase with time as the deep channel cut through civilization becomes a definite boundary line. Although the shores of the chasm are actually separated by four years, today bridged by the more persistent of the older school and the more reflective of the new, yet gradually they will coalesce. On the hither side will lie the domain of the modern.

At the end of the nineteenth century, conventions of the Victorian age ruled America no less than England. Immigration waves had not beaten violently against our land with the steady sweep that later demanded the bulwark of the quota. Movement from farm to city, by which limits of rural life and urban life were sharply delineated, was barely under way. Promotion of labor-saving devices through electricity was only just begun. Not until the twentieth century was well advanced had the gasoline engine revolutionized travel through the automobile, later through the airplane. Not by two decades had the motion picture business swelled to the fourth largest industry of the earth. Mrs. Catt and her sisters, fighting in the rear-guard of valiant pioneers, had not yet won the battle for woman suffrage. Carrie Nation's hatchet had smashed the first saloon, but closing of all saloons was yet to find place in the Constitution alongside the abolition of slaves and the right of women to vote. The negro, roused from his long African sleep by the whip of slavery, and freed but a generation before into a world not realized, was only glimpsing his self-revelation in fiction. Dr. Freud's maleficent star, destined to be the lode of not a few novelists, was hidden behind the horizon. The dollar still had a purchasing value; division of a growing middle class had not yet separated the fabulously wealthy from the respectably poor; an aristocracy built on a mere hundred years held itself aloof from the lower social scale. The German Emperor patiently perfected a war machine, the day for whose operation was far off.

In the epoch of peace after the Civil War, peace ruffled briefly by the Spanish-Cuban episode, America grew in literary self-consciousness. Cooper, first historian of the frontier, himself a scion of Scott, had his descendants of the late nineteenth and early twentieth centuries in Hamlin Garland, Owen Wister, Mary Johnston, Gertrude Atherton, Stewart Edward White, and

Jack London. These, and others, told the sagas of pioneering extended through the years, whether in Virginia, the mid-West, the far West, or Alaska — sagas of the settler's life in Dakota or Minnesota, grimly realistic, or of the gold-seeker along the Yukon, stirringly romantic. Hawthorne and Poe, who owed something to the tale-of-terror school in England, but whose stories of fantasy and mystery are distinctively American, had been succeeded by no worthy descendants in the direct line but were to be represented by a collateral kinsman who, at the beginning of the century, was in his literary cradle — James Branch Cabell. The detective story, in the strictest sense America's one contribution to the types of English fiction, was renascent after a flourishing growth of Poe's poor offspring, the dime novel, in the tales of Anna Katharine Green and Melville Davisson Post. The novel of characterization, social life, and manners, heritage from Miss Burney and eighteenth-century England, was the greatest of American assets in the work of Henry James and William Dean Howells, already hard-pressed for supremacy by Edith Wharton, Booth Tarkington, and Ellen Glasgow, with no inconsiderable claims by Margaret Deland, Alice Brown, and others. The abundant humor of Mark Twain, the whimsicality of Stockton, and the gentle laughter of Joel Chandler Harris were passing, to be succeeded by the satirical fun-making of George Ade ('Fables in Slang,' 1902). Most distinguished of local colorists was Mary Wilkins (later, Mrs. Freeman), before whom Sarah Orne Jewett had painted delicate pastels of New England, and George W. Cable had framed glowing splashes of Creole Louisiana.

When the first decade of the new century swung round the corner, a host of writers was at work. An age of comparative leisure had produced them; forces suggested above were now moving them to expression, while stimulation of the magazine and book trade by demands of advertisers summoned them with a golden wand. Steady lights were climbing to noon or declining with greater or lesser effulgence toward the west. The year 1910 [1] was the year of Winston Churchill's 'A Modern Chronicle,' Irving Bacheller's 'The Master,' Robert W. Chambers' 'Ailsa Paige,' Harold Bell Wright's 'The Uncrowned King,' Arthur Train's 'C. Q., or In the Wireless House,' Emerson Hough's 'The Young Alaskans,' Gertrude Atherton's 'The Tower of Ivory,' Richard Harding Davis' 'Once Upon a Time,' James Brendan Connolly's 'Open Water,' Jack London's 'Burning Daylight' (and two other books), Basil King's 'Wild Olive,' Meredith Nicholson's 'The Siege of the Seven Suitors,' Melville Davisson Post's 'The Gilded Chair,' Helen R. Martin's 'Crossways,' Anna Katharine Green's 'The House of the Whispering Pines,' Edith Wharton's 'Tales of Men and Ghosts,' Alice Brown's 'Country Neighbors,' Mary Wilkins Freeman's 'The Green Door,' Albert Payson Terhune's 'The New Mayor,' Robert Herrick's 'A Life for a Life,' and too many

[1] The year of book publication. Some of these works were serialized earlier.

others to record.[2] The year 1911 was that of Hamlin Garland's 'Victor Olnee's Discipline,' Mary Johnston's 'The Long Roll,' Jean Webster's 'Just Patty,' Theodore Dreiser's 'Jennie Gerhardt,' Booth Tarkington's 'Beauty and the Jacobin,' Ellen Glasgow's 'The Miller of Old Church,' Eleanor Hallowell Abbott's 'The Sick-a-Bed Lady,' Kate Douglas Wiggin's 'Mother Carey's Chickens,' Carolyn Wells' 'The Gold Bag,' Samuel Hopkins Adams' 'Average Jones,' and Margaret Deland's 'The Iron Woman.' For some of these authors, the works mentioned are near the middle of their long lists; for others, near the end; from others the best was yet to come. From a survey of their novels, the pertinent deduction is that these men and women — today's older generation — were carrying on, for the most part, in traditional subject and style. Arthur Train's 'In the Wireless House' marks a new invention; Dreiser's 'Jennie Gerhardt,' with 'Sister Carrie' which had preceded it ten years earlier, drew into the realms of literature quite frankly a subject relegated, after Hawthorne made Hester Prynne immortal, to the background and dregs of American letters.

With the authors named above, and they are by no means all, who began to express themselves in the nineties or in the early nineteen hundreds, a number of new ones take their places. Zona Gale, in 'Friendship Village' (1908, 1909), does for Wisconsin what Mary Wilkins had done earlier for Vermont and Massachusetts, Alice Brown for New Hampshire, and Alice Hegan Rice for the Cabbage Patch of Louisville, Kentucky. Oliver Curwood, American engaged by the Canadian Government as exploratory and descriptive writer, published in 1908 'The Courage of Captain Plum,' first of twenty-five volumes he was to complete before his death in 1927. His descriptions of the vast Northland and his stirring narratives of the men who conquer it follow the trail of Jack London. Irvin S. Cobb, a reporter in New York, starred his birthplace, Paducah, Kentucky, with 'Back Home Sketches' (1912) and 'The Escape of Mr. Trim' (1913). The detective story found new exponents in Mary Roberts Rinehart, whose 'Circular Staircase' (1908) inaugurated her story-telling career (she has thirty or so volumes to her credit); and in Natalie Sumner Lincoln, whose 'Trevor Case' (1912) heads nearly

[2] With the tales of O. Henry (William Sydney Porter), who died in 1910, a new era of the short story was advanced. Although many of O. Henry's successors who wore fragments of his mantle fain would rid themselves of it, they could do so no more than they could set forward or backward their birth dates. His was the greatest influence on the short story of the remainder of this period under consideration, and that influence was toward democracy. His four million in Bagdad-on-the-Subway were substituted speedily for the old four hundred; servant girl, shop girl, and tramp became subject for romance or realism. He popularized the short story, both in subject matter and style. Edna Ferber, first among his followers, with 'Buttered Side Down' (1912) preceded only two years Fannie Hurst's 'Just Around the Corner' (1914); through both these women the O. Henry tradition is best and longest preserved. They have been affected through causes unforeseen by the man from whom they learned, but they are the most active of his earlier descendants, of those who bridge the years between 1914 and 1918.

a score of books. Kathleen Norris, to achieve first rank as writer of sentiment by the year 1920, appeared with 'Mother' in 1911. Peter B. Kyne, who was to evoke after 1920 the humor and the pathos of the Great War, published 'Three Godfathers' in 1913. Novels of characterization and manners, a number of them bordering on the problem novel, were written by Dorothy Canfield Fisher ('The Squirrel Cage,' 1912), by Charles G. Norris, husband of Kathleen and brother of Frank ('The Amateur,' 1915), and by Harry Leon Wilson, who after his 'Zig-Zag Tales' (1896) became recrudescent in 'Bunker Bean' (1912) and 'Ruggles of Red Gap' (1915).

With increasing emphasis on the child's right to be heard as well as seen, an unprecedented vogue of books about children, for adult reading, arose. Frances Hodgson Burnett's 'Little Lord Fauntleroy,' as remote as 1886, and Kate Douglas Wiggin's 'The Birds' Christmas Carol' (1888) had pointed the way, sentimentally enough; through Josephine Dodge Daskam's 'Madness of Philip' (1902) was contributed the needed element of humor, of which Mrs. Wiggin availed herself in 'Rebecca' (1903). Myra Kelly's 'Little Citizens' (1904) endeared the immigrant school-child to his fellow-townsmen of New York and to much of America besides. But of all fiction about pre-adolescents Booth Tarkington's Penrod and Sam tales are most mellow and most enduring; his village boys of the Middle West are rooted in the soil as are his young men and women of 'Seventeen' (1916) and 'Alice Adams' (1921).

By all these writers, old subjects and traditions were extended, adapted entertainingly, sometimes brilliantly, to the social, political, and ethical background of their day. With them, however, a few authors rose to prophesy certain things, to accomplish certain other things. Foremost among them Willa Cather, whose 'Troll Garden' (1905) was followed by 'Alexander's Bridge' (1912), revealed a depth of taste, simplicity of subject, and beauty of style, with no little of that originality associated with genius. 'O Pioneers!' (1913) and 'My Antonia' (1918) recount in epic fashion struggles with the soil, and the latter book introduces the immigrant in the biographical study of Antonia Cuzak. 'The Song of the Lark' (1915) again approaches biography in its carefully detailed study of Thea Kronberg and the attempt to explain her greatness. 'One of Ours,' which pursues the fortunes of Claude Wheeler from his western home to the front of war and his death in battle, won the Pulitzer Prize in 1922 — a prize annually awarded to the novel which best "presents the wholesome atmosphere of American life, and the highest standard of American manners and manhood." These first novels, augmented by 'The Professor's House' (1923) and 'Death Comes for the Archbishop' (1927) glow, through western and Mexican settings, with the author's appreciation of beauty and her respect for struggle, without which no drama can exist. Miss Cather's failure lies in not grasping as a whole the meaning of America. She catches fragmentary glimpses of the vision; she does not see it perfectly, completely. She who, from her early life in Virginia, her girlhood on the western plains, her years in Pennsylvania as teacher, her work in New York as editor, and her mature cosmopolitan years as writer, should be well endowed to gather into one volume the material of a greater epic, is limited to the individual scene and conflict. Within her limits she is superb.

James Branch Cabell, who in his earlier novels and stories relied upon the conventions of romance, turned (1913) to the search for and interpretation of a new beauty that never was on sea or land but existent, for him, in the scenes of his invention. His 'Domnei' (1920), first published as 'The Soul of Mellicent' (1913) and followed by 'Jurgen' (1919), 'Figures of Earth' (1921), and other fiction, grew from his desire to write perfectly of beautiful happenings, and his surrender of actuality, past or present, "because even the unobservant literary genius may notice that this life for the most part consists of ugly and stupid persons doing foolish things." His non-actual world is a "vastly superior place where the Dream is realized and everything which we knew was possible comes true . . . a world we have all glimpsed . . . have not entered, and have not ever forgotten." In his desire to preserve the glories of the Dream untarnished and to recreate them for the awakening of joy and magnanimity, Cabell is caviar to the general. He has cast off too many shackles of the real world to be followed easily by those who must live in it. He believes, with Gautier, that everything passes but art; he believes that clarity, beauty, and symmetry with tenderness, truth, and urbanity contribute to literary stability. If ideal love, ideal beauty, and a dream world belong to the romanticist, Cabell today stands supreme among romantic writers. Yet he has failed, in his failure to be god-like; for he casually scoffs, with a smile of cynicism, at his own creations and so betrays himself the idealist grown old. His own dream world appears to fail him: "Life may become symmetrical, well plotted, coherent, and rational"; but he has not found life so in the actual world; he has not found it so even in his vision.

Joseph Hergesheimer, after practising the art of writing for fourteen years, published (1914) 'The Lay Anthony,' first of a dozen volumes that place him with Willa Cather and James Branch Cabell as the first three artists in contemporary American literature. The struggles of Hergesheimer's characters are between the spirit and the flesh, with victory for the spirit, says the author himself, a victory which makes his books happy books. In the words of his friend Cabell, however, not one of Hergesheimer's five first novels varies from the formula of men laboring toward the unattainable, and a high questing foiled. In 'Mountain Blood' (1915), Makimmon makes a vain effort to atone; the heroes of 'The Three Black Pennys' (1917) flounder toward the beauty of a defiant carnal passion; the five persons of 'Java Head' (1919) know their failure foredoomed, "toward the capturing of one or another evincement of beauty, with the resultant bodily demolishment of three of them and the spiritual maiming of the others." 'Linda Condon' (1919), a story of "the service of beauty, of the old gesture toward the stars," is a story of beauty here never won nor realized. In connection with his spiritual themes, the author celebrates various ages of industry in America. There are the days of long clipper-ship voyages to China, early days of steel and iron in Pennsylvania, days of the Argonauts heading, in '49, for California. In his details of setting, dress, and speech, Hergesheimer's accuracy is an index to his backward reincarnation and to his identification of himself with his heroes of the past. He succeeds in making vivid that past, through an artistry peculiar to his own age.

From these three authors, who have declared explicitly or implicitly their desire to write beautifully about beautiful things, who point the way to a promised land they do not quite attain, a swift turn is necessary for a glance at Sinclair Lewis. Most pungent of present-day satirists, perhaps the first satirist American fiction has produced, Lewis preluded with 'Our Mr. Wren' (1914) the unmelodious bursts which have made common coinage of his self-minted "babbitt," and conferred peculiar significance upon the term, "main street." In satirizing the fatuously blatant business man and in striking at the foibles, weaknesses, and pretensions of the small town, Lewis chiefly won admiration. In 'Elmer Gantry' (1927), which turns the protestant cleric upon a spit and roasts him to a nice turn, he has played too mischievously with his Promethean gift. He has fractured if not broken the laws of good taste; to the Comstockians he has proclaimed his infamy. Of his power to see through hypocrisy, meanness, and cant there is no doubt; of his ability to display these sins, there is no doubt; of his essential fairness, sympathy, and greatness of spirit, there is grave doubt.

Mentioned above are most of the men and women of note who were fictionizing in America, if not always America, when the war broke. Many of these published throughout the war, their books reflecting the turbulence of the period. Some of them reported events at the front — Cobb, for example. Others near the scene fictionized the great conflict: Richard Harding Davis, in 'Somewhere in France' (1915) and 'The Deserter' (1917); Edith Wharton, in 'The Marne' (1918); Dorothy Canfield, in 'Home Fires in France' (1918). Since the war, the following continue their interpretations of the ever-changing present or reconstructions of the past with the freshness and skill demanded by the modern reader: Booth Tarkington, Hamlin Garland, Mary Johnston, Owen Wister, Robert W. Chambers, Gertrude Atherton, Mary Austin, James Branch Cabell, Mary Roberts Rinehart, Henry Kitchell Webster (with his not infrequent collaborator, Samuel Merwin), Albert Payson Terhune, Edith Wharton, Willa Cather, Dorothy Canfield, Edna Ferber, Fannie Hurst, the Norrises (Charles and Kathleen), Harold Bell Wright, Bess Streeter Aldrich, Theodore Dreiser, Sinclair Lewis, William Allen White, George Ade, Ellis Parker Butler, the Irwins (Wallace, Will, and Inez Haynes), and Irvin S. Cobb.

To the period after the war belong these and others of the earlier writers; separated from them, yet existing with them, is the clamant group labeled the younger generation. Time is unripe for appraising this new group which, in its radicalism, but manifests itself a part of the time spirit in the most chaotic time the world has ever experienced. Whether the newer fiction is to be buried as rubbish under its own swift crumbling and decay, or whether it is to originate subjects, thoughts, and styles different from any preceding, and persistently different, one must wait a half century to know.

What are the characteristics of this decade after the treaty of peace? How are they reflected in fiction? The first and greatest characteristic is lawlessness, lawlessness rooted primarily in the war and fertilized by the Eighteenth Amendment, lawlessness abetted by and abetting the break-up of moral, ethical, and religious standards. Old standards were tottering before 1914, their trembling was not wholly uncontributory to the war; reciprocally, the war threatened them with temporary abolishment or permanent destruction. More specifically, the decade following the war was the age of the gunman; the age of the single sex-standard; the age of the bootlegger, the hi-jacker, and the speak-easy. In fiction, the reflectors of these and their kindred are F. Scott Fitzgerald, Sherwood Anderson, Anita Loos, Ernest Hemingway, Percy Marks, Ben Hecht, Floyd Dell, Carl Van Vechten, John Dos Passos, and Viña Delmar. The novel of revolt and escape, long familiar, had been popularized by Upton Sinclair, Robert Herrick, Theodore Dreiser, and William Allen White. To it, Sherwood Anderson made a fresh contribution in 1916 with his first novel, 'Windy McPherson's Son,' and in succeeding works, which emphasize lawlessness in sex. Anderson is realistic, sober even to bitterness provoked by a sense of futility. Anita Loos's 'Gentlemen Prefer Blondes' accepts humorously an age-old sex relation which until 1925 hardly could have been treated so casually nor accepted so frankly and gratefully by a world that needed to laugh. Viña Delmar's 'Bad Girl' (1928) traces in detail the life of a prospective mother through the period of gestation; though it would have been barred from print a score of years ago, in April, 1928, it was chosen by the Literary Guild as the "book of the month." Floyd Dell, apostle of sex equality, is, by his own statement, the patriarch of the break-down of the family. 'An Unmarried Father' (1927) is logically sane in its implications; there is no reason why an unmarried father should not take care of the child deserted by the mother. The idea, worth considering, long had remained unconsidered. In 'Janet March' (1923) the wholesale sex profligacy is pointless enough, save as it reflects a not improbable condition among the young men and women indicated by the time and place of action. F. Scott Fitzgerald, with 'This Side of Paradise' (1920), betrayed the hitherto unconventional relations between flappers and collegians; Percy Marks, with 'The Plastic Age' (1924), gave answer to "What is wrong with the colleges?" by implied charges of dishonesty, drunkenness, and social leprosy. Ernest Hemingway's 'The Sun Also Rises' (1927) and 'The

Killers' (1928) appal through their nonchalant acceptance of crime, crime to which actors and victims are fatally indifferent.

Carl Van Vechten is not only a commentator but, like Ben Hecht, a satirist of the new day. Hecht's 'Count Bruga' (1926), while incidentally holding the mirror to a phase of contemporary life, pierces the too elaborately and therefore thinly disguised ego of a well-known poet type. Van Vechten, in 'Peter Whiffle' (1922), is concerned with the study of a would-be writer whose attempt to do something that he should not have attempted met with failure. The author's interest in Peter, however, ultimately converts satire into serious analysis; for as Peter himself is made to say, "And so I have learned that I cannot write. Is a little experience too much to pay for knowing oneself? I think not, and that is why, now, I feel more like a success than a failure, because finally I do know myself, and because I have left no bad work." . . . 'Spider Boy' (1928), half-picture of life in Hollywood, wholly satire of the movie kingdom, transfixes with blunt shafts the waste of wealth, lack of business honesty, and crimes in the name of art. 'The Blind Bow-Boy' (1923) had already taken a shot at the motion-picture world and elaborately travestied the triflings of the moneyed classes and the visiting titular great. Satirizing the literary ego, Anne Parrish's 'All Kneeling' (1928) exaggerates less than 'Count Bruga' or 'Peter Whiffle,' and therefore achieves, through scarcely more than an outline, a more convincing portrait as well as a more pertinent criticism.

Though satire begins its reign, sentiment is not dead: Margaret Widdemer, Nalbro Bartley, Sophie Kerr, Fannie Heaslip Lea, and others younger — many ephemeral as the day — prove the statement; Harold Bell Wright and Kathleen Norris continue to prove it. A return to American history and American biography, for subjects, is a wholesome breeze blowing across the miasma of sex novels, Freudian complexes, and libido quagmires. Honoré Willsie Morrow's 'We Must March' (1925), recounting the hazardous and tragic struggle of missionaries to the Oregon Indians around 1840; her 'Forever Free' (1926) and 'With Malice toward None' (1928), in their sympathetic studies of Lincoln, cannot but offset the biography of a transitory Harlem couple, and purge the present of fleeting agonies — agonies in a world arranged better than ever to make life worth living. Perhaps the most serious post-war "escape" novelist is Louis Bromfield, who undertakes in 'The Green Bay Tree' (1924), 'Possession' (1925), 'Early Autumn' (Pulitzer Prize novel of 1926), and 'A Good Woman' (1927) to create a screen of four panels depicting American family life. In the opinion of some critics, the most promising artist is Glenway Wescott, whose prize novel, 'The Grandmothers' (1927), was followed by a volume of stories, 'Good-bye Wisconsin' (1928). Both Bromfield and Wescott illustrate in their lives and works the growing literary interrelation of France and America that was strengthened by the war.

Through Americanization of foreigners from many lands, the native literature is modified and strengthened. Achmed Abdullah, from Afghanistan;

Konrad Bercovici, from Roumania; and Anzia Yezierska, from Russia — these have widened the sympathy and understanding of Pilgrim and Cavalier descendants. Through development of the negro race American literature receives also a tributary element: the short stories of Eric Walrond, Jean Toomer, and Arthur Huff Fauset — many of them found worthy of perpetuation in anthologies — have added color and richness to the Anglo-Saxon stream. The Jewish race, augmented by incoming numbers, has provided not a few of the writers listed above, and continues to complement the Gentile stock with shrewdness, humor, and philosophy. Among recent discussions of the Jewish race problem, mention should be made of Ludwig Lewisohn's 'The Island Within' (1928), which treats the subject from a wholly sympathetic point of view, and arrives at just conclusions. Political changes, including immigrant, negro and Jew, include also woman, whose shifting status as a result of constitutional amendment is best indicated in the stories of Margaret Culkin Banning. Humor, continued in the works of Cobb, Butler, and Ade, finds a new outlet in the whimsies of Don Marquis, whose 'When the Turtles Sing' (1928) is characteristic of his ways and means to provoke laughter; in the reportorial realism of Ring Lardner, at its best in 'How to Write Short Stories' (1924) and 'The Love Nest' (1926); and in the playful dalliance of Christopher Morley, notably in 'Where the Blue Begins' (1922), who recalls the delightful inconsequentialities of the author of 'Alice in Wonderland.' Besides these, two other humorists full-grown since the war have pleased millions of short story readers: Octavus Roy Cohen, by his dark-town folk of Birmingham, and H. C. Witwer, by his telephone girls and their kin, of New York City.

What has the new writer gained in style? Foremost of all, he has learned economy; he had to learn it, to serve his age; for despite all leisure-saving devices, the age lacks leisure. The novelist, for example, has taken a hint from the brief story writer in limitation of time and place; he has taken a further lesson from the longer stories as well as shorter stories of Henry James, who knew and practised perfectly adherence to a single point of view. To the acquirement of this technique the "stream of consciousness" novel owes its origin. He has produced a new form by combining the technique of the short story and the novel; for example, Thornton Wilder's 'The Bridge of San Luis Rey' (Pulitzer Prize novel, 1928) and Louis Bromfield's 'The Strange Case of Miss Annie Spragg' (1928). The writer of today describes in a sentence rather than a paragraph, in a phrase rather than a sentence. He writes, on occasion, lists of words which, controlled by some guiding principle, serve instead of sentences. He creates staccato effects which, unmelodious as they are, perhaps because they are, contribute to rapid reading. He is not static, but dynamic.[3] Gertrude Stein's experiments in word connotation have

[3] One current mechanical oddity is that appearing in the books of Van Vechten and a few others, a lack of quotation marks. Actually, this innovation contributes not to economy but to confusion; the step is regressive, toward the unpunctuated medieval manuscript.

operated to brevity; her disciples, Dorothy Richardson and May Sinclair, have extended her example; Carl Van Vechten, Fannie Hurst, and Edna Ferber have used it to smiting advantage. Among the extreme radicals is a straining for strangeness and a search for oddity. Ethel Kelly's 'Wings' (1924) begins with the end of the story; the final division of the book shows the beginning, and in a way vastly different from the mere reversal of chronological order. John Dos Passos' 'Manhattan Transfer' (1925), in its not unpraiseworthy attempt to portray agglomerative New York, leaps abruptly from one person, one fact, one incident to another person, fact, or incident apparently unrelated; yet by his agility and his suggestive glimpses of intercommunication, he compels the reader to see and to understand, in a measure, the many-faceted city.

By way of brief summary, our latest fiction is a realistic mirror of the present age; if the realism itself is an abortion or exaggeration, the mirror produces an effect of perverted romanticism. Current fiction reports life, but the work of no writer reports more than a small part of a single phase of life. The fictionist today does not, like Arnold's Sophocles, see life steadily or see it whole. If he describes a metropolitan night-club, he does so superbly; but that night-club is, after all, only a small part and a momentary part of the cosmic scene. Realism exists in unprecedented quantity and extremity; reality does not exist. The contemporary writer's relation to the American spirit is local rather than national; his vision is acute and clear for the immediate in time and place, hazy and blurred for the grand total of America past and present. He appears to lack a sense of comparison; he accepts the cash of the day and lets go the credit of the future. And this is to say that although he is an excellent time server, he lacks vision.

Freud's theories underlie, inevitably, most of these new writers. Joined with the staccato brevity of realism is a derivative psychology attempting, sometimes superficially enough, to account for the springs of behavior.[4] The first rule of the modern is "Be different"; if he is radical, "Be different at any cost." His second rule is "Obey no authority; smash the conventions." He forgets that by being ultra-this or ultra-that he places himself in a category no less highly conventionalized than that of the writers in the Classic Age of Dryden.

BLANCHE COLTON WILLIAMS

[4] A legitimate sphere for the operation of Freudian psychology is the detective novel. The most intellectual of all detective-story writers who have appeared since Poe is Willard Huntington Wright (S. S. Van Dine, pseudonym), whose 'Benson Murder Case' (1927) followed by 'The Canary Murder Case' (1927), 'The Greene Murder Case' (1928), and 'The Bishop Murder Case' (1929) all rely on scientific, psychological, and philosophical information, not obviously trumped up for the exploitation of a straw-man detective's knowledge, but growing out of the writer's deep acquaintance with science and philosophy.

MODERN AMERICAN DRAMA

THE contemporary drama in America has at length escaped from the leading strings of Europe. In the theater of Bronson Howard may be seen the transition from the rhetorical entertainment of a Dion Boucicault to the play that dispenses with outworn conventions, simplifies its technique, and finds inspiration in native sources. If a little too sensational or sentimental, he was in the main veracious and humorous. Humor, sentiment, and observation were combined, also, in the crude but effective entertainments of Harrigan and Hart and Charles E. Hoyt, and with far greater skill in the dramas of James A. Herne, whose 'Shore Acres' and 'Sag Harbor' are in the tradition of Denman Thompson's 'Old Homestead,' but simpler, stronger, more sincere.

Like Thompson and Herne, Augustus Thomas has made local color a point of departure for his plot in such plays as 'Alabama,' 'In Mizzoura,' 'The Hoosier Doctor,' 'Arizona,' and 'Colorado.' Thomas is versatile in accomplishment, stimulating in ideas, less concerned with the analysis of character than with its consistency, and the appropriate functioning of each in a general scheme. In precept and by example, he has commended the potency of deed and gesture apart from word. Of the score of plays that have come from his pen since 1890, some are semi-farcical, some are light legitimate comedy, like 'Mrs. Leffingwell's Boots,' and several are serious dramas, the best being 'The Witching Hour' and 'As a Man Thinks.' These and 'The Harvest Moon' rely in part upon belief in mental telepathy, and show their maker's theory that the theater should visualize notions "at the time in the public mind."

Clyde Fitch, the writer of some forty original pieces and a dozen adaptations, had no philosophy to impart, but his instinct for the picturesque, the amusing, and the locally characteristic was unerring. He had the historic imagination and the feeling for character to breathe life into historical personages and periods, as in 'Beau Brummell,' 'His Grace de Grammont,' and 'Barbara Frietchie.' He might draw now and then from the German or the French, but he was most happy in describing his countrymen abroad or at home. It was above all the New Yorker in his habitat that Fitch delighted to portray, the metropolitan now of an earlier period, as in 'Captain Jinks of the Horse Marines,' and now of the present, as in 'The Climbers,' 'The Truth,' and 'The City.'

William Gillette has written some sixteen pieces exploiting varied material, the best being his Civil War dramas, the most popular his 'Sherlock Holmes,' and the most amusing his farce comedies. He is a careful craftsman, and a master of rapid-fire dialogue, intent upon plot rather than character, but agreeable in his avoidance of the sentimental. More expert as a technician is David Belasco, who has produced singly and in collaboration a remarkable series of stage successes. Of his own work the best example is 'The Return of Peter Grimm.' To these plays, as to those that he has merely staged, Belasco has applied extraordinary skill in the arts of decoration, atmosphere, and lighting, carrying the mechanism of the theater to the highest point of calculated illusion. His influence has largely molded his associates, Warfield, Ditrichstein, De Mille, and Klein. The melodramas of Charles Klein in particular are devised with exact knowledge of just what settings, situations, words, and actions will keep the waves of emotion surging in the hearts of an eager audience. His most agreeable play is 'The Music Master,' his play of greatest strength and promise is 'The Lion and the Mouse.' In Klein's manner are George Broadhurst's study of political storm and stress, 'The Man of the Hour,' and of marital adjustment, 'Bought and Paid For.'

Somewhat richer, although cut from the same cloth, are such dramas as Eugene Walter's 'Paid in Full,' 'The Easiest Way,' and 'Fine Feathers,' treating journalistic subjects with a violent and unliterary directness. Zest in reproducing the form and pressure of the time may be observed, also, in the plays of Edward Sheldon, who, at twenty-two, took the public by storm with his vigorous representation of counter-currents in the city slums, 'Salvation Nell.' 'The Nigger' was more ambitious in its exhibition of racial antagonisms in the South. Sheldon's later works — 'Princess Zim-Zim,' 'Egypt,' 'The Song of Songs,' 'The Garden of Paradise,' and 'The Lonely Heart' — have scarcely realized the expectations aroused by his first efforts; but 'The Boss' and 'The Highroad' are excellent studies of character against a political background, and 'Romance' has achieved phenomenal success at home and abroad with its story of a clergyman's love for an opera singer acted out in retrospect as the former tells it to a youth who would marry an actress.

William Vaughn Moody will be remembered for a single play, 'The Great Divide,' a fortunate study of contrasts between two civilizations and codes of conduct. Admirable in conception, setting, and language, it suffers in execution from anti-climax and a psychology not thoroughly established. In 'The Faith Healer,' Moody endeavored to suggest the potency of love to restore faith and of faith to restore health, dealing with problems already considered in a spirit more sceptical by Björnson; but his ideal is one better suited to exposition in a novel than a play. His poetic imagination, yoked with realism in these two dramas, was given free rein in a metrical trilogy. But for the versified play adapted to theatrical performance, one must look to 'The Piper,' by Josephine Peabody (Mrs. Lionel Marks). Though given wide currency, its flagging movement after the first act, and its substitution for the dramatic of pictorial, lyrical, and spiritual appeal, could ensure it no continued run.

Another aspirant for poetic honors upon the stage is Percy MacKaye. His interest in theatrical reform has found expression in critical essays and experiments in pageantry, the most elaborate being 'Caliban by the Yellow Sands.' His delight in spectacle was earlier evidenced in 'The Canterbury Pilgrims,' and his poetic gifts in 'Fenris the Wolf,' 'Jeanne D'Arc,' and 'Sappho and Phaon.' In 'Mater' and 'Anti-Matrimony' appears a vein of satiric humor which turns to joyous fantasy in 'A Thousand Years Ago.' 'To-Morrow' has more of substance, but is less characteristic than his 'Yankee Fantasies' and 'The Scarecrow,' the last a clever adaptation of a tale by Hawthorne which has reached the French and the German theater. Interesting as an experiment in localized drama is 'This Fine Pretty World,' depicting an unscrupulous dreamer of the Kentucky mountains, a piece to be compared with such other plays of the provinces as Hatcher Hughes's 'Hell-Bent fer Heaven' and 'Ruint,' Lulu Vollmer's 'Sun-Up,' 'Shame Woman,' and 'Dunce Boy,' and Paul Green's 'Last of the Lowries,' 'Fixins,' 'The No 'Count Boy,' 'The Field God,' and 'In Abraham's Bosom.'

Dramatic romance, native and foreign, has been exploited by Milton Royle in 'The Squaw Man,' 'The Struggle Everlasting,' and 'Lancelot and Elaine'; by Booth Tarkington in 'Monsieur Beaucaire'; by Richard Walton Tully, in the Hawaiian 'Bird of Paradise,' the Persian 'Omar the Tent Maker,' and the Mexican 'Flame'; by George Hazelton and Harry Benrimo in the Chinese 'Yellow Jacket,' employing Oriental stage conventions; by Benrimo and Harrison Rhodes in the Japanese 'Willow Tree'; by Edward Knoblock in his 'Arabian Nights' fantasy 'Kismet'; by Philip Moeller, reviving interest in historical personalities with 'Madame Sand,' 'Molière,' and 'Sophie'; and by Edward Carpenter and Michael Flavin in 'The Cinderella Man,' 'Pipes of Pan,' 'Children of the Moon,' and 'Lady of the Rose.'

Several women have evinced marked dramatic talent, Zona Gale adapting for the stage two of her novels in 'Miss Lulu Bett' and 'Mr. Pitt'; Eleanor Gates writing an effective dream play, 'The Poor Little Rich Girl,' as well as 'We Are Seven'; and Zoë Akins revealing her originality in 'The Magical City,' 'Papa,' 'Daddy's Gone a-Hunting,' and 'The Texas Nightingale,' employing also the movie "cut-back" in 'The Varying Shore,' and scoring her principal success in 'Déclassée.' Susan Glaspell has satirized the Freudians in 'Suppressed Desires,' and shown the alternations of conservatism and radicalism in 'The Inheritors.' She has demonstrated her uncanny skill at analyzing motives of heroines unseen in her brief 'Trifles' and longer 'Berenice'; and, in 'The Verge,' she has produced a remarkable study of a neurasthenic heroine going mad. Clare Kummer, in such pieces as 'Good Gracious Annabelle,' 'Be, Calm, Camilla,' and 'Rollo's Wild Oat,' has exhibited her talents as a writer of the comedy of manners.

Most accomplished of all these women playwrights is Rachel Crothers, adroit in depicting locale in 'The Three of Us,' 'Once Upon a Time,' 'A Little Journey,' and 'Old Lady 39,' and also interested in ideas. Thus, 'A Man's World' considers the double standard; 'He and She' sets forth the dangers of professional rivalry between husband and wife; 'Young Wisdom' criticizes trial marriage; 'Nice People' thrusts at the post-war morals of the young; and 'Expressing Willie' laughs at the Freudian faith professed by esthetic poseurs.

Of male playwrights the name is legion. Langdon Mitchell and Jesse Lynch Williams have specialized in social comedy, the former dramatizing Thackeray in 'Becky Sharp' and 'Pendennis,' and doing an original play dealing with divorce in 'The New York Idea'; the latter, in 'Why Marry?' 'Why Not?' and 'Lovely Lady,' treating family life with humorous sanity. George Ade and Booth Tarkington have emphasized types, directing good-natured satire at American traits and conditions, Ade producing the 'County Chairman,' 'The College Widow,' 'Just Out of College,' and 'Father and the Boys,' and Tarkington presenting 'The Man from Home,' 'Getting a Polish,' 'Mr. Antonio,' 'The Country Cousin,' 'Clarence,' 'The Intimate Strangers,' 'Rose Briar,' and, with Harry Leon Wilson, an amusing defense of capital against labor in 'The Gibson Upright.'

George M. Cohan, equally a dramatist of types, has written merely to entertain, and achieves his purpose well in 'Forty-five Minutes from Broadway,' 'Get-Rich-Quick Wallingford,' 'Seven Keys to Baldpate,' and 'The Song and Dance Man.' The comedy of types has been cultivated, also, by James Forbes, Winchell Smith, and Frank Craven. Craven is the author of 'The First Year' and other amusing comedies. Forbes, after exploiting theatrical life in 'The Chorus Lady' and 'The Show Shop,' grew satiric, and in 'The Famous Mrs. Fair' poked fun at women war-workers, released by the Armistice yet restlessly carrying on to the neglect of their husbands and children. Smith, having won popularity in 'The Fortune Hunter,' 'The Boomerang,' 'Turn to the Right,' and 'Thank You,' broke all records for commercial success with 'Lightnin',' the living picture of a kindly "old soak" in the Rip Van Winkle tradition. This play ran nearly thirteen hundred consecutive nights in New York. It has since been far outdistanced by Anne Nichols' 'Abie's Irish Rose,' which, by reason of its plea for religious tolerance, its representation of romantic and paternal love, its contrast of familiar comic types, and its use of all the old jokes about Jews and Irishmen, has struck a chord responsive in the hearts of simple-minded millions.

George Kaufman and Marc Connelly have celebrated in collaboration the adorably stupid wife in 'Dulcy,' the winningly clever wife in 'To the Ladies,' and the movie-struck youth in 'Merton of the Movies.' They have drawn upon Continental inspiration for the technique of their imaginative dream satire, 'Beggar on Horseback,' which ranks high among such American ventures in expressionism as Elmer Rice's 'Adding Machine' and 'The Subway,' John Howard Lawson's 'Processional,' 'Roger Bloomer,' and 'Nirvana,' and certain of the later pieces of Eugene O'Neill. A touch of native fantasy colors the work of A. E. Thomas, Philip Barry, and Austin Strong — Thomas writing 'Just Suppose' and 'Come Out of the Kitchen'; Barry writing 'You and I,' 'In a Garden,' 'White Wings,' 'Paris Bound,' and 'Holiday'; and Strong writing 'Seventh Heaven' and 'A Play Without a Name,' one scene of which in expressionistic wise discloses to the audience the inside of the hero's cranium.

Character is the principal concern of certain other dramatists now in the public eye. Thus, Gilbert Emery exhibits it in his careful studies of domestic life, 'The Hero,' 'Tarnish,' and 'Episode'; and Owen Davis, author of numberless melodramas and of jolly farces like 'The Nervous Wreck,' has turned fairly serious in two character plays, 'The Detour' and 'Ice Bound.' Maxwell Anderson, author of a Dakotan tragedy of loneliness and jealousy, 'White Desert,' and of a tramp play, 'Beggars of Life,' and a domestic comedy, 'Saturday's Children,' has collaborated with Laurence Stallings in two historical romances, 'First Flight' and 'Buccaneer.' Earlier they wrote the most vivid of all indictments of militarism, 'What Price Glory,' expressing the disillusion following upon the World War and the instinctive heroism of certain rough bad men engaged in it. George Kelly and Sidney Howard are two other prominent creators of character in plays gay and grave. Kelly, in 'The Torch Bearers,' pays his respects to those who would attain social eminence through the Little Theater, and in 'The Show Off' he draws inimitably the bumptious, self-satisfied ass who triumphs in love and business by his very conceit. In 'Craig's Wife' he deepens his character study in drawing a selfish woman who values her husband less than the house he has given her. In 'Daisy Mayme' Kelly has displayed the rescue through marriage of a youth ignored and abused by his sisters. Sidney Howard, who began by adapting Melchior Lengyel's 'Sancho Panza' and writing a medieval play in verse called 'Swords,' has turned realistic in several character dramas. The first was 'They Knew What They Wanted,' which shocked the conservative by allowing a husband to accept as his own the child of his wife's chance lover. But the extenuating circumstances were ample; the California background and the portraits of an elderly Italian vine-grower, his young waitress bride, and his disloyal tramp friend proved delightful. Howard's later work includes 'Lucky Sam McCarver,' 'Ned McCobb's Daughter,' and 'The Silver Cord,' all sketching local conditions as incidental to the most careful painting of character.

Adept and versatile as are many of these dramatists, none can compete in originality or world-wide recognition with Eugene O'Neill. Beginning as a maker of one-act plays of the sea produced by the Provincetown Players, he first tried the long form in 'Beyond the Horizon,' an acute study of two brothers, one practical, and one a dreamer, both in love with the same girl yet devoted to each other. There followed such pieces short and long of lesser interest as 'Diff'rent,' 'The Straw,' 'The First Man,' and 'Gold.' Then came two striking successes, 'Anna Christie' and 'Desire Under the Elms.' The first is a comedy of character depicting a Scandinavian sailor-man afraid of "that ole Davil sea" and his erstwhile immoral daughter regenerated by love of the sea and the Irish castaway it brings her. The second is a grim and acrid tragedy of lust for the land and for woman giving the lie profanely to the pretty pictures of New England drawn by Whittier, Longfellow, Aldrich, and Mary Wilkins Freeman.

In wholly different vein, O'Neill, in 'The Fountain,' has written a symbolic romance based on Ponce de Leon's quest for eternal youth, and, in 'Marco Millions,' a poetic satire upon the obtuse Babbitt of Cathay, who, thinking only of gain, fails to appreciate the love of the princess whom he conducts to Persia. In 'Lazarus Laughed' O'Neill has grown lyrical over his hero's contempt for death, declaring that nothing that has been can cease to be. Although the critics at first had thought of O'Neill as a realist, he has defied all classification. He is a poet who uses reality freely only to transfigure it, lending a pulsing rhythm to the language of even his lowest characters, and in certain pieces adopting the methods of Continental expressionism to externalize symbolically mental processes. Thus, in 'The Emperor Jones,' 'The Hairy Ape,' 'The Great God Brown,' 'All God's Chillun Got Wings,' and 'Dynamo,' he departs from fidelity to appearance, allowing ideas to distort and stylize his pictures. He employs masks in a novel way in 'Brown' and in 'Lazarus,' spectral shapes in the 'Ape,' and projected thoughts in the constantly interpolated soliloquies of 'Strange Interlude.' Like his master Strindberg, he shows people obsessed or repressed, driven by inner urges that cannot be satisfied. He scorns mere happiness, finding in Greek and Elizabethan tragedy "a tremendous lift," that rouses to a deeper understanding of life. "I don't love life because it's pretty," he has said. "Prettiness is only clothes-deep. I am a truer lover than that. I love it naked." He confesses to finding the transfiguring nobility of tragedy "in seemingly the most ignoble, detested lives," and he seeks "to interpret Life in terms of lives, never just lives in terms of character." In short, O'Neill possesses the mystic's faith in a great unseen Force and would show in his plays "man in his glorious, self-destructive struggle to make the Force express him, instead of being, as an animal is, an infinitesimal incident in its expression." So, our most distinctive dramatist is not only an expert playwright but also a philosopher.

Frank W. Chandler

RECENT AMERICAN HISTORICAL WRITING

IN the year 1891 Professor J. Franklin Jameson published a little book of 160 pages on 'The History of Historical Writing in America.' George Bancroft had been in his grave but a few months. Francis Parkman had just completed his 'Montcalm and Wolfe,' that brilliant series of works on the French and the English in North America which he had begun forty years earlier with 'The Conspiracy of Pontiac.' Two years before (in 1889) there had appeared the final volume of Justin Winsor's monumental 'Narrative and Critical History of America,' with its graceful dedication to the editor's classmate, President Eliot of Harvard — the first serious work in the scientific collation of the source material in American history since the interrupted or frustrated labors of Sparks, Clark, and Force several decades before. It was the centennial year of the foundation of the Massachusetts Historical Society, but the American Historical Association was only seven years old and had as yet given little indication of stimulating and co-ordinating scientific historical work in the country. The publication of the first number of the American Historical Review was to wait for the year 1895, and Professor Jameson, who, until his recent resignation, presided so ably over the management of that Review for many years, wrote pathetically in 1891: "Meanwhile the scientific workers may find an avenue of publication through the hospitable columns of the new English Historical Review, since the prospect of having one of their own is exceedingly remote."

Professor Jameson proved to be a better prophet in his forecast of the trend of historical writing in America toward the close of the nineteenth century than he did in his fear that the prospect of an American review was "exceedingly remote." And we may conveniently take his prognostications as the point of departure for the discussion of some modern tendencies in American historiography. The features which Professor Jameson predicted a generation ago would be of increasing importance in American historical writing may be stated briefly as follows: first, the growth of a professional class of historians, with improved scientific technique and training, due to the closer co-ordination between the teaching and the writing of history; second, the multiplication of works of collaboration, to which various specialists contribute simultaneous volumes dealing with their "field," in place of the long sustained labor of a single scholar to cover long periods of our history in a half a dozen or more volumes, appearing at quinquennial intervals; and third, an increasing emphasis upon economic, social, and cultural factors in our history, as over against the purely political narrative or the institutional analysis.

The most distinguished American historians of the early and middle years of the nineteenth century were great literary artists rather than scientific investigators. Not that men like Bancroft, Sparks, Irving, Prescott, and Motley were not diligent searchers and collectors of documents, omnivorous readers, and tireless composers and compilers. But their aim was the production of a literary masterpiece, and they selected and adapted their material to that end. They handled their documents as an artist handles the masses of color in a landscape or as a dramatist handles his *personæ,* rejecting this feature and heightening that feature for the total effect to be produced. They were quite unashamed of their partisanships and prejudices. History in their eyes was a work of edification, of exhortation to liberty and republican virtues. Motley's volumes on the Dutch Republic are a panegyric on William of Orange, with the Duke of Alva, Margaret of Parma, and Requescens figuring as the dark villains of the drama, the foils to set off the virtues of the hero. Emulating Nelson on the occasion of the famous signal for retreat, Prescott turned his blind eye only to the constructive and civilizing work of the Spaniards in the New World. Bancroft's theme was the American Republic, destined by Providence to be the evangelist of freedom, democracy, and civic virtue to a world groaning under the accumulated tyrannies of ages. There is an apocalyptic quality in his writing. America bursts on the world like a revelation. So rapt is the author in contemplating the glorious destiny of America that he cannot come down from the mount of vision to the plains of reality. One would gather from his pages that the founders of the republic got their inspiration directly from the Goddess of Liberty; for he takes little note of the actual historical sources of their emancipating doctrine in the works and deeds of the great seventeenth-century apostles of liberty across the water — the Miltons, Lockes, and Sidneys; the Eliots, Pyms, and Hampdens. Preferring to deal with abstract themes like the onward march of freedom or the unfolding designs of Providence, which lent themselves to flights of oratory, the author had little inclination to investigate with prosaic patience such fundamental factors in the relations between England and the American colonies as the organs of administration in the British empire or the economic ramifications of the navigation policy. Finally, the modern canon of disinterestedness in historical writing exercised no chastening authority over Bancroft's mind. In spite of the warning of his brother-in-law, "Honest John" Davis (on the appearance of the first volume of the 'History of the United States') to beware of indulging prejudiced and partisan opinions, Bancroft continued to write his great work as an apology for the Democratic party. His volumes, says Jameson, "voted for Jackson." Washington Irving even went so far as to rebuke the scientific research historian for the method which we regard as not only the merit but the indispensable duty of the scholar today. In his 'Life of Columbus' he complains of "certain meddlers who in the name of learned research go nosing into the traces of history," thus disturbing traditions and opinions which have become fixed in the popular mind.

In a word, few of ths historians of the middle period had any real training in the school of history. They were quite often men who had studied for the ministry or prepared themselves to teach the classics. Sometimes they were authors who had won a reputation in the literary field and who turned to some attractive and picturesque epoch of history as a fine theme for the exercise of their gift of narrative. They produced best sellers and reaped financial harvests from their subscription lists and from eager publishers. Irving received $42,000 for his 'Life of Columbus,' 'Conquest of Granada,' and 'The Alhambra,' with $24,000 more for the English rights. Fifteen thousand sets of Motley's 'Rise of the Dutch Republic' were sold the first year after publication. Prescott was paid $7500 for 'The Conquest of Peru' the day the work was put on sale. Sparks and Bancroft grew rich on royalties. These great literary historians undoubtedly made an appeal to a wider reading public than their more scientific successors were able to reach. Compare, for example, the 15,000 sets of Motley's 'Dutch Republic' sold in the first year with the meager reception of Professor Herbert L. Osgood's authoritative volumes on 'The History of the American Colonies in the Seventeenth Century' (1907). Indeed, Professor Osgood's subsequent four-volume work on the Colonies in the eighteenth century was not published until six years after the author's death in 1918, because no house was willing to risk the loss anticipated. It was only when a certain man of means, who had been a student of the distinguished professor, underwrote the expense of publication that the volumes appeared. Within the last decade only there have been hopeful signs that the historian is recapturing an audience among the general reading public. The success of such works as Breasted and Robinson's 'The Human Adventure' and the Beards' 'The Rise of American Civilization' is an encouraging witness to the fact that the results of unimpeachable scholarship and strict scientific method can be presented in such attractive form as to make best sellers.

Whether or not history can be called a science is a question which we need not discuss here. Certain it is that history, like every other discipline, has felt the influence of the scientific spirit and has undergone a decided transformation as a result of that influence. The publication of Droysen's famous essay in the ninth volume of the Historische Zeitschrift, in 1863, on 'The Elevation of History to the Rank of a Science' was a summons to the historian to treat his material with the same objectivity and disinterestedness that the zoölogist uses in his laboratory. There was to be an end of "loose talk" in history, as John Richard Green put it. Instead of rhetoric the historian must cultivate research; in the place of propaganda he must put proof; documentation must succeed declamation. At the same time the doctrine of evolution was working mightily in the minds of the scholars of the last generation of the nineteenth century to replace the cataclysmic and arbitrary doctrine of the course of history by the conception of the continuity of history, and hence to emphasize origins and trends and the power of long established customs and institutions at the expense of tyrannical innovators or revolutionary plots. This scientific-genetic spirit, pervading the field of history, as it did every other field of human study, bore fruit in the establishment of graduate schools and seminars for the training of professional historians. Professor Charles Kendall Adams of Michigan introduced the seminar method into America, as practised by Ranke in Germany, Duruy in France, and Stubbs in England. Around the dull red-covered table of Professor Herbert Baxter Adams' seminar at Johns Hopkins sat a group of young American scholars, including Richard Ely, J. Franklin Jameson, Albert Shaw, Davis R. Dewey, Albion Small, and Woodrow Wilson. In these and like professional schools the students learned to weigh evidence, to sift sources, to judge the value of documents, to eschew prepossessions and prejudices, to dismiss partisan zeal and personal enthusiasms — in short, to search with single-minded diligence for the facts and to report them as faithfully as possible.

That history suffered an artistic decline at the hands of the professional writers of the later years of the nineteenth century cannot be denied. In their reaction against the "loose talk" of their predecessors, these men too often neglected or scorned the legitimate adornments of style. Because writers of a former generation had drawn too heavily on their imagination, the new school of scientific historians were inclined to taboo the imagination altogether. Because rhetoric had tempted their predecessors into unwarranted statements, they shunned the devices of antithesis, alliteration, and climax as tricks of the stump orator. Their pages bristled with tiny figures referring to learned footnotes. They excluded any suspicion of humor as they would from a funeral sermon. A tradition seemed to be getting established that if an historical work was readable it must be superficial. The dry-as-dust historian, of whom Carlyle complained so bitterly, had his day. But it is an encouraging fact that he has also largely ceased to be. His work was necessary, if not entertaining to the public. Before a newer and truer historical narrative could appear the way had to be prepared by diligent research into the sources and by the publication of countless monographs setting forth the results of this research. Before the structure could be reared the foundations had to be laid. If the scientific historian was busier with pick and spade, plumb-line, and blue-print than with marquetry floors, carved mantels, and decorative wall-paper, it was because he discovered that many of the imposing structures of the earlier builders rested on poor foundations and contained "jerry" material, whose unsoundness was disguised by the florid ornamentation of rhetoric and the popular appeal to prejudice.

Every reputable historian of today would be pained rather than flattered to have his writings serve as propaganda for any party, race, or sect. For he knows that the very essence of propaganda is false emphasis and perspective — the historical astigmatism which he is concerned to remedy. Compare, for example, the elaborate panegyric on the virtues of the Puritans, in John Gorham Palfrey's four-volume 'History of New England,' with the recent trilogy 'The Founding of New England,' 'Revolutionary New England,' and 'New England in the Republic' by James Truslow Adams. Palfrey paints a community of saints. Adams describes a society of men (and women) characterized by the mingled virtues and vices to which the human race is heir: courageous idealism and sordid materialism, broad vision and narrow prejudice, sturdy self-reliance and nagging persecution. Palfrey's work is an apology; Adams' is a history. Or compare the treatment of the slavery question in two elaborate histories of the middle years of the last century, Hermann von Holst's 'Constitutional and Political History of the United States' and James Ford Rhodes' 'History of the United States since the Compromise of 1850.' The eighth and last volume of the English translation of Von Holst's work appeared in the same year (1892) as the first of the seven volumes of Rhodes. Von Holst wrote an anti-slavery tract; Rhodes, an impartial and scrupulously documented history.

In no other epoch of American history, perhaps, are the results of the scientific spirit and method more evident (and more disturbing to a class of people who confuse patriotism with a blind worship of the fathers of the republic) than in the writing of the American Revolution and the founding of the national government. Due partially to an inherited and persistent animosity against Great Britain and partially to a just pride in the wonderful achievements of men like Washington, Franklin, Madison, Jefferson, and Hamilton, the older historians portrayed the Revolution as the spontaneous uprising of a wholly virtuous people, imbued with an unprecedented passion for liberty, against the minions of a brutal tyrant. It is true that a few of the more sober scholars, like Richard Hildreth, protested against so partial an interpretation of the Revolutionary epoch; but the protests had little effect on writers who found it both congenial and profitable to cater to the popular demand for "twisting the lion's tail." With no less respect for the fathers, but with far more respect for the facts, the scientific historians investigated the prosaic records of colonial officials' reports and ships' bills of lading, as well as the impassioned speeches of patriots and Tories. Professor Osgood's study of colonial institutions, based on a thorough search of the documents in our state archives and in the British Record Office, laid the foundation (hard and dry, as foundations should be) for a just comprehension of th[e] complex questions at issue between the American colonies and the mothe[r] country. Osgood's student, Professor George Louis Beer, in a series of boo[ks] on 'The Origins of the British Colonial System' (1578–1660), 'The O[ld] Colonial System' (1660–1754), and 'British Colonial Policy' (1754–176[5] showed how difficult was the problem of reconciling the colonial ideas of the freedom of trade with the mercantile theories of the seventeenth and eighteenth centuries prevalent among all the maritime nations of Europe. Professor A. M. Schlesinger's 'The Colonial Merchant and the American Revolution' demonstrated the truth of old John Adams' remark that molasses was an essential ingredient in that historic struggle. Other trained historians, like Professors A. C. McLaughlin, C. M. Andrews, G. E. Howard, and C. H. Van Tyne, studied the structure and functions of the British Empire in the eighteenth century, revealing the significance for the American colonies of the interplay of factional groups at Westminster and the problems involved in the attempt to preserve the loyalty of distant and freedom-loving subjects without sacrificing imperial unity. Every fair-minded student of the documentary evidence which the trained historians have adduced knows that the traditional interpretation of the American Revolution is not true to the facts. It is based on the psychology of the pamphleteer and the orator; and these men are the very worst guides for the historian, because their object is to prove a case by the arbitrary selection of data and the deliberate distortion of emphasis.

The scientific method in history, with its canons of objectivity, impartiality, and fidelity to authenticated sources, has rendered forever obsolete, among historians deserving the name, propagandist tracts and apologetic treatises. Such works will, of course, continue to be written; but they will fall afoul of deserved censure in the first notice taken of them by a competent reviewer. That there will always be those who prefer legend to fact goes without saying. They will, however, find their mental pabulum furnished by writers whose lack of training corresponds to their own lack of discrimination. Even with the spread of democratic education, there will probably always be far more readers of Weems's caricature of Washington than of Rupert Hughes's portraiture of Washington. But for the wise and judicious it is a matter for congratulation that Professor Jameson's prophecy of a school of professional historians, trained in historical method and historical conscience, is being so signally fulfilled in our day.

The second tendency that Professor Jameson noted in American historiography was the multiplication of co-operative works. More than a century and a half ago (1769) the indefatigable Scottish historian William Robertson wrote: "The term of life is too short for the study or even the perusal of the materials with which science and the art of printing have filled Europe." What, then, would he say today! The list of books recommended for collateral reading at the end of a single chapter in many a college textbook would occupy the student's time for his whole college course. A few scholars in our generation, undismayed by the accumulating masses of material to be examined, have devoted years to the many-volumed type of history covering long period of time, which was the customary production of the older historians, like Bancroft, Hildreth, Prescott, and Parkman. The first of James Schouler's seven volumes on the history of our country from 1783 to 1877 appeared in 1880 and the last in 1913. Professor John B. McMaster, beginning at the same point as Schouler, devoted thirty years of unremitting labor to his 'History of the People of the United States,' completing the eighth volume (to the Civil War) in 1913. He has more recently (in 1927) added a ninth volume on President Lincoln's administration. Professor Edward Channing of Harvard has undertaken to cover the whole period of our history from the discovery of America to the present. He published the first volume of this comprehensive 'History of the United States' almost a quarter of a century ago (1905), and the sixth volume on 'The War for Southern Independence,' in 1925. He is now at work on the Reconstruction period. The late James Ford Rhodes wrote seven volumes (1892–1906) on 'The History of the United States since the Compromise of 1850,' bringing the story down to the end of the Reconstruction period in 1877. An eighth volume, 'From Hayes to McKinley' was published in 1919, and a ninth on 'The McKinley and Roosevelt Administrations,' three years later. Ellis P. Oberholzer is now at work on a comprehensive 'History of the United States since the Civil War.' In the decade 1917–1927 he has published the first three volumes, which cover the period from 1865 to 1878. At the same rate of production Oberholzer would reach the end of Roosevelt's first administration by 1947, and the entrance of America into the World War by 1957.

Many years ago the value of co-operative histories was recognized, both for the scope which such works give to presentation of expert views on specific subjects or epochs of history and for the opportunity of getting the volumes before the public within a comparatively short space of time. Reference has been made at the beginning of this article to Justin Winsor's 'Narrative and Critical History of America,' which was published during the years 1884–1889 in eight large octavo volumes. It was a veritable mine of historical and antiquarian information, profusely illustrated, and dealing not only with the history of the United States from the days of the aboriginal tribes down to the middle of the nineteenth century, but with Spanish, Portuguese, French, and English history in both the American continents. The editor contributed more than twenty of the historical chapters and critical essays on the authorities himself; and called to his assistance thirty-eight expert collaborators. Hubert Howe Bancroft's twenty-one volumes on 'The History of the Pacific States of North America,' with fourteen more on 'The Native Races of the Pacific States,' 'The History of Central America,' and 'The History of Mexico,' published between 1874 and 1890, were, like Winsor's volumes, rather an encyclopedia than a carefully balanced historical work. Bancroft employed a large number of assistants for the collection of materials, which he published with rather profuse haste. His collected works, acquired by the library of the University of California in 1905, contain an immense amount of valuable matter for the history of the Far West, but they leave much to be desired from the point of view of scientific historiography.

It is not, however, in encyclopedic works like Winsor's and Bancroft's that recent co-operative efforts have taken form. They are rather the connected story of our history, divided into longer or shorter "epochs," each of which is handled by a special student of the field. The 'American History Series' in seven volumes, covering the period from 1450 to 1877, was the first of such works to appear (1892–1902). The last four volumes, dealing with 'The Middle Period' (1817–1859), 'The Civil War' (two volumes), and 'The Reconstruction Period,' were written by that distinguished authority on our political and constitutional history, Professor John W. Burgess. A briefer set, entitled, 'Epochs of American History,' edited by Professor A. B. Hart, was originally published early in the 1890's, with revisions of all the volumes in 1910 and the addition of a new volume in 1927 ('Expansion and Reform') by the late Professor J. S. Bassett, covering the years from 1889 to 1926. This little set of duodecimo volumes, one of which was written by Woodrow Wilson, has enjoyed a remarkable popularity for more than thirty years. Early in the present century Professor Hart undertook the editorship of a much more extensive co-operative history of our country from the pre-Columbian days to the present, under the title of 'The American Nation.' The work consists of twenty-eight good-sized volumes, each written by a recognized expert in the period treated. Indeed, the names of the authors would constitute a bead-roll of the best known American historians at the beginning of the twentieth century. Among these names are Bourne, Thwaites, Tyler, McLaughlin, Garrison, Chadwick, Dunning, Sparks, Latané, and Ogg. The volumes, averaging about 350 pages in length, were all published during the years 1904–1908, and, in spite of their subordination of economic and cultural factors to political history, they are still probably the most useful set of American history for the college and university student. About ten years after 'The American Nation' came the 'Riverside History of the United States,' in four volumes, edited by Professor W. E. Dodd, with Carl Becker, Allen Johnson, and F. L. Paxson as the other contributors. And just at the close of the second decade of the twentieth century the Yale University Press began the publication of a co-operative history (under the competent editorship of Professor Allen Johnson) in fifty volumes, entitled 'The Chronicles of America.' Both in form and in content the Chronicles are a work of art. The volumes, small enough to go in one's coat pocket, are beautifully bound and illustrated. They supplement the American Nation series on the cultural side, devoting a good deal of attention to manners and customs, religion, education, art, and letters. They have been recognized as so faithful a picture of American life that they have been adapted to the screen, under the skilful supervision of Arthur H. Brook, Professors N. M. Stephenson and D. R. Fox, and others, and shown widely in the schools and movie theaters of the country. Two other important co-operative works in American history are now in process of publication. 'The Pageant of America,' also produced by the Yale University Press, is a magnificent work in large volumes profusely illustrated with the most carefully selected cuts, representing every phase of our cultural development. Each volume is complete in itself, dealing with some important topic, such as the history of American agriculture and industry, the American Revolution, or American architecture. Finally, there appeared from the Macmillan press in 1927 the first four volumes of a twelve-volume co-operative 'History of American Life,' edited by Professors A. M. Schlesinger and D. R. Fox. These volumes ('The First Americans, 1607–1690,' by Professor T. J. Wertenbaker; 'Provincial Society, 1690–1763,' by James Truslow Adams; 'The Rise of the Common Man, 1830–1850,' by Professor C. R. Fish; and 'The Emergence of Modern America, 1865–1878,' by Professor Allan Nevins) are as utter a denial of Freeman's famous dictum that "history is past politics" as could be imagined. They leave political, military, diplomatic, and constitutional questions entirely untouched, to explore the subjects to which the major share of any people's attention in any age or clime is directed: food, shelter, dress, amusements, occupations, beliefs, acquisitions, social ambitions, and the like. Professor Nevins writes a book of over 400 pages on the period usually called 'The Reconstruction Era' without finding it necessary to mention the name of Thaddeus Stevens! Surely the scrapping of political history could be no more complete. Spinning wheels, pots, kettles, agricultural machinery, and buggies replace attitudinizing statesmen and facsimiles of acts of Congress in the illustrations — a change, perhaps, as shocking to the orthodox historians as was the substitution of carrots, rakes, and watering-pots for the saints of the Church in the calendar of revolutionary France.

The mention of this refreshingly iconoclastic 'History of American Life' offers an easy transition to the third of Professor Jameson's prognostications as to the trend of modern American historiography: namely the increasing emphasis on cultural and economic as against political factors in history. This emphasis is noticeable in three manifestations. First, the present-day historians are including, even in narratives chiefly political, a far greater proportion of economic material than did their predecessors of a generation ago. So thoroughly has the influence permeated the historical guild that even the textbook writer knows that he can have no hope that his book will sell unless he states in the preface (and redeems his promise in the text) that "economic and social factors will receive due consideration." In the second place, there is a tendency to attribute to economic causes much of the development of institutions, the course of legislation, and the motives of diplomacy, which former historians assumed to be due to some inherent quality of the state *quâ* state or the "physics of politics." Some scholars, in their reaction against the older type of political and constitutional history, have gone to the extreme Marxian position of economic determinism, which, perhaps, is as great a temptation to distortion as the "filio-pietistic" bias. An outstanding example of a sane application of the economic method is Professor C. A. Beard's 'An Economic Interpretation of the Constitution of the United States' (1913), in which the author shows by incontrovertible evidence drawn from the Treasury books how important a rôle the struggle between the public security-holders and the farmer-debtor class played in the formation and the operation of the new Constitution. In his 'Economic Origins of Jeffersonian Democracy' (1915), Professor Beard continues the history of this struggle through the closing decade of the eighteenth century. A third sign of increasing emphasis on economic factors in the historical writings of recent years is the large number of books dealing with the industrial, agricultural, commercial, and financial development of America. Katherine Coman's 'Industrial History of the United States' (1911), E. L. Bogart's 'Economic History of the United States' (1918), Isaac Lippincott's 'Economic Development of the United States' (1921), and H. U. Faulkner's 'American Economic History' (1924) are general surveys of the colonial and national periods of our history. Other scholars have given us special treatises on different sections of the country, like W. B. Weeden's 'Economic and Social History of New England,' P. A. Bruce's 'Economic History of Virginia in the Seventeenth Century,' and E. D. Fite's 'Social and Industrial Conditions in the North During the Civil War.'

Not even the briefest sketch of recent tendencies in American historical writing should fail to note the attention paid to the West. The official announcement of the disappearance of the American frontier, in the Census of 1890, furnished the text for a remarkable article by Professor Frederick J. Turner of Wisconsin on 'The Significance of the Frontier in American History' (American Historical Association, Annual Report, 1893). The standard works of Rhodes, Schouler, Dunning, and Burgess on the period immediately following the Civil War had taken little notice of the agrarian West; but Turner showed that the ever westward-moving frontier had been the most constant influence in development of the American spirit. Turner's essays on the subject, published in various magazines and historical journals, were collected in a volume entitled 'The Frontier in American History' (1920). The nearest thing to a "school" of American history that we have had grew out of the work of Professor Turner and of the late Professor C. W. Alvord, the distinguished historian of the Mississippi Valley. A group of younger writers, including Carl Becker, Carl Russell Fish, Frederick L. Paxson, and Solon J. Buck, followed Turner's lead. Paxson's scholarly 'History of the American Frontier' was recently awarded the Pulitzer prize for the outstanding work on American history for the year. Buck's 'The Granger Movement' and 'The Agrarian Crusade,' together with F. E. Haynes' 'Third Party Movements since the Civil War,' give us the first adequate treatment of the influence of the farmer on our national politics. If space permitted, we could dwell on the value for American historiography of several other types of work which have been conspicuous in the last two or three decades. A great number of source documents have been made available by such publications as 'Original Narratives of Early American History' (edited by Professor Jameson) in eighteen volumes; 'American History Told by Contemporaries,' by Professor A. B. Hart, in four volumes, and various source-books and readings in American history, by MacDonald, Morison, Johnson, and others. Our historical knowledge has also been enriched by a number of rather elaborate two-volume biographies and collections of letters of important statesmen. J. B. Bishop's 'Theodore Roosevelt and his Time,' Charles Seymour's 'The Intimate Papers of Colonel House,' Burton Hendrick's 'Life and Letters of Walter H. Page,' Robert M. McElroy's 'Grover Cleveland, the Man and the Statesman,' T. C. Smith's 'Life of Abraham Garfield,' Wandell and Minnegerode's 'Aaron Burr,' W. C. Bruce's 'John Randolph,' and Allan Nevins' 'John C. Frémont' are some examples of the recent type of biography, which contrast favorably in scope and style with the jejune volumes of the American Statesmen series published in the last generation. Still more elaborate biographies, like Rupert Hughes' 'Life of Washington' and Ray Stannard Baker's 'Life of Woodrow Wilson' (of each of which the first two volumes have appeared) are in process of composition. Finally, we have had in recent years at least a score of historical memoirs and reminiscences by cabinet officers, newspaper men, and other persons close to the incumbents of high political office. No fewer than five of the members of Wilson's cabinet, for example (Bryan, Lansing, Lane, Daniels, and Houston), in addition to his private secretary Tumulty, have left us more or less valuable material for the interpretation of President Wilson's personality and policies.

The most promising of the tendencies in our historical writing today is the emphasis which our best authors are placing on a new synthesis of the political, economic, and cultural elements in our past. If American history is enjoying something of a renewal of the popularity which it had in the days of Bancroft and Parkman, it means that the stage of necessary but rather dull labor of the scientific pioneers is being superseded by essays in the interpretation of American life. It is not without significance that the Pulitzer prize for the best work in American history for the year 1927 was awarded to a professor of English, Vernon L. Parrington, for his 'Main Currents of American Thought.' And certainly the jury must have had no easy task in deciding between this work and the Beards' magnificent interpretation of 'The Rise of American Civilization.' This does not mean, of course, that our historians will abandon the scientific attitude and lose sight of the importance of the genetic method, the economic factors, and the truth of the continuity of history; but rather that they will take these principles up into their synthesis, and, adding the gains of science to the gifts of art, will rewrite our history with ever increasing approximation to the truth.

David Saville Muzzey

THE NEW ART OF BIOGRAPHY

DESPITE the fact that our own age is rather naïvely certain that it holds the secret of biographical writing; though it loves to speak, with a faint scorn unhampered by knowledge of past achievement, of biographies by "moderns" and "in the modern manner"; though, when it boasts that it has reclaimed the realm of biography for literature, it forgets (if it ever knew) that the Muse was scarcely absent when Plutarch or Johnson or Macaulay wrote the biographical essay, or Boswell or Lockhart or Froude the more extended life: despite the frequency of such jaunty boasts and provincial pride, the twentieth century promises, nevertheless, to be the age of biography. Just as what we loosely call Elizabethan England found its most characteristic expression in the drama and the last century in the novel, so we of today are witnessing a multiplication of books about particular men and women, and books of a temper and abundance unparalleled in the history of the world.

This contemporary interest in human personality is not only encouraging in the appearance of a wealth of journals, diaries, confessions, memoirs, imaginary lives, literary portraits, historical novels, autobiographies, and jottings of gossip and conversation; but, to meet a popular craving, we seem launched upon a campaign to rewrite every "Life" we have inherited from the past. Not only this: but, by way of original contribution, we are commemorating in volumes and essays the careers of the curious, the criminal, and the quaint of vaguer memory. In the rear of the parade, but celebrants in the same worship and orgy, the "True Story" magazines provoke the question: May it not be that as fiction has grown increasingly "realistic," we have, in our growing passion for "biography," but disguised our craving for romance? Nowadays, no "fact" is too fantastic to be credible; correspondingly, we have grown in scepticism towards the world of fiction. In a "true story," as in a "biography," we can be brought to believe anything; in novels, we demand more and more a kind of literalness and logic that less and less we impute to life itself.

Now, as never before, the proper study of mankind is man. We have outgrown the taste for fairy-tales, we like to say; we have smoked out the comfortable myths and delusions of our superstitious forebears; we are the people, and ours is the belated courage to take a square look at ourselves and our ancestors; and we are done with mysteries and veils. Though this is a widespread and fashionable orthodoxy, accepted largely in blind faith, and a faith prolific in self-deception, it is, nevertheless, at the basis of what is best — as well as of what is worst — in the welter of contemporary "biographies." At its best this creed has provoked the attempt to isolate biography; to give it an independent existence and a distinct identity; to free it from the entanglements by which it has been obstructed and obscured; to differentiate it from history, fiction, the pious tale, and the extended epitaph; to clear it of the questionable repute of its shabby relatives and its mixed ancestry; and to accord it a name and a dignity of its own.

For an account of 'The Development of English Biography' the reader is especially recommended to Harold Nicolson's book of that title. As Nicolson has taken pains to show, the history of biography has been a story of arrested development; and even today, biography as a distinct branch of the art of writing is still in its infancy. It was scarcely thought of, it had not even a name, before 1683; its legitimacy was hardly recognized before 1791; it possesses a most unfortunate heredity; it suffers from many congenital defects; and its less legitimate manifestations behave with such frequent vulgarity as to bring it into disrepute.

Nicolson's studies have convinced him that no form of literary composition has been more sensitive than biographical writing to the "spirit of the age"; over no form of literary composition have the requirements of the reading public exercised so marked and immediate an influence. And the development of biography has been primarily the development of a taste for biography.

Few are likely to contradict Nicolson's statement that "biography was invented to satisfy the commemorative instinct" — born of the same impulse that built the pyramids. The family wished to commemorate the dead, and we had elegies, laments, runic inscriptions, and the sons of Cain telling their children stories of their ancestors. The Church wished to commemorate its founders, and we had the Gospels and the Saints' Lives — "an honor to the virtuous dead, and a lesson in magnanimity to those who shall succeed them." Until the age of Chaucer, curiosity largely expended itself in vague wonderings about the supernatural rather than in any realistic interest in the lives and characters of human beings. By 1387, however, with Chaucer's conception of the 'Canterbury Tales,' there existed an audience with a definite if limited taste for realism; but the fourteenth and fifteenth centuries failed to exploit the Chaucerian vein. This early spring of robust native curiosity was quenched in the sands of unreality; it was not until the sixteenth century that it revived. The books of Roper and Cavendish, though marred by vestiges of their commemorative and didactic heredity, are indications that psychological curiosity — the desire, that is, to learn a man's character rather than his exploits — still existed. In the memoirs of the seventeenth century, above all in Aubrey and the Duchess of Newcastle, this native stream of actuality can still be recognized; but the main current had already been diverted by the drama, and the trickle that survived was trapped by external influences — by pietism, by

Puritanism, by metaphysics, by the passion for Plutarch, Theophrastus, and the rest. Before our own, the eighteenth century was the great age of biography: then were North and Mason, and Johnson and Boswell, and the same tradition gave us Moore and Lockhart. But by the middle of the nineteenth century moral earnestness again intervened.

Between the last quarter of the eighteenth century and the middle of the nineteenth, both England and America had grown from national danger to great personal perplexity. In England, the French Revolution and the Napoleonic wars had left an abiding horror of excess and a distaste for adventure. England was tired of romance, disillusioned of idealism. And to the Victorians, both in England and by contagion and imitation here, peace and prosperity — a domestic, enlightened, and sane existence — was the sum and goal of virtue and well-being. All the while, disturbing intimations were in the air: disquieting findings in geology and astronomy, and uneasy hints of evolution. And after that the deluge, science seeming to sweep away every dike of orthodoxy and to revolutionize every flattering myth of man, the universe, and God. With militant agnosticism the generation of Thomas Huxley preached the "unfathomable injustice" of creation: the essential criminal nature of man they viewed as an intimate product of the criminal nature of the cosmic process. Thomas Huxley's generation, in a merciless vendetta of ideas, strove to establish justice in a universe conceived as being otherwise without justice. That was three generations ago. The fighting scepticism of Huxley's generation has bequeathed to us a scientific determinism that has abolished the idea of good and evil, vitriol and sugar, as virtue and vice, equally by-products of blind necessity. They bequeathed to us a corrosive and paralyzing spirit of analysis, a malicious psychology that pretends to destroy all values whose origins it can probe. The fruits of lusty moral earnestness of the fathers has set on edge the teeth of the third generation.

The Victorians, both here and abroad, were incorrigible hero-worshipers. The more the scientists shook their belief in God, the more they invested their leading contemporaries with divine attributes. Their divinities took kindly to apotheosis; and the postures expected of them became the very attitudes which they happened, quite naturally and sincerely, to adopt. "The history of mankind," according to Carlyle, "is the history of its great men"; and the appropriate business of posterity is "to find out these, clean the dirt from them, and place them on their proper pedestals." Lack of truth in biography was thus given the authority of a moral law; and biographers sought to palliate their expurgations by an appeal to such considerations as "loyalty," or "discretion," or "reverence." Longfellow, in telling us of what the lives of great men should remind us, but echoed the Victorian sentiment on this side of the Atlantic. But whether here or abroad, the Victorian sentiment which branded as "cruel and vulgar" any attempt at complete and ungarnished portraiture, was, by implication, a libel upon human greatness: as if no man nakedly viewed could be other than an object of shame; as if a taint of depravity and meanness infected all human greatness.

It is sobering to remember that there lived in those belated Victorian days a young man who contributed a life of St. Neot to Newman's 'Lives of the Saints.' After the publication of this life, however, the young man described the whole business as "nonsense," and consoled himself by writing an improper novel under the pseudonym of "Zeta," and a few months later a 'Nemesis of Faith,' under the name of Froude.

On the death of Carlyle, Froude found himself the sole surviving executor; he found himself in a stronger position even than Boswell. Carlyle in a letter to Sterling once described himself as a "poor concrete reality, very offensive now and then." Carlyle had defended Lockhart against the charges of unkindliness and disloyalty in his life of Scott. Froude had to choose between the alternative of giving a truthful and as such a disagreeable representation of Carlyle, or else of writing no biography at all. He chose the former alternative. Between 1881 and 1884 Froude published nine fat volumes which stirred up a whirlwind of disapprobation. Tennyson boomed, and Mrs. Oliphant wrote a long article on the ethics of biography. Froude was charged with desecrating the sanctities of private life, with revealing secrets that should have remained forever hidden in the grave — disturbing, unpleasant, positively heartless. Amid all this dust and shouting there was one point, however, that escaped attention: it was not noticed that Froude had introduced a new element into the art of English biography — an element that had not occurred to Boswell, and that is wholly absent from Lockhart's 'Life of Scott.' If the ironic detachment of 'Eminent Victorians' is a trait peculiar to "modern" biography, then "modern" biography is to be dated from 1881, and its originator was Froude.

Since the time when Froude's discovery was in 1917 brilliantly utilized by Strachey while turning an inquiring eye upon four of Froude's contemporaries, a varying degree of disrespect has enjoyed the widest vogue. Superficially viewed, one of the most striking characteristics of our "modern" manner in biography seems to be studied irreverence. It is now hopelessly antiquated to think of ourselves or our forebears as being (except in a cynical sense) little lower than the angels. All things biological, rather, are viewed as one great fraternity, and we like to pose as viewing the human animal with the same detachment with which we observe the oyster or the louse. No reputable scientist can study a louse without dispassionate piety; in biography it is the mode to regard one's specimen with disrespect — with a curious arching of the eyebrows, with an impertinent stare, with rudely pointed fingers, and even with ribald exclamations. But, as Philip Guedalla asks: "Is it not dreadfully significant that Thackeray's dismissal of the Georges was dismissed a few decades later by Mr. Max Beerbohm with the comment that its style was 'a trifle 1860' in prose that is even now a trifle 1894? For the conscious superiority of the next generation may often yield amusing reading; but it is rarely readable for more than twenty years. Then time moves on again; and to the succeeding generation the ironist himself becomes ridiculous. The priest of such a cult must hold his dignity by an uncertain tenure; he is indeed

The priest who slays the slayer
And shall himself be slain.

Such suicidal irony may be (perhaps it is) the 'modern' mode. If so, its contributions to biography can scarcely hope to be enduring. For, however exquisitely 1928 to us, we may be sure that one day they will be preposterously 1928 to others."

If there is indeed any note in "modern" biography that is at once enduring and characteristic of our time, it must be something other than supercilious amusement at our ancestors.

There is a school of biographers today who view their problem as being, in essence, that of the dramatist or novelist: to invoke in another's fancy a sequence of images that take on the strange potency of life and give one the illusion of having experienced a profoundly moving adventure, of having touched the flesh and heard the heart-beat of what is, after all, but a world of ghosts.

"The duties of a biographer," according to one of the most brilliant of modern practitioners, "however infrequently performed, are easily defined. They are, if I am not mistaken, to produce a living record of men who were themselves once living. Other forms of commemoration may be preferred — the recumbent statue and its literary equivalent, the official Life, the simple obituary notice, the panegyric, or the lampoon. Each has its merits. At least one masterpiece of English biographical writing was produced as an official life; the lapidary inscription has, at best, a simple dignity; and as for the posthumous lampoon, it enjoys increasing prestige in an unchivalrous age which appears to derive unlimited enjoyment from gay onslaughts upon the unprotected dead. But, whatever else these may be, they are not biography."

The Oxford Dictionary, if less vivacious than Guedalla, is, if anything, even more drastic in limitation. For, in defining biography as "the history of lives of individual men as a branch of literature" it excludes by implication all narrative that is untruthful, that does not deal primarily with individuals, or that is not composed with conscious and competent artistic purpose. Such exclusion might be applied with cruel consequence to the majority of all biographies both past and present.

The exclusion of the untruthful, for example. In the past, for a biographer to be instigated primarily by a drastic and austere piety for truth, has been so rare as to be negligible. If not by truth, he has been instigated by other pieties extraneous to strict biography — the commemorative instinct, for example; the cenotaphy urge, which has falsified the art of biography, "replacing the clinical arc-lamp by the muffled candles of the mortuary"; or the didactic strain, an equally pregnant source of biography not strictly true. These pious tales can never achieve truth merely by the avoidance of misstatements: "white-washing is as nefarious as malignant, and inaccuracy of representation is as culpable as inaccuracy of fact."

If a biography is, in any genuine sense, to be a "history" of a life, it must first of all conform to the highest standards of accuracy. And accuracy connotes research, a rigorous exploitation of all printed and unprinted sources of information. There is, however, implicit in this doctrine a double danger. On the one hand is the abuse of the deep-seated human weakness to believe a bore. Few things can be more wearisome than minute, relentless mere erudition; and there is still among us a strange delusion that dullness is a symptom and guarantee of accuracy; that tedium, in some mysterious way, is one of the testimonies of truth. This in some quarters has brought veracity itself in disrepute; on the other hand, it has tended to cast suspicion upon all vivacity. In consequence, much of contemporary biography is perhaps a shade unscientific, and Philip Guedalla's comment is completely just: "Its masters, whose deftness compels our admiration, rarely admit the necessity for more than a hasty glance at the best-known published authorities upon their subject before embarking, for our pleasure, upon their gay, inimitable comments. Their documentary foundation is often absurdly slight; and one may well fear for the future of the edifices, however graceful, reared upon such slight foundations, when the harsh winds of scholarship begin to blow."

Though accuracy is a prime prerequisite of all good biography, accuracy alone is not enough. Perfect veracity, after all, is not synonymous with truth. To quote again from Guedalla: "Accuracy itself requires that biography should attain a high degree of animation. Of the two alternatives presented by the poet Gray, the 'storied urn' may satisfy a group of sorrowing relatives; but the true biographer will surely aim at the 'animated bust.' His duty, in the very cause of accuracy, is to reproduce a man and not a mummy. For if the record fails to live, it is untrue to its original. He, after all, was once alive; and his biographer's first duty is to make him live again." And the yawn is one evidence that a biographer has failed in his duty no less drastically than the cruder criminal of false dates and misquotations. For biography is more than a noble storehouse of inexpugnable facts. By the requirement of the definition quoted from the Oxford Dictionary, biography is a "branch of literature." And the biographer, after satisfying the cruel exigencies of exact scholarship, must be an artist as well. Every biographer, before becoming an artist, must first have been a scholar, and have patiently assembled his materials. But once they are assembled, as André Maurois has expressed it, the biographer who is an artist follows the course of an architect who builds a house: he takes down his scaffolding and offers the reader only the finished work.

Of the enormous yearly outpouring of biographies in this country, all of them, whether Victorian or "modern," have been instigated by foreign models. Strachey, a decade ago, set the fashion in ironic detachment with his 'Eminent Victorians'; in 1921 he defied the world with his 'Queen Victoria,' a miracle of constructive excellence. And most of the "modern" biography in this country has been an unintended parody of Strachey's achievements. We still have, of course, our supply of ready-made biographies which the journeymen of letters provide for the literary public; we still have our "life-and-times"; we still have the two-volume obituary biography, the official life, the standard work of reference; the "Character" (rechristened by Gamaliel Bradford as "psychography" — an old thing now enjoying a wide popularity under a new name): these, and the other traditional variants of biographical writing. There is, besides, at the present day, and exerting an influence not second even to that of Strachey, a fashion derived from Freud and his successors.

In 1910, Freud published his study of a childhood recollection of Leonardo da Vinci, which appeared in English in this country in 1916. Tennyson, in his own time, had spoken of the "abysmal depths of personality"; and if, with the horror with which he viewed posthumous lives of himself, he could have had a prevision of Freudian enterprise, his years would have been shortened. To the Victorians, prowling about in the private life of a public man was "vulgar and cruel"; all the proprieties demanded that to a decent biographer his subject be always clothed and in his right mind. But to prowl about shamelessly in a man's consciousness! — even worse, to go probing and dredging into a man's unconsciousness, imputing to him motives and qualities that not even he himself knew anything about! — that, by comparison, would have made poking about in the pantry of one's host without leave seem the acme of gentility. Despite the vivid distaste which Freud's study still provokes in many readers, it is true nevertheless that the 'Da Vinci' set a new ideal of decency for biographers, as well as a model of modesty which Freudian converts have not always emulated. Freud himself denies all claim that psychoanalysis can explain why Leonardo was an artist; at best, it can help us to understand a little better the manifestations and limitations of his art. He also says: "If my deductions should provoke, even among the friends and followers of psychoanalysis, the opinion that I have written only a psychoanalytic romance, I can only reply that I do not myself exaggerate the certitude of my results."

Though there is appearing in this country a school of psychoanalytic biographers of varying degree of temerity, competence, and art, the influence of Freud upon writers not avowedly psychoanalytic has been enormous. Just as earlier attempts at a scientific approach to the analysis of character — medicine with its "humors," astrology, physiognomy, phrenology — so psychoanalysis has enriched our vocabulary and enlarged our concepts. It has, too, quickened our realization of the bewildering and incredible complexity of the human spirit. And though psychoanalysis has tempted some novelists and biographers to over-simplify, to convert a personality into a diagram or a caricature, the time seems safely passed when it was merely an appalling craze, and writers either succumbed to it as to an epidemic of influenza or reacted against it with blind and ridiculous animosity. If the best of psychoanalysis — and the best is not so minute a part of it, after all — cannot be taken up into the mental equipment of the biographers of today and tomorrow, so much the worse for biography.

If, ideally, biography be "the history of lives of individual men as a branch of literature"; if, for excellence in biography, we insist on the three elements of truth, individuality, and art: then, we must not be discouraged or misled because, of the hundreds of biographies produced yearly in this country, most are either erudite compilations, shallow and amiable tributes, imaginary lives, or the short-lived progeny of Strachey's none too sedulous apes.

"With us," Strachey said in the preface to 'Eminent Victorians,' "the most delicate and humane of all the branches of the art of writing has been relegated to the journeymen of letters; we do not reflect that it is perhaps as difficult to write a good life as to live one." Consider the supreme difficulty of the problem of the biographer — to achieve at one and the same time the scrupulousness of science, the enchantment of art, the palpable truth of fiction and the lying "veracity" of history. This is a synthesis rarely even approximated; as nearly realized as is humanly possible, perhaps, by James Boswell. But we do not always consider the extraordinarily unusual concatenation of circumstances necessary for that event: a Boswell, and a Johnson, and an eighteenth century. It could happen only once.

Though in the English language there are, among biographies, a few masterpieces, there has never been a great biographical tradition; and in America there has not yet appeared a biography of pre-eminence. And yet, despite the torrents of inferior and even contemptible work, there are surely being now produced in this country biographies of an excellence never known here before. Lloyd Morris' 'The Rebellious Puritan,' Van Wyck Brooks's 'The Pilgrimage of Henry James,' Thomas Beer's 'Stephen Crane,' Joseph Wood Krutch's 'Edgar Allan Poe' are typical of a small but distinguished company. The first volume of the 'Dictionary of American Biography' seems a hopeful prognostication. This volume is written not only with thoroughness (which, in the nature of the case, is nothing remarkable), but much of it is written with art (or at least a will to art) as well. If such things as this continue, and the demand grows that biographers be artists indeed, then we may yet live to enjoy a foretaste of the day of judgment. For the whole duty of every biographer is to re-enact the miracle of the resurrection of the dead.

RAYMOND WEAVER

GENERAL INDEX

	VOL.	PAGE
A		
À Rebours, Huysmans	7	353
Ab Gwilym, Dafydd	4	266
Abbé le Monnier, Letter to the, Diderot	6	366
Abbey of Thelema, The, Rabelais	6	51
Abbott, Allan, on American Poetry since 1900	18	515
Abélard, Pierre	4	487
Abélard, Letter to, Héloïse	4	497
Abolishing of Christianity, The, Swift	12	53
Abou Ben Adhem, Hunt	13	299
Abraham Lincoln: a History, Hay	18	126
Abraham Lincoln, On the Life-Mask of, Gilder	18	507
Absalom and Achitophel, Dryden	11	622
Absence, Minnesingers	4	465
Abu 'l-'Ata of Sind	1	237
Abu Muhammad the Lazy, Arabian Nights	1	245
Abu Sakhr	1	237
Acaranga-Sutra, Indian Literature	1	439
Acharnians, The, Aristophanes	2	221, 222
Acropolis of Athens and Its Temples, The, Pausanias	2	508
Ad Amphoram, Horace	3	202
Adages, Erasmus	8	325
Adam Bede, Eliot	14	643, 652
Adams, Henry	18	135
Adams, John	16	156
Adams, John Quincy	16	244
Adapa Myth, The, Babylonian Literature	1	82
Addison, Joseph	12	84
Address of the President of the United States, April 2, 1917, Wilson	18	378
Address to the American People, D'Annunzio	5	505
Address to the Beloved, An, Abu 'l-'Ata of Sind	1	237
Addresses to the German Nation, Fichte	9	211
Adieu! Thou Proud but Lovely One, Bredero	8	351
Admission of Michigan, Speech on the, Calhoun	16	300
Adonais, Shelley	13	408
Adventure of the Cloak, The, Petronius	3	328
Adventurer and the Singer, The, Hofmannsthal	9	600, 602
Adventures, The, Mandeville,	4	525, 527
Æneid, Vergil	3	181, 185, 186
Æschines	2	364
Æschylus	2	146
Æsop	2	58
Affairs round the Village Green, Browne	17	396
After the Hunt, Liliencron	9	429
After Three Years, Verlaine	7	284
Afterwards, Scott, D. C.	8	495
Agamemnon, Æschylus	2	158
Agamemnon, Alfieri	5	310
Agathias	2	582
Agathon, Woodberry	18	370
Age, Anacreon	2	122
Age of Homespun, The, Bushnell	16	509
Agincourt, The Ballad of, Drayton	11	131
Agricola, Tacitus	3	350, 351
Agriculture. See also Nature		
Chants du Paysan, Déroulède	7	246
De Agricultura, Cato	3	24
Epitaph for a Husbandman, An, Roberts	8	491
Growth of the Soil, Hamsun	10	282
Letters from an American Farmer, Crèvecœur	16	104
Northern Farmer (Old Style), Tennyson	14	316
Palamedes, Vondel	8	336
Walden, Thoreau	17	315

	VOL.	PAGE
Ainger, Alfred, on Lamb	13	205
Airs from Arcady, Bunner	18	358
Akhad ha-'Am	2	215
Akhenaten	1	52
Akhmatova, Anna	10	331
Aladdin, Oehlenschläger	10	66, 68, 89
Alcæus	2	111
Alcestis' Farewell to Her Home, Account of, Euripides	2	211
Alciphron	2	514
Alcott, Louisa May	17	379
Alcuin	4	483
Aldrich, Thomas Bailey	18	66
Aleman, Mateo	8	60
Alexander's Feast; or the Power of Music, Dryden	11	630
Alexandrian Library, The, Gibbon	12	448
Alexis and Dora, Goethe	9	167
Alfieri, Vittorio	5	308
Alfonso the Wise	8	18
Alfred the Great	4	340
Alfred's Preface to His Version of Pope Gregory's 'Pastoral Care,' Alfred the Great	4	340
Alhambra, The, Irving	16	374
al-Hariri of Basra, see Hariri, al-, of Basra		
Alice's Adventures in Wonderland, Carroll	15	142, 144, 146, 152
al-Kharizi, Judah, see Judah al-Kharizi		
All the Hills and Vales Along, Sorley	15	617
Allegory. See also Fables		
Bestiaries and Lapidaries	4	510
Everyman, Medieval Drama	4	161
Faery Queen, The, Spenser	11	66, 67, 72
Gesta Romanorum	4	502
Pearl, The, Middle English Poetry	4	538
Piers Plowman, The Vision of William Concerning, Middle English Poetry	4	532, 534, 536
Pilgrim's Progress, The, Bunyan	11	593, 594, 597, 600
Romance of the Rose, The, Jean de Meung	4	387
Allen, James Lane	18	329
Alleyne, Letter to John, Franklin	16	95
Allingham, William	14	482
"Alma Felice, che Sovente Torni," Petrarch	5	101
Althea from Prison, To, Lovelace	11	464
Amateur of Lying, The, Lucian of Samosata	2	528
America, see United States		
America, Dobell	14	482
America, Gilder	18	506
America, Expectations of, Hakluyt	11	22
America, The Mission of, Adams, J. Q.	16	250
American Commonwealth, The, Bryce	15	189
American Flag, The, Drake	16	448
American Literature		
American Literature in the Colonial Period	16	11
American Poetry since 1900	18	515
The Early New Yorkers	16	327
The First American Poets — The Indians	16	1
Modern American Drama	18	538
Modern Fiction	18	528
The New Art of Biography	18	555
The New England Group	17	1
The New York Group	17	400
Recent American Historical Writing	18	544
The South and West	17	514
American of the Future and Other Essays, The, Matthews	18	342
American Ornithological Biography, The, Audubon	16	290
American Ornithology, Wilson	16	232, 235
American Revolution, The, Everett	16	438
Americans. See also United States		
American of the Future and Other Essays, The, Matthews	18	342
At Home and Abroad, Fuller	17	229
Certain Condescension in Foreigners, On a, Lowell	17	355
Clockmaker, The, Haliburton	8	506, 508
Militarism, Ferrero	5	540
Outre-Mer, Bourget	7	402
Amor Mundi, Rossetti, C. G.	14	475

	VOL.	PAGE
Amphitruo, Plautus	3	49
An Thou Were My Ain Thing, Ramsay	12	201
Anabasis, Xenophon	2	282, 283
Anacreon	2	120
Anacreon's Grave, Antipater of Sidon	2	575
Anatomy of Melancholy, The, Burton	11	114
Ancelmus the Emperour, Gesta Romanorum	4	506
Anciens Canadiens, Les, de Gaspé	8	526, 528
Ancient Authors, On, Quintilian	3	309
Ancient Mariner, The Rime of the, Coleridge	13	76
Ancient Régime, The, Taine	7	145, 148
Ancient Sindbad, An, Avesta	1	319
And the Heavens Shall Yield Their Dew, Gabirol	1	166
Andersen, Hans Christian	10	100
Andrea del Sarto, Browning	14	355
Andreyev, Leonid Nikolayevich	10	473
Andromaque, Racine	6	233
Aneirin	4	252
Angel, Newman	14	43
Angel, The, Lermontov	10	316
Angel, The, Pushkin	10	338
Angel in the House, The, Patmore	14	479
Angel of Divine Obedience, The, Avesta	1	317
Angelus, Yehoash	8	640
Anglo-Saxon Literature	4	312
Animals, see Nature		
Animals Sick of the Plague, The, La Fontaine	6	131
An-Nabighah	1	235
Anna Karenina, Tolstoy	10	416, 421
Annabel Lee, Poe	17	575
Annals, Ennius	3	34, 35, 36, 37, 38
Annals, Tacitus	3	357, 358, 359
Anno Domini 1812, Dehmel	9	578
Annunzio, Gabriele d'	5	489
Ant, The, Bestiaries	4	514
'Antar	1	283
Anthropology. See also Evolution; Science		
Descent of Man, The, Darwin	14	535
Descent of Man, On Our Present Knowledge of the, Haeckel	9	483
Hereditary Genius, Galton	14	574
Anthropomorphism On, Sa'adia Ga'on	1	173
Antipater of Sidon	2	575
Antique Medal, On an, Hérédia	7	257
Antiquities, Josephus	1	129, 131
Antony and Cleopatra, Ferrero	5	536
Antony and Cleopatra, Plutarch	2	491
Antony and Cleopatra, Shakespeare	11	313, 314
Anvar-i-Suhaili, or Lights of Canopus, Iranian Literature	1	305
Anxious Mother, Letter from an, Alciphron	2	517
Any	1	59
Anzengruber, Ludwig	9	485
Aphrodite and Selene, Lucian of Samosata	2	523
Aphrodite, To, Sappho	2	109
Apocalypse Revealed, The, Swedenborg	10	149
Apocrypha, Jewish, see Old Testament and the Jewish Apocrypha		
Apollo, Hymn to Delian, Homeric Hymns	2	72
Apologia pro Vita Sua, Newman	14	21
Apology, The, Plato	2	320
Appeal to Ahura Mazda, the Lord, for Knowledge, An, Avesta	1	316
Approach, The, Blok	10	328
Apuleius, Lucius	3	397
Aquinas, St. Thomas	5	25
Arabia Deserta, Doughty	14	678, 680, 681, 683
Arabian Nights, The	1	242
Arabic Literature	1	219
Arbitrants, The, Menander	2	356
Arblay, Madame d', see Burney, Frances		
Arcadia, The Arrival in, Sidney	11	48
Archias	2	574
Archias, Oration for the Poet, Cicero	3	76
Areopagitica, Milton	11	461
Arethusa, Shelley	13	404

	VOL.	PAGE
Ariel's Songs, Shakespeare	11	266
Ariosto, Ludovico	5	189
Aristophanes	2	213
Aristotle	2	335
Armenia, A Prose Elegy on, Moses of Khorni	1	393
Armenian Literature	1	386
Armenians, The Second Battle of the, Elisaeus	1	395
Arnaut de Maroill, Provençal Literature	4	404
Arne, Björnson	10	238, 247
Arnljot Gelline, Björnson	10	239
Arnold, Matthew	14	412
Arrow and the Song, The, Longfellow	17	135
Art and Architecture		
Acropolis of Athens and Its Temples, The, Pausanias	2	508
Andrea del Sarto, Browning	14	355
Art Criticism, Landor	13	259
Breviary of Æsthetic, The, Croce	5	510
Casting of the Perseus, The, Cellini	5	222
Crown of Wild Olive, The, Ruskin	13	612
Dürer Painting the Saviour's Head, Machar	10	568
Elgin Marbles, On Seeing the, Keats	13	458
Esthetic Education of Man, On the, Schiller	9	196
Laocoön, Lessing	9	88, 89
Madonna of the Future, The, James, Henry	18	234
Natural History, Pliny the Elder	3	287
Ode on a Grecian Urn, Keats	13	449
Psalm of Montreal, A, Butler	15	167
Refinement in the Arts, On, Hume	12	301
Renaissance in Italy, The, Symonds	15	218
Seven Lamps of Architecture, The, Ruskin	13	593
Sodoma's 'Christ Scourged,' Woodberry	18	369
Stones of Venice, The, Ruskin	13	598, 603
Sunken Bell, The, Hautmann	9	545
Tamagatsuma, Motoöri	1	568
Temple of Zeus at Olympia, The, Pausanias	2	510
Art Criticism, Landor	13	259
Art of Grandfatherhood, The, Hugo	6	497
Art of Poetry, The, Boileau-Despréaux	6	224, 226
Art of Poetry, The, Horace	3	209
Artemus Ward: His Travels, Browne	17	397
Arthur, see Legends of Arthur and the Round Table		
Arthur's Coronation, Geoffrey of Monmouth	4	75
Arthur's Fight with Colgrim, Layamon	4	77
As I Laye A-thynkynge, Barham	13	461
As the Flowers of the Field, Strato	2	576
As You Like It, Shakespeare	11	259, 260, 274
Ascham, Roger	11	13
Ash, Scholem	8	632
Ash-Shanfara of Azd	1	233
Asia, see Orient		
Asian Birds, Bridges	15	554
Asinaria, Plautus	3	49
Asolando, Epilogue to, Browning	14	397
Aspatia's Song, Beaumont and Fletcher	11	395
Aspects of the Pines, Hayne	17	616
Ass and the Little Dog, The, Æsop	2	63
Ass and the Little Dog, The, La Fontaine	6	134
Ass Eating Thistles, The, Æsop	2	61
Ass in the Lion's Skin, The, Æsop	2	60
Assignation, The, Poe	17	568
Assyrian Literature	1	61
Astarotte and Rinaldo, Pulci	5	165
Astor, Letter to Francis, Newton	11	640
Astronomy, see Science		
Astrophel and Stella, Sidney	11	54
At Home and Abroad, Fuller	17	229
Atala, Chateaubriand	6	419
Atalanta in Calydon, Swinburne	15	108
Aten, Hymn to the, Akhenaten	1	52
Atharva-Veda, The, Indian Literature	1	436

	VOL.	PAGE
Athenæus	2	545
Athenian Dead at Platæa, On the, Simonides	2	572
Athens, Heroism of, during the Persian Invasion, Herodotus	2	254
Atsumori, A *No No Utai*, Seami	1	553
Attack on the Mill, The, Zola	7	302
Attic Nights, Gellius	3	411
Attic Nights (Cato), Gellius	3	25
Atticus, Letter to, Cicero	3	87
Au Bord de l'Eau, Sully-Prudhomme	7	272
Aucassin and Nicolette, Medieval French Literature	4	374
Audubon, John James	16	289
Augier, Émile	7	152
Augustine of Hippo, St.	3	440
Auld House, The, Nairne	12	618
Aurelius Antoninus, Marcus	3	421
Ausonius, Decimus Magnus	3	456
Austen, Jane	13	174
Author Unknown, Provençal Literature	4	413
Author's Ambition, The, Persius	3	293
Author's Resolution in a Sonnet, The, Wither	11	145
Authorship, On, Schopenhauer	9	289
Autobiography, Franklin	16	80
		82, 84, 97
Autobiography, Trollope	14	182
Autobiography, The, Mill	13	642
Autocrat of the Breakfast-Table, The, Holmes	17	218
Autumn, Watson	15	563
Autumn Dirge, An, Ou-yang Hsiu	1	515
Autumn Leaves, Hugo	6	498
Autumn, To, Keats	13	452
Avesta, The	1	307
Awakening of Cupid, The, Apuleius	3	406
Away, Riley	18	318
Axel and Valborg, Oehlenschläger	10	69
Ayres, H. M., on		
Gibson	15	603
The Middle Ages	4	1
Moore, George	15	381
Aytoun, William Edmonstoune	13	504

B

	VOL.	PAGE
Babylon; or the Bonnie Banks o' Fordie, Medieval Literature	4	42
Babylonian Literature	1	61
Babylonian Wisdom, Ut-Napishtim	1	95
Bacchæ, The, Euripides	2	197
Bacchus, The Invocation of, Ivanov	10	330
Bacchylides	2	99
Back to Methuselah, Shaw	15	510
Bacon, Francis	11	88
Bacon, Francis, on Browne	11	521
Bacourt, Pierre de, on		
Barrès	7	444
Bourget	7	395
Huysmans	7	349
de Régnier	7	517
Bagehot, Walter	14	596
Baillie, Joanna	12	574
Baker, F. T., on Crèvecœur	16	102
Baker, R. P., on Canadian Literature	8	482
Bakhya ibn Pakuda	1	176
Balaustion's Adventure (from Euripides), Browning	2	211
Balfour, Arthur James	15	238
Ballad, The, Medieval Literature	4	11
Ballad Made at the Request of His Mother, Villon	6	37
Ballad of Dead Ladies, The, Villon	6	30
Ballad of Human Life, Beddoes	13	494
Ballad of the Outer Life, Hofmannsthal	9	605
Ballad to Queen Elizabeth, A, Dobson	14	498
Ballad upon a Wedding, Suckling	11	173
Ballads		
Agincourt, The Ballad of, Drayton	11	131
Babylon; or the Bonnie Banks o' Fordie, Medieval Literature	4	42
Ballad, The, Medieval Literature	4	11
Ballad Made at the Request of His Mother, Villon	6	37
Ballad of Dead Ladies, The, Villon	6	30
Ballad to Queen Elizabeth, A, Dobson	14	498
Ballad upon a Wedding, Suckling	11	173
Barbarossa, Rückert	9	412
Belle Dame Sans Merci, La, Keats	13	457

	VOL.	PAGE
Bessie Bell and Mary Gray, Medieval Literature	4	38
Binnorie, Medieval Literature	4	51
Bonnie George Campbell, Medieval Literature	4	37
Bonny Earl of Murray, The, Medieval Literature	4	34
Calendau, Mistral	7	210
Childe Maurice, Medieval Literature	4	43
Death of Ivo, The, Slavonic Literature	10	602
Edward, Medieval Literature	4	40
Elfin-King, The, Goethe	9	164
Epitaph in the Form of a Ballad, The, Villon	6	33
Fall of the Serbian Empire, The, Slavonic Literature	10	599
Frederick Redbeard, Geibel	9	423
Hunting of the Cheviot, The, Medieval Literature	4	24
Lenora, Bürger	9	109
Lord Randal, Medieval Literature	4	40
Lorelei, Eichendorff	9	296
Luck of Edenhall, The, Uhland	9	408
Mary Hamilton, Medieval Literature	4	35
Robin Hood and Guy of Gisborne, Medieval Literature	4	17
Sir Patrick Spens, Medieval Literature	4	33
Sweet William's Ghost, Medieval Literature	4	49
Things Known and Unknown, Ballad of, Villon	6	34
Those Who Missay of France, Ballad against, Villon	6	35
Three Ravens, The, Medieval Literature	4	39
Villon in Prison, Ballad of, Villon	6	36
Wife of Usher's Well, The, Medieval Literature	4	48
Women of Paris, Ballad of the, Villon	6	31
Balladyna, Slowacki	10	512
Balmont, Konstantin	10	327
Balzac, Honoré de	6	551
Bancroft, George	17	11
Banks o' Doon, The, Burns	12	612
Banquet Song, A, Alcæus	2	113
Banville, Théodore de	7	286
Barbara Frietchie, Whittier	17	164
Barbarossa, Rückert	9	412
Barber of Seville, The, Beaumarchais	6	373
Barchester Towers, Trollope	14	165
Bard, The, Gray	12	341
Barefoot Boy, The, Whittier	17	171
Barham, Richard Harris	13	460
Barlow, Joel	16	206
Barnes, William	13	505
Barnouw, A. J., on		
Bilderdijk	8	371
Bredero	8	350
Cats	8	347
Hildebrand	8	373
Hooft	8	345
Huygens	8	353
The Imitation of Christ	4	474
Middle Dutch Literature	4	467
Modern Dutch Literature	8	396
Multatuli	8	384
Reinaert the Fox	4	470
Vondel	8	334
Barrès, Maurice	7	444
Barrie, Sir James Matthew	15	316
Baruch of Mayence, Tchernichowsky	1	207
Bataille de Dames, Scribe	6	535
Battenhouse, H. M., on the New Testament	2	422
Battle of Blenheim, The, Southey	13	117
Battle of Ivry, The, Macaulay	13	541
Battle-Field, The, Bryant	16	427
Baucis and Philemon, Ovid	3	252
Baudelaire, Charles	7	18
Beaconsfield, Lord	14	44
Beaumarchais	6	371
Beaumont, Francis	11	374
Beauty, see Esthetics		
Beauty, Baudelaire	7	29
Beauty Unadorned, Propertius	3	234
Beauty Which Decayeth, The, Cohen	1	205
Bed in Summer, Stevenson	15	274
Beddoes, Thomas Lovell	13	492
Bede	4	341 343
Before the Storm, Dehmel	9	577
Beggar's Opera, The, Gay	12	119
Beholding of God in His Footsteps in This Sensible World, On the, St. Bonaventura	5	22
Being, Of, Edwards	16	63
Beleaguered City, The, Longfellow	17	118

	VOL.	PAGE
Belfrey of Bruges, The, Longfellow	17	130
Believe It Not, Tolstoy	10	324
Believe Me, If All Those Endearing Young Charms, Moore	13	290
Belle Dame Sans Merci, La, Keats	13	457
Belle of the Ball, The, Praed	13	498
Belloc, Hilaire	15	600
Bells, The, Poe	17	572
Belly and the Members, The, Æsop	2	62
Beloved, To the, Sappho	2	110
Beloved Youth Gains Fame from the Poet's Songs, The, Theognis	2	117
Benavente, Jacinto	8	241
Benefits, Lessing	9	78
Bennett, Arnold	15	430
Bennett, C. E., on Tacitus	3	345
Bentham, Jeremy	12	562
Bentzon, Th. (Madame Thérèse Blanc), on Sand	7	30
Beowulf, Anglo-Saxon Literature	4	325
Béranger, Jean-Pierre de	6	524
Bérenger, Henry, on François Rabelais	6	39
Bergson, Henri Louis	7	459
Berkeley, George	12	42
Bernard de Ventadour, Provençal Literature	4	401
Bertrand d'Alamanon, Provençal Literature	4	413
Bessie Bell and Mary Gray, Medieval Literature	4	38
Bessy Bell and Mary Gray, Ramsay	12	199
Bestiaries and Lapidaries	4	510
Betrothed, The, Manzoni	5	350
	359,	364
Better Answer, A, Prior	12	39
Between Heaven and Earth, Ludwig	9	355
Beyle, Marie-Henri (Stendhal)	6	539
Bezruč, Petr	10	566
Bhagavad Gita, Indian Literature	1	452
Bhartrihari	1	454
Bialik, Khayyim Nakhman	1	211
Bigelow, John, on Franklin	16	68
Biglow Papers, The, Lowell	17	339
Bilderdijk, Willem	8	371
Bill and Joe, Holmes	17	203
Bingham, J. F., on Pellico	5	377
Petrarch	5	84
Tasso	5	234
Binnorie, Medieval Literature	4	51
Biography. See also Characterizations		
Abraham Lincoln: a History, Hay	18	126
American Literature: The New Art of Biography	18	555
Annals, Tacitus	3	358
Antony and Cleopatra, Ferrero	5	536
Antony and Cleopatra, Plutarch	2	491
Autobiography, Franklin	16	80
	82, 84,	97
Caligula's Madness, Suetonius	3	391
Catiline's Conspiracy, History of, Sallust	3	144
Causeries du Lundi, Sainte-Beuve	6	627
Charles II, The Character of, Macaulay	13	529
Confessions, Augustine	3	442
		443
Confessions of an English Opium-Eater, De Quincey	13	367
		372
Constantine, Character of, Gibbon	12	435
Coriolanus, Plutarch	2	479
Description of Himself, D'Alembert	6	369
Easy Chair, The, Curtis	17	475
England, History of, Froude	14	621
Essais, Montaigne	6	83
Estimate of Himself, Lessing	9	91
Father and Son, Gosse	15	635
Gibbon, Strachey	15	678
Goncourts, The, de Gourmont	7	441
Herbert, Life of Mr. George, Walton	11	509
Heroes and Hero-Worship, Carlyle	13	558
History, Sze-ma Ch'ien	1	508
Hooker, Life of Mr. Richard, Walton	11	507
Illustrious Ladies, Lives of, Brantôme	6	78
Johnson, Life of Samuel, Boswell	12	281
Julian, Death of, Gibbon	12	438
Letters, Burney	12	470

	VOL.	PAGE
Letters from My Windmill, Daudet	7	225
Life and Opinions, Ewald	10	54
Mahomet's Death and Character, Gibbon	12	443
Memoirs, Adams, J. Q.	16	247
		248, 249
Memoirs, Fuller	17	227
		231
Memoirs, Saint-Simon	6	283
My Childhood, Gorky	10	464
My Recollections, D'Azeglio	5	368
		371, 374
My Sister Henriette, Renan	7	116
Narrative of His Religious History, Edwards	16	60
Nero, Cowardice and Death of, Suetonius	3	393
Of Myself, Cowley	11	480
Pericles, Plutarch	2	468
Personal Memoirs, Grant	17	601
Petrarch's Laura, Foscolo	5	333
Philip II, History of, Prescott	16	472
Philosophers, Lives and Sayings of the, Diogenes Laërtius	2	535
Plutarch on Himself, Plutarch	2	490
Portraits of Men, Sainte-Beuve	6	629
Prigioni, Le Mie, Pellico	5	379
Raphael Sanzio, Vasari	5	261
Renaissance, The, Michelet	6	654
Roger Williams: The Prophet of Religious Freedom, Eggleston	18	84
Rome, History of, Levy	3	218
Rome, History of, Mommsen	9	433
Rousseau, Morley	15	202
Savonarola, Life and Times of, Villari	5	413
Struggle against Illness and Assassins, The, Mussolini	5	574
Toussaint l'Ouverture, Phillips	16	496
United States, History of the, Bancroft	17	19
		21
Valedictory to the Senate, The, Clay	16	274
Vitellius, Suetonius	3	395
Worthies of England, The, Fuller	11	546
		547
Biography, The New Art of	18	555

	VOL.	PAGE
Biology, see Science		
Bion	2	406
Bion, The Lamentation for, Moschus	2	411
Birds, see Nature		
Birds, The Aristophanes	2	230
Birds in the Night, Verlaine	7	283
Birth of Christ, The, New Testament	2	429
Birthday, A, Rossetti, C. G.	14	471
Bishop of Beauvais and Joan of Arc, The, De Quincey	13	378
Bishop of Rum-Ti-Foo, The, Gilbert	14	499
Bishop, W. H., on Pereda	8	186
Bittersweet, Holland	17	429
		430
Björnson, Björnstjerne	10	230
Björnstjerne Björnson, Brandes	10	126
Blackmwore Maidens, Barnes	13	506
Blake, William	12	630
Blanche-Taque, Of the Battle of, Froissart	6	20
Blasco Ibañez, see Ibañez, Blasco		
Blessèd Damozel, The, Rossetti	14	459
Blind Men and the Elephant, The, Sama'i	1	300
Blindness, On His, Milton	11	449
Bloch, Joshua, on		
Medieval Hebrew Literature	1	152
Modern Hebrew Literature	1	195
Blok, Alexander	10	328
Blot of Shame, The, Anzengruber	9	487
Boccaccio	5	105
Bôcher, Ferdinand, on Montaigne	6	80
Boëthius	3	460
Boileau-Despréaux, Nicholas	6	222
Bojer, Johan	10	286
Bolingbroke, Henry St. John, Viscount	12	101
Bon Gaultier Ballads, Aytoun	13	504
Bonaventura, St.	5	20
Bonds of Interest, The, Benavente	8	244
Bonduca, Fletcher	11	390
Bonnie George Campbell, Medieval Literature	4	37
Bonny Dundee, Scott	13	151
Bonny Earl of Murray, The, Medieval Literature	4	34
Book of My Friend, The, France	7	369

	VOL.	PAGE
Book of Poetry, The, Chinese Literature	1	509
Book of the Dun (Cow), Medieval Irish Literature	4	228
Books and Reading, see Literature		
Books and Reading, On, Schopenhauer	9	284
Bore, The, Horace	3	205
Boris Godunov, Pushkin	10	339
Borrow, George	13	644
Bossuet, Jacques Bénigne	6	217
Boswell, James	12	277
Botany, see Nature		
Bourdeille, Pierre de, see Brantôme		
Bourget, Paul	7	395
Bourget, Paul, on Flaubert	7	53
Boynton, H. W., on		
British Fiction in the Twentieth Century	15	368
Galsworthy	15	444
Brandes, Georg	10	122
Branding-Ground, The, Farrukhi	1	295
Brandon House, The, Jewett	18	301
Brantôme, Abbé de (Pierre de Bourdeille)	6	75
Break, Break, Break, Tennyson	14	276
Bredero, Gerbrand Adriaenszoon	8	350
Breviary of Æsthetic, The, Croce	5	510
Brewster, Dorothy, on		
Carpenter	15	225
Lagerlöf	10	182
Brewster, W. T., on Gil Vicente	8	274
Březina, Otakar	10	565
Bridge, The, Longfellow	17	132
Bridge of Sighs, The, Hood	13	468
Bridges, Robert	15	551
Bridges, Robert (Droch), on Stevenson	15	252
Brief Is Pain, Carpenter	15	231
Briefness of Life, The, Drummond	11	141
Brieux, Eugène	7	476
Bright Star! Would I Were Steadfast as Thou Art, Keats	13	459
Brightest and Best of the Sons of the Morning, Heber	12	573
Brignall Banks, see Rokeby		
Brihadaranyaka Upanishad, Indian Literature	1	437
Bristowe Tragedie, The, Chatterton	12	370
Broken Bell, The, Baudelaire	7	27
Broken Heart, The, Ford	11	407 409
Broken Music, Aldrich	18	69
Broken Ring, The, Eichendorff	9	297
Brontë, Charlotte	14	218
Brontë, Emily	14	218
Brooding, Machar	10	568
Brook, The, Tennyson	14	292
Brooke, Rupert	15	610
Brother's Grave, A, Catullus	3	161
Brown, C. N., on		
Greek Literature (The Glory That Was Greece)	2	1
Modern Greek Literature	8	645
Brown, Charles Brockden	16	255
Brown, R. C. E., on		
Ingersoll	17	618
Wilson, Woodrow	18	372
Browne, Charles Farrar (Artemus Ward)	17	390
Browne, Sir Thomas	11	521
Browne, William	11	142
Brownell, W. C., on Thackeray	14	68
Browning, Elizabeth Barrett	14	399
Browning, Robert	14	324
Bruce, J. D., on Spenser	11	58
Bruce to His Men at Bannockburn, Burns	12	610
Brunetière, Ferdinand	7	420
Brunetière, Ferdinand, on		
Renan	7	107
Taine	7	132
Bruno, Giordano	5	266
Bruyère, Jean de La, see La Bruyère		
Bryant, William Cullen	16	417
Bryce, James	15	188
Buchner, E. F., on Fichte	9	209
Buckle, Henry Thomas	14	582
Buddenbrooks, Mann	9	610 613
Buddhistic Literature	1	440
Buffon, George Louis le Clerc	6	333
Bulgarian Literature	10	572
Bull, The, Hodgson	15	621
Bulwer-Lytton, Edward	14	52
Bunker Hill Monument, Oration on Laying the Corner-Stone of the, Webster	16	312
Bunner, Henry Cuyler	18	356
Bunyan, John	11	589
Burden of the Desert, The, Simms	17	535
Bürger, Gottfried August	9	107
Burial of Sir John Moore at Corunna, The, Wolfe	13	484

	VOL.	PAGE
Burke, Edmund	12	404
Burlingame, E. L., on Browning	14	324
Burney, Frances (Madame d'Arblay)	12	464
Burns, Robert	12	582
Burns, Whittier	17	183
Burrill, E. W., on De Morgan	15	400
Burroughs, John	18	89
Burroughs, John, on		
Thoreau	17	297
Whitman	17	402
Burton, Richard, on		
Field	18	509
Heine	9	313
Lanier	18	193
Burton, Sir Richard F.	14	665
Burton, Robert	11	113
Bushnell, Horace	16	505
Busybodies, Plautus	3	49
But Little Here Below, Martial	3	343
Butler, Nicholas Murray, on the Columbia University Course in Literature	1	1
Butler, Samuel	11	489
Butler, Samuel	15	154
Byron, Lord	13	306
Byron, Miller	18	192

C

	VOL.	PAGE
Cabell, I. C., on Beaconsfield	14	44
Cable, George W.	18	262
Cælius	3	96
Cæsar, Caius Julius	3	106
Cæsar and Cleopatra, Shaw	15	495
Çakuntala; or, The Lost Ring, Kalidasa	1	464
Calderon, Pedro	8	130
Calderon y su Teatro, Menendez y Pelayo	8	228
Calendau, Mistral	7	208
		210, 213
Calhoun, John Caldwell	16	294
Caligula's Madness, Suetonius	3	391
"Call Me Not Dead," Gilder	18	507
Caller Herrin', Nairne	12	617
Callimachus	2	386
Calpurnius Siculus	3	454
Calverley, Charles Stuart	14	492
Calvin, John	6	58
Camera Obscura, Hildebrand	8	373
Camoens, Luiz Vaz de	8	282
Campaspe, Lyly	11	192
		200
Campbell, Thomas	13	260
Campbell, Wilfred	8	494
Campion, Thomas	11	136
Canadian Literature	8	482
Canadians, The Rights of, Howe	8	502
Candida, Shaw	15	490
Candide: or All for the Best, Voltaire	6	311
		312, 319, 320, 321
Canfield, A. G., on Pascal	6	196
Cannibalism, Martial	3	341
Canning, George	13	235
Canterbury Tales, Prologue to the, Chaucer	4	563
Canticle of the Shining Ones, Bruno	5	270
Canticle of the Sun, The, St. Francis of Assisi	5	18
Cantigas, Alfonso the Wise	8	23
Canzone to La Pietra, Dante	5	81
Čapek, Karel	10	561
Captain and the Mermaids, The, Gilbert	14	502
Captives, The, Plautus	3	49
		50
Card-Dealer, The, Rossetti	14	463
Carducci, Giosuè	5	429
Carew, Thomas	11	168
Carlyle, Thomas	13	544
Carlyle, On, Mazzini	5	407
Carman, Bliss	8	495
Carmen, Mérimée	6	618
Carnations, The, Herrick	11	166
Carpenter, Edward	15	225
Carpenter, G. R., on		
De Quincey	13	362
Whittier	17	151
Carpenter, W. H., on		
Alcuin	4	483
The Eddas	4	273
Ibsen	10	205
Carroll, Lewis	15	140
Cary, Edward, on Curtis	17	465
Caryatids, The, de Banville	7	287
Casanova	5	320
Casas, Bartolomeo de Las, see Las Casas, Bartolomeo de		
Casina, Plautus	3	47
		50
Cassandra, To, Ronsard	6	71
Castiglione, Baldassare	5	182
Castile, The Spirit of, Unamuno	8	237
Casting Away of Mrs. Lecks and Mrs. Aleshine, The, Stockton	18	2
Casting of the Perseus, The, Cellini	5	222

	VOL.	PAGE
Castle of Indolence, The, Thomson	12	314
Castle Rackrent, Edgeworth	13	121
		124
Cat, the Weasel, and the Young Rabbit, The, La Fontaine	6	129
Çatapatha Brahmana, Indian Literature	1	437
Catiline's Conspiracy, History of, Sallust	3	144
		146
Cato the Censor	3	22
Cats, Jacob	8	347
Catullus, Valerius	3	155
Caucasus, Pushkin	10	335
Causeries du Lundi, Sainte-Beuve	6	627
Cazamian, Louis, on French Literature from 1848 to the Present Day — a General View	7	1
Celia, Song to, Jonson	11	352
Cellini, Benvenuto	5	214
Celtic Literature		
Medieval Irish Literature	4	192
Modern Irish Literature in Gaelic	8	557
Other Celtic Literatures	4	270
Welsh Literature	4	243
Cenci, The, Shelley	13	387
Centaur, The, de Guérin	6	532
Centennial Hymn, Whittier	17	176
Certain Condescension in Foreigners, On a, Lowell	17	355
Cervantes	8	82
Chadwick, J. W., on		
Lecky	15	178
Parker	17	233
Chambered Nautilus, The, Holmes	17	197
Chandler, F. W., on		
Modern American Drama	18	538
Twentieth-Century Drama in England	15	460
Changed, Calverley	14	493
Changeling, The, Lowell	17	328
Channing, William Ellery	16	281
Chants du Paysan, Déroulède	7	246
Chapman, George	11	318
Chapman's Homer, see On First Looking into Chapman's Homer		
Chapter on Ears, A, Lamb	13	209
Characterizations. See also Biography		
Absalom and Achitophel, Dryden	11	622
Characters, La Bruyère	6	247
Corsica, An Account of, Boswell	12	280
Daniel Gray, Holland	17	431
Death of 'Abdallah, The, Duraid	1	232
Euphues and His England, Lyly	11	190
Ichabod, Whittier	17	170
Isaac Ashford, Crabbe	12	626
Italy, Heine	9	335
Jean-Christophe, Rolland	7	535
Last Leaf, The, Holmes	17	194
Laudator Temporis Acti, Petronius	3	332
Letters, Pliny the Younger	3	377
		380
Mann, Letter to Sir Horace, Walpole	12	347
Master of the Feast, The, Petronius	3	333
Memoirs, Saint-Simon	6	284
		288
Michael, Wordsworth	13	31
Milton, John, Macaulay	13	526
Old Gentlemen, The, Hunt	13	302
Old Lady, The, Hunt	13	300
Pencillings by the Way, Willis	17	104
Phædo, Plato	2	317
Prue and I, Curtis	17	472
Redburn, Melville	17	443
Return of the Native, The, Hardy	15	83
Spectator, The, Addison	12	93
Talisman, The, Scott	13	169
Trimalchio's Reminiscences, Petronius	3	331
Village Corsican, A, Boswell	12	281
Characters, La Bruyère	6	244
		247
Charbonnel, Victor, on		
Schérer	7	98
Verlaine	7	276
Charge of the Light Brigade, The, Tennyson	14	306
Charge to Keep I Have, A, Charles Wesley	12	547
Charity, Doctrine of, Swedenborg	10	151
Charlemagne, A Letter to, Alcuin	4	486
Charles, Duke of Byron, Tragedy of, Chapman	11	322
Charles IV, The Court of, Galdos	8	202

	VOL.	PAGE
Charles II, The Character of, Macaulay	13	529
Chastisements, Hugo	6	500, 501
Chateaubriand, François René Auguste	6	418
Chattahoochee, Song of the, Lanier	18	197
Chatterton, Thomas	12	367
Chaucer, Geoffrey	4	552
Chaucer, Longfellow	17	142
Chekhov, Anton Pavlovich	10	451
Chemineau, Le, Richepin	7	292
Chemistry, see Science		
Chénier, André	6	400
Cherry Orchard, The, Chekhov	10	457
Chesterfield, Lord	12	255
Chesterton, Gilbert Keith	15	642
"Chi Vuol Veder Quantunque Può Natura," Petrarch	5	103
"Chiare, Fresche e Dolci Acque," Petrarch	5	98
Child Jesus, The, New Testament	2	431
Child of Quality, To a, Prior	12	36
Child-Songs, Whittier	17	180
Child's Future, A, Swinburne	15	127
Childe Harold's Pilgrimage, Byron	13	318, 319, 321, 322, 324
Childe Maurice, Medieval Literature	4	43
Children. See also Education		
Art of Grandfatherhood, The, Hugo	6	497
Autumn Leaves, Hugo	6	498
Barefoot Boy, The, Whittier	17	171
Bed in Summer, Stevenson	15	274
Bittersweet, Holland	17	429
Book of My Friend, The, France	7	369
Buddenbrooks, Mann	9	613
Changeling, The, Lowell	17	328
Child of Quality, To a, Prior	12	36
Child-Songs, Whittier	17	180
Child's Future, A, Swinburne	15	127
Contemplations, Hugo	6	502, 503
Cossack Cradle Song, The, Lermontov	10	316
Countess of Bute, Letters to the, Montagu	12	252
Cry of the Children, The, Browning, E. B.	14	403
Dream-Children: a Revery, Lamb	13	231
Dutch Lullaby, Field	18	511
Education: Intellectual, Moral, and Physical, Spencer	14	694, 701
Eton College, On a Distant Prospect of, Gray	12	338
Étude Réaliste, Swinburne	15	127
From Childhood, Liliencron	9	429
Good-by to Childhood, Greek Anthology	2	579
Hartley Coleridge, To, Wordsworth	13	50
In School Days, Whittier	17	166
Letter to His Father, at the Age of Ten, Adams, J. Q.	16	246
Little Orphant Annie, Riley	18	315
Little Women, Alcott	17	383
Menaphon, Greene	11	209
My Boy, Rosenfeld	8	639
My Children, Yamagami no Okura	1	542
My Lost Youth, Longfellow	17	135
My Recollections, D'Azeglio	5	368
Old Wives' Tale, The, Bennett	15	438
Oratory, A Dialogue on, Tacitus	3	349
Out to Old Aunt Mary's, Riley	18	311
Parental Ode to My Son, A, Hood	13	465
Parzival, Wolfram von Eschenbach	4	444
Passing Saint, To the, Field	18	51
Penrod, Tarkington	18	4
Pépa, To, Musset	6	47
Picture of Little T. C., The, Marvell	11	47
Prescience, Aldrich	18	71
Quest, The, Eeden	8	404
Registre of Hystories, A, Ælianus Claudius	3	416
Reminiscences of Childhood, Bentham	12	566
Retreat, The, Vaughan	11	473
Rocking Hymn, A, Wither	11	143
Salt of the Earth, The, Swinburne	15	126
Satires, Juvenal	3	374
Schoolmaster, The, Ascham	11	14
She Came and Went, Lowell	17	328
Swann's Way, Proust	7	567

	VOL.	PAGE
Toys, The, Patmore	14	478
What the Moon Saw, Andersen	10	115
Children of the World, Heyse	9	466
Chinese and Roman Artists, The, Jalal ad-Din Rumi	1	371
Chinese Literature	1	494
Chiushingura, Japanese Literature	1	564
Chloe, To, Horace	3	199
Choice, The, Rossetti	14	467
Christ before Pilate, New Testament	2	444
Christ, Excellency of, Edwards	16	64
Christabel, Coleridge	13	94
Christian Morals, Browne	11	535
Christian Poetry, Armenian Literature	1	391
Christmas Carol, A, Wither	11	146
Christmas Purchases, Schnitzler	9	561
Chrysostom, St. John	2	551
Chuang Tzu	1	502
Cicero, Marcus Tullius	3	68
Cicero, Letter to, Cæsar	3	95
Cicero, Letter to, Cælius	3	96
Cicero, Letter to, Matius	3	97
Cid, The	8	8
Cid, The, Corneille	6	107, 109
Cid, The Poem of My, Spanish Literature	8	14
Cinque Port, A, Davidson	15	540
Circles, Emerson	17	46
Citizenship, see Government		
Citizenship in a Republic, Roosevelt	18	390
City of Chandu, and the Kaan's Palace There, Of the, Marco Polo	4	522
City of Dreadful Night, The, Thomson	14	505
City of God, The, Augustine	3	444
Civilization, see Sociology		
Civilization in Europe, General History of, Guizot	6	644
Clapp, E. B., on Plutarch	2	465
Classicism. See also Literature		
French Literature: The Classical Tradition	6	90
French Literature: The Decline of Classicism	6	254
Jonson, Ben	11	338
Renaissance, The, Italian Literature	5	128
Claudianus, Claudius	3	458
Claudius, Ælianus	3	415
Clay, Henry	16	265
Cleanthes	2	384
Clemens, Samuel Langhorne (Mark Twain)	18	27
Clifton Chapel, Newbolt	15	572
Clockmaker, The, Haliburton	8	506, 508
Cloister and the Hearth, The, Reade	14	187
Cloud, The, Shelley	13	399
Cloud Confines, The, Rossetti	14	465
Clouds, The, Aristophanes	2	227
Clough, Arthur Hugh	14	445
Cobbler's Last, The, Martial	3	343
Coester, Alfred, on Latin-American Literature since 1888	8	309
Cohen, Jacob	1	204
Cohn, Adolphe, on		
Brunetière	7	420
Hugo	6	488
Voltaire	6	304
Coleridge, Samuel Taylor	13	67
Colette Baudoche, Barrès	7	455
Collar, The, Herbert	11	156
Collected Essays, Huxley	14	558, 564, 565
Collins, F. H., on Spencer	14	684
Collins, William	12	325
Colonial Period, see American Literature in the Colonial Period		
Columbia University Course in Literature, The	1	1
Come, Holy Spirit, Heavenly Dove, Watts	12	193
Come, Rest in This Bosom, Moore	13	290
Comedy. See also Drama		
Aristophanes	2	213
Goldoni	5	286
Molière	6	137
Philemon, Menander, etc.	2	345
Plautus, Titus Maccius	3	39
Terence	3	52
Comenius, see Komensky		
Common Lot, The, Greek Anthology	2	577
Compensation, Bruno	5	274
Compensation, Emerson	17	42
Complete Angler, The, Walton	11	510
Comrade, To a, Musset	6	477
Comte, Auguste	6	657
Comtesse de Die, Provençal Literature	4	411

	VOL.	PAGE
Comus, Milton	11	443
Conciliation with America, Speech on, Burke	12	412
Concord Hymn, Emerson	17	64
Condla the Red, Adventures of, Medieval Irish Literature	4	220
Conduct of Life, The, Croce	5	527
Confessio Amantis, Gower	4	544
Confession of Sloth, The, Piers Plowman	4	534
Confessions, Augustine	3	442
		443
Confessions, Browning	14	382
Confessions of an English Opium-Eater, De Quincey	13	367
		372
Confucius	1	505
Congreve, William	11	646
Congreve, To My Dear Friend Mr., Dryden	11	627
Connecticut Yankee in King's Arthur's Court, A, Clemens	18	55
Conqueror's Grave, The, Bryant	16	425
Conquerors, The, Hérédia	7	256
Conquest of England by the Normans, History of the, Thierry	6	639
Conquest of Mexico, The, Prescott	16	453
Conquest of Peru, The, Prescott	16	466
Conrad, Joseph	15	345
Consider It Again, Clough	14	454
Constance, Letter from, Hus	10	553
Constant Lover, The, Suckling	11	175
Constantine, Character of, Gibbon	12	435
Consulate of Stilicho, The, Claudianus	3	458
Contemplations, Hugo	6	502
		503
Conversation of the Herdsman Dhaniya with the Buddha, Buddhistic Literature	1	441
Conversations with Eckermann, Goethe	9	172
Conversion of the Giant Morgante, The, Pulci	5	160
Convito, The, Dante	5	57
Conviviality		
Ad Amphoram, Horace	3	202
Banquet Song, A, Alcæus	2	113
Drinking, Anacreon	2	121
Epicure, The, Anacreon	2	122
Ideal Trio, An, Li Po	1	512
Invitation, An, Alcæus	2	113
Mæcenas, An Invitation to, Horace	3	203
Poet's Choice, The, Anacreon	2	125
Song, Beaumont and Fletcher	11	394
Thaliarchus, To, Horace	3	198
Cook Well Done, The, Martial	3	342
Cooke, J. G., on		
Le Sage	6	266
Trollope	14	162
Cooper, F. T., on Beyle	6	539
Cooper, James Fenimore	16	383
Cooper Institute, Speech at the, Lincoln	17	586
Copernicus	10	494
Coppée, François	7	259
Coquette, To a, Campion	11	138
Coral, Bestiaries	4	517
Corinna's Parrot, On the Death of, Ovid	3	248
Corinna's Singing, Of, Campion	11	137
Corinne, de Staël	6	412
Coriolanus, Plutarch	2	479
Cormac Mac Culennain Sang This, Medieval Irish Literature	4	242
Corneille, Pierre	6	103
Cornelia, Propertius	3	239
Correggio, Oehlenschläger	10	88
Correspondence, Erasmus	8	329
Corsica, An Account of, Boswell	12	280
Cortegiano, Il, Castiglione	5	185
Cossack Cradle Song, The, Lermontov	10	316
Cotter's Saturday Night, The, Burns	12	593
Coulanges, Letter to Her Cousin, M. de, de Sévigné	6	210
Coulanges, Letter to M. de, de Sévigné	6	211
Count Gismond, Browning	14	334
Counterfeiters, The, Gide	7	551
		556
Countess of Bute, Letters to the, Montagu	12	252
		253, 254
Countess of Mar, Letter to the, Montagu	12	249
Country Life, On the Pleasures of a, Tibullus	3	224
Country Mouse and the City Mouse, The, Æsop	2	64
Countryman and the Snake, The, Æsop	2	61

	VOL.	PAGE
Couperus, Louis	8	411
Courtin', The, Lowell	17	345
Courting of T'nowhead's Bell, The, Barrie	15	325
Cowley, Abraham	11	478
Cowper, William	12	394
Coy Maiden, To a, Greek Anthology	2	580
Crabbe, George	12	624
Cradle Song, A, Blake	12	638
Crainquebille, Putois, Riquet, and Other Profitable Tales, France	7	377
Cranford, Gaskell	14	243 249
Crawford, Lindsay, on Modern Irish Literature in Gaelic	8	557
Creation, Noyes	15	578
Creation, The, Ovid	3	251
Creative Evolution, Bergson	7	467
Cressey, Of the Battle of, Froissart	6	24
Crèvecœur, Hector Saint John de	16	102
Cricket, The, Cowper	12	397
Crime of Sylvestre Bonnard, The, France	7	365
Crimean Sonatas, Mickiewicz	10	508
Crisis, The, Paine	16	165
Criticism. See also Literature		
Art of Poetry, The, Boileau-Despréaux	6	224 226
Art of Poetry, The, Horace	3	209
Conversations with Eckermann, Goethe	9	172
Criticism, On, Schopenhauer	9	286
Dickens, Charles, Chesterton	15	648
Essay on Criticism, Pope	12	141
Every Man in His Humor, Jonson	11	352
Flaubert, Correspondence with, Sand	7	47
Frogs, The, Aristophanes	2	237
Heroic Enthusiasts, The, Bruno	5	268
Journal, Goncourts	7	85
Knights, The, Aristophanes	2	225
Nouveaux Lundis, Sainte-Beuve	6	623
One Book More, Laforgue	7	293
Popular Playwrights, Heywood	11	367
Problems of Modern Democracy, Godkin	17	494
Shakespeare, On, Jonson	11	342
Shakespeare, To the Memory of, Jonson	11	343
Terentius, Epigram on, Cæsar	3	129
Criticism, On, Schopenhauer	9	286
Critique of Pure Reason, The, Kant	9	69
Croakers, The, Drake	16	441
Croce, Benedetto	5	507
Crocodile, The, Bestiaries	4	515
Crossing the Bar, Tennyson	14	323
Crowded Street, The, Bryant	16	423
Crown of Wild Olive, The, Ruskin	13	612
Cry of the Children, The, Browning, E. B.	14	403
Cuarto Poder, El, Valdes	8	223
Cuckoo, To the, Wordsworth	13	53
Culprit Fay, The, Drake	16	442
Culture and Anarchy, Arnold	14	421
Cunlife, J. W., on		
The Age of Milton	11	418
British Essayists in the Twentieth Century	15	626
The Elizabethan Theater	11	177
English Literature: Eighteenth Century Survey	12	1
English Literature: The Romantic Revival	13	1
Mille	7	525
The Revolt from Victorianism	15	1
Shakespeare to Dryden	11	1
The Victorian Era	14	1
Cupid and Campaspe, Lyly	11	200
Cupid Mistaken, Prior	12	39
Curious Scythian Customs, Herodotus	2	249
Curious Youth, Letter from a, Alciphron	2	517
Curse of Kehama, The, Southey	13	114
Curtis, George William	17	465
Customs, see Manners and Customs		
Cuvier	6	425
Cyclic Poets and the Homeric Hymns, The	2	66
Cymbeline, Shakespeare	11	263
Cynthia, To, Propertius	3	236
Cynthia's Revels, Jonson	11	355
Cyrano de Bergerac, Rostand	7	494
Cyriack Skinner, To, Milton	11	450
Cyropedia, Xenophon	2	287
Czechoslovak Literature	10	550
Czechoslovak Poetry	10	565

	VOL.	PAGE
D		
Dadu Panthis, Bible of the, Indian Literature	1	459
Daffodils, To, Herrick	11	165
Dafydd ab Gwilym, see Ab Gwilym, Dafydd		
D'Alembert, Jean le Rond	6	368
Dame Care, Sudermann	9	519
		521
Dana, Richard Henry, Junior	17	290
Daniel Gray, Holland	17	431
Danish Literature	10	13
Danish National Song, The, see King Christian		
D'Annunzio, Gabriele, see Annunzio, Gabriele d'		
Danny Deever, Kipling	15	312
Dante	5	33
Daphnis and Chloe, Longus	2	566
Darest Thou Now, O Soul, Whitman	17	426
Darwin, Charles Robert	14	510
Daudet, Alphonse	7	215
Daughter of Iorio, The, D'Annunzio	5	501
David and Absalom, Willis	17	106
David and Bethsabe, Peele	11	203
David Copperfield, Dickens	14	119
124, 131, 136, 141, 147,	149,	155
Davidson, John	15	534
Davidson, Thomas, on		
Abélard	4	487
Aristotle	2	335
Nairne	12	614
St. Bonaventura	5	20
Sappho	2	103
Dawn of Spring, Hofmannsthal	9	604
Day Is Coming, The, Morris	15	137
Day Is Done, The, Longfellow	17	133
Day of Pentecost, The, New Testament	2	447
Days, Emerson	17	58
D'Azeglio, Massimo	5	367
De Agricultura, Cato	3	24
De Amicis, Edmondo	5	468
"De Gustibus—," Browning	14	373
De Morgan, William Frend	15	400
De Quincey, Thomas	13	362
Deacon's Masterpiece, The, or, The Wonderful "One-Hoss Shay," Holmes	17	198
Dead, The, Verhaeren	8	445
Dead Love, Sonnet to His, Camoens	8	292
Death. See also Epitaphs		
Apology, The, Plato	2	320
Away, Riley	18	318
Brother's Grave, A, Catullus	3	161
Card-Dealer, The, Rossetti	14	463
Charles, Duke of Byron, Tragedy of, Chapman	11	322
Cornelia, Propertius	3	239
Crossing the Bar, Tennyson	14	323
Dead, The, Verhaeren	8	445
Death of Thomson, Ode on the, Collins	12	329
Duchess of Malfi, The, Webster	11	357
Death, The Nothingness of, Lucretius	3	140
Earth-Bound, Noyes	15	580
End of All, The, Lucretius	3	141
Epitaph in the Form of a Ballad, The, Villon	6	33
Fragment on Mummies, A, Browne	11	542
Funeral Oration on Henrietta of France, Bossuet	6	218
Garden of Proserpine, The, Swinburne	15	115
Hydriotaphia, or Urn-Burial, Browne	11	538
Katha Upanishad, Indian Literature	1	439
King—and Death, The, Mahmud of Ghazna	1	297
Lament on His Father's Death, A, Liu Heng	1	511
Letter to His Wife on Their Daughter's Death, Plutarch	2	497
Letters, Pliny the Younger	3	382
Miss Tempy's Watchers, Jewett	18	293
Morning Thought, A, Sill	18	185
O Captain! My Captain, Whitman	17	425
Old Age, Dialogue on, Cicero	3	83
Pilgrimage, The, Herbert	11	158
Porter, Mrs. Lucy, Letter to, Johnson	12	268
Prospice, Browning	14	383
Rambler, The, Johnson	12	274
Rubaiyat	1	343
Rules and Exercises of Holy Dying, Taylor	11	559
Strange, Sill	18	186
Sulpicius Consoles Cicero after His Daughter Tullia's Death, Sulpicius	3	88
Thanatopsis, Bryant	16	421

	VOL.	PAGE
They Are All Gone, Vaughan	11	475
Tombs in Westminster, On the, Beaumont	11	396
When Lilacs Last in the Door-Yard Bloomed, Whitman	17	418
Death Agony, The, Sully-Prudhomme	7	274
Death and the Fool, Hofmannsthal	9	606
Death and the Woodcutter, La Fontaine	6	127
Death of 'Abdallah, The, Duraid	1	232
Death of Ivo, The Slavonic Literature	10	602
Death of the Flowers, The, Bryant	16	424
Death of the Poor, The, Baudelaire	7	26
Death of Thomson, Ode on the, Collins	12	329
Death, The Nothingness of, Lucretius	3	140
Deborah Outwits the Cossack, Ash	8	632
Declaration of Independence, The, Jefferson	16	180
Decoration Day Oration, Ingersoll	17	621
Dedication for a Volume of Lyrics, Catullus	3	157
Dedication Hymn, Willis	17	108
Defendant, The, Chesterton	15	653
Defense of His Dictatorship, Solon	2	128
Deffaud, Letter to Mme. du, Voltaire	6	330
Defoe, Daniel	12	16
Dehmel, Richard	9	574
Deirdre's Farewell to Scotland, Medieval Irish Literature	4	236
Dejection: An Ode, Coleridge	13	106
Dekker, Eduard Douwes, see Multatuli		
Dekker, Thomas	11	324
Delavigne, Jean François Casimir	6	529
Deloney, Thomas	11	78
Demeter, Hymn to, Homeric Hymns	2	73
Democracy, see Government		
Democracy, Lowell	17	352
Democracy in America, de Tocqueville	6	667, 669, 670, 671
Demon, The, Lermontov	10	318
Demosthenes	2	368
Deor's Lament, Anglo-Saxon Literature	4	329
Déroulède, Paul	7	245
Desbordes-Valmore, Madame	6	527
Descartes, René	6	96
Descent into the Maelström, A, Poe	17	539
Descent of Man, The, Darwin	14	535
Descent of Man, On Our Present Knowledge of the, Haeckel	9	483
Description, see Travel		
Description of Himself, D'Alembert	6	369
Desert, a Beggar Born, Theognis	2	119
Deserted Village, The, Goldsmith	12	515
Destiny, Aldrich	18	68
Devil and the Deep Sea, The, Leacock	8	514
Deyssel, Lodewijk van	8	410
Dhammapada, Buddhistic Literature	1	440
Dialogue, Wieland	9	102
Diamond Cut Diamond, Martial	3	342
Diamond Lens, The, O'Brien	17	479
Diamond Necklace, The, de Maupassant	7	342
Diaries. See also Biography		
Diary, Adams, John	16	159
Diary, Evelyn	11	563
Diary, Pepys	11	576
Journal, Goncourts	7	85
Journal, Woolman	16	144
Diary, Adams, John	16	159
Diary, Evelyn	11	563
Diary, Pepys	11	576
Diaz, Bernal	8	44
Dibdin, Charles	12	569
Dickens, Charles	14	106
Dickens, Charles, Chesterton	15	648
Dickens in Camp, Harte	18	171
Diderot, Denis	6	361
Diet of Worms, Reply at the, Luther	9	18
Dilemma, A, Andreyev	10	479
Diogenes Laërtius	2	534
Dionysus and the Pirates, Homeric Hymns	2	71
Directors of Amsterdam, To the, Huygens	8	355
Dirge, Beddoes	13	494
Dirge for Two Veterans, Whitman	17	417

	VOL.	PAGE
Disappointment, Shenstone	12	321
Discourse Delivered before the Congregational Ministers of Massachusetts, Channing	16	283
Discourse on Method, Descartes	6	99
		100
Discourse upon Universal History, Bossuet	6	220
Discourses, Epictetus	2	458
Discovery, see Exploration and Discovery		
Dispute of the Heart and Body, The, François Villon	6	32
Disraeli, Benjamin, see Beaconsfield		
Dissertation upon Roast Pig, A, Lamb	13	213
Distich, The, Schiller	9	191
Distinguished Men and Great Captains, Lives of, Brantôme	6	79
Divan, An-Nabighah	1	235
Divan, Labid	1	231
Divan, Nasir-i-Khusru	1	299
Diverting Scrape, A, Martial	3	342
Divina Commedia, Longfellow	17	143
Divine and Moral Songs, Campion	11	138
Divine Providence, Swedenborg	10	149
Do You Not See, Beloved? Solovyev	10	327
Dobell, Sydney	14	481
Dobson, Austin	14	494
Doctor and Divinity, Greek Anthology	2	576
Doctor Faustus, Marlowe	11	222
Doctor's Dilemma, The, Shaw	15	505
Dodgson, Charles Lutwidge, see Carroll, Lewis		
Dog and the Wolf, The, Æsop	2	65
Dogs, Smith	13	249
Dole, N. H., on		
Goncharov	10	383
Omar Khayyam	1	337
Verga	5	443
Doll's House, A, Ibsen	10	218
Dominant Note of the Law, The, Japanese Literature	1	561
Don Juan, Byron	13	315
328, 329, 331, 332,		334
Don Quixote, Cervantes	8	88
92, 96, 99, 104,		108
Doña Perfecta, Galdos	8	204
Donne, John	11	148
Dora Versus Rose, Dobson	14	496
Dorothy Q., Holmes	17	205
Dostoyevsky, Feodor Mikhailovich	10	427
Doughty, Charles Montagu	14	676
Dover Beach, Arnold	14	431
Dowden, Edward, on		
Goethe	9	117
Shakespeare	11	229
Dragon-Fly, The, Gautier	6	682
Drake, Joseph Rodman	16	440
Drake in California, Hakluyt	11	32
Drake, On the Death of Joseph Rodman, Halleck	17	416
Drake, Song from, ("N'Oserez Vous"), Noyes	15	576
Drake's Drum, Newbolt	15	570
Drama. See also Tragedy; Comedy		
Casina, Plautus	3	47
Drama in England, Twentieth-Century	15	460
Dramatic Art and Literature, Lectures on, Schlegel, A. W. von	9	234
Dramatic Poesy, An Essay of, Dryden	11	618
Elizabethan Theater, The	11	177
Every Man in His Humor, Jonson	11	352
Hamlet, Thoughts on, Lemaître	7	427
Ibsen, Henrik	10	205
Medieval Drama, The	4	146
Modern American Drama	18	538
Opera and Drama, Wagner	9	373
Shakespeare, William	11	229
Shaw, Bernard, and the Theatre Guild	15	480
Spectator, The, Addison	12	95
Tom Jones, Fielding	12	187
Dramatic Art and Literature, Lectures on, Schlegel, A. W. von	9	234
Dramatic Poesy, An Essay of, Dryden	11	618
Drayton, Michael	11	130
Dream of Fair Women, A, Tennyson	14	276
Dream of Gerontius, The, Newman	14	41
Dream of Scipio, The, Cicero	3	99
Dream-Children: a Revery, Lamb	13	231
Dream-Pedlary, Beddoes	13	495
Dream Pictures, Heine	9	325
Dreaming, Petöfi	8	599
Dreams, On, Petronius	3	334
Dreyfus Case, On the, Dunne	18	468

	VOL.	PAGE
Drink to Me Only with Thine Eyes, see Celia, Song to		
Drinking, Anacreon	2	121
Droste-Hülshoff, Annette Elisabeth von	9	415
Drummond, William	11	139
Drummond, William Henry	8	497
Dryden, John	11	605
Duchess of Malfi, The, Webster	11	357
Duffield, Pitts, on		
Sidney	11	45
Smollett	12	238
Duke of Ferrara, To the, Tasso	5	257
Dumas, Alexandre, Junior	7	167
Dumas, Alexandre, Senior	6	589
Dun (Cow), Book of the, see Book of the Dun (Cow)		
Dunciad, Pope	12	160
Dunne, Finley Peter	18	464
Duraid of Jusharn	1	232
Dürer Painting the Saviour's Head, Machar	10	568
Dutch Literature		
Dutch Literature	8	314
Middle Dutch Literature	4	467
Modern Dutch Literature since 1880	8	396
Dutch Lullaby, Field	18	511
Duty, Ode to, Wordsworth	13	56
Dynasts, The, Hardy	15	91

E

	VOL.	PAGE
E Pluribus Unus, Martial	3	343
E. W. Montagu, Esq., Letter to, Montagu	12	248
Each and All, Emerson	17	52
Eagle, The, Bestiaries	4	513
Earl of Hertford, Letter to the, Walpole	12	348
Earnest Suit to His Unkind Mistress, An, Wyatt	11	126
Earth in Spring, The, Judah ha-Levi	1	184
Earth-Bound, Noyes	15	580
Earth's Enigmas, Roberts	8	511
Earthly Paradise, The, Morris	15	133
Earthquake at Nishapur, The Cause of the, Fasihi Khvafi	1	298
East, see Orient		
Easter Day, Clough	14	449
Easy Chair, The, Curtis	17	475
Eaton, W. P., on Bernard Shaw and the Theatre Guild	15	480

	VOL.	PAGE
Ecclesiastical History, Bede	4	341, 343
Echegaray y Eizaguirre, José	8	174
Echo, Rossetti, C. G.	14	472
Eclogue, The First, Vergil	3	176
Economics		
America, Expectations of, Hakluyt	11	22
Autobiography, The, Mill	13	642
Cry of the Children, The, Browning, E. B.	14	403
Federalist, The, Hamilton	16	222
French Revolution, History of the, Thiers	6	649
Lombard Street, Bagehot	14	610
Lord Kames, Letter to, Franklin	16	95
Morals and Legislation, An Introduction to the Principles of, Bentham	12	564
Political Economy, Mill	13	635
Progress and Poverty, George	18	154, 160
Spirit of Laws, The, Montesquieu	6	300, 301
United States, The, Ferrero	5	540
Virginia Legislature, Speech in the, Henry	16	139
Wealth of Nations, The, Smith	12	379, 382
Economist, The, Xenophon	2	278
Eddas, The, Old Norse Literature	4	273
Edgeworth, Maria	13	120
Education. See also Sociology		
Ancient Régime, The, Taine	7	145
Charlemagne, A Letter to, Alcuin	4	486
Countess of Bute, Letters to the, Montagu	12	252, 253
Culture and Anarchy, Arnold	14	421
Cyropedia, Xenophon	2	287
Democracy in America, de Tocqueville	6	667
Education: Intellectual, Moral, and Physical, Spencer	14	691, 694, 701
Education, Of, Joubert	6	395
Education of Women, The, Smith	13	243

	VOL.	PAGE
Education, Treatise on, Milton	11	459
Émile, Rousseau	6	350
Essays in Criticism, Arnold	14	425
Esthetic Education of Man, On the, Schiller	9	196
Gargantua, The Education of, Rabelais	6	43
Holy and Profane State, The, Fuller	11	547
Human Understanding, Essay Concerning, Locke	11	637
Idea of a University, The, Newman	14	25
Institutes, Quintilian	3	302
Knowledge, In Praise of, Bacon	11	110
Little Son Hans, Aged Six, Letter to His, Luther	9	24
Mothers and Nurses, Plutarch	2	503
Need of Good Schoolmasters, The, Plutarch	2	502
Oratory, Dialogue on, Cicero	3	84
Oratory, A Dialogue on, Tacitus	3	349
Orbis Pictus, Komenský	10	557
Politics, Aristotle	2	343
Satires, Juvenal	3	374
Schoolmaster, The, Ascham	11	14
Education: Intellectual, Moral, and Physical, Spencer	14	691
		694, 701
Education, Of, Joubert	6	395
Education of Women, The, Smith	13	243
Education, Treatise on, Milton	11	459
Edward, Medieval Literature	4	40
Edward the Second, Marlowe	11	224
Edwards, Jonathan	16	57
Edwin Forrest as Othello, Browne	17	393
Eeden, Frederik van	8	404
Eekhoud, Georges	8	452
Egan, M. F., on		
Calderon	8	130
Hérédia	7	255
Lope de Vega	8	114
Manzoni	5	347
St. Francis of Assisi	5	14
Eggleston, Edward	18	82
Egyptian Literature	1	21
Eichendorff, Joseph von	9	295
Eighteenth Century, The, Schérer	7	100
Eleazar ha-Kalir	1	162
Elegies. See also Poetry		
Adonais, Shelley	13	408
Bion, The Lamentation for, Moschus	2	411
Death of Thomson, Ode on the, Collins	12	329
Decoration Day Oration, Ingersoll	17	621
Elegy, Nibi	1	543
Elegy on Franklin, The, Mirabeau	6	392
Elegy Written in a Country Churchyard, Gray	12	333
In Memoriam, Tennyson	14	298
Life of Jesus, Dedication to the, Renan	7	123
Lycidas, Milton	11	445
Rose and the Ring, The, Locker-Lampson	14	490
Threnody, Bion	2	407
Threnody, Emerson	17	61
When Lilacs Last in the Door-Yard Bloomed, Whitman	17	418
Elegy, Nibi	1	543
Elegy on Franklin, The, Mirabeau	6	392
Elegy Written in a Country Churchyard, Gray	12	333
Elfin-King, The, Goethe	9	164
Elgin Marbles, On Seeing the, Keats	13	458
Eliot, George	14	632
Elisaeus	1	395
Elixir, The, Herbert	11	157
Eliza, To, Krasiński	10	526
Eloa, de Vigny	6	456
Elsie Venner, Holmes	17	210
		214
Ely, R. T., on		
Mill	13	628
Smith	12	375
Emerson, Ralph Waldo	17	26
Emigrants in Bermudas, The, Marvell	11	468
Émigré, L', Bourget	7	405
Émile, Rousseau	6	350
Emma, Austen	13	200
Empedocles	2	296
Emptied Quiver, The, Greek Anthology	2	580
Enchiridion, Epictetus	2	462
Encyclopedia, The, Diderot	6	363
End of All, The, Lucretius	3	141
End of the Play, The, Thackeray	14	103
Endymion, Keats	13	433

	VOL.	PAGE
England		
Candide: or All for the Best, Voltaire	6	320
Drake's Drum, Newbolt	15	570
England, Inge	15	662
England, History of, Macaulay	13	516
		518, 523, 525
England, Notes on, Taine	7	140
		142
Gibraltar, At, Woodberry	18	368
Historical Essays, Freeman	14	628
Home-Thoughts from Abroad, Browning	14	345
Homes of England, The, Hemans	13	481
Midas, Lyly	11	196
Purple East, The, Watson	15	559, 560
Recessional, Kipling	15	314
South Country, The, Belloc	15	601
Tono-Bungay, Wells	15	423
Volland, Letter to Mlle., Diderot	6	365
England, Inge	15	662
England, History of, Froude	14	621
England, History of, Macaulay	13	516
		518, 523, 525
England, History of Civilization in, Buckle	14	585
England, Notes on, Taine	7	140
		142
English Constitution, The, Bagehot	14	606
English Literature		
The Age of Milton	11	418
Anglo-Saxon Literature	4	312
British Essayists in the Twentieth Century	15	626
British Fiction in the Twentieth Century	15	368
British Poetry in the Twentieth Century	15	512
Corinne, de Staël	6	412
Eighteenth-Century Survey	12	1
The Elizabethan Theater	11	177
The Literatures of France, England, and Germany, Brunetière	7	423
The Medieval Drama	4	146
Middle English Poetry	4	530
Modern Irish Literature in English	8	529
The Revolt from Victorianism	15	1
The Romantic Revival	13	1
Shakespeare to Dryden	11	1
Twentieth-Century Drama in England	15	460
English People, History of the, Green	15	176
Englishmen at Cressy, Of the Order of the, Froissart	6	22
Enemy, The, Baudelaire	7	28
Ennius	3	27
Eötvös, Josef	8	584
Ephemera; An Emblem of Human Life, The, Franklin	16	93
Epic. See also Poetry		
Beowulf, Anglo-Saxon Literature	4	325
Cid, The Poem of My, Spanish Literature	8	14
Homer	2	27
Lusiads, The, Camoens	8	287
Mahabharata, Indian Literature	1	450
Nibelungenlied, Medieval German Literature	4	428
Roland, Song of, Medieval French Literature	4	355
Epic of Creation, The, Babylonian Literature	1	72
Epic Hexameter, The, Schiller	9	191
Epictetus	2	456
Epicure, The, Anacreon	2	122
Epigram, Callimachus	2	389
Epigram, Lessing	9	78
Epigrams		
Benefits, Lessing	9	78
Distich, The, Schiller	9	191
Epic Hexameter, The, Schiller	9	191
Epigram, Callimachus	2	389
Epigram, Lessing	9	78
Greek Wit and Wisdom, Examples of, Diogenes Laërtius	2	541
Kant and His Interpreters, Schiller	9	191
My Creed, Schiller	9	191
On Mr. R——, Lessing	9	78
Epilogue, Greek Anthology	2	575
Episode under the Terror, An, Balzac	6	565
Epistle to Dr. Arbuthnot, Pope	12	158
Epistles, Holberg	10	44
		46
Epitaph, Callimachus	2	390
Epitaph, An, Pickthall	8	501
Epitaph for a Husbandman, An, Roberts	8	491

	VOL.	PAGE
Epitaph in the Form of a Ballad, The, Villon	6	33
Epitaph on Himself, Plautus	3	51
Epitaph upon Himself, Callimachus	2	390
Epitaphs		
Athenian Dead at Platæa, On the, Simonides	2	572
Drake, On the Death of Joseph Rodman, Halleck	16	416
Epitaph, Callimachus	2	390
Epitaph for a Husbandman, An, Roberts	8	491
Epitaph on Himself, Plautus	3	51
Epitaph upon Himself, Callimachus	2	390
Favorite Hunting Dog, Epitaph on a, Petronius	3	335
Heraclitus, Epitaph on, Callimachus	2	390
Lacedæmonian Dead at Platæa, Simonides	2	572
Living Author, Epitaph on a, Cowley	11	484
Meleager's Own Epitaph, Meleager	2	575
Mother's Epitaph, A, Ausonius	3	457
My First Daughter, On, Jonson	11	354
Nameless Grave, A, Greek Anthology	2	582
Pembroke, On the Countess Dowager of, Browne	11	142
Poet's Epitaph, A, Greek Anthology	2	573
Requiem, Stevenson	15	275
Resignation, Greek Anthology	2	578
Salathiel Pavy, An Epitaph on, Jonson	11	354
Service of God, The, Greek Anthology	2	579
Trumbal, Epitaph on Sir William Pope	12	163
Young Hero's Epitaph, A, Greek Anthology	2	580
Young Wife, The, Greek Anthology	2	578
Equals Added to Equals, Martial	3	342
"Erano i Capei d' Oro all' Aura Sparsi," Petrarch	5	99
Erasmus	8	314
Erasmus Montanus, Holberg	10	35
Erewhon, Butler	15	168
Errors and Entanglements, Fontane	9	451
Erskine, John, on		
British Poetry in the Twentieth Century	15	512
Woodberry	18	367
Escape from Prison, The, Cellini	5	218
Escapes of Casanova and Latude from Prison, The, Casanova	5	322
Eschenbach, Wolfram von, see Wolfram von Eschenbach		
Essais, Montaigne	6	83, 84, 85, 88
Essashi Juo [The Bird-Catcher in Hell], Japanese Literature	1	559
Essay, see Literature		
Essay on Criticism, Pope	12	141
Essay on Man, Pope	12	151
Essays, Bacon	11	100, 101, 102, 104, 106
Essays in Criticism, Arnold	14	425
Essences, On, Aristotle	2	342
Esther Waters, Moore, George	15	384
Esthetic Education of Man, On the, Schiller	9	196
Esthetics. See also Art and Architecture		
Breviary of Æsthetic, The, Croce	5	510
Crown of Wild Olive, The, Ruskin	13	612
Seven Lamps of Architecture, The, Ruskin	13	593
Treasure of the Humble, The, Maeterlinck	8	474
Yusuf and Zulaikha, Jami	1	382
Estimate of Himself, Lessing	9	91
Estrella de Sevilla, Lope de Vega	8	117
Eternal Goodness, The, Whittier	17	168
Ethics. See also Religion; Philosophy		
Acaranga-Sutra, Indian Literature	1	439
Apocalypse Revealed, The, Swedenborg	10	149
Autobiography, Franklin	16	97
Charity, Doctrine of, Swedenborg	10	151
Chinese and Roman Artists, The, Jalal ad-Din Rumi	1	371
Collected Essays, Huxley	14	565

	VOL.	PAGE
Compensation, Emerson	17	42
Dhammapada, Buddhistic Literature	1	440
Education: Intellectual, Moral, and Physical, Spencer	14	701
Endymion, Keats	13	433
England, History of Civilization in, Buckle	14	585
Essais, Montaigne	6	88
Essays, Bacon	11	100
		101, 102
Faith and Patience of the Saints, Taylor	11	554
Fragment, Avesta	1	321
Garden of Perfume, The, Sa'di	1	361
		362, 363
Gorgias, Plato	2	325
Guide of the Perplexed, Maimonides	1	192
Improvement of the Understanding, The, Spinoza	8	363
Luxury, The Foolishness of, Lucretius	3	139
Maimonides' Will, Extract from, Maimonides	1	190
Meditations, Aurelius	3	427
Merchant of Venice, The, Shakespeare	11	269
Orthodoxy, Chesterton	15	650
Passions, Of the, Joubert	6	395
Past and Present, Carlyle	13	582
Personality, Tagore	1	490
Philosophy of History, Hegel	9	272
Positive Polity, Comte	6	662
Raku-Kun, Kaibara Yekken	1	563
Rambler, The, Johnson	12	271
Refinement in the Arts, On, Hume	12	301
Romance of the Rose, Jean de Meung	4	387
Rules and Exercises of Holy Dying, Taylor	11	555
		556, 558, 559
Sartor Resartus, Carlyle	13	554
Self-Reliance, Emerson	17	48
Table-Talk, Selden	11	118
Takhkemoni, Judah al-Kharizi	1	178
Teaching of Virtue, The, Plutarch	2	501
Thus Spake Zarathustra, Nietzsche	9	506
Treasure of the Humble, The, Maeterlinck	8	474
Virginia, Notes on, Jefferson	16	187
Virtue and Morality, Of, Joubert	6	395
War, The Moral Equivalent of, James, William	18	207
Will to Power, Nietzsche	9	509
Wise Man, The, Avesta	1	319
Eton College, On a Distant Prospect of, Gray	12	338
Étude Réaliste, Swinburne	15	127
Eumenides, The, Æschylus	2	161
Euphues and His England, Lyly	11	190
Euripides	2	191
European Morals, History of, Lecky	15	183
Evangeline, Longfellow	17	146
		147, 150
Evans, E. P., on		
Lessing	9	74
Richter	9	215
Schiller	9	178
Eve, Hodgson	15	619
Eve of St. Agnes, The, Keats	13	434
Evelina, Burney	12	467
Evelyn, John	11	561
Even-Song, An, Medieval Irish Literature	4	237
Evening Hymn, Keble	13	486
Evening Song, Lanier	18	199
Everett, Edward	16	433
Everlasting Mercy, The, Masefield	15	588
Every Man in His Humor, Jonson	11	352
Everybody's Business Is Nobody's Business, Defoe	12	32
Everyman, Medieval Drama	4	161
Evgeny Onyegin, Pushkin	10	344
Evolution. See also Religion; Philosophy; Science		
Back to Methuselah, Shaw	15	510
Claims of Science, The, Tyndall	14	542
Collected Essays, Huxley	14	558
		564, 565
Creative Evolution, Bergson	7	467
Descent of Man, On Our Present Knowledge of the, Haeckel	9	483
Erewhon, Butler	15	168
Higher Man, The, Nietzsche	9	511
Inevitable March of Improvement, The, Everett	16	436
Life and Letters, Darwin	14	517
Origin of Species, The, Darwin	14	519
		521, 524, 526, 528, 533

	VOL.	PAGE
Evolution, Martial	3	339
Ewald, Johannes	10	48
Ex-Voto, Eekhoud	8	453
Excelente Balade of Charitie, An, Chatterton	12	372
Except the Lord Build the House, Carpenter	15	229
Exile of Erin, The, Campbell	13	264
Exile's Hymn at Sunset on the Sea, An, Slowacki	10	516
Existence of a Creator, On the, Sa'adia Ga'on	21	172
Exploration and Discovery. See also Travel		
American Literature in the Colonial Period	16	11
Conquerors, The, Hérédia	7	256
Conquest of Mexico, The, Prescott	16	453
Conquest of Peru, The, Prescott	16	466
Drake in California, Hakluyt	11	32
Farthest North, Nansen	10	262, 263, 264, 266
Guiana, Discovery of, Raleigh (Hakluyt)	11	35
Lusiads, The, Camoens	8	287
Mexico, The Grim Idols of, Diaz	8	47
Relation of the First Voyage, A, Las Casas	8	41
United States, History of the, Bancroft	17	16
Voyages, Hakluyt	11	19
Exquisite Hour, Verlaine	7	285
Ezra, Moses ibn, see Moses ibn Ezra		

F

	VOL.	PAGE
Fables		
Ancelmus the Emperour, Gesta Romanorum	4	506
Animals Sick of the Plague, The, La Fontaine	6	131
Ass and the Little Dog, The, Æsop	2	63
Ass and the Little Dog, The, La Fontaine	6	134
Ass Eating Thistles, The, Æsop	2	61
Ass in the Lion's Skin, The, Æsop	2	60
Belly and the Members, The, Æsop	2	62
Cat, the Weasel, and the Young Rabbit, The, La Fontaine	6	129
Country Mouse and the City Mouse, The, Æsop	2	64
Countryman and the Snake, The, Æsop	2	61
Death and the Woodcutter, La Fontaine	6	127
Dog and the Wolf, The, Æsop	2	65
Fables, Gay	12	113, 115
Fox and the Lion, The, Æsop	2	60
Grasshopper and the Ant, The, La Fontaine	6	129
Hog, the Goat, and the Sheep, The, La Fontaine	6	135
Lion and the Other Beasts, The, Æsop	2	63
Oak and the Reed, The, La Fontaine	6	128
Satyr and the Traveler, The, Æsop	2	62
Theodosius the Emperoure, Gesta Romanorum	4	504
Wolf and the Dog, The, La Fontaine	6	133
Wolf in Sheep's Clothing, The, Æsop	2	61
Fables, Gay	12	113, 115
Fabre, Jean-Henri	7	198
Faery Queen, The, Spenser	11	66, 67, 72
Faguet, Émile	7	434
Fair Ines, Hood	13	467
Fair Maid of the Exchange, The, Heywood	11	366
Fair-Haired Eckbert, The, Tieck	9	240
Fairclough, H. R., on Tyrtæus, Archilochus, etc.	2	76
Fairy Tales and Folk Stories		
Abu Muhammad the Lazy, Arabian Nights	1	245
Anvar-i-Suhaili, or Lights of Canopus, Iranian Literature	1	305
Blind Men and the Elephant, The, Sana'i	1	300
Fair-Haired Eckbert, The, Tieck	9	240
Hitopadeça, Indian Literature	1	449
Household Tales, Grimm	9	275, 278
How the Devil Took to Himself an Old Wife, Sachs	9	49

	VOL.	PAGE
Jatakas, Indian Literature	1	444
Liao-chai Chi-i, Chinese Literature	1	516
Lovers, The, Andersen	10	115
Lovers of the Banu Udhrah, The, Arabian Nights	1	263
Manyoshu, Japanese Literature	1	539
Merchant and the Parrot, The, Jalal ad-Din Rumi	1	369
Pancatantra, Indian Literature	1	446
Setna, The Story of, Egyptian Literature	1	37
Shipwrecked Sailor, The, Egyptian Literature	1	26
Shu Ching [Book of History], Chinese Literature	1	503
Sindbad the Sailor, The Fourth Voyage of, Arabian Nights	1	256
Snow Queen, The, Andersen	10	117
Teapot, The, Andersen	10	106
Tin Soldier, The Steadfast, Andersen	10	103
Treasure, The, Peretz	8	630
Two Brothers, The, Egyptian Literature	1	29
Ugly Duckling, The, Andersen	10	107
Valor of 'Antar, The, Arabic Literature	1	286
Faith and Patience of the Saints, Taylor	11	554
Faith and the Future, Mazzini	5	404
Faithful Shepherdess, The, Fletcher	11	380
Faithfulness, Petőfi	8	599
Faithless Sally Brown, Hood	13	463
Fall of Rome, The, Gibbon	12	441
Fall of the House of Usher, The, Poe	17	551
Fall of the Serbian Empire, The, Slavonic Literature	10	599
Fancy, Keats	13	450
Fantasia, Serao	5	485
Far from the Madding Crowd, Hardy	15	72
Far from the World, Lamartine	6	453
Farce, see Humor		
Farewell, Landor	13	259
Farewell, A, Kingsley	14	208
Farewell, The, Whittier	17	174
Farewell Address, Washington	16	124
Farewell to Folly, Greene	11	212
Farewell to His Fellow-Officers, Catullus	3	162
Farewell to His Mother's Aged Servant, Johnson	12	267
Farewell to Italy, Landor	13	259
Farrukhi	1	295
Farthest North, Nansen	10	262
		263, 264, 266
Fascist Italy, Governmental Policies of, Mussolini	5	577
Fasihi Khvafi	1	298
Father, The, Björnson	10	249
Father, The, Gibson	15	607
Father and Son, Gosse	15	635
Fathers and Children, Turgenev	10	371
Faun, The, Verlaine	7	283
Faun with the Mirror, The, de Régnier	7	521
Faust, Goethe	9	127
		128
Favorite Hunting Dog, Epitaph on a, Petronius	3	335
Federal Convention, Speech in the, in Favor of Opening Its Sessions with Prayer, Franklin	16	90
Federalist, The, Hamilton	16	217
		218, 219, 220, 221, 222, 223, 225, 227
		228, 229
Federalist, The, Madison	16	200
		204
Female Phaeton, The, Prior	12	41
Fénelon	6	249
Ferdinand and Isabella, Prescott	16	460
Ferrero, Guglielmo	5	532
Festival of Adonis, The, Theocritus	2	402
Fet, A. (Afanasy Afanasyevich Shenshin)	10	326
Fêtes Galantes, Verlaine	7	278
		280
Feuillerat, Albert, on French Literature (Old France and the Revolution)	6	1
Feuilles Volantes, Les, Fréchette	8	525
Fichte, Johann Gottlieb	9	209
"Fickle and Changeable Ever," Catullus	3	165
Fiction. See also Literature; Realism		
American Literature: Modern Fiction	18	528
British Fiction in the Twentieth Century	15	368
Flaubert, Faguet	7	436

	VOL.	PAGE
Guardian, The, Steele	12	82
Picaresque Novel, The	8	51
Skipwith, Letter to Robert, Jefferson	16	186
Field, Eugene	18	509
Field Full of Folk, The, Piers Plowman	4	532
Fielding, Henry	12	164
Fields, Mrs. J. T., on Holmes	17	189
Fife, R. H., on German Literature (The German Mind)	9	1
Fight at Maldon, The, Anglo-Saxon Literature	4	338
Filon, Augustin, on Daudet	7	215
Final Struggle in the Harbor of Syracuse, The, Thucydides	2	272
Finance, see Economics		
Fine Frenzy, Martial	3	343
Finnish Literature	8	609
Fir-Tree, The, Freiligrath	9	420
Firdausi	1	321
Fire, To the, Avesta	1	317
Fires, Gibson	15	605
First Flower Piece, Richter	9	220
First Love Again Remembered, Greek Anthology	2	583
Fish-Hawk, or Osprey, The, Wilson	16	242
Fishermen's Luck, Plautus	3	51
Fishers, The, Ewald	10	55
Fisher's Boy, The, Thoreau	17	305
Fisher's Hut, The, Heine	9	322
Fitzgerald, Edward	1	343
Five Towns, The, Bennett	15	442
Flanders Fields, In, McCrae	8	502
Flats, The, Lanier	18	202
Flaubert, Gustave	7	53
Flaubert, Faguet	7	436
Flaubert, Correspondence with, Sand	7	47
Fletcher, J. B., on		
Butler	15	154
Dunne	18	464
Italian Literature (The Voice of Italy)	5	1
Lorenzo de' Medici	5	140
Poliziano	5	147
Pulci	5	155
The Renaissance	5	128
Fletcher, John	11	374
Flora Mac-Ivor's Song (from 'Waverley'), Scott	13	153
Florence, History of, Machiavelli	5	176
Florus, Annius	3	452
Flos Mercatorum ('Tales of the Mermaid Tavern'), Noyes	15	574
Flower, Fruit, and Thorn Pieces, Richter	9	218
Flowers, see Nature		
Fogazzaro, Antonio	5	449
Folk-Song, Medieval Literature	4	112
Folk-Songs, The, Slavonic Literature	10	599
Folk Stories, see Fairy Tales and Folk Stories		
Fontaine, La, Jean de, see La Fontaine		
Fontane, Theodor	9	443
Fool's Prayer, The, Sill	18	184
For Annie, Poe	17	565
Ford, John	11	404
Ford, P. L., on Jefferson	16	173
Forecast, A, Lampman	8	493
Forsaken Garden, A, Swinburne	15	123
Fortier, Alcée, on Lamartine	6	445
Fortunes of Men, The, Anglo-Saxon Literature	4	335
Foscolo, Ugo	5	330
Foundation of Constantinople, Gibbon	12	429
Four Million, The, Porter	18	428
Four Principles of Democracy, The, Sun Yat Sen	1	518
Fowler, On a, Greek Anthology	2	581
Fox and the Lion, The, Æsop	2	60
Fragment, Avesta	1	321
Fragment on Mummies, A, Browne	11	542
Fragments, Epictetus	2	463
Fragments, Heraclitus	2	290
France		
Candide: or All for the Best, Voltaire	6	319
Chastisements, Hugo	6	500, 501
Dreyfus Case, On the, Dunne	18	468
France, 1870, Meredith	15	55
Illustrious Ladies, Lives of, Brantôme	6	78
Travels in France, Young	12	388
France, Anatole	7	358
France, 1870, Meredith	15	55
Francis of Assisi, St.	5	14
Francke, Kuno, on		
Herder	9	92
Klopstock	9	55

	VOL.	PAGE
Franklin, Benjamin	16	68
"Frater Ave Atque Vale," Tennyson	14	322
Fraternity, Galsworthy	15	449
Fray Luis de Leon	8	78
Fréchette, Louis Honoré	8	523
Frederick of the Alberighi and His Falcon, Boccaccio	5	112
Frederick Redbeard, Geibel	9	423
Free Life of the Bird, The, Pushkin	10	338
Free Will, On, Sa'adia Ga'on	1	175
Freedom of the Will, Inquiry into the, Edwards	16	63
Freeman, Edward Augustus	14	624
Freeman, Mary Wilkins	18	433
Freiligrath, Ferdinand	9	420
French Literature		
The Classical Tradition	6	90
Corinne, de Staël	6	412
The Decline of Classicism	6	254
The Drama of Today	7	506
French Literature from 1848 to the Present Day — a General View	7	1
The Growth of Realism	7	8
Historians and Publicists	6	636
The Literatures of France, England, and Germany, Brunetière	7	423
Main Currents in the Literature of the Nineteenth Century, Brandes	10	128
The Medieval Drama	4	146
Medieval French Literature	4	346
Old France and the Revolution	6	1
Provençal Literature	4	397
The Revival of Learning	6	6
The Rise of Romanticism	6	433
The Third French Republic	7	233
French Republic, The Third	7	233
French Revolution, The, Carlyle	13	565, 572, 578
French Revolution, History of the, Thiers	6	649
French Revolution, On the, Burke	12	416
Frenchmen at Cressy, The Order of the, Froissart	6	23
Frenssen, Gustav	9	584
Freytag, Gustav	9	377
Friar's Song, The, Peacock	13	477
Friedland, L. S., on Scandinavian Literature	10	1
Friend of Humanity and the Knife-Grinder, The, Canning	13	240
Friend, To a, Arnold	14	426
Friend, To a, Hitomaru	1	543
Friendship		
Bill and Joe, Holmes	17	203
Comrade, To a, Musset	6	477
Essais, Montaigne	6	84
Essays, Bacon	11	106
Friend, To a, Hitomaru	1	543
Friendship, Emerson	17	38
Friendship, Hooft	8	346
Friendship, Dialogue on, Cicero	3	81
"We Twa," Persius	3	294
When Ivy Twines, Cats	8	349
Friendship, Emerson	17	38
Friendship, Hooft	8	346
Friendship, Dialogue on, Cicero	3	81
Frogs, The, Aristophanes	2	233, 237
Froissart	6	15
From Childhood, Liliencron	9	429
From Greenland's Icy Mountains, Heber	12	572
Frost Song, Pickthall	8	500
Froude, James Anthony	14	613
Frug, Semion	8	629
Fuji-Yama, Ode to, Japanese Literature	1	544
Fuller, Sarah Margaret (Marchioness Ossoli)	17	224
Fuller, Thomas	11	545
Funeral Oration on Henrietta of France, Bossuet	6	218
Future Life, The, Bryant	16	431
"Fuzzy-Wuzzy," Kipling	15	310

G

	VOL.	PAGE
Gabirol, Solomon ibn	1	165
Galahad at the Grail Castle and at Sarras, Malory	4	92
Galdos, Benito Perez	8	198
Gallathea, Lyly	11	197
Gallic War, The, Cæsar	3	114, 122, 128
Galsworthy, John	15	444
Galton, Francis	14	573
Ga'on, Sa'adia, see Sa'adia Ga'on		
Garden, The, Marvell	11	466
Garden of Epicurus, The, France	7	372
Garden of Perfume, The, Sa'di	1	358, 361, 362, 363

	VOL.	PAGE
Garden of Proserpine, The, Swinburne	15	115
Gardens, see Nature		
Gargantua, The Education of, Rabelais	6	43
Garland, Hamlin, on Grant	17	595
Garnett, Richard, on Emerson	17	26
Garret, The, Béranger	6	526
Gaskell, Elizabeth Stevenson	14	242
Gaspé, Philippe Aubert de	8	526
Gautier, Théophile	6	673
Gawain and the Green Knight, Legends of Arthur and the Round Table	4	87
Gay, John	12	110
Gay Marigold, Bridges	15	556
Gayley, C. M., on Goldsmith	12	498
Geese, The Flight of the, Roberts	8	490
Geibel, Emanuel	9	423
Gellius, Aulus	3	410
Genji Monogatari, Murasaki	1	550
Gentle Craft, The, Deloney	11	81
Gentle Jesus, Meek and Mild, Wesley, Charles	12	544
Gentle Shepherd, The, Ramsay	12	198
Genung, C. H., on		
Kleist	9	248
Mickiewicz	10	498
Petöfi	8	595
Sachs	9	31
Sienkiewicz	10	528
Wagner	9	368
Geoffrey of Monmouth	4	75
Geology, see Science		
George, Henry	18	150
George Montagu, Esq., Letters to, Walpole	12	349 350
Georgics, Vergil	3	179
Gerig, J. L., on Medieval Irish Literature	4	192
German Literature		
Between Dusk and Dawn	9	10
German Historians	9	432
The German Mind	9	1
The Literatures of France, England, and Germany, Brunetière	7	423
Lyrics Voices of the Nineteenth Century	9	406
Main Currents in the Literature of the Nineteenth Century, Brandes	10	128
Medieval German Literature	4	415
A New Dawn	9	52
Power, Prosperity, and Pride	9	440
The Romantic School in Germany	9	230
Sunshine and Shadow	9	207
Germania, Tacitus	3	352
Germany, On, de Staël	6	408
Gesta Romanorum	4	502
Get You Gone, Verhaeren	8	451
Getting Married, Shaw	15	510
Gettysburg Address, The, Lincoln	17	593
Gezelle, Guido	8	431
Ghazals or Odes, Selected, Hafiz	1	375
Giaour, The. Byron	13	313
Gibbon, Edward	12	422
Gibbon, Edward, Bagehot	14	602
Gibbon, Strachey	15	678
Gibraltar, At, Woodberry	18	368
Gibson, Wilfrid Wilson	15	603
Giddings, F. H., on Bridges	15	551
Gide, André	7	545
Gil Blas, Le Sage	6	268 275
Gil Vicente	8	274
Gilbert, William Schwenck	14	499
Gilder, Richard Watson	18	504
Gildersleeve, B. L., on Pindar	2	131
Gilgamesh, Epic of, Babylonian Literature	1	85
Gilman, D. C., on Hamilton	16	212
Gingillino, Giusti	5	399
Giovine Italia, Mazzini	5	406
Girdle, On a, Waller	11	485
Gissing, George Robert	15	276
Giusti, Giuseppe	5	398
"Gli Occhi Miei Vaghi Delle Cose Belle," Michelangelo	5	212
Gluck, J. F., on Aurelius	3	421
Go, Lovely Rose, Waller	11	486
God and Woman, Bojer	10	288
God of the World, Nagara	1	171
Goddess of the Waters, The, Avesta	1	318
Godkin, E. L., on Burke	12	404
Godkin, Edwin Lawrence	17	493
Godlike, The, Goethe	9	165
Gododdin, The, Welsh Literature	4	252
Goethe, Johann Wolfgang	9	117
Goethe, Visit to, Heine	9	337
Gogol, Nikolay Vasilyevich	10	351
Going to a Fight, Hazlitt	13	272
Gold, Anacreon	2	123
Golden Age, The, Tasso	5	255
Goldfinch, The, Dehmel	9	581
Goldoni	5	286

	VOL.	PAGE
Goldsmith, Oliver	12	498
Goliardic Poetry, Medieval Literature	4	132
Goncharov, Ivan Aleksandrovich	10	383
Goncourt, Edmond de	7	82
Goncourt, Jules Huot de	7	82
Goncourts, The, de Gourmont	7	441
Good Counsel, Ronsard	6	74
Good Hope, The, Heijermans	8	421
Good Samaritan, The, New Testament	2	437
Good Steward, The, Wesley, John	12	538
Good-by to Childhood, Greek Anthology	2	579
Gordon, Judah Loeb	1	202
Gorgias, Plato	2	325
Gorky, Maxim (Aleksyey Maksimovich Pyeshkov)	10	462
Gosse, Edmund	15	629
Gottfried von Strassburg	4	454
Gottheil, Gustav, on Maimonides	1	186
Gottheil, Richard, on		
Arabian Nights	1	242
Arabic Literature	1	219
Judah ha-Levi	1	179
Gourmont, Remy de	7	439
Government		
Adages, Erasmus	8	325
Admission of Michigan, Speech on the, Calhoun	16	300
Areopagitica, Milton	11	461
Cicero, Letter to, Cælius	3	96
Cicero, Letter to, Matius	3	97
Citizenship in a Republic, Roosevelt	18	390
Conciliation with America, Speech on, Burke	12	412
Cooper Institute, Speech at the, Lincoln	17	586
Crisis, The, Paine	16	165
Declaration of Independence, The, Jefferson	16	180
Defense of His Dictatorship, Solon	2	128
Democracy, Lowell	17	352
Democracy in Amercia, de Tocqueville	6	670, 671
Dr. Styles, Letter to, Jefferson	16	190
Dreyfus Case, On the, Dunne	18	468
English Constitution, The, Bagehot	14	606
Farewell Address, Washington	16	124
Federalist, The, Hamilton	16	217, 218, 219, 220, 221, 222, 223, 225, 227, 228, 229
Federalist, The, Madison	16	200, 204
Four Principles of Democracy, The, Sun Yat Sen	1	518
French Revolution, History of the, Thiers	6	649
French Revolution, On the, Burke	12	416
Gettysburg Address, The, Lincoln	17	593
Government, A Disquisition on, Calhoun	16	302
Greek Struggle for Independence, On the, Clay	16	273
Idea of a Patriot King, The, Bolingbroke	12	102
Inaugural Address, The First, Lincoln	17	589
Jewish Wars, Josephus	1	133
Justification of His Patriotic Policy, Demosthenes	2	382
License of Speech, Invective against, Demosthenes	2	381
Madison, Letter to, James Jefferson	16	192
March on Rome, The, Mussolini	5	564
Memoirs, Adams, J. Q.	16	247, 248
Missouri Compromise, Urging the Repeal of the, Calhoun	16	303
Napoleon Bonaparte, The Life and Character of, Channing	16	282
Nullification, Adams, J. Q.	16	252
Orations and Addresses, Curtis	17	474
Our Cuban Allies, Dunne	18	466
Peel, Sir Robert, Bagehot	14	605
Perpetuation of Our Political Institutions, The, Lincoln	17	585
Philippic, The Third, Demosthenes	2	373
Physics and Politics, Bagehot	14	607
Prince, The, Machiavelli	5	179, 180
Problems of Modern Democracy, Godkin	17	494

	VOL.	PAGE
Public Spirit in Politics, Clay	16	272
Reflections on Revolution, Thucydides	2	270
Right of Petition, The, Adams, J. Q.	16	251
Right of Petition, Remarks on the, Calhoun	16	296
Siete Partidas, Las, Alfonso the Wise	8	21
Social Contract, The, Rousseau	6	353
		358
Solon Speaks His Mind to the Athenians, Solon	2	129
South American Independence as Related to the United States, Clay	16	273
Speech in the National Assembly, Mirabeau	6	388
Spirit of Laws, The, Montesquieu	6	296
		298
Statesman, The, Plato	2	332
Vacillation in the Civil War, Cicero	3	92
Virginia Convention, Speech in the, Henry	16	137
Government, A Disquisition on, Calhoun	16	302
Gower, John	4	542
Gracian, Baltasar	8	145
Grammar of the Stars, The, Heine	9	323
Grammarian's Funeral, A, Browning	14	365
Gran Conquista de Ultramar, La, Alfonso the Wise	8	22
Grant, Ulysses S.	17	595
Grantchester, see The Old Vicarage, Grantchester		
Grasshopper, The, Anacreon	2	124
Grasshopper and the Ant, The, La Fontaine	6	129
Gray, L. H., on		
Armenian Literature	1	386
Iranian Literature	1	292
Oriental Literature	1	8
Other Celtic Literatures	4	270
Gray, Thomas	12	331
Great Assize, The, Wesley, John	12	542
Great Go-Between, The, Echegaray	8	182
Great Mysteries, The, Greek Anthology	2	576
Great River of Badashan, Of the, Marco Polo	4	521

	VOL.	PAGE
Grecian Urn, Ode on a, Keats	13	449
Greece		
Don Juan, Byron	13	315
Giaour, The, Byron	13	313
Hellas, Shelley	13	421
Philosophy of History, The, Hegel	9	268
Siege of Corinth, The, Byron	13	315
Temple of Zeus at Olympia, The, Pausanias	2	510
Greek Anthology, The	2	570
Greek Literature		
The Glory That Was Greece	2	1
The Greek Lyric	2	76
Modern Greek Literature	8	645
On Ancient Authors, Quintilian	3	309
Greek Struggle for Independence, On the, Clay	16	273
Greek Wit and Wisdom, Examples of, Diogenes Laërtius	2	541
Green, John Richard	15	175
Green Grow the Rashes, Burns	12	599
Greene, Robert	11	207
Gregersen, Halfdan, on The Spanish Romances	8	24
Griffith, F. L., on Egyptian Literature	1	21
Griffith, K. B., on Egyption Literature	1	21
Grignan, Letter to Her Daughter, Madame de, de Sévigné	6	212
	213, 214,	216
Grillparzer, Franz	9	304
Grimm, Jakob	9	274
Grimm, Wilhelm	9	274
Griselda, The Story of, Boccaccio	5	120
Groatsworth of Wit, A, Greene	11	213
Grotius, To Hugo, Hooft	8	346
Growth of Love, The, Bridges	15	554
Growth of the Soil, Hamsun	10	276
		282
Gruesome Lover, A, Ovid	3	257
Guardian, The, Steele	12	80
		82
Guardian Spirits, Avesta	1	318
Guérin, Maurice de	6	531
Guiana, Discovery of, Raleigh (Hakluyt)	11	35
Guide of the Perplexed, Maimonides	1	192

	VOL.	PAGE
Guillaume de Cabestaing, Provençal Literature	4	406
Guillaume de Poitiers, Provençal Literature	4	410
Guiney, L. I., on Keats	13	429
Guiraud le Roux, Provençal Literature	4	401
Guiraut de Borneil, Provençal Literature	4	405
Guizot, François	6	642
Gulliver's Travels, Swift	12	55
		61, 64, 70
Gummere, F. B., on		
The Ballad	4	11
Folk-Song	4	112
Guzman de Alfarache, Aleman	8	60

H

	VOL.	PAGE
ha-'Am, Akhad, see Akhad ha-'Am		
ha-Kalir, Eleazar, see Eleazar ha-Kalir		
ha-Levi, Judah, see Judah ha-Levi		
Hadloub, Johann	4	466
Hadrian, The Emperor	3	452
Haeckel, Ernst	9	473
Hafiz	1	372
Haggadoth, Three, Talmud	1	149
Haig, R. M., on George	18	150
Hail! Holy, Holy, Holy Lord, Wesley, Charles	12	546
Hajdamaki, The, Shevchenko	10	486
Hakluyt, Richard	11	17
Hakon Jarl, Oehlenschläger	10	81
		85
Hale, Edward Everett	17	358
Haliburton, Thomas Chandler	8	506
Hall, Leland, on		
Conrad	15	345
Fabre	7	198
London	18	470
Rolland	7	533
Woolman	16	141
Halleck, Fitz-Greene	16	412
Hamasah, Abu Sakhr	1	237
Hamilton, Alexander	16	212
Hamilton, Clayton, on		
Brieux	7	476
Shaw	15	475
Hamlet, Shakespeare	11	290
		295, 296
Hamlet, Thoughts on, Lemaître	7	427
Hamsun, Knut	10	269
Hand of Lincoln, The, Stedman	17	504
Hanging of the Crane, The, Longfellow	17	142
Hannele, Hauptmann	9	533
Hapgood, I. F., on		
Dostoyevsky	10	427
Gogol	10	351
Pushkin	10	332
Happy He Who Saw of Old, Gabirol	1	165
Happy Life, The Means to Attain, Surrey	11	127
Happy Warrior, Character of the, Wordsworth	13	57
Hard Times, Dickens	14	114
Hardenberg, Friedrich von, see Novalis		
Hardy, Thomas	15	59
Hariri, al-, of Basra	1	238
Harp that Once through Tara's Halls, The, Moore	13	294
Harper, G. M., on		
Froissart	6	15
La Fontaine	6	123
Harper, The Song of the, Egyptian Literature	1	55
Harris, Joel Chandler	18	279
Harris, W. T., on Hegel	9	260
Harrison, Caskie, on Martial	3	336
Harryings of Annwn, The, Legends of Arthur and the Round Table	4	74
Hart, Samuel, on St. Augustine	3	440
Harte, Francis Bret	18	164
Hartley Coleridge, To, Wordsworth	13	50
Hartranft, C. D., on Luther	9	13
Harz Journey, The, Heine	9	328
		331
Hasty Pudding, Barlow	16	208
Hauptmann, Gerhart	9	526
Hawthorne, Julian, on		
Borrow	13	644
Bulwer-Lytton	14	52
Cooper	16	383
Hawthorne, Nathaniel	17	67
Hay, John	18	125
Hayes, C. J. H., on		
Balfour	15	238
Newman	14	15
Hayne, Paul Hamilton	17	613
Hayne, Reply to, Webster	16	318
		319
Hazlitt, William	13	269
He Remembers Forgotten Beauty, Yeats	8	538
Hearn, Lafcadio	18	320

	VOL.	PAGE
Heart Knoweth Its Own Bitterness, The, Rossetti, C. G.	14	476
Heart of Mid-Lothian, The, Scott	13	155, 160
Heat, Lampman	8	492
Heathen Chinee, The, see Plain Language from Truthful James		
Heaven and Hell, Swedenborg	10	152
Heaven Hath Its Stars, Greek Anthology	2	581
Hebbel, Christian Friedrich	9	338
Hebe, Lowell	17	327
Heber, Reginald	12	571
Hebrew Literature		
Medieval Hebrew Literature	1	152
Modern Hebrew Literature	1	195
The Old Testament and the Jewish Apocrypha	1	97
The Talmud	1	138
Yiddish Literature	1	619
Hecuba Hears the Story of Her Daughter's Death, Euripides	2	203
Hegel, Georg Wilhelm Friedrich	9	260
Heijermans, Herman	8	421
Heine, Heinrich	9	313
Heir in His Old Age, An, Chinese Literature	1	519
Helen, To, Poe	17	578
Heliodorus	2	559
Hell, Dante	5	59
Hellas, Shelley	13	421
Héloïse	4	497
Héloïse, Answer to, Abélard	4	500
Helvétius, Letter to Madame, Franklin	16	92
Hemans, Felicia Dorothea	13	480
Henderson, Brooks, on		
Noyes	15	573
Tagore	1	485
Watson	15	556
Henley, William Ernest	15	531
Henry Esmond, The History of, Thackeray	14	76, 79
Henry, O., see Porter, William Sydney		
Henry, Patrick	16	136
Henry of Auë, Hauptmann	9	550
Henry VIII (Shakespeare), see King Henry VIII		
Henry VIII, Character of, see History of England (Froude)		
Henry IV, see King Henry IV		
Heraclitus	2	289
Heraclitus	2	574
Heraclitus, Epitaph on, Callimachus	2	390
Herbert, George	11	155
Herbert, Life of Mr. George, Walton	11	509
Hercules Furens, Seneca	3	273
Herder, Johann Gottfried von	9	92
Hérédia, José-Maria de	7	255
Hereditary Genius, Galton	14	574
Heriot, Thomas	11	31
Hernani, Hugo	6	504
Herod and Mariamne, Hebbel	9	340
Herodotus	2	240
Heroes and Hero-Worship, Carlyle	13	558
Heroic Enthusiasts, The, Bruno	5	268
Herrick, Robert	11	160
Hertha, Swinburne	15	118
Hertz, Henrik	10	91
Hervé Riel, Browning	14	390
Hesiod	2	52
Hesper, Bion	2	409
Heyse, Paul	9	465
Heywood, John	11	182
Heywood, Thomas	11	364
Hiawatha, The Song of, Longfellow	17	144
Higginson, T. W., on		
Epictetus	2	456
Joubert	6	393
Taylor	11	551
High-Handed Outrage at Utica, Browne	17	395
Higher Man, The, Nietzsche	9	511
Highland Lassie, The, Ramsay	12	203
Highland Mary, Burns	12	611
Highway of the Upright, The, Luzzatto	1	178
Hildebrand	8	373
Hill, G. B., on Johnson	12	258
Hillard, Katharine, on		
Leopardi	5	391
Ronsard	6	64
Hind and the Panther, The, Dryden	11	624
Hindu Literature, see Indian Literature		
Hinsdale, B. A., on Komensky	10	555
Hippolytus, Euripides	2	199
Hippolytus' Disaster, Euripides	2	201
His Lady's Tomb, Ronsard	6	72

	VOL.	PAGE
Historians, German	9	432
Historical Essays, Freeman	14	628
Historical Writing, Recent American	18	544
Histories, Polybius	2	417
		419, 420
History		
Discourse upon Universal History, Bossuet	6	220
Gibbon, Edward	12	422
Herodotus	2	240
Historical Writing, Recent American	18	544
History, Emerson	17	50
Poetics, Aristotle	2	340
Short Studies on Great Subjects, Froude	14	618
Thucydides	2	257
History, Emerson	17	50
History, Sze-ma Ch'ien	1	508
Hitomaru	1	543
Hitopadeça, Indian Literature	1	449
Hobbes, Thomas	11	496
Hodgins, J. C., on Yeats	8	529
Hodgson, Ralph	15	618
Hodous, Lewis on Chinese Literature	1	494
Hofmannsthal, Hugo von	9	598
Hog, the Goat, and the Sheep, The, La Fontaine	6	135
Hogg, James	12	578
Hohenlinden, Campbell	13	262
Hojoki, Japanese Literature	1	551
Holberg, Ludvig	10	18
Holden, E. S., on		
'Antar	1	283
Copernicus	10	494
Hölderlin, Friedrich	9	407
Holland, Josiah Gilbert	17	428
Holland and Its People, De Amicis	5	469
Holmes, Oliver Wendell	17	189
Holy and Profane State, The, Fuller	11	547
		549
Holy, Holy, Holy! Lord God Almighty! Heber	12	573
Holy Russia, Tyutchev	10	322
Holy Thursday, Blake	12	637
Home, Gibson	15	608
Home, Sill	18	183
Home to Sirmio, Catullus	3	159
Homer	2	27
Homeric Hymns, see Cyclic Poets		
Homer's Odyssey, Translation of, Chapman	11	319
Home-Thoughts from Abroad, Browning	14	345
Homes of England, The, Hemans	13	481
Homily VIII, Chrysostom	2	557
Homme Libre, L', Barrès	7	453
Honest Lover, The, Suckling	11	174
Hood, Thomas	13	462
Hooft, Pieter Corneliszoon	8	345
Hooker, Life of Mr. Richard, Walton	11	507
Hope and Experience, Greek Anthology	2	579
Hopkins, E. W., on Indian Literature	1	403
Hopkinson, Letter to Mr., Jefferson	16	189
Horace (Quintus Horatius Flaccus)	3	191
Horace, Corneille	6	111
Horace's Farm, Horace	3	207
Horatian Ode upon Cromwell's Return from Ireland, An, Marvell	11	471
Horatius, Macaulay	13	533
Horrida Tempestas, Horace	3	204
Hospital Sketches, Alcott	17	381
Hostile Confederacy, The, Welsh Literature	4	256
Hound of Heaven, The, Thompson	15	543
House of the Righteous, The, Greek Anthology	2	578
House of the Seven Gables, The, Hawthorne	17	90
Household Tales, Grimm	9	275
		278
Housman, Alfred Edward	15	565
How an Anchoress Was Tempted by the Devil, Gesta Romanorum	4	509
How Doth the Little Busy Bee, Watts	12	196
How Sleep the Brave, Collins	12	326
How the Devil Took to Himself an Old Wife, Sachs	9	49
How the Old Man Came by His End, Marco Polo	4	521
How the Old Man Used to Train His Assassins, Marco Polo	4	520
How to Preserve the Health, Athenæus	2	548
How to Succeed, 'Ubaid Zakani	1	304
Howadji in Syria, Curtis	17	469
Howard, Henry, Earl of Surrey	11	127

	VOL.	PAGE
Howe, Joseph	8	502
Howe, W. D., on Riley	18	303
Howells, William Dean	18	102
Howells, W. D., on Tolstoy	10	393
Hsiao Yen	1	511
Hudibras Described, Butler	11	490
Hudson, W. H., on Harte	18	164
Hughes, E. A., on Strachey	15	674
Hughes, H. H., on Sardou	7	190
Hugo, Victor	6	488
Human Nature, Hobbes	11	498
Human Understanding, Essay Concerning, Locke	11	635, 637
Humble-Bee, The, Emerson	17	54
Hume, David	12	297
Humor		
Alice's Adventures in Wonderland, Carroll	15	142, 144, 146, 152
Artemus Ward: His Travels, Browne	17	397
As You Like It, Shakespeare	11	274
Astarotte and Rinaldo, Pulci	5	165
Beggar's Opera, The, Gay	12	119
Belle of the Ball, The, Praed	13	498
Betrothed, The, Manzoni	5	350
Bishop of Rum-Ti-Foo, The, Gilbert	14	499
Bon Gaultier Ballads, Aytoun	13	504
Bore, The, Horace	3	205
Camera Obscura, Hildebrand	8	373
Captain and the Mermaids, The, Gilbert	14	502
Casting Away of Mrs. Lecks and Mrs. Aleshine, The, Stockton	18	2
Chapter on Ears, A, Lamb	13	209
Clockmaker, The, Haliburton	8	506, 508
Connecticut Yankee in King Arthur's Court, A, Clemens	18	55
Constant Lover, The, Suckling	11	175
Cook Well Done, The, Martial	3	342
Courting of T'nowhead's Bell, The, Barrie	15	325
Culprit Fay, The, Drake	16	442
Deacon's Masterpiece, The, Holmes	17	198
Devil and the Deep Sea, The, Leacock	8	514
Diamond Cut Diamond, Martial	3	342
Dissertation upon Roast Pig, A, Lamb	13	213
Diverting Scrape, A, Martial	3	342
Dogs, Smith	13	249
Don Quixote, Cervantes	8	92, 96
Dora Versus Rose, Dobson	14	496
Dreyfus Case, On the, Dunne	18	468
Earl of Hertford, Letter to the, Walpole	12	348
Edwin Forrest as Othello, Browne	17	393
Ephemera; An Emblem of Human Life, The, Franklin	16	93
Faithless Sally Brown, Hood	13	463
Four Million, The, Porter	18	428
Frogs, The, Aristophanes	2	237
George Montagu, Esq., Letters to, Walpole	12	349, 350
Gil Blas, Le Sage	6	268, 275
Gingillino, Giusti	5	399
Guardian, The, Steele	12	80, 82
Guzman de Alfarache, Aleman	8	60
Hard Times, Dickens	14	114
Hasty Pudding, Barlow	16	208
High-Handed Outrage at Utica, Browne	17	395
Hudibras Described, Butler	11	490
Hunting of the Snark, The, Carroll	15	150
Inspector, The, Gogol	10	355
Invitation to Dinner, An, Catullus	3	161
Joseph Vance, De Morgan	15	402
Jumping Frog of Calaveras County, The Notorious, Clemens	18	36
King Henry IV, Shakespeare	11	279, 282, 283
Knickerbocker History of New York, The, Irving	16	346
Last Trousers, The, Scheffel	9	427
Lazarillo de Tormes, Mendoza	8	56
Legend of Sleepy Hollow, The, Irving	16	352
Letter of Advice, A, Praed	13	501

	VOL.	PAGE
Life on the Mississippi, Clemens	18	41
Little Billee, Thackeray	14	102
Little Minister, The, Barrie	15	340
Locandiera, La, Goldoni	5	289
Love for Love, Congreve	11	648
		650
Love-Letters of Smith, The, Bunner	18	358
Mann, Letter to Sir Horace, Walpole	12	347
Margutte's Confession, Pulci	5	163
Master Paul, Petőfi	8	597
Master Pierre Patelin, The Farce of, Medieval Drama	4	184
Miles Gloriosus [The Braggart Soldier], Plautus	3	44
Mrs. Battle's Opinions on Whist, Lamb	13	224
Morning Call, A, Catullus	3	158
Much Ado about Nothing, Shakespeare	11	272
Old Creole Days, Cable	18	264
Our Cuban Allies, Dunne	18	466
Pablos de Segovia, Quevedo	8	63
Pardoner's Story, The, Heywood	11	184
Parental Ode to My Son, A, Hood	13	465
Penrod, Tarkington	18	494
Plain Language from Truthful James, Harte	18	169
Playboy of the Western World, The, Synge	8	549
Poet at the Breakfast-Table, The, Holmes	17	207
Reinaert the Fox, Middle Dutch Literature	4	471
Rivals, The, Sheridan	12	477
		480, 483
Saint Patrick, Maginn	13	488
School for Scandal, The, Sheridan	12	488
		493
Schoolmistress, The, Shenstone	12	323
She Stoops to Conquer, Goldsmith	12	520
Silent Woman, The, Jonson	11	349
Society upon the Stanislaus, The, Harte	18	168
Sorrows of Werther, The, Thackeray	14	101
Spectator, The, Steele	12	77
Tam o' Shanter, Burns	12	604
Tartarin of Tarascon, Daudet	7	222
		224
Tatler, The, Steele	12	75
Teutoburger Battle, The, Scheffel	9	425
Through the Looking-Glass, Carroll	15	147
To His Book, Horace	3	208
Ulysses von Ithacia, Holberg	10	26
Uncle Remus and His Friends, Harris	18	281
		284, 288
Uncle Tom's Cabin, Stowe	17	258
Under the Greenwood Tree, Hardy	15	65
Verses, Suckling	11	176
What I Know about Gardening, Warner	17	489
Hundred Pipers, The, Nairne	12	616
Hungarian Literature	8	583
Hunger, Hamsun	10	272
Hunt, Leigh	13	295
Hunt, M. L., on		
Wharton	18	448
Wister	18	406
Hunting of the Cheviot, The, Medieval Literature	4	24
Hunting of the Snark, The, Carroll	15	150
Hus, Jan	10	552
Husband and Wife, Japanese Literature	1	542
Hushed Be the Camps Today, Whitman	17	426
Hutton, Laurence, on, Dickens	14	106
Huxley, Aldous	15	667
Huxley, Thomas Henry	14	549
Huygens, Constantijn	8	353
Huysmans, Joris Karl	7	349
Hyacinth, The, Hayne	17	617
Hydriotaphia, or Urn-Burial, Browne	11	538
Hymn, Oehlenschläger	10	89
Hymn for Children at Christmas, A, Luther	9	22
Hymns		
And the Heavens Shall Yield Their Dew, Gabirol	1	166
Apollo, Hymn to Delian, Homeric Hymns	2	72
Aten, Hymn to the, Akhenaten	1	52
Atharva-Veda, The, Indian Literature	1	436
Brightest and Best of the Sons of the Morning, Heber	12	573
Centennial Hymn, Whittier	17	176

	VOL.	PAGE
Charge to Keep, I Have, A, Charles Wesley	12	547
Come, Holy Spirit, Heavenly Dove, Watts	12	193
Dedication Hymn, Willis	17	108
Demeter, Hymn to, Homeric Hymns	2	73
Dominant Note of the Law, The, Japanese Literature	1	561
Evening Hymn, Keble	13	486
From Greenland's Icy Mountains, Heber	12	572
Gentle Jesus, Meek and Mild, Wesley, Charles	12	544
God of the World, Nagara	1	171
Hail! Holy, Holy, Holy Lord, Wesley, Charles	12	546
Holy, Holy, Holy! Lord God Almighty! Heber	12	573
Hymn, Oehlenschläger	10	89
Hymn for Children at Christmas, A, Luther	9	22
Jesus, Lover of My Soul, Wesley, Charles	12	547
Jesus Shall Reign Where'er the Sun, Watts	12	192
Jupiter, Hymn to, Callimachus	2	387
Latin Hymns, Medieval Literature	4	99
Lead, Kindly Light, Newman	14	41
Love Divine, All Love Excelling, Wesley, Charles	12	543
Mercury, Hymn to, Homeric Hymns	2	68
Nannar, Hymn to, Babylonian Literature	1	93
Our God, Our Help in Ages Past, Watts	12	191
Palms and Myrtles, Eleazar ha-Kalir	1	164
Raghuvança, Kalidasa	1	463
Rig-Veda, Hymns from the, Indian Literature	1	428
Safe Stronghold Our God Is Still, A, Luther	9	21
Shamash, Hymns to, Babylonian Literature	1	91
Spectator, The, Addison	12	100
Sun-Day Hymn, A, Holmes	17	201
There Is a Land of Pure Delight, Watts	12	194
Usertesen III, Hymn to, Egyptian Literature	1	49
Venus, Hymn to, Homeric Hymns	2	70
Vesper Hymn, The, Abélard	4	501
Virtue, Hymn to, Aristotle	2	344
Welcome, Sweet Day of Rest, Watts	12	193
When I Survey the Wondrous Cross, Watts	12	194
Zeus, Hymn to, Cleanthes	2	384
Hyperion, Keats	13	454
Hyperion's Song of Fate, Hölderlin	9	407

I

	VOL.	PAGE
I Came into This World to See the Sunlight, Balmont	10	327
I Heard You Solemn-Sweet Pipes of the Organ, Whitman	17	408
I Remember, I Remember, Hood	13	473
I Traveled among Unknown Men, Wordsworth	13	28
I Wandered Lonely as a Cloud, Wordsworth	13	54
I Weep Not for the Life, Schneor	1	213
Ibañez, Blasco	8	253
Ibrahim ibn Kunaif of Nabhan	1	236
Ibsen, Henrik	10	205
Iceland Fisherman, An, Loti	7	386
Icelandic Literature, see Old Norse Literature		
Icelandic Sagas, Old Norse Literature	4	297
Ichabod, Whittier	17	170
Idea of a Patriot King, The, Bolingbroke	12	102
Idea of a University, The, Newman	14	25
Ideal Trio, An, Li Po	1	512
Identity, Aldrich	18	69
Idiot, The, Dostoyevsky	10	435
Idyl of the Roses, Ausonius	3	456
Idyl, The Second, Theocritus	2	397
Idyl, The Seventh, Theocritus	2	398
If You but Knew, Sully-Prudhomme	7	273
Il Penseroso, Milton	11	438
Iliad, Homer	2	35, 36, 37, 39, 40, 41
Illustrious Ladies, Lives of, Brantôme	6	78
Imaginary Correspondence of Pericles and Aspasia, Landor	13	255
Imaginary Verses of Alexander Selkirk, Cowper	12	400
Imbecile, The, Pirandello	5	551

	VOL.	PAGE
Imitation of Christ, The, Middle Dutch Literature	4	474
(selections 477, 479, 481)		
Immanuel ben Solomon of Rome	1	172
Immensee, Storm	9	398
Immensity, Of, Bruno	5	271
Immortality of Genius, The, Propertius	3	238
Impatience, Thaxter	18	80
Impeachment of Night, The, Michelangelo	5	210
Imperfect Sympathies, Lamb	13	218
Impressions and Memories, Hearn	18	325
Impromptu of Chopin, To an, D'Annunzio	5	500
Improvement of the Understanding, The, Spinoza	8	363
Imr al-Kais	1	229
In a Drear-Nighted December, Keats	13	456
In a Winter Night, Liliencron	9	430
In a Year, Browning	14	380
In Memoriam, Tennyson	14	298
In School Days, Whittier	17	166
In the Fisher's Cabin, Heine	9	322
In the Spring a Young Man's Fancy, Meleager	2	582
In Time of Peace Prepare for War, Sumner	16	483
Inaugural Address, The First, Lincoln	17	589
Inaugural Address, The Second, Lincoln	17	593
Inchcape Rock, The, Southey	13	115
Incident of the French Camp, Browning	14	338
Inconsistency, Seneca	3	268
Independence in Action, Seneca	3	267
India, D'Annunzio	5	500
Indian Literature	1	403
Indian Serenade, The, Shelley	13	420
Indian Summer, Campbell	8	494
Indians (American)		
American Literature in the Colonial period	16	11
American Ornithological Biography, The, Audubon	16	290
Drake in California, Hakluyt	11	32
Guiana, Discovery of Raleigh (Hakluyt)	11	35
Hiawatha, The Song of, Longfellow	17	144
Indians — the First American Poets, The	16	1
Jesuits in North America in the Seventeenth Century, The, Parkman	17	369
Journal, Woolman	16	144
Last of the Mohicans, The, Cooper	16	400
Mémoires d'Outre-Tombe, Chateaubriand	6	420
Mexico, The Grim Idols of, Diaz	8	47
"Noche Triste, La" [The Night of Sorrows], Diaz	8	48
Relation of the First Voyage, A, Las Casas	8	41
Specimen Jones, Wister	18	407
United States, History of the, Bancroft	17	18
Virginia, A Report of, Heriot (Hakluyt)	11	31
Yemassee, The, Simms	17	524
Indians — the First American Poets, The	16	1
Indifference, Petöfi	8	600
Inevitable March of Improvement, The, Everett	16	436
Inge, Dean	15	658
Ingersoll, Robert Green	17	618
Inner Voices, Hugo	6	499
Insects, see Nature		
Insects and the National Holiday, Fabre	7	201
Inspector, The, Gogol	10	355
Inspiration, Thoreau	17	302
Institutes, Quintilian	3	300
302, 303, 304, 306		
Institutes, Prefatory Address to the, Calvin	6	61
Intellectual Beauty, Hymn to, Shelley	13	385
Intimations of Immortality from Recollections of Early Childhood, Wordsworth	13	59
Invisible Links, Lagerlöf	10	194
Invitation, An, Alcæus	2	113
Invitation to Dinner, An, Catullus	3	161
Invocation to Rain, Avesta	1	320
Ion's Song, Euripides	2	198
Ipswich, Field	18	513
Iranian Literature	1	292
Iridion, Krasiński	10	521
Irish Literature		
Medieval Irish Literature	4	192
Modern Irish Literature in English	8	529

	VOL.	PAGE
Modern Irish Literature in Gaelic	8	557
Irreparable Loss, Michelangelo	5	211
Irving, Washington	16	338
Is There for Honest Poverty? Burns	12	600
Isaac Ashford, Crabbe	12	626
Ishtar Myth, The, Babylonian Literature	1	77
Ishtar, Prayer to, Babylonian Literature	1	93
Isolation, Arnold	14	427
Israel Nagara, see Nagara, Israel		
It Is a Beauteous Evening, Calm and Free, Wordsworth	13	48
It Is Not to Be Thought of, Wordsworth	13	50
It Was on a Morn When We Were Thrang, Baillie	12	575
"Italia Mia, Benchè 'l Parlar Sia Indarno," Petrarch	5	92
Italian in England, The, Browning	14	340
Italian Literature		
Corinne, de Staël	6	412
Italy in the Middle Ages	5	8
Modern Italian Literature	5	275
The Renaissance	5	128
The Voice of Italy	5	1
Italy		
Cortegiano, Il, Castiglione	5	185
"De Gustibus —," Browning	14	373
Farewell to Italy, Landor	13	259
Fascist Italy, Governmental Policies of, Mussolini	5	577
"Italia Mia, Benchè 'l Parlar Sia Indarno," Petrarch	5	92
Italian in England, The, Browning	14	340
Italy and Florence, Indictment of, Dante	5	72
Prince, The, Machiavelli	5	180
Toccata of Galuppi's, A, Browning	14	361
Italy, Heine	9	335
Itinerarium, Numatianus	3	459
Ivanov, Vyacheslav	10	330

J

	VOL.	PAGE
Jack, Daudet	7	227
Jackson, A. V. W., on		
The Avesta	1	307
Firdausi	1	321
Hafiz	1	372
Jalal ad-Din Rumi	1	366
Jami	1	380
Jayadeva	1	480
Kalidasa	1	459
Nizami	1	350
Sa'di	1	356
Jaffár, Hunt	13	298
Jakšić, Mileta	10	588
Jalal ad-Din Rumi	1	366
James Boswell, Esq., Letter to, Johnson	12	269
James, Henry	18	218
James, Henry, on		
Hawthorne	17	67
Lowell	17	320
Turgenev	10	366
James, William	18	204
Jameson, J. F., on Motley	17	267
Jami	1	380
Jane Eyre, Brontë, Charlotte	14	224
January Morning, A, Lampman	8	493
Japanese Literature	1	530
Jatakas, Indian Literature	1	444
Jayadeva	1	480
Jealous Husband, The, Ab Gwilym	4	268
Jean-Christophe, Rolland	7	535
Jean de Meung	4	387
Jefferies, Richard	15	232
Jefferson, Thomas	16	173
Jerusalem Delivered, Tasso	5	240
Jessie Lee, Barnes	13	508
Jester's Plea, The, Locker-Lampson	14	401
Jesting Pilate, Huxley	15	671
Jesuits in North America in the Seventeenth Century, The, Parkman	17	369
Jesus, Dedication to the Life of, Renan	7	123
Jesus, Lover of My Soul, Wesley, Charles	12	547
Jesus Shall Reign Where'er the Sun, Watts	12	192
Jew Converted to Christianity by Going to Rome, The, Boccaccio	5	116
Jew of Malta, The, Marlowe	11	227
Jewels, The, Heine	9	324
Jewett, Sarah Orne	18	291
Jewish Wars, Josephus	1	133, 135
Jews		
Jew Converted to Christianity by Going to Rome, The, Boccaccio	5	116

	VOL.	PAGE
Jew of Malta, The, Marlowe	11	227
Jewish Wars, Josephus	1	133
		135
Medieval Hebrew Literature	1	152
Merchant of Venice, The, Shakespeare	11	268
Modern Hebrew Literature	1	195
Nathan the Wise, Lessing	9	81
Old Testament and the Jewish Apocrypha, The	1	97
Priest and Prophet, Akhad ha'Am	1	215
Semitic People in the History of Civilization, The Share of, Renan	7	123
Table-Talk, Selden	11	118
Talmud, The	1	138
Yiddish Literature	8	617
Jim, Harte	18	167
Jim Bludso of the Prairie Belle, Hay	18	133
Jock o' Hazeldean, Scott	13	147
John Anderson, My Jo, Burns	12	598
John Bull's Other Island, Shaw	15	498
Johnson, C. F., on		
Boswell	12	277
Browne	17	390
Defoe	12	16
Froude	14	613
Longfellow	17	111
Johnson, Samuel	12	258
Johnson, Life of Samuel, Boswell	12	281
Jókai, Maurice	8	601
Jonson, Ben	11	338
Joseph Andrews, Fielding	12	174
		177
Joseph Vance, De Morgan	15	402
Josephus	1	127
Joubert, Joseph	6	393
Journal, Goncourts	7	85
Journal, Woolman	16	144
Journals, see Diaries		
Juan de la Cruz, Sañ, see San Juan de la Cruz		
Juana, Musset	6	480
Judah al-Kharizi	1	178
Judah ha-Levi	1	179
Judgment of Paris, The, Lucian of Samosata	2	524
Judith, Anglo-Saxon Literature	4	336
Julian, Death of, Gibbon	12	438
Julius Cæsar, Shakespeare	11	287
Jumping Frog of Calaveras County, The Notorious, Clemens	18	36
Jupiter, Hymn to, Callimachus	2	387
Justification of His Patriotic Policy, Demosthenes	2	382
Juvenal	3	362

K

	VOL.	PAGE
Kaibara Yekken	1	563
Kalevala, The, Finnish Literature	8	613
Kalidasa	1	459
Kallen, H. M., on James, William	18	204
Kant, Immanuel	9	62
Kant and His Interpreters, Schiller	9	191
Katha Upanishad, Indian Literature	1	439
Katharina, Heine	9	320
Keats, John	13	429
Keble, John	13	485
Keller, Gottfried	9	386
Kelsey, F. W., on Ovid	3	242
Khayyam, Omar	1	337
Kilmer, Joyce, on Thompson	15	541
King, A. Huygens	8	354
King — and Death, The, Mahmud of Ghazna	1	297
King and the Philosopher, The, Herodotus	2	245
King Christian, Ewald	10	52
King, Grace, on		
Baudelaire	7	18
Mérimée	6	615
de Vigny	6	454
de Vogüé	7	415
King Henry IV, Shakespeare	11	279
		282, 283
King Henry VIII, Shakespeare	11	265
King Lear, Shakespeare	11	300
		302
King of Yvetot, The, Béranger	6	524
King René's Daughter, Hertz	10	93
		97
King Rhampsinitus and the Robber, Herodotus	2	252
Kingsley, Charles	14	204
Kiokutei Bakin	1	567
Kipling, Rudyard	15	289
Kiss Refused, The, Maykov	10	373
Kitab al-Khazari, Judah ha-Levi	1	184
Kitchen, The, Verhaeren	8	444
Klaus Hinrich Baas, Frenssen	9	586

	VOL.	PAGE
Kleist, Heinrich von	9	248
Klopstock, Friedrich Gottlieb	9	55
Knee-Deep in June, Riley	18	308
Knickerbocker History of New York, The, Irving	16	346
Knight Toggenburg, The, Schiller	9	186
Knights, The, Aristophanes	2	225
Knowledge, In Praise of, Bacon	11	110
Kojiki, Japanese Literature	1	538
Kokinshu, Japanese Literature	1	544
Komenský, Jan Amos (Comenius)	10	555
Konrad von Würzburg	4	465
Konrad Wallenrod, Mickiewicz	10	501
Kosmos, Parmenides	2	295
Kraeling, E. G. H., on the Literature of Babylonia and Assyria	1	61
Krasiński, Żygmunt	10	519
Kubla Khan, Coleridge	13	110
Kubler, E. A., on Swiss Literature	8	562
Kuhns, L. O., on		
Alfieri	5	308
Ariosto	5	189
Bestiaries and Lapidaries	4	510
Kulikovo, On the Field of, Blok	10	329
Kwannon, The Temple of, Hearn	18	326

L

	VOL.	PAGE
Labid	1	231
La Bruyère, Jean de	6	243
Lacedæmonian Dead at Platæa, On the, Simonides	2	572
La Chartreuse de Parme, Beyle	6	543
Lachesis Lapponica, Linnæus	10	161, 163
Ladies of St. James's, The, Dobson	14	494
Lady of Shalott, The, Tennyson	14	263
Lady of the Lake, The, Scott	13	140, 146
Lady, To a, Prior	12	37
Lady, To a, Voltaire	6	331
La Fontaine, Jean de	6	123
Laforgue, Jules	7	293
Lagerlöf, Selma	0	182
L'Aiglon, Rostand	7	495
Laila and Majnun, Nizami	1	351
Laird o' Cockpen, The, Nairne	12	620
Lake of B —, Ode to the, Lamartine	6	451
L'Allegro, Milton	11	435
Lamartine, Alphonse de Prat de	6	445
Lamb, Charles	13	205
Lament, Walther von der Vogelweide	4	460
Lament, A, Shelley	13	428
Lament for Israel, A, Eleazar ha-Kalir	1	162
Lament on His Father's Death, A, Liu Hang	1	511
Lament, Song of, Petőfi	8	598
Lamentation of Gudrun over Sigurd Dead, Of the, Old Norse Literature	4	293
Lampman, Archibald	8	492
Land o' the Leal, The, Nairne	12	615
Landing of the Pilgrim Fathers in New England, The, Hemans	13	482
Landor, Walter Savage	13	250
Lang, Andrew, on		
Dumas	6	589
Scott	13	129
Lang, H. R., on Camoens	8	282
Langland, William, see Piers Plowman		
Lanier, Sidney	18	193
Lankester, E. R., on		
Darwin	14	510
Huxley	14	549
Laocoön, Lessing	9	88, 89
Lape, E. E., on Frenssen	9	584
Lapidaries, see Bestiaries and Lapidaries		
Lark Ascending, The, Meredith	15	51
La Rochefoucauld, François	6	115
Las Casas, Bartolomeo de	8	40
Last Chronicle of Barset, The, Trollope	14	174
Last Days of Pompeii, The, Bulwer-Lytton	14	57
Last Eve of Summer, The, Whittier	17	187
Last Fight of the Revenge, The, Raleigh	11	41
Last Leaf, The, Holmes	17	194
Last Letter to His Aged Mother, Johnson	12	267
Last of the Mohicans, The, Cooper	16	400
Last of the Vikings, The, Bojer	10	291

	VOL.	PAGE
Last Ride Together, The, Browning	14	369
Last Rose of Summer, see 'Tis the Last Rose of Summer		
Last Trousers, The, Scheffel	9	427
Late, Raisen	8	636
Lathrop, G. P., on		
Bryant	16	417
Gray	12	331
Latin-American Literature before 1888	8	293
Latin-American Literature since 1888	8	309
Latin Hymns, Medieval Literature	4	99
Latin Literature		
Goliardic Poetry	4	132
The Grandeur That Was Rome	3	1
Latin Hymns	4	99
Roman Poets of the Later Empire	3	447
The Scholar and His Public	4	483
Laudator Temporis Acti, Petronius	3	332
Laura, The Death-Bed of, Petrarch	5	100
Lavengro, Borrow	13	648
Law. See also Government		
Attic Nights, Aulus Gellius	3	411
Institutes, Quintilian	3	306
Poet at the Breakfast Table, The, Holmes	17	207
Red Robe, The, Brieux	7	485
Trial of Warren Hastings, The, Macaulay	13	530
Village Communities in the East and West, Maine	14	593
Lawton, W. C., on		
Cicero	3	68
Ennius	3	27
Euripides	2	191
Goldoni	5	286
Hesiod	2	52
Landor	13	250
Livy	3	212
Menander	2	352
Philemon, Menander, etc.	2	345
Statius	3	313
Vergil	3	167
Xenophon	2	275
Lay of the Last Minstrel, The, Scott	13	135
Lay of the Two Lovers, The, Marie de France	4	384
Layamon	4	77
Lazarillo de Tormes, Mendoza	8	56
Lazarus, Andreyev	10	475
Leacock, Stephen	8	514
Leacock, Stephen, on Porter	18	423
Lead, Kindly Light, Newman	14	41
Leandro's Song, Fletcher	11	395
Lear, see King Lear		
Learning by Doing, Martial	3	341
Least of Evils, The, Martial	3	340
Lecky, William Edward Hartpole	15	178
Lecky, W. E. H., on Gibbon	12	422
Leconte de Lisle, Charles Marie René	7	250
Legend of Sleepy Hollow, The, Irving	16	352
Légende d'un Peuple, La, Fréchette	8	523
Legends of Arthur and the Round Table, The	4	65
Leisure, On, Seneca	3	269
Lélia, Sand	7	38
Lemaître, Jules	7	426
Lending a Punch-Bowl, On, Holmes	17	196
Lenora, Bürger	9	109
Leonidas of Tarentum	2	573
Leopardi, Giacomo	5	391
Lermontov, Mikhail Yurevich	10	316
Le Sage, Alain René	6	265
Lesbia, Last Word to, Catullus	3	165
Lesbia's Sparrow, Elegy on, Catullus	3	164
Lessing, Gotthold Ephraim	9	74
Let Dogs Delight to Bark and Bite, Watts	12	195
L'Étrangère, Dumas, Junior	7	180
Letter of Advice, A, Praed	13	501
Letter to His Father, at the Age of Ten, Adams, J. Q.	16	246
Letter to His Wife on Their Daughter's Death, Plutarch	2	497
Letteris, Meir Halevi	1	201
Letters		
Abélard, Letter to, Héloïse	4	497
Alleyne, Letter to John, Franklin	16	95
Astor, Letter to Francis, Newton	11	640
Atticus, Letter to, Cicero	3	87
Charlemagne, A Letter to, Alcuin	4	486
Cicero, Letter to, Cælius	3	96
Cicero, Letter to, Cæsar	3	95
Cicero, Letter to, Matius	3	97
Constance, Letter from, Hus	10	553
Coulanges, Letter to Her Cousin, M. de, de Sévigné	6	210

	VOL.	PAGE
Coulanges, Letter to M. de, de Sévigné	6	211
Countess of Bute, Letters to the, Montagu	12	252
		253, 254
Countess of Mar, Letter to the, Montagu	12	249
Deffand, Letter to Mme. du, Voltaire	6	330
E. W. Montagu, Esq., Letter to, Montagu	12	248
Earl of Hertford, Letter to the, Walpole	12	348
Ephemera; An Emblem of Human Life, The, Franklin	16	93
Farewell to His Mother's Aged Servant, Johnson	12	267
George Montagu, Esq., Letters to, Walpole	12	349
		350
Grignan, Letters to Her Daughter, Madame de, de Sévigné	6	212
		213, 214, 216
Héloïse, Answer to, Abélard	4	500
Helvétius, Letter to Madame, Franklin	16	92
Hopkinson, Letter to Mr., Jefferson	16	189
James Boswell, Esq., Letter to, Johnson	12	269
Last Letter to His Aged Mother, Johnson	12	267
Letter to His Father, at the Age of Ten, Adams, J. Q.	16	246
Letters, Burney	12	470
Letters, Pliny the Younger	3	377
		378, 379, 380, 382, 383, 386, 387, 388
Letters from an American Farmer, Crèvecœur	16	104
		111
Letters to His Son, Chesterfield	12	256
Lisbon Earthquake, Letter on the, Voltaire	6	331
Lord Chesterfield, Letter to, as to the 'Dictionary,' Johnson	12	266
Lord Kames, Letter to, Franklin	16	95
Madison, Letter to James, Jefferson	16	192
Mann, Letter to Sir Horace, Walpole	12	347
Newton, Letter to Rev. John, Cowper	12	402
Olympias, Letters to, Chrysostom	2	554
Perkins, Letter to Mr., Johnson	12	269
Porter, Letter to Mrs. Lucy, in Lichfield, Johnson	12	268
Rousseau, Letter to, Voltaire	6	328
Santa Teresa, From the Correspondence of	8	73
Skipwith, Letter to Robert, Jefferson	16	186
Styles, Letter to Dr., Jefferson	16	190
Sulpicius Consoles Cicero after His Daughter Tullia's Death, Sulpicius	3	88
Sulpicius, Reply to, Cicero	3	91
Terentia, Letter to, Cicero	3	87
Thrale, Letter to Mrs., Johnson	12	270
Tiro, Letter to, Cicero	3	86
Unwin, Letter to, William, Cowper	12	402
Vacillation in the Civil War, Cicero	3	92
Volland, Letter to Mlle., Diderot	6	365
Letters, Burney	12	470
Letters from an American Farmer, Crèvecœur	16	104
		111
Letters from My Windmill, Daudet	7	225
Letters, Pliny the Younger	3	377
		378, 379, 380, 382, 383, 386, 387, 388
Letters to His Son, Chesterfield	12	256
Leuconoë, To, Horace	3	198
Leva, La, Pereda	8	189
Levia Gravia, Carducci	5	432
		433, 434
Leviathan, Hobbes	11	499
		501
Lewis, C. T., on Bacon	11	88
Lewisohn, Ludwig, on		
Dehmel	9	574
Hauptmann	9	526
Strindberg	10	167
Li Po	1	512
Li Tai Po	1	514
Liao-chai Chi-i, Chinese Literature	1	516
Libation-Pourers, The, Æschylus	2	160

	VOL.	PAGE
Libertine of Seville, The, Tirso de Molina	8	126
Liberty of Prophesying, The, Taylor	11	553
License of Speech, Invective against, Demosthenes	2	381
Lie, Jonas	10	252
Lieberman, Herman, on Yiddish Literature	8	617
Life, Procter	13	479
Life, Santa Teresa	8	71
Life, A, de Maupassant	7	331
Life and Letters, Darwin	14	517
		536, 537
Life and Opinions, Ewald	10	54
Life and Song, Lanier	18	200
Life for Song, Bruno	5	274
Life Lesson, A, Riley	18	317
Life on the Mississippi, Clemens	18	41
		44, 46, 50, 52
Life Well Lost, Bruno	5	271
Life's Wandering, A, Greek Anthology	2	581
Light Conceits of Lovers, Campion	11	138
Light o' Love, Schnitzler	9	568
Liliencron, Detlev von	9	428
Limbo, Delavigne	6	530
Lincoln, Abraham	17	580
Lindsay, T. B., on		
Juvenal	3	362
Terence	3	52
Lines, Woodberry	18	369
Lines: When the Lamp Is Shattered, Shelley	13	426
Linnæus	10	155
Lion, The, Bestiaries	4	512
Lion and the Other Beasts, The, Æsop	2	63
Lisbon Earthquake, Letter on the, Voltaire	6	331
L'Isle-Adam, Villiers de, see Villiers de l'Isle-Adam		
Literature. See also Drama; Poetry; Fiction; Epic; etc.		
Aladdin, Oehlenschläger	10	66
Ancient Authors, On, Quintilian	3	309
Archias, Oration for the Poet, Cicero	3	76
Art of Poetry, The, Horace	3	209
Authorship, On, Schopenhauer	9	289
Autobiography, Trollope	14	182
Björnstjerne Björnson, Brandes	10	126
Books and Reading, On, Schopenhauer	9	284
Chaucer, Longfellow	17	142
Congreve, To My Dear Friend Mr., Dryden	11	627
Conversations with Eckermann, Goethe	9	172
Corinne, de Staël	6	412
Countess of Bute, Letters to the, Montagu	12	254
Crime of Sylvestre Bonnard, The, France	7	365
Deffand, Letter to Mme. du, Voltaire	6	330
Divina Commedia, Longfellow	17	143
Essais, Montaigne	6	85
Flaubert, Faguet	7	436
Flaubert, Correspondence with, Sand	7	47
Friend, To a, Arnold	14	426
Gibbon, Edward, Bagehot	14	602
Goncourts, The, de Gourmont	7	441
Hamlet, Thoughts on, Lemaître	7	427
Holy and Profane State, The, Fuller	11	549
Journal, Goncourts	7	85
Letters, Pliny the Younger	3	379
		386
Levia Gravia, Carducci	5	432
		433, 434
Life and Letters, Darwin	14	536
Literature and Civilization	1	3
Literature of the Nineteenth Century, Main Currents in the, Brandes	10	128
Literatures of France, England, and Germany, The, Brunetière	7	423
Magazine in America, The, Paine	16	170
Memorial Verses, Arnold	14	429
Milton, Longfellow	17	143
Milton's Portrait, Lines Printed under, Dryden	11	629
My Recollections, D'Azeglio	5	374
Northanger Abbey, Austen	13	185
Phi Beta Kappa Oration, Sumner	16	491
Pierre, Melville	17	458
Prose, Of, van Deyssel	8	410
Qualities of the Writer, Of the, Joubert	6	397
Reading, The Pleasures of, Balfour	15	245

	VOL.	PAGE
Realistic Literature, de Vogüé	7	417
Revolt from Victorianism, The	15	1
Rousseau, Letter to, Voltaire	6	328
Shakespeare, On, Milton	11	448
Shakespeare, the Man, Bagehot	14	601
Shakespeare, To the Memory of, Jonson	11	343
Style, Of, Joubert	6	397
Terentius, Epigram on, Cæsar	3	129
Truth about an Author, The, Bennett	15	436
Wilhelm Meister's Apprenticeship, Goethe	9	158
Literature and Civilization	1	3
Literature of Babylonia and Assyria, The	1	61
Literature of the Nineteenth Century, Main Currents in the, Brandes	10	128
Literatures of France, England, and Germany, The, Brunetière	7	423
Little Bateese, Drummond	8	498
Little Billee, Thackeray	14	102
Little Black Boy, The, Blake	12	638
Little Flowers, The, St. Francis of Assisi	5	19
Little Lac Grenier, Drummond	8	497
Little Minister, The, Barrie	15	340
Little Orphant Annie, Riley	18	315
Little Poems in Prose, Baudelaire	7	23
Little Son Hans, Aged Six, Letter to His, Luther	9	24
Little Women, Alcott	17	383
		389
Liu Heng	1	511
Live Without Dining, Martial	3	344
Living Author, Epitaph on a, Cowley	11	484
Livingston, Arthur, on		
D'Annunzio	5	489
Croce	5	507
Ferrero	5	532
Fogazzaro	5	449
Modern Italian Literature	5	275
Pirandello	5	547
Provençal Literature	4	397
Livy (Titus Livius)	3	212
Loafer, A, Davidson	15	539
Locandiera, La, Goldoni	5	289
"Loch Achray," The Yarn of the, see Salt Water Ballads		
Lochaber No More, Ramsay	12	200
Lochinvar, Scott	13	138
Locke, John	11	634
Locker-Lampson, Frederick	14	484
Locksley Hall, Tennyson	14	269
Locusts and Wild Honey, Burroughs	18	92
Lodge, Gonzales, on Plautus	3	39
Lodge, Thomas	11	128
Lodging for the Night, A, Stevenson	15	260
Lombard Street, Bagehot	14	610
Lomer, G. R., on		
English Literature: Eighteenth Century Survey	12	1
English Literature: The Romantic Revival	13	1
Shakespeare to Dryden	11	1
The Victorian Era	14	1
London		
Composed upon Westminster Bridge, Wordsworth	13	47
London, Davidson	15	539
London, Verhaeren	8	444
Plague in London, History of the, Defoe	12	23
Worthies of England, The, Fuller	11	549
London, Davidson	15	539
London, Jack	18	470
London, 1802, Wordsworth	13	49
London, Verhaeren	8	444
Longfellow, Henry Wadsworth	17	111
Longing for Jerusalem, Judah ha-Levi	1	183
Longus	2	565
Loomis, R. S., on		
The Legends of Arthur and the Round Table	4	65
Welsh Literature	4	243
Lope de Vega	8	114
Lord Chesterfield, Letter to, as to the 'Dictionary,' Johnson	12	266
Lord Jim, Conrad	15	357
Lord Kames, Letter to, Franklin	16	95
Lord Ormont and His Aminta, Meredith	15	43
Lord Randal, Medieval Literature	4	40
Lord Ullin's Daughter, Campbell	13	265
Lorelei, Eichendorff	9	296
Lorelei, The, Heine	9	318
Lost Leader, The, Browning	14	344

	VOL.	PAGE
Lost Manuscript, The, Freytag	9	380
Loti, Pierre	7	384
Lounsbury, T. R., on		
Chaucer	4	552
Cowley	11	478
Dryden	11	605
Pope	12	128
Love		
Abélard, Letter to, Héloïse	4	497
Getting Married, Shaw	15	510
Heaven and Hell, Swedenborg	10	152
Human Nature, Hobbes	11	498
Love, Emerson	17	44
Love in a Cottage, Willis	17	110
Love, the Life-Giver, Michelangelo	5	211
Modern Love, Meredith	15	56
New Life, The, Dante	5	53
One Word More, Browning	14	374
Universal Love, Mo Ti	1	507
Valediction Forbidding Mourning, A, Donne	11	151
Venus, Hymn to, Homeric Hymns	2	70
Yusuf and Zulaikha, Jami	1	381
Love, Emerson	17	44
Love, Greek Anthology	2	574
Love, Herbert	11	157
Love, Lodge	11	130
Love among the Ruins, Browning	14	363
Love Divine, All Love Excelling, Wesley, Charles	12	543
Love for Love, Congreve	11	648, 650
Love in a Cottage, Willis	17	110
Love in the Country, Tibullus	3	230
Love in the Valley, Meredith	15	48
Love Is All, Catullus	3	164
Love of Animals for Man, The, Athenæus	2	549
Love Poems, Rabi'a	1	234
Love Song, A, Saïat Nova	1	392
Love Songs, Egyptian Literature	1	47
Love Songs, Heine	9	319
Love, the Life-Giver, Michelangelo	5	211
Lovelace, Richard	11	463
Love-Letters of Smith, The, Bunner	18	358
Lovely Mary Donnelly, Allingham	14	483
Lovers, The, Anderson	10	115
Lover's Melancholy, The, Ford	11	407
Lover's Sigh, A, Anacreon	2	126
Lovers of Gudrun, The, Morris	15	134
Lovers of the Banu Udhrah, The, Arabian Nights	1	263
Love's Ferriage, Agathias	2	582
Love's Growth, Donne	11	153
Love's Immortality, Strato	2	576
Love's Labor's Lost, Shakespeare	11	250
Love's Parting, Minuchihri	1	297
Love's Young Dream, Moore	13	288
Low Tide on Grand Pré, Carman	8	495
Lowell, Amy, on Verhaeren	8	438
Lowell, James Russell	17	320
Lower Depths, The, Gorky	10	468
Lucasta Going to the Wars, To, Lovelace	11	463
Lucasta, To, Lovelace	11	465
Lucian of Samosata	2	519
Lucifer, Vondel	8	337, 343
Luck of Edenhall, The, Uhland	9	408
Luck of Roaring Camp, The, Harte	18	172
Lucretius (Titus Lucretius Carus)	3	130
Ludwig, Otto	9	353
Luis de Leon, Fray, see Fray Luis de Leon		
Lun Yü, Confucius	1	505
Lusatian Literature	10	570
Lusiads, The, Camoens	8	287
Luther, Martin	9	13
Luxury, The Foolishness of, Lucretius	3	139
Luzzatto, Moses Khayyim	1	178
Lycidas, Milton	11	445
Lyly, John	11	189
Lyra Apostolica, Newman	14	40
Lyric, A, Kalidasa	1	479
Lyric Fragment, A, Firdausi	1	337
Lyrics, Bhartrihari	1	454
Lytton, Lord, see Bulwer-Lytton		

M

	VOL.	PAGE
Mabie, H. W., on		
Addison	12	84
Lincoln	17	580
Warner	17	485
Mabinogion, Welsh Literature	4	259
Mac Datho's Pig, The Story of, Medieval Irish Literature	4	222
Macaulay, Thomas Babington	13	511

	VOL.	PAGE
Macbeth, Shakespeare	11	305
		306, 309, 310
MacCauley, Clay, on Japanese Literature	1	530
McCrae, John	8	502
McGiffert, A. C., on Calvin	6	58
Machar, J. S.	10	568
Machiavelli, Niccolò	5	168
Mackail, J. W., on		
Catullus	3	155
Theocritus	2	391
Mackenzie, J. K., on		
Belloc	15	600
Brooke	15	610
Huxley	15	667
Meynell	15	547
Mackery End in Hertfordshire, Lamb	13	227
McMaster, J. B., on		
Freeman	14	624
Macaulay	13	511
MacMechan, Archibald	8	521
Macpherson, James	12	352
Madame Bovary, Flaubert	7	61
		67, 71
Madison, James	16	197
Madison, Letter to, James, Jefferson	16	192
Madman or Saint? Echegaray	8	178
Madonna of the Future, The, James, Henry	18	234
Madrigal, Drummond	11	140
Madrigal, A, Ronsard	6	73
Mæcenas, An Invitation to, Horace	3	203
Mæcenas, Caius Clinius, To, Propertius	3	237
Maeterlinck, Maurice	8	463
Magazine in America, The, Paine	16	170
Magda ('Heimat'), Sudermann	9	515
Magi, The, New Testament	2	430
Maginn, William	13	487
Maha-Parinibbana-Sutta, Buddhistic Literature	1	442
Mahabharata, Indian Literature	1	450
Mahaffy, J. P., on Sophocles	2	162
Mahmud of Ghazna	1	297
Mahomet's Death and Character, Gibbon	12	443
Maid of Athens, Byron	13	312
Maid of Honor, The, Massinger	11	400
Maid's Tragedy, The, Beaumont and Fletcher	11	387
Maiden from Afar, The, Schiller	9	184
Maiden of Tarentum, The, Chénier	6	405
Maidenhood, Longfellow	17	123
Maiden's Lament, A, Sakanoe	1	541
Maimonides, Moses	1	186
Maimonides' Will, Extract from, Maimonides	1	190
Maine, Sir Henry	14	591
Makamat, al-Hariri of Basra	1	238
Makura no Soshi, Sei Shonagon	1	549
Mallarmé, Stéphane	7	513
Malone, John, on St. John Chrysostom	2	551
Malory, Sir Thomas	4	92
Man and Superman, Shaw	15	497
Man, Of, Joubert	6	394
Man without a Country, The, Hale	17	359
Mandalay, Kipling	15	313
Mandeville, Sir John	4	523
Mandragora, The, Bestiaries	4	516
Mangan, James Clarence	13	491
Mann, Thomas	9	608
Mann, Letter to Sir Horace, Walpole	12	347
Manners and Customs. See also Anthropology; Sociology		
Adventure of the Cloak, The, Petronius	3	328
Age of Homespun, The, Bushnell	16	509
Amateur of Lying, The, Lucian of Samosata	2	528
American Literature in the Colonial Period	16	11
Anciens Canadiens, Les, de Gaspé	8	526
Ancient Régime, The, Taine	7	145
		148
Anxious Mother, Letter from an, Alciphron	2	517
Casina, Plautus	3	50
Characters, La Bruyère	6	244
Cortegiano, Il, Castiglione	5	185
Coulanges, Letter to Her Cousin, M. de, de Sévigné	6	210
Coulanges, Letter to M. de, de Sévigné	6	211
Countess of Mar, Letter to the, Montagu	12	249
Cranford, Gaskell	14	243
		249
Curious Scythian Customs, Herodotus	2	249

	VOL.	PAGE
Diary, Adams, John	16	159
Diary, Evelyn	11	563
Diary, Pepys	11	576
Drake in California, Hakluyt	11	32
Earl of Hertford, Letter to the, Walpole	12	348
Eighteenth Century, The, Schérer	7	100
Émigré, L', Bourget	7	405
Evelina, Burney	12	467
Everybody's Business Is Nobody's Business, Defoe	12	32
Ex-Voto, Eekhoud	8	453
Festival of Adonis, The, Theocritus	2	402
Gallic War, The, Cæsar	3	122
Gentle Craft, The, Deloney	11	81
Germania, Tacitus	3	352
Germany, On, de Staël	6	408
Gran Conquista de Ultramar, La, Alfonso the Wise	8	22
Grignan, Letter to Her Daughter, Madame de, de Sévigné	6	213
Guardian, The, Steele	12	80
Guiana, Discovery of, Raleigh (Hakluyt)	11	35
History of England, Macaulay	13	516, 518, 523
How to Preserve the Health, Athenæus	2	548
Knickerbocker History of New York, The, Irving	16	346
Lazarillo de Tormes, Mendoza	8	56
Letters, Pliny the Younger	3	378
Letters to His Son, Chesterfield	12	256
Makura no Soshi, Sei Shonagon	1	549
Mercenary Girl, Letter from a, Alciphron	2	516
Metamorphoses, Apuleius	3	399
Mirgorod, Gogol	10	359
M. Poirier's Son-in-Law, Augier	7	154, 157, 158, 164
Mysteries, Jakšić	10	588
Necklace of Pearls, A, Cellini	5	228
Necromancy, An Adventure in, Cellini	5	231
Pleasures of Athens, The, Alciphron	2	516
Protagoras, Plato	2	313
Rape of the Lock, The, Pope	12	147
Reflections on Society, La Rochefoucauld	6	121
Registre of Hystories, A, Ælianus Claudius	3	417, 419, 420
Rustic in the Amphitheater, The, Calpurnius	3	454
Santa Teresa, From the Correspondence of	8	73
Shoemaker's Holiday, A, Dekker	11	327
Silvæ, Statius	3	321
Spectator, The, Addison	12	98
Spectator, The, Steele	12	77
Travels in France, Young	12	388
Under the Yoke, Vasov	10	578
Virginia, A Report of, Heriot (Hakluyt)	11	31
Manning, C. A., on		
Andreyev	10	473
Capek	10	561
Chekhov	10	451
Czechoslovak Literature	10	550
Gorky	10	462
Hus	10	552
Polish Literature	10	490
Reymont	10	544
Russian Literature	10	301
Russian Poetry	10	314
Shevchenko	10	485
Slowacki	10	511
The Ukraine	10	484
Yugoslav Literature	10	586
Mansfield Park, Austen	13	190, 192, 195, 198
Manyoshu, Japanese Literature	1	539
Manzoni, Alessandro	5	347
Marble Faun, The, Hawthorne	17	99
March on Rome, The, Mussolini	5	564
Marco Bozzaris, Halleck	16	413
Marco Polo	4	518
Marco Polo, Ser, Prologue to the Book of, Travelers' Tales	4	518
Marcus Aurelius Antoninus, see Aurelius Antoninus, Marcus		
Marduk, Prayer to, Babylonian Literature	1	92
Margolis, Max, on the Talmud	1	138
Margutte's Confession, Pulci	5	163
Mariana, Tennyson	14	260

	VOL.	PAGE
Marie, Ronsard	6	70
Marie de France	4	384
Marius the Epicurean, Pater	15	210
Mark Twain, see Clemens, Samuel Langhorne		
Marlowe, Christopher	11	214
Marriage		
Alleyne, Letter to John, Franklin	16	95
Doll's House, A, Ibsen	10	218
Economist, The, Xenophon	2	278
Heaven and Hell, Swedenborg	10	152
Husband and Wife, Japanese Literature	1	542
John Anderson, My Jo, Burns	12	598
Man and Superman, Shaw	15	497
Marriage, Gibson	15	607
Marriage Ring, The, Taylor	11	557
Maxims, Richter	9	221
Memoirs, Saint-Simon	6	280
My Childhood, Gorky	10	464
New Household, The, Longfellow	17	142
Peregrine Pickle, Smollett	12	243
Poet's Song to His Wife, The, Procter	13	480
Pride and Prejudice, Austen	13	178
Princess, The, Tennyson	14	295
Prothalamion; or, A Spousall Verse, Spenser	11	61
Subjection of Women, The, Mill	13	637
Table-Talk, Luther	9	25
Table-Talk, Selden	11	118
Marriage, Gibson	15	607
Marriage of Figaro, The, Beaumarchais	6	379
Marriage Ring, The, Taylor	11	557
Marsh, The, Gautier	6	681
Marshes of Glynn, The, Lanier	18	200
Marta y Maria, Valdes	8	218
Martial (Marcus Valerius Martialis)	3	336
Martyrdom of Saint Hiztibuzit, The, Armenian Literature	1	397
Marvell, Andrew	11	465
Mary Hamilton, Medieval Literature	4	35
Masefield, John	15	581
Massacre in Piedmont, On the Late, Milton	11	449
Massinger, Philip	11	399
Master of the Feast, The, Petronius	3	333

	VOL.	PAGE
Master Paul, Petőfi	8	597
Master Pierre Patelin, The Farce of, Medieval Drama	4	184
Matters Pertaining to Religion, A Discourse of, Parker	17	237
Matthews, Brander	18	339
Matthews, Brander, on		
Beaumarchais	6	371
Clemens	18	27
Molière	6	137
Roosevelt	18	385
Sheridan	12	474
Matius	3	97
Maud, Tennyson	14	308
Maud Muller, Whittier	17	161
Maupassant, Guy de	7	326
Max Havelaar, Multatuli	8	386
Maxims. See also Philosophy; Ethics		
Babylonian Wisdom, Ut-Napishtim	1	95
Discourses, Epictetus	2	458
Enchiridion, Epictetus	2	462
Fragments, Epictetus	2	463
Hope and Experience, Greek Anthology	2	579
James Boswell, Esq., Letter to, Johnson	12	269
Letters to His Son, Chesterfield	12	256
Man, Of, Joubert	6	394
Maxims, La Rochefoucauld	6	116
Maxims, Richter	9	221
Maxims and Descriptions, Heine	9	326
Maxims and Reflections, Goethe	9	171
Maxims of Any	1	59
Miscellaneous Sayings, Fuller	11	550
Miscellaneous Works, Chesterfield	12	257
Nature of Minds, Of the, Joubert	6	394
Oraculo Manual, Gracian	8	149
Pamphlets, Voltaire	6	325
Perkins, Letter to Mr., Johnson	12	269
Poor Richard's Almanac, Franklin	16	86
		87
Pure in Heart, The, Greek Anthology	2	579
Sayings of Luther, Luther	9	28
Table-Talk, Luther	9	25
Table-Talk, Selden	11	118
Thoughts, Pascal	6	198

	VOL.	PAGE
Water of Purity, The, Greek Anthology	2	580
Works and Days, Hesiod	2	56
Maxims, La Rochefoucauld	6	116
Maxims, Richter	9	221
Maxims and Descriptions, Heine	9	326
Maxims and Reflections, Goethe	9	171
Maxims of Any	1	59
May-Night, Petöfi	8	599
Maykov, Appollon Nikolayevich	10	323
Mazzini, Giuseppe	5	402
Meadows, To, Herrick	11	167
Means, D. M., on Maine	14	591
Measure for Measure, Shakespeare	11	263
Medea Resolving to Slay Her Children, Euripides	2	204
Medici, Lorenzo de'	5	140
Medicine, see Science		
Medieval Drama, The	4	146
Meditation, Baudelaire	7	26
Meditations, Aurelius	3	427
Meghaduta, or Cloud Messenger, Kalidasa	1	476
Melancholy, Ode on, Keats	13	453
Melancholy, Ode to, Fletcher	11	397
Meleager	2	575
		582
Meleager's Own Epitaph	2	575
Melville, Herman	17	434
Mémoires d' Outre-Tombe, Chateaubriand	6	420
Memoirs, see Biography		
Memoirs, Adams, J. Q.	16	247
		248, 249
Memoirs, Fuller	17	227
		231
Memoirs, Saint-Simon	6	283
		284, 288
Memorabilia, Browning	14	372
Memorial Verses, Arnold	14	429
Memory, Aldrich	18	71
Men of Gotham, The, Peacock	13	475
Menander	2	352
Menaphon, Greene	11	209
Mencius	1	506
Mendoza, Diego Hurtado de	8	56
Menendez y Pelayo, Marcelino	8	225
Mercenary Girl, Letter from a, Alciphron	2	516
Merchant and the Parrot, The, Jalal ad-Din Rumi	1	369
Merchant of Venice, The, Shakespeare	11	257
		268, 269, 270
Mercury, Hymn to, Homeric Hymns	2	68
Meredith, George	15	19
Mérimée, Prosper	6	615
Mermaid Tavern, Lines on the, Keats	13	446
Merriam, G. S., on Stowe	17	245
Messiah, The, Klopstock	9	58
Metamorphoses, Apuleius	3	399
Metaphysics. See also Philosophy; Religion		
Being, Of, Edwards	16	63
Brihadaranyaka Upanishad, Indian Literature	1	437
Critique of Pure Reason, The, Kant	9	69
Essences, On, Aristotle	2	342
Freedom of the Will, Inquiry into the, Edwards	16	63
Nan Hua Chen Ching, Chuang Tzu	1	502
Physics and Metaphysics, Russell	15	687
Principia Rerum Naturalium, Swedenborg	10	142
		144
Prolegomena, Kant	9	71
Republic, The, Plato	2	328
Metric System, The, Adams, J. Q.	16	254
Mexico, The Grim Idols of, Diaz	8	47
Meyer, Konrad Ferdinand	9	455
Meynell, Alice	15	547
Michael, Wordsworth	13	31
Michael Kramer, Hauptmann	9	555
Michelangelo	5	208
Michelet, Jules	6	652
Mickiewicz, Adam	10	498
Midas, Lyly	11	196
Middle Ages, The (Medieval Song and Story)	4	1
Midsummer Days and Nights, Ballade of, Henley	15	532
Midsummer Night's Dream, A, Shakespeare	11	251
		254, 256
Mikkelsen, M. A., on Hume	12	297
Miles Gloriosus [The Braggart Soldier], Plautus	3	44
Military Servitude and Grandeur, de Vigny	6	457
Milkèn Time, Barnes	13	508
Mill, John Stuart	13	628
Mill on the Floss, The, Eliot	14	658

	VOL.	PAGE
Mille, Pierre	7	525
Miller, Joaquin	18	187
Miller, The, Verhaeren	8	447
Milton, John	11	423
Milton, Longfellow	17	143
Milton, John, Macaulay	13	526
Milton's Portrait, Lines Printed under, Dryden	11	629
Minister's Wooing, The, Stowe	17	262 265
Minna von Barnhelm, Lessing	9	79
Minnesingers, The, Medieval German Literature	4	461 462, 463, 464, 465, 466
Minstrel's Curse, The, Uhland	9	410
Minuchihri	1	297
"Mio Rifugio, Il," Michelangelo	5	212
Mirabeau	6	385
Miraculous Story about the Holy Rabbi Elimelech of Lizensk, A, Rabbi Ramas	8	627
Mirèio, Mistral	7	207
Mirgorod, Gogol	10	359
Misanthrope, The, Callimachus	2	390
Miscellaneous Sayings, Fuller	11	550
Miscellaneous Works, Chesterfield	12	257
Misérables, Les, Hugo	6	518
Mishna, The, Talmud	1	147
Miss Tempy's Watchers, Jewett	18	293
Missal, The, Sully-Prudhomme	7	271
Missouri Compromise, Urging the Repeal of the, Calhoun	16	303
Mr. Dooley, see Dunne, Finley Peter		
Mr. Hosea Biglow to the Editor of the Atlantic Monthly, Lowell	17	348
Mistral, Frédéric	7	205
Mrs. Battle's Opinions on Whist, Lamb	13	224
Mrs. Jenny Treibel, Fontane	9	445
Mitchell, E. K., on Josephus	1	127
Mo Ti	1	507
Moby-Dick, Melville	17	448 452
Modern Life, Some Changes in, Sumner	16	487
Modern Love, Meredith	15	56
Modern Painters, Ruskin	13	609 610
Molière	6	137
Molina, Tirso de, see Tirso de Molina		
Mommsen, Theodor	9	433
Monk and His Pet Cat, The, Medieval Irish Literature	4	240
Monk's Wedding, The, Meyer	9	457
M. Poirier's Son-in-Law, Augier	7	154 157
Montagu, Lady Mary Wortley	12	247
Montague, W. P., on		
Bergson	7	459
Nietzsche	9	495
Montaigne, Michel Eyquem de	6	80
Montcalm and Wolfe, Parkman	17	374
Montesquieu	6	292
Moore, George	15	381
Moore, Thomas	13	285
Morals, see Ethics		
Morals and Legislation, An Introduction to the Principles of, Bentham	12	564
Morgan, B. Q., on		
Anzengruber	9	485
Fontane	9	443
German Literature: Between Dusk and Dawn	9	10
German Literature: Lyric Voices of the Nineteenth Century	9	406
German Literature: A New Dawn	9	52
German Literature: Power, Prosperity, and Pride	9	440
German Literature: Sunshine and Shadow	9	207
Hebbel	9	338
Hofmannsthal	9	598
Ludwig	9	353
Mann	9	608
Meyer	9	455
The Romantic School in Germany	9	230
Sudermann	9	513
Morgan, Forrest, on Bagehot	14	596
Mörike, Eduard	9	417
Morley, John	15	200
Morning, Keble	13	485
Morning Call, A, Catullus	3	158
Morning Thought, A, Sill	18	185
Morris, L. R., on Synge	8	541
Morris, William	15 4	129 296
Morse, E. W., on Irving	16	338
Morte d'Arthur, Tennyson	14	285
Morungen, Heinrich von	4	462

	VOL.	PAGE
Moschus	2	410
Moses, de Vigny	6	456
Moses ibn Ezra	1	169
Moses of Khorni	1	393
Mosses from an Old Manse, Hawthorne	17	95
Mothers and Nurses, Plutarch	2	503
Mother's Epitaph, A, Ausonius	3	457
Motley, John Lothrop	17	267
Motoöri	1	568
Mountain Daisy, To a, Burns	12	602
Mountains, The, Cohen	1	204
Mountains of California, The, Muir	18	20
Mourning Bride, The, Congreve	11	653
Mourning Garment, The, Greene	11	210
Mouse, To a, Burns	12	601
Mower to the Glow-Worms, The, Marvell	11	469
Mower's Song, The, Marvell	11	469
Mu'allakat, Imr al-Kais	1	229
Mu'allakat, Zuhair	1	229
Much Ado about Nothing, Shakespeare	11	258, 272
Mufaddaliyat, Ash-Shanfara of Azd	1	233
Muir, John	18	19
Muir, John, on Linnæus	10	155
Muller, H. F., on Medieval French Literature	4	346
Multatuli	8	384
Munger, T. T., on Bushnell	16	505
Murasaki no Shikihi	1	550
Muse, To the, Propertius	3	238
Music. See also Hymns		
Alexander's Feast; or the Power of Music, Dryden	11	630
Impromptu of Chopin, To an, D'Annunzio	5	500
Hopkinson, Letter to Mr., Jefferson	16	189
Jean-Christophe, Rolland	7	535
King Henry VIII, Shakespeare	11	265
Music, Baudelaire	7	27
Music of Wagner, The, Ingersoll	17	627
Opera and Drama, Wagner	9	373
Swann's Way, Proust	7	570
Toccata of Galuppi's, A, Browning	14	361
Value and Power of Music, The, Luther	9	24
With a Guitar, to Jane, Shelley	13	424
Work and Play, Bushnell	16	514
Music, Baudelaire	7	27
Music of Wagner, The, Ingersoll	17	627
Musketaquid, Emerson	17	58
Musobioye Kosho Monogatari, Kiokutei Bakin	1	567
Musset, Alfred de	6	473
Mussolini, Benito	5	563
Muzzey, D. S., on Recent American Historical Writing	18	544
My Books, Longfellow	17	138
My Boy, Rosenfeld	8	639
My Childhood, Gorky	10	464
My Children, Yamagami no Okura	1	542
My Creed, Schiller	9	191
My First Daughter, On, Jonson	11	354
My Grandmother, To, Locker-Lampson	14	488
My Heart Leaps Up When I Behold, Wordsworth	13	47
My Heart with Hidden Tears Is Swelling, Heine	9	319
My Heart's in the Highlands, Burns	12	612
My Lamp, To, Lamartine	6	448
My Last Duchess, Browning	14	333
My Lost Youth, Longfellow	17	135
My Mother, To, Neruda	10	567
My Neighbor Rose, Locker-Lampson	14	485
My Recollections, D'Azeglio	5	368, 371, 374
My Sister Henriette, Renan	7	116
My Star, Browning	14	369
My Summer in a Garden, Warner	17	488
Myers, F. W. H., on		
Poe	17	536
Wordsworth	13	18
Myself, Of, Cowley	11	480
Mysteries, Jakšić	10	588
Mysterious Nature, Hsiao Yen	1	511
Mystics, The Spanish	8	66
Mythology. See also Religion; Hymns		
Adapa Myth, The, Babylonian Literature	1	82
Ancient Sindbad, An, Avesta	1	319
Angel of Divine Obedience, The, Avesta	1	317
Apollo, Hymn to Delian, Homeric Hymns	2	72

	VOL.	PAGE
Appeal to Ahura Mazda, the Lord, for Knowledge, An, Avesta	1	316
Arethusa, Shelley	13	404
Atharva-Veda, The, Indian Literature	1	436
Awakening of Cupid, The, Apuleius	3	406
Baucis and Philemon, Ovid	3	252
Catapatha Brahmana, Indian Literature	1	437
Centaur, The, de Guérin	6	532
Demeter, Hymn to, Homeric Hymns	2	73
Dionysus and the Pirates, Homeric Hymns	2	71
Epic of Creation, Babylonian Literature	1	72
Faun with the Mirror, The, de Régnier	7	521
Frogs, The, Aristophanes	2	233
Goddess of the Waters, The, Avesta	1	318
Gruesome Lover, A, Ovid	3	257
Guardian Spirits, Avesta	1	318
Harryings of Annwn, The, Legends of Arthur and the Round Table	4	74
Hyperion, Keats	13	454
Ishtar Myth, The, Babylonian Literature	1	77
Ishtar, Prayer to, Babylonian Literature	1	93
Jupiter, Hymn to, Callimachus	2	387
Kojiki, Japanese Literature	1	538
Maiden of Tarentum, The, Chénier	6	405
Marduk, Prayer to, Babylonian Literature	1	92
Mercury, Hymn to, Homeric Hymns	2	68
Nannar, Hymn to, Babylonian Literature	1	93
Nihongi, Japanese Literature	1	539
Ode, First Pythian, Pindar	2	141
Odes, Olympian, Pindar	2	134 137, 139
Orpheus and Eurydice, Ovid	3	261
Pan, Hymn of, Shelley	13	407
Pheidippides, Browning	14	394
Poèmes Antiques, Leconte de Lisle	7	253
Poetic Edda, The, Old Norse Literature	4	289
Raghuvança, Kalidasa	1	463
Rape of Proserpine, The, Claudianus	3	458
Rig-Veda, Hymns from the, Indian Literature	1	428
Shamash, Hymns to, Babylonian Literature	1	91
Snorra Edda, The, Old Norse Literature	4	282
Sun-God's Palace, The, Ovid	3	260
Theogony, Hesiod	2	55
Tosa Nikki, Japanese Literature	1	547
Transformation, A, Ovid	3	261
Venus, Hymn to, Homeric Hymns	2	70
Works and Days, Hesiod	2	53
Zeus, Hymn to, Cleanthes	2	384

N

	VOL.	PAGE
Nagara, Israel	1	171
Nairne, Lady (Carolina Oliphant)	12	614
Nameless Grave, A, Greek Anthology	2	582
Nameless One, The, Mangan	13	491
Names, Lessing	9	77
Nan Hua Chen Ching, Chuang Tzu	1	502
Nannar, Hymn to, Babylonian Literature	1	93
Nansen, Fridtjof	10	261
Napoleon Bonaparte, The Life and Character of, Channing	16	282
Narrative of His Religious History, Edwards	16	60
Nasir-i-Khusru	1	299
Nathan the Wise, Lessing	9	81
Nativity, The Hymn on the, Milton	11	432
Natural History, Buffon	6	334 335
Natural History, Pliny the Elder	3	285 287, 289
Naturalism, see Realism		
Nadal, E. S., on Milton	11	423
Nature. See also Sea		
American Ornithology, Wilson	16	232 235
Anabasis, Xenophon	2	282
Arne, Björnson	10	247
Asian Birds, Bridges	15	554
Aspects of the Pines, Hayne	17	616
Atala, Chateaubriand	6	419
Autumn, Watson	15	563

	VOL.	PAGE
Autumn Dirge, An, Ou-yang Hsiu	1	515
Autumn, To, Keats	13	452
Branding-Ground, The, Farrukhi	1	295
Brook, The, Tennyson	14	292
Calendau, Mistral	7	208, 213
Campaspe, Lyly	11	200
Carnations, The, Herrick	11	166
Caryatids, The, de Banville	7	287
Caucasus, Pushkin	10	335
Chambered Nautilus, The, Holmes	17	197
Chants du Paysan, Déroulède	7	246
Chattahoochee, Song of the, Lanier	18	197
Cloud, The, Shelley	13	399
Complete Angler, The, Walton	11	510
Country Life, On the Pleasures of a, Tibullus	3	224
Cricket, The, Cowper	12	397
Crimean Sonatas, Mickiewicz	10	508
Cuckoo, To the, Wordsworth	13	53
Daffodils, To, Herrick	11	165
Daphnis and Chloe, Longus	2	566
Dawn of Spring, Hofmannsthal	9	604
Death of the Flowers, The, Bryant	16	424
Don Juan, Byron	13	329
Dragon-Fly, The, Gautier	6	682
Earth in Spring, The, Judah ha-Levi	1	184
Earth's Enigmas, Roberts	8	511
Ecologue, The First, Vergil	3	176
Fêtes Galantes, Verlaine	7	278
Fir-Tree, The, Freiligrath	9	420
Fish-Hawk, or Osprey, The, Wilson	16	242
Flats, The, Lanier	18	202
Forsaken Garden, A, Swinburne	15	123
Fuji-Yama, Ode to, Japanese Literature	1	544
Garden, The, Marvell	11	466
Gay Marigold, Bridges	15	556
Geese, The Flight of the, Roberts	8	490
Georgics, Vergil	3	179
Goldfinch, The, Dehmel	9	581
Grasshopper, The, Anacreon	2	124
Heat, Lampman	8	492
Horace's Farm, Horace	3	207
Humble-Bee, The, Emerson	17	54
Hyacinth, The, Hayne	17	617
I Wandered Lonely as a Cloud, Wordsworth	13	54
Idyl of the Roses, Ausonius	3	456
Idyl, The Seventh, Theocritus	2	398
Indian Summer, Campbell	8	494
Insects and the National Holiday, Fabre	7	201
January Morning, A, Lampman	8	493
Knee-Deep in June, Riley	18	308
Kokinshu, Japanese Literature	1	544
Kosmos, Parmenides	2	295
Lachesis Lapponica, Linnæus	10	161, 163
Letters, Pliny the Younger	3	383, 387
Letters from an American Farmer, Crèvecœur	16	104
Locusts and Wild Honey, Burroughs	18	92
Love's Labor's Lost, Shakespeare	11	250
Maiden from Afar, The, Schiller	9	184
Marsh, The, Gautier	6	681
Marshes of Glynn, The, Lanier	18	200
Meadows, To, Herrick	11	167
Meghaduta, or Cloud Messenger, Kalidasa	1	476
Mémoires d' Outre-Tombe, Chauteaubriand	6	420
Memoirs, Adams, J. Q.	16	249
Modern Painters, Ruskin	13	609, 610
Mountain Daisy, To a, Burns	12	602
Mountains of California, The, Muir	18	20
Mouse, To a, Burns	12	601
Mu'allakat, Imr al-Kais	1	229
Musketaquid, Emerson	17	58
My Summer in a Garden, Warner	17	488
Mysterious Nature, Hsiao Yen	1	511
Natural History, Buffon	6	334, 335
Natural History, Pliny the Elder	3	285, 289
Nature, Emerson	17	40

	VOL.	PAGE
Nature, Goethe	9	172
Nature, Introduction to the Poem on, Parmenides	2	293
Nature, Other Fragments from the Poem on, Empedocles	2	301
Nature, Poem on, Empedocles	2	299
Night, Hymn to the, Longfellow	17	117
Night, To, Shelley	13	422
Nightingale, The, Verlaine	7	284
Nightingale, Ode to a, Keats	13	447
Our Hundred Days in Europe, Holmes	17	222
Palace Garden, The, Greek Anthology	2	577
Pan, Hymn of, Shelley	13	407
Panegyric to the Summer, Ab Gwilym	4	266
Pastel (to Julius Zeyer), Vrchlický	10	569
Peace, The, Aristophanes	2	228 229
Pervigilium Veneris, Roman Poetry	3	453
Pine-Tree, The, Vazov	10	576
Prairie, The, Cooper	16	395 407
Primroses Filled with Morning Dew, To, Herrick	11	166
Rest at Noon, Meleager	2	575
Retirement, Vaughan	11	477
Return of the Native, The, Hardy	15	80
Rhodora, The, Emerson	17	53
Robert of Lincoln, Bryant	16	429
Roses, Florus	3	452
Sandpiper, The, Thaxter	18	79
Scholar, Gipsy, The, Arnold	14	432
Seasons, The, Thomson	12	312
Sensitive Plant, The, Shelley	13	396
Singing Reed, The, Greek Anthology	2	578
Skylark, The, Hogg	12	579
Skylark, To a, Shelley	13	401
Small Celandine, To the, Wordsworth	13	65
Snow, The, Ab Gwilym	4	267
Snow-Bound, Whittier	17	177
Song of Summer, Medieval Irish Literature	4	237
Song of Winter, A, Medieval Irish Literature	4	239
Songs of the Orient, Hugo	6	498
Sparrow's Nest, The, Wordsworth	13	46
Spring, Timrod	17	610
Spring, The, Carew	11	171
Spring, Ode on the, Gray	12	337
Spring on the Coast, Leonidas of Tarentum	2	573
Spring, The Song of, Vicente	8	277
Spring Waters, Tyutchev	10	321
Spring, Wherein Each Thing Renews, Description of, Surrey	11	128
Story of My Heart, The, Jefferies	15	233
Summer-Time, For, Wither	11	147
Sunbeams and Shadows, Hugo	6	500
Sunset, Hérédia	7	257
Swallow, The, Anacreon	2	125
Tampa Robins, Lanier	18	199
Task, The, Cowper	12	397
Telling the Bees, Whittier	17	159
Thyrsis, The Song of, Theocritus	2	395
Tintern Abbey, Lines Composed a Few Miles above, Wordsworth	13	23
'Tis Noon; the Light Is Fierce, Hérédia	7	258
To Daisies, Not to Shut So Soon, Herrick	11	165
Two Noble Kinsmen, The, Shakespeare and Fletcher	11	397
Union of Seasons, Kalidasa	1	478
Violets, To, Herrick	11	167
Visit to Ceylon, A, Haeckel	9	476 479
Vita Nuova, Watson	15	564
Walden, Thoreau	17	306 309, 315
West Wind, Ode to the, Shelley	13	393
Westminster Bridge, Sonnet Composed upon, Wordsworth	13	47
When o'er the Yellowing Corn, Lermontov	10	318
Wild Geese, Thaxter	18	80
Woods of Westermain, The, Meredith	15	54
World Is Too Much with Us, The, Wordsworth	13	55
Worship in Spring, Theætetus	2	573
Yellow Flowers, Sova	10	565
Nature, Emerson	17	40
Nature, Goethe	9	172

	VOL.	PAGE
Nature, Introduction to the Poem on, Parmenides	2	293
Nature of Minds, Of the, Joubert	6	394
Nature of Things, Opening Lines of the (Spenser's Imitation from 'The Faery Queen'), Lucretius	3	137
Nature of True Virtue, The, Edwards	16	66
Nature, Other Fragments from the Poem on, Empedocles	2	301
Nature, Poem on, Empedocles	2	299
"Nè Mai Pietosa Madre al Caro Figlio," Petrarch	5	103
Near East, see Orient		
Necklace of Pearls, A, Cellini	5	228
Necromancy, An Adventure in, Cellini	5	231
Need of Good Schoolmasters, The, Plutarch	2	502
Negative Confession, The, Egyptian Literature	1	56
Neill, C. P., on Machiavelli	5	168
Nekrasov, N. A.	10	322
Neptune, A Hymn in Praise of, Campion	11	137
Nero, Cowardice and Death of, Suetonius	3	393
Neruda, Jan	10	567
Never Too Late, Greene	11	211
Nevins, Allan, on		
Bennett	15	430
Gissing	15	276
New Birth, The, Wesley, John	12	537
New Day, The, Gilder	18	505
		508
New Grub Street, Gissing	15	283
New England		
Brandon House, The, Jewett	18	301
House of the Seven Gables, The, Hawthorne	17	90
Miss Tempy's Watchers, Jewett	18	293
Mosses from an Old Manse, Hawthorne	17	95
Musketaquid, Emerson	17	58
New England, Discourse in Commemoration of the First Settlement of, Webster	16	321
Pilgrim Fathers, The Emigration of the, Everett	16	435
Revolt of "Mother," The, Freeman	18	435
Roger Williams: The Prophet of Religious Freedom, Eggleston	18	84
Scarlet Letter, The Hawthorne	17	74
New England, Discourse in Commemoration of the First Settlement of, Webster	16	321
New Jerusalem, Heavenly Doctrine of the, Swedenborg	10	148
New Life, The, Dante	5	53
New Testament, The	2	422
New Way to Pay Old Debts, A, Massinger	11	401
New York		
Four Million, The, Porter	18	428
Knickerbocker History of New York, The, Irving	16	346
Love-Letters of Smith, The, Bunner	18	358
Pan in Wall Street, Stedman	17	507
Their Wedding Journey, Howells	18	110
Newbolt, Sir Henry	15	569
Newcomes, The, Thackeray	14	92
		98
Newman, John Henry	14	15
Newton, Sir Isaac	11	639
Newton, Letter to Rev. John, Cowper	12	402
Never Is, but Always to Be, Martial	3	341
Nibelungenlied, Medieval German Literature	4	428
Nibi	1	543
Nietzsche, Friedrich	9	495
Night, Bialik	1	211
Night, Blake	12	635
Night Attack on Platæa, The, Thucydides	2	263
Night, Hymn to the, Longfellow	17	117
Night, Hymns to the, Novalis	9	226
Night in Venice, Hay	18	133
Night Piece — to Julia, The, Herrick	11	168
Night-Song of a Wandering Asian Shepherd, Leopardi	5	395
Night Thoughts, Young	12	197
Night, To, Shelley	13	422
Nightingale, Ode to a, Keats	13	447
Nightingale, The, Verlaine	7	284
Nihongi, Japanese Literature	1	539

	VOL.	PAGE
Nine Singers, The Song of the, Bruno	5	272
Nizami	1	350
Njalssaga, Old Norse Literature	4	303
No Trifling with Love, Musset	6	481
Noad, A. S., on		
Benavente	8	241
Diaz	8	44
Faguet	7	434
Foscolo	5	330
French Literature: The Drama of Today	7	506
Gide	7	545
Gracian	8	145
Ibañez	8	253
Mallarmé	7	513
Musset	6	473
The Picaresque Novel	8	51
Proust	7	559
Santa Teresa	8	68
Spain and France	8	152
Spain's European Greatness and Decline	8	31
Spanish Literature	8	1
Spanish Romanticism	8	157
Thierry	6	637
Tirso de Molina	8	124
Unamuno	8	233
Valéry	7	576
Noah's Flood, Medieval Drama	4	150
Noble Nature, The, Jonson	11	355
"Noche Triste, La" [The Night of Sorrows], Diaz	8	48
Noiseless Patient Spider, A, Whitman	17	427
Nombres de Cristo, De Los, Fray Luis de Leon	8	80
Non Sine Dolore, Gilder	18	508
"Non So se s'è la Desiata Luce," Michelangelo	5	213
Nora Creina, Moore	13	291
Nora's Vow, Scott	13	149
Norris, Frank	18	481
Norse Literature, see Old Norse Literature		
Norse Love Story, A, Lie	10	253
Northanger Abbey, Austen	13	185
Northern Farmer (Old Style), Tennyson	14	316
Norton, C. E., on		
Clough	14	445
Dante	5	33
Italy in the Middle Ages	5	8
Norwegian Literature	10	200
Nothin' to Say, Riley	18	319

	VOL.	PAGE
Nouveaux Lundis, Sainte-Beuve	6	623
Nova Scotia-ness of Nova Scotia, The, MacMechan	8	521
Novalis	9	223
Novel, see Fiction		
Noyes, Alfred	15	573
Nullification, Adams, J. Q.	16	252
Numatianus, Claudius Rutilius	3	439
Nun's Priest's Tale, The, Chaucer	4	578
Nut-Brown Maid, The, Medieval Literature	4	54
Nymphidia, the Court of Faery, Drayton	11	134
Nymph's Reply to the Shepherd, The, Raleigh	11	40

O

	VOL.	PAGE
O Captain! My Captain, Whitman	17	425
Oak and the Reed, The, La Fontaine	6	128
Oberon, Wieland	9	103
Oblomov, Goncharov	10	385
O'Brien, Fitz-James	17	478
Obscure Night of the Soul, The, San Juan de la Cruz	8	77
Octopus, The, Norris	18	483
Odd Number, The, de Maupassant	7	336
Ode, Chénier	6	404
Ode, Emerson	17	65
Ode, Keats	13	443
Ode, An, Prior	12	38
Ode, First Pythian, Pindar	2	141
Ode: The Dying Christian to His Soul, Pope	12	162
Odelette I, de Régnier	7	524
Odes, Olympian, Pindar	2	134, 137, 139
Odi Barbare, Carducci	5	440
Odyssey, Homer	2	42
Œdipus the King, Sophocles	2	187, 189
Oehlenschläger, Adam Gottlob	10	60
Of Old Sat Freedom on the Heights, Tennyson	14	282
Of Such Is the Kingdom of Heaven, Swinburne	15	126
Oft, in the Stilly Night, Moore	13	292
Oh! Breathe Not His Name, Moore	13	293
Oh, May I Join the Choir Invisible, Eliot	14	663

	VOL.	PAGE
"Oh, Time and Change," Henley	15	533
Oh, to Be in England, see Home Thoughts from Abroad		
Old Age. See also Death		
Aurelia as a Grandmother, Curtis	17	470
Bill and Joe, Holmes	17	203
Daniel Gray, Holland	17	431
Last Eve of Summer, The, Whittier	17	187
Last Leaf, The, Holmes	17	194
My Grandmother, To, Locker-Lampson	14	488
Newcomes, The, Thackeray	14	98
Old Age, Peele	11	203
Old Age, Dialogue on, Cicero	3	81 83
Rabbi Ben Ezra, Browning	14	384
Rambler, The, Johnson	12	274
Tatler, The, Steele	12	75
Old Age, Peele	11	203
Old Age, Dialogue on, Cicero	3	81 83
Old and Young Women, Nietzsche	9	508
Old Antony's Son, Tavčar	10	594
Old Creole Days, Cable	18	264
Old Familiar Faces, The, Lamb	13	208
Old Gentleman, The, Hunt	13	302
Old House Unroofed by an Autumn Gale, An, Tu Fu	1	513
Old Ironsides, Holmes	17	193
Old Judge, The, Haliburton	8	510
Old Lady, The, Hunt	13	300
Old Man of the Mountain, Concerning the, Marco Polo	4	519
Old Norse Literature	4	273
Old People and the Things That Pass, Couperus	8	411
Old Testament and the Jewish Apocrypha, The	1	97
Old Vicarage, Grantchester, The, Brooke	15	612
Old Wives' Tale, The, Bennett	15	438
Oliphant, Carolina, see Nairne		
Olympias, Letters to, Chrysostom	2	554
Omar Khayyam, see Khayyam, Omar		
On First Looking into Chapman's Homer, Keats	13	432
On Mr. R——, Lessing	9	78
On the Tower, Droste-Hülshoff	9	415
On This Day I Complete My Thirty-Sixth Year, Byron	13	354
One Book More, Laforgue	7	293
One-Hoss Shay, The, see Deacon's Masterpiece, The		
One Little Hour ere Day, Mörike	9	418
One Word More, Browning	14	374
Onis, F. de, on		
Echegaray	8	174
Menendez	8	225
Opera and Drama, Wagner	9	373
Opportunity, Sill	18	183
Oraculo Manual, Gracian	8	149
Oration against Ctesiphon, Æschines	2	365
Orations		
Address of the President of the United States, April 2, 1917, Wilson	18	378
Admission of Michigan, Speech on the, Calhoun	16	300
America, The Mission of, Adams, J. Q.	16	250
American Revolution, The, Everett	16	438
Archias, Oration for the Poet, Cicero	3	76
Bunker Hill Monument, Oration on Laying the Corner-Stone of the, Webster	16	312
Catiline's Conspiracy, History of, Sallust	3	146
Cooper Institute, Speech at the, Lincoln	17	586
Decoration Day Oration, Ingersoll	17	621
Discourse Delivered before the Congregational Ministers of Massachusetts, Channing	16	283
Farewell Address, Washington	16	124
Federal Convention, Speech in the, in Favor of Opening Its Sessions with Prayer, Franklin	16	90
Funeral Oration on Henrietta of France, Bossuet	6	218
Gettysburg Address, The, Lincoln	17	593
Greek Struggle for Independence, On the, Clay	16	273
Hayne, Reply to, Webster	16	318 319

	VOL.	PAGE
Inaugural Address, The First, Lincoln	17	589
Inaugural Address, The Second, Lincoln	17	593
Jewish Wars, Josephus	1	133
Julius Cæsar, Shakespeare	11	287
Justification of His Patriotic Policy, Demosthenes	2	382
License of Speech, Invective against, Demosthenes	2	381
Missouri Compromise, Urging the Repeal of the, Calhoun	16	303
New England, Discourse in Commemoration of the First Settlement of, Webster	16	321
Nullification, Adams, J. Q.	16	252
Oration against Ctesiphon, Æschines	2	365
Pericles' Memorial Oration over the Athenian Dead, Thucydides	2	265
Phi Beta Kappa Oration, Sumner	16	491
Philippic, The Third, Demosthenes	2	373
Pilgrim Fathers, The Emigration of the, Everett	16	435
Public Spirit in Politics, Clay	16	272
Retirement to Private Life, Speech on, Clay	16	277
Right of Petition, Remarks on the, Calhoun	16	296
South American Independence as Related to the United States, Clay	16	273
Speech in the National Assembly, Mirabeau	6	388
True Grandeur of Nations, The, Sumner	16	489
Valedictory to the Senate, The, Clay	16	274
Virginia Convention, Speech in the, Henry	16	137
Virginia Legislature, Speech in the, Henry	16	139
War against Jugurtha, History of the, Sallust	3	151
Orations and Addresses, Curtis	17	474
Oratory		
Demosthenes	2	368
Institutes, Quintilian	3	300
		303, 304
Oratory, A Dialogue on, Tacitus	3	349
Oratory, Dialogue on, Cicero	3	84
Oratory, A Dialogue on, Tacitus	3	349
Oratory, Dialogue on, Cicero	3	84
Orbeck, Anders, on		
Bojer	10	286
Danish Literature	10	13
Hamsun	10	269
Norwegian Literature	10	200
Swedish Literature	10	133
Orbis Pictus, Komenský	10	557
Ordeal of Richard Feverel, The, Meredith	15	33
		40
Order, St. Francis of Assisi	5	17
Orient		
Howadji in Syria, Curtis	17	469
Impressions and Memories, Hearn	18	325
India, D'Annunzio	5	500
Kwannon, The Temple of, Hearn	18	326
Lord Jim, Conrad	15	357
Mandalay, Kipling	15	313
Orient, My First Day in the, Hearn	18	321
Samurai, The, Hérédia	7	256
Without Benefit of Clergy, Kipling	15	293
Orient, My First Day in the, Hearn	18	321
Oriental Literature	1	8
Origin of Species, The, Darwin	14	519
		521, 524, 526, 528, 533
Orlando Furioso, Ariosto	5	192
		198, 201
Ornament, The, Vaughan	11	474
Orpheus and Eurydice, Ovid	3	261
Orpheus, The Fable of, Poliziano	5	152
Orthodoxy, Chesterton	15	650
Ossian, Poems of, Macpherson	12	360
		363, 365
Ossian, The Death-Song of, Macpherson	12	366
Ossoli, Marchioness, see Fuller, Sarah Margaret		
Ostrava, Bezruč	10	566
Othello, Shakespeare	11	299
Other Celtic Literatures	4	270
Our Cuban Allies, Dunne	18	466
Our God, Our Help in Ages Past, Watts	12	191
Our Hundred Days in Europe, Holmes	17	222

	VOL.	PAGE
Our Lady's Juggler, France	7	373
Out of the Life of a Good-for-Nothing, Eichendorff	9	298
"Out of the Night That Covers Me," Henley	15	533
Out to Old Aunt Mary's, Riley	18	311
Outre-Mer, Bourget	7	402
Ou-yang Hsiu	1	515
Ovid (Publius Ovidius Naso)	3	242
Ozymandias, Shelley	13	387

P

	VOL.	PAGE
Pablos de Segovia, Quevedo	8	63
Pace, E. A., on St. Thomas Aquinas	5	25
"Padre del Ciel, Dopo i Perduti Giorni," Petrarch	5	102
Page, C. H., on		
France	7	358
Rostand	7	488
Paine, Thomas	16	162
Pakuda, Bakhya ibn, see Bakhya ibn Pakuda		
Palace, The, Alcæus	2	112
Palace Garden, The, Greek Anthology	2	577
Palamedes, Vondel	8	336
Palmer, G. H., on Empedocles	2	296
Palm-Tree, The, Vaughan	11	477
Palms and Myrtles, Eleazar ha-Kalir	1	164
Pamela, Richardson	12	206
Pamphlets, Voltaire	6	325
Pan, Hymn of, Shelley	13	407
Pan in Wall Street, Stedman	17	507
Pan of the Sea-Cliff, Archias	2	574
Pancatantra, Indian Literature	1	446
Panegyric to My Lord Protector, A, Waller	11	486
Panegyric to the Summer, Ab Gwilym	4	266
Paradise, Dante	5	79
Paradise Lost, Milton	11	450
		452, 454, 455, 456, 458
Pardo-Bazan, Emilia	8	208
Pardoner's Story, The, Heywood	11	184
Pardoner's Tale, The, Chaucer	4	571
Parental Ode to My Son, A, Hood	13	465
Parish Workhouse and Apothecary, The, Crabbe	12	627
Parker, E. P., on Bunyan	11	589
Parker, Theodore	17	233
Parkman, Francis	17	366
Parmenides	2	293
Parnassus Within, Bruno	5	273
Parzival, Wolfram von Eschenbach	4	444
Pascal, Blaise	6	196
Pascoli, Giovanni	5	477
"Passato è 'l Tempo Omai, Lasso! Che Tanto," Petrarch	5	101
Passing of Arthur, The, Malory	4	96
Passing Saint, To the, Field	18	510
Passion in the Desert, A, Balzac	6	578
Passionate Shepherd to His Love, The, Marlowe	11	217
Passions, The, Collins	12	326
Passions, Of the, Joubert	6	395
Past and Present, Carlyle	13	582
Pastel (to Julius Zeyer), Vrchlický	10	569
Pastels in Prose, Mallarmé	7	516
Pastoral. See also Literature		
Arcadia, The Arrival in, Sidney	11	48
Eclogue, The First, Vergil	3	176
Faithful Shepherdess, The, Fletcher	11	380
Mourning Garment, The, Greene	11	210
Orpheus, The Fable of, Poliziano	5	152
Passionate Shepherd to His Love, The, Marlowe	11	217
Robin and Marion, Medieval Drama	4	182
Shepherd's Song, Heywood	11	367
Theocritus	2	391
Pastoral Ballad, Shenstone	12	320
Pater, Walter	15	207
Patience, Ibrahim ibn Kunaif of Nabhan	1	236
Patient Grissil, Dekker	11	325
		327
Patmore, Coventry	14	477
Patriot, The, Fogazzaro	5	454
Patriotism. See also Government		
Address to the American People, D'Annunzio	5	505
Addresses to the German Nation, Fichte	9	211
Æneid, Vergil	3	186
American Flag, The, Drake	16	448
American Revolution, The, Everett	16	438
Armenia, A Prose Elegy on, Moses of Kharni	1	393
Barbara Frietchie, Whittier	17	164

	VOL.	PAGE
Centennial Hymn, Whittier	17	176
Chastisements, Hugo	6	500
		501
Crisis, The, Paine	16	165
Concord Hymn, Emerson	17	64
Declaration of Independence, The, Jefferson	16	180
Decoration Day Oration, Ingersoll	17	621
Discourse upon Universal History, Bossuet	6	220
Fishers, The, Ewald	10	55
Hayne, Reply to, Webster	16	318
		319
It Is Not to Be Thought of, Wordsworth	13	50
"Italia Mia, Benchè 'l Parlar Sia Indarno," Petrarch	5	92
King Christian, Ewald	10	52
Man without a Country, The, Hale	17	359
Marco Bozzaris, Halleck	16	413
Midas, Lyly	11	196
New England, Discourse in Commemoration of the First Settlement of, Webster	16	321
Ode, Emerson	17	65
Old Ironsides, Holmes	17	193
Pericles' Memorial Oration over the Athenian Dead, Thucydides	2	265
Pilgrim Fathers, The Emigration of the, Everett	16	435
Pleasures of Hope, The, Campbell	13	261
Retirement to Private Life, Speech on, Clay	16	277
Seer, The, Whittier	17	182
Sir John Norris and Sir Francis Drake, A Farewell to, Peele	11	205
Song of the Sea, Maginn	13	490
"Spirto Gentil che Quelle Membra Reggi," Petrarch	5	95
Those Who Missay of France, Ballad against, Villon	6	35
Virginia Convention, Speech in the, Henry	16	137
What Is the Serbian Native Land? Zeiler	10	570
Ye Mariners of England, Campbell	13	263
Patterson, F. A., on		
Goliardic Poetry	4	132
Latin Hymns	4	99

	VOL.	PAGE
Paul at Rome, New Testament	2	450
Paul before Agrippa, New Testament	2	448
Paul Revere's Ride, Longfellow	17	138
Pausanias	2	505
Payne, W. M., on		
Björnson	10	230
Brandes	10	122
Ewald	10	48
Holberg	10	18
Morris	15	129
Oehlenschläger	10	60
Rossetti, C. G.	14	470
Rossetti, D. G.	14	455
Schopenhauer	9	281
Swinburne	15	105
Peace, The, Aristophanes	2	228
		229
Peacock, Thomas Love	13	474
Pearl, The, Middle English Poetry	4	537
		538
Peasants, The, Reymont	10	545
Peck, H. T., on		
Æsop	2	58
Alciphron	2	514
Peel, Sir Robert, Bagehot	14	605
Peele, George	11	202
Peer Gynt, Ibsen	10	224
Pelican, The, Bestiaries	4	512
Pellico, Silvio	5	377
Pembroke, On the Countess Dowager of, Browne	11	142
Pencillings by the Way, Willis	17	104
Penguin Island, France	7	380
Penitential Prayer, Moses ibn Ezra	1	169
Penrod, Tarkington	18	494
Pépa, To, Musset	6	479
Pepita Jimenez, Valera	8	166
		167, 169, 170, 171
Pepys, Samuel	11	572
Père Antoine's Date-Palm, Aldrich	18	71
Pereda, José Maria de	8	186
Peregrine Pickle, Smollett	12	243
Peretz, Judah Leib	8	630
Pericles, Plutarch	2	468
Pericles' Memorial Oration over the Athenian Dead, Thucydides	2	265
Perkin Warbeck, Ford	11	405
Perkins, Letter to Mr., Johnson	12	269
Perlesvaus, Legends of Arthur and the Round Table	4	83

	VOL.	PAGE
Perpetuation of our Political Institutions, The, Lincoln	17	585
Perrin, Bernadotte, on Pausanias	2	505
Persian Literature, see Iranian Literature		
Persius (Aulus Persius Flaccus)	3	292
Personal Memoirs, Grant	17	601
		605
Personality, Tagore	1	490
Pervigilium Veneris, Roman Poetry	3	453
Peskett, A. G., on Pepys	11	572
Petition to Time, A, Procter	13	479
Petöfi, Alexander	8	595
Petrarch	5	84
Petrarch's Laura, Foscolo	5	333
Petronius Arbiter	3	325
Phædo, Plato	2	317
Phædrus, Plato	2	322
Pharisee and the Publican, The, New Testament	2	439
Phèdre, Racine	6	236
		240
Pheidippides, Browning	14	394
Phi Beta Kappa Oration, Sumner	16	491
Phidyle, To, Horace	3	202
Philaster, or Love Lies A-Bleeding, Beaumont and Fletcher	11	383
Philemon, Menander, etc.	2	345
Philip II, History of, Prescott	16	472
		476
Philippic, Ninth, Cicero	3	80
Philippic, Third, Demosthenes	2	373
Phillips, Wendell	16	493
Philomela, Greene	11	212
Philosophers, Lives and Sayings of the, Diogenes Laërtius	2	535
Philosophical Dictionary, Voltaire	6	323
Philosophy. See also Religion; Ethics; Metaphysics		
Abbé le Monnier, Letter to the, Diderot	6	366
Aristotle	2	335
Circles, Emerson	17	46
Conduct of Life, The, Croce	5	527
Convito, The, Dante	5	57
Creative Evolution, Bergson	7	467
Discourse on Method, Descartes	6	99
		100
Dream of Scipio, The, Cicero	3	99
Encyclopedia, The, Diderot	6	363
Flower, Fruit, and Thorn Pieces, Richter	9	218
Fragments, Heraclitus	2	290
Free Will, On, Sa'adia Ga'on	1	175
Hojoki, Japanese Literature	1	551
Inconsistency, Seneca	3	268
Independence in Action, Seneca	3	267
Leisure, On, Seneca	3	269
Lisbon Earthquake, Letter on, Voltaire	6	331
Lun Yü, Confucius	1	505
Meditations, Aurelius	3	427
Mencius	1	506
Musobioye Kosho Monogatari, Kiokutei Bakin	1	567
Mysterious Nature, Hsiao Yen	1	511
Philosophy, On, Aristotle	2	342
Philosophy, Praises of the Rival School in, Seneca	3	268
Philosophy, The Consolations of, Boëthius	3	462
		467
Plato	2	303
Savoyard Vicar's Creed, The, Rousseau	6	344
Thought and Existence, Parmenides	2	294
Tsure-zure gusa, Japanese Literature	1	552
Vanity of Human Wishes, The, Johnson	12	264
Philosophy of History, The, Hegel	9	268
		269, 271, 272
Philosophy of the History of Man, Herder	9	95
Philosophy, On, Aristotle	2	342
Philosophy, Praises of the Rival School in, Seneca	3	268
Philosophy, The Consolations of, Boëthius	3	462
		466, 467
Phoenix, The, Bestiaries	4	513
Physical Basis of Life, On the, Huxley	14	567
Physician in Spite of Himself, The, Molière	6	147
Physics and Metaphysics, Russell	15	687
Physics and Politics, Bagehot	14	607
Pibroch of Donuil Dhu (Highland Song), Scott	13	148

	VOL.	PAGE
Picaresque Novel, The	8	51
Pickthall, Marjorie L. C.	8	500
Picture of Little T. C., The, Marvell	11	470
Pierre, Melville	17	458
Piers Plowman, The Vision of William Concerning, Middle English Poetry	4	531
Piers the Plowman's Pardon, Piers Plowman	4	536
Pigeon, The, Galsworthy	15	455
Pilgrim at Rome, The, Medieval Irish Literature	4	241
Pilgrim before St. Just, The, Platen-Hallermünde	9	413
Pilgrim Fathers, The Emigration of the, Everett	16	435
Pilgrimage, The, Herbert	11	158
Pilgrimage to El Medinah and Meccah, A, Burton	14	667
		670
Pilgrim's Progress, The, Bunyan	11	593
		594, 597, 600
Pillar of the Cloud, The, see Lead, Kindly Light		
Pindar	2	131
Pine and Palm, Heine	9	318
Pine-Tree, The, Vazov	10	576
Pinnace, The, Catullus	3	159
Piper and the Child, The, Blake	12	636
Pippa Passes, Browning	14	331
Pirandello, Luigi	5	547
Pitkin, W. B., on Haeckel	9	473
Plague in London, History of the, Defoe	12	23
Plain Language from Truthful James, Harte	18	169
Platen-Hallermünde, August Graf von	9	413
Plato	2	303
Plato (Greek Anthology)	2	572
Plautus, Titus Maccius	3	39
Playboy of the Western World, The, Synge	8	549
Pleasures of Athens, The, Alciphron	2	516
Pleasures of Hope, The, Campbell	13	261
Pliny the Elder (Caius Plinius Secundus)	3	283
Pliny the Younger (Caius Plinius Cæcilius Secundus)	3	375
Plutarch	2	465
Plutarch on Himself, Plutarch	2	490
Poe, Edgar Allan	17	536
Poèmes Antiques, Leconte de Lisle	7	253
Poèmes Barbares, Leconte de Lisle	7	252
		254
Poèmes Militaires, Déroulède	7	247
		248, 249
Poèmes Saturniens, Verlaine	7	278
Poesie, Carducci	5	431
		432, 433, 434
Poet at the Breakfast-Table, The, Holmes	17	207
Poet, To the, Pushkin	10	336
Poetic Edda, The, Old Norse Literature	4	289
Poetics, Aristotle	2	340
Poetry. See also Literature; Epic; Lyric; etc.		
Acharnians, The, Aristophanes	2	222
American Literature: American Poetry since 1900	18	515
Art of Poetry, The, Boileau-Despréaux	6	224
		226
British Poetry in the Twentieth Century	15	512
Distich, The, Schiller	9	191
Dramatic Poesy, An Essay of, Dryden	11	618
Epic Hexameter, The, Schiller	9	191
Heroic Enthusiasts, The, Bruno	5	268
Laocoön, Lessing	9	88
		89
Mermaid Tavern, Lines on the, Keats	13	446
Old Testament and the Jewish Apocrypha, The	1	97
On First Looking into Chapman's Homer, Keats	13	432
Poet, To the, Pushkin	10	336
Poetics, Aristotle	2	340
Poetry, Of, Joubert	6	396
Poetry of the Present Day, Wilson	13	357
Poets of America, Stedman	17	509
Shakespeare, William	11	229
Tyrtæus, Archilochus, etc.	2	76
Vowels, Rimbaud	7	292
Poetry, Of, Joubert	6	396
Poetry of the Present Day, Wilson	13	357
Poet's Choice, The, Anacreon	2	125
Poet's Epitaph, A, Greek Anthology	2	573

	VOL.	PAGE
Poet's Fame, The, Ovid	3	262
Poet's Song to His Wife, The, Procter	13	480
Poets of America, Stedman	17	509
Polish Literature	10	490
Political Economy, Mill	13	635
Political Pewterer, The, Holberg	10	29
Politics, see Government		
Politics, Aristotle	2	343
Poliziano	5	147
Polybius	2	415
Polyeucte, Corneille	6	113
Poor Fisherman, The, Alcæus	2	114
Poor Jack, Dibdin	12	569
Poor People, Dostoyevsky	10	431
Poor Richard's Almanac, Franklin	16	86, 87
Pope, Alexander	12	128
Popular Playwrights, Heywood	11	367
Porter, Letter to Mrs. Lucy, in Lichfield, Johnson	12	268
Porter, William Sydney (O. Henry)	18	423
Portraits of Men, Sainte-Beuve	6	629
Portuguese Literature	8	264
Positive Philosophy, Comte	6	660, 661
Positive Polity, Comte	6	662, 663
Post Office, The, Tagore	1	488
Potts, William, on John and Charles Wesley	12	533
Poverty, Alcæus	2	115
Poverty, Hayne	17	616
Poverty Parts Good Company, Baillie	12	577
Praed, Winthrop Mackworth	13	496
Prairie, The, Cooper	16	395, 407
Praise of Folly, The, Erasmus	8	326
Prayer for Healing, A, Avesta	1	320
Prayer for Strength, A, Michelangelo	5	210
Prayers		
Fire, To the, Avesta	1	317
Invocation to Rain, Avesta	1	320
Ishtar, Prayer to, Babylonian Literature	1	93
Marduk, Prayer to, Babylonian Literature	1	92
Prayer for Healing, A, Avesta	1	320
Private Prayer, A, Johnson	12	271
Suppliants, The, Æschylus	2	155
Trinity, The, Augustine	3	445
Universal Prayer, The, Pope	12	161
Pre-Christian Poems, Fragments of, Armenian Literature	1	389
Preliminary Discourse, D'Alembert	6	368
Prescience, Aldrich	18	71
Prescott, William Hickling	16	450
Preston, H. W., on		
Horace	3	191
Mistral	7	205
Petronius	3	325
Quintilian	3	295
Roman Poets of the Later Empire	3	447
Pretenders, The, Ibsen	10	215
Priapus of the Shore, To, Greek Anthology	2	577
Pride and Prejudice, Austen	13	178, 182, 184
Priest and Prophet, Akhad ha-'Am	1	215
Prigioni, Le Mie, Pellico	5	379
Primroses Filled with Morning Dew, To, Herrick	11	166
Prince, The, Machiavelli	5	179, 180
Prince and the Pauper, The, Clemens	18	60
Prince Mikhailo Repnin, Tolstoy	10	324
Prince of Homburg, The, Kleist	9	250
Princess, The, Björnson	10	242
Princess, The, Tennyson	14	293, 295
Princesses of Ferrara, To the, Tasso	5	258
Principia, Newton	11	642
Principia Rerum Naturalium, Swedenborg	10	142, 144
Prior, Matthew	12	34
Prisoner of Chillon, The, Byron	13	326
Private Prayer, A, Johnson	12	271
Problem, The, Emerson	17	56
Problems of Modern Democracy, Godkin	17	494
Procter, Bryan Waller	13	477
Procter, J. R., on Clay	16	265
Prodigal Father, A, Dumas, Junior	7	173
Prodigal Son, The, New Testament	2	438
Professional Diner-Out, Letter from a, Alciphron	2	517

	VOL.	PAGE
Progress, see Government; Sociology; etc.		
Progress and Poverty, George	18	154 160
Prolegomena, Kant	9	71
Prometheus, Goethe	9	162
Prometheus Bound, Æschylus	2	153
Prometheus Unbound, Shelley	13	391
Proper Subjects of Study, On the, Bakhya ibn Pakuda	1	176
Propertius, Sextus	3	232
Property, Verga	5	444
Prophet, The, Nekrasov	10	323
Prose, Of, van Deyssel	8	410
Prospect of Planting Arts and Learning in America, On the, Berkeley	12	45
Prospice, Browning	14	383
Protagoras, Plato	2	313
Protestation, The, Carew	11	170
Prothalamion; or a Spousall Verse, Spenser	11	61
Proust, Marcel	7	559
Provençal Literature	4	397
Provençal Lovers — Aucassin and Nicolette, Stedman	17	505
Prue and I, Curtis	17	470 471, 472
Psalm of Montreal, A, Butler	15	167
Psychology. See also Science		
Anatomy of Melancholy, The, Burton	11	114
Dilemma, A, Andreyev	10	479
Dreams, On, Petronius	3	334
Human Understanding, Essay Concerning, Locke	11	635
Leviathan, Hobbes	11	499
Superstition and Fear, Spinoza	8	367
Value of Personality, The, Schopenhauer	9	292
Public Spirit in Politics, Clay	16	272
Pulci, Luigi	5	155
Pulci's Aspiration, Pulci	5	166
Pulley, The, Herbert	11	159
Puppets, Verlaine	7	279
Pure in Heart, The, Greek Anthology	2	579
Purgatory, Dante	5	72
Purifications, The Poem of, Empedocles	2	302
Purple East, The, Watson	15	559 560, 561
Pushkin, Alexander Sergyeyevich	10	332
Putnam, E. J., on Lucian of Samosata	2	519
Pyeshkov, Aleksyey Maksimovich, see Gorky		

Q

	VOL.	PAGE
Quæstiones Disputatæ, Aquinas	5	30 31
Qualities of the Writer, Of the, Joubert	6	397
Quatrains, Persian Literature	1	301
Quest, The, van Eeden	8	404
Question, The, Gibson	15	606
Quevedo y Villegas, Francisco Gomez de	8	63
"Qui Reposan Quei Caste e Felici Ossa," Petrarch	5	104
Quintilian, Marcus Fabius	3	295
Quintus Dellius, To, Horace	3	201
Qur'an, The	1	268
Qur'an, Selections from the	1	273

R

	VOL.	PAGE
R. U. R., Čapek	10	561
Rabbi Ben Ezra, Browning	14	384
Rabbi Ramas	8	627
Rabelais, François	6	39
Racine, Jean	6	230
Radha and Krishna, Jayadeva	1	481
Raghuvança, Kalidasa	1	463
Raimon de Miravai, Provençal Literature	4	409
Rain, The, Verhaeren	8	446
Raining, Gibson	15	606
Rainy Day, The, Longfellow	17	130
Raisen, Abraham	8	636
Raising of Lazarus, The, New Testament	2	442
Raku-Kun, Kaibara Yekken	1	563
Raleigh, Sir Walter	11	38
Ramayana, Indian Literature	1	454
Rambler, The, Johnson	12	271 274
Ramsay, Allan	12	197
Ramsey, M. M., on Latin-American Literature before 1888	8	293
Ranke, Leopold von	9	432
Rape of Lucrece, The, Heywood	11	365
Rape of Proserpine, The, Claudianus	3	458
Rape of the Lock, The, Pope	12	147
Raphael Sanzio, Vasari	5	261
Raven, The, Poe	17	569
Reade, Charles	14	184

	VOL.	PAGE
Reading, see Literature		
Reading, The Pleasures of, Balfour	15	245
Realism. See also Literature; Fiction		
Flaubert, Gustave	7	53
Growth of Realism, The, French Literature	7	8
Maupassant, Guy de	7	326
Realistic Literature, de Vogüé	7	417
Zola, Émile	7	295
Realistic Literature, de Vogüé	7	417
Reason and Feeling, Drummond	11	141
Recessional, Kipling	15	314
Red Hanrahan's Song about Ireland, Yeats	8	539
Red Robe, The, Brieux	7	485
Redburn, Melville	17	443
Reef, The, Wharton	18	450
Refinement in the Arts, On, Hume	12	301
Reflections on Revolution, Thucydides	2	270
Reflections on Society, La Rochefoucauld	6	121
Refusal of Aid Between Nations, On, Rossetti	14	469
Registre of Hystories, A, Ælianus Claudius	3	416
417, 418,	419,	420
Régnier, Henry de	7	517
Regrets Too Late, Rudagi	1	296
Reich, Emil, on Jókai	8	601
Reinaert the Fox, Middle Dutch Literature	4	470
Relation of the First Voyage, A, Las Casas	8	41
Religio Medici, Browne	11	524
Religion. See also Philosophy; Ethics; Hymns; Sermons; etc.		
Alfred's Preface to His Version of Pope Gregory's 'Pastoral Care,' Alfred the Great	4	340
Ancelmus the Emperour, Gesta Romanorum	4	506
Anthropomorphism, On, Sa'adia Ga'on	1	173
Apologia pro Vita Sua, Newman	14	21
Approach, The, Blok	10	328
Aten, Hymn to the, Akhenaten	1	52
Avesta, The	1	307
Beholding of God in His Footsteps in This Sensible World, On the, St. Bonaventura	5	22
Bhagavad Gita, Indian Literature	1	452
Canticle of the Sun, The, St. Francis of Assisi	5	18
Cantigas, Alfonso the Wise	8	23
Christ, Excellency of, Edwards	16	64
Christian Morals, Browne	11	535
Christian Poetry, Armenian Literature	1	391
City of God, The, Augustine	3	444
Collar, The, Herbert	11	156
Collected Essays, Huxley	14	564
Complete Angler, The, Walton	11	510
Confessions, Augustine	3	442
		443
Constance, Letter from, Hus	10	553
Correspondence, Erasmus	8	329
Dadu Panthis, Bible of the, Indian Literature	1	459
Defendant, The, Chesterton	15	653
Diet of Worms, Reply at the, Luther	9	18
Divine Providence, Swedenborg	10	149
Dream of Scipio, The, Cicero	3	99
Dürer Painting the Saviour's Head, Machar	10	568
Easter Day, Clough	14	449
Ecclesiastical History, Bede	4	341
		343
Emigrants in Bermudas, The, Marvell	11	468
Eternal Goodness, The, Whittier	17	168
Existence of a Creator, On the, Sa'adia Ga'on	1	172
Faith and the Future, Mazzini	5	404
Federal Convention, Speech in the, in Favor of Opening Its Session with Prayer, Franklin	16	90
Free Will, On, Sa'adia Ga'on	1	175
Garden of Perfume, The, Sa'di	1	358
Guide of the Perplexed, Maimonides	1	192
Heart Knoweth Its Own Bitterness, The, Rossetti, C. G.	14	476
Héloise, Answer to, Abélard	4	500

	VOL.	PAGE
Hind and the Panther, The, Dryden	11	624
Home, Sill	18	183
Homily VIII, Chrysostom	2	557
Hound of Heaven, The, Thompson	15	543
How an Anchoress Was Tempted by the Devil, Gesta Romanorum	4	509
Hydriotaphia, or Urn-Burial, Browne	11	538
Imitation of Christ, The, Middle Dutch Literature	4	474
Institutes, Prefatory Address to the, Calvin	6	61
Intimations of Immortality from Recollections of Early Childhood, Wordsworth	13	59
Kitab al-Khazari, Judah ha-Levi	1	184
Leviathan, Hobbes	11	501
Liberty of Prophesying, The, Taylor	11	553
Life, Santa Teresa	8	71
Life and Letters, Darwin	14	537
Lion, The, Bestiaries	4	512
Longing for Jerusalem, Judah ha-Levi	1	183
Love, Herbert	11	157
Massacre in Piedmont, On the Late, Milton	11	449
Matters Pertaining to Religion, A Discourse of, Parker	17	237
Messiah, The, Klopstock	9	58
Narrative of His Religious History, Edwards	16	60
Nativity, The Hymn on the, Milton	11	432
Nature of True Virtue, The, Edwards	16	66
New Jerusalem, Heavenly Doctrine of the, Swedenborg	10	148
New Testament, The	2	422
Nombres de Cristo, De los, Fray Luis de Leon	8	80
Non Sine Dolore, Gilder	18	508
Obscure Night of the Soul, The, San Juan de la Cruz	8	77
Old Testament and the Jewish Apocrypha, The	1	97
Olympias, Letters to, Chrysostom	2	554
Order, St. Francis of Assisi	5	17
Palm-Tree, The, Vaughan	11	477

	VOL.	PAGE
Paradise, Dante	5	79
Phædrus, Plato	2	322
Philosophy of History, Hegel	9	269
		271
Philosophy, The Consolations of, Boëthius	3	466
Physical Basis of Life, On the, Huxley	14	567
Pilgrim's Progress, The, Bunyan	11	593
		594, 597, 600
Praise of Folly, The, Erasmus	8	326
Principia, Newton	11	642
Proper Subjects of Study, On the, Bakhya ibn Pakuda	1	176
Pulley, The, Herbert	11	159
Purple East, The, Watson	15	561
Quæstiones Disputatæ, Aquinas	5	30
		31
Qur'an, Selections from the	1	273
Religio Medici, Browne	11	524
Repentance, On, Bakhya ibn Pakuda	1	177
Revival, The, Vaughan	11	476
Sacred Scriptures, The Doctrine of the, Swedenborg	10	146
Saul, Browning	14	345
Savoyard Vicar's Creed, The, Rousseau	6	344
Science, The Claims of, Tyndall	14	542
Simchas Torah, Gordon	1	202
Sodoma's 'Christ Scourged,' Woodberry	18	369
Song of the "Marner," Minnesingers	4	464
Song of the Reed, or Divine Affections, The, Jalal ad-Din Rumi	1	367
Soul, On the, Sa'adia Ga'on	1	174
Soul, The, Swedenborg	10	144
Spirit of Laws, The, Montesquieu	6	302
Spiritual Freedom, Discourse on, Channing	16	285
Spiritual Letters, Fénelon	6	252
Summa Theologica, Aquinas	5	29
Table-Talk, Selden	11	118
That Real Wealth Is from Within, Chrysostom	2	552
Theodosius the Emperoure, Gesta Romanorum	4	504
Thirteen Articles of Faith, The, Maimonides	1	191

	VOL.	PAGE
Thoughts, Pascal	6	198
Trees and the Master, A Ballad of, Lanier	18	202
True Christian Religion, Swedenborg	10	154
Universal Love, Mo Ti	1	507
Variation of Animals and Plants under Domestication, The, Darwin	14	534
Vesper Hymn, The, Abélard	4	501
Waterfowl, To a, Bryant	16	428
Remember, Rossetti, C. G.	14	471
Remembrance, For, Scott, D. C.	8	494
Reminiscences of Childhood, Bentham	12	566
Remorse, Platen-Hallermünde	9	414
Remy, A. F. J., on Medieval German Literature	4	415
Renaissance, The, Italian Literature	5	128
Renaissance, The, Michelet	6	654
Renaissance in Italy, The, Symonds	15	218
Renan, Ernest	7	107
Renée Mauperin, Goncourts	7	94
Renouncement, Meynell	15	550
Repentance, On, Bakhya ibn Pakuda	1	177
Republic, The, Plato	2	328
Requiem, Stevenson	15	275
Resignation, Greek Anthology	2	578
Resolution and Independence, Wordsworth	13	42
Responses, Březina	10	565
Rest at Noon, Meleager	2	575
Retirement, Vaughan	11	477
Retirement to Private Life, Speech on, Clay	16	277
Retreat, The, Vaughan	11	473
Return of the Native, The, Hardy	15	80
		83
Revenge, The, Tennyson	14	319
Revival, The, Vaughan	11	476
Revival of Learning, The, French Literature	6	6
Revolt from Victorianism, The	15	1
Revolt of "Mother," The, Freeman	18	435
Reymont, Wladyslaw Stanislaw	10	544
Reynard the Fox, Masefield	15	598
Rhodora, The, Emerson	17	53
Rhys, Ernest, on Hunt	13	295
Rich Man and Lazarus, The, New Testament	2	439
Richard Cœur de Lion, Provençal Literature	4	403
Richardson, Samuel	12	204
Richepin, Jean	7	292
Richter, Jean Paul	9	215
Riders to the Sea, Synge	8	545
Right of Petition, The, Adams, J. Q.	16	251
Right of Petition, Remarks on the, Calhoun	16	296
Rig-Veda, Hymns from the, Indian Literature	1	428
Riley, James Whitcomb	18	303
Rimbaud, Arthur	7	291
Rise of the Dutch Republic, The, Motley	17	273
Rivals, The, Sheridan	12	477
		480, 483
Roast Pig, A Dissertation upon, see Dissertation upon Roast Pig, A		
Robert of Lincoln, Bryant	16	429
Roberts, Charles G. D.	8	490
		511
Roberts, C. G. D., on Parkman	17	366
Robin and Marion, Medieval Drama	4	182
Robin Hood, Keats	13	444
Robin Hood and Guy of Gisborne. Medieval Literature	4	17
Robinson Crusoe, Defoe	12	19
Rochefoucauld, La, François, see La Rochefoucauld		
Rocking Hymn, A, Wither	11	143
Rod, Edouard, on Rousseau	6	339
Roderick Random, Smollett	12	239
Roger Williams: The Prophet of Religious Freedom, Eggleston	18	84
Rokeby, Scott	13	150
Roland, Song of, Medieval French Literature	4	355
Rolland, Romain	7	533
Romance of the Mummy, The, Gautier	6	675
Romance of the Rose, Jean de Meung	4	387
Romances, Heine	9	321
Romanticism. See also Literature		
Charles IV, The Court of, Galdos	8	202
Dramatic Art and Literature, Lectures on, Schlegel, A. W. von	9	234
English Literature: The Romantic Revival	13	1

	VOL.	PAGE
French Literature: The Rise of Romanticism	6	433
Oehlenschläger, Adam Gottlob	10	60
Romantic School in Germany, The	9	230
Rome		
Childe Harold's Pilgrimage, Byron	13	318
		319
Itinerarium, Numatianus	3	459
Poesie, Carducci	5	431
Rome, History of, Livy	3	214
		218, 219
Rome, The Final Ruin of, Gibbon	12	450
Rome, History of, Livy	3	214
		218, 219
Rome, History of, Mommsen	9	433
Rome, The Final Ruin of, Gibbon	12	450
Romeo and Juliet, Shakepeare	11	286
Rondeau, Hunt	13	299
Ronsard, Pierre	6	64
Ronsard to His Mistress, Ronsard	6	69
Roosbroeck, G. L. van, on Gezelle	8	431
Roosevelt, Theodore	18	385
Rosalind's Madrigal, Lodge	11	129
Rose, The, Ronsard	6	70
Rose and the Ring, The, Locker-Lampson	14	490
Rose and Thorn, Greek Anthology	2	581
Rose Aylmer, Landor	13	258
"Rose-Dark the Solemn Sunset," Gilder	18	505
Rose-Garden, The, Sa'di	1	364
		365, 366
Roses, Florus	3	452
Roses, Ronsard	6	73
Roses of Saadi, The, Desbordes-Valmore	6	529
Rose-Wreath, The, Klopstock	9	58
Rosenfeld, Morris	8	639
Rossetti, Christina Georgina	14	470
Rossetti, Dante Gabriel	14	455
Rostand, Edmond	7	488
Roumanian Literature	8	641
Rousseau, Jean-Jacques	6	339
Rousseau, Morley	15	202
Rousseau, Letter to, Voltaire	6	328
Rovers, The, Canning	13	238
Royal Banquet, A, Statius	3	316
Royal George, On the Loss of the, Cowper	12	399
Royce, Josiah, on		
Kant	9	62
Spinoza	8	356
Roz, Firmin, on		
de Maupassant	7	326
Sully-Prudhomme	7	269
Rubaiyat (Selected Quatrains from Fitzgerald's Version)	1	343
Rückert, Friedrich	9	412
Rudagi	1	296
Rugby Chapel, Arnold	14	439
Ruit Hora, Carducci	5	442
Rule, Britannia, Thomson	12	311
Rules and Exercises of Holy Dying, Taylor	11	555
		556, 558, 559
Rumi, Jalal ad-Din, see Jalal ad-Din Rumi		
Runkle, L. G., on Hood	13	462
Rural Deities, The, Tibullus	3	229
Rusk, R. L., on American Literature in the Colonial Period	16	11
Ruskin, John	13	586
Russell, Bertrand	15	684
Russian Poetry	10	314
Russian Literature		
Russian Literature	10	301
Russian Poetry	10	314
The Ukraine	10	484
Russian Scene, Fet	10	326
Russian Soldier, The, Nekrasov	10	322
Rustic in the Amphitheater, The, Calpurnius	3	454
Ruth, Hood	13	466
Ruusbroec, Jan van	4	474

S

	VOL.	PAGE
Sa'adia Ga'on	1	172
Sachs, Hans	9	31
Sacred Scriptures, The Doctrine of the, Swedenborg	10	146
Sa'd	1	237
Sa'di	1	356
Safe Stronghold Our God Is Still, A, Luther	9	21
Sage, Alain René Le, see Le Sage		
Sagesse, Verlaine	7	279
Saïat Nova	1	392
St. Augustine, see Augustine of Hippo, St.		
Saint Patrick, Maginn	13	488
Saint's Tragedy, The, Kingsley	14	208

	VOL.	PAGE
Saint-Simon, Louis de Rouvroy, Duke of	6	280
Sainte-Beuve, Charles Augustin	6	621
Sakanoe, Lady	1	541
Saladin and the Jew Usurer, The Story of, Boccaccio	5	119
Salathiel Pavy, An Epitaph on, Jonson	11	354
Sallust (Gaius Sallustius Crispus)	3	142
Salt of the Earth, The, Swinburne	15	126
Salt Water Ballads, Masefield	15	592
		594, 595
Samurai, The, Hérédia	7	256
San Juan de la Cruz	8	76
San Lorenzo Giustiniani's Mother, Meynell	15	549
Sana'i	1	300
Sand, George	7	30
Sand and Stars, Frug	8	629
Sanderson, Robert, on		
Coppée	7	259
Gautier	6	673
Sandpiper, The, Thaxter	18	79
Sands of Dee, The, Kingsley	14	207
Sang, A, Ramsay	12	202
Sanskrit Literature, see Indian Literature		
Santa Teresa	8	68
Santa Teresa, From the Correspondence of	8	73
Santayana, George, on Cervantes	8	82
Sapphire, Bestiaries	4	517
Sappho	2	103
Sappho, Grillparzer	9	306
		310
Sappho and Phao, Lyly	11	201
Sappho's Letter to Phaon, Ovid	3	249
Sarcey, Francisque, on Dumas, Junior	7	167
Sardou, Victorien	7	190
Sartor Resartus, Carlyle	13	554
Satire. See also Literature		
Abolishing of Christianity, The, Swift	12	53
Absalom and Achitophel, Dryden	11	622
Aphrodite and Selene, Lucian of Samosata	2	523
Birds, Aristophanes	2	230
Candide: or All for the Best, Voltaire	6	311
		312, 319, 320, 321
Cannibalism, Martial	3	341
Cobbler's Last, The, Martial	3	343
Don Quixote, Cervantes	8	88
		99, 104
E Pluribus Unus, Martial	3	343
Erasmus Montanus, Holberg	10	35
Evolution, Martial	3	339
Fine Frenzy, Martial	3	343
Gulliver's Travels, Swift	12	55
		61, 64, 70
John Bull's Other Island, Shaw	15	498
Judgment of Paris, The, Lucian of Samosata	2	524
Learning by Doing, Martial	3	341
Least of Evils, The, Martial	3	340
Lucian of Samosata	2	519
Max Havelaar, Multatuli	8	386
Penguin Island, France	7	380
Psalm of Montreal, A, Butler	15	167
Satires, Juvenal	3	370
		372, 374
Shah Namah, Firdausi	1	334
Ship of Hell, The, Vicente	8	277
Sic Vos Non Vobis, Martial	3	339
Silence Is Golden, Martial	3	340
Similia Similibus, Martial	3	341
So Near and Yet So Far, Martial	3	340
Steam-Guillotine, The, Giusti	5	400
Tartuffe, Molière	6	170
		178, 186, 192
Tertium Quid, Martial	3	341
Thou Reason'st Well, Martial	3	340
Two Things Needful, The, Martial	3	344
Unkindest Cut, The, Martial	3	339
Vale of Tears, Martial	3	339
Vision of Judgment, The, Byron	13	345
Satires, Juvenal	3	370
		372, 374
Satyr and the Traveler, The, Æsop	2	62
Saul, Browning	14	345
Savage Prayer, A, Theognis	2	119
Savonarola, Life and Times of, Villari	5	413
Savoyard Vicar's Creed, The, Rousseau	6	344
Say Not, the Struggle Naught Availeth, Clough	14	453
Sayings of Luther, Luther	9	28

	VOL.	PAGE
Scandinavian Literature		
Danish Literature	10	13
Norwegian Literature	10	200
Old Norse Literature	4	273
		297
Scandinavian Literature	10	1
Swedish Literature	10	133
Scarlet Letter, The, Hawthorne	17	74
		77, 79, 84
Scheffel, Joseph Viktor von	9	425
Schérer, Edmond	7	98
Schiller, Johann Christoph Friedrich	9	178
Schlegel, August Wilhelm von	9	232
Schlegel, Friedrich von	9	232
Schneor, Zalman	1	213
Schnitzler, Arthur	9	559
Scholar Gipsy, The, Arnold	14	432
School for Scandal, The, Sheridan	12	488
		493
Schoolmaster, The, Ascham	11	14
Schoolmistress, The, Shenstone	12	323
Schopenhauer, Arthur	9	281
Schurz, Carl, on Webster	16	305
Science. See also Evolution		
Collected Essays, Huxley	14	558
		564, 565
Discourse on Method, Descartes	6	99
		100
Erewhon, Butler	15	168
Metric System, The, Adams, J. Q.	16	254
Physical Basis of Life, On the, Huxley	14	567
Physics and Metaphysics, Russell	15	687
Positive Philosophy, Comte	6	660
		661
Principia, Newton	11	642
Science, The Claims of, Tyndall	14	542
Siris, Berkeley	12	46
Styles, Letter to Dr., Jefferson	16	190
Theory of the Earth, The, Cuvier	6	427
Visit to Ceylon, A, Haeckel	9	476
		479
Science, The Claims of, Tyndall	14	542
Scott, Austin, on Bancroft	17	11
Scott, Duncan Campbell	8	494
Scott, R. D., on		
Macpherson's "Ossian"	12	352
Medieval Irish Literature	4	192
Scott, Sir Walter	13	129
Scrap of Paper, A, Sardou	7	192
Scribe, Augustin Eugène	6	535
Scribe, The, Medieval Irish Literature	4	241
"Se Lamentar Augelli o Verdi Fronde," Petrarch	5	100
Sea. See also Nature		
Break, Break, Break, Tennyson	14	276
David Copperfield, Dickens	14	155
Dover Beach, Arnold	14	431
Good Hope, The, Heijermans	8	421
Hervé Riel, Browning	14	390
Iceland Fisherman, An, Loti	7	386
Inchcape Rock, The, Southey	13	115
Last Fight of the Revenge, The, Raleigh	11	41
Last of the Vikings, The, Bojer	10	291
Lord Jim, Conrad	15	357
Moby-Dick, Melville	17	452
Old Ironsides, Holmes	17	193
Pinnace, The, Catullus	3	159
Poor Jack, Dibdin	12	569
Robinson Crusoe, Defoe	12	19
Roderick Random, Smollett	12	239
Salt Water Ballads, Masefield	15	592
		594, 595
Sea, The, Procter	13	478
Sea Wolf, The, London	18	472
Seafarer, The, Anglo-Saxon Literature	4	333
Sir Patrick Spens, Medieval Literature	4	33
Summer Sailing, Greek Anthology	2	576
Tom Bowling, Dibdin	12	570
Two Years Before the Mast, Dana	17	295
United Netherlands, History of the, Motley	17	281
		286
United States, History of the, Adams, Henry	18	146
Water-Witch, The, Cooper	16	390
Westward Ho! Kingsley	14	208
Wreck of the Hesperus, The, Longfellow	17	126
Sea, The, Procter	13	478
Sea Child, A, Carman	8	497
Sea Wolf, The, London	18	472
Seafarer, The, Anglo-Saxon Literature	4	333

	VOL.	PAGE
Seami	1	553
Seasons, The, Thomson	12	312
Seaward, Thaxter	18	78
Secret in Words, The, Calderon	8	133
Sedge Songs, Strehlenau	9	416
Seer, The, Whittier	17	182
Sei Shonagon	1	549
Sejanus, Jonson	11	345, 348
Selden, John	11	117
Seldwyla Folk, Keller	9	387
Self-Reliance, Emerson	17	48
Self-Tormentor, The, Terence	3	60
Semitic People in the History of Civilization, The Share of, Renan	7	123
Seneca	3	263
Sennacherib, The Destruction of, Byron	13	325
Sensitive Plant, The, Shelley	13	396
Sentimental Journey, A, Sterne	12	231, 232, 235
"Sento l' Aura Mia Antica e i Dolci Colli," Petrarch	5	102
Separation, Eichendorff	9	296
Separation, Judah ha-Levi	1	183
Separation, Sully-Prudhomme	7	273
Serao, Matilde	5	484
Serenade, Pickthall	8	500
Sermon on the Mount, The, New Testament	2	432
Sermon on the Mount, The First Discourse upon the, Wesley, John	12	540
Sermons. See also Religion		
Faith and Patience of the Saints, Taylor	11	554
Good Steward, The, Wesley, John	12	538
Great Assize, The, Wesley, John	12	542
Homily VIII, Chrysostom	2	557
New Birth, The, Wesley, John	12	537
Sermon on the Mount, The First Discourse upon the, Wesley, John	12	540
Service of God, The, Greek Anthology	2	579
Servus Reginae, Blok	10	328
Sesame and Lilies, Ruskin	13	592
Setna, The Story of, Egyptian Literature	1	37
Seven against Thebes, The, Æschylus	2	157
Seven Lamps of Architecture, The, Ruskin	13	593
Seven Who Were Hanged, The, Andreyev	10	481
Sévigné, Madame Marie de	6	208
Sewall, Frank, on		
Carducci	5	429
Mazzini	5	402
Swedenborg	10	137
Seymour, T. D., on Homer	2	27
Shah Namah, Firdausi	1	324, 330, 333, 334
Shakespeare, William	11	229
Shakespeare, On, Jonson	11	342
Shakespeare, On, Milton	11	448
Shakespeare, the Man, Bagehot	14	601
Shakespeare, To the Memory of, Jonson	11	343, 235
Shamash, Hymns to, Babylonian Literature	1	91
Sharing of the Earth, The, Schiller	9	183
Sharp, Robert, on		
Anglo-Saxon Literature	4	312
Demosthenes	2	368
Sharp, William, on		
Icelandic Sagas	4	297
Maeterlinck	8	463
Shaw, George Bernard	15	475
Shaw, Bernard, and the Theatre Guild	15	480
Shaw's Socialism, Note on	15	489
She Came and Went, Lowell	17	328
She Dwelt among the Untrodden Ways, Wordsworth	13	28
She Stoops to Conquer, Goldsmith	12	520
She Walks in Beauty, Byron	13	325
She Was a Phantom of Delight, Wordsworth	13	51
Shelley, Percy Bysshe	13	380
Shenshin, Afanasy Afanasyevich, see Fet, A.		
Shenstone, William	12	318
Shepherd's Song, Heywood	11	367
Sherburn, George, on American Literature: The New England Group	17	1
Sheridan, Richard Brinsley	12	474
Sherman, S. P., on		
Chesterton	15	642
James, Henry	18	218
Shevchenko, Taras	10	485
Shintō Faith, The, Hearn	18	327
Ship of Hell, The, Vicente	8	277
Ship of State, To the, Horace	3	199

	VOL.	PAGE
Shipwrecked Sailor, The, Egyptian Literature	1	26
Shoemaker's Holiday, A, Dekker	11	327
Sholl, A. M., on		
Hardy	15	59
Meredith	15	19
Montagu	12	247
Pater	15	207
Swift	12	49
Shorey, Paul, on		
Aristophanes	2	213
Lucretius	3	130
Plato	2	303
Short Story, see Literature; Fiction		
Short Studies on Great Subjects, Froude	14	618
Shropshire Lad, A, Housman	15	566
Shu Ching [Book of History], Chinese Literature	1	503
Sic Vos Non Vobis, Martial	3	339
Siculus, Calpurnius, See Calpurnius Siculus		
Sidney, Sir Philip	11	45
Siege of Corinth, The, Byron	13	315
Sienkiewicz, Henryk	10	528
Siete Partidas, Las, Alfonso the Wise	8	21
Sigurd Slembe, Björnson	10	241 243
Sigurd the Völsung, The Story of (Morris), Old Norse Literature	4	296
Silence Is Golden, Martial	3	340
Silent Woman, The, Jonson	11	349
Sill, Edward Rowland	18	181
Silvæ, Statius	3	318 321
Silver Age, The, Heywood	11	365
Simchas Torah, Gordon	1	202
Simile, A, Prior	12	40
Similia Similibus, Martial	3	341
Simms, William Gilmore	17	522
Simon, Sand	7	44
Simonides	2	572
Sindbad the Sailor, The Fourth Voyage of, Arabian Nights	1	256
Singing Reed, The, Greek Anthology	2	578
Sir Charles Grandison, Richardson	12	215
Sir Galahad, Tennyson	14	283
Sir John Norris and Sir Francis Drake, A Farewell to, Peele	11	205
Sir Patrick Spens, Medieval Literature	4	33
Siren, The, Bestiaries	4	515
Siris, Berkeley	12	46
Sister Philomène, de Goncourts	7	91
Skeleton in Armor, The, Longfellow	17	119
Skeleton in the Cupboard, The, Locker-Lampson	14	484
Skinner, C. L., on the First American Poets — the Indians	16	1
Skipis, Sotiris, on Modern Greek Literature	8	645
Skipper Ireson's Ride, Whittier	17	156
Skipwith, Letter to Robert, Jefferson	16	186
Skylark, The, Hogg	12	579
Skylark, To a, Shelley	13	401
Slab of Rose Marble, On a, Musset	6	478
Slaughter, G. E. T., on		
Hardy	15	87
Meredith	15	19
Pascoli	5	477
Slave and Philosopher, Greek Anthology	2	583
Slavery. See also Government; Sociology		
Cooper Institute, Speech at the, Lincoln	17	586
Farewell, The, Whittier	17	174
Inaugural Address, The Second, Lincoln	17	593
Right of Petition, Remarks on the, Calhoun	16	296
Spirit of Laws, The, Montesquieu	6	299
Uncle Tom's Cabin, Stowe	17	250
Virginia, Notes on, Jefferson	16	187
Slavonic Literature		
Bulgarian Literature	10	572
Czechoslovak Literature	10	550 565
Lusatian Literature	10	570
Polish Literature	10	490
Russian Literature	10	301 314
Ukrainian Literature	10	484
Yugoslavian Literature	10	586
Sleep, Ode to, Hayne	17	614
Sleeping Satyr, On a, Plato	2	572
Słowacki, Juljusz	10	511
Slumber Did My Spirit Seal, A, Wordsworth	13	30

	VOL.	PAGE
Small Celandine, To the, Wordsworth	13	65
Smalley, G. W., on Phillips	16	493
Smith, Adam	12	375
Smith, C. S., on the Cid	8	8
Smith, H. P., on the Qur'an	1	268
Smith of His Own Fortunes, The, Keller	9	390
Smith, Sydney	13	242
Smoke, Thoreau	17	305
Smollett, Tobias George	12	238
Smyth, E. C., on Edwards	16	57
Smyth, H. W., on Thucydides	2	257
Snorra Edda, The, Old Norse Literature	4	282
Snow, The, Ab Gwilym	4	267
Snow-Bound, Whittier	17	177
Snow Queen, The, Andersen	10	117
So Near and Yet So Far, Martial	3	340
Social Contract, The, Rousseau	6	353, 358
Society, see Manners and Customs		
Society upon the Stanislaus, The, Harte	18	168
Sociology		
Civilization in Europe, General History of, Guizot	6	644
Day Is Coming, The, Morris	15	137
Hereditary Genius, Galton	14	574
Higher Man, The, Nietzsche	9	511
Philosophy of the History of Man, Herder	9	95
Positive Polity, Comte	6	662
Semitic People in the History of Civilization, The Share of, Renan	7	123
Thus Spake Zarathustra, Nietzsche	9	506
Times, The, Emerson	17	36
Variety, Valéry	7	581
Sodoma's 'Christ Scourged,' Woodberry	18	369
Soldier, The, Brooke	15	616
Soldier's Bride (Laodamia), A, Ovid	3	250
Soldier's Dream, The, Campbell	13	265
Solitary Reaper, The, Wordsworth	13	52
Solomon ibn Gabirol, see Gabirol, Solomon ibn		
Solomon, Immanuel ben, see Immanuel ben Solomon		
Solon	2	127
Solon Speaks His Mind to the Athenians, Solon	2	129
Solovyev, Vladimir	10	327
Song, Beddoes	13	493
Song, Carew	11	170
Song, Hadloub	4	466
Song, von Morungen	4	462
Song, Prior	12	37
Song, Rossetti, C. G.	14	472
Song, Shenstone	12	321
Song, Steinmar	4	463
Song, Suckling	11	172
Song, von Toggenburg	4	462
Song, von Veldeke	4	461
Song, Walther von der Vogelweide	4	459
Song, von Würzburg	4	465
Song, A, Carew	11	169
Song, A, Riley	18	308
Song of Summer, Medieval Irish Literature	4	237
Song of the Bell, The, Schiller	9	188
Song of the Bower, Rossetti	14	466
Song of the Marches, A, Li Tai Po	1	514
Song of the "Marner," Minnesingers	4	464
Song of the Open Road, Whitman	17	408
Song of the Reed, or Divine Affections, The, Jalal ad-Din Rumi	1	367
Song of the Sea, Maginn	13	490
Song of the Shirt, The, Hood	13	471
Song of Winter, A, Medieval Irish Literature	4	239
Songs		
An Thou Were My Ain Thing, Ramsay	12	201
Ariel's Songs, Shakespeare	11	266
As You Like It, Shakespeare	11	259, 260
Banks o' Doon, The, Burns	12	612
Believe Me, If All Those Endearing Young Charms, Moore	13	290
Bessy Bell and Mary Gray, Ramsay	12	199
Bonny Dundee, Scott	13	151
Bruce to His Men at Bannockburn, Burns	12	610
Caller Herrin', Nairne	12	617
Celia, Song to, Jonson	11	352
Come, Rest in This Bosom, Moore	13	290
Cymbeline, Shakespeare	11	263
Drink to Me Only with Thine Eyes, see Celia, Song to		

	VOL.	PAGE
Faust, Goethe	9	132 137, 149
Fisher's Hut, The, Heine	9	322
Flora Mac-Ivor's Song (from 'Waverley'), Scott	13	153
Folk-Song, Medieval Literature	4	112
Gentle Shepherd, The, Ramsay	12	198
Goliardic Poetry, Medieval Literature	4	132
Grammar of the Stars, The, Heine	9	323
Green Grow the Rashes, Burns	12	599
Harp that Once through Tara's Halls, The, Moore	13	294
Highland Lassie, The, Ramsay	12	203
Highland Mary, Burns	12	611
How Doth the Little Busy Bee, Watts	12	196
Hundred Pipers, The, Nairne	12	616
In the Fisher's Cabin, Heine	9	322
Jock o' Hazeldean, Scott	13	147
King Henry VIII, Shakespeare	11	265
King of Yvetot, The, Béranger	6	524
Land o' the Leal, The, Nairne	12	615
Let Dogs Delight to Bark and Bite, Watts	12	195
Lochaber No More, Ramsay	12	200
Lochinvar, Scott	13	138
Lorelei, The, Heine	9	318
Love's Labor's Lost, Shakespeare	11	250
Love Songs, Heine	9	319
Lovely Mary Donnelly, Allingham	14	483
Love's Young Dream, Moore	13	288
Maid of Athens, Byron	13	312
Measure for Measure, Shakespeare	11	263
Merchant of Venice, The, Shakespeare	11	257
Midsummer Night's Dream, A, Shakespeare	11	256
Much Ado about Nothing, Shakespeare	11	258
My Heart's in the Highlands, Burns	12	612
Nymph's Reply to the Shepherd, The, Raleigh	11	40
Oft, in the Stilly Night, Moore	13	292
Oh! Breathe Not His Name, Moore	13	293
Passionate Shepherd to His Love, The, Marlowe	11	217
Pibroch of Donuil Dhu (Highland Song), Scott	13	148
Pippa Passes, Browning	14	331
Princess, The, Tennyson	14	293
Rokeby, Scott	13	150
Rule, Britannia, Thomson	12	311
Sands of Dee, The, Kingsley	14	207
Sound the Loud Timbrel, Moore	13	294
Tempest, The, Shakespeare	11	267
'Tis the Last Rose of Summer, Moore	13	293
Twelfth Night, Shakespeare	11	261 262
Two Gentlemen of Verona, Shakespeare	11	251
Weary Pund o' Tow, The, Baillie	12	576
Wha'll Be King but Charlie? Nairne	12	621
When Maggy Gangs Away, Hogg	12	578
When the Kye Comes Hame, Hogg	12	580
Wilhelm Meister's Apprenticeship, Goethe	9	156 160, 161
Will She Come? Heine	9	320
Will Ye No Come Back Again? Nairne	12	622
Winter's Tale, The, Shakespeare	11	264 265
Songs, Beaumont and Fletcher	11	394
Songs, Blake	12	633 634
Songs, Donne	11	152 154
Songs of the Orient, Hugo	6	498
Songs of the Sierras, Miller	18	188
Songs of Twilight, Hugo	6	499
Sonnet, Drayton	11	131
Sonnet, Immanuel ben Solomon of Rome	1	172
Sonnet, Slowacki	10	518
Sonnet, Timrod	17	612
Sonnet, The, Gilder	18	506
Sonnets, Masefield	15	595
Sonnets from the Portuguese, Browning, E. B.	14	408
Sonnets to His Mother, Heine	9	324
Sonnica, Ibañez	8	257

	VOL.	PAGE
Sophocles	2	162
Sorley, Charles Hamilton	15	616
Sorrow, Thaxter	18	77
Sorrow and Joy, Petöfi	8	600
Sorrow's Barren Grave, Heraclitus	2	574
Sorrows of Werther, The, Thackeray	14	101
Sotileza, Pereda	8	192
Soul, The, Swedenborg	10	144
Soul, On the, Sa'adia Ga'on	1	174
Sound the Loud Timbrel, Moore	13	294
Source of Strength, The, Bialik	1	212
South American Independence as Related to the United States, Clay	16	273
South Country, The, Belloc	15	601
Southern United States, see United States, Southern		
Southey, Robert	13	112
Sova, Antonín	10	556
Spanish Literature		
The Picaresque Novel	8	51
Spain and France	8	152
Spain's European Greatness and Decline	8	31
Spanish Literature	8	1
Spanish Mystics	8	66
The Spanish Romances	8	24
Spanish Romanticism	8	157
Spanish Rodomontades, Brantôme	6	77
Spanish Student, The, Longfellow	17	125
Sparrow's Nest, The, Wordsworth	13	46
Specimen Jones, Wister	18	407
Spectator, The, Addison	12	93
		95, 98, 100
Spectator, The, Steele	12	77
Speech in the National Assembly, Mirabeau	6	388
Spell, The, Verlaine	7	283
Spencer, Herbert	14	684
Spenser, Edmund	11	58
Spinoza, Benedict	8	356
Spirit of Laws, The, Montesquieu	6	296
		298, 299, 300, 301, 302
Spiritual Freedom, Discourse on, Channing	16	285
Spiritual Letters, Fénelon	6	252
"Spirto Gentil che Quelle Membra Reggi," Petrarch	5	95
Spring, Timrod	17	610
Spring, Ode on the, Gray	12	337
Spring on the Coast, Leonidas of Tarentum	2	573
Spring, The, Carew	11	171
Spring, The Song of, Vicente	8	277
Spring Waters, Tyutchev	10	321
Spring, Wherein Each Thing Renews, Description of, Surrey	11	128
Squire, J. C., on Gosse	15	629
Staël, Madame de	6	406
Stage-Coach, The, Irving	16	378
Stanzas Written in Dejection, Shelley	13	427
Stanzas Written in My Library, Southey	13	119
State, The, Alcæus	2	114
Statesman, The, Plato	2	332
Statius, Publius Papinius	3	313
Steam-Guillotine, The, Giusti	5	400
Stedman, Edmund Clarence	17	502
Steele, Sir Richard	12	72
Steinmar	4	463
Stella, Sonnets to, Sidney	11	55
Stendhal, see Beyle, Marie-Henri		
Stephen, Leslie	15	197
Stephen, Leslie, on		
Carlyle	13	544
Fielding	12	164
Sterne, Laurence	12	221
Stevenson, Robert Louis	15	252
Stillman, W. J., on Boccaccio	5	105
Stock Exchange, The, Verhaeren	8	449
Stockton, Francis Richard	18	1
Stoddard, R. H., on Burns	12	582
Stones of Venice, The, Ruskin	13	598
		603
Stops of Various Quills, Howells	18	108
		109
Storm, Theodor	9	397
Storm, The, Alcæus	2	114
Story of Gösta Berling, The, Lagerlöf	10	185
Story of My Heart, The, Jefferies	15	233
Stowe, Harriet Beecher	17	245
Strachey, Lytton	15	674
Strange, Sill	18	186
Strange Fits of Passion Have I Known, Wordsworth	13	27
Strassburg, Gottfried von, see Gottfried von Strassburg		
Strato	2	576
Strehlenau, Nikolaus Niembsch von	9	416

	VOL.	PAGE
Strindberg, August	10	167
Struggle against Illness and Assassins, The, Mussolini	5	574
Style, Of, Joubert	6	397
Styles, Letter to Dr., Jefferson	16	190
Subjection of Women, The, Mill	13	637
Success, see Ethics; Sociology; etc.		
Such a One as He Would Love, A Description of, Wyatt	11	126
Such Stuff as Dreams Are Made of, Calderon	8	140
		144
Suckling, Sir John	11	171
Sudden Hope, Dehmel	9	576
Sudermann, Hermann	9	513
Suetonius	3	391
Sully-Prudhomme	7	269
Sulpicius Consoles Cicero after His Daughter Tullia's Death, Sulpicius	3	88
Sulpicius, Reply to, Cicero	3	91
Sultzer, Kenneth, on		
Davidson	15	534
Deloney	11	78
Summa Theologica, Aquinas	5	29
Summer in Arcady, Allen	18	330
Summer Is Gone, Medieval Irish Literature	4	239
Summer Night, The, Klopstock	9	58
Summer Sailing, Greek Anthology	2	576
Summer-Time, For, Wither	11	147
Summons, The, Whittier	17	186
Sumner, Charles	16	481
Sun Yat Sen	1	518
Sunbeams and Shadows, Hugo	6	500
Sun-Day Hymn, A, Holmes	17	201
Sun-God's Palace, The, Ovid	3	260
Sunken Bell, The, Hauptmann	9	545
Sunrise, Tyutchev	10	321
Sun's Darling, The, Dekker	11	326
Sunset, Hérédia	7	257
Superscription, A, Rossetti	14	469
Superstition and Fear, Spinoza	8	367
Superstition, On the Evil of, Lucretius	3	139
Suppliants, The, Æschylus	2	155
Surprise, The, Barnes	13	507
Surrey, Earl of, see Howard, Henry		
Suum Cuique, Mörike	9	418
Swallow, The, Anacreon	2	125
Swan of Vilamorta, The, Pardo-Bazan	8	210
Swann's Way, Proust	7	567
		570
Swedenborg, Emanuel	10	137
Swedish Literature	10	133
Sweet William's Farewell to Black-Eyed Susan, Gay	12	116
Sweet William's Ghost, Medieval Literature	4	49
Sweetness and Light, see Culture and Anarchy		
Swift, Jonathan	12	49
Swinburne, Algernon Charles	15	105
Swiss Literature	8	562
Sylvia, Leopardi	5	393
Symonds, John Addington	15	216
Synge, John Millington	8	541
Sze-ma Ch'ien	1	508

T

	VOL.	PAGE
Table-Talk, Luther	9	25
Table-Talk, Selden	11	118
Tacitus, Publius Cornelius	3	345
Tagore, Rabindranath	1	485
Tain Bo Cualnge [Cattle-Raid of Cooley], Medieval Irish Literature	4	210
Taine, Hippolyte Adolphe	7	132
Taketori Monogatari, Japanese Literature	1	547
Takhkemoni, Judah al-Kharizi	1	178
Tale of Troy, The, Greek Anthology	2	574
Tales of the Mermaid Tavern, see Flos Mercatorum		
Taliessin	4	256
Talisman, The, Pushkin	10	337
Talisman, The, Scott	13	169
Talmud, The	1	138
Tam o'Shanter, Burns	12	604
Tamagatsuma, Motoöri	1	568
Tamburlaine, Marlowe	11	217
		218, 220
Tampa Robins, Lanier	18	199
Tarkington, Booth	18	493
Tartarin of Tarascon, Daudet	7	222
		224
Tartuffe, Molière	6	170
		178, 186, 192
Task, The, Cowper	12	397
Tasso	5	234
Tatler, The, Steele	12	75
Tavčar, Ivan	10	594
Taylor, Jeremy	11	551
Tchernichowsky, Saul	1	207

	VOL.	PAGE
Teaching of Virtue, The, Plutarch	2	501
Teapot, The, Andersen	10	106
Tears Fall within My Heart, Verlaine	7	282
Telemachus, Fénelon	6	251
		253
Tellez, Gabriel, see Tirso de Molina		
Telling the Bees, Whittier	17	159
Tempest, The, Shakespeare	11	267
Temple of Zeus at Olympia, The, Pausanias	2	510
Ten Tales, Coppée	7	261
Ten Virgins, The, New Testament	2	440
Tennyson, Alfred	14	255
Tennyson, Aldrich	18	70
Terence	3	52
Terentia, Letter to, Cicero	3	87
Terentius, Epigram on, Cæsar	3	129
Teresa, see Santa Teresa		
Tertium Quid, Martial	3	341
Teutoburger Battle, The, Scheffel	9	425
Thackeray, William Makepeace	14	68
Thaliarchus, To, Horace	3	198
Thanatopsis, Bryant	16	421
Thanksgiving, A, Herrick	11	162
That Real Wealth Is from Within, Chrysostom	2	552
That Women Are but Men's Shadows, Jonson	11	353
Thaxter, Celia	18	76
Theætetus	2	573
Theagenes and Cariclea, Heliodorus	2	560
		562
Theatre Guild, see Shaw, Bernard and the Theatre Guild		
Their Wedding Journey, Howells	18	110
Theocritus	2	391
Theodosius the Emperoure, Gesta Romanorum	4	504
Theognis	2	116
Theogony, Hesiod	2	55
Theory of the Earth, The, Cuvier	6	427
There Are Crimes and Crimes, Strindberg	10	170
There Is a Land of Pure Delight, Watts	12	194
There Is No Devil, Jókai	8	602
Thesmophoriazusæ, The, Aristophanes	2	232
They Are All Gone, Vaughan	11	475
Thierry, Augustin	6	637
Thiers, Adolphe	6	647
Things Known and Unknown, Ballad of, Villon	6	34
Thirteen Articles of Faith, The, Maimonides	1	191
Thirty Bob a Week, Davidson	15	536
Thomas à Kempis	4	474
Thomas of Britain	4	80
Thompson, Francis	15	541
Thomson, James (1700–1748)	12	309
Thomson, James (1834–1882)	14	505
Thoreau, Henry D.	17	297
Thoreau's Flute, Alcott	17	388
Thorndike, A. H., on		
Beaumont	11	374
Fletcher	11	374
Literature and Civilization	1	3
Raleigh	11	38
Thorpe, F. N., on		
Mirabeau	6	385
Montesquieu	6	292
Prescott	16	450
Those Who Missay of France, Ballad against, Villon	6	35
Thou Didst Delight My Eyes, Bridges	15	555
Thou Reason'st Well, Martial	3	340
Though Treasures Unbounded, Bredero	8	352
Thought and Existence, Parmenides	2	294
Thoughts, Pascal	6	198
Thrale, Letter to Mrs., Johnson	12	270
Three Daughters of Monsieur Dupont, The, Brieux	7	480
Three Enemies, The, Rossetti, C. G.	14	473
Three Musketeers, The, Dumas	6	596
		602
Three Ravens, The, Medieval Literature	4	39
Three Years She Grew in Sun and Shower, Wordsworth	13	29
Threnody, Bion	2	407
Threnody, Emerson	17	61
Through the Looking-Glass, Carroll	15	147
Through the Night, Dehmel	9	578
Thucydides	2	257
Thunder, Lessing	9	78
Thus Spake Zarathustra, Nietzsche	9	506

	VOL.	PAGE
Thyrsis, The Song of, Theocritus	2	395
Tibullus, Albius	3	222
Tieck, Johann Ludwig	9	239
Tiger, The, Blake	12	639
Time I've Lost in Wooing, The, Moore	13	289
Time Wasted, Seneca	3	266
Times, The, Emerson	17	36
Timrod, Henry	17	609
Tin Soldier, The Steadfast, Andersen	10	103
Tintagiles, The Death of, Maeterlinck	8	470
Tintern Abbey, Lines Composed a Few Miles above, Wordsworth	13	23
Tiro, Letter to, Cicero	3	86
Tirso de Molina	8	124
'Tis Noon; the Light Is Fierce, Hérédia	7	258
'Tis the Last Rose of Summer, Moore	13	293
To ——, Shelley	13	423
To Daisies, Not to Shut So Soon, Herrick	11	165
To Find God, Herrick	11	164
To His Book, Horace	3	208
To His Soul, Hadrian	3	452
To M——, Mickiewicz	10	509
Toccata of Galuppi's, A, Browning	14	361
Tocqueville, Alexis de	6	664
Toggenburg, Count Kraft von	4	462
Tolstoy, Count Aleksyey Konstantinovich	10	324
Tolstoy, Lyev Nikolayevich	10	393
Tom Bowling, Didbin	12	570
Tom Jones, Fielding	12	181, 185, 187
Tomb of Burns, The, Watson	15	561
Tombs in Westminster, On the, Beaumont	11	396
Tomorrow, and Tomorrow, Greek Anthology	2	577
Tono-Bungay, Wells	15	423
Tosa Nikki, Japanese Literature	1	547
Toujours Amour, Stedman	17	506
Toussaint l'Ouverture, Phillips	16	496
Toussaint l'Ouverture, To, Wordsworth	13	49
Toy, C. H., on the Old Testament and the Jewish Apocrypha	1	97
Toys, The, Patmore	14	478
Tragedy. See also Drama		
Æschylus	2	146
Alfieri	5	308
Amphitruo, Plautus	3	49
Euripides	2	191
Hamlet, Thoughts on, Lemaître	7	427
Racine, Jean	6	230
Shakespeare	11	229
Seneca	3	263
Sophocles	2	162
Transformation, A, Ovid	3	261
Transmigration, Menander	2	353
Travel and Description. See also Exploration and Discovery		
Alhambra, The, Irving	16	374
American Ornithological Biography, The, Audubon	16	290
Arabia Deserta, Doughty	14	678, 680, 683
Astor, Letter to Francis, Newton	11	640
Émile, Rousseau	6	350
Essays, Bacon	11	104
Harz Journey, The, Heine	9	328, 331
History of England, Macaulay	13	518
Holland and Its People, De Amicis	5	469
Howadji in Syria, Curtis	17	469
Italy, Heine	9	335
Journal, Woolman	16	144
Orient, My First Day in the, Hearn	18	321
Pilgrimage to El Medinah and Meccah, A, Burton	14	667, 670
Prue and I, Curtis	17	471
Stage-Coach, The, Irving	16	378
Their Wedding Journey, Howells	18	110
Traveler's Letters, A, Sand	7	41
Travelers' Tales, Medieval Literature	4	518, 523
Travels in France, Young	12	388
Two Years before the Mast, Dana	17	295
Venetian Life, Howells	18	118
Voyages, Hakluyt	11	19
Traveler's Letters, A, Sand	7	41
Travelers' Tales, Medieval Literature	4	518
Travels in France, Young	12	388
Treasure, The, Peretz	8	630
Treasure of the Humble, The, Maeterlinck	8	474

	VOL.	PAGE
Trees and the Master, A Ballad of, Lanier	18	202
Trent, W. P., on		
Balzac	6	551
Calhoun	15	294
Tribesman's Valor, A, Sa'd	1	237
Trimalchio's Reminiscences, Petronius	3	331
Trinity, The, Augustine	3	445
Trinummus, Plautus	3	48
Tristan, Thomas	4	80
Tristan and Isolde, Gottfried von Strassburg	4	454
Tristram Shandy, The Life and Opinions of, Sterne	12	224
Triumph of Death, The, D'Annunzio	5	493
Trojan Women, The, Euripides	2	206
Trollope, Anthony	14	162
Trotter, Spencer, on		
Buffon	6	333
Wilson, Alexander	16	231
Trousseau, The, Chekhov	10	453
Troyes, Chrestien de	4	365
True Beauty, Beaumont and Fletcher	11	395
True Christian Religion, Swedenborg	10	154
True Grandeur of Nations, The, Sumner	16	489
True Lent, To Keep a, Herrick	11	163
Trumbal, Epitaph on Sir William, Pope	12	163
Truth, Chaucer	4	595
Truth about an Author, The, Bennett	15	436
Tryst, Fet	10	326
Tsure-zure gusa, Japanese Literature	1	552
Tu Fu	1	513
Tullus, To, Propertius	3	235
Turgenev, Ivan Sergyeyevich	10	366
Turmoil, The, Tarkington	18	498
Turnstile, The, Barnes	13	509
Turtle-Dove, The, Bestiaries	4	516
Twain, Mark, see Clemens, Samuel Langhorne		
Twelfth Night, Shakespeare	11	261
		262
Twenty-Eight and Twenty-Nine, Praed	13	497
Two Brothers, The, Egyptian Literature	1	29
Two Chords, Catullus	3	165
Two Gentlemen of Verona, Shakespeare	11	251
Two Lives, Dehmel	9	581
Two Lovers, Mörike	9	419
Two Noble Kinsmen, The, Shakespeare and Fletcher	11	397
Two Songs, The, Blake	12	634
Two Things Needful, The, Martial	3	344
Two Years before the Mast, Dana	17	291
		295
Tyndall, John	14	541
Typee, Melville	17	440
Tyrant's Fortune, A, Herodotus	2	248
Tyrtæus, Archilochus, etc.	2	76
Tyutchev, Fedor Ivanovich	10	321

U

	VOL.	PAGE
'Ubaid Zakani	1	304
Ugly Duckling, The, Andersen	10	107
Uhland, Johann Ludwig	9	408
Ukraine, The, Russian Literature	10	484
Ulalume, Poe	17	576
Ulysses, Tennyson	14	267
Ulysses von Ithacia, Holberg	10	26
'Umar ibn Rabi'a	1	234
Unamuno, Miguel de	8	233
Uncle Remus and His Friends, Harris	18	281
		284, 288
Uncle Tom's Cabin, Stowe	17	250
		258
Under the Greenwood Tree, Hardy	15	65
Under the Moon, Yeats	8	540
Under the Yoke, Vazov	10	578
Undertaking, The, Donne	11	150
Union of Seasons, Kalidasa	1	478
United Netherlands, History of the, Motley	17	281
		286
United Netherlands, History of the Revolt of the, Schiller	9	195
United States. See also Americans		
Address to the American People, D'Annunzio	5	505
America, Dobell	14	482
America, Gilder	18	506
America, Expectations of, Hakluyt	11	22
America, The Mission of, Adams	16	250
American Commonwealth, The, Bryce	15	189

	VOL.	PAGE
American Literature in the Colonial Period	16	11
Bunker Hill Monument, Oration on Laying the Corner-Stone of the, Webster	16	312
Citizenship in a Republic, Roosevelt	18	390
Conciliation with America, Speech on, Burke	12	412
Democracy in America, de Tocqueville	6	667
Indians — The First American Poets, The	16	1
Landing of the Pilgrim Fathers in New England, The, Hemans	13	482
Letters from an American Farmer, Crèvecœur	16	111
Prospect of Planting Arts and Learning in America, On the, Berkeley	12	45
Purple East, The, Watson	15	560
United States, Annexation to the, Howe	8	504
United States, The, Ferrero	5	540
United States, To the, Keble	13	486
United States, Annexation to the, Howe	8	504
United States, History of the, Adams, Henry	18	137
		141, 146
United States, History of the, Bancroft	17	16
		18, 19, 21
United States, Southern		
Aspects of the Pines, Hayne	17	616
Chattahoochee, Song of the, Lanier	18	197
Feuilles Volantes, Les, Fréchette	8	525
Marshes of Glynn, The, Lanier	18	200
Old Creole Days, Cable	18	264
Père Antoine's Date-Palm, Aldrich	18	71
Spring, Timrod	17	610
Summer in Arcady, Allen	18	330
Tampa Robins, Lanier	18	199
Uncle Remus and His Friends, Harris	18	281
		284, 288
Yemassee, The, Simms	17	524
United States, The, Ferrero	5	540
United States, To the, Keble	13	486
United States, Western		
Dickens in Camp, Harte	18	171
Jim, Harte	18	167
Jumping Frog of Calaveras County, The Notorious, Clemens	18	36
Luck of Roaring Camp, The, Harte	18	172
Mountains of California, Muir	18	20
Octopus, The, Norris	18	483
Songs of the Sierras, Miller	18	188
Specimen Jones, Wister	18	407
Universal Love, Mo Ti	1	507
Universal Prayer, The, Pope	12	161
Universe, The, Drummond	11	142
Unkindest Cut, The, Martial	3	339
Unlike Children of Eve, The, Sachs	9	34
Unlucky Luck, Alciphron	2	518
Unmarked Festival, An, Meynell	15	550
Unseen Spirits, Willis	17	109
Unwin, Letter to William, Cowper	12	402
Up-Hill, Rossetti, C. G.	14	474
Usertesen III, Hymn to, Egyptian Literature	1	49
Ut-Napishtim	1	95

V

	VOL.	PAGE
Vacillation in the Civil War, Cicero	3	92
Valdes, Armando Palacio	8	215
Vale of Tears, Martial	3	339
Valediction Forbidding Mourning, A, Donne	11	151
Valedictory to the Senate, The, Clay	16	274
Valera, Juan	8	163
Valéry, Paul	7	576
Vallier, Robert, on Zola	7	295
Valor of 'Antar, The, Arabic Literature	1	286
Value and Power of Music, The, Luther	9	24
Value of Personality, The, Schopenhauer	9	292
Van Doren, Carl, on		
Howells	18	102
Norris	18	481
Van Dyke, Henry, on		
Tennyson	14	255
Walton	11	503
Van Dyke, J. C., on Ruskin	13	586
Vanity Fair, Thackeray	14	85
		90
Vanity of Human Wishes, The, Johnson	12	264

	VOL.	PAGE
Variation of Animals and Plants Under Domestication, The, Darwin	14	534
Variety, Valéry	7	581
Vasari, Giorgio	5	259
Vase, The, de Régnier	7	522
Vaughan, Henry	11	472
Vaughan, S. E., on		
Inge	15	658
Masefield	15	581
Russell	15	684
Vazov, Ivan	10	574
Vega, Lope de, see Lope de Vega		
Veldeke, Heinrich von	4	461
Venetian Life, Howells	18	118
Venetian Republic, On the Extinction of the, Wordsworth	13	48
Venice		
Childe Harold's Pilgrimage, Byron	13	321
Night in Venice, Hay	18	133
Stones of Venice, The, Ruskin	13	598
		603
Toccata of Galuppi's, A, Browning	14	361
Traveler's Letters, A, Sand	7	41
Venetian Life, Howells	18	118
Venetian Republic, On the Extinction of the, Wordsworth	13	48
Venus, Hymn to, Homeric Hymns	2	70
Venus, Invocation to, Lucretius	3	138
Verga, Giovanni	5	443
Vergil	3	167
Vergil, To, Horace	3	200
Vergiss Mein Nicht, Musset	6	476
Verhaeren, Émile	8	438
Verlaine, Paul	7	276
Verses, Suckling	11	176
Verses from an Epithalamium, Catullus	3	162
Vesper Hymn, The, Abélard	4	501
Vicar of Wakefield, The, Goldsmith	12	506
		512
Victorian Era, The	14	1
Victory, Conrad	15	364
Vida Es Sueno, La, see Such Stuff as Dreams Are Made of		
Vigil, Dehmel	9	576
Vigny, Alfred de	6	454
Viking Terror, The, Medieval Irish Literature	4	242
Village Blacksmith, The, Longfellow	17	128
Village Communities in the East and West, Maine	14	593
Village Corsican, A, Boswell	12	281
Village Notary, The, Eötvös	8	586
Villari, Pasquale	5	411
Villiers de l'Isle-Adam, Jean Marie Mathias Philippe Auguste, Comte de	7	288
Villon, François	6	28
Villon in Prison, Ballad of, Villon	6	36
Vindication of the Rights of Women, A, Wollstonecraft	12	552
Violets, To, Herrick	11	167
Virginia, A Report of, Heriot (Hakluyt)	11	31
Virginia Convention, Speech in the, Henry	16	137
Virginia Legislature, Speech in the, Henry	16	139
Virginia, Notes on, Jefferson	16	187
Virtue, Herbert	11	160
Virtue and Morality, Of, Joubert	6	395
Virtue, Hymn to, Aristotle	2	344
Viscount of Bragelonne, The, Dumas	6	612
Vision of Judgment, The, Byron	13	345
Vision of Sir Launfal, The, Lowell	17	330
Visit to Ceylon, A, Haeckel	9	476
		479
Vita Nuova, Watson	15	564
Vitaï Lampada, Newboldt	15	571
Vitellius, Suetonius	3	395
Vittoria Corombona, Webster	11	363
Vivian Grey, Beaconsfield	14	48
Vogelweide, Walther von der, see Walther von der Vogelweide		
Vogüé, Eugène-Melchior de	7	415
Voice in the Darkness, Dehmel	9	578
Voiceless, The, Holmes	17	202
Volland, Letter to Mlle., Diderot	6	365
Volpone, Jonson	11	353
Voltaire (François Marie Arouet)	6	304
Vondel, Joost van den	8	334
Vow, A, Petőfi	8	600
Vowels, Rimbaud	7	292
Vox Populi, Villiers de l'Isle-Adam	7	288

	VOL.	PAGE
Voyages, Hakluyt	11	19
Vrchlický, Jaroslav	10	569

W

	VOL.	PAGE
Wagner, Richard	9	368
Waiting, Burroughs	18	101
Walden, Thoreau	17	306
		309, 315
Wallenstein's Death, Schiller	9	192
Waller, Edmund	11	484
Walpole, Horace	12	345
Walsh, Thomas, on Moore	13	285
Walston, Charles, on Eliot	14	632
Walther von der Vogelweide	4	459
Walton, Izaak	11	503
Wanderer, The, Anglo-Saxon Literature	4	330
Wanderer's Night Songs, Goethe	9	164
Wandering Ængus, The Song of, Yeats	8	538
Wanted, Holland	17	431
War		
Acharnians, The, Aristophanes	2	221
Address of the President of the United States, April 2, 1917, Wilson	18	378
Æneid, Vergil	3	181
Agincourt, The Ballad of, Drayton	11	131
All the Hills and Vales Along, Sorley	15	617
Anabasis, Xenophon	2	283
Annals, Tacitus	3	357
Anno Domini 1812, Dehmel	9	578
Armenians, The Second Battle of the, Eliasaeus	1	395
Attack on the Mill, The, Zola	7	302
Attic Nights (Cato), Gellius	3	25
Battle of Blenheim, The, Southey	13	117
Battle of Ivry, The, Macaulay	13	541
Blanche-Taque, Of the Battle of, Froissart	6	20
Burial of Sir John Moore at Corunna, The, Wolfe	13	484
Charge of the Light Brigade, The, Tennyson	14	306
Childe Harold's Pilgrimage, Byron	13	322
Cid, The, Corneille	6	109
Conquest of England by the Normans, History of the, Thierry	6	639
Conquest of Mexico, The, Prescott	16	453
Cressy, Of the Battle of, Froissart	6	24
Danny Deever, Kipling	15	312
Dirge for Two Veterans, Whitman	17	417
Discourse Delivered before the Congregational Ministers of Massachusetts, Channing	16	283
Dynasts, The, Hardy	15	91
English People, History of the, Green	15	176
Englishmen at Cressy, Of the Order of the, Froissart	6	22
Fall of the Serbian Empire, The, Slavonic Literature	10	509
Father, The, Gibson	15	607
Fight at Maldon, The, Anglo-Saxon Literature	4	338
Final Struggle in the Harbor of Syracuse, The, Thucydides	2	272
Flanders Fields, In, McCrae	8	502
French Revolution, The, Carlyle	13	565
Frenchmen at Cressy, The Order of the, Froissart	6	23
Gallic War, The, Cæsar	3	114
		128
Gibraltar, At, Woodbury	18	368
Gododdin, The, Welsh Literature	4	252
Hervé Riel, Browning	14	390
Hohenlinden, Campbell	13	262
Horatius, Macaulay	13	533
Hunting of the Cheviot, The, Medieval Literature	4	24
In a Winter Night, Liliencron	9	430
In Time of Peace Prepare for War, Sumner	16	483
Incident of the French Camp, Browning	14	338
Kulikovo, On the Field of, Blok	10	329
Last Fight of the Revenge, The, Raleigh	11	41
Mr. Hosea Biglow to the Editor of the Atlantic Monthly, Lowell	17	348
Montcalm and Wolfe, Parkman	17	374

	VOL.	PAGE
Night Attack on Platæa, The, Thucydides	2	263
"Noche Triste, La" [The Night of Sorrows], Diaz	8	48
Personal Memoirs, Grant	17	605
Philosophical Dictionary, Voltaire	6	323
Poèmes Militaires, Déroulède	7	247
		248, 249
Question, The, Gibson	15	606
Raining, Gibson	15	606
Revenge, The, Tennyson	14	319
Rome, History of, Livy	3	214
		219
Sir John Norris and Sir Francis Drake, A Farewell to, Peele	11	205
Soldier, The, Brooke	15	616
Telemachus, Fénelon	6	251
		253
True Grandeur of Nations, The, Sumner	16	489
United States, History of, Adams, Henry	18	137
		141, 146
United States, History of the, Bancroft	17	18
War against Jugurtha, History of the, Sallust	3	147
War and Peace, Tolstoy	10	403
War and Warriors, Nietzsche	9	507
War, On, Franklin	16	91
War, The Moral Equivalent of, James, William	18	207
Who Knows Where, Liliencron	9	428
Wife of Flanders, The, Chesterton	15	656
With Fire and Sword, Sienkiewicz	10	531
War against Jugurtha, History of the, Sallust	3	147
		151
War and Peace, Tolstoy	10	403
War and Warriors, Nietzsche	9	507
War, On, Franklin	16	91
War, The Moral Equivalent of, James, William	18	207
Ward, Artemus, see Browne, Charles Farrar		
Warner, Charles Dudley	17	485
Warner, C. D., on Byron	13	306
Warren, F. M., on		
Corneille	6	103
Racine	6	230
Warren Hastings, Trial of, Macaulay	13	530
War-Song of Dinas Vawr, The, Peacock	13	475
Washington, George	16	122
Water of Purity, The, Greek Anthology	2	580
Water Song, Gabirol	1	168
Waterfowl, To a, Bryant	16	428
Water-Witch, The, Cooper	16	390
Watson, Sir William	15	556
Watts, Isaac	12	191
Waves, The, Letteris	1	201
We Read in Books, Cats	8	348
"We Twa," Persius	3	294
Wealth of Nations, The, Smith	12	379
		382
Weary Pund o' Tow, The, Baillie	12	576
Weaver, R. M., on		
Melville	17	434
The New Art of Biography	18	555
Weavers, The, Hauptmann	9	529
Webster, Daniel	16	305
Webster, John	11	356
Welcome, Sweet Day of Rest, Watts	12	193
Wells, B. W., on		
Andersen	10	100
Jacob and Wilhelm Grimm	9	274
Sainte-Beuve	6	621
Wells, Herbert George	15	412
Welsh Literature	4	243
Wendell, Barrett, on Jonson	11	338
Wesley, Charles	12	533
Wesley, John	12	533
West Wind, Ode to the, Shelley	13	393
Westcott, J. H., on Cæsar	3	106
Western Wall, The, Cohen	1	206
Westminster Bridge, Sonnet Composed upon, Wordsworth	13	47
Westward Ho! Kingsley	14	208
Whale, The, Bestiaries	4	515
Wha'll Be King but Charlie? Nairne	12	621
Wharton, Edith	18	448
What D'Ye Call It? Gay	12	117
What Have You Done with It? Desbordes-Valmore	6	527
What I Know about Gardening, Warner	17	489
What Is the Serbian Native Land? Zeiler	10	570
What Mr. Robinson Thinks, Lowell	17	343

	VOL.	PAGE
What the Moon Saw, Andersen	10	115
Wheeler, B. I., on Herodotus	2	240
When I Have Fears that I May Cease to Be, Keats	13	459
When I Survey the Wondrous Cross, Watts	12	194
When Ivy Twines, Cats	8	349
When Lilacs Last in the Door-Yard Bloomed, Whitman	17	418
When Maggy Gangs Away, Hogg	12	578
When o'er the Yellowing Corn, Lermontov	10	318
When Phyllis Laughs, Hay	18	132
When She Comes Home, Riley	18	307
When the Frost Is on the Punkin, Riley	18	316
When the Kye Comes Hame, Hogg	12	580
When the Lamp Is Shattered, see Lines: When the Lamp Is Shattered		
Whicher, G. M., on		
Propertius	3	232
Tibullus	3	222
While Here, Krasinski	10	527
White, A. D., on Erasmus	8	314
White, J. W., on Æschylus	2	146
Whitman, Walt	17	402
Whittier, John Greenleaf	17	151
Who Knows Where, Liliencron	9	428
Why the Nile Overflows, Athenæus	2	548
Widow's Mite, The, New Testament	2	440
Wieland, Christoph Martin	9	100
Wieland's Statement, Brown	16	258
Wife, The, Pickthall	8	501
Wife of Bath's Tale, The, Chaucer	4	571
Wife of Flanders, The, Chesterton	15	656
Wife of Pythes, The, Plutarch	2	500
Wife of Sir Isaac Harman, The, Wells	15	417
Wife of Usher's Well, The, Medieval Literature	4	48
Wild Geese, Thaxter	18	80
Wild Mare in the Desert, The, Musset	6	479
Wilhelm Meister's Apprenticeship, Goethe	9	155, 158, 160, 161
Will She Come? Heine	9	320
Will to Power, Nietzsche	9	509
Will Ye No Come Back Again? Nairne	12	622
William Tell, Schiller	9	197
Williams, B. C., on Modern Fiction	18	528
Williams, Talcott, on the Greek Anthology	2	570
Willis, Nathaniel Parker	17	103
Wilson, Alexander	16	231
Wilson, John	13	356
Wilson, Woodrow	18	372
Windmill, The, Verhaeren	8	444
Winter's Tale, The, Shakespeare	11	264, 265
Wisdom of Our Ancestors, Smith	13	248
Wise Man, The, Avesta	1	319
Wishing, Greek Anthology	2	583
Wister, Owen	18	406
With a Guitar, to Jane, Shelley	13	424
With Fire and Sword, Sienkiewicz	10	531
Wither, George	11	143
Without Benefit of Clergy, Kipling	15	293
Wolf and the Dog, The, La Fontaine	6	133
Wolf in Sheep's Clothing, The, Æsop	2	61
Wolfe, Charles	13	483
Wolfram von Eschenbach	4	444
Wollstonecraft, Mary	12	549
Woman Killed with Kindness, A, Heywood	11	367, 368
Woman of Samaria, The, New Testament	2	441
Women. See also Education; Sociology		
American Commonwealth, The, Bryce	15	189
Ballad of Dead Ladies, The, Villon	6	30
Countess of Bute, Letters to the, Montagu	12	253
Democracy in America, de Tocqueville	6	667
Doll's House, A, Ibsen	10	218
Dream of Fair Women, A, Tennyson	14	276
Economist, The, Xenophon	2	278
Education of Women, The, Smith	13	243
Epistles, Holberg	10	46
European Morals, History of, Lecky	15	183

	VOL.	PAGE
Genji Monogatari, Murasaki	1	550
Marriage Ring, The, Taylor	11	557
Mufaddaliyat, Ash-Shanfara of Azd	1	233
Nut-Brown Maid, The, Medieval Literature	4	54
Old and Young Women, Nietzsche	9	508
Poèmes Saturniens, Verlaine	7	278
Positive Polity, Comte	6	663
Princess, The, Tennyson	14	295
Sesame and Lilies, Ruskin	13	592
Subjection of Women, The, Mill	13	637
Thesmophoriazusæ, The, Aristophanes	2	232
Vindication of the Rights of Women, A, Wollstonecraft	12	552
Women of Paris, Ballad of the, Villon	6	31
Worth of Women, Schiller	9	184
Women of Paris, Ballad of the, Villon	6	31
Wonderful Magician, The, Calderon	8	135
Woodberry, George Edward	18	367
Woodberry, G. E., on		
Arnold	14	412
Coleridge	13	67
Shelley	13	380
Woods of Westermain, The, Meredith	15	54
Wooing of Etain, The, see Book of the Dun (Cow)		
Woolman, John	16	141
Wordsworth, William	13	18
Wordsworth's Grave, Watson	15	562
Work and Play, Bushnell	16	512, 514
Working Man, The, Dehmel	9	580
Works and Days, Hesiod	2	53, 56
World Is Too Much with Us, The, Wordsworth	13	55
World War		
Address of the President of the United States, April 2, 1917, Wilson	18	378
Address to the American People, D'Annunzio	5	505
All the Hills and Vales Along, Sorley	15	617
Father, The, Gibson	15	607
Flanders Fields, In, McCrae	8	502
Question, The, Gibson	15	606
Raining, Gibson	15	606
Soldier, The, Brooke	15	616
Variety, Valéry	7	581
Wife of Flanders, The, Chesterton	15	656
Worldly Wisdom, Theognis	2	118
Worship in Spring, Theætetus	2	573
Worth of Women, Schiller	9	184
Worthies of England, The, Fuller	11	546, 547, 549
Would You Be Young Again? Nairne	12	623
Wounded Crane, The, Akhmatova	10	331
Wreck of the Hesperus, The, Longfellow	17	126
Wright, E. H., on		
Matthews	18	339
Shakespeare	11	235
Stephen	15	197
Wells	15	412
Written in Sickness at Corcyra, Tibullus	3	226
Written on a Blank Leaf in 1723, Edwards	16	62
Würzburg, Konrad von, see Konrad von Würzburg		
Wuthering Heights, Brontë, Emily	14	232
Wyatt, Sir Thomas	11	125

X

	VOL.	PAGE
Xenophon	2	275

Y

	VOL.	PAGE
Yamagami no Okura	1	542
Yamato Monogatari, Japanese Literature	1	545
Ye Mariners of England, Campbell	13	263
Yeats, William Butler	8	529
Yehoash	8	640
Yellow Flowers, Sova	10	565
Yemassee, The, Simms	17	524
Yiddish Literature	8	617
You Ask Me Why, Though Ill at Ease, Tennyson	14	281
Young, Arthur	12	386
Young, Edward	12	196
Young, Karl, on the Medieval Drama	4	146
Young Captive, The, Chénier	6	402
Young Hero's Epitaph, A, Greek Anthology	2	580

	VOL.	PAGE
Young Lady, To a, Wordsworth	13	55
Young Wife, The, Greek Anthology	2	578
Youth and Age, Kingsley	14	207
Youth and Calm, Arnold	14	427
Youth and Riches, Greek Anthology	2	579
Youths and Theseus, The, Bacchylides	2	99
Yugoslav Literature	10	586
Yusuf and Zulaikha, Jami	1	381
Yvain, Chrestien de Troyes	4	365

Z

	VOL.	PAGE
Zeiler, Handrij	10	570
Zeus, Hymn to, Cleanthes	2	384
Zion, Ode to, Judah ha-Levi	1	181
Zola, Émile	7	295
Zoölogy, see Science		
Zuhair	1	229